SAUNDERS MATHEMATICS BOOKS

Consulting Editor

BERNARD R. GELBAUM, University of California

CORRELATION THEORY OF STATISTICALLY OPTIMAL SYSTEMS

N. I. ANDREYEV

Translated by Scripta Technica, Inc.
Edited by Wendell H. Fleming

W. B. SAUNDERS COMPANY 1969
Philadelphia   London   Toronto

W. B. Saunders Company: West Washington Square
Philadelphia, Pa. 19105

12 Dyott Street
London W.C. 1

1835 Yonge Street
Toronto 7, Ontario

Originally published as *Korrlyatsionnaya Teoriya Statisticheski Optimal 'nykh Sistem* by Nauka Press, Moscow.

Correlation Theory of Statistically Optimal Systems

Preface to the English Translation

This is an account of work in stochastic control by the author, Pugachev, and other scientists in the Soviet Union. The general problem is to design systems that produce from noise-corrupted input signals outputs that are best according to some statistical criterion. However, to obtain meaningful results some more specific formulation of the problems must be treated. The central question considered in this book is to find among systems with known block diagram, and with known statistical properties of the input signal and noise, one that is best. The criterion used for comparing such systems is often the variance (or second moment) of error between the output of the system and an " ideal " output at some instant of time. Another criterion considered is the probability that the error exceeds given limits; in that case errors are assumed to be normally distributed. In mathematical terms the problem of finding a system that minimizes the criterion becomes one of calculus of variations.

The book is intended for mathematically inclined engineers working in the field of automatic control. The emphasis is on the part of the theory that can actually be implemented in engineering problems with the aid of computing devices. Various ways of approximately calculating the minimum are described.

The author draws upon a number of parts of mathematics—calculus of variations, probability, game theory, statistical decision theory, and nonlinear programming. The background in each of these topics is outlined at the point in the exposition where it is needed. This makes the book nearly self-contained. The level of exposition makes it accessible to graduate students in engineering and to advanced under-

v

graduates. We believe that the book will be a welcome addition to the growing literature in the field of automatic-control.

Wendell H. Fleming
Brown University

Preface

The operation of any automatic-control system in practice is subject to random influences. Therefore, it is impossible to study the operation of automatic-control systems under actual conditions without bringing in probabilistic methods. At the present time, probabilistic methods in the theory of automatic control seem most promising. They are widely used both in analysis and in synthesis of automatic systems. An important part in the synthesis is the determination of optimal systems with respect to statistical criteria. The theory of optimal systems with respect to statistical criteria has been expounded by numerous authors [Refs. 1, 3–7, 10, 15, 21–23, 38, 39, 46–48, 52, 56]. Features of the present book include (1) a systematic and more complete exposition of the methods of determining optimal systems with respect to complex statistical criteria (the probability that the error will not exceed given limits, and the like), (2) a single overall procedure for obtaining the necessary conditions for maximization or minimization of a given statistical criterion, and (3) clarification of the close relationship between optimal and adaptive systems.

The book is divided into nine chapters. The first chapter discusses briefly the statistical dynamics of automatic-control systems and presents some information from the calculus of variations. In particular, we present Euler's equation for the double integral of a weight function of a system. We use Euler's equation to obtain necessary conditions for maximization or minimization of various statistical criteria in the remaining chapters of the book. We also prove theorems on necessary conditions for maximization or minimization of more complicated functionals.

In Chapter 2, we pose the problem of determining the optimal system with respect to a statistical criterion. Here, we give a description of how the initial data influence the system, of criteria for comparing two systems, and of classes of admissible systems. In Chapter

3, we expound methods of determining optimal linear continuous systems with respect to minimum mean square error and other criteria that are quadratic functionals of the weight function of the system. In Chapter 4, we present methods of determining optimal linear continuous systems with respect to a criterion of a general form. This criterion is an arbitrary given function of quadratic functionals of the weight function of the system. An example of such a criterion is the probability that the error of the system will not exceed allowed limits. Chapter 5 is devoted to methods of determining optimal linear discrete systems with respect to the criteria just mentioned. In Chapter 6, we consider certain methods of achieving systems that are nearly optimal and we expound one of the methods of determining an optimal system under supplementary restrictions imposed on the class of admissible systems.

Chapter 7 is devoted to methods of determining optimal nonlinear systems with respect to statistical criteria of a general form. In Chapter 8, we present methods for determining optimal systems with decision elements. These systems are, by their very nature, adaptive, since they operate when we have incomplete initial information about the influences. Supplementary information obtained by the system in the course of its operation is processed by a special decision element that estimates the values of the parameters of the system. Such systems are considered in a separate chapter, since the methods of investigating them are considerably different from the methods of investigating other adaptive systems. In Chapter 9, we treat certain problems concerned with the investigation of systems of extremal regulation, which is one of the most important classes of adaptive systems. Moreover, we show the close connection between systems of extremal regulation and optimal systems, and we look at the problem of calculating a statistical criterion when the system is in operation and the problem of finding the maximum or minimum for this criterion in several typical cases.

The purpose of the present book is to systematize the existing methods of determining optimal automatic-control systems with respect to statistical criteria. It is intended for technicians and engineers who work in the field of automatic control. The exposition of the material of the book follows essentially References 2 though 10 with supplementary material by the author.

The author considers it a pleasant duty to express his deep appreciation to V. S. Pugachev for valuable advice used in the preparation of the book and to V. D. Sedov for suggestions made to the author regarding the content of the manuscript. The author also expresses his deep appreciation to I. Ya. Andreyeva for her great help in preparing the manuscript for printing.

Moscow, September 17, 1965   N. I. ANDREYEV

CONTENTS

Chapter VI

Chapter VII

Chapter VIII

Chapter IX

Chapter 1

FUNDAMENTALS OF THE STATISTICAL DYNAMICS OF AUTOMATIC-CONTROL SYSTEMS AND OF THE CALCULUS OF VARIATIONS

1. SOME PROBABILITY THEOREMS

At the present time, it is impossible to make a very deep compre-
hensive study of automatic control systems without bringing in probabilistic (statistical) methods. Therefore, before we begin our actual
study of automatic-control systems, we must review the basic concepts
and theorems of probability theory. In this section, we present a brief
sketch of the concepts and formulas that we shall use in the remainder
of the book. For more detailed information on probability theory and
mathematical statistics, the reader is referred to the books [Refs. 18, 22,
23, 47, 56].*

At the basis of probability theory, just as in every science, are experimental facts. The results of each experiment can be characterized
qualitatively and quantitatively. A qualitative result of an experiment
is called an **event**. For example, the presence of a useful signal at the
input of a system at a given instant is an event. The absence of a useful
signal at the input of the system at a given instant is also an event.

An arbitrary quantitative characteristic of an experiment, one that
can assume any of a number of possible values as a result of the experiment, is called a **random variable**. An example is the amount of useful
signal at the input of a system at a given instant of time. With each
random variable we can associate an event; for example, the event in

---

* The following presentation is intuitive and not axiomatic. It is designed to
bring the reader to a state of familiarity with the problems and tools in probability, Ed.

1

which the random variable assumes a value less than some specified number. With each event we can associate a random variable; for example, the number of occurrences of each event when $k(\geqslant 1)$ experiments are performed.

An event is said to be **certain** if it cannot fail to happen as the result of a given experiment. An event is said to be **impossible** if it cannot occur as the result of a given experiment. An event that can either happen or fail to happen as the result of an experiment is called a **random event**.

The **probability** $P(A)$ of an event A under the given conditions of an experiment is defined as the theoretical frequency of the event A about which the actual frequency of the event shows a tendency to fluctuate as the experiment is repeated. Obviously, we always have

$$0 \leqslant P(A) \leqslant 1. \tag{1.1}$$

In particular, for the case of a certain event we have $P(A) = 1$, and for the case of an impossible event we have $P(A) = 0$.

Let $A_1, \cdots, A_n$ denote events. The event in which at least one of these events occurs is called the **sum** of the events $A_1, \cdots, A_n$. The event in which all occur is called the **product** of these events.

The events $A_1, \cdots, A_n$ are said to be **mutually exclusive** if no two of them can occur as the result of a given experiment. *The probability of the sum of an arbitrary set (finite or infinite) of mutually exclusive events is equal to the sum of the probabilities of the individual events:*

$$P(A) = \sum_{i=1}^{n} P(A_i). \tag{1.2}$$

A set of events $A_1, \cdots, A_n$ is said to be **complete** if at least one of them must occur as the result of an experiment. Obviously, in this case,

$$\sum_{i=1}^{n} P(A_i) = 1. \tag{1.3}$$

Two mutually exclusive events constituting a complete set are said to be **opposite**. For example, the presence and absence of a useful signal at the input of a system are opposite events. We denote the event opposite to the event A by $\bar{A}$. On the basis of (1.3), we may write

$$P(A) + P(\bar{A}) = 1. \tag{1.4}$$

Let us suppose that under certain conditions we carry out a sequence of experiments in which an event A may occur or fail to occur in each experiment, and let us suppose that the probability of its occurrence is $P(A)$. At this stage, we call this probability the **unconditional probability**. Let us then, suppose that as a result of each of these experiments another event B may occur or fail to occur, and that the probability of its occurrence is $P(B)$. Out of all n experiments, let us consider only those results in which the event B occurred. Suppose that the number of such experiments is n_B. Out of these n_B experiments, let $n_{A/B}$ denote the number of experiments in which the event A occurred. We define the **conditional frequency** of the event A relative to the event B as the ratio of the number of experiments $n_{A/B}$ in which both events A and B occurred to the number n_B in which B occurred; that is, this conditional frequency is $n_{A/B}/n_B$. As we let n approach ∞, the conditional frequency of A relative to B approaches a number $P(A/B)$. We call this number the **conditional probability** of the event A relative to the event B. The number of experiments $n_{A/B}$ is equal to the number of experiments in which the event AB occurred. Consequently, the frequencies of the events AB, A/B (A relative to B), and B are equal respectively to

$$\frac{n_{A/B}}{n}, \; \frac{n_{A/B}}{n_B}, \; \frac{n_B}{n} \; .$$

As one can easily see, these numbers are related by

$$\frac{n_{A/B}}{n} = \frac{n_{A/B}}{n_B} \frac{n_B}{n} \; .$$

The corresponding probabilities of these three events are related by

$$P(AB) = P(A/B)P(B) \; .$$

By analogy, we obtain

$$P(AB) = P(B/A)P(A) \; .$$

Consequently,

$$P(AB) = P(A/B)P(B) = P(B/A)P(A) \; . \tag{1.5}$$

Thus, the conditional probability of A relative to B is equal to

$$P(A/B) = \frac{P(AB)}{P(B)} \; . \tag{1.6}$$

If $P(A/B) \neq P(A)$, the event A is said to be **dependent** on B. If $P(A/B) = P(A)$, the event A is said to be **independent** of B. From these definitions, it follows that the probability of joint occurrence of independent events is equal to the product of the probabilities of these events:

$$P(AB) = P(A)P(B) \; . \tag{1.7}$$

If we apply successively formula (1.5), we can obtain the following formula for the probability of the product of the events $A_1, \cdots, A_n$:

$$P(A_1 A_2 \cdots A_n) = P(A_1)P(A_2/A_1) \cdots P(A_n/A_1 A_2 \cdots A_{n-1}) \; . \tag{1.8}$$

In this case, the order in which we number the events is immaterial, and for independent events formula (1.8) takes the form

$$P(A_1 A_2 \cdots A_n) = P(A_1)P(A_2) \cdots P(A_n) \; . \tag{1.9}$$

Let $A_1, \cdots, A_n$ denote the incompatible events that constitute a complete set. Then, the event $A = A_1, + \cdots, + A_n$ is the certain event, and the probability of any other event B can be written as

$$P(B) = P(B[A_1 + \cdots + A_n]) = P(BA_1 + \cdots + BA_n) = \sum_{i=1}^{n} P(BA_i).$$

From this, we obtain by using formula (1.5)

$$P(B) = \sum_{i=1}^{n} P(A_i) P(B/A_i). \tag{1.10}$$

This formula is called the **formula for complete probability.**

From (1.5) and (1.10), we can obtain an expression for the conditional probability of the event A_k relative to B:

$$P(A_k/B) = \frac{P(A_k) P(B/A_k)}{P(B)} = \frac{P(A_k) P(B/A_k)}{\sum_{i=1}^{n} P(A_i) P(B/A_i)}. \tag{1.11}$$

This formula is known as **Bayes' formula** and it is used to calculate so-called *a posteriori* probabilities; that is, probabilities determined by the result of some experiment. Let us suppose that the probabilities of events A_i before an experiment—the *a priori* **probabilities**—are respectively $P(A_i)$, and that as a consequence of an experiment the event B occurs. By using this new information, we can determine the conditional probabilities $P(A_i/B)$ relative to the event B. These probabilities are called the *a posteriori* **probabilities.** Bayes' formula enables us to calculate the *a posteriori* probabilities $P(A_i/B)$ from the given *a priori* probabilities $P(A_i)$ and $P(B/A_i)$.

In accordance with the foregoing definition, a random variable is any quantity that assumes one and only one of a set of possible values as the result of an experiment. We shall denote random variables by capital letters and their possible values by the corresponding lower-case letters. In order to characterize a random variable completely, we need to give the set of its possible values and a means of determining the probabilities of these values. Such a characteristic of a random variable is called its **distribution law.** The distribution law of a random variable can be given in various forms. For example, for a discontinuous random variable X in which the set of possible values is either finite or countably infinite, the distribution law can be given in the form of a sequence of the possible values $x_1, x_2, x_3, \cdots$, and the corresponding probabilities can be given as

$$P_i = P(X = x_i), \quad i = 1, 2, 3, \cdots. \tag{1.12}$$

Here, the probabilities P_i must satisfy the condition

$$\sum_i P_i = 1, \tag{1.13}$$

since, in accordance with the definition of a random variable, the events

$X = x_i$ are mutually exclusive and constitute a complete set. However, the distribution law cannot be represented by equations of the form (1.12) for all random variables. For example, it is impossible to give the distribution law of a continuous random variable in the form (1.12), since the set of possible values of such a variable is uncountable.

The most general form for giving the distribution law of a random variable X is the distribution function or the integral distribution law $F(x)$; that is, the probability that $X < x$, where x is a variable quantity:

$$F(x) = P(X < x). \tag{1.14}$$

Every distribution function is a nondecreasing function of x; that is,

$$F(x') \leqslant F(x'') \text{ if } x' < x''.$$

Obviously,

$$F(-\infty) = 0, \quad F(+\infty) = 1. \tag{1.15}$$

If we know the distribution function $F(x)$, we can determine the probability in which the random variable X will fall in the interval $\alpha \leqslant X < \beta$. Specifically, the event $X < \beta$ is the sum of the mutually exclusive events $X < \alpha$ and $\alpha \leqslant X < \beta$. Therefore,

$$P(X < \beta) = P(X < \alpha) + P(\alpha \leqslant X < \beta).$$

Consequently,

$$P(\alpha \leqslant X < \beta) = F(\beta) - F(\alpha). \tag{1.16}$$

Taking the limit as $\beta \to \alpha$, we obtain

$$P(X = \alpha) = F(\alpha + 0) - F(\alpha).$$

If the distribution function is continuous at the point $x = \alpha$, then $P(X = \alpha) = 0$ and formula (1.16) can be rewritten in the form

$$P(\alpha < X < \beta) = F(\beta) - F(\alpha). \tag{1.17}$$

If the distribution function $F(x)$ is continuous and suitably differentiable on the entire real axis, the corresponding random variable X is said to be a **continuous random variable**. In this case, the derivative

$$f(x) = \frac{dF(x)}{dx} \tag{1.18}$$

is called **probability density** or the **differential distribution law** of the random variable X. Since the distribution function is a nondecreasing function, it follows that the probability density is a nonnegative function:

$$f(x) \geqslant 0 \tag{1.19}$$

Formula (1.17) can now be rewritten in the form

$$P(\alpha < X < \beta) = \int_{\alpha}^{\beta} f(x)dx. \tag{1.20}$$

Here, if we set $\alpha = -\infty$ and $\beta = x$, we obtain

$$F(x) = \int_{-\infty}^{x} f(x)dx. \tag{1.21}$$

Since $f(\infty) = 1$, we have

$$\int_{-\infty}^{\infty} f(x)dx = 1. \tag{1.22}$$

For example, if the random variable is uniformly distributed on the interval $a \leqslant X \leqslant b$, we have

$$f(x) = \begin{cases} \dfrac{1}{b-a} & \text{for} \quad a \leqslant x \leqslant b, \\ 0 & \text{for} \quad x < a, x > b; \end{cases}$$

$$F(x) = \begin{cases} 0 & \text{for} \quad x < a, \\ \dfrac{x-a}{b-a} & \text{for} \quad a \leqslant x \leqslant b, \\ 1 & \text{for} \quad x > b. \end{cases}$$

An arbitrary random variable, whether continuous, discrete, or mixed, has a distribution function. The probability density defined by formula (1.18) exists only for a continuous random variable if we confine ourselves to the class of ordinary functions. If we consider the δ-function (a special case of a generalized function [Ref. 17]) and differentiation of step functions, then an arbitrary random variable also has a probability density [Refs. 18, 47].

The distribution function $F(x)$ and the probability density $f(x)$ are both complete characteristics of a random variable. However, it is sometimes impossible or laborious to obtain these characteristics. In such cases, we need to confine ourselves to less complete probabilistic characteristics. Furthermore, in a number of problems it is possible to confine ourselves to a less complete characteristic of a random variable; for example, certain moments of the random variable.

The moment of order k of a random variable X is defined as the integral

$$a_k = \int_{-\infty}^{\infty} x^k f(x)dx, \quad k = 1, 2, \cdots, \tag{1.23}$$

where $f(x)$ is the probability density of the random variable X. The first two moments α_1 and α_2 are of particular importance. The first-order moment α_1 is called the **mathematical expectation** or the **mean** of the random variable. We denote by M the operator for obtaining the mathematical expectation, and we denote the value of the mathematical expectation itself by m_x. Thus, we may write

$$m_x = M[X] = \int_{-\infty}^{\infty} xf(x)dx. \tag{1.24}$$

Generalizing formula (1.24), we define the mathematical expectation of an arbitrary function $\varphi(X)$ of a random variable X by

$$m_\varphi = M[\varphi(X)] = \int_{-\infty}^{\infty} \varphi(x)f(x)dx. \tag{1.25}$$

The mathematical expectation characterizes only the mean value of a random variable; it does not characterize the spread of the possible values of the random variable about that mean value. The extent of this spread can be characterized by the central moments of the random variable. The **central moment of order k** of a random variable X is defined as the kth-order moment of the difference $(X - m_x)$; that is, the deviation of the random variable X from its mathematical expectation:

$$\mu_k = M[(X - m_x)^k] = \int_{-\infty}^{\infty} (x - m_x)^k f(x)dx, \quad k = 1, 2, \cdots \tag{1.26}$$

It is easy to see that $\mu_1 = 0$.

Of especial importance is the second-order central moment, known as the **variance** of the random variable. The variance is defined by

$$D_x = M[(X - m_x)^2] = \int_{-\infty}^{\infty} (x - m_x)^2 f(x)dx. \tag{1.27}$$

It characterizes the spread of values of a random variable about its mean value. The greater the variance, the greater is this spread.

To solve certain problems in probability theory, it is sufficient to know the mathematical expectation and the variance of a random variable. Sometimes, instead of the variance, we use the **mean square deviation** of a random variable. This is defined as the nonnegative square root of the variance:

$$\sigma_x = \sqrt{D_x}. \tag{1.28}$$

The central moments of a random variable can be expressed in terms of its moments α_k. To distinguish these from the central moments, one often calls them **initial moments.** In particular, the variance can be expressed in terms of the second initial moment and the mathematical expectation as follows:

$$D_x = \alpha_2 - m_x^2. \tag{1.29}$$

Thus, knowing the pair of moments m_x and D_x is equivalent to knowing the pair m_x and α_2. In each particular problem, we use whichever pair we find more convenient.

The distribution law of a random variable that is most widely used in practice is what is known as a **normal** or **Gaussian** distribution law. For this law, the probability density is given by the formula

$$f(x) = \frac{1}{\sqrt{2\pi D_x}} \exp\left\{-\frac{(x - m_x)^2}{2D_x}\right\} \tag{1.30}$$

Here, m_x and D_x are numbers equal respectively to the mathematical expectation and the variance of the random variable X. This can easily be verified from formulas (1.24) and (1.27).

For a normal law, the distribution function can be obtained from formulas (1.21) and (1.30):

$$F(x) = \frac{1}{\sqrt{2\pi D_x}} \int_{-\infty}^{x} \exp\left\{-\frac{(x-m_x)^2}{2D_x}\right\} dx$$

$$= \frac{1}{\sqrt{2\pi}} \int_{-\infty}^{\frac{x-m_x}{\sigma_x}} \exp\left\{-\frac{x^2}{2}\right\} dx. \tag{1.31}$$

In probability theory, one encounters the function

$$\Phi(u) = \frac{1}{\sqrt{2\pi}} \int_{0}^{u} \exp\left\{-\frac{t^2}{2}\right\} dt, \tag{1.32}$$

which is known as " Gauss's function." Tables have been compiled for this function (cf. Appendix 1). From (1.32) it is obvious that the function $\Phi(u)$ is an odd function:

$$\Phi(-u) = -\Phi(u),$$

and that $\Phi(\infty) = 1/2$. In view of what we have said, by using equation (1.31) we can write, for a normal distribution law,

$$F(x) = \frac{1}{2} + \Phi\left(\frac{x-m_x}{\sigma_x}\right). \tag{1.33}$$

We can obtain from (1.17) and (1.33) a formula for the probability expressing that a random variable with a normal distribution will fall in the interval $\alpha < X < \beta$:

$$P(\alpha < X < \beta) = \Phi\left(\frac{\beta-m_x}{\sigma_x}\right) - \Phi\left(\frac{\alpha-m_x}{\sigma_x}\right). \tag{1.34}$$

In many problems, we need to consider several random variables simultaneously. For example, in artillery practice, we need to consider the coordinates of the point at which a shell lands or, in measuring a complicated object, we need to consider the errors made in the various measurements. A set of random variables $X_1, \cdots, X_n$ can be regarded as the Cartesian coordinates of the point or as components of a random vector $X = (X_1, \cdots, X_n)$ in n-dimensional space. Let us first look at the case in which $n = 2$; that is, $X = (X_1, X_2)$. The **joint distribution function** of the random variables X_1 and X_2 or the distribution function of the two-dimensional random vector with components X_1 and X_2 is defined as the probability of the satisfaction of both the inequalities $X_1 < x_1$ and $X_2 < x_2$:

$$F(x_1, x_2) = P(X_1 < x_1, X_2 < x_2), \tag{1.35}$$

where x_1 and x_2 are variable quantities. Here,

$$F(-\infty, x_2) \equiv 0, \quad F(x_1, -\infty) \equiv 0,$$
$$F(\infty, x_2) \equiv F_2(x_2), \quad F(x_1, \infty) \equiv F_1(x_1), \quad F(\infty, \infty) = 1.$$

One can easily show that the distribution function $F(x_1, x_2)$ is a non-decreasing function of each variable for a fixed value of the other one, and that the probability that a random point (X_1, X_2) will fall in a given rectangle can be computed from the formula

$$P(\alpha \leqslant X_1 < \beta, \gamma \leqslant X_2 < \delta)$$
$$= F(\beta, \delta) - F(\alpha, \delta) - F(\beta, \gamma) + F(\alpha, \gamma). \tag{1.36}$$

The **distribution function** of an n-dimensional random vector $X = (x_1, \cdots, x_n)$ is defined as the probability that all the inequalities $X_k < x_L$, for $k = 1, \cdots, n$, will be satisfied:

$$F(x) = F(x_1, \cdots, x_n) = P(X_k < x_k), \quad k = 1, \cdots, n. \tag{1.37}$$

The properties of the distribution function of a two-dimensional random vector are easily generalized to the distribution function of an n-dimensional random vector. The distribution functions are sufficiently general characteristics of random vectors. Sometimes it is convenient to use the probability density of random vectors.

The **probability density** of an n-dimensional random vector is defined as the mixed partial derivative of order n of the distribution function

$$f(x) = f(x_1, \cdots, x_n) = \frac{\partial^n F(x_1, \cdots, x_n)}{\partial x_1, \cdots, \partial x_n}. \tag{1.38}$$

The probability that the vector X will fall in a region Ω of n-dimensional space is

$$P(X \in \Omega) = \int_\Omega f(x_1, \cdots, x_n) dx_1 \cdots dx_n = \int_\Omega f(x) dx. \tag{1.39}$$

From this it follows that

$$\int_{-\infty}^{\infty} \cdots \int_{-\infty}^{\infty} f(x_1, \cdots, x_n) dx_1 \cdots dx_n = 1. \tag{1.40}$$

If we integrate the probability density of the n-dimensional vector with respect to the variables $x_{m+1}, \cdots, x_n$ for some $m \leqslant n - 1$, we obtain the probability density of the random variables corresponding to the remaining variables:

$$= \int_{-\infty}^{\infty} \cdots \int_{-\infty}^{\infty} f(x_1, \cdots, x_m, \cdots, x_n) dx_{m+1} \cdots dx_n. \tag{1.41}$$

If the components X_1 and X_2 of a two-dimensional random vector X are dependent, then fixing a value of one of them influences the probability distribution of the other. Suppose that $f(x_1/x_2) dx_1$ is the probability that a random variable X_1 will assume a value in a fixed interval $[x_1, x_1 + dx_1]$ under the condition that the random variable X_2 has a fixed value x_2. The probability density $f(x_1/x_2)$ for X_1 with fixed $X_2 = x_2$ is called the **conditional probability density.** If we know the joint probability density $f(x_1, x_2)$, we can easily find the conditional probability density $f(x_1/x_2)$. Specifically, on the basis of the theorem for multiplying probabilities, we can easily write the approximate equation

$$f(x_1, x_2)dx_1dx_2 \approx [f(x_1)dx_1]\left[f\left(\frac{x_2}{x_1}\right)dx_2\right]$$

$$\approx [f(x_2)dx_2]\left[f\left(\frac{x_1}{x_2}\right)dx_1\right].$$

The smaller the values of dx_1 and dx_2, the more accurate will be this approximation. Therefore, by letting dx_1 and dx_2 approach 0, we see that

$$f(x_1, x_2) = f(x_1)f\left(\frac{x_2}{x_1}\right) = f(x_2)f\left(\frac{x_1}{x_2}\right). \tag{1.42}$$

Formula (1.42) can easily be generalized to an *n*-dimensional random vector.

If we are studying simultaneously several random variables, we may need to use, in addition to their separate moments, the mixed moments of these random variables. The **mixed moment** of order $p + s$ of two random variables X_1 and X_2 is defined as the mathematical expectation of the random variable $X_1^p X_2^s$:

$$\alpha_{ps} = M[X_1^p X_2^s]. \tag{1.43}$$

The **mixed central moment of order** $p + s$ of these variables is defined as the mathematical expectation of the quantity $(X_1 - m_{x_1})^p(X_2 - m_{x_2})^s$:

$$\mu_{ps} = M[(X_1 - m_{x_1})^p(X_2 - m_{x_2})^s]. \tag{1.44}$$

Of the mixed moments, of especial significance is the second-order mixed central moment μ_{11}, commonly known as the **correlation moment.** We denote it by $K_{x_1 x_2}$:

$$K_{x_1 x_2} = \mu_{11} = M[(X_1 - m_{x_1})(X_2 - m_{x_2})], \tag{1.45}$$

or

$$K_{x_1 x_2} = \int_{-\infty}^{\infty}\int_{-\infty}^{\infty}(x_1 - m_{x_1})(x_2 - m_{x_2})f(x_1, x_2)dx_1dx_2$$

$$= \alpha_{11} - m_{x_1}m_{x_2}. \tag{1.46}$$

The correlation moment characterizes the dependence between the two random variables X_1 and X_2. If X_1 and X_2 are independent, we have $f(x_1, x_2) = f(x_1)f(x_2)$ and $K_{x_1 x_2} = 0$. Instead of the correlation moment of random variables, we frequently use the **correlation coefficient**

$$r_{x_1 x_2} = \frac{K_{x_1 x_2}}{\sqrt{D_{x_1}D_{x_2}}} = \frac{K_{x_1 x_2}}{\sigma_{x_1}\sigma_{x_2}}. \tag{1.47}$$

This quantity is always a dimensionless one. Both the correlation coefficient and the correlation moment of two independent variables are always equal to 0. The converse of this statement does not hold: The correlation coefficient and the correlation moment can be equal to 0 even in the case of dependent random variables. A sufficient condition for the vanishing of the correlation moment of two random variables X_1 and X_2 is that the probability density $f(x_1, x_2)$ be symmetric about one of the straight lines $x_1 = m_{x_1}$, $x_2 = m_{x_2}$ (cf. (1.46)).

Two random variables X_1 and X_2 are said to be **correlated** if their correlation moment is nonzero, and they are said to be **uncorrelated** if their correlation moment is zero.

The mathematical expectation of an arbitrary function of n random variables $X_1, \cdots, X_n$ is defined by

$$m_\varphi = M[\varphi(X_1, \cdots, X_n)]$$
$$= \int_{-\infty}^{\infty} \cdots \int_{-\infty}^{\infty} \varphi(x_1, \cdots, x_n) f(x_1, \cdots, x_n) dx_1 \cdots dx_n. \quad (1.48)$$

If we set

$$\varphi(X_1, \cdots, X_n) = X_1^{p_1} \cdots X_n^{p_n},$$

in (1.48), we obtain the moment of the n-dimensional random vector $X = (X_1, \cdots, X_n)$ of order $p_1 + \cdots + p_n$:

$$\alpha_{p_1 \cdots p_n} = M[X_1^{p_1} \cdots X_n^{p_n}]. \quad (1.49)$$

The central moment of an n-dimensional random vector X of order $p_1 + \cdots + p_n$ is defined by

$$\mu_{p_1, \cdots p_n} = M[\overset{0}{X}_1^{p_1} \cdots \overset{0}{X}_n^{p_n}]. \quad (1.50)$$

The notation $\overset{0}{X}_\nu$ stands (here and in the remainder of the book) for the deviation of the random variable X_ν from its mathematical expectation:

$$\overset{0}{X}_\nu = X_\nu - m_{x_\nu}.$$

The **mathematical expectation** of a random vector $X = (X_1, \cdots, X_n)$ is defined as the n-dimensional vector $m_x = m_{x_1}, \cdots, m_{x_n})$, the components of which are equal to the mathematical expectations of the corresponding components $X_1, \cdots, X_n$. The correlation moments of the components of the vector $X_1, \cdots, X_n$ are defined by

$$K_{\nu\mu} = M[\overset{0}{X}_\nu \overset{0}{X}_\mu], \quad \nu, \mu = 1, \cdots, n. \quad (1.51)$$

For $\mu = \nu$, this formula yields the variances of the random variables $X_1, \cdots, X_n$:

$$D_{x_\nu} = K_{\nu\nu} = M[\overset{0}{X}_\nu^2]. \quad (1.52)$$

The set of correlation moments of the components of a random vector constitutes the **correlation matrix** of that vector as follows:

$$K = \begin{Vmatrix} K_{11} & K_{12} & \cdots & K_{1n} \\ K_{21} & K_{22} & \cdots & K_{2n} \\ \cdots\cdots\cdots\cdots\cdots \\ \cdots\cdots\cdots\cdots\cdots \\ K_{n1} & K_{n2} & \cdots & K_{nn} \end{Vmatrix}. \tag{1.53}$$

This matrix is symmetric, since we always have $K_{\nu\mu} = K_{\mu\nu}$ as is obvious from formula (1.51).

Sometimes, a random vector can be characterized merely by its mathematical expectation and correlation matrix. For example, the mathematical expectation m_n and the correlation matrix (1.53) of a normally distributed random vector completely determine its probability density. The multidimensional probability density is expressed in this case in terms of m_x and $K_{\nu\mu}$ [Refs. 18, 47] as follows:

$$f(x_1, \cdots, x_n)$$
$$= \frac{1}{\sqrt{2^n \pi^n |K|}} \exp\left\{ -\frac{2}{2|K|} \sum_{\nu,\mu=1}^{n} K^{\nu\mu}(x_\nu - m_{x_\nu})(x_\mu - m_{x_\mu}) \right\}, \tag{1.54}$$

where $|K|$ is the determinant of the matrix K, and $K^{\nu\mu}$ is the cofactor of the element $K_{\nu\mu}$ in the determinant of the correlation matrix K.

A more complicated object is a **random function,** defined as a mapping that maps each member of its domain of definition into a random variable. The argument of a random function can be of an arbitrary nature. In the cases most commonly encountered in practice, the argument is time. As the result of an experiment, a random function may assume various specific forms. These possible values of the random function are called its **sample functions.** In the following examination, we shall denote random functions by capital letters of the Roman alphabet: $X(t)$, $Y(t)$. And we shall denote their sample functions by the corresponding lower-case letters: $x(t)$, $y(t)$.

As a subject of mathematical investigation, a random function is considerably more complicated than an ordinary random variable, since it is equivalent to an infinite (uncountable in fact) set of random variables.

For every value of the argument t, the value of the random function $X(t)$ is a random variable. Therefore, a complete probabilistic characteristic of $X(t)$ for every given value of t is the distribution law of the value of the random function $X(t)$ for that value of t. This distribution law $f_1(x, t)$ is called the **one-dimensional distribution law** of the random function $X(t)$. In the general case, it depends on t (treated as a parameter). The one-dimensional distribution law is sufficient for solving those problems in which the values of the random function for different values of the argument are treated separately from each other. On the other hand, to consider simultaneously the values of the random function at two or more values of the argument, we introduce the joint distribution laws of the values of the random function for several values of the argument. The **two-dimensional distribution law** of a random function $X(t)$ is defined as the joint distribution law of its values $X(t_1)$ and $X(t_2)$ for any two values of the argument t. The **n-dimensional distribution law** of the random function $X(t)$ is defined as the distribution law of the set of values $X(t_1), \cdots, X(t_n)$ of the random variable $X(t)$ for n arbitrary values $t_1, \cdots, t_n$ of the argument t. Ordinarily, an n-dimensional distribution law of a random function $X(t)$ is completely characterized by its n-dimensional probability density $f_n(x_1, \cdots, x_n, t_1, \cdots, t_n)$, which depends in the general case on the values $t_1, \cdots, t_n$ of the argument t. These values are treated as parameters.

If the values of a random function $X(t)$ are independent random variables for arbitrary distinct values of the argument $t_1, \cdots, t_n$, then the n-dimensional probability density of the random function $X(t)$ is, in accordance with (1.9) and the definition of independence of random variables, expressed for arbitrary n in terms of its one-dimensional probability density according to the formula

$$f_n(x_1, \cdots, x_n, t_1, \cdots, t_n) = f_1(x_1, t_1) \cdots f_1(x_n, t_n). \qquad (1.55)$$

This formula states that an exhaustive characteristic of a random function with independent values is its one-dimensional distribution law.

For normally distributed random functions, an exhaustive characteristic is the two-dimensional distribution law. We assume that a random function is normally distributed if the set of its values $X(t_1)$, $\cdots, X(t_n)$ constitutes, for arbitrary $t_1, \cdots, t_n$, a normally distributed random vector. It was previously shown that an n-dimensional normal distribution law is completely determined by the mathematical expectation and the correlation moments of the random variables [cf. (1.54)]. However, the mathematical expectations of the random variables $X(t_1)$, $\cdots, X(t_n)$ are completely determined by the one-dimensional distribution law of the random variable $X(t)$, and their correlation moments are completely determined by the two-dimensional distribution law of the random function $X(t)$. Consequently, a two-dimensional distribution law of a normally distributed random function completely determines its n-dimensional distribution law for arbitrary n, and hence it is an exhaustive characteristic of that random function.

Markov random processes [Ref. 47] constitute a second example of random functions for which the two-dimensional distribution law is an exhaustive characteristic.

In other cases, to get a complete characteristic of a random function, we need to know the n-dimensional distribution law, in which n is a large number or possibly for all n.

Many-dimensional distribution laws of several random functions are defined analogously.

Distribution laws of a random function $X(t)$ are more or less complete characteristics of a random function, but, in actual investigations of automatic-control systems, they prove to be quite complicated. Therefore, it is expedient to consider simpler characteristics of random functions; namely, the mathematical expectation and the correlation function.

The **mathematical expectation** $m_x(t)$ of a random function $X(t)$ is defined by

$$m_x(t) = M[X(t)] = \int_{-\infty}^{\infty} x f_1(x, t)dx. \tag{1.56}$$

It is a sort of mean function about which all possible sample functions of the random function are grouped.

The **correlation function** $K_x(t_1, t_2)$ of a random function $X(t)$ is defined as the correlation moment of the values $X(t_1)$ and $X(t_2)$:

$$\begin{aligned} K_x(t_1, t_2) &= M[\overset{0}{X}(t_1)\overset{0}{X}(t_2)] \\ &= M[\{X(t_1) - m_x(t_1)\}\{X(t_2) - m_x(t_2)\}]. \end{aligned} \tag{1.57}$$

In accordance with formula (1.46), the correlation function of a random function $X(t)$ can be expressed in terms of its two-dimensional probability density $f_2(x_1, x_2; t_1, t_2)$:

$$\begin{aligned} &K_x(t_1, t_2) \\ &= \int_{-\infty}^{\infty}\int_{-\infty}^{\infty} [x_1 - m_x(t_1)][x_2 - m_x(t_2)]f_2(x_1, x_2; t_1, t_2)dx_1dx_2. \end{aligned} \tag{1.58}$$

The variance of a random function can be defined as the value of the correlation function for $t_1 = t_2 = t$:

$$\begin{aligned} D_x(t) &= K_x(t, t) = M[\{\overset{0}{X}(t)\}^2] \\ &= \int_{-\infty}^{\infty}\int_{-\infty}^{\infty} [x - m_x(t)]^2 f_1(x, t)dx, \end{aligned} \tag{1.59}$$

where

$$f_1(x, t) = f_2(x, x; t, t).$$

The **joint correlation function** of two random functions $X(t)$ and $Y(t)$, denoted by $K_{xy}(t_1, t_2)$, is defined as the correlation moment of the values $X(t_1)$ and $Y(t_2)$ of these two functions:

$$K_{xy}(t_1, t_2) = M[\overset{0}{X}(t_1)\overset{0}{Y}(t_2)]. \tag{1.60}$$

If $K_{xy}(t_1, t_2) \equiv 0$, then the random functions $X(t)$ and $Y(t)$ are said to be **uncorrelated.** On the other hand, if $K_{xy}(t_1, t_2)$ is not identically equal to zero, then $X(t)$ and $Y(t)$ are said to be **correlated.**

In accordance with (1.60), the mutual correlation function of two random functions $X(t)$ and $Y(t)$ can be expressed in terms of their two-dimensional probability density $f_2(x, y; t_1, t_2)$:

$$K_{xy}(t_1,\ t_2)$$
$$= \int_{-\infty}^{\infty}\int_{-\infty}^{\infty} [x - m_x(t)][y - m_y(t_2)] f_2(x,\ y;\ t_1,\ t_2)\,dx\,dy. \quad (1.61)$$

The mathematical expectation and the correlation function are less complete characteristics of a random function than are its distribution laws. However, the mathematical expectation and the correlation function are sometimes exhaustive characteristics of a random function; for example, if the random function has a normal distribution law.

In certain cases, instead of a correlation function, we use the normalized correlation function. The **normalized correlation function** $R_x(t_1,\ t_2)$ of a random function $X(t)$ is defined as the correlation coefficient of its values for various values of the argument:

$$R_x(t_1,\ t_2) = \frac{K_x(t_1,\ t_2)}{\sqrt{K_x(t_1,\ t_1)\,K_x(t_2,\ t_2)}}. \quad (1.62)$$

Analogously, the **normalized joint correlation function** of two random functions $X(t)$ and $Y(t)$ is defined as the correlation coefficient of their values for arbitrary values of their arguments:

$$R_{xy}(t_1,\ t_2) = \frac{K_{xy}(t_1,\ t_2)}{\sqrt{K_x(t_1,\ t_1)\,K_y(t_2,\ t_2)}}. \quad (1.63)$$

The **initial second-order moment** $\Gamma_x(t_1,\ t_2)$ of a random function $X(t)$ is defined as the initial second-order moment of its values for arbitrary values of the argument:

$$\Gamma_x(t_1,\ t_2) = M[X(t_1)X(t_2)] = K_x(t_1,\ t_2) + m_x(t_1)m_x(t_2). \quad (1.64)$$

Let us enumerate certain properties, which can be easily proved, of the correlation functions.

(1) A correlation function is symmetric, that is,

$$K_x(t_1,\ t_2) = K_x(t_2,\ t_1). \quad (1.65)$$

(2) The absolute value of a correlation function for values of the arguments t_1 and t_2 does not exceed the goemetric mean of the values of the variances $D(t_1) = K_x(t_1,\ t_1)$ and $D(t_2) = K_x(t_2,\ t_2)$:

$$|K_x(t_1,\ t_2)| \leqslant \sqrt{K_x(t_1,\ t_1)\,K_x(t_2,\ t_2)}. \quad (1.66)$$

(3) The correlation function of a random function remains invariant if we add to the random function an arbitrary nonrandom function.

(4) The two correlation functions K_{xy} and K_{yx} are related by

$$K_{xy}(t_1,\ t_2) = K_{yx}(t_2,\ t_1). \quad (1.67)$$

(5) The joint correlation function $K_{xy}(t_1,\ t_2)$ does not exceed in absolute value the geometric mean of the variances $D_x(t_1) = K_x(t_1,\ t_1)$ and $D_y(t_2) = K_y(t_2,\ t_2)$:

$$K_{xy}(t_1,\ t_2) \leqslant \sqrt{K_x(t_1,\ t_1)\,K_y(t_2,\ t_2)}. \quad (1.68)$$

(6) A normalized correlation function does not exceed unity under absolute value:

$$|R_x(t_1, t_2)| \leqslant 1.$$

In practice, we often encounter random functions that are sums of several other random functions:

$$Z(t) = \sum_{\nu=1}^{n} X_\nu(t). \tag{1.69}$$

In this case, the mathematical expectation $m_z(t)$ and the correlation function $K_z(t_1, t_2)$ can be determined by

$$m_z(t) = \sum_{\nu=1}^{n} m_{x_\nu}(t), \tag{1.70}$$

$$K_z(t_1, t_2) = \sum_{\nu,\mu=1}^{n} K_{\nu\mu}(t_1, t_2), \tag{1.71}$$

where

$$m_{x_\nu}(t) = M[X_\nu(t)],$$

$$K_{\nu\mu}(t_1, t_2) = M[\overset{0}{X}_\nu(t_1)\overset{0}{X}_\mu(t_2)], \quad \nu, \mu = 1, \cdots, n.$$

If the random functions $X_\nu(t)$ are not correlated, formula (1.71) becomes simplified:

$$K_z(t_1, t_2) = \sum_{\nu=1}^{n} K_{\nu\nu}(t_1, t_2) = \sum_{\nu=1}^{n} K_{x_\nu}(t_1, t_2). \tag{1.72}$$

In investigating random functions, one often finds it convenient to use canonical decompositions of random functions [Refs. 46, 47]. A **canonical decomposition** of a random function $X(t)$ is defined as any representation of that function as the sum of its mathematical expectation $m_x(t)$ and mutually uncorrelated elementary random functions $V_\nu x_\nu(t)$:

$$X(t) = m_x(t) + \sum_\nu V_\nu x_\nu(t), \tag{1.73}$$

where the $x_\nu(t)$ are nonrandom functions, the V_ν are mutually uncorrelated random variables whose mathematical expectations are zero, and the $V_\nu x_\nu(t)$ are elementary random functions. In this case, the correlation function $K_x(t_1, t_2)$ can be defined by the formula

$$K_x(t_1, t_2) = M[\overset{0}{X}(t_1)\overset{0}{X}(t_2)] = M\left[\sum_\nu V_\nu x_\nu(t_1) \sum_\nu V_\nu x_\nu(t_2)\right]$$

$$= \sum_\nu D_\nu x_\nu(t_1) x_\nu(t_2), \tag{1.74}$$

where $D_\nu = M[x_\nu^2]$ is the variance of the random variable V_ν.

In formulas (1.73) and (1.74), the index of summation ν can vary over either finite or infinite domains. A canonical decomposition for an individual random function is not unique, for each random function has infinitely many canonical decompositions.

A special form of random function is a stationary random function. A random function $X(t)$ is said to be **stationary in the wide sense** if its mathematical expectation is constant and the correlation function depends only on the difference in the arguments:

$$K_x(t_1,\ t_2) = K_x(t_2 - t_1) = K_x(\tau), \tag{1.75}$$

where $\tau = t_2 - t_1$. A random function $X(t)$ is said to be **stationary in the strict sense** if its n-dimensional distribution law depends for arbitrary n on the intervals $[t_i,\ t_j]$ and not on the position of these intervals on the t-axis. In what follows, when we speak of stationary random functions, we shall always mean stationary in the wide sense.

One can easily see that, for any stationary random function $X(t)$,

(1) $D_x(t) = K_x(t,\ t) = K_x(0) = \text{const},$

(2) $K_x(\tau) = K_x(-\tau),$

(3) $|K_x(\tau)| < K_x(0).$

In the literature on the statistical dynamics of automatic systems, one often uses the concept of an ergodic random function. Let us give some of the basic facts of such functions. Pugachev [Ref. 47] gives a proof of the following (ergodic) theorem:

If the mathematical expectation of a random function is constant and the correlation function satisfies the equation

$$\lim_{T \to \infty} \frac{1}{T^2} \int_0^T \int_0^T K_x(t_1,\ t_2)\,dt_1\,dt_2 = 0, \tag{*}$$

then the mean-square limit of the mean value of the random function over the region T is the mathematical expectation of the random function. Conversely, if the mean-square limit of the mean value over the region T of a random function with constant mathematical expectation is equal to the mathematical expectation of the random function, its correlation function satisfies condition (*).

One can easily see that a sufficient condition for (*) is that the correlation function $K_x(t_1,\ t_2)$ approach zero as the absolute value of the difference in the arguments $|t_2 - t_1|$ becomes infinite.

A random function satisfying the hypothesis of the ergodic theorem is called an **ergodic random function**. The ergodic theorem as applied to a stationary random function can be formulated as follows:

For the relation

$$\lim_{T \to \infty} \frac{1}{T} \int_0^T X(t)\,dt = m_x \tag{1.76}$$

to be satisfied, it is necessary and sufficient that the correlation function $K_x(\tau)$ of a stationary random function $X(t)$ satisfy the condition

$$\lim_{T \to \infty} \frac{1}{T} \int_0^T \left(1 - \frac{\tau}{T}\right) K_x(\tau) d\tau = 0. \qquad (**)$$

Equation (1.76) is satisfied with probability 1. It follows from the relation (**) that a stationary random function X is ergodic if its correlation function $K_x(\tau)$ decreases in absolute value to zero as $|\tau|$ becomes infinite.

One can easily see that the condition (**) is satisfied by the correlation functions

$$K_x(\tau) = D_x e^{-\alpha|\tau|}, \qquad (a)$$
$$K_x(\tau) = D_x \delta(\tau), \qquad (b)$$
$$K_x(\tau) = D_x \cos \omega\tau, \qquad (c)$$

where D_x, α, and ω are constants. However, a correlation function of the form

$$K_x(\tau) = D_x. \qquad (d)$$

does not satisfy that condition.

Thus, if a random function is ergodic, its mathematical expectation can be determined from formula (1.76); that is, by taking the time average of a sufficiently protracted sample function.

The following question now arises: Is it not also possible to obtain the correlation function of a stationary random function from a single sample function? It turns out that, for the relation

$$K_x(\tau) = \lim_{T \to \infty} \frac{1}{T} \int_0^T \overset{0}{X}(t) \overset{0}{X}(t + \tau) dt \qquad (1.77)$$

to be valid, it is necessary and sufficient that the correlation function $K_x(\tau)$ of a normally distributed stationary random function $X(t)$ satisfy the condition

$$\lim_{T \to \infty} \frac{1}{T} \int_0^\infty \left(1 - \frac{\tau}{T}\right) [K_x^2(\tau) + K_x(\tau + \tau_0) K_x(\tau - \tau_0)] d\tau = 0. \quad (***)$$

Equation (1.77) is satisfied with probability 1. A stationary random function for which the relation (***) is satisfied is said to be **ergodic with respect to the correlation function.**

It follows from the condition (***) that a normally distributed stationary random function is ergodic with respect to the correlation function if its correlation function $K_x(\tau)$ decreases in absolute value to zero as $|\tau| \to \infty$. One can easily see that the correlation functions (a) and (b) previously defined satisfy condition (***), but that the correlation functions (c) and (d) do not.

Formulas (1.76) and (1.77) are of great practical importance. They enable us to curtail the amount of experimental labor and to simplify the experimental procedure in determining the mathematical expectation and the correlation function of the random function $X(t)$ being studied. Sometimes, these functions are also quite convenient in theoretical investigations.

Two stationary random functions $X(t)$ and $Y(t)$ are said to be **stationarily connected** if their joint correlation function K_{xy} depends only on the difference $t_2 - t_1$:

$$K_{xy}(t_1, t_2) = K_{xy}(t_2 - t_1) = K_{xy}(\tau).$$

The Fourier transform of the correlation function $K_x(\tau)$ of a stationary random function $X(t)$

$$S_x(\omega) = \int_{-\infty}^{\infty} K_x(\tau) e^{-j\omega\tau} d\tau \tag{1.78}$$

is called the **spectral density** of that random function. By means of the inverse Fourier transformation, we can obtain the correlation function $K_x(\tau)$ from the spectral density:

$$K_x(\tau) = \frac{1}{2\pi} \int_{-\infty}^{\infty} S_x(\omega) e^{j\omega\tau} d\omega. \tag{1.79}$$

Formulas (1.78) and (1.79) can be rewritten in another form by using Euler's familiar formulas:

$$S_x(\omega) = 2 \int_0^{\infty} K_x(\tau) \cos \omega\tau \, d\tau, \tag{1.78a}$$

$$K_x(\tau) = \frac{1}{\pi} \int_0^{\infty} S_x(\omega) \cos \omega\tau \, d\omega. \tag{1.79a}$$

Analogously, the Fourier transform of the joint correlation function $K_{xy}(\tau)$

$$S_{xy}(\omega) = \int_{-\infty}^{\infty} K_{xy}(\tau) e^{-j\omega\tau} d\tau \tag{1.80}$$

is called the **joint spectral density** of the random functions $X(t)$ and $Y(t)$.

A random function for which $S(\omega) = S_0$ is constant is called a **white noise**. The correlation function of a white noise $K_x(\tau)$ is equal to

$$K_x(\tau) = S_0 \delta(\tau), \tag{1.81}$$

where $\delta(\tau)$ is the unit δ-function defined by

$$\delta(\tau) = \begin{cases} 0 & \text{for } \tau \neq 0, \\ \infty & \text{for } \tau = 0, \end{cases} \quad \int_{-\varepsilon}^{+\varepsilon} \delta(\tau) d\tau = 1 \quad \text{for arbitrary } \varepsilon > 0.$$

2. TRANSFORMATION OF A RANDOM FUNCTION BY A DYNAMICAL SYSTEM AND ITS PROBABILISTIC CHARACTERISTICS

One of the most important practical problems in the theory of random functions is the problem of transforming a random function by means of an automatic-control system. An automatic-control system transforms an input variable into an output variable. From a mathematical point of view, an automatic-control system maps one time function into another time function. By each particular system, given functions at the input of the system are put in correspondence with specific functions at the output of the system. In mathematics, a symbol mapping each function of a given set into a function of another set is called an **operator.** The concept of an operator is a natural generalization of the concepts of function and functional.

A **functional** is defined as a mapping that assigns to every member of a given set of functions a member of a given set of numbers. A **function** is a mapping that assigns to every member of a given set of numbers a member of another set of numbers. Thus, a function sets up a correspondence between elements of two sets of numbers, a functional sets up a correspondence between a set of functions and a set of numbers, and an operator sets up a correspondence between two sets of functions. Examples of operators are differentiation, (indefinite) integration, (the unique) solution of differential, integral, and other functional equations.

The correspondence between two functions $x(t)$ and $y(s)$ that is set up by an operator A is written as

$$y(s) = Ax(t) \tag{1.82}$$

or

$$y(s) = A\{x(t), s\}. \tag{1.83}$$

The arguments of the functions x and y can, in the general case, be different quantities (scalar or vector). In automatic-control theory, the arguments t and s are quite often two different values of the same variable; for example, time. An automatic control system and the operator corresponding to it can be either linear or nonlinear.

An operator A is said to be **linear** if

$$A \sum_{k=1}^{n} C_k x_k(t) = \sum_{k=1}^{n} C_k A x_k(t), \tag{1.84}$$

where the C_k are arbitrary numbers and the $x_k(t)$ are arbitrary functions in a given class.

In applications, we sometimes have occasion to deal with a **nonhomogeneous linear operator** L defined by

$$y(s) = Lx(t) = Ax(t) + \varphi(s), \tag{1.85}$$

where A is a linear operator and $\varphi(s)$ is a function independent of the argument function $x(t)$.

The following are examples of linear operators:
(a) The differentation operator

$$y(t) = \frac{d}{dt}x(t),$$

(b) a linear integral operator corresponding to a given weight function $w(s, t)$ of the system:

$$y(s) = \int_0^s w(s, t)\, x(t)\, dt.$$

A nonlinear operator is one that does not satisfy the identity (1.84). The following are examples of nonlinear operators:

(a) $$y(t) = x(t)\frac{dx(t)}{dt},$$

(b) a nonlinear integral operator of the form

$$y(s) = \int_0^T \varphi[x(t),\, t,\, s]\, dt, \tag{1.86}$$

where $\varphi(x, t, s)$ is a given function that is nonlinear in x.

The laws of transformation of probabilistic characteristics of random functions are quite simple in the case of linear transformations. In certain cases, the theory of linear transformations can be applied to the approximate determination of probabilistic characteristics of random functions obtained as the result of nonlinear transformations. Therefore, it is expedient for us to study first linear transformations of random functions.

Of great practical interest is the problem of finding the probabilistic characteristics of the output variable of a linear system when the probabilistic characteristics of the input variable are given. The most complete probabilistic characteristic of a random function $X(t)$ is the set of multidimensional probability densities $f_n(x_1, \cdots, x_n; t_1, \cdots, t_n)$. However, in practical problems the mathematical expectation and the correlation function are often sufficient probability characteristics of a random function.

Let us suppose (1) that we are given the mathematical expectation $m_x(t)$ and the correlation function $K_x(t_1, t_2)$ of a random function $X(t)$ and (2) that we know the operator A of the linear system connecting the output variable $Y(t)$ and the input variable $X(t)$ of the system.

$$Y(t) = AX(t). \tag{1.87}$$

If we know the weight function of the system $w(t, \tau)$ corresponding to a given influence, then the linear operator A can be represented in the following specific form:

$$AX(t) = \int_0^\infty w(t, \tau)\, X(\tau)\, d\tau$$

(we neglect characteristic motion of the system).

We assume that the operator A and the mathematical-expectation operator commute, which is the case for almost all linear operators. Let us determine the mathematical expectation of the output variable of the system:

$$m_y(t) = M[Y(t)] = M[AX(t)] = AM[X(t)] = Am_x(t).$$

Thus, there exists a simple relationship between the mathematical expectations of the input and output of the system:

$$m_y(t) = Am_x(t). \tag{1.88}$$

Since A is linear, we obtain from (1.87) and (1.88)

$$\overset{0}{Y}(t) = A\overset{0}{X}(t), \tag{1.89}$$

where $\overset{0}{X}(t)$ and $\overset{0}{Y}(t)$ are the centralized components of the random functions $X(t)$ and $Y(t)$ respectively. On the basis of (1.89) and the commutativity of the operator A with the mathematical-expectation operator, we can write the following relations that determine the correlation function of the output of the system:

$$\begin{aligned}
K_y(t_1, t_2) &= M[\overset{0}{Y}(t_1)\,\overset{0}{Y}(t_2)] = M[A_{t_1}\overset{0}{X}(t_1)\,A_{t_2}\overset{0}{X}(t_2)] \\
&= M[A_{t_1}A_{t_2}\overset{0}{X}(t_1)\,\overset{0}{X}(t_2)] = A_{t_1}A_{t_2}M[\overset{0}{X}(t_1)\,\overset{0}{X}(t_2)] \\
&= A_{t_1}A_{t_2}K_x(t_1, t_2).
\end{aligned}$$

Consequently, the correlation function of the output variable of the system is connected with the correlation function of the input variable by

$$K_y(t_1, t_2) = A_{t_1}A_{t_2}K_x(t_1, t_2). \tag{1.90}$$

The subscript on A means that this operator is applied to the function of the given argument with fixed values of the other arguments. The operators A_{t_1} and A_{t_2} in (1.90) can be reversed.

Thus, *to find the correlation function of the output variable of a system, we transform the correlation function of the input variable with the aid of the operator A, first with respect to one argument and then with respect to the other, the order being immaterial.*

EXAMPLE 1.   The linear system is an amplifying component; that is, $Y(t) = AX(t) = kX(t)$. In this case,

$$m_y(t) = km_x(t), \qquad K_y(t_1, t_2) = k^2 K_x(t_1, t_2).$$

EXAMPLE 2.   The linear system is a differentiating component; that is, $Y(t) = AX(t) = dX(t)/dt$. In accordance with formulas (1.88) and (1.90), we find

$$m_y(t) = \frac{d}{dt}m_x(t), \qquad K_y(t_1, t_2) = \frac{d}{dt_1}\frac{d}{dt_2}K_x(t_1, t_2).$$

If

$$K_x(t_1, t_2) = K_x(t_1 - t_2) = e^{-\alpha(t_1 - t_2)^2},$$

then

$$K_y(t_1, t_2) = \frac{d}{dt_1}[2\alpha(t_1 - t_2)\exp\{-\alpha(t_1 - t_2)^2\}]$$

$$= 2\alpha\exp\{-\alpha(t_1 - t_2)^2\} - 4\alpha^2(t_1 - t_2)^2\exp\{-\alpha(t_1 - t_2)^2\}$$

$$= 2\alpha[1 - 2\alpha(t_1 - t_2)^2]\exp\{-\alpha(t_1 - t_2)^2\} = K_y(t_1 - t_2).$$

A random function can be characterized in another way. In the general case, an arbitrary random function $X(t)$ can be represented by its canonical decomposition (1.73):

$$X(t) = m_x(t) + \sum_\nu V_\nu x_\nu(t)$$

with given variances D_ν of the uncorrelated random variables V_ν. Let us show how we can determine the canonical decomposition of the output variable of the system $Y(t)$ in this case. We use the fact that A is a linear operator and we write

$$Y(t) = AX(t) = A\{m_x(t) + \sum_\nu V_\nu x_\nu(t)\}$$

$$= Am_x(t) + \sum_\nu V_\nu Ax_\nu(t). \tag{1.91}$$

(In the case of a nonhomogeneous linear transformation (1.85), we need to add to the canonical decomposition (1.91) the canonical decomposition of the random function φ.)

The canonical decomposition of the output variable of a system can be obtained by applying the operator A to the mathematical expectation of the input variable and to each coordinate function $x_\nu(t)$ individually.

After we obtain the canonical decomposition of the output variable, we can easily calculate the correlation function of the output variable:

$$K_y(t_1, t_2) = M[\overset{0}{Y}(t_1)\overset{0}{Y}(t_2)] = M\left[\sum_{\nu,\mu} V_\nu V_\mu Ax_\nu(t_1)Ax_\nu(t_2)\right]$$

$$= \sum_{\nu,\mu} M[V_\nu V_\mu]Ax_\nu(t_1)Ax_\nu(t_2) = \sum_\nu D_\nu Ax_\nu(t_1)Ax_\nu(t_2), \tag{1.92}$$

since

$$M[V_\nu V_\mu] = \begin{cases} D_\nu & \text{for } \nu = \mu, \\ 0 & \text{for } \nu \neq \mu. \end{cases}$$

Obtaining a linear transformation of coordinate functions $x_\nu(t)$ is considerably simpler than obtaining an analogous transformation of the correlation function $K_x(t_1, t_2)$ in accordance with formula (1.90). Therefore, if we have obtained the canonical decomposition of the input variable, then it is easier to use formula (1.92) rather than formula (1.90) in order to obtain the correlation function of the output variable.

Here, we have considered systems with a single input $X(t)$ and a single output $Y(t)$ (one-dimensional systems). In practice, we often encounter systems with several inputs $X_i(t)$ and several outputs $Y_i(t)$ (multidimensional systems). The procedure for obtaining the probabilistic characteristics of a vector-valued output variable $Y(t) = Y_1(t)$, $\cdots$, $Y_n(t)$ from the probabilistic characteristics of a vector-valued input variable $X(t) = X_1(t)$, $\cdots$, $X_n(t)$ is analogous to procedure previously expounded, though it involves more complicated and laborious transformations. A systematic exposition of the theory in this more complicated case is given in [Ref. 47].

Frequently, investigations of a quantity being sought involve the error of the system; that is, the difference between the output variable $Y(t)$ and the desired (ideal) output variable $H(t)$ of the system:

$$E(t) = Y(t) - H(t).$$

Figure 1.1 shows a block diagram clarifying the formation of the output variable $Y(t)$ and the error $E(t)$ of the system. The portion of the diagram enclosed in the dashed rectangle is, of course, absent from the system. The operator B represents an ideal operator reflecting the purpose of the system, and we assume that it is linear. We express the error E in terms of the input signals and the operators A and B:

$$E(t) = AX(t) - BG(t).$$

Remembering the linearity of the operators A and B and the fact that they commute with the mathematical-expectation operator, we can write the following expressions for the probabilistic characteristics of the error of the system:

$$m_E(t) = M[E(t)] = M[AX(t) - BG(t)] = Am_x(t) - Bm_g(t), \quad (1.93)$$

$$
\begin{aligned}
K_E(t_1, t_2) &= M[\overset{0}{E}(t_1)\,\overset{0}{E}(t_2)] \\
&= M[\{A\overset{0}{X}(t_1) - B\overset{0}{G}(t_1)\}\{A\overset{0}{X}(t_2) - B\overset{0}{G}(t_2)\}] \\
&= M[A_{t_1}A_{t_2}\overset{0}{X}(t_1)\overset{0}{X}(t_2) - A_{t_1}B_{t_2}\overset{0}{X}(t_1)\overset{0}{G}(t_2) \\
&\quad - B_{t_1}A_{t_2}\overset{0}{G}(t_1)\overset{0}{X}(t_2) + B_{t_1}B_{t_2}\overset{0}{G}(t_1)\overset{0}{G}(t_2)] \\
&= A_{t_1}A_{t_2}K_x(t_1, t_2) - A_{t_1}B_{t_2}K_{xg}(t_1, t_2) - A_{t_2}B_{t_1}K_{gx}(t_1, t_2) \\
&\quad + B_{t_1}B_{t_2}K_g(t_1, t_2).
\end{aligned}
\quad (1.94)
$$

If the operators A and B are the linear integral operators

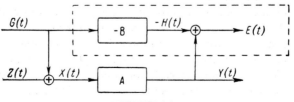

FIGURE 1.1

$$AX(t) = \int_0^\infty X(\tau) w(t, \tau) d\tau,$$

$$BG(t) = \int_0^\infty G(\tau) v(t, \tau) d\tau,$$

then

$$m_E(t) = \int_0^\infty m_x(\tau) w(t, \tau) d\tau - \int_0^\infty m_g(\tau) v(t, \tau) d\tau, \qquad (1.95)$$

$$K_E(t_1, t_2) = \int_0^\infty \int_0^\infty K_x(\tau_1, \tau_2) w(t_1, \tau_1) w(t_2, \tau_2) d\tau_1 \, d\tau_2$$

$$- \int_0^\infty \int_0^\infty K_{xg}(\tau_1, \tau_2) w(t_1, \tau_1) v(t_2, \tau_2) d\tau_1 \, d\tau_2$$

$$- \int_0^\infty \int_0^\infty K_{gx}(\tau_1, \tau_2) w(t_1, \tau_1) v(t_2, \tau_2) d\tau_1 \, d\tau_2$$

$$+ \int_0^\infty \int_0^\infty K_g(\tau_1, \tau_2) v(t_1, \tau_1) v(t_2, \tau_2) d\tau_1 \, d\tau_2. \qquad (1.96)$$

In the special case in which the random functions $G(t)$, $Z(t)$, $X(t)$, and $E(t)$ and the operators A and B are stationary, the computations with the aid of the formulas given here are simplified. For example, formulas (1.95) and (1.96) then take the forms

$$m_E = m_x \int_0^\infty w(\tau) d\tau - m_g \int_0^\infty v(\tau) d\tau, \qquad (1.95a)$$

$$K_E(\tau) = \int_0^\infty \int_0^\infty w(\tau_1) w(\tau_2) K_x(\tau - \tau_2 + \tau_1) d\tau_1 \, d\tau_2$$

$$- 2 \int_0^\infty \int_0^\infty K_{xg}(\tau - \tau_2 + \tau_1) w(\tau_1) v(\tau_2) d\tau_1 \, d\tau_2$$

$$+ \int_0^\infty \int_0^\infty K_g(\tau - \tau_2 + \tau_1) v(\tau_1) v(\tau_2) d\tau_1 \, d\tau_2. \qquad (1.96a)$$

These last formulas are easily obtained if we take into account the stationariness of the random functions and the system (both the real one and the ideal one). To determine the output variables of the systems, we use the formulas

$$Y(t) = \int_0^\infty X(t - \tau_1) w(\tau_1) d\tau_1, \qquad H(t) = \int_0^\infty G(t - \tau_2) v(\tau_2) d\tau_2. \qquad (1.96b)$$

If we set $v(\tau) \equiv 0$ in formula (1.96a), we obtain a formula for determining the correlation function of the output variable $Y(t)$:

$$K_y(\tau) = \int_0^\infty \int_0^\infty K_x(\tau - \tau_2 + \tau_1) w(\tau_1) w(\tau_2) d\tau_1 \, d\tau_2. \qquad (1.97)$$

This formula enables us to obtain by means of double integration the correlation function of the stationary output variable of the system if we know the correlation function of the stationary input variable and the weight function of the stationary linear system.

If we take the Fourier transforms of the correlation functions and the weight functions, we can obtain formulas relating the spectral densities of stationary input and output variables. To do this, we take the Fourier transform of (1.97):

$$S_y(\omega) = \int_{-\infty}^{\infty} K_y(\tau)e^{-j\omega\tau}\,d\tau$$

$$= \int_{-\infty}^{\infty} e^{-j\omega\tau}\,d\tau \int_0^{\infty} w(\tau_1)\,d\tau_1 \int_0^{\infty} w(\tau_2)\,K_x(\tau - \tau_2 + \tau_1)\,d\tau_2$$

$$= \int_0^{\infty} w(\tau_1)\,d\tau_1 \int_0^{\infty} w(\tau_2)\,d\tau_2 \int_{-\infty}^{\infty} K_x(\tau - \tau_2 + \tau_1)e^{-j\omega\tau}\,d\tau$$

$$= \int_0^{\infty} w(\tau_1)e^{j\omega\tau_1}\,d\tau_1 \int_0^{\infty} w(\tau_2)e^{-j\omega\tau_2}\,d\tau_2$$

$$\times \int_{-\infty}^{\infty} K_x(\tau - \tau_2 + \tau_1)e^{-j\omega(\tau - \tau_2 + \tau_1)}\,d\tau$$

$$= W(-j\omega)\,W(j\omega)S_x(\omega) = |W(j\omega)|^2 S_x(\omega),$$

where $W(p)$ is the operator transfer function of the linear system, $|W(j\omega)|^2$ is the square of the amplitude-frequency characteristic of the system, and $S_x(\omega)$ and $S_y(\omega)$ are the spectral densities of the input and output variables of the system. Thus, we obtain

$$S_y(\omega) = |W(j\omega)|^2 S_x(\omega). \tag{1.98}$$

The spectral density of the output variable is equal to the spectral density of the input variable multiplied by the square of the amplitude-frequency characteristic of the system.

The simplicity of formula (1.98) brings out certain convenient features of the spectral method of investigating stationary processes. It follows from formulas (1.79) and (1.98) that the variance of an output variable is given in this case by the simple formula

$$D_y = K_y(0) = \frac{1}{2\pi}\int_{-\infty}^{\infty} S_y(\omega)\,d\omega$$

$$= \frac{1}{\pi}\int_0^{\infty} |W(j\omega)|^2 S_x(\omega)\,d\omega. \tag{1.99}$$

In an analogous manner, we can obtain formulas for the spectral density of the error S_E and for the variance of the error D_E:

$$S_E(\omega) = |W(j\omega)|^2 S_x(\omega) - 2W(j\omega)V(-j\omega)S_{xg}(\omega) + |V(j\omega)|^2 S_g(\omega), \tag{1.98a}$$

$$D_E = \frac{1}{2\pi}\int_{-\infty}^{\infty} S_E(\omega)\,d\omega, \tag{1.99a}$$

where $S_{xg}(\omega)$ is the joint spectral density of X and G and where $S_g(\omega)$ is the spectral density of the useful signal G.

The simplicity of the formulas giving the probabilistic characteristics of the output variables in the cases that we have been considering is due to the fact that we have been considering only linear systems. The transition to nonlinear systems is associated with a sharp increase in the complexity of the computational formulas. Therefore, in applications, we quite frequently resort to linearization of nonlinearities; that is, we try to reduce the problem to a linear one. Here, we shall not investigate in detail the transformation of random functions by means of nonlinear systems. We refer the reader interested in these questions to the books [Refs. 20, 31, 33, 40, 47]. We shall consider only one form of nonlinear transformation, which we shall use later. Specifically, let us consider a nonlinear integral transformation, which is a generalization of a linear integral operator. We write it in the form

$$Y(t) = \int_0^T \varphi[X(\tau),\ \tau,\ t]d\tau, \tag{1.100}$$

where $X(t)$ and $Y(t)$ are the input and output variables of the system and $\varphi(x, \tau, t)$ is an arbitrary function known as the **characteristic function** of the nonlinear operator. (When we were considering linear operators, this function had the special form $\varphi(x, \tau, t) = x(\tau)w(t, \tau)$.)

The mathematical expectation of the random function $Y(t)$ is equal to

$$m_y(t) = \int_0^T M[\varphi\{X(\tau),\ \tau,\ t\}]d\tau$$
$$= \int_0^T \int_{-\infty}^{\infty} \varphi(x,\ \tau,\ t)f_1(x,\ \tau)dx\ d\tau, \tag{1.101}$$

where $f_1(x, t)$ is the one-dimensional probability density of the random function $X(t)$. We now determine the initial second-order moment of the random function $Y(t)$:

$$\Gamma_y(t_1,\ t_2) = M[Y(t_1)\ Y(t_2)]$$
$$= M\left[\int_0^T \int_0^T \varphi\{X(\tau_1),\ \tau_1,\ t_1\}\varphi\{X(\tau_2),\ \tau_2,\ t_2\}d\tau_1\ d\tau_2\right]$$
$$= \int_0^T \int_0^T M[\varphi\{X(\tau_1),\ \tau_1,\ t_1\}\varphi\{X(\tau_2),\ \tau_2,\ t_2\}]d\tau_1\ d\tau_2$$
$$= \int_0^T \int_0^T \int_{-\infty}^{\infty} \int_{-\infty}^{\infty} \varphi(x_1,\ \tau_1,\ t_1)\varphi(x_2,\ \tau_2,\ t_2)f_2(x_1,\ x_2;\ \tau_1,\ \tau_2)$$
$$\times\ dx_1\ dx_2\ d\tau_1\ d\tau_2, \tag{1.102}$$

where $f_2(x_1, x_2; t_1, t_2)$ is the two-dimensional probability density of the random function $X(t)$. From formulas (1.64), (1.101), and (1.102), we can obtain an expression for the correlation function Y:

$$K_y(t_1,\ t_2) = \Gamma_y(t_1,\ t_2) - m_y(t_1)m_y(t_2)$$
$$= \int_0^T \int_0^T \int_{-\infty}^{\infty} \int_{-\infty}^{\infty} \varphi(x_1,\ \tau_1,\ t_1)\varphi(x_2,\ \tau_2,\ t_2)[f_2(x_1,\ x_2,\ \tau_1,\ \tau_2)$$
$$-\ f_1(x_1,\ \tau_1)f_1(x_2,\ \tau_2)]\ dx_1\ dx_2\ d\tau_1\ d\tau_2. \tag{1.103}$$

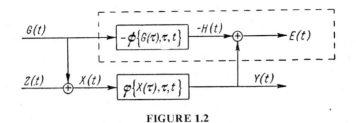

FIGURE 1.2

The formulas that we have obtained here for determining the mathematical expectation of the correlation function and the second initial moment of the output variable of a nonlinear system demonstrate the necessity of knowing the probability densities of the input variable in order to obtain the moments of the output function. Knowing the moments of the input variable is not enough to obtain the corresponding moments of the output variable. It is also important to note that knowing the first and second moments of the output variable does not give a complete probabilistic characteristic of this random function since it usually has a nonnormal distribution law.

Frequently, it is not the output variable itself of the system, but the error of the system (that is, the difference between this variable Y and some ideal output variable H) that interests us (see Fig. 1.2). Let us suppose that an actual nonlinear operator is characterized by a function $\varphi\{X(\tau), \tau, t\}$ and that the ideal operator is characterized by the function $\phi\{G(\tau), \tau, t\}$. Let us determine the first and second moments of the error of the system.

The mathematical expectation of the error is equal to

$$
\begin{aligned}
m_E(t) = M[E(t)] &= M[Y(t) - H(t)] \\
&= M\left[\int_0^T \varphi\{X(\tau), \tau, t\}d\tau - \int_0^T \phi\{G(\tau), \tau, t\}d\tau\right] \\
&= \int_0^T M[\varphi\{X(\tau), \tau, t\}]d\tau - \int_0^T M[\phi\{G(\tau), \tau, t\}d\tau] \\
&= \int_0^T \int_{-\infty}^\infty \varphi(x, \tau, t) f_1(x, \tau) dx\, d\tau \\
&\quad - \int_0^T \int_{-\infty}^\infty \phi(g, \tau, t)\eta_1(g, \tau) dg\, d\tau,
\end{aligned}
\tag{1.104}
$$

where $f_1(x, \tau)$ and $\eta_1(g, \tau)$ are one-dimensional probability densities of the random functions $X(t)$ and $G(t)$. Let us determine the initial second-order moment of the error:

$$
\begin{aligned}
\Gamma_E(t_1, t_2) = M[E(t_1)E(t_2)] &= M[\{Y(t_1) - H(t_1)\}\{Y(t_2) - H(t_2)\}] \\
&= M[Y(t_1)Y(t_2) - H(t_1)Y(t_2) - Y(t_1)H(t_2) + H(t_1)H(t_2)] \\
&= \int_0^T \int_0^T M[\varphi\{X(\tau_1), \tau_1, t_1\}\varphi\{X(\tau_2), \tau_2, t_2\}]d\tau_1\, d\tau_2
\end{aligned}
$$

$$-\int_0^T\int_0^T M[\phi\{G(\tau_1),\,\tau_1,\,t_1\}\varphi\{X(\tau_2),\,\tau_2,\,t_2\}]d\tau_1\,d\tau_2$$

$$-\int_0^T\int_0^T M[\varphi\{X(\tau_1),\,\tau_1,\,t_1\}\phi\{G(\tau_2,\,\tau_2,\,t_2)\}]d\tau_1\,d\tau_2$$

$$+\int_0^T\int_0^T M[\phi\{G(\tau_1),\,\tau_1,\,t_1\}\phi\{G(\tau_2),\,\tau_2,\,t_2\}]d\tau_1\,d\tau_2$$

$$=\int_0^T\int_0^T\Big[\int_{-\infty}^\infty\int_{-\infty}^\infty \varphi(x_1,\,\tau_1,\,t_1)\varphi(x_2,\,\tau_2,\,t_2)\,f_2(x_1,\,x_2;\,\tau_1,\,\tau_2)dx_1\,dx_2$$

$$-\int_{-\infty}^\infty\int_{-\infty}^\infty \phi(x,\,\tau_1,\,t_1)\varphi(g,\,\tau_2,\,t_2)\chi_2(x,\,g;\,\tau_1,\,\tau_2)dx\,dg$$

$$-\int_{-\infty}^\infty\int_{-\infty}^\infty \varphi(x,\,\tau_1,\,t_1)\phi(g,\,\tau_2,\,t_2)\chi_2(g,\,x,\,\tau_1,\,\tau_2)dx\,dg$$

$$+\int_{-\infty}^\infty\int_{-\infty}^\infty \phi(g_1,\,\tau_1,\,t_1)\phi(g_2,\,\tau_2,\,t_2)\eta_2(g_1,\,g_2;\,\tau_1,\,\tau_2)dg_1\,dg_2\Big]$$

$$\times\,d\tau_1\,d\tau_2, \tag{1.105}$$

where the quantities

$$f_2(x_1,\,x_2;\,\tau_1,\,\tau_2),\quad \chi_2(x,\,g;\,\tau_1,\,\tau_2),\quad \eta_2(g_1,\,g_2;\,\tau_1,\,\tau_2)$$

are two-dimensional probability densities of the random functions $X(t)$ and $G(t)$.

The correlation function of the error is equal to

$$K_E(t_1,\,t_2) = \Gamma_E(t_1,\,t_2) - m_E(t_1)m_E(t_2). \tag{1.106}$$

3. DETERMINATION OF THE EXTREMA OF A FUNCTIONAL OF THE TYPE

$$I = \int_{x_2}^{x_1} F[x,\,y,\,y^{(1)},\,\cdots,\,y^{(n)}]dx.$$

The basic problem in the calculus of variations [Refs. 32, 50] is the determination of extrema of functionals.

$I\{y(x)\}$ is a functional of a function $y(x)$ belonging to a given class if to every function of that class there corresponds a number $I\{y(x)\}$.

The class of the functions $y(x)$, on which the functional is defined, is called the **domain of definition** of the functional. The following are examples of classes of admissible functions $y(x)$:

(a) the class of all continuous functions,

(b) the class of all bounded continuous functions,

(c) the class of all piecewise-continuous functions $y(x)$ such that $y(x) \leqslant C$, where C is a given number.

A very simple example of a functional is a definite integral of the form

$$I\{y(x)\} = \int_{x_0}^{x_1} y(x)dx.$$

Let us pose a very simple problem from the calculus of variations. Find an extremum of the functional

$$I = \int_{x_0}^{x_1} F(x, y, y')dx, \tag{1.107}$$

where F is a given single-valued continuously differentiable function of its arguments x, y, $y' = dy/dx$ for all values of x and y in a region R of the xy-plane and the numbers x_0 and x_1 are given limits of integration. The function $y = y(x)$ is single valued and continuously differentiable in the interval $[x_0, x_1]$ (that is, it belongs to the class C^1). We shall consider curves $y = y(x)$ to be admissible if they belong to the class C^1, if they lie entirely inside the region R, and if they pass through given points (x_0, y^0) and (x_1, y^1), where $y^0 = y(x_0)$ and $y^1 = y(x_1)$. The problem then is as follows: Out of all admissible curves $y(x)$, find the one that minimizes (or maximizes) the value of the integral (1.107).

We can easily obtain a condition that the function $y_0 = y_0(x)$ must satisfy if it is to be the solution to this problem. Suppose that $y_0(x)$ is the function sought. Consider another function "close" to it:

$$y = y_0(x) + \Delta \cdot Z(x), \tag{1.108}$$

where $Z(x)$ is an arbitrary function in the class C^1 that vanishes at the end-points of the interval $[x_0, x_1]$:

$$Z(x_0) = Z(x_1) = 0, \tag{1.109}$$

and Δ is a small number. Thus, the function y defined by equation (1.108) is admissible. The increment $\Delta \cdot Z(x)$ plays the same role in this problem as the increment Δx plays in the solution of problems of finding an extremum of a function $f(x)$ of an argument x. When we substitute (1.108) into (1.107), the functional I becomes a function of the number Δ:

$$I(\Delta) = \int_{x_0}^{x_1} F[x, y_0(x) + \Delta \cdot Z(x), y_0'(x) + \Delta \cdot Z'(x)]dx. \tag{1.110}$$

Let us expand $I(\Delta)$ in a series of powers of Δ:

$$I(\Delta) = I(\Delta)|_{\Delta=0} + \Delta\frac{\partial I}{\partial \Delta}\bigg|_{\Delta=0} + \frac{\Delta^2}{2!}\frac{\partial^2 I}{\partial \Delta^2}\bigg|_{\Delta=0} + \cdots \tag{1.111}$$

The derivatives of I with respect to Δ

$$\frac{\partial I}{\partial \Delta}\bigg|_{\Delta=0}, \qquad \frac{\partial^2 I}{\partial \Delta^2}\bigg|_{\Delta=0}$$

are called respectively the **first** and **second variations** of the integral I and they are denoted by δI and $\delta^2 I$. In investigations of extrema of a functional, the first and second variations play a role analogous to that of the first and second derivatives in the investigation of extrema of functions.

One can easily see that if the function $y_0(x)$ corresponds to an extremum of the functional I, we must have

$$\delta I = \frac{\delta I\{y_0(x) + \Delta \cdot Z(x)\}}{\delta \Delta}\bigg|_{\Delta = 0} = 0 \qquad (1.112)$$

for an *arbitrary* function $Z(x)$ belonging to the class C^1 and satisfying conditions (1.109). If we differentiate the integrand in (1.110) with respect to Δ and then set $\Delta = 0$, we obtain

$$\delta I = \frac{\delta I\{y_0(x) + \Delta \cdot Z(x)\}}{\partial \Delta}\bigg|_{\Delta = 0}$$

$$= \int_{x_0}^{x_1}\left[\frac{\partial F}{\partial y}Z(x) + \frac{\partial F}{\partial y'}Z'(x)\right]dx. \qquad (1.113)$$

Let us break the integral on the right into two integrals and integrate the second one by parts:

$$\int_{x_0}^{x_1}\frac{\partial F}{\partial y'}Z'(x)\,dx = \left[Z(x)\frac{\partial F}{\partial y'}\right]_{x_0}^{x_1} - \int_{x_0}^{x_1}Z(x)\frac{d}{dx}\left(\frac{\partial F}{\partial y'}\right)dx$$

$$= -\int_{x_0}^{x_1}Z(x)\frac{d}{dx}\left(\frac{\partial F}{\partial y'}\right)dx. \qquad (1.114)$$

Combining this result with (1.113), we obtain

$$\delta I = \int_{x_0}^{x_1}Z(x)\left[\frac{\partial F}{\partial y} - \frac{d}{dx}\left(\frac{\partial F}{\partial y'}\right)\right]dx. \qquad (1.115)$$

It follows from (1.112) and (1.115) that the integral of the product of the two functions $Z(x)$ and $[\partial F/\partial y - d/dx(\partial F/\partial y')]$ vanishes for an arbitrary function $Z(x)$ in the class C^1. One can easily show [Ref. 32] that this is possible only when

$$\frac{\partial F}{\partial y} - \frac{d}{dx}\left(\frac{dF}{dy'}\right) = 0, \qquad x_0 \leqslant x \leqslant x_1. \qquad (1.116)$$

Equation (1.116), known as **Euler's equation,** is a *necessary* condition for the function $y = y_0(x)$ in the representation of the extremum of the functional (1.107). In the general case, it is an ordinary nonlinear differential equation. Solutions of Euler's equation are called **extremals.** We then need to seek a solution of the problem among the extremals.

We note that, whereas condition (1.116) is a necessary condition, it is not in the general case sufficient. Therefore, every solution of equation (1.116) must be checked to see whether it actually is an extremum of the functional (1.107). To do this, we may, for example, use the sufficient conditions for an extremum of the functional I [Refs. 32, 50]. However, these conditions are very complicated and are not as a rule convenient for practical use. In certain practical problems, one can show by simple verification that an extremal is a solution of the problem. Sometimes, it is clear from physical considerations that the functional has an extremum. In such a case, a solution of equation (1.116), if it exists and is unique, is the solution of the problem. Of course, there are cases when equation (1.116) does not have a solution in the class of admissible functions. For example, if $F = F(x, y)$, then equation (1.116) is of the form

$$\frac{\partial F(x, y)}{\partial y} = 0.$$

This algebraic or transcendental equation enables us to express y as a function of x:

$$y = y(x),$$

and the solution does not contain arbitrary constants. In the general case, the extremal $y = y(x)$ does not pass through the boundary values y^{00} and y^{01}. Consequently, in such a case, the problem does not usually have a solution. On the other hand, if we do not require satisfaction of given boundary conditions, a given particular problem will often have a solution.

To derive another necessary condition for a minimum (or maximum) of the functional (1.107), let us consider the second variation $\delta^2 I$ (in analogy with the procedure for obtaining an additional necessary condition for a minimum of a function of x by considering the second derivative of that function with respect to x). It is shown in [Ref. 32] that such an additional necessary condition for minimization of the functional is that the inequality

$$F_{y'y'} \geq 0 \tag{1.117}$$

hold along the extremal. (For maximization, the direction of the inequality is reversed.)

The variational problem is easily generalized to the case in which the function F constituting the integrand depends on derivatives of higher orders:

$$I = \int_{x_0}^{x_1} F[x, y, y', \cdots, y^{(n)}] dx. \tag{1.118}$$

In this case, it is natural to require that the admissible functions $y(x)$ belong to the class C^n; that is, to the class of single-valued continuous functions with continuous derivatives of the first n orders. Furthermore, the boundary values of the function y and of its $n - 1$ derivatives are given: $y^{(i)}(x_0) = y^{0i}$, $y^{(i)}(x_1) = y^{1i}$ for $i = 0, 1, \cdots, n - 1$. If we set the first variation $\delta I = 0$ and integrate by parts, we obtain a necessary condition for an extremum of the functional (1.118):

$$\frac{\partial F}{\partial y} - \frac{d}{dx}\left(\frac{\partial F}{\partial y'}\right) + \cdots + (-1)^n \frac{d^n}{dx^n}\left(\frac{\partial F}{\partial y^{(n)}}\right) = 0. \tag{1.119}$$

We assume that the function F is differentiable an appropriate number of times with respect to the variables $x, y, y^{(1)}, \cdots, y^{(n)}$. If a function belonging to the class C^n corresponds to an extremum of the functional (1.118), it must satisfy equation (1.119).

In the general case, equation (1.119) is a nonlinear ordinary differential equation. In the particular case in which the function

$$F = F[x, y, y^{(1)}, \cdots, y^{(n)}]$$

is a bilinear form of $y^{(i)}$ (that is, when

$$F = \sum_{i, j = 0}^{n} f_{ij}(x) y^{(i)} y^{(j)}, \tag{1.120}$$

for certain $f_{ij}(x)$), equation (1.119) will be linear.

Suppose that the functional I depends on several functions $y_1, \cdots, y_k$ of a single variable:

$$I = \int_{x_0}^{x_1} F(x, y_1, \cdots, y_k, y_1', \cdots, y_k') dx, \tag{1.121}$$

and that boundary conditions $y_1(x_0), \cdots, y_k(x_0), y_1(x_1), \cdots, y_k(x_1)$ are given. By momentarily fixing all the functions except $y_s(x)$, we obtain the necessary condition

$$\frac{\partial F}{\partial y_s} - \frac{d}{dx}\left(\frac{\partial F}{\partial y_s'}\right) = 0, \quad s = 1, \cdots, k. \tag{1.122}$$

We frequently encounter calculus-of-variations problems with additional conditions imposed on the solutions. Suppose, for example, that we are required to find an extremum of the functional (1.107) in the class of functions C^1 that satisfy the additional conditions

$$\int_{x_0}^{x_1} F_i(x, y, y') dx = d_i, \quad i = 1, 2, \cdots, m. \tag{1.123}$$

This problem reduces to the problem of finding an unconditional extremum of the functional

$$I^* = \int_{x_0}^{x_1}\left(F + \sum_{i=1}^{m} \lambda_i F_i\right) dx. \tag{1.124}$$

The Lagrange multipliers λ_i, as yet undetermined, can be found from conditions (1.123).

Moreover, other forms of additional conditions imposed on the solution are possible. Let us suppose that we are required to find curves $y_1, \cdots, y_k$ corresponding to an extremum of the functional (1.121) and subject to the additional conditions

$$\varphi_i(x, y_1, \cdots, y_k, y_1', \cdots, y_k') = 0, \quad i = 1, \cdots, m. \tag{1.125}$$

To find the solution, we again use the method of Lagrange multipliers. To do this, we find the unconditional extremum of the functional

$$I^* = \int_{x_0}^{x_1} \left[F + \sum_{i=1}^{m} \lambda_i(x)\varphi_i \right] dx. \qquad (1.126)$$

This functional I^* is not in principle different from the functional (1.121). Instead of the system of equations (1.122), we set up an analogous system of equations by replacing the function F with the function $F^* = F + \sum_{i=1}^{m} \lambda_i(x)\varphi_i$:

$$\frac{\partial F^*}{\partial y_s} - \frac{d}{dx}\left(\frac{\partial F^*}{\partial y'_s}\right) = 0, \quad s = 1, \cdots, k. \qquad (1.127)$$

The system of $m + k$ equations (1.125) and (1.127) enables us, in the general case, to determine $m + k$ unknown functions $y_1, \cdots, y_k, \lambda_1, \cdots, \lambda_m$.

Up to now, all our admissible curves have been curves passing through two fixed points. In a more general statement of the problem, the boundary points are not fixed but belong to certain regions G_0 and G_1, which in particular cases can be curved surfaces. This problem can be solved by finding the solution of Euler's equations in the general form. The unknown arbitrary constants are determined from the condition that the boundary points of the extremals are on the surfaces G_0 and G_1 as well as from the so-called transversality conditions [Refs. 32, 50].

4. DETERMINATION OF THE EXTREMA OF A FUNCTIONAL OF THE TYPE

$$I = \int_{t_0}^{t_1}\int_{t_0}^{t_1} \Phi[t, s, y(t), y(s), y^{(1)}(t), y^{(1)}(s), \cdots, y^{(n)}(t), y^{(n)}(s)]\,dt\,ds$$

It should be noted that the set of functionals (1.107), (1.118), and (1.121) commonly studied in classical calculus of variations [Refs. 32, 50] does not include all functionals that are used as criteria in the theory of optimal systems. For example, the second initial moment of error of a system is a functional of a different type. This criterion and numerous others that are used in the choice of optimal automatic control systems are functionals of the type

$$I = \int_{t_0}^{t_1}\int_{t_0}^{t_1} \Phi[t, s, y(t), y(s), y'(t), y'(s)]\,dt\,ds. \qquad (1.128)$$

We note that the functional (1.107) previously considered is a special case of the functional (1.128). Specifically, if we set

$$\Phi[t, s, y(t), y(s), y'(t), y'(s)] = F[t, y(t), y'(t)]$$

in (1.128), we obtain

$$I = \int_{t_0}^{t_1}\int_{t_0}^{t_1} F[t, y(t), y'(t)]dt\,ds = (t_1 - t_0)\int_{t_0}^{t_1} F[t, y(t), y'(t)]dt.$$

Except for the insignificant constant factor $(t_1 - t_0)$, this is a functional of the form (1.107).

Let us formulate the simplest problems of the calculus of variations as applied to the functional (1.128).

Suppose that we seek an extremum of the functional (1.128), where Φ is a given single-valued continuously differentiable function, $(t, y(t))$ belongs to some region R, and t_0 and t_1 are given limits of integration. The function $y = y(t)$ (or $y = y(s)$) is single-valued and continuously differentiable in the interval $[t_0, t_1]$; that is, it belongs to the class C^1. We shall consider curves $y = y(t)$ (or $y = y(s)$) admissible if they belong to the class C^1, if they lie entirely in the region R, and if they pass through the points (t_0, y^0) and (t_1, y^1), where $y^0 = y(t_0)$ and $y^1 = y(t_1)$. From all admissible curves $y(t)$ (or $y(s)$, which amounts to the same thing), find the one that minimizes (or maximizes) the functional (1.128).

Let us obtain a necessary condition that the function $y_0 = y_0(t)$ must satisfy to be a solution of this problem. Let $y_0(t)$ denote the function we are seeking. Just as we did in investigating the functional (1.107), let us consider another function

$$y(t) = y_0(t) + \Delta \cdot Z(t) \quad (\text{or } y(s) = y_0(s) + \Delta \cdot Z(s)), \qquad (1.108a)$$

where $Z(t)$ is an arbitrary function in the class C^1 that satisfies condition (1.109):

$$Z(t_0) = Z(t_1) = 0$$

and where Δ is a small number. Consequently, the function $y(t)$ so defined is admissible. When we substitute this $y(t)$ into (1.128), the functional I becomes a function of the number Δ:

$$I(\Delta) = \int_{t_0}^{t_1}\int_{t_0}^{t_1} \Phi[t, s, y_0(t) + \Delta \cdot Z(t), y_0(s) + \Delta \cdot Z(s), y_0'(t)$$
$$+ \Delta \cdot Z'(t), y_0'(s) + \Delta \cdot Z'(s)]dt\,ds. \qquad (1.129)$$

Let us expand $I(\Delta)$ in a series of powers of Δ:

$$I(\Delta) = I(\Delta)|_{\Delta=0} + \Delta\,\frac{\partial I}{\partial \Delta}\Big|_{\Delta=0} + \frac{\Delta^2}{2!}\,\frac{\partial^2 I}{\partial \Delta^2}\Big|_{\Delta=0} + \cdots. \qquad (1.130)$$

One can easily see that if the function $y_0(t)$ corresponds to an extremum of the functional I, the first variation of the functional I must vanish:

$$\delta I = \frac{\partial I\{y_0 + \Delta \cdot Z\}}{\partial \Delta}\bigg|_{\Delta=0} = 0,$$

for an arbitrary function $Z(t) \in C^1$ that satisfies conditions (1.109).

If we differentiate with respect to Δ under the integral sign in (1.129) and then set $\Delta = 0$, we obtain

$$\delta I = \int_{t_0}^{t_1}\int_{t_0}^{t_1}\left[\frac{\partial\Phi}{\partial y_t}Z(t) + \frac{\partial\Phi}{\partial y_s}Z(s)\right.$$
$$\left. + \frac{\partial\Phi}{\partial y'_t}Z'(t) + \frac{\partial\Phi}{\partial y'_s}Z'(s)\right]dt\,ds, \qquad (1.131)$$

where

$$y_t = y(t),\ y_s = y(s),\ y'_t = y'(t),\ y'_s = y'(s).$$

If we integrate by parts the terms containing the derivative Z', we get

$$\int_{t_0}^{t_1}\int_{t_0}^{t_1}\left[\frac{\partial\Phi}{\partial y'_t}Z'(t) + \frac{\partial\Phi}{\partial y'_s}Z'(s)\right]dt\,ds$$

$$= \int_{t_0}^{t_1}\left[Z(t)\frac{\partial\Phi}{\partial y'_t}\right]_{t_0}^{t_1}ds - \int_{t_0}^{t_1}\int_{t_0}^{t_1}Z(t)\frac{d}{dt}\left(\frac{\partial\Phi}{\partial y'_t}\right)dt\,ds$$

$$+ \int_{t_0}^{t_1}\left[Z(s)\frac{\partial\Phi}{\partial y'_s}\right]_{t_0}^{t_1}dt - \int_{t_0}^{t_1}\int_{t_0}^{t_1}Z(s)\frac{d}{ds}\left(\frac{\partial\Phi}{\partial y'_s}\right)dt\,ds$$

$$= -\int_{t_0}^{t_1}\int_{t_0}^{t_1}\left[Z(t)\frac{d}{dt}\left(\frac{\partial\Phi}{\partial y'_t}\right) + Z(s)\frac{d}{ds}\left(\frac{\partial\Phi}{\partial y'_s}\right)\right]dt\,ds. \quad (1.132)$$

From (1.112), (1.131), and (1.132), we obtain

$$\delta I = \int_{t_0}^{t_1}Z(t)\left\{\int_{t_0}^{t_1}\left[\frac{\partial\Phi}{\partial y_t} + \frac{\overline{\partial\Phi}}{\partial y_s} - \frac{d}{dt}\left(\frac{\partial\Phi}{\partial y'_t}\right)\right.\right.$$

$$\left.\left. - \frac{\overline{d}}{ds}\left(\frac{\partial\Phi}{\partial y'_s}\right)\right]ds\right\}dt = 0. \qquad (1.133)$$

Here, the derivatives

$$\frac{\overline{\partial\Phi}}{\partial y_s} \quad \text{and} \quad \frac{\overline{d}}{ds}\left(\frac{\partial\Phi}{\partial y'_s}\right)$$

are obtained by differentiating with respect to the variables y_s and y'_s and then reversing the positions of the arguments t and s. It follows from (1.133) that the integral of the product of $Z(t)$ and the braced expression vanishes for arbitrary admissible $Z(t)$. This is possible only if the expression in the braces vanishes identically [Refs. 32, 50]; that is, only if

$$\int_{t_0}^{t_1}\left[\frac{\partial\Phi}{\partial y_t} + \frac{\overline{\partial\Phi}}{\partial y_s} - \frac{d}{dt}\left(\frac{\partial\Phi}{\partial y'_t}\right) - \frac{\overline{d}}{ds}\left(\frac{\partial\Phi}{\partial y'_s}\right)\right]ds = 0,$$

$$t_0 \leqslant t \leqslant t_1. \qquad (1.134)$$

Equation (1.134) is a *necessary condition* so that the function $y = y_0(t)$ represents an extremum of the functional (1.128). This equation is, in the general case, a nonlinear integro-differential equation. Let us call its solutions **extremals.** Finally, we seek the solution of the problem among the extremals.

This variational problem can easily be generalized to the case in which the integrand contains derivatives of higher orders:

$$I = \int_{t_0}^{t_1} \int_{t_0}^{t_1} \Phi[t, s, y(t), y(s), \cdots, y^{(n)}(t), y^{(n)}(s)] dt \, ds. \qquad (1.135)$$

Admissible functions $y(t)$ must belong to the class C^n, and must satisfy the conditions

$$y^i(t_0) = y^{0i}, \quad y^i(t_1) = y^{1i}, \quad i = 0, 1, \cdots, n-1 \qquad (1.135a)$$

at the end-points. If we set the first variation δI equal to 0 and integrate by parts, we obtain a necessary condition for an extremum of the functional (1.135):

$$\int_{t_0}^{t_1} \left[\frac{\partial \Phi}{\partial y_t} + \overline{\frac{\partial \Phi}{\partial y_s}} - \frac{d}{dt}\left(\frac{\partial \Phi}{\partial y'_t}\right) - \overline{\frac{d}{ds}\left(\frac{\partial \Phi}{\partial y'_s}\right)} + \right.$$
$$\left. \cdots + (-1)^n \frac{d^n}{dt^n}\left(\frac{\partial \Phi}{\partial y_t^{(n)}}\right) + (-1)^n \overline{\frac{d^n}{ds^n}\left(\frac{\partial \Phi}{\partial y_s^{(n)}}\right)} \right] ds = 0. \qquad (1.136)$$

$$t_0 \leqslant t \leqslant t_1.$$

In deriving condition (1.136), we assume that the function Φ is differentiable the necessary number of times with respect to $y_t^{(i)}$ and $y_s^{(i)}$. The results that we have obtained can be formulated as

THEOREM 1. *For an admissible function $y(t)$ belonging to the class C^n and satisfying condition $(1.135a)$ to represent an extremum of the functional (1.135), it is necessary that it satisfy equation (1.136).*

Equation (1.136) is in the general case a nonlinear integro-differential equation. We note that if the function Φ is symmetric about its arguments, that is, if

$$\Phi[t, s, y(t), y(s), \cdots, y^{(n)}(t), y^{(n)}(s)]$$
$$= \Phi[s, t, y(s), y(t), \cdots, y^{(n)}(s), y^{(n)}(t)],$$

then

$$\overline{\frac{d^i}{ds^i}\left(\frac{\partial \Phi}{\partial y_s^{(i)}}\right)} = \frac{d^i}{dt^i}\left(\frac{\partial \Phi}{\partial y_t^{(i)}}\right), \quad i = 1, \cdots, n$$

(the positions of the variables t and s need to be reversed in the derivatives). Consequently, equation (1.136) can be rewritten in the simpler form

$$\int_{t_0}^{t_1} \left[\frac{\partial \Phi}{\partial y_t} - \frac{d}{dt}\left(\frac{\partial \Phi}{\partial y'_t}\right) + \cdots + (-1)^n \frac{d^n}{dt^n}\left(\frac{\partial \Phi}{\partial y_t^{(n)}}\right) \right] ds = 0. \qquad (1.136a)$$

In the special case in which the function Φ is a bilinear form in $y^{(i)}$:

$$\Phi = \sum_{i,j=0}^{n} f_{ij}(t, s) y^{(i)}(t) y^{(j)}(s), \qquad (1.137)$$

equation (1.136) is a linear equation.

EXAMPLE.   Suppose that

$$\Phi = f_{00}(t, s)\, y(t)\, y(s) + f_{11}(t, s)\, y'(t)\, y'(s)$$

$$+ \frac{1}{t_1 - t_0} f_0(t)\, y^2(t) + \frac{1}{t_1 - t_0} f_1(t)[y'(t)]^2 + \frac{1}{t_1 - t_0} \varphi(t)\, y(t),$$

where $f_{00}(t, s)$, $f_{11}(t, s)$, $f_0(t)$, $f_1(t)$, and $\varphi(t)$ are given functions of their arguments. Let us also suppose that $f_{00}(t, s) = f_{00}(s, t)$ and that $f_{11}(t, s) = f_{11}(s, t)$. Finally, let us suppose that we have the following boundary conditions for the functions y:

$$y(t_0) = y^{00}, \quad y(t_1) = y^{01}.$$

In this case, equation (1.136) takes the form

$$\int_{t_0}^{t_1} \left[f_{00}(t, s)\, y(s) - \frac{df_{11}}{dt} y'(s) + \frac{1}{t_1 - t_0} f_0(t)\, y(t) \right.$$

$$\left. - \frac{1}{t_1 - t_0} f_1(t)\, y''(t) - \frac{1}{t_1 - t_0} \frac{df_1}{dt} y'(t) + \frac{1}{2(t_1 - t_0)} \varphi(t) \right] ds = 0.$$

It can be rewritten as

$$\int_{t_0}^{t_1} \left[f_{00}(t, s)\, y(s) - \frac{df_{11}}{dt} (t, s)\, y'(s) \right] ds$$

$$+ f_0(t)\, y(t) - \frac{df_1}{dt} y'(t) - f_1(t)\, y''(t) + \frac{1}{2} \varphi(t) = 0. \quad \text{(1.138)}$$

$$t_0 \leqslant t \leqslant t_1.$$

The solution of this linear integro-differential equation depends on two arbitrary constants, which can be determined from the boundary conditions. If $f_{00} \equiv f_{11} \equiv 0$, equation (1.137) is an ordinary differential equation. If $f_1 \equiv 0$, equation (1.137) is an integral equation.

The problem of finding an extremum of the functional (1.135) can be posed in a different way. We have thus far required that the admissible functions $y(t)$ satisfy the boundary conditions (1.135a). In certain cases, the problem may hinge around free end-points of the function $y(t)$. Consequently, in such cases we need to find an extremum of the functional (1.135) without the conditions (1.135a). Of course, the solutions of this problem must be sought among the extremals; that is, among the solutions of equation (1.136). However, in the present case, these solutions depend on $2n$ arbitrary constants; for example, on the values of the function y and its $2n - 1$ derivatives at $t = t_0$; that is, on the numbers $y^{(i)}(t_0)$, where $i = 0, 1, \cdots, 2n - 1$ (in the general case, the highest derivative in equation (1.136) is of order $2n$). To find the value of these arbitrary constants that maximize or minimize the functional (1.135), we can substitute the solution of equation (1.136), expressed in terms of these arbitrary constants, into (1.135) and then find the extremum of I by treating it as a function of the parameters

$y^{(i)}(t_0)$. Thus, in the present case, when we have found the form of the extremals, we need to seek the extremum of a function of several variables.

Of practical interest is the special case of the functional (1.128) when the function Φ depends only on t, s, $y(t)$, and $y(s)$ and is independent of the derivatives $y^{(i)}(t)$ and $y^{(i)}(s)$. Then, the functional I is of the form

$$I = \int_{t_0}^{t_1}\int_{t_0}^{t_1}\Phi[t, s, y(t), y(s)]\,dt\,ds. \qquad (1.139)$$

An example of such a functional is the second initial moment of the error of an automatic-control system.

The extremals of the functional (1.139) satisfy the equation (cf. (1.134))

$$\int_{t_0}^{t_1}\left(\frac{\partial\Phi}{\partial y_t} + \frac{\overline{\partial\Phi}}{\partial y_s}\right)ds = 0, \quad t_0 \leqslant t \leqslant t_1. \qquad (1.140)$$

This integral equation has a solution that, in the general case, does not pass through preassigned boundary values of the function $y_0(t)$. On the other hand, if we do not require that the function $y_0(t)$ assume given values at $t = t_0$ and $t = t_1$, then, in the general case, we can find the solution of this problem. Its solution does not always belong to the class of continuous functions.

If the function Φ satisfies the condition

$$\Phi[t, s, y(t), y(s)] = \Phi[s, t, y(s), y(t)], \qquad (1.140a)$$

then the equation determining the extremal $y_0 = y_0(t)$ is of the form

$$\int_{t_0}^{t_1}\frac{\partial\Phi}{\partial y_t}ds = 0, \quad t_0 \leqslant t \leqslant t_1. \qquad (1.140b)$$

If a symmetric function Φ is a bilinear form in $y(t)$ and $y(s)$, then equation (1.140b) is a linear integral equation. To see this, suppose that

$$\Phi = f_1(t, s)\,y(t)\,y(s) + \frac{f_2(t)\,y^2(t)}{2(t_1 - t_0)} + \frac{f_2(s)\,y^2(s)}{2(t_1 - t_0)}$$

$$+ \frac{f_3(t)\,y(t)}{(t_1 - t_0)} + \frac{f_3(s)\,y(s)}{(t_1 - t_0)} + \varphi(t, s).$$

Then, equation (1.140b) may be written as (we assume that $f_1(t, s) = f_1(s, t)$)

$$\int_{t_0}^{t_1}[f_1(t, s)\,y(s)]ds + f_2(t)\,y(t) + f_3(t) = 0, \qquad (1.141)$$

$$t_0 \leqslant t \leqslant t_1.$$

In the general case, this Fredholm integral equation of the second kind has a solution in the class of continuous functions. If $f_2(t) \equiv 0$, equation (1.141) is a Fredholm integral equation of the first kind and its solution belongs, in the general case, to the class of discontinuous functions and possibly including the δ-functions.

In addition to this problem of finding an unconditional extremum of the functional (1.135), it is also possible to pose the problem of finding the *conditional extremum* of the functional. This problem is posed as follows: Find the function $y(t)$ corresponding to an extremum of the functional

$$I_1 = \int_{t_0}^{t_1} \int_{t_0}^{t_1} \Phi_1 \, dt \, ds$$

under the condition that the functional I_2 of the same form assumes a given value d_2:

$$I_2 = \int_{t_0}^{t_1} \int_{t_0}^{t_1} \Phi_2 \, dt \, ds = d_2. \qquad (1.142)$$

Let us show that the function $y_0(t)$ that we are seeking must correspond to the unconditional extremum of the functional

$$I = I_1 + \lambda_2 I_2,$$

where λ_2 is a Lagrange multiplier, which can be determined from condition (1.142). Let G denote the region in the $I_1 I_2$-plane that covers the locus of the point (I_1, I_2) as $y(t)$ ranges over all possible values (see Fig. 1.3). The functional I_1 attains its extreme (minimum in Fig. 1.3) value I_{1e} at the point A of intersection of the straight line $I_2 = d_2$ with the boundary L of the region G. But how can we find this point A and the function $y_0(t)$ corresponding to it? We propose the following method: Let us draw a straight line a through the coordinate origin at an angle α to the I_2-axis and let us find the point in the region G that is closest to the line a. Of course, this point is on the boundary L (the region G is closed and hence contains its boundary). It can be found geometrically by drawing a tangent b to the boundary L parallel to a. (If the boundary L has several tangents parallel to a, we simply choose the one closest to a.)   However, we are interested in an analytical method of finding the closest point of G to the line a. Let us find an expression for the distance from an arbitrary point C of G to the line a in terms of the coordinates I_1 and I_2 and the angle α. This distance can be represented as the projection OO_1 of the segment OC onto the line N drawn through the coordinate origin and perpendicular to a. Figure 1.4 shows the supplementary constructions, which enable us to determine the form of the dependence of OO_1 on I_1, I_2, and α. In this drawing,

$$CE \perp OE, \quad CO_1 \perp NN \text{ and } CD \,\|\, NN.$$

From a consideration of the triangle CDE, we see that

$$CD = CE \sin \alpha = I_2 \sin \alpha.$$

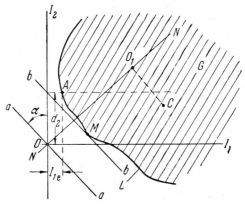

FIGURE 1.3

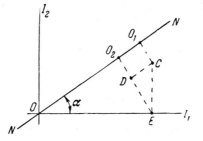

FIGURE 1.4

From a consideration of the triangle OO_2E we see that

$$OO_2 = OE \cos \alpha = I_1 \cos \alpha.$$

Consequently,

$$OO_1 = OO_2 + O_2O_1 = OO_2 + CD = I_1 \cos \alpha + I_2 \cos \alpha.$$

Thus, the distance of an arbitrary point in the region $G(I_1, I_2)$ from the line a can be expressed in terms of the coordinates I_1 and I_2 and the angle α in the following manner:

$$OO_1 = I_1 \cos \alpha + I_2 \sin \alpha = \cos \alpha (I_1 + I_2 \tan \alpha).$$

The minimum (extremum) of this distance for fixed α corresponds to the minimum (extremum) of the expression

$$I_\lambda = I_1 + I_2 \tan \alpha = I_1 + \lambda_2 I,$$

where $\lambda_2 = \tan \alpha$ is an as yet undetermined multiplier.

The function $y_\lambda(t, \lambda_2)$ corresponding to the minimum (extremum) of the functional I_λ determines the values of the functionals I_1 and I_2, which are the coordinates of the point M closest to the line a. If we now assign different values to the factor $\lambda_2 = \tan \alpha$, we can obtain different points of the boundary L. The desired point A corresponds to some value of the multiplier λ_2. This value λ_2 can be found by substituting into equation (1.142) the function $y_\lambda(t, \lambda_2)$ found from the condition for the functional I to be minimized and by solving this equation for λ.

This procedure of proof enables us to clarify the meaning of Lagrange's undetermined multiplier λ_2: This coefficient represents the tangent of the angle α formed by the line a—or the line b tangent to the boundary L at the point M—and the ordinate.

We have considered the simplest case, when the region G is simply-connected and lies to the right of the ordinate. However, the proof is not essentially changed in the general case when the region G is multiply-connected and occupies an arbitrary position in the $I_1 I_2$ -plane. In the general case, the functional I can have several extrema for fixed λ_2 (or α).

One can easily show by induction that if, instead of the supplementary condition (1.142), we have the condition

$$I_2 = \int_{t_0}^{t_1}\int_{t_0}^{t_1} \Phi_2\, dt\, ds = d_2, \left.\begin{array}{c} \\ \\ \end{array}\right\}$$

$$\dots\dots\dots\dots\dots\dots \qquad\qquad (1.142a)$$

$$I_k = \int_{t_0}^{t_1}\int_{t_0}^{t_1} \Phi_k\, dt\, ds = d_k, \left.\begin{array}{c} \\ \\ \end{array}\right.$$

then the problem of determining an extremum of the functional I_1 reduces to the problem of determining the unconditional extremum of the functional

$$I_\lambda = I_1 + \sum_{i=2}^{k} \lambda_i I_i. \qquad\qquad (1.143)$$

Here, the factors λ_i, for $i = 2, \cdots, k$, can be determined if we substitute into (1.142a) the function $y_\lambda(t, \lambda_2, \cdots, \lambda_k)$ corresponding to an extremum (minimum) of the functional I_λ. From $k - 1$ equations, we can determine the $k - 1$ unknowns $\lambda_2, \cdots, \lambda_k$.

EXAMPLE.   Determine the function $y(t)$ that minimizes the functional

$$I_1 = \int_0^1\int_0^1 e^{-\alpha|t-s|} y(t)\, y(s)\, dt\, ds \qquad\qquad (a)$$

with the conditions

$$I_2 = \int_0^1 y^2(t)\, dt = 1, \qquad\qquad (b)$$

$$y(0) = 0, \quad y(1) = 1. \qquad\qquad (c)$$

In accordance with the general procedure previously expounded, we need to find the function $y_\lambda(t, \lambda_2)$ corresponding to the unconditional minimum of the functional (1.143), which in the present example is of the form

$$I_\lambda = I_1 + \lambda_2 I_2 = \int_0^1 \int_0^1 e^{-\alpha|t-s|} y(t)\, y(s)\, dt\, ds + \lambda_2 \int_0^1 y^2(t)\, dt$$

$$= \int_0^1 \int_0^1 e^{-\alpha|t-s|} y(t)\, y(s)\, dt\, ds + \lambda_2 \int_0^1 \int_0^1 \frac{[y^2(t) + y^2(s)]}{2}\, dt\, ds. \qquad (d)$$

By using the formula (1.140b), we can write the necessary condition for minimization of the functional (d):

$$\int_0^1 e^{-\alpha|t-s|} y_\lambda(s, \lambda)\, ds + \lambda_2 y_\lambda(t, \lambda_2) = 0, \quad 0 \leqslant t \leqslant 1. \qquad (e)$$

The function $y_\lambda(t, \lambda_2)$ corresponds to the minimum of the functional I_λ. It depends on λ_2 as a parameter. To find this function, we need to solve the homogeneous Fredholm integral equation (e). In the present particular case, we proceed to find the solution of this equation in the following manner: We rewrite it in the equivalent form

$$\int_0^1 e^{-\alpha(t-s)} y_\lambda(s, \lambda_2)\, ds + \int_t^1 e^{-\alpha(s-t)} y_\lambda(s, \lambda_2)\, ds + \lambda_2 y_\lambda(t, \lambda_2) = 0, \qquad (f)$$

$$0 \leqslant t \leqslant 1.$$

Differentiating both sides of this last equation twice with respect to t, we obtain

$$\alpha^2 \left[\int_0^t e^{-\alpha(t-s)} y_\lambda(s, \lambda_2)\, ds + \int_t^1 e^{-\alpha(s-t)} y_\lambda(s, \lambda_2)\, ds \right]$$
$$- 2\alpha y_\lambda(t, \lambda_2) + \lambda_2 \ddot{y}_\lambda(t, \lambda_2) = 0. \qquad (g)$$

From (e)-(g), we obtain

$$\ddot{y}_\lambda(t, \lambda_2) - \left(\alpha^2 + \frac{2\alpha}{\lambda_2} \right) y_\lambda(t, \lambda_2) = 0.$$

The general solution of this equation is

$$y_\lambda(t, \lambda_2) = C_1 e^{kt} + C_2 e^{-kt}, \qquad (h)$$

where $k = \sqrt{\alpha^2 + \dfrac{2\alpha}{\lambda_2}}$.

The constants C_1 and C_2 can be expressed in terms of the Lagrange multiplier λ_2 by substituting the solution (h) into the condition (c):

$$C_1 = -C_2 = C = \frac{1}{\exp\sqrt{\alpha^2 + \dfrac{2\alpha}{\lambda_2}} + \exp\left(\sqrt{\alpha^2 + \dfrac{2\alpha}{\lambda_2}}\right)}.$$

The required value of the constant λ_2 can be determined by substituting the solution (h) into the condition (b).

Sometimes, the solution of equation (1.136) or equation (1.137) can be obtained in closed form. In the general case, the solutions of these equations can be obtained by some sort of approximate method [Refs. 19, 31, 41, 47]. In particular, we can use the method of fastest descent [Refs. 7, 19]. Let us briefly discuss the essentials of this method as applied to the problem of minimizing the functional (1.128). This given method is a method of successive approximations. Let $y_1(t)$ denote the first approximation of the unknown function $y(t)$. We then determine the direction of the gradient in a normed space of the function $y(t)$; that is, the direction, in that space, in which the functional I changes the most rapidly. As a norm for the function $y(t)$, we take

$$||y(t)|| = \int_{t_0}^{t_1} y^2(t)\,dt. \tag{1.144}$$

The function $Z_1(t)$ corresponding to the direction of the gradient must minimize the quantity

$$\frac{\partial}{\partial \Delta} I\{y_1(t) + \Delta \cdot Z_1(t)\}\Big|_{\Delta = 0} \tag{1.145}$$

(i.e., maximize its absolute value) under the condition that

$$\int_0^{t_1} Z_1^2(t)\,dt = 1. \tag{1.146}$$

The quantity (1.145) is the first variation of the functional I at $y(t) = y_1(t)$. It is a functional of $Z_1(t)$ and, it accordance with (1.133), it can be determined from the formula

$$\delta I_{y=y_1}$$

$$= \int_{t_0}^{t_1} Z_1(t) \left\{ \int_{t_0}^{t_1} \left[\frac{\partial \Phi}{\partial y_t} + \overline{\frac{\partial \Phi}{\partial y_s}} - \frac{d}{dt}\left(\frac{\partial \Phi}{\partial y_t'}\right) - \overline{\frac{d}{ds}\left(\frac{\partial \Phi}{\partial y_s'}\right)} \right]_{y=y_1} ds \right\} dt. \tag{1.147}$$

The problem of minimizing this functional under condition (1.146) reduces to finding the unconditional minimum of the functional

$$\int_{t_0}^{t_1} Z_1(t) \left\{ \int_{t_0}^{t_1} \left[\frac{\partial \Phi}{\partial y_t} + \overline{\frac{\partial \Phi}{\partial y_s}} - \frac{d}{dt}\left(\frac{\partial \Phi}{\partial y_t'}\right) - \overline{\frac{d}{ds}\left(\frac{\partial \Phi}{\partial y_s'}\right)} \right]_{y=y_1} ds \right\} dt$$

$$+ \lambda \int_{t_0}^{t_1} Z_1^2(t)\,dt, \tag{1.148}$$

where λ is a Lagrange multiplier that can be determined from condition (1.146).

Euler's equation for the functional (1.148) is of the form

$$\int_{t_0}^{t_1} \left[\frac{\partial \Phi}{\partial y_t} + \overline{\frac{\partial \Phi}{\partial y_s}} - \frac{d}{dt}\left(\frac{\partial \Phi}{\partial y_t'}\right) - \overline{\frac{d}{ds}\left(\frac{\partial \Phi}{\partial y_s'}\right)} \right]_{y=y_1} ds + 2\lambda Z_1(t) = 0.$$

Consequently, the function $Z_1(t)$ is, up to the factor $1/2\lambda$, equal to

$$Z_1(t) = \int_{t_0}^{t_1} \left[\frac{\partial \Phi}{\partial y_t} + \overline{\frac{\partial \Phi}{\partial y_s}} - \frac{d}{dt}\left(\frac{\partial \Phi}{\partial y_s'} \right) - \overline{\frac{d}{ds}\left(\frac{\partial \Phi}{\partial y_s'} \right)} \right]_{y=y_1} ds.$$

As our second approximation of the function $y(t)$, we take

$$y_2(t) = y_1(t)$$
$$+ v_1 \int_{t_0}^{t_1} \left[\frac{\partial \Phi}{\partial y_t} + \overline{\frac{\partial \Phi}{dy_s}} - \frac{d}{dt}\left(\frac{\partial \Phi}{\partial y_t'} \right) - \overline{\frac{d}{ds}\left(\frac{\partial \Phi}{\partial y_s'} \right)} \right]_{y=y_1} ds,$$

$$(1.149)$$

where the factor v is determined from the condition that the function

$$\xi(v) = I\{y_1(t) + vZ_1(t)\} \qquad (1.150)$$

is minimized at $v = v_1$.

The third and subsequent approximations are determined analogously. The most tedious operation in this method is, in the general case, that of minimizing the function $\xi(v)$. However, in the special case (frequently encountered in practice) when the function Φ is a symmetric bilinear form in $y(t)$, $y(s)$, $y'(t)$, and $y'(s)$:

$$\Phi = f_{00}(t, s)\, y(t)\, y(s) + f_{11}(t, s)\, y'(t)\, y'(s)$$
$$+ f_0(t)\, y(t) + f_1(t)\, y'(t),$$

and the functional I is a quadratic functional, this operation is relatively simple. In such a case,

$$I\{y_1(t) + vZ_1(t)\} = C_0 + 2C_1 v + C_2 v^2, \qquad (1.151)$$

where

$$C_0 = I\{y_1(t)\}, \quad C_1 = \frac{1}{2}\int_0^{t_1} Z_1^2(t)\, dt,$$

$$C_2 = \int_{t_0}^{t_1}\int_{t_0}^{t_1} [f_{00} Z_1(t)\, Z_1(s) + f_{11} Z_1'(t)\, Z_1'(s)]\, dt\, ds$$

is independent of v. Here, the desired value v_1 is easily determined. From (1.151) it follows that this value is

$$v_1 = -\frac{C_1}{C_2}$$

$$= -\frac{\displaystyle\int_{t_0}^{t_1} Z_1^2(t)\, dt}{2\displaystyle\int_{t_0}^{t_1}\int_{t_0}^{t_1}\left[\frac{\partial^2 \Phi}{\partial y_t \partial y_s} Z_1(t)\, Z_1(s) + \frac{\partial^2 \Phi}{\partial y_t' \partial y_s'} Z_1'(t)\, Z_1'(s) \right] dt\, ds}.$$

$$(1.152)$$

All the calculations involved in the use of the method of fastest descent can easily be programmed for machine calculation. This method always ensures sufficiently rapid convergence of the calculations.

5. DETERMINATION OF THE EXTREMA OF A FUNCTIONAL THAT IS A GIVEN FUNCTION OF OTHER FUNCTIONALS

In the foregoing, we considered a functional I (cf. (1.128)) that takes care of many criteria encountered in practice; for example, the variance of the error of a system or the second initial moment of the error of the system. However, a criterion such as the probability P that the error of the system will lie within allowed limits is already an example of a criterion that cannot be represented in the form (1.128). In the case in which the error has a normal distribution law, this criterion is a function of the mathematical expectation and variance of the error of the system. Consequently, the probability P that the error will lie within allowed limits can be represented as a function of two functionals I_1 and I_2 of the type (1.128). In practice, one can encounter yet other criteria similar to the probability P. Of interest in this connection is the problem of finding an extremum of a functional that is a given function of two functionals of the type (1.128):

$$I = f(I_1, I_2) = f[I_1\{y(t)\}, \quad I_2\{y(t)\}, \tag{1.153}$$

where

$$\begin{aligned}
I_1 &= \int_{t_0}^{t_1}\int_{t_0}^{t_1} \Phi_1[t, s, y(t), y(s), y'(t), y'(s)]\,dt\,ds, \\
I_2 &= \int_{t_0}^{t_1}\int_{t_0}^{t_1} \Phi_2[t, s, y(t), y(s), y'(t), y'(s)]\,dt\,ds.
\end{aligned} \right\} \tag{1.154}$$

We denote by Y the class of admissible functions $y(t)$. Consequently, $y(t) \in Y$. In the present case, the functional I can be regarded as a function of the two parameters I_1 and I_2. The region G of values of the parameters (functionals) I_1 and I_2 is determined by the class Y of admissible functions. Two cases are possible: (1) The function $f(I_1, I_2)$ attains an extremum inside the region G; (2) this function does not attain an extremum in the region G.

In the first case, the extremum of the functional I coincides with an extremum of the function f. This extremum can be determined from the condition

$$\frac{\partial f}{\partial I_1} = 0, \quad \frac{\partial f}{\partial I_2} = 0. \tag{1.155}$$

If the function f is not differentiable everywhere in the region G, then one or both of conditions (1.155) can be replaced with the conditions

$$\frac{\partial f}{\partial I_1} \quad \text{does not exist,}$$

$$\frac{\partial f}{\partial I_2} \quad \text{does not exist.}$$

If we solve the system of equations (1.155), we can determine the value of the functionals $I_1 = I_{10}$ and $I_2 = I_{20}$, which correspond to an extremum of the functional I. We then need to determine the function $y_0(t)$ corresponding to values of the functionals $I_1 = I_{10}$ and $I_2 = I_{20}$. In the general case, the system (1.155) does not have a unique solution and the function corresponding to $I_1 = I_{10}$ and $I_2 = I_{20}$ is also not unique. The first case is not often encountered in practice, since the optimality criterion $I = f(I_1, I_2)$ is usually chosen in such a way that the function f attains its extrema outside the region G of values of the parameters I_1 and I_2.

The basic case is case (2), in which an extremum of the function f lie outside the region G. We now prove a theorem that will be important in what follows [Refs. 3, 4, 7].

THEOREM 2. *For a function $y(t)$ belonging to the class Y of admissible functions to represent an extremum of the functional* (1.153), *it is necessary that it correspond to an extremum of the reduced functional*

$$I_\theta = \theta I_1\{y(t)\} + I_2\{y(t)\} \tag{1.156}$$

for some value of the parameter θ.

We shall call this parameter the **harmonizing parameter** or the **harmonizing factor** (it harmonizes the results obtained when we use the criteria I and I_θ).

We present two proofs of this theorem.

First proof. Let us make the additional assumptions that the function $f(I_1, I_2)$ is everywhere differentiable in the region G and that the class Y of admissible functions $y(t)$ is a linear space; that is, that the relations $y_1(t) \in Y$ and $y_2(t) \in Y$ imply that

$$K_1 y_1(t) + K_2 y_2(t) \in Y, \tag{1.157}$$

where K_1 and K_2 are arbitrary real numbers.

This proof is of an analytic nature. We use the fundamental proposition of the calculus of variations, which states that a necessary condition for an extremum of a functional is that its first variation vanish. Let us write the expression for the first variation of the functional (1.153) and let us set it equal to 0:

$$\delta I = \left. \frac{\partial I\{y_0 + \Delta \cdot Z\}}{\partial \Delta} \right|_{\Delta = 0} = 0.$$

Remembering the form of the functional (1.153), for an arbitrary function $Z \in Y$ we may write

$$\delta I = \left. \frac{\partial f(I_1\{y_0 + \Delta \cdot Z\}, I_2\{y_0 + \Delta \cdot Z\})}{\partial \Delta} \right|_{\Delta = 0}$$

$$= \left. \frac{\partial f}{\partial I_1} \frac{\partial I_1\{y_0 + \Delta \cdot Z\}}{\partial \Delta} \right|_{\Delta = 0} + \left. \frac{\partial f}{\partial I_2} \frac{\partial I_2\{y_0 + \Delta \cdot Z\}}{\partial \Delta} \right|_{\Delta = 0} = 0.$$

This equation is satisfied if

$$\frac{\partial f}{\partial I_1} = \frac{\partial f}{\partial I_2} = 0;$$

that is, if the function f attains an extremum inside the region G (case (1)). We have already agreed to consider the second case the basic one; that is, the case in which the function f does not attain an extremum in the region G and hence the two partial derivatives $\partial f/\partial I_1$ and $\partial f/\partial I_2$ do not vanish anywhere simultaneously in G. Without loss of generality, we may assume that

$$\frac{\partial f}{\partial I_2} \neq 0.$$

Then, the last equation can be rewritten

$$\frac{\dfrac{\partial f}{\partial I_1}}{\dfrac{\partial f}{\partial I_2}} \frac{\partial I_1\{y_0 + \Delta \cdot Z\}}{\partial \Delta}\bigg|_{\Delta=0} + \frac{\partial I_2\{y_0 + \Delta \cdot Z\}}{\partial \Delta}\bigg|_{\Delta=0} = 0. \quad \text{(1.158)}$$

In this equation, the factor

$$\frac{\dfrac{\partial f(I_1, I_2)}{\partial I_1}}{\dfrac{\partial f(I_1, I_2)}{\partial I_2}}\bigg|_{y=y_0}$$

is an unknown number θ_0:

$$\frac{\dfrac{\partial f}{\partial I_1}}{\dfrac{\partial f}{\partial I_2}}\bigg|_{y=y_0} = \theta_0. \quad \text{(1.159)}$$

Consequently, equation (1.158) can be rewritten in the form

$$\theta_0 \frac{\partial I_1\{y_0 + \Delta \cdot Z\}}{\partial \Delta}\bigg|_{\Delta=0} + \frac{\partial I_2\{y_0 + \Delta \cdot Z\}}{\partial \Delta}\bigg|_{\Delta=0} = 0$$

or

$$\frac{\partial I_\theta\{y_0 + \Delta \cdot Z\}}{\partial \Delta}\bigg|_{\Delta=0} = 0. \quad \text{(1.160)}$$

where

$$I_\theta = \theta_0 I_1 + I_2.$$

Equation (1.160) is a necessary condition for the functional I_θ to have an extremum at some value of the parameter $\theta = \theta_0$. From this it follows that Theorem 2 may be considered as proved. We note that the

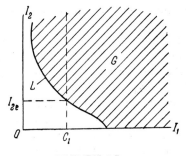

FIGURE 1.5

linearity of the space Y was used here only in the determination of the first variation of the functional I. In the evaluation of I we use the admissible function

$$y_0(t) + \Delta \cdot Z(t),$$

where $Z(t)$ is an arbitrary function in the class Y. The differentiability of the function f with respect to I_1 and I_2 is also used in obtaining an expression for the first variation of the functional I.

  Second proof. In this proof, we shall not require that the set Y be a linear space or that the function f be everywhere differentiable.

  The functional I, defined by (1.153), of the function $y(t)$ can be regarded as a function of the variables I_1 and I_2 with values in some region G (see Fig. 1.5). Since the function f is assumed to have no extrema inside G, it follows that an extremum of the functional I (if it exists) must coincide with the greatest or smallest value of the function f. Its greatest or smallest value lies on the boundary L of the region G. Consequently, to find an extremum of the functional I, we first need to find the functions $y(t)$ corresponding to the boundary L. These functions $y(t)$ constitute a set of functions that depend on a single parameter. Then, we need to find the value of this parameter that corresponds to the greatest or smallest value of the function f, and hence to the extremum of the functional I.

  To find the function $y(t)$ corresponding to the boundary L of the region G, we proceed as follows: Consider a particular value of the functional

$$I_1 = C_1$$

and, under this condition, let us determine the extremum I_{2e} of the functional I_2. As was previously shown, the problem of finding the conditional extremum reduces to the problem of finding an unconditional extremum of the functional

$$I_\theta\{y\} = \theta I_1\{y\} + I_2\{y\}.$$

By considering different values of C_1 or different values of the parameter

θ, we can obtain all points of the boundary L. For some value of the harmonizing parameter $\theta = \theta_0$, we obtain the function $y(t)$ corresponding to the greatest or lowest value of the function f, and hence to an extremum of the functional I. Thus, the function $y(t)$ corresponding to an extremum of the functional I must correspond to an extremum of the functional I_θ for $\theta = \theta_0$.

Our second proof was carried out under more general assumptions than the first proof. Here, we removed the restrictions imposed in the first proof on the set Y of admissible functions $y(t)$ and on the function f; that is, we did not require that the set Y be a linear space or that the function f be differentiable.

On the basis of Theorem 2, we may conclude that the function $y^0(t)$ corresponding to an extremum of the functional (1.153) should be sought among the functions $y_0(t, \theta)$ corresponding to the extrema of the functionals $I_\theta = \theta I_1 + I_2$.

As yet, we have not answered the question as to how to determine the value of the harmonizing parameter $\theta = \theta_0$ corresponding to an extremum of the functional (1.153). However, if we can determine the value of the harmonizing parameter $\theta = \theta_0$, then the function $y^0(t)$ corresponding to an extremum of the functional (1.153) can be obtained in accordance with the formula

$$y^0(t) = y_0(t, \theta_0). \tag{1.161}$$

Let us show how we can determine the value of the parameter θ_0 corresponding to an extremum of the functional (1.153) when we know the function $y_0(t, \theta)$ corresponding to an extremum of the functional (1.156).

First method of determining the harmonizing parameter θ_0. This method is based on the use of equation (1.159). Let us substitute the function $y_0(t, \theta)$ into the left-hand member of that equation. Obviously, equation (1.159) is satisfied for $\theta = \theta_0$:

$$\frac{\dfrac{\partial f(I_1, I_2)}{\partial I_1}}{\dfrac{\partial f(I_1, I_2)}{\partial I_2}} = \theta_0.$$

Here, the partial derivatives are evaluated at the values of the functionals

$$I_1 = I_1\{y_0(t, \theta_0)\}, \quad I_2 = I_2\{y_0(t, \theta_0)\}.$$

The ratio of the partial derivatives on the left is a function of the parameter θ:

$$\left. \frac{\dfrac{\partial f}{\partial I_1}}{\dfrac{\partial f}{\partial I_2}} \right|_{y = y_0(t, \theta_0)} = F(\theta_0).$$

Thus, the desired value of the parameter θ_0 is a solution of the equation

$$F(\theta_0) = \theta_0. \tag{1.162}$$

In the general case, this equation is a nonlinear algebraic or transcendental equation. It may have several roots, and we need to use the method of comparison to determine that root that corresponds to the extremum of the functional (1.153) that we are seeking.

Second method of determining the harmonizing parameter θ_0. With this method, the function $y_0(t, \theta)$ corresponding to the extremum of the functional (1.156) is substituted into the functional (1.153):

$$I = f[I_1\{y_0(t, \theta)\}, \quad I_2\{y_0(t, \theta)\}] = \Phi(\theta), \tag{1.163}$$

which in the present case is a function Φ of the parameter θ. We need to determine the extremum (minimum or maximum) in question of the function $\Phi(\theta)$. The value of the parameter θ corresponding to this extremum of the function Φ is the sought value θ_0. The extremum that we have found for the function $\Phi_e = \Phi(\theta_0)$ is the extremum I_e we are seeking of the functional (1.153) (see Fig. 1.6). In many cases encountered in practice, this second method of determining the value of the parameter θ_0 corresponding to an extremum of the functional (1.153) is more convenient, since it does not necessitate solving the complicated equation (1.162).

Thus, the complicated problem of finding an extremum of the functional (1.153) is reduced to solving two simpler problems. The first of these is the problem of finding the function $y_0(t, \theta)$ corresponding to an extremum of the functional (1.156). The second problem is the problem of determining the value of the harmonizing parameter θ_0 that maximizes or minimizes the functional $I = I\{y_0(t, \theta)\}$.

By reasoning in an analogous manner, we can prove the following theorem [Refs. 3, 4, 8]:

THEOREM 2a. *In order for a function $y(t)$ belonging to the class Y of admissible functions to represent an extremum of the functional*

$$I = f(I_1, I_2, \cdots, I_{n+1}) = f[I_1\{y(t)\}, \cdots, I_{n+1}\{y(t)\}], \tag{1.164}$$

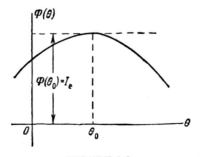

FIGURE 1.6

it is necessary that it correspond to an extremum of the reduced functional

$$I_\theta = \theta_1 I_1 + \theta_2 I_2 + \cdots + \theta_n I_n + I_{n+1} \tag{1.165}$$

for certain values of the harmonizing parameters $\theta_1, \cdots, \theta_n$.
    Let us denote by

$$y_0(t, \theta_1, \cdots, \theta_n) \tag{1.166}$$

the function corresponding to the extremum of the functional (1.164). Of course, this function depends on the n harmonizing parameters θ_i. The values of the harmonizing parameters $\theta_1 = \theta_{10}, \cdots, \theta_n = \theta_{n0}$ corresponding to an extremum of the functional (1.164) can also be determined by two methods. In the first method, the parameters $\theta_{10}, \cdots, \theta_{n0}$ are determined from the following equations:

$$\left. \frac{\dfrac{\partial f}{\partial I_i}}{\dfrac{\partial f}{\partial I_{n+1}}} \right|_{y(t)\,=\,y_0(t,\theta_{10},\cdots,\theta_{n0})} = F_i(\theta_{10}, \cdots, \theta_{n0}) = \theta_{i0}, \tag{1.167}$$

$$i = 1, \cdots, n.$$

With the second method, we need to substitute into the functional (1.164) the function (1.166) determined from the condition for an extremum of the functional (1.165). In this case, the functional (1.164) is a function Φ of the n parameters θ_i:

$$I\{y_0(t, \theta_1, \cdots, \theta_n)\} = \Phi(\theta_1, \cdots, \theta_n). \tag{1.168}$$

    We then need to find by some method or other an extremum of the function Φ and the corresponding values of the harmonizing parameters $\theta_{10}, \cdots, \theta_{n0}$:

$$\Phi_e = \Phi(\theta_{10}, \cdots, \theta_{n0}).$$

The values of the parameters θ_{i0} corresponding to the extremum of the function Φ can be determined analytically from the system of equations

$$\left. \frac{\partial \Phi}{\partial \theta_i} \right|_{\theta_j = \theta_{j0}} = \theta_{i0}, \quad i, j = 1, \cdots, n, \tag{1.169}$$

or by some other method; for example, graphically. The extreme value Φ_e is an extremum of the functional (1.164):

$$I_e = \Phi_e = \Phi(\theta_{10}, \cdots, \theta_{n0}),$$

and the function

$$y^0(t) = y_0(t, \theta_{10}, \cdots, \theta_{n0}) \tag{1.170}$$

corresponds to this extremum of the functional (1.164).
    In the general case, solutions of this problem are not unique. In such cases, from the maxima of the functional (1.164), we need to choose the maximum maximorum (or the minimum minimorum).

In the general case, the systems (1.167) and (1.169) also have non-unique solutions. The following question arises: Do the solutions of these systems of equations coincide? If a combination of the parameters $\theta_{10}, \cdots, \theta_{n0}$ corresponds to an extremum of the functional (1.164), then this combination is a solution of both the system (1.167) and of the system (1.169), since each of these systems is a necessary condition for maximization or minimization of the functional (1.164) by the function $y^0(t) = y_0(t, \theta_{10}, \cdots, \theta_{n0})$. Under the additional assumption (usually satisfied) that

$$
\begin{vmatrix}
\dfrac{\partial I_1}{\partial \theta_1}, & \cdots, & \dfrac{\partial I_n}{\partial \theta_1} \\
\cdots\cdots\cdots \\
\dfrac{\partial I_1}{\partial \theta_n}, & \cdots, & \dfrac{\partial I_n}{\partial \theta_n}
\end{vmatrix}_{\theta_j = \theta_{j0}} \neq 0, \quad j = 1, \cdots, n,
$$

one can show [Refs. 4, 7] that, if a combination of the parameters $\theta_{10}, \cdots, \theta_{n0}$ (not necessarily corresponding to an extremum of the functional (1.164)) satisfies the system (1.167), then it also satisfies the system (1.169) and that, conversely, if the combination of the parameters $\theta_{10}, \cdots, \theta_{n0}$ satisfies the system (1.169), it satisfies the system (1.167).

In the foregoing, we proved the necessary conditions for an extremum of the functional (1.164). We shall now say a few words regarding sufficient conditions for minimization or maximization of that functional. Here, we shall use the interpretation of the functional (1.164) as a function of $n + 1$ variables $I_1, \cdots, I_{n+1}$ that vary in some region G with boundary L (cf., for example, Fig. 1.5).

Sufficient conditions for maximization or minimization of (1.164) by a function $y^0(t) = y_0(i, \theta_{10}, \cdots, \theta_{n0})$ must include

(a) sufficient conditions for maximization or minimization of the reduced functional I_θ (cf. (1.165)) by $y_0 = y_0(t, \theta_1, \cdots, \theta_n)$ in some small region of variation of the parameters

$$
|\theta_i - \theta_{i0}| < \varepsilon, \quad \varepsilon > 0, \tag{1.171}
$$

including the point $\theta_i = \theta_{i0}$ for $i = 1, \cdots, n$,

(b) sufficient conditions for the function $\Phi = \Phi(\theta_1, \cdots, \theta_n)$ (cf. (1.168)) to attain a minimum or maximum on the boundary L of the region G at the point $(\theta_{10}, \cdots, \theta_{n0})$,

(c) sufficient conditions for displacement from the point $(\theta_{10}, \cdots, \theta_{n0})$ inside the region G along the normal to the boundary L to increase or decrease the value of the functional (1.164).

Let us look at these three features of sufficient conditions for an extremum of the functional (1.164). The sufficient conditions for the functional I_θ to be maximized or minimized must be verified not only for $\theta_i = \theta_{i0}$, where $i = 1, \cdots, n$, but throughout the region (1.171), because, when we are investigating the behavior of the function $\Phi(\theta_1,$

$\cdots$, θ_n) on the boundary L, it is necessary that this boundary exist in a neighborhood of the point $(\theta_{10}, \cdots, \theta_{n0})$. A sufficient condition for existence of a boundary L in some region containing the point $(\theta_{10}, \cdots, \theta_{n0})$ is (a). We shall not formulate sufficient conditions for maximization or minimization of the functional I_θ in the region (1.171). In the general case, these conditions are quite complicated and difficult to verify [Refs. 32, 50]. In the particular cases encountered in practical problems, these conditions are often easily determined and verified [Refs. 31, 47, 52]. Examples of such cases will be presented in Chapter III.

Sufficient conditions in order for the function $\Phi(\theta_1, \cdots, \theta_n)$ to have a minimum at the point $(\theta_{10}, \cdots, \theta_{n0})$ can be expressed by the relations

$$
\left.\begin{array}{c}
\left.\dfrac{\partial \Phi}{\partial \theta_i}\right|_{\theta_j = \theta_{j0}} = 0, \\[2mm]
\left.\dfrac{\partial^2 \Phi}{\partial \theta_i \partial \theta_j}\right|_{\theta_k = \theta_{k0}} \begin{cases} > 0, & \text{if } i = j, \\ = 0, & \text{if } i \ne j, \end{cases} \\[2mm]
i, j, k = 1, \cdots, n.
\end{array}\right\} \tag{1.172}
$$

In order for Φ to have a maximum at that point, we need to replace the sign $>$ with $<$.

The validity of (b) is easily verified if there exists a relationship $\Phi = \Phi(\theta_1, \cdots, \theta_n)$ in a neighborhood of the point $(\theta_{10}, \cdots, \theta_{n0})$. Verification of conditions (1.172) of (b) enables us to distinguish the point $(\theta_{10}, \cdots, \theta_{n0})$ corresponding to a minimum of the function Φ from a point corresponding to a maximum or a point of inflection (or a saddle point) of that function.

If sufficient conditions for the displacement of the point $(\theta_{10}, \cdots, \theta_{n0})$ inside the region G along the normal to the boundary L to increase (respectively decrease) the value of the functional I are satisfied, then displacement of the point

$$
[I_{10}, \cdots, I_{n+1,0}] = [I_1(\theta_{10}, \cdots, \theta_{n0}), \cdots, I_{n+1}(\theta_{10}, \cdots, \theta_{n0})]
$$

in an arbitrary direction inside the region G increases (respectively decreases) the functional I. One can easily see that in this case (when (a) and (b) are also satisfied) the point $(I_{10}, \cdots, I_{n+1,0})$ corresponds to the smallest (respectively greatest) value of the function $f(I_1, \cdots, I_{n+1})$ in the region G.

The boundary L of the region G of possible values of the variables $I_1, \cdots, I_{n+1}$ is defined by equations in parametric form

$$
I_i = I_i\{y_0(t, \theta_1, \cdots, \theta_n)\} = \varphi_i(\theta_1, \cdots, \theta_n), \quad i = 1, \cdots, n. \tag{1.173}
$$

In this case, the equation for the normal to the surface L at the point $I_i = I_{i0} = \varphi_i(\theta_{10}, \cdots, \theta_{n0})$ is written as [Ref. 50]

$$\frac{I_1 - I_{10}}{v_1} = \cdots = \frac{I_{n+1} - I_{n+1,0}}{v_{n+1}}, \tag{1.174}$$

where

$$v_k = \begin{vmatrix} \dfrac{\partial \varphi_1}{\partial \theta_1} & \cdots & \dfrac{\partial \varphi_1}{\partial \theta_n} \\ \cdots \cdots \cdots \cdots \\ \dfrac{\partial \varphi_{k-1}}{\partial \theta_1} & \cdots & \dfrac{\partial \varphi_{k-1}}{\partial \theta_n} \\ \dfrac{\partial \varphi_{k+1}}{\partial \theta_1} & \cdots & \dfrac{\partial \varphi_{k+1}}{\partial \theta_n} \\ \cdots \cdots \cdots \cdots \\ \dfrac{\partial \varphi_{n+1}}{\partial \theta_1} & \cdots & \dfrac{\partial \varphi_{n+1}}{\partial \theta_n} \end{vmatrix}_{\theta_i = \theta_{i0}} , \quad k = 1, \cdots, n+1. \tag{1.175}$$

The values of the functional (1.164) on the straight line (1.174) can be expressed in terms of a varying parameter α, which characterizes the distance of a variable point on the normal from the point $(I_{10}, \cdots, I_{n+1,0})$, in the following manner:

$$f\left(I_{10} + \frac{\alpha}{v_1}, \cdots, I_{n+1,0} + \frac{\alpha}{v_{n+1}}\right) = \varphi(\alpha). \tag{1.176}$$

Investigation of the behavior of the function $\varphi(\alpha)$ in a neighborhood of the value of the argument $\alpha = 0$ enables us in particular cases to conclude that (c) is satisfied. In the particular case in which $n = 1$ and $I_\theta = \theta_1 I_1 + I_2$, formulas (1.174)-(1.176) take the forms

$$v_1 = \frac{\partial I_2(\theta_1)}{\partial \theta_1}\bigg|_{\theta_1 = \theta_{10}}, \quad v_2 = \frac{\partial I_1(\theta_1)}{\partial \theta_1}\bigg|_{\theta_1 = \theta_{10}}, \tag{1.174a}$$

$$\frac{I_1 - I_{10}}{\dfrac{\partial I_2}{\partial \theta_1}} = \frac{I_2 - I_{20}}{\dfrac{\partial I_1}{\partial \theta_1}}, \tag{1.175a}$$

$$f\left(I_{10} + \frac{\alpha}{\dfrac{\partial I_2}{\partial \theta_1}}, \quad I_{20} + \frac{\alpha}{\dfrac{\partial I_1}{\partial \theta_1}}\right) = \varphi(\alpha). \tag{1.176a}$$

Chapter 2

OPTIMAL SYSTEMS

6. THE MEANING OF THE THEORY OF OPTIMAL SYSTEMS

In recent years, a great deal of attention has been given in Russian and foreign literature to optimal automatic-control systems. By an optimal system, we mean a system that is "best" in some sense or other. To choose the "best" system out of a number of systems, we need to have a method of comparing these systems quantitatively; that is, we need to have some criterion for comparing them. The criterion needs to be expressed by a number depending on the characteristics of the systems. If we have such a criterion, *we consider a system optimal if it maximizes or minimizes the criterion chosen.* Depending on the specific form of the criterion, the "optimal system" may either minimize or maximize that criterion. For example, if we choose as our criterion for comparing different systems the amount of energy used up or the mean square error of the system, that system is considered optimal that ensures minimum expenditure of energy in the first case and minimum mean square error in the second. On the other hand, if our criterion is the probability that the error of the system will lie within prescribed limits or the probability that the system will operate without failure for a given length of time, then that system is optimal that maximizes the probability that the error will lie within the prescribed limits in the first case and the probability of failure-free operation for the required length of time in the second.

People have always tried to find optimal systems, or optimal designs. However, until recently, an approximation of optimal characteristics was achieved experimentally by "groping around." For example, it was from experiment that one recommended a certain length of axe handle or the diameter of a cartwheel, or that one chose a certain gear when driving an automobile, and so on. The amount of experimental material, the great diversity in technological tools, and the development of mathematical methods of finding extrema of functions and function-

56

als have enabled us to solve theoretically problems concerned with the determination of optimal characteristics of systems in cases that are important in practice.

A characteristic feature of any problem of determining an optimal system is the existence of contradictory factors. These factors influence in different ways the criterion used in comparing different systems. Therefore, change in the parameter(s) of the system leads to two types of change in the criterion: To a change in the criterion due to the presence of the first factor and to a change in the criterion due to the presence of the second factor. The problem of choosing the optimal value of a parameter of the system consists in determining what value maximizes or minimizes the criterion in question. If there are no contradictory factors, it is not meaningful to pose a problem over the determination of the optimal system.

The theory of optimal systems deals essentially with the study of the dialectic law of struggle of contradictions from a quantitative point of view. A thorough study of the contradictory factors influencing the operation of a system, a quantitative estimate of their influence on the criterion, and the search for optimal characteristics of the system enable us to indicate the path for improving existing systems; that is, to indicate the direction of progress of these systems.

In practice, it is not always possible to carry out all the recommendations of the theory of optimal systems. Questions concerned with the methods for carrying out these recommendations constitute the subject matter of the synthesis of optimal systems. At the present time, the high level of precision instruments, the high quality of automatization elements, and the successful development of related fields of technology enable us in many cases to realize systems that are close to optimal.

The determination of optimal systems and the construction of systems nearly optimal have always constituted and will always constitute very real problems in scientific investigations in all fields of technology. The results of technological investigations on the determination of optimal systems can be used in the construction of high-quality systems, in the adjustment and completion of new high-quality systems, in the development of new principles of constructing high-quality systems, in the development of engineering problems dealing with projected systems, in the estimation of specific systems (with regard to their closeness to the optimal systems), and in evaluating the prospects of their completion.

The problem of determining an optimal system includes four important problems: (1) The choice of a criterion for comparing two systems and the obtaining of a mathematical description of that criterion, (2) the study and mathematical description of the information on the influences on the system, (3) the determination and mathematical description of classes of admissible automatic-control systems, and (4) the finding of an extremum of the criterion and of the characteristics of the system that correspond to it.

7.   CRITERIA FOR COMPARISON OF AUTOMATIC-CONTROL SYSTEMS

A criterion for comparison of automatic-control systems must, to some degree or other, reflect the nature of the operation of these systems, their efficiency, the results of their application under given conditions, the extent to which they solve the problem for which they were designed, and so on. Thus, a criterion must approximate as nearly as possible the qualities of the system from several points of view. As a rule, it is desirable for the criterion to reflect the accuracy of operation of the system, its reliability, its technology, its cost, its weight, its dimensions, and the like. However, it is usually impossible to have a single criterion that reflects all these properties of a system and to find a mathematical relationship between these qualities and the parameters of the system. Therefore, we need to choose the most important quality (or the two or three most important qualities) and use it (or them) as a criterion. The importance of each criterion is relative. Under one set of conditions, a criterion may be acceptable whereas under another set of conditions the same criterion may be clearly unsatisfactory. If we take this approach, when one of the qualities of the system is used as a criterion and the other qualities are not taken into account, we implicitly assume that change in the values of the parameters of the system in the neighborhood of their optimal values with respect to the criterion chosen causes only insignificant changes in the other properties of the system (for example, its weight). This assumption is quite frequently satisfied.

Of course, there is no such thing as an all-purpose criterion, one that will be suitable in all cases. In each particular case, it is expedient to use whatever criterion is most appropriate for that case. In some cases we can use familiar criteria and in others we need to develop a new criterion.

Let us look at some examples of various criteria. In the following exposition, we shall always assume that the systems in question are subject to random influences. Therefore, it is expedient to choose for our criteria certain probabilistic characteristics of the quantities characterizing the operation of the system.

In many cases, precision is an important element of the operation of a system. Therefore, in what follows, our criteria will be probabilistic characteristics (of some form or other) of the error of the system.

1. The variance of the error of a system

If we know that the mathematical expectation $m_E(t) = M[E(t)]$ of the error $E(t)$ is equal to 0, we can sometimes take for our criterion the variance of the error at a certain instant of time t_1:

$$D_E(t_1) = M[\overset{0}{E}^2(t_1)].$$

The positive side of this criterion is its simplicity. Of all probabilistic criteria that are of practical value, the variance in the error of the system is the simplest both from the point of view of its calculation and from the point of view of determining the optimal system. (The mathematical expectation is an even simpler probabilistic characteristic, but we rule it out since it cannot be used as a criterion for comparing systems subject to random influences.)

However, in a number of cases, the variance does not reflect the purpose of the system and is not immediately connected with the problems the system is intended to solve. This defect is to some extent mitigated by the fact that in an important particular case, the minimum of the variance in the error corresponds to the maximum of the probability that the error of the system is small. This will be the case when the error of the system is subject to a normal distribution law. Consequently, in this particular case, the variance in the error of the system does indeed reflect the purpose of the system.

2. The second initial moment of the error of a system or the mean square error of the system

If the mathematical expectation of the error of a system is nonzero, then the variance in the error of the system cannot be an acceptable criterion. In this case, we may take as our criterion the second initial moment of the error of the system (that is, the mean square error of the system) at some instant of time

$$\Gamma_E(t_1) = M[E(t_1)E(t_1)] = D_E(t_1) + m_E^2(t_1).$$

If the mathematical expectation of the error $m_E(t)$ is zero, then

$$\Gamma_E(t) = D_E(t).$$

Consequently, the second criterion $\Gamma_E(t_1)$ is more general than the first $D_E(t_1)$, which it includes as a special case. As a criterion, the mean square error of the system $\Gamma_E(t_1)$ has the advantage of being a simple probabilistic characteristic that is convenient in solving problems of choice of optimal systems. A defect in it is that, in many cases, it is not directly connected with the problems that the systems are designed to solve and does not reflect well enough the purpose of the systems.

The simplicity of these two criteria has determined their widespread use in the theory of optimal systems.

3. A function of the mathematical expectation and variance in the error of a system

As we have already emphasized, a very real defect in both the preceding criteria is the fact that, in a number of cases, they do not reflect the purpose of the system. Let us try to choose a criterion that will reflect this purpose for a rather large class of systems.

We know that many systems are designed to ensure some law of change of the output variable. For example, a reproducing system is designed to reproduce the input signal, an extrapolator is designed to reproduce the input signal with prediction, and so on. Ordinarily, we want as small an error in absolute value as possible. If we take the variance as a comparison criterion, the degree of undesirability of the error is considered proportional to the square of the value of the error. This is a rather artificial estimate of the undesirability of the error. For example, a control system for a reproducing lathe that turns out manufactured objects with a specified accuracy must be evaluated according to some other criterion. In such cases, all the errors that do not exceed a certain tolerated value are equally acceptable (the manufactured object is suitable for use), and the errors exceeding this tolerance are also equally acceptable (the object is not suitable for use). In this case, a suitable criterion, one that reflects the purpose of the system quite well is the probability P that the error of the system will lie within specified tolerated limits. If the error is subject to a normal distribution law, this probability is equal to

$$P = P(C_1 \leqslant E \leqslant C_2) = \frac{1}{\sqrt{2\pi D_E}} \int_{C_1}^{C_2} \exp\left[-\frac{(m_E - E)^2}{2D_E}\right] dE,$$

where $m_E(t_1)$ and $D_E(t_1)$ are respectively the mathematical expectation and the variance of the error of the system at the given instant t_1, and C_1 and C_2 are given tolerated errors (ordinarily, $C_1 < 0$ and $C_2 > 0$).

In all cases in which it is expedient to keep the error of the system within given limits, the probability that the error will be within those limits is a good criterion. If the probability density of the error is determined by the first two moments; that is, the mathematical expectation and the variance, then the probability that the error of the system will fall within given limits is a function of these probabilistic moments:

$$P = f(m_E, D_E).$$

Sometimes, instead of the function $f(m_E, D_E)$, it is more convenient to consider either the function

$$f_1(m_E, \Gamma_E) = f(m_E, \Gamma_E - m_E^2)$$

which is a function of the mathematical expectation and the mean square error, or else the function

$$f_2(m_E^2, D_E) = f(\sqrt{m_E^2}, D_E)$$

which is a function of the square of the mathematical expectation and the variance of the error of the system.

The criterion $f(m_E, D_E)$ may have an interpretation other than the probability $P = P(C_1 \le E \le C_2)$. This criterion includes the probability P as a special case.

4. A given function of the values of the mathematical expectation and the correlation function at different instants of time

In the preceding subsection, we considered the quality of operation of a system at an instant t_1. Sometimes, it is required that the system operate with a sufficiently high degree of accuracy over the course of a certain interval of time. The probability that the error of a system will not exceed certain limits during the period from 0 to T can be calculated approximately if the error obeys a normal law. This probability is a function of the values of the mathematical expectation of the error m_E at the instants $0, \Delta t, 2\Delta t, \cdots, n\Delta t$, where $\Delta t = T/n$, and the values of the correlation function of the error $K_E(i\Delta t, j\Delta t) = K_{ij}$, where $i, j = 0, 1, \cdots, n$.

Thus, in such cases, the comparison criterion of the system is a function of the values of the mathematical expectation of the error $m_E(i\Delta t)$ at the instants $i\Delta t$ for $i = 0, 1, \cdots, n$, and the values of the correlation function of the error $K_E(i\Delta t, j\Delta t)$:

$$P = f[m_E(i\Delta t), K_E(i\Delta t, j\Delta t)] = f(m_i, K_{ij}).$$

5. The mathematical expectation of a given function of the error of the system

This criterion is of the following form: $M[\varphi(E)]$, where φ is a given function. In the special cases in which $\varphi = E^2$, this criterion is either the variance of the error of the system (if $m_E = 0$) or the mean square error of the system (if $m_E \ne 0$).

In the case in which

$$\varphi(E) = \begin{cases} 0, & \text{if } E > C_2 \text{ or } E < C_1, \\ 1, & \text{if } C_1 \le E \le C_2, \end{cases}$$

our criterion is the probability that the error of the system will fall within tolerated limits:

$$M[\varphi(E)] = P(C_1 \leqslant E \leqslant C_2).$$

For different specific functions $\varphi(E)$, the criterion $M[\varphi(E)]$ has different physical interpretations.

It should be noted that the fourth of the criteria that we have just considered includes the third as a special case, and that the third includes the second as a special case, and that the second includes the first as a special case. The fifth criterion includes the second as a special case and in some cases it coincides with the third criterion (specifically, when the third criterion means the probability that the error will fall within specified limits).

Of course, there are yet other criteria. In each specific case, we need to choose the most suitable criterion for comparing systems. In certain cases, this will be the second initial moment (variance) of the error; in other cases, it will be the probability that the error will not exceed tolerated limits or some other criterion.

The more completely and accurately the criterion reflects the purpose of the system, the more complicated it is likely to be and the more difficult will be its use in determining an optimal system. Therefore, in choosing a comparison criterion, we also need to solve the problem for the optimum, keeping two contradictory factors in mind; namely, the complexity of the criterion and the completeness and accuracy with which the criterion reflects the purpose of the system. The more powerful the computational technology at the disposal of the investigator and the higher the level reached by the theory of optimal systems, the more complicated the criterion may be and the more it will reflect the purpose of the system, and hence the higher will be the quality of the system that can be obtained.

8. INFLUENCES ON AN AUTOMATIC-CONTROL SYSTEM. THE CLASS OF ALLOWED SYSTEMS

At the present time, any serious investigation of the analysis and synthesis of automatic-control systems must take into account the stochastic (statistical) nature of the signals. Therefore, in determining the optimal system, we need to remember that, in the general case, random influences are exerted on an automatic-control system at different points. A complete probabilistic characteristic of a random influence that is a random function is an n-dimensional distribution law. In the following examination, we shall usually use less complete characteristics, such as the mathematical expectation and the correlation function of a random influence, without considering the distribution law or assuming that it is given; for example, assuming that the distribution law of the random influence is a normal one.

Let us first consider a single random influence $X(t)$ of which we need to know something about the probabilistic characteristics.

The mathematical expectation of this influence (useful signal or noise) is a known function of the time:*

$$m_x = M[X] = m_x(t).$$

The vanishing of the mathematical expectation of the inputs and outputs of a system simplifies study of the system and the search for its optimal characteristics. The more complicated the form of the function $m_x(t)$, the more complicated will the investigations of the system be. The functions $m_x(t)$ that are obtained in practice are usually continuous and they can be approximated by polynomials:

$$m_x(t) = \sum_{i=0}^{p} G_i t^i.$$

The correlation function $K_x(t_1, t_2)$ of a random influence $X(t)$ is a function of two variables and can be determined from formula (1.57):

$$K_x(t_1, t_2) = M[\{X(t_1) - m_x(t_1)\}\{X(t_2) - m_x(t_2)\}]$$
$$= M[\overset{0}{X}(t_1), \overset{0}{X}(t_2)],$$

where

$$\overset{0}{X}(t) = X(t) - m_x(t)$$

is a centralized random function; that is, a random function whose mathematical expectation is zero.

Sometimes we need to consider several random signals simultaneously, let us say the signals $X_1(t)$ and $X_2(t)$. Then we need to consider the correlation function between the two random functions $X(t)$ and $Y(t)$ (cf. (1.60)):

$$K_{xy}(t_1, t_2) = M[\overset{0}{X}(t_1)\,\overset{0}{Y}(t_2)].$$

The more complicated the form of the functions K_x and K_{xy}, the more complicated will be the problem of determining the optimal system.

The simplest to solve is the problem of finding the optimal system when the random signals are stationary or stationarily connected. In this case, the corresponding correlation functions depend only on the difference in the arguments $\tau = t_2 - t_1$ (more precisely, on the absolute value of the difference $|\tau| = |t_2 - t_1|$):

$$K_x = K_x(\tau) = K_x(t_2 - t_1),$$
$$K_{xy} = K_{xy}(\tau) = K_{xy}(t_2 - t_1).$$

---

* Here and in what follows, we take time as the argument of the random function. However, all that we shall have to say will also be valid for random functions of arbitrary arguments.

The mathematical expectations and the correlation functions of the influences on the system can be obtained by either experiment or calculation.

Let us give some examples of correlation functions of stationary influences:

1)
$$K_x(\tau) = \delta(\tau),$$ (2.1)

where $\delta(\tau)$ is the delta-function. This correlation function corresponds to what is called "white noise"; that is, an ideal random process whose values are unconnected at arbitrarily close instants of time t_1 and t_2. A physical approximate analogue of such a process is the velocity of a molecule in Brownian motion. Sometimes, a real random influence can be represented approximately as white noise. The variance of a white noise is infinite, which reflects the unrealness of such a process.

2)
$$K_x(\tau) = D_x e^{-\alpha|\tau|} = D_x e^{-\alpha|t_2 - t_1|},$$ (2.2)

where $D_x = K_x(0)$ is the variance of a random signal X and α is a positive number. Figure 2.1 (curve a) shows the graph of such a correlation function. The greater the parameter α, the more rapidly (that is, for the smaller value of τ) will the dependence between the values of the random signal at different instants of time t_2 and t_1 disappear. For a given value of the parameter α, the relationship between two values $X(t_1)$ and $X(t_2)$ of the signal decreases monotonically with increase in the interval $\tau = t_2 - t_1$.

3)
$$K_x(\tau) = D_x e^{-\alpha|\tau|} \cos \beta\tau,$$ (2.3)

where α and β are positive parameters with dimension 1/sec. Figure 2.1 (curve b) shows the graph of such a correlation function. Here, just as in the preceding case, $K_x(\tau) \to 0$ as $\tau \to \infty$. In contrast with the preceding case, the correlation function $K_x(t)$ assumes negative as well as positive values. Such a correlation function has a more general form

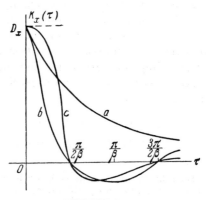

FIGURE 2.1

and hence it can correspond to a broader class of random functions.

4)
$$K_x(\tau) = D_x e^{-\alpha \tau^2} \cos \beta \tau, \tag{2.4}$$

where α and β are position parameters with dimensions $1/\text{sec}^2$ and $1/\text{sec}$ respectively. This correlation function approaches 0 more rapidly than do the others as $\tau \to \infty$. In contrast with the preceding correlation functions, this one is differentiable at $\tau = 0$, which is typical of correlation functions of several continuous random processes. Figure 2.1 (curve c) shows the graph of such a correlation function.

All three graphs in Figure 2.1 are drawn only for $\tau > 0$. For $\tau < 0$, the graphs are the mirror images about the ordinate of those shown in the figure.

These four forms of correlation function take care of many random processes that are of interest. We need also to remember that it is possible to construct new correlation functions by combining those that we have listed. For example, we often use a correlation function that is the sum of exponential functions:

5)
$$K_x(\tau) = D_1 e^{-\alpha_1 |\tau|} + \cdots + D_p e^{-\alpha_p |\tau|}, \tag{2.5}$$

where the D_i and the α_i are positive. An arbitrary continuous correlation function can be approximated with any desired degree of accuracy by a function of this form with a sufficient number p of terms [Ref. 31].

A centralized component $\overset{0}{X}(t)$ of a random process $X(t)$ can be characterized by other things than the correlation function $K_x(t_1, t_2)$. In the case in which $\overset{0}{X}(t)$ is a stationary process, it can be characterized by the spectral density $S_y(\omega)$ [Refs. 31, 33, 47, 52, 57]. The spectral density $S_x(\omega)$ and the correlation function $K_x(\tau)$ of a stationary process are connected by the following relations:

$$\left. \begin{aligned} S_x(\omega) &= \int_{-\infty}^{\infty} K_x(\tau) e^{-j\omega\tau} d\tau = \int_{-\infty}^{\infty} K_x(\tau) \cos \omega\tau \, d\tau \\ &= 2 \int_0^{\infty} K_x(\tau) \cos \omega\tau \, d\tau, \\ K_x(t) &= \frac{1}{2\pi} \int_{-\infty}^{\infty} S_x(\omega) e^{j\omega\tau} d\omega = \frac{1}{\pi} \int_0^{\infty} S_x(\omega) \cos \omega\tau \, d\omega. \end{aligned} \right\} \tag{2.6}$$

For example, corresponding to a process with correlation function $K_x(\tau) = D_x e^{-\alpha |\tau|}$ is the spectral density

$$S_x(\omega) = \frac{2\alpha}{\omega^2 + \alpha^2}, \tag{2.7}$$

and corresponding to a process with correlation function $K_x(\tau) = D_x e^{-\alpha \tau^2} \cos \beta \tau$ is the spectral density

$$S_x(\omega) = \frac{1}{2}\sqrt{\frac{\pi}{\alpha}} \left[e^{-\frac{(\beta-\omega)^2}{4\alpha}} + e^{-\frac{(\beta+\omega)^2}{4\alpha}} \right]. \tag{2.8}$$

The correlation function of a nonstationary process can be interpreted as a surface in three-dimensional space. Sometimes, it can be represented in analytical form as follows:

$$K_x(t_1,\ t_2) = \sigma_x(t_1)\sigma_x(t_2)\,R_x(\tau) = \sigma_x(t_1)\sigma_x(t_2)\,R_x(t_2 - t_1), \qquad (2.9)$$

where $\sigma_x(t) = \sqrt{D_x(t)}$ is the mean square deviation of the random function $X(t)$, which is equal to the square root of the variance D_x, and $R_x(\tau)$ is the normalized correlation function:

$$R_x(\tau) = R_x(t_2 - t_1) = \frac{K_x(t_1,\ t_2)}{\sigma_x(t_1)\sigma_x(t_2)}. \qquad (2.10)$$

In the present special case, this function depends only on the interval of time $\tau = t_2 - t_1$.

The process of determining optimal systems also depends on the class of admissible systems. The class of admissible automatic-control systems is restricted by the following considerations:

In the first place, we have at our disposal only a finite number of elements possessing certain characteristics. For example, if we have only linear elements, the class of admissible systems must consist only of linear systems.

In the second place, the criterion for comparison does not include all qualities of the control system. Therefore, it is sometimes expedient to include in the restrictions on the class of admissible systems qualities not taken into account by the criterion. For example, in choosing an optimal automatic-control system subject to stationary random influences (optimal according to minimum mean square error criterion), the time required for regulation of the system is not considered. The time required for regulation can be quite great in the optimal system, and this is ordinarily not acceptable. To avoid such cases in the formulation of the problem of choosing the optimal system we restrict the class of admissible systems to linear systems with regulating time not exceeding a given value T.

In the third place, with an eye to simplifying the problem of determining the optimal systems, we sometimes extend or restrict the class of admissible systems. For example, if we wish to avoid a very complicated problem of choosing a nonlinear optimal system, we sometimes make a choice of optimal system on the class of linear systems.

The following are fairly typical classes of admissible automatic-control systems:

(1)   all nonlinear automatic-control systems,
(2)   all linear automatic-control systems,
(3)   linear automatic-control systems with regulating time not exceeding T,
(4)   all linear systems with constant parameters,

(5) linear automatic-control systems with a given structure,

(6) linear automatic-control systems described by ordinary differential equations of order not exceeding n,

9. FORMULATION OF THE PROBLEM OF DETERMINING OPTIMAL AUTOMATIC-CONTROL SYSTEMS

Various formulations of problems of determining optimal automatic-control systems are possible. They differ from each other in form of comparison criterion, class of admissible systems, form of probabilistic characteristics of random influences, and purpose of the system (purpose of the control). The basic features differentiating the problems of determining optimal systems are the comparison criterion and the class of admissible systems. The form of the probabilistic characteristics of the random influences and the purpose of the control usually affect only the complexity or simplicity of the operations performed in obtaining a solution. Let us look at some formulations of the problem of determining optimal systems.

1. Determination of an optimal system over the class of all linear systems with respect to the criterion of minimization of the mean square error

Suppose that a random signal $X(t)$ is applied to the input of a system and that this random signal $X(t)$ is the sum of a useful signal $G(t)$ and a noise $Z(t)$. The probabilistic characteristics $m_g(t)$, $m_z(t)$, $K_g(t_1, t_2)$, $K_z(t_1, t_2)$, and $K_{gz}(t_1, t_2)$ are assumed known. Let us characterize the linear system with a weight function $w(t, \tau)$ (see Fig. 2.2). The output variable of the system $Y(t)$ is also a random function. The purpose of the control is to ensure closeness of the output variable $Y(t)$ to the ideal output variable $H(t)$. We assume that this ideal output variable $H(t)$ is the result of application of a linear operator L to the useful signal $G(t)$:

$$H(t) = L\{G(t)\}. \tag{2.11}$$

Figure 2.2 shows diagramatically a component with ideal weight function $v(t, \tau)$. Thus, we assume that the ideal output variable can be represented as the result of application of a linear integral operator to the useful signal:

$$H(t) = \int_0^t G(\tau) v(t, \tau) d\tau. \tag{2.12}$$

The representation of the purpose of the control, that is, of an ideal output variable of the system, in the form (2.11) or (2.12) is of a rather

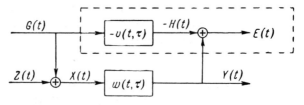

FIGURE 2.2

general nature and it takes care of many cases that are of interest in practice. Let us look at some particular examples.

(a) A reproducing system:

$$v(t, \tau) = \delta(t - \tau),$$
$$H(t) = G(t).$$

(b) An extrapolating system:

$$v(t, \tau) = \delta(t - \tau + T_e),$$
$$H(t) = G(t + T_e),$$

where T_e is the interval of extrapolation.

(c) An integrating system:

$$v(t, \tau) = 1(\tau),$$
$$H(t) = \int_0^t G(\tau) d\tau.$$

(d) A differentiating system:

$$v(t, \tau) = \dot{\delta}(t - \tau),$$
$$H(t) = \dot{G}(t).$$

The error of the system $E(t)$ (see Fig. 2.2) is equal to the difference between the real output variable and the ideal output variable:

$$E(t) = Y(t) - H(t). \tag{2.13}$$

We note that the portion of the scheme enclosed in Figure 2.2 by the dashed rectangle does not exist in actuality. This portion of the scheme is drawn only to clarify the concept of error of the system $E(t)$.

Our criterion, the mean square error of the system at a fixed instant t, is, in the present case, of the form

$$\Gamma_E(t) = M[E^2(t)] = M[\{Y(t) - H(t)\}^2]$$
$$= M\left[\left\{\int_0^t X(\tau) w(t, \tau) d\tau - \int_0^t G(\tau) v(t, \tau) d\tau\right\}^2\right]. \tag{2.14}$$

The problem now reduces to determining the function $w(t, \tau)$ minimizing (2.14); that is, minimizing the functional $\Gamma_{E_{(t)}} = \Gamma_E\{w(t, \tau)\}$ of the function $w(t, \tau)$ for fixed t.

2. Determination of an optimal system over the class of nonlinear automatic-control systems

Suppose that the w and v in Figure 2.2 represent not weight functions of linear systems but certain nonlinear operators of a real and ideal system respectively. Suppose that we choose for our criterion a criterion of the form

$$M[\varphi(E)],$$

where $\varphi(E)$ is a given function of the error. For a mathematical formulation of the problem, we need to express the error $E(t) = Y(t) - H(t)$ in terms of the operator of the real system, the known operator of the ideal system, and the known distribution laws of the random functions $G(t)$, $Z(t)$, and $X(t)$. We then need to find the operator of the desired nonlinear system that will minimize or maximize the criterion chosen.

In view of what was previously said, we may note that, when we have chosen the criterion and the class of admissible systems, the solving of the problem of the determination of an optimal system needs to be divided into the following stages:

(1) a mathematical description of the required probabilistic characteristics of the random influences and the purpose of the control,

(2) the obtaining of a mathematical expression for the criterion in terms of the characteristics of the system (in terms of the weight function), and

(3) the finding of an extremum of the criterion and the characteristics of the system that correspond to it.

Figure 2.2 represents a system with a single input $X(t)$ and a single output $Y(t)$. We may encounter cases in which several input signals $X_i(t)$ have an influence on the system and the system has several outputs $Y_j(t)$. In such cases (of investigation of multi-dimensional systems), we need to determine several optimal systems connecting the ith input $X_i(t)$ with the jth output $Y_j(t)$.

In the foregoing, we assumed that all the necessary probabilistic characteristics of the random influences are known. Cases are possible in which these characteristics are incompletely known; for example, we may not know the variance of the noise D_z. In such cases, we need to shift from an optimal system to an adaptive system. Even when we have only incomplete *a priori* information regarding the probabilistic characteristics of the random influences, an adaptive system can maintain the characteristics of the system about those values that correspond to an extremum of the criterion.

Solution of the problem of determining an optimal automatic-control system subject to random influences requires knowledge of certain material from the statistical dynamics of automatic systems and the calculus of variations. Minimal information of this kind was given in Chapter 1.

Chapter 3

DETERMINATION OF AN OPTIMAL LINEAR CONTINUOUS SYSTEM IN TERMS OF MINIMUM MEAN SQUARE ERROR OR SIMILAR CRITERIA

In this chapter, we shall expound methods for determining the optimal system that is chosen in accordance with the criterion of minimum mean square error (the second initial moment of error) for that system. A special case of this criterion is the variance of the error of a system. We first consider the simpler case in which the influences on the system and the chosen system are stationary. We then turn to nonstationary influences on the system and to nonstationary systems. Such a shift from the simpler situation to the more complicated one seems to us to be expedient in the present case. As a rule, a linear system is characterized, in the exposition of the material, by its weight function. In a few cases, we shall use a frequency characteristic or the block diagram of the system.

The basic works in the field of optimal transformations of random processes are those by academician A. N. Kolmogorov [Refs. 22, 23]. Important contributions in this field as applied to stationary systems were made by Wiener [Ref. 55], Zadeh and Ragazzini [Ref. 59], and other authors. Wiener relied heavily on the results of Kolmogorov's article [Ref. 23]. Very important contributions to the study of nonstationary signals and systems have been made and are still being made by Professor V. S. Pugachev [Refs. 42–45, 47].

At the end of the chapter, we consider criteria of a more general nature; linear forms in the values of the correlation function at different instants of time and in the mathematical expectation of the error. These criteria are quadratic functionals [Ref. 36] of the weight function of the system.

10. DETERMINATION OF THE OPTIMAL WEIGHT FUNCTION OF A STATIONARY AUTOMATIC-CONTROL SYSTEM WHICH PROVIDES FOR A MINIMUM ERROR VARIANCE

1. Determination of an optimal stationary system when the useful signal and the noise are stationary and stationarily connected and the mathematical expectations of the useful signal and noise are zero

The block diagram for this case is shown in Figure 3.1. Here, $w(\tau)$ denotes the weight function of the optimizing system and $v(\tau)$ denotes the weight function of the ideal system. The input signal into the optimizing system is $X(t)$. This signal is the sum of the useful signal $G(t)$ and the noise $Z(t)$. The probabilistic characteristics of $G(t)$ and $Z(t)$ are

$$m_g(t) = m_z(t) = 0,$$

$$K_g = K_g(\tau), \quad K_z = K_z(\tau), \quad K_{gz} = K_{gz}(\tau),$$

and are also the given correlation functions. It follows that

$$m_x(t) = 0, \quad K_x = K_x(\tau) = K_g(\tau) + K_z(\tau) + 2K_{gz}(\tau).$$

The output signal of the system $Y(t)$ and the ideal (desired) output signal $H(t)$, are, in this instance, determined in accordance with formula (1.96b).

The mathematical expectation of the error can be determined from formula (1.95a), which in the present case states that $m_E = 0$. The variance of the error D_E can be determined in accordance with formula (1.96a), in which we need to set the interval τ equal to 0:

$$D_E = K_E(0) = \int_0^\infty \int_0^\infty w(\tau_1) w(\tau_2) K_x(\tau_1 - \tau_2) d\tau_1 d\tau_2$$

$$- 2 \int_0^\infty \int_0^\infty K_{xg}(\tau_1 - \tau_2) w(\tau_1) v(\tau_2) d\tau_1 d\tau_2$$

$$+ \int_0^\infty \int_0^\infty K_g(\tau_1 - \tau_2) v(\tau_1) v(\tau_2) d\tau_1 d\tau_2. \tag{3.1}$$

Making the change of variables ($\tau_1 \to \tau$ and $\tau_2 \to \lambda$), and keeping equation (1.90) and the relation

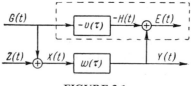

FIGURE 3.1

$$\int_0^\infty G(t - \tau)v(\tau)d\tau = H(t)$$

in mind, we can write formula (3.1) in the more convenient form

$$D_E = \int_0^\infty \int_0^\infty w(\tau)w(\lambda)K_x(\tau - \lambda)d\tau\,d\lambda$$
$$- 2\int_0^\infty K_{xh}(\tau)w(\tau)d\tau + D_h. \tag{3.2}$$

For the class of admissible weight functions $w(\tau)$, let us consider the set of all functions that are integrable on the interval $[0, T]$ and that vanish for $\tau < 0$ and $\tau > T$, where T is a fixed period of time bounding the regulation time of the system. If the weight function $w(\tau)$ of the optimizing system vanishes for $\tau < 0$ and $\tau > T$, then formula (3.2) can be written in the form

$$D_E = \int_0^T \int_0^T w(\tau)w(\lambda)K_x(\tau - \lambda)d\tau\,d\lambda$$
$$- 2\int_0^T K_{xh}(\tau)w(\tau)d\tau + D_h. \tag{3.3}$$

The criterion that we have chosen for comparing the systems (3.3) is a functional of the system's weight function $w(\tau)$. This functional is a special case of the functional (1.139) previously considered. In fact, (3.3) can be written in the form

$$D_E = \int_0^T \int_0^T \left\{ w(\tau)w(\lambda)K_x(\tau - \lambda) \right.$$
$$\left. - \frac{1}{T}[w(\tau)K_{xh}(\tau) + w(\lambda)K_{xh}(\lambda)] \right\} d\tau\,d\lambda + D_h. \tag{3.4}$$

The term D_h is independent of the function $w(\tau)$, and hence has no effect on the choice of the optimal weight function. Comparing (3.4) with (1.139), we conclude that corresponding to the function $y(t)$ in the expression (1.139) is the function $w(\tau)$ in the expression (3.4). The function Φ in the functional (3.4) has the following specific form:

$$\Phi[\tau, \lambda, w(\tau), w(\lambda)] = K_x(\tau - \lambda)w(\tau)w(\lambda)$$
$$- \frac{1}{T}[K_{xh}(\tau)w(\tau) + K_{xh}(\lambda)w(\lambda)]. \tag{3.5}$$

(The variables of integration t, s, τ, and λ are of no significance.) The integrand (3.5) is a symmetric bilinear form in $w(\tau)$ and $w(\lambda)$. This means that the optimal weight function $w_0(\tau)$ must satisfy condition (1.141), which, in view of (3.5), may be written as

$$\int_0^T \left[K_x(\tau - \lambda)w_0(\lambda) - \frac{1}{T}K_{xh}(\tau) \right] d\lambda = 0, \quad 0 \leqslant \tau \leqslant T.$$

Finally, this equation can be written as

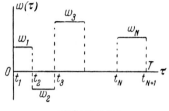

FIGURE 3.2

$$\int_0^T K_x(\tau - \lambda) w_0(\lambda) d\lambda - K_{xh}(\tau) = 0, \quad 0 \leqslant \tau \leqslant T. \tag{3.6}$$

Equation (3.6) is a Fredholm linear integral equation of the first kind [Refs. 41, 50].

In the general case, the solution of equation (3.6) can be pursued by some sort of approximating method. For example, we can use the method of canonical decompositions (canonical representations), which was developed by Pugachev. This method is expounded in detail in the book [Ref. 47]. We can also use an approximate substitution of a system of linear algebraic equations for the integral equation (3.6). Let us show how this can be done.

Let us partition the interval $[0, T]$ into N subintervals with endpoints $t_1 = 0 < t_2 < t_3 <' \cdots < t_{N+1} = T$. Let us seek the weight function $w(\tau)$ in the class of piecewise-constant functions; that is, let us assume that $w(\tau) = w_i$ for $t_i \leq \tau \leq t_{i+1}$ (see Fig. 3.2). Since the weight function $w(\tau)$ is now determined by the values of the N parameters w_i, equation (3.6) can be satisfied for N values of the variable τ. Suppose that these values are $\tau = t_1, t_2, \cdots, t_N$. Then, equation (3.6) is replaced by the following system of equations

$$\sum_{i=1}^N w_{i0} \int_{t_i}^{t_{i+1}} K_x(t_j - \lambda) d\lambda - K_{xh}(t_j) = 0, \quad j = 1, 2, \cdots, N. \tag{3.7}$$

The system of N linear algebraic equations (3.7) enables us to determine N values w_{i0} of the weight function that is close to the optimal one. If the number N is sufficiently great and the maximum interval $t_{s+1} - t_s$ is sufficiently small, then the piecewise-constant function determined by the system of equations (3.7) is close to the optimal weight function $w_0 = w_0(\tau)$ defined by equation (3.6). If all the intervals $t_{s+1} - t_s$ are sufficiently small and equal to each other, that is, if $t_{s+1} - t_s = \Delta t$, for $s = 1, \cdots, N$, the system (3.7) can be replaced with the following system of approximate equations:

$$\sum_{i=1}^N K_x(t_j - t_i) w_{i0} \Delta t - K_{xh}(t_j) = 0, \quad j = 1, 2, \cdots, N. \tag{3.7a}$$

The solution of the system (3.7) can be easily obtained on any computing machine. In certain cases, one can obtain an exact solution of equation (3.6) in closed form [Refs. 38, 47, 48, 52, 57]. Suppose, for example, that the correlation functions of both the useful signal and the noise are linear combinations of exponential functions:

$$K_g(\tau) = \sum_{i=1}^{m} A_i e^{-\alpha_i|\tau|}, \quad K_z(\tau) = \sum_{j=1}^{l} B_j e^{-\beta_j|\tau|}, \tag{3.8}$$

and that the correlation function of the useful signal and the noise is 0:

$$K_{gz}(\tau) = 0.$$

In this case, the correlation function of G and H is equal to

$$K_{gh}(\tau) = \sum_{i=1}^{m} H_i e^{-\alpha_i \tau}, \quad 0 < \tau \leqslant T,$$

where the coefficients H_i are uniquely determined for a given ideal output variable of the system $H(t)$. For example, in the case in which $H(t) = G(t + t_e)$, the coefficients H_i are given by the formula

$$H_i = A_i e^{-\alpha_i t_e}.$$

Correlation functions of the type (3.8) are often encountered in practice. Moreover, for sufficiently many terms (m or l), it is possible to represent an arbitrary correlation function [Ref. 31] by a function of the type (3.8) to an arbitrary degree of accuracy.

In the present case, it is natural to seek an optimal weight function of the form

$$w_0(\tau) = \sum_{s=1}^{N} D_s e^{-d_s \tau} + D_0 \delta(\tau) + D_T \delta(\tau - T), \tag{3.9}$$

where Re $d_s > 0$. This function, which is the sum of damped exponential functions, damped sinusoids and cosinusoids, and δ-functions, is the reaction of some linear system with constant parameters to a unit impulse. The coefficients d_s and D_s, for $s = 1, \cdots, N$, and D_0 and D_T are as yet undetermined. To see that the function (3.9) satisfies equation (3.6) for some N and certain values of the coefficients d_s, D_s, D_0, and D_T, we need to substitute (3.6) into this equation and find the number N and those values of the coefficients d_s, D_s, D_0, and D_T that satisfy this equation identically for all $0 \leq \tau \leq T$. In view of the relation

$$\int_0^T e^{-\alpha_i|\tau-\lambda|} e^{-d_s\lambda} d\lambda$$

$$= \frac{e^{-\alpha_i\tau}}{d_s - \alpha_i} - \frac{2\alpha_i}{d_s^2 - \alpha_i^2} e^{-d_s\tau} - \frac{e^{-(\alpha_i+d_s)T}}{\alpha_i + d_s} e^{\alpha_i\tau},$$

$$\int_0^T e^{-\alpha_i|\tau-\lambda|} \delta(\lambda) d\lambda = e^{-\alpha_i\tau},$$

$$\int_0^T e^{-\alpha_i|\tau-\lambda|} \delta(\lambda - T) d\lambda = e^{-\alpha_i T} e^{\alpha_i\tau},$$

and analogous relationships in which we have β_j instead of α_i, we obtain, when we make the foregoing substitution,

$$
\sum_{s=1}^{N} D_s \left[\sum_{i=1}^{m} A_j \left(\frac{e^{-\alpha_i \tau}}{d_s - \alpha_i} - \frac{e^{-(\alpha_i + d_s)T}}{\alpha_i + d_s} e^{\alpha_i \tau} + \frac{2\alpha_i e^{-d_s \tau}}{\alpha_i^2 - d_s^2} \right) \right.
$$
$$
\left. + \sum_{j=1}^{l} B_j \left(\frac{e^{-\beta_j \tau}}{d_s - \beta_j} - \frac{e^{-(\beta_j + d_s)T}}{\beta_j + d_s} e^{\beta_j \tau} + \frac{2\beta_j e^{-d_s \tau}}{\beta_j^2 - d_s^2} \right) \right]
$$
$$
+ D_0 \left(\sum_{i=1}^{m} A_i e^{-\alpha_i \tau} + \sum_{j=1}^{l} B_j e^{-\beta_j \tau} \right)
$$
$$
+ D_T \left(\sum_{i=1}^{m} A_i e^{-\alpha_i T} e^{\alpha_i \tau} + \sum_{j=1}^{l} B_j e^{-\beta_j T} e^{\beta_i \tau} \right) - \sum_{i=1}^{m} H_i e^{-\alpha_i \tau} = 0.
$$

$$(3.10)$$

For equation (3.10) to be satisfied identically for all $0 \leq \tau \leq T$, it is necessary that the coefficients of the functions

$$e^{-\alpha_i \tau}, \ e^{\alpha_i \tau}, \ e^{-d_s \tau}, \ e^{-\beta_j \tau}, \ e^{\beta_j \tau}$$

vanish. By setting the coefficients of these functions equal to zero, we obtain $2m + 2l + N$ equations for determining the $2N + 2$ unknowns d_s, D_s, D_0, and D_T. It is necessary that the number of equations be equal to the number of unknowns; that is, that

$$2m + 2l + N = 2N + 2.$$

Solving for N, we find

$$N = 2(m + l - 1).$$

In the special case in which $T = \infty$, all the terms containing T in equation (3.10) vanish. In this case, the coefficients of all functions for the form $e^{\alpha_i \tau}$ and $e^{\beta_j \tau}$ automatically vanish. In the function (3.9), the term $D_T \delta(\tau - T)$ vanishes. Consequently, the number of equations is equal to $m + l + N$ and the number of unknowns is $2N + 1$. This means that, in the case we are considering,

$$N = m + l - 1.$$

One can use the method of fastest descent (cf. Chapter I) to find the solution of equation (3.6) or the function $w_0(\tau)$ minimizing the variance of the error (3.3).

Let $w_1(\tau)$ denote a first approximation of the unknown function $w_0(\tau)$. In accordance with formula (1.149), the second approximation, by virtue of (3.5), can be taken as

$$
w_2(\tau) = w_1(\tau) + v_1 \cdot 2 \int_0^T \left[K_x(\tau - \lambda) w_1(\lambda) - \frac{1}{T} K_{hx}(\tau) \right] d\lambda
$$
$$
= w_1(\tau) + 2v_1 \left[\int_0^T K_x(\tau - \lambda) w_1(\lambda) d\lambda - K_{hx}(\tau) \right], \qquad (3.11)
$$

where v_1 is defined in accordance with formula (1.152). In the present case, v_1 can be written as

$$v_1 = -\frac{\int_0^T w_1^2(\tau)\,d\tau}{2\int_0^T\int_0^T K_x(\tau - \lambda)w_1(\tau)w_1(\lambda)\,d\tau\,d\lambda}. \qquad (3.12)$$

The third approximation $w_3(\tau)$ is equal to

$$w_3(\tau) = w_2(\tau) + 2v_2\left[\int_0^T K_x(\tau - \lambda)w_2(\lambda)\,d\lambda - K_{hx}(\tau)\right],$$

where

$$v_2 = -\frac{\int_0^T w_2^2(\tau)\,d\tau}{2\int_0^T\int_0^T K_x(\tau - \lambda)w_2(\tau)w_2(\lambda)\,d\tau\,d\lambda}.$$

Subsequent approximations are determined analogously.

We have shown that condition (3.6) is necessary in order that the function $w_0(\tau)$ will minimize the variance of the error (3.3). Let us show that condition (3.6) is not only a necessary but also a sufficient condition in order for the weight function satisfying it to minimize the variance of the error (3.3). To do this, let us show that, if $w_0(\tau)$ satisfies condition (3.6), then

$$D_E\{w_0(\tau) + \kappa(\tau)\} \geqslant D_E\{w_0\}$$

for an arbitrary function $\kappa(\tau)$.

Let us give the expanded expression for the variance D_E of the system with the arbitrary weight function $w_0(\tau) + \kappa(\tau)$:

$$D_E\{w_0 + \kappa\} = D_E\{w_0\}$$
$$+ 2\int_0^T \kappa(\tau)\left[\int_0^T K_x(\tau - \lambda)w_0(\lambda)\,d\lambda - K_{xh}(\tau)\right]d\tau$$
$$+ \int_0^T\int_0^T K_x(\tau - \lambda)\kappa(\tau)\kappa(\lambda)\,d\tau\,d\lambda.$$

By virtue of condition (3.6), this last expression can be rewritten as

$$D_E\{w_0 + \kappa\} = D_E\{w_0\} + \int_0^T\int_0^T K_x(\tau - \lambda)\kappa(\tau)\kappa(\lambda)\,d\tau\,d\lambda.$$

Here, the last term is the variance of the system's output variable with weight function $\kappa(\tau)$ on the input by which a random function $X(t)$ is defined. The variance is everywhere nonnegative. Consequently,

$$D_E\{w_0 + \kappa\} \geq D_E\{w_0\},$$

and the sufficiency of condition (3.6) is proved.

After the optimal weight function $w_0(\tau)$ is determined, we can determine the minimal variance of the error $D_{E\,min}$, which corresponds to the optimal weight function

$$D_{E\,min} = D_E\{w_0\}.$$

To do this, we use formula (3.3). It turns out that, in determining $D_{E\,min}$, formula (3.3) is considerably simplified. Specifically, by virtue of condition (3.6), formula (3.3) can be written as

$$D_{E\,min} = D_h - \int_0^T K_{xh}(\tau)w_0(\tau)d\tau. \tag{3.13}$$

Suppose that

$$K_g(\tau) = 3e^{-2|\tau|},$$
$$K_z(\tau) = 2e^{-|\tau|},$$
$$K_x(\tau) = 3e^{-2|\tau|} + 2e^{-|\tau|},$$
$$m_g = m_z = 0, \quad \text{and}$$
$$H(t) = G(t).$$

Let us determine the exact solution (that is, let us determine exactly $w_0(\tau)$). In the present case,

$$m = l = 1, \; N = 1, \; A_1 = 3, \; \alpha_1 = 2, \; B_1 = 2, \; \beta_1 = 1, \\ H_1 = 1, \; w_0(\tau) = D_1 e^{-\alpha_1 \tau} + D_0\delta(\tau). \tag{3.14}$$

Let us substitute (3.14) into (3.6). Then, we obtain

$$\int_0^\infty (3e^{-2|\tau-\lambda|} + 2e^{-|\tau-\lambda|})[D_1 e^{-\alpha_1\lambda} + D_0\delta(\lambda)]d\lambda - 3e^{-2\tau} = 0,$$
$$0 \leqslant \tau \leqslant \infty,$$

or

$$D_1\left[\frac{3}{d_1 - 2}e^{-2\tau} + \frac{3 \cdot 2 \cdot 2}{2^2 - d_1^2}e^{-d_1\tau} + \frac{2^{-\tau}}{d_1 - 1}e + \frac{2 \cdot 2}{1 - d_1^2}e^{-d_1\tau}\right]$$
$$+ 3D_0 e^{-2\tau} + 2D_0 e^{-\tau} = 0, \quad 0 \leqslant \tau \leqslant \infty.$$

Let us rewrite this equation, collecting similar terms:

$$\left(\frac{3D_1}{d_1 - 2} + 3D_0 - 3\right)e^{-2\tau} + \left(\frac{2D_1}{d_1 - 1} + 2D_0\right)e^{-\tau}$$
$$+ D_1\left(\frac{12}{4 - d_1^2} + \frac{4}{1 - d_1^2}\right)e^{-d_1\tau} = 0.$$

If we now set the coefficients of the functions $e^{-d_1\tau}$, $e^{-\tau}$, and $e^{-2\tau}$ equal to zero, we obtain the three equations

$$D_1\left(\frac{12}{4 - d_1^2} + \frac{4}{1 - d_1^2}\right) = 0,$$

$$\frac{2D_1}{d_1 - 1} + 2D_0 = 0,$$

$$\frac{3D_1}{d_1 - 2} + 3D_0 - 3 = 0.$$

From the first equation, we obtain

$$d_1 = \frac{\sqrt{7}}{2} \simeq 1.32.$$

Furthermore, from the second and third equations, we obtain

$$D_0 = 0.68 \quad \text{and} \quad D_1 = -0.22.$$

The optimal weight function is therefore

$$w_0(\tau) = -0.22e^{-1.32\tau} + 0.68\delta(\tau). \tag{3.15}$$

Corresponding to this weight function is the block diagram of the system, which is shown in Figure 3.3. The minimal variance of the error $D_{E\,min}$ is determined from formula (3.13):

$$D_{E\,min} = 3 - \int_0^\infty 3e^{-2\tau}[-0.22e^{-1.32\tau} + 0.68\delta(\tau)]d\tau$$

$$= 3 + \frac{3 \cdot 0.22}{3.32} - 3 \cdot 0.68 = 1.2.$$

It is of interest to note that, in the present case, the optimal system ensures that the variance in the error of the system is less than the variance in the noise. The optimal system contains an aperiodic and an amplifying component. The aperiodic component is realized without difficulty. An ideal amplifying component cannot be realized exactly in electromechanical systems. In realizing a system close to an optimal one, we need to insert, in place of an ideal amplifying component, a real aperiodic component with the same coefficient of amplification 0.68 and with small constant time.

Let us consider the special case of initial data when the input variable X is white noise; that is, when $K_x(t) = D\delta(t)$. In this case, equation (3.6) can, by virtue of the properties of the δ-function, be written as

$$Dw_0(\tau) - K_{xh}(\tau) = 0$$

or

$$w_0(\tau) = K_{xh}(\tau)\frac{1}{D}, \quad 0 \leqslant \tau \leqslant T. \tag{3.16}$$

FIGURE 3.3

Thus, when the sum of the irregular portion of the useful signal and noise constitute a white noise, the integral equation (3.6) leads to the linear algebraic equation (3.16). Consequently, on the interval [0, T] of observation, the optimal weight function is easily determined by use of formula (3.16). Outside that interval, it must be set equal to 0.

In determining an optimal stationary linear system, it is sometimes expedient to use frequency characteristics. We shall look at the application of frequency methods in an important particular case.

2. Determination of an optimal stationary system in the case of stationary and stationarily connected useful signal and noise, and in the case of an infinite interval of observation

The statement of the problem of this subsection differs from that of the preceding section only in that, instead of an arbitrary interval of observation T, we take an infinite interval of observation; that is, we take $T = \infty$.

To obtain a solution of this problem, we use formula (3.16), and for this formula we transform the input variable X into white noise. This transformation can be achieved according to the diagram shown in Figure 3.4. The random function X is applied at the input of the component with weight function $w_1(\tau)$ and with corresponding transfer function $W_1(p)$. The component must be chosen in such a way that at its output will be a signal X_1 representing unit white noise. To do this, we need to represent the spectral density of the input X in the form

$$S_x(\omega) = |\Phi(j\omega)|^2, \tag{3.17}$$

and set

$$W(j\omega) = \frac{1}{\Phi(j\omega)}, \tag{3.18a}$$

or

$$W(p) = \frac{1}{\Phi(p)}. \tag{3.18b}$$

The substitution of (3.18a) and (3.17) into formula (1.98) enables us to conclude that a white noise X_1 is formed at the output of the circuit with transfer function (3.18b) and that $S_{x1}(\omega) = 1$.

Let us denote by $w_{20}(\tau)$ the optimal weight function for the case of white noise X_1 at the input of the system. Then, we obtain an optimal

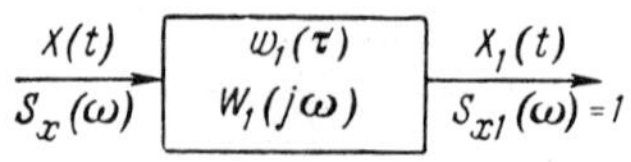

FIGURE 3.4

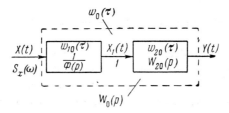

FIGURE 3.5

weight function for the input random variable X by subsequently join-ing the system with weight function $w_{10}(\tau)$ (with transfer function $1/\Phi$ (p)) and with weight function $w_{20}(\tau)$ (see Fig. 3.5).

The weight function $w_{20}(\tau)$ can be determined in accordance with formula (3.16), in which we need to take not $K_{xh}(\tau)$ but $K_{x_1h}(\tau)$ and in which we see $D = 1$:

$$
\begin{aligned}
w_{20}(\tau) &= K_{x_1h}(\tau), \quad 0 \leqslant \tau \leqslant \infty, \\
w_{20}(\tau) &= 0, \qquad \tau < 0.
\end{aligned}
\tag{3.19}
$$

The transfer function $W_{20}(p)$ corresponding to (3.19) is determined as the Laplace transform of $w_{20}(\tau)$:

$$
W_{20}(p) = \int_0^\infty K_{x_1h}(\xi) e^{-p\xi} d\xi.
\tag{3.20}
$$

Since the transfer function of components connected in series is equal to the product of the transfer functions of these circuits, the transfer function of the desired optimal system for the input random function X is equal to

$$
W_0(p) = W_{10}(p) W_{20}(p) = \frac{W_{20}(p)}{\Phi(p)}.
\tag{3.21}
$$

We shall have the complete solution if we can determine the joint correlation function K_{x_1h} of the white noise X_1 and the desired output signal H. First, let us determine the joint spectral density of the white noise X_1 and the desired output signal H:

$$
\begin{aligned}
S_{x_1h}(\omega) &= \int_{-\infty}^{\infty} K_{x_1h}(\tau) e^{-j\omega\tau} d\tau = \int_{-\infty}^{\infty} M[X_1(t) H(t + \tau)] e^{-j\omega\tau} d\tau \\
&= \int_{-\infty}^{\infty} M\left[\int_0^\infty X(t - \xi) w_1(\xi) d\xi H(t + \tau)\right] e^{-j\omega\tau} d\tau \\
&= \int_{-\infty}^{\infty} \left\{\int_0^\infty M[X(t - \xi) H(t + \tau)] w_1(\xi) d\xi\right\} e^{-j\omega\tau} d\tau \\
&= \int_{-\infty}^{\infty} \left\{\int_0^\infty K_{xh}(\tau - \xi) w_1(\xi) d\xi\right\} e^{-j\omega\tau} d\tau \\
&= \int_0^\infty w_1(\xi) e^{j\omega\xi} d\xi \int_{-\infty}^{\infty} K_{xh}(\tau - \xi) e^{-j\omega(\tau - \xi)} d\tau
\end{aligned}
$$

$$= W_1(-j\omega)S_{xh}(\omega) = \frac{1}{\Phi(-j\omega)}S_{xh}(\omega).$$

The joint spectral density $S_{x_1h}(\omega)$ of the white noise X_1 and the desired output signal H is determined as the product of the joint spectral density $S_{xh}(\omega)$ and the function $W_1(-j\omega)$ of the conjugate frequency characteristic $W_1(+j\omega)$. According to the familiar formula (1.79) in probability theory, we obtain the desired correlation function $K_{x_1h}(\tau)$:

$$K_{x_1h}(\tau) = \frac{1}{2\pi}\int_{-\infty}^{\infty}S_{x_1h}(\omega)e^{j\omega\tau}d\omega = \frac{1}{2\pi}\int_{-\infty}^{\infty}\frac{S_{xh}(\omega)}{\Phi(-j\omega)}e^{j\omega\tau}d\omega. \quad (3.22)$$

From the relations (3.19), (3.20), and (3.22), we obtain the following formula for determining the optimal transfer function of a linear system in the present case:

$$W_0(p) = \frac{1}{2\pi\Phi(p)}\int_0^{\infty}e^{-p\xi}\int_{-\infty}^{\infty}\frac{S_{xh}(\omega)}{\Phi(j-\omega)}e^{j\omega\xi}d\omega\,d\xi. \quad (3.23)$$

This formula is the basic formula in the theory of optimal stationary processes [Refs. 47, 52, 57].

The double integral in formula (3.23) is usually not difficult to evaluate. For example, if the ratio $S_{xh}(\omega)/\Phi(-j\omega)$ is a rational function, this formula is considerably simplified. Let us consider this case, which is important for applications. Thus, suppose that the function $S_{xh}(\omega)/\Phi(-j\omega)$ can be represented in the form

$$\frac{S_{xh}(\omega)}{\Phi(-j\omega)} = \frac{Q_1(\omega)}{Q_2(\omega)},$$

where Q_1 and Q_2 are polynomials in ω, and let us suppose that the degree m of the polynomial Q_1 is less than the degree n of the polynomial Q_2. For the moment, let us suppose that the polynomial Q_2 has no repeated factors. Then, the fraction on the right has the partial-fraction decomposition

$$\frac{Q_1(\omega)}{Q_2(\omega)} = \sum_{k=1}^{n}\frac{a_k}{\omega - \omega_k}.$$

To evaluate the inner integral in formula (3.23) for each of the simple fractions in the summation, we can use the theory of residues [Ref. 50]. The contour of integration should be taken in the upper half-plane; that is, we should have ω vary from $-R$ to $+R$ along the upper semicircle of radius R and then we should let R approach ∞. Since for $\xi > 0$ the integral over the upper semicircle approaches 0 as $R \to \infty$, we have

$$\int_{-\infty}^{\infty}\frac{a_k e^{j\omega\xi}}{\omega - \omega_k}d\omega = \begin{cases} 2\pi j a_k e^{j\omega_k\xi} & \text{for } \text{Im}\{\omega_k\} > 0, \\ 0 & \text{for } \text{Im}\{\omega_k\} < 0. \end{cases}$$

Thus, for an arbitrary zero ω_k of the polynomial Q_2 contained in the upper half-plane and for an arbitrary value of S such that $\text{Im } S > \text{Im } \omega_k$,

$$\frac{1}{2\pi}\int_0^\infty e^{-jS\xi}d\xi\int_{-\infty}^\infty \frac{a_k e^{-j\omega\xi}}{\omega - \omega_k}d\omega = ja_k\int_0^\infty e^{j(\omega_k - S)\xi}d\xi = \frac{a_k}{S - \omega_k},$$

and, for an arbitrary zero ω_k in the lower half-plane,

$$\frac{1}{2\pi}\int_0^\infty e^{-jS\xi}d\xi\int_{-\infty}^\infty \frac{a_k e^{-j\omega\xi}}{\omega - \omega_k}d\omega = 0.$$

This result can be written as

$$W_0(jS) = \frac{1}{\Phi(jS)}\sum_k \frac{a_k}{S - \omega_k}.$$

Here, the summation is taken only over those indices k such that the root ω_k lies in the upper half-plane. This last relation is usually written as

$$W_0(jS) = \frac{1}{\Phi(jS)}\left[\frac{S_{xh}(S)}{\Phi(-jS)}\right]_+,$$

where the subscript $+$ means that the expression in the square brackets should be decomposed into partial fractions, and only those fractions kept that correspond to poles lying in the upper half-plane. The variable S can be replaced in the last expression for W_0 with the usual variable ω:

$$W_0(j\omega) = \frac{1}{\Phi(j\omega)}\left[\frac{S_{xh}(\omega)}{\Phi(-j\omega)}\right]_+. \qquad (3.23a)$$

One can easily show [Ref. 47] that formula (3.23) remains valid when the polynomial Q_2 has repeated factors.

Formula (3.23a) enables us to obtain immediately a complex frequency characteristic of the optimal system. To determine the transfer function $W_0(p)$, we need to replace $j\omega$ in formula (3.23a) with the variable p. This enables us to obtain the following equation:

$$W_0(p) = \frac{1}{\Phi(p)}\left[\frac{S_{xh}(-jp)}{\Phi(-p)}\right]_+. \qquad (3.23b)$$

It is possible to solve the problem that we have been considering by using the time characteristics (the weight functions) instead of the frequency characteristics. However, the shift to frequency characteristics in this case makes the computations simpler.

EXAMPLE. Suppose that

$$K_g(\tau) = 3e^{-2|\tau|}, \quad K_z(\tau) = \delta(\tau),$$

$$K_x(\tau) = 3e^{-2|\tau|} + \delta(\tau), \quad m_g = m_z = m_x = 0, \quad H(t) = G(t).$$

Use the method expounded above to find the optimal linear system.

Let us find the spectral density of the input signal X:

$$S_x(\omega) = S_g(\omega) + S_z(\omega) = 3 \cdot \frac{2 \cdot 2}{2^2 + \omega^2} + 1 = \frac{4^2 + \omega^2}{2^2 + \omega^2}.$$

We represent it in the form

$$S_x(\omega) = \left| \frac{4 + j\omega}{2 + j\omega} \right|^2 = |\Phi(j\omega)|^2.$$

Consequently, the transfer function of a stationary linear system that transforms the random function $X(t)$ into white noise is expressed by the formula

$$W_1(p) = \frac{1}{\Phi(p)} = \frac{2 + p}{4 + p}.$$

The joint spectral density of the random functions $X(t)$ and $H(t) = G(t)$ is equal to

$$S_{xh}(\omega) = S_g(\omega) = 3 \cdot \frac{4}{4 + \omega^2}.$$

Now, we can determine the integrand in (3.22):

$$\frac{S_{xh}(\omega)}{\Phi(-j\omega)} = 3 \frac{4}{4 + \omega^2} \cdot \frac{2 - j\omega}{4 - j\omega} = \frac{12}{(2 + j\omega)(4 - j\omega)}$$

$$= \frac{2}{j} \left(\frac{1}{\omega - j \cdot 2} - \frac{1}{\omega + j \cdot 4} \right).$$

The pole $-j \cdot 4$ of the second fraction lies in the lower half-plane. Therefore, we can discard this fraction. Integration of the first fraction and division by $\Phi(p)$ yields the result

$$W_0(j\omega) = \frac{2}{4 + j\omega}.$$

Consequently, the desired optimal transfer function is of the form

$$W_0(p) = 2 \cdot \frac{1}{4 + p}.$$

The problems that we previously considered for determining optimal systems enable us to draw the following conclusions with respect to the order of solution of these problems. After we have obtained a mathematical description of the probabilistic characteristics of the influences and a mathematical expression for the criterion, we seek optimal characteristics of the system (the weight function, the transfer function) by using variational methods. An exact solution of the problem is possible only in special cases. In the general case, we seek an approximate solution by one of the known methods (method of canonical decompositions, the method of fastest descent, replacement of a linear integral equation with a system of linear algebraic equations). The method of fastest descent can be applied immediately to the criterion and does not require a shift to Euler's equation. The specific form of the criterion and its complexity depend not only on the probabilistic characteristics of the useful signal and the noise, but on the class of admissible systems as well. The conclusions that we have drawn here remain valid in other similar cases, as we shall presently see.

11. DETERMINATION OF THE OPTIMAL WEIGHT FUNCTION OF A STATIONARY AUTOMATIC-CONTROL SYSTEM WHICH ENSURES AN EXTREMUM OF THE CRITERION $I_2 = m_E + \theta_1 K_E(\tau_1) + \cdots + \theta_n K_E(\tau_n)$

Our block diagram remains as before (cf. Fig. 3.1). However, the probabilistic characteristics of the influences and the comparison criterion are different. Let us suppose that the mathematical expectation of the useful signal is $m_g = M[G] = G_0$, where G_0 is a constant. The mathematical expectation of the noise is equal to zero: $m_z = 0$. The correlation functions $K_g = K_{g(\tau)}$, $K_z = K_{z(\tau)}$, and $K_{gz} = K_{gz(\tau)}$ of stationary and stationarily connected processes are given.

As a criterion, let us take the functional

$$I_2 = m_E + \theta_1 K_E(\tau_1) + \cdots + \theta_n K_E(\tau_n), \tag{3.24}$$

where m_E is the mathematical expectation of the error of the system, and $K_E(\tau_i)$ is the value of the correlation function of a stationary error of the signal for a fixed interval τ_i, for $i = 1, \cdots, n$. As a particular case, we may take $\tau_1 = 0$, $\tau_2 = \Delta$, $\tau_3 = 2\Delta$, $\cdots$, $\tau_n = (n - 1)\Delta$, where Δ is a given fixed interval.

A criterion of the type (3.24) can be used as an approximate characteristic of the quality of the system for certain values of the factors $\theta_1, \cdots, \theta_n$ or as an intermediate criterion in the case in which a complicated basic criterion is a function of m_E, $K_E(\tau_i)$ (cf. Chapters 1 and 4). From a mathematical point of view, the criterion (3.24) is close to the variance and the second initial moment of error. Therefore, we shall examine it in this chapter. For admissible weight functions $w(\tau)$, we take functions that are integrable over the interval $[0, T]$ and that vanish outside that interval.

Let us express the criterion in terms of initial conditions. The mathematical expectation of the error can be determined from formula (1.95a):

$$m_E = m_x \int_0^\infty w(\tau)d\tau - m_g \int_0^\infty v(\tau)d\tau = m_g \int_0^T w(\tau)d\tau - m_h, \tag{3.25}$$

where m_h is the mathematical expectation of the desired output variable H. The correlation function of the error of the system $K_E(\tau_i)$ is determined from formula (1.96a), in which τ_1 and τ_2 are replaced with τ and λ respectively:

$$K_E(\tau_i) = \int_0^\infty \int_0^\infty K_x(\tau_i - \lambda + \tau) w(\tau) w(\lambda) d\tau \, d\lambda$$

$$- 2 \int_0^\infty \int_0^\infty K_{xg}(\tau_i - \lambda + \tau) w(\tau) v(\lambda) d\tau \, d\lambda$$

$$+ \int_0^\infty \int_0^\infty K_g(\tau_i - \lambda + \tau) v(\tau) v(\lambda) d\tau \, d\lambda.$$

Remembering that $w(\tau) = 0$ for $\tau < 0$ and $\tau > T$ and that

$$H(t) = \int_0^\infty G(t - \tau) L(\tau) d\tau,$$

we rewrite the expression for $K_E(\tau_i)$ in the form

$$K_E(\tau_i) = \int_0^T \int_0^T K_x(\tau_i - \lambda + \tau) w(\tau) w(\lambda) d\tau \, d\lambda$$

$$- 2 \int_0^T K_{xh}(\tau_i + \tau) w(\tau) d\tau_1 + K_h(\tau_i). \qquad (3.26)$$

Now, the criterion I_2 can be represented in the form

$$I_2 = m_g \int_0^T w(\tau) d\tau - m_h$$

$$+ \sum_{i=1}^n \theta_i \left[\int_0^T \int_0^T K_x(\tau_i - \lambda + \tau) w(\tau) w(\lambda) d\tau \, d\lambda \right.$$

$$\left. - 2 \int_0^T K_{xh}(\tau_i + \tau) w(\tau) d\tau + K_h(\tau_i) \right]. \qquad (3.27)$$

The terms $-m_h$, $K_h(\tau_1)$, $\cdots$, $K_h(\tau_n)$ are independent of the weight function $w(\tau)$ and hence they do not affect the choice of the optimal weight function. As one can see from (3.27), the criterion I_2 is a functional of the weight function $w(\tau)$ of a system of the type (1.139). Corresponding to the function $y(t)$ in the expression (1.139) is the weight function $w(\tau)$ in the expression (3.27). The function Φ in the functional (3.27) has the following particular form:

$$\Phi[\tau, \lambda, w(\tau), w(\lambda)] = \sum_{i=1}^n \theta_i K_x(\tau_i - \lambda + \tau) w(\tau) w(\lambda)$$

$$- \frac{1}{T} \sum_{i=1}^n \theta_i [K_{xh}(\tau_i + \tau) w(\tau) + K_{xh}(\tau_i + \lambda) w(\lambda)]$$

$$+ \frac{m_g}{2T} [w(\tau) + w(\lambda)]. \qquad (3.28)$$

The integrand (3.28) is a symmetric bilinear form in $w(\tau)$ and $w(\lambda)$. This means that the optimal weight function $w_0(\tau)$ must satisfy condition (1.141), which, by virtue of (3.28), may be written as

$$\int_0^T \sum_{i=1}^n \theta_i K_x(\tau_i - \lambda + \tau) w_0(\lambda) d\lambda$$

$$- \sum_{i=1}^n \theta_i K_{xh}(\tau_i + \tau) + \frac{m_g}{2} = 0, \quad 0 \leqslant \tau \leqslant T. \tag{3.29}$$

Equation (3.29) is the same linear Fredholm integral equation of the first kind as is equation (3.6). The only difference is that, in the general case, equation (3.29) contains more complicated analytical expressions of the free function

$$\sum_{i=1}^n \theta_i K_{xh}(\tau_i + \tau) + \frac{m_g}{2}$$

and the kernel

$$\sum_{i=1}^n \theta_i K_x(\tau_i - \lambda + \tau).$$

There are no theoretical differences between the two equations.

We can find a solution of equation (3.29) by the methods described for equation (3.6).

The necessary condition (3.29) for maximization or minimization of the criterion I_2 is also sufficient, as can be proved in a manner analogous to the proof of the sufficiency of condition (3.6). However, the condition (3.29) can correspond either to a minimum or a maximum of the criterion I_2. Particular values of the parameter θ_i determine whether a minimum or maximum of the criterion I_2 exists.

After we have determined the optimal weight function $w_0(\tau)$ satisfying condition (3.29), we can easily determine an extremum of the criterion I_2. It follows from (3.29) that

$$\int_0^T \sum_{n=1}^n \theta_i K_x(\tau_i - \lambda + \tau) w_0(\lambda) d\lambda = \sum_{i=1}^n \theta_i K_{xh}(\tau_i + \tau) - \frac{m_g}{2}.$$

From this we easily obtain the relation

$$\int_0^T \int_0^T \sum_{i=1}^n \theta_i K_x(\tau_i - \lambda + \tau) w_0(\lambda) w_0(\tau) d\lambda d\tau$$

$$= \int_0^T \sum_{i=1}^n \theta_i K_{xh}(\tau_i + \tau) w_0(\tau) d\tau - \frac{m_g}{2} \int_0^T w_0(\tau) d\tau.$$

When we substitute this last expression for the double integral into (3.27), we obtain a simple formula for determining an extremum of the criterion I_{2e}:

$$I_{2e} = \sum_{i=1}^n \theta_i \left[K_h(\tau_i) - \int_0^T K_{xh}(\tau_i + \tau) w_0(\tau) d\tau \right]$$

$$+ \frac{m_g}{2} \int_0^T w_0(\tau) d\tau - m_h. \tag{3.30}$$

Let us suppose that the mathematical expectations of the useful signal G and the noise Z are equal to 0, that the noise and the useful signal are uncorrelated, that the desired output variable is the useful signal (that is, that the system is designed for reproduction of the useful signal), and that the correlation functions of the signal and the noise are exponential functions. Thus, the given conditions are

$$m_g = m_z = m_x = 0, \quad K_g(\tau) = 3e^{-2|\tau|}, \quad K_z(\tau) = 2e^{-|\tau|},$$
$$K_x(\tau) = 3e^{-2|\tau|} + 2e^{-|\tau|}, \quad H(t) = G(t), \quad K_{xh}(\tau) = K_g(\tau).$$

Let us consider the time of observation to be infinite; that is, $T = \infty$.

As a criterion, let us take a functional of the following specific form:

$$I_2 = K_E(0) + 5K_E(1).$$

The conditions of this problem coincide with the conditions of the problem of the preceding section in every respect in the form of the criterion. Here, instead of the variance of the error $D_E = K_E(0)$, we take the criterion I_2, which is the sum of the variance of the error and the weighted value of the correlation function K_E at $\tau = 1$ sec.

In the present case, equation (3.29) does not differ in principle from equation (3.6). Therefore, we can follow exactly the procedure adopted in the first subsection of section 10 to obtain an exact solution.

We note that, in the present example,

$$m = l = 1, \quad N = 1, \quad A_1 = 3, \quad \alpha_1 = 2, \quad B_1 = 2,$$
$$\beta_1 = 1, \quad H_1 = 1, \quad w_0(\tau) = D_1 e^{-d_1 \tau} + D_0 \delta(\tau). \tag{3.31}$$

We need to find the values of the coefficients D_1, d_1, and D_0. In the present case, equation (3.29) takes the form

$$\int_0^\infty [3e^{-2|\tau-\lambda|} + 2e^{-|\tau-\lambda|} + 5(3e^{-2|1+\tau-\lambda|} + 2e^{-|1+\tau-\lambda|})]$$
$$\times w_0(\lambda) d\lambda - 3e^{-2\tau} - 15e^{-2(1+\tau)} = 0, \quad 0 \leqslant \tau \leqslant \infty. \tag{3.32}$$

When we substitute (3.31) into (3.32), we obtain an identity that is satisfied for arbitrary $\tau \in [0, \infty]$:

$$\int_0^T [3e^{-2|\tau-\lambda|} + 2e^{-|\tau-\lambda|} + 5(3e^{-2|1+\tau-\lambda|} + 2e^{-|1+\tau-\lambda|})]$$
$$\times [D_1 e^{-d_1 \tau} + D_0 \delta(\tau)] d\lambda - 3e^{-2\tau} - 15e^{-2(1+\tau)} = 0.$$

If we partition the interval of integration into two intervals $[0, 1 + \tau]$ and $[1 + \tau, \infty]$, we can carry out the integrations in elementary functions. We obtain the following result:

$$D_1 \left[\frac{3(1 + 5e^2)}{d_1 - 2} e^{-2\tau} + \frac{3 \cdot 2 \cdot 2(1 + 5e^{-2})}{2^2 - d_1^2} e^{-d_1 \tau} \right.$$

$$+ \frac{2(1 + 5e^{-1})}{d - 1} e^{-\tau} + \frac{2 \cdot 2(1 + 5e^{-1})}{1 - d_1^2} e^{-d_1 \tau} \Bigg]$$
$$+ 3D_0(1 + 5e^{-2})e^{-2\tau} + 2D_0(1 + 5e^{-1})e^{-\tau}$$
$$- 3(1 + e^{-2})e^{-2\tau} = 0, \quad 0 \leqslant \tau \leqslant \infty.$$

Collecting terms of like powers, we rewrite this identity in the form

$$(1 + 5e^{-2})\left(\frac{3D_1}{d_1 - 2} + 3D_0 - 3\right)e^{-2\tau}$$

$$+ (1 + 5e^{-1})\left(\frac{2D_1}{d_1 - 1} + 2D_0\right)e^{-\tau}$$

$$+ 4D_1 \left[\frac{3(1 + 5e^{-2})}{4 - d_1^2} + \frac{1 + 5e^{-1}}{1 - d_1^2}\right]e^{-d_1\tau} = 0, \quad 0 \leqslant \tau \leqslant \infty.$$

Setting the coefficients of the functions $e^{-d_1\tau}$, $e^{-\tau}$, and $e^{-2\tau}$ equal to 0, we obtain three equations for determining the three unknowns D_1, d_1, and D_0:

$$4D_1\left(3\frac{1 + 5e^{-2}}{4 - d_1^2} + \frac{1 + 5e^{-1}}{1 - d_1^2}\right) = 0,$$

$$2(1 + 5e^{-1})\left(\frac{D_1}{d_1 - 1} + D_0\right) = 0,$$

$$3(1 + 5e^{-2})\left(\frac{D_1}{d_1 - 2} + D_0 - 1\right) = 0.$$

From the first equation, we obtain

$$D_1 = 0 \quad \text{or} \quad 3\frac{1 + 5e^{-2}}{4 - d_1^2} + \frac{1 + 5e^{-1}}{1 - d_1^2} = 0.$$

The root $D_1 = 0$ is superfluous, as one can easily verify; from the second possibility, we have $d_1 = 1.42$. We can then easily determine the coefficients $D_0 = 0.59$, $D_1 = -0.25$. In the present problem, the optimal weight function is then shown to be

$$w_0(\tau) = -0.25e^{-1.42\tau} + 0.59\delta(\tau). \tag{3.33}$$

This weight function corresponds to the block diagram shown in Figure 3.3 as applied to the problem of section 10. The only difference between the optimal function (3.32) and the optimal function (3.15) consists in the values of the coefficients D_1, d_1, and D_0.

Let us now determine the minimum value of the criterion I_2 corresponding to the optimal weight function $w_0(\tau)$. To do this, we use formula (3.30), which in the present case is of the form

$$I_{2e} = 3 - \int_0^\infty 3e^{-2\tau}[-0.25e^{-1.42\tau} + 0.59\delta(t)]d\tau$$

$$+ 5 \left\{ 3e^{-2 \cdot 1} - \int_0^\infty 3e^{-2|1+\tau|} [-0.25e^{-1.42\tau} + 0.59\delta(t)] d\tau \right\}$$

$$= 3 + 3 \cdot \frac{0.25}{3.42} - 3 \cdot 0.59$$

$$+ 5 \left(3 \cdot 0.13 + 3 \cdot 0.13 \frac{0.25}{3.42} - 3 \cdot 0.13 \cdot 0.59 \right) = 2.38.$$

12. DETERMINATION OF THE OPTIMAL PARAMETERS OF A STATIONARY SYSTEM WHOSE BLOCK DIAGRAM IS GIVEN

In the preceding sections, we took as our admissible systems linear stationary systems prossessing an integrable weight function that is nonzero on a time interval $[0, T]$. Moreover, we imposed no restrictions on the structure of the system. This type of exposition of the problem is expedient when the problem is to determine the best of all possible linear systems. This type of exposition can be used, for example, in working out a tactical-technical problem for a newly developed system. However, there are other ways of posing problems. For example, we may need to pose the problem of determining optimal parameters of a system whose block diagram is given. Such a problem arises if the block diagram has already been chosen on the basis of some consideration or other (or if it has been set up in a specific working system) and we need to determine the parameters of the elements in it in such a way as to minimize or maximize the criterion chosen. A complicated present-day control system usually contains several parameters (coefficients of amplification of the components, time constants of the components, and the like) that can easily be varied. The choice of optimal parameters of a system with a given structure differs essentially from the choice of the optimal weight function of an arbitrary structure.

Let us formulate the statement of the problem. Suppose that the block diagram of the system is given. In this diagram, we can let n parameters $q_1, \cdots, q_n$ vary in a given region Q. A useful signal $G(t)$ and a noise $Z(t)$ act on the system (see Fig. 3.6). The system has a transfer function $W = W(p, q_1, \cdots, q_n)$ depending on the n parameters q_i. The transfer function W is determined by the block diagram of the

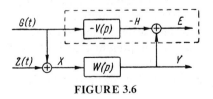

FIGURE 3.6

system and is a given function of the complex variable p and the parameters $q_1, \cdots, q_n$. We denote by $V = V(p)$ the ideal (desired) transfer function of the system and we denote by H the ideal (desired) output variable. The portion of Figure 3.6 enclosed in the dashed rectangle does not appear in the system and is shown in the diagram only to illustrate the procedure. The signal G and the noise Z are stationary and stationarily connected. As criterion, we take the variance of the stationary error of the system. In this case, the variance of the error D_E can be determined by substituting (1.98a) into (1.99a):

$$D_E = D_E(q_1, \cdots, q_n) = \frac{1}{2\pi} \int_{-\infty}^{\infty} [\,|\,W(j\omega, q_1, \cdots, q_n)\,|^2 S_x(\omega)$$
$$- 2W(j\omega, q_1, \cdots, q_n)\,V(-j\omega)\,S_{xg}(\omega) + |V(j\omega)|^2 S_g(\omega)\,]\,d\omega,$$
$$(3.34)$$

where $S_x(\omega)$ and $S_g(\omega)$ are the spectral densities of the input variable X and the useful signal G, and where $S_{xg}(\omega)$ is the joint spectral density of the input variable X and the useful signal G.

Formula (3.34) can be written in another form:

$$D_E = D_E(q_1, \cdots, q_n) = \frac{1}{2\pi} \int_{-\infty}^{\infty} [\,|\,W(j\omega, q_1, \cdots, q_n)\,|^2 S_x(\omega)$$
$$- 2W(j\omega, q_1, \cdots, q_n)\,S_{xh}(\omega) + S_h(\omega)\,]\,d\omega, \qquad (3.35)$$

where $S_h(\omega)$ is the spectral density of the desired output variable and $S_{xh}(\omega)$ is the joint spectral density of the input variable and the desired output variable. We need to use whichever of the two formulas (3.34), (3.35) is more convenient under specific given conditions.

When the useful signal and the noise are uncorrelated and $H = G$, formula (3.35) takes the form

$$D_E = \frac{1}{\pi} \int_0^{\infty} [\,|\,W(j\omega, q_1, \cdots, q_n)\,|^2 S_x(\omega) + S_g(\omega)\,]\,d\omega. \qquad (3.35a)$$

Examination of the expressions (3.34) and (3.35) enable us to conclude that the criterion D_E is, from a mathematical point of view, a known function of several variables $q_1, \cdots, q_n$.

We have considered a method of expressing the variance of the error in terms of the parameters $q_1, \cdots, q_n$ of the system by using the frequency characteristics of the system and the influences on it. We can obtain expressions for the variance of the error of a system by using the weight function of the system and the correlation functions of the influences. In this last case, we need to use not Figure 3.6 but Figure 2.2 and, instead of formulas (3.34) and (3.35), we need to use formula (1.96a) with $\tau = 0$. By virtue of (1.96b), we can write formula (1.96a) with $\tau = 0$ in the form

$$D_E = K_E(0) = \int_0^{\infty}\!\!\int_0^{\infty} K_x(\tau_2 - \tau_1)\,w(\tau_1, q_1, \cdots, q_n)$$

$$\times w(\tau_2, q_1, \cdots, q_n) d\tau_1 d\tau_2$$

$$- 2 \int_0^\infty \int_0^\infty K_{xh}(\tau_1) w(\tau_1, q_1, \cdots, q_n) d\tau_1 + D_h, \qquad (3.35b)$$

where $w(\tau_1, q_1, \cdots, q_n)$ is the weight function of the system whose block diagram is characterized by the parameters $q_1, \cdots, q_n$.

As one can see from formula (3.35b), the variance of the error $D_E = D_E(q_1, \cdots, q_n)$ is a known function of the variables $q_1, \cdots, q_n$.

To obtain the dependence $D_E = D_E(q_1, \cdots, q_n)$, we may use both formulas (3.34), (3.35) and formulas (1.96a) and (3.35b). In any particular case, we choose whichever of these pairs of formulas enables us to obtain the desired dependence $D_E = D_E(q_1, \cdots, q_n)$ in the simpler and more economical manner. Thus, the problem of finding the minimum of the variance in the error of the system when we have a given block diagram of the system reduces to the problem of finding the minimum of a function of several variables.

The problem of finding a minimum can always be reduced to a problem of finding a maximum and vice versa. In what follows, we shall encounter the problem of finding the maximum of a function of several variables. Moreover, the exposition of the procedure for finding the maximum of a function of several variables is somewhat more convenient from a methodological point of view. Therefore, let us turn to an exposition of methods of finding the maximum of a function $F(q_1, \cdots, q_n)$ of several variables.

If the number n of variables is small, the finding of a maximum of the function F is not a difficult problem. When n is large, the problem of finding the maximum of a complicated function F is associated with considerable difficulties.

As we know, a necessary condition for a maximum of the function $F(q_1, \cdots, q_n)$ can be written

$$\frac{\partial F}{\partial q_i} = 0, \quad i = 1, \cdots, n. \qquad (3.36)$$

Equations (3.36), as applied to an automatic-control system, are usually complicated nonlinear algebraic equations. Therefore, the problem of finding a solution of the system (3.36) is usually a quite difficult one. Therefore, some other approach is necessary in order to find the maximum of the function F. Ordinarily, some sort of approximation method is used. We shall consider two of these: (1) the method of successive choice of the parameters and (2) the method of fastest descent.

1.   The method of successive choice of the parameters

The crux of this method is as follows: First, we choose first approximations $q_{11}, q_{21}, \cdots, q_{n1}$ on some basis or other; for example, on the basis of previous experiment in projecting similar automatic-control systems. Then, we determine a second approximation $q_{12}, q_{22}, \cdots, q_{n2}$. To do this, we fix the parameters $q_2 = q_{21}, \cdots, q_n = q_{n1}$ and we choose the value of the parameter $q_1 = q_{12}$ by requiring that the function $F_1(q_1)$ $= F(q_1, q_{21}, \cdots, q_{n1})$ be maximized. We then fix the values of the parameters $q_1 = q_{12}, q_3 = q_{31}, \cdots, q_n = q_{n1}$, and we choose the value of the parameter $q_2 = q_{22}$ by requiring that the function $F_2(q_2) = F(q_{12}, q_2, q_{31}, \cdots, q_{n1})$ be maximized. In the same way, we define $q_{32}, \cdots, q_{n2}$. Consequently, to determine the second approximation $q_{12}, \cdots, q_{n2}$, we carry out successively the operations according to the choice of the second approximations of each parameter. We define the third and subsequent approximations

$$(q_{13}, \cdots, q_{n3}), \quad (q_{14}, \cdots, q_{n4}), \quad \cdots$$

in an analogous manner.

We complete the computational operations when the values of the function F corresponding to two successive approximations cease to differ appreciably.

This method is attractive by virtue of its simplicity. The search for the kth approximation of the ith parameter does not present great difficulties (if worse comes to worse, we can perform this operation graphically). However, this method does usually require a large number of approximations. Also, each approximation is done in n stages. It would be desirable to have a method in which the calculations are organized in a more convenient manner. An example of such a method is that of fastest descent. In sections four and ten, this method is expounded as it is used in choosing a function. Here, we shall expound the method as applied to choice of parameters.

2.   The method of fastest descent

We shall clarify the idea of this method by using an example. Suppose that the criterion is a function $F(q_1, q_2)$ of two parameters. In order to give the problem a visual aspect, let us interpret F as the altitude of the surface of the earth above sea level and let us interpret q_1 and q_2 as longitude and latitude respectively. The curves (contour lines) on the map (Fig. 3.7) are the level curves of the altitude function F, that is, the curves described by the equations $F(q_1, q_2) = C$, where C is a constant. The different curves correspond to different values of C. What we have then is a topographical map. The problem is posed as follows: How can one get from a given point A_1 with coordinates (q_{11}, q_{21}) to the maximum value of the function F (on the top of some hill)? We assume that the speed at which one travels is constant throughout the $q_1 q_2$-plane. This means that corresponding to the quickest path to the maximum of the function F is the greatest gradient of the function F (the greatest steepness of the path of ascent). The desired route to the maximum F can be arranged as follows. At the starting point A_1, we determine the direction of the greatest gradient of the function F (the direction of greatest steepness at that point). This direction coincides with the normal to the level curve at the point A_1. We then proceed in this direction until we reach the maximum value of F on the line determined by this direction. Let A_2 denote this point. On a topographical map, this point can be determined as a point of tangency between the line in which one is moving and some contour line. We then find the direction corresponding to the gradient of the function F at the point A_2. We then proceed in this direction to the point A_3 representing a maximum of the function F on the line determined by that direction, and so forth. One continues along this broken line until the difference between two successive points A_i and A_{i+1} is negligibly small.

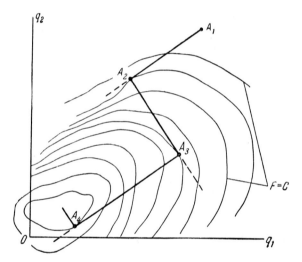

FIGURE 3.7

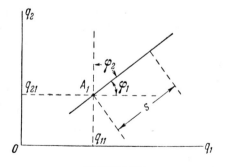

FIGURE 3.8

We need to express this simple visually clear idea quantitatively; that is, we need to give a mathematical description of the process of successive approximations to the maximum of the function F. Again, we shall do this for the case in which the number of parameters is 2. It will then be easy to show how the method can be extended to an arbitrary number of parameters.

Suppose that $F(q_1, q_2)$ is a given differentiable function of two parameters. Suppose that we need to find the maximum of that function.

Let us make a first approximation of the variables $q_1 = q_{11}$ and $q_2 = q_{21}$ (see Fig. 3.8) and hence a first approximation of the function $F = F(q_{11}, q_{21})$. Here, we need to find the direction in the $q_1 q_2$-plane in which the function F increases the most rapidly, that is, the direction of the gradient. To do this, we first write the equation of an arbitrary line passing through the point (q_{11}, q_{21}):

$$q_1 = q_{11} + \cos \varphi_1 s,$$
$$q_2 = q_{21} + \cos \varphi_2 s,$$

where $\cos \varphi_1$ and $\cos \varphi_2$ are the direction cosines and s is a parameter representing the distance from the point (q_{11}, q_{21}) to an arbitrary point on that line.

The position of this line will be determined if we know the angles φ_1 and φ_2 or the direction cosines $\cos \varphi_1 = \theta_1$ and $\cos \varphi_2 = \theta_2$. The numbers θ_1 and θ_2 are related by

$$\theta_1^2 + \theta_2^2 = 1. \tag{3.37}$$

The values of the function F on a given straight line can be written as

$$F(q_{11} + \theta_1 s, q_{21} + \theta_2 s).$$

To determine the direction of fastest increase in the function F at the point (q_{11}, q_{21}), we need to determine the values $\theta_1 = \theta_{11}$ and $\theta_2 = \theta_{21}$ that maximize the derivative of $F(q_{11} + \theta_1 s, q_{21} + \theta_2 s)$ with respect to s. The value of this derivative at the point (q_{11}, q_{21}) is

$$\frac{dF(q_{11} + \theta_1 s, q_{21} + \theta_2 s)}{ds} \bigg|_{s=0}$$

$$= \frac{\partial F(q_1, q_2)}{\partial q_1} \bigg|_{\substack{q_1 = q_{11} \\ q_2 = q_{21}}} \theta_1 + \frac{\partial F(q_1, q_2)}{\partial q_2} \bigg|_{\substack{q_1 = q_{11} \\ q_2 = q_{21}}} \theta_2.$$

We need to find the maximum of this expression with θ_1 and θ_2 subject to the constraint (3.37). As we know, this problem of finding the conditional maximum reduces to the problem of finding the unconditional maximum of the function

$$f(\theta_1, \theta_2) = \frac{\partial F}{\partial q_1} \theta_1 + \frac{\partial F}{\partial q_2} \theta_2 + \gamma (\theta_1^2 + \theta_2^2). \tag{3.38}$$

Let us write the necessary condition for a maximum of the function f:

$$\frac{\partial f}{\partial \theta_1} = 0, \qquad \frac{\partial f}{\partial \theta_2} = 0$$

or, in expanded form,

$$\frac{\partial F}{\partial q_1} + 2\gamma\theta_1 = 0, \qquad \frac{\partial F}{\partial q_2} + 2\gamma\theta_2 = 0.$$

From this we determine the values of the direction cosines θ_{11} and θ_{21}:

$$\theta_{11} = -\frac{1}{2\gamma}\frac{\partial F}{\partial q_1}, \qquad \theta_{21} = -\frac{1}{2\gamma}\frac{\partial F}{\partial q_2}, \qquad (3.39)$$

where the partial derivatives of the function F are evaluated at $q_1 = q_{11}$ and $q_2 = q_{21}$. The Lagrange multiplier γ can be determined by substituting (3.39) into (3.37). However, we do not need to determine this multiplier.

Thus, the direction of fastest increase in the function F at the point (q_{11}, q_{21}) is determined. Now, let us look at the values of the function F on the line determined by the conditions (3.39), that is, on the line of fastest increase in the function F:

$$F\left(q_{11} - \frac{s}{2\gamma}\frac{\partial F}{\partial q_1}, \qquad q_{21} - \frac{s}{2\gamma}\frac{\partial F}{\partial q_2}\right).$$

We define $v = -s/2\gamma$. Then, the values of the function F on the line chosen may be written as

$$F\left(q_{11} - v\frac{\partial F}{\partial q_1}, \qquad q_{21} + v\frac{\partial F}{\partial q_2}\right) = \mu(v), \qquad (3.40)$$

where v is a variable parameter differing from the parameter s only by the constant factor $-1/2\gamma$. The value of the factor $v = v_1$ that maximizes the function F on this straight line (that is, corresponding to the point A_2) can be determined from the condition

$$\mu(v_1) = F\left(q_{11} + v_1\frac{\partial F}{\partial q_1}, \qquad q_{21} + v_1\frac{\partial F}{\partial q_2}\right) = \max_v \mu(v).$$

Consequently, the value of the parameter $v = v_1$ can be determined from the condition

$$\frac{d\mu(v)}{dv} = 0$$

or with the aid of the graph of the function $\mu(v)$ (see Fig. 3.9). A second approximation of the parameters q_1 and q_2 is determined from the formulas

$$q_{12} = q_{11} + v_1\frac{\partial F}{\partial q_1}, \qquad q_{22} = q_{21} + v_1\frac{\partial F}{\partial q_2}.$$

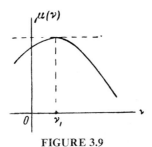

FIGURE 3.9

The second approximation of the function F is $F(q_{12}, q_{22})$. The third and subsequent approximations are determined analogously.

Let us list in order the calculations performed according to the method of fastest descent (for the case of two variables q_1 and q_2):

(1) Choice of the first approximation of the parameters q_{11} and q_{12}.

(2) Determination of the first approximation of the criterion $F(q_{11}, q_{21})$.

(3) Evaluation of the partial derivatives $\partial F/\partial q_1$ and $\partial F/\partial q_2$ at the values $q_1 = q_{11}, q_2 = q_{21}$.

(4) Determination of the value of the auxiliary parameter $v = v_1$ from the condition $\mu(v_1) = \max\limits_{v} \mu(v)$.

(5) Calculation of the second approximation of the parameters

$$q_{12} = q_{11} + v_1\frac{\partial F}{\partial q_1}, \quad q_{22} = q_{21} + v_1\frac{\partial F}{\partial q_2}.$$

(6) Calculation of the second approximation of the criterion $F(q_{12}, q_{22})$.

The third and subsequent approximations are determined in the same order. The calculations stop when the difference

$$F(q_{1, k+1}, q_{2, k+1}) - F(q_{1k}, q_{2k})$$

is sufficiently small.

If the criterion F depends on n parameters $q_1, \cdots, q_n$ of the system, then, by shifting from 2-dimensional $q_1 q_2$-space to n-dimensional $q_1 \cdots q_n$-space, we easily obtain an analogous method for determining the maximum of the function $F(q_1, \cdots, q_n)$.

The order of carrying out the calculations in the n-dimensional case is as follows:

(1) Choice of first approximation of the parameters $q_{11}, \cdots, q_{n1}$.

(2) Calculation of the first approximation of the criterion $F(q_{11}, \cdots, q_{n1})$.

(3) Evaluation of the partial derivatives $\partial F/\partial q_1, \cdots, \partial F/\partial q_n$ at $q_1 = q_{11}, \cdots, q_n = q_{n1}$.

(4) Determination of the value of the auxiliary parameter $v = v_1$ from the condition

$$\mu(v_1) = F\left(q_{11} + v_1\frac{\partial F}{\partial q_1}, \cdots, q_{n1} + v_n\frac{\partial F}{\partial q_n}\right) = \max_v \mu(v).$$

(5) Calculation of the values of the parameters of the second approximation

$$q_{12} = q_{11} + v_1\frac{\partial F}{q\partial_1}, \cdots, q_{n2} = q_{n1} + v_1\frac{\partial F}{\partial q_n}.$$

(6) Calculation of the second approximation of the criterion $F(q_{12}, \cdots, q_{n2})$.

The third and successive approximations are calculated in the same order. The calculations are terminated when the difference

$$F(q_{1,k+1}, \cdots, q_{n,k+1}) - F(q_{1k}, \cdots, q_{nk})$$

becomes negligibly small.

The values of the partial derivatives $\partial F/\partial q_1, \cdots, \partial F/\partial q_n$ in determining the $(k+1)$st approximation are calculated from the values of the variables $q_{1k}, \cdots, q_{nk}$ of the kth approximation. These derivatives can be evaluated approximately as a ratio of finite differences:

$$\left.\begin{aligned}
&\frac{\partial F}{\partial q_1}\bigg|_{q_i=q_{ik}} \\
&\quad \simeq \frac{F(q_{1k} + \Delta q_1, q_{2k}, \cdots, q_{nk}) - F(q_{1k}, \cdots, q_{nk})}{\Delta q_1}, \\
&\cdots\cdots\cdots\cdots\cdots\cdots\cdots\cdots\cdots\cdots\cdots\cdots \\
&\frac{\partial F}{\partial q_n}\bigg|_{q_i=q_{ik}} \\
&\quad \simeq \frac{F(q_{1k}, \cdots, q_{n-1,k}, q_{nk} + \Delta q_n) - F(q_{1k}, \cdots, q_{nk})}{\Delta q_n}, \\
&\quad i = 1, \cdots, n.
\end{aligned}\right\} \quad \text{(3.41)}$$

The value of the finite increment Δq_s must be chosen sufficiently small. However, we need to keep in mind that, for very small values of Δq_s, quite large errors can be made in the process of evaluating the fractions (3.41).

The function $\mu_k(v)$ used to determine v_k as we go from the kth to the $(k+1)$st approximation is of the form

$$\mu_k(v) = F\left(q_{1k} + v\frac{\partial F}{\partial q_1}, \cdots, q_{nk} + v\frac{\partial F}{\partial q_n}\right),$$

where the derivatives $\partial F/\partial q_1, \cdots, \partial F/\partial q_n$ are calculated from the values of the arguments $q_{1k}, \cdots, q_{nk}$ of the kth approximation. In the general case, the function $\mu_k(v)$ can have several maxima. We need to examine all values of the auxiliary parameter v corresponding to these different maxima of the function $\mu_k(v)$.

The method of fastest descent usually ensures rapid convergence of the sequence of approximations.

We have noted that the problem of finding the minimum of the function $F(q_1, \cdots, q_n)$ can always be reduced to the problem of finding the maximum of the function $-F(q_1, \cdots, q_n)$. However, it is possible to organize all the calculations for immediate application to the problem of finding the minimum of the function $F(q_1, q_n)$. The order of the calculations remains essentially the same. Insignificant differences consist only in the fact that, in determining the value of the parameter $v = v_k$, we need to find not the maximum of the function $\mu_k(v)$ but the minimum of that function. When we are seeking the minimum of the function $F(q_1, \cdots, q_n)$, motion in the $q_1 \cdots q_n$-space at the beginning of any one of the approximations proceeds in the direction of fastest decrease of the function F (that is, in the direction of fastest descent on a topographic map). It is from this that the name of the method originated.

The order that we have given for the calculations remains valid only when the function $\mu_k(v)$ attains its maximum or minimum inside the region Q of variation of the parameters $q_1, \cdots, q_n$. If the function $\mu_k(v)$ does not attain its maximum or minimum inside this region, the value of the auxiliary parameter v_k is determined from the fact that the point

$$\left(q_{1k} + v\frac{\partial F}{\partial q_1}, \cdots, q_{nk} + v\frac{\partial F}{\partial q_n} \right)$$

must fall on the boundary of the region Q. Subsequent motion in the $q_1 \cdots q_n$-space is made on the boundary of the region Q.

It should be noted that the problem of finding optimal parameters of a system with a given structure involves laborious calculations when the number of parameters $q_1, \cdots, q_n$ is great.

Suppose that a system is an aperiodic component with coefficient of amplification k and constant time T. Suppose that a signal $X(t)$ is applied to the input of this system and that $X(t)$ is the sum of two uncorrelated influences: a useful signal $G(t)$ and a noise $Z(t)$. The mathematical expectations $m_g(t)$ and $m_z(t)$ are equal to 0. The correlation functions of the stationary influences have the following forms:

$$K_g(\tau) = 3e^{-2|\tau|}, \quad K_z(\tau) = \delta(\tau).$$

Consequently, the correlation function of the input signal $X(t)$ is

$$K_x(\tau) = 3e^{-2|\tau|} + \delta(\tau).$$

The desired output variable is equal to the useful signal: $H(t) = G(t)$ and hence $K_{xh}(\tau) = K_g(\tau)$. We need to determine the optimal parameters k and T that minimize the variance of the error D_E of the system.

We go back to the notations previously used. We denote by q_1 the coefficient of amplification K and we donote by q_2 the constant time T. Then, we obtain an expression for the variance of the error of the system D_E in terms of the parameters q_1 and q_2. To do this, we use formula (3.35b). The weight function of the system in the given case is of the form

$$w(\tau) = \frac{k}{T}e^{-\tau/T} = \frac{q_1}{q_2}e^{-\tau/q_2}.$$

The variance of the error D_E is equal to

$$D_E = \int_0^\infty \int_0^\infty [3e^{-2|\tau-\lambda|} + \delta|\tau-\lambda|]\frac{q_1}{q_2}e^{-\lambda/q_2}\frac{q_1}{q_2}e^{-\lambda/q_2}d\lambda\,d\tau$$

$$- 2\int_0^\infty 3e^{-\tau}\frac{q_1}{q_2}e^{-\tau/q_2}d\tau + 3.$$

The single integral is easily evaluated. In the case of the iterated integral, we need to partition in the first integration (for example, with respect to the variable λ) the interval of integration into two intervals $[0, \tau]$ and $[\tau, \infty)$. Then, the absolute value in the exponent can be replaced with $\tau - \lambda$ in the first interval and with $\lambda - \tau$ in the second. Thus, evaluation of the double integral reduces to elementary operations, which yield the following results:

$$\int_0^\infty e^{-2|\tau-\lambda|}e^{-\lambda/q_2}d\lambda = \int_0^\tau e^{-2(\tau-\lambda)}e^{-\lambda/q_2}d\lambda + \int_\tau^\infty e^{2(\tau-\lambda)}e^{-\lambda/q_2}d\lambda$$

$$= \frac{4}{4-\frac{1}{q_2^2}}e^{-\tau/q_2} - \frac{1}{2-\frac{1}{q_2}}e^{-2\tau},$$

$$\int_0^\infty \delta|\tau-\lambda|e^{-\lambda/q_2}d\lambda = e^{-\tau/q_2},$$

$$D_E = \frac{q_1^2}{q_2^2}\left(\frac{3q_2^2}{1+2q_2} + \frac{q_2}{2}\right) - \frac{6q}{1+2q_2} + 3.$$

Elementary transformations enable us to write the expression for the variance of the error in the following form:

$$D_E = \frac{(1+8q_2)q_1^2 - 12q_2q_1}{2q_2(1+2q_2)} + 3 = F(q_1, q_2).$$

To calculate the different approximations, we obtain analytical expressions for the partial derivatives of the criterion F with respect to the parameters q_1 and q_2:

$$\frac{\partial F}{\partial q_1} = \frac{q_1 - 2q_2(3-4q_1)}{q_2(1+2q_2)},$$

$$\frac{\partial F}{\partial q_2} = \frac{4q_1(2q_1-3)}{2q_2(1+2q_2)} - \frac{(1+4q_2)[q_2^2(1+8q_2) - 12q_1q_2]}{2q_2^2(1+2q_2)^2}.$$

The order of the calculations is as follows:

(1) We choose a first approximation of the parameters $q_{11} = 1$, $q_{21} = 1$.

(2) We determine the first approximation of the criterion: $F(1, 1) = 2.5$.

(3) We evaluate the partial derivatives of the criterion with respect to the parameters q_1 and q_2 at $q_1 = q_{11} = 1$, $q_2 = q_{21} = 1$:

$$\frac{\partial F}{\partial q_1} = 1, \quad \frac{\partial F}{\partial q_2} = \frac{1}{6}.$$

(4) We write the expression for the function $\mu_1(v)$:

$$\mu_1(v) = \frac{(1 + v)^2\left[1 + 8\left(1 + \frac{1}{6}v\right)\right] - 12(1 + v)\left(1 + \frac{1}{6}v\right)}{2\left(1 + \frac{1}{6}v\right)\left[1 + 2\left(1 + \frac{1}{6}v\right)\right]} + 3,$$

and we determine the value of the auxiliary parameter $v = v_1$ from the condition

$$\mu_1(v_1) = \min_v \mu_1(v).$$

One can easily see that, in determining v_1, we need in the present case to consider negative values of v. Calculations show that, with accuracy up to 0.1, we need to take $v_1 = -0.3$.

(5) We calculate the values of the second approximation of the parameters q_1 and q_2:

$$q_{12} = q_{11} - 0.3 \cdot 1 = 0.7, \quad q_{22} = 1 - 0.3 \cdot \frac{1}{6} = 0.95.$$

(6) We calculate the second approximation of the function $F(q_{12}, q_{22})$:

$$F(0.7, 0.95) = 2.21.$$

(7) We evaluate the partial derivatives of the criterion F with respect to the parameters q_1 and q_2 at $q_1 = q_{12} = 0.7$, $q_2 = q_{22} = 0.95$:

$$\frac{\partial F}{\partial q_1} = 0.13, \quad \frac{\partial F}{\partial q_2} = 0.39.$$

(8) We write the expression for the function $\mu_2(v)$:

$$\mu_2(v) = \frac{(0.7 + 0.13v)^2[1 + 8(0.95 + 0.39v)] - 12(0.7 + 0.13v)(0.95 + 0.39v)}{2(0.95 + 0.39v)[1 + 2(0.95 + 0.39v)]} + 3,$$

and we determine the value of the auxiliary parameter $v = v_2$ from the condition

$$\mu_2(v_2) = \min_v \mu_2(v).$$

Calculations show that we need to take $v_2 = -1.7$.

(9) We calculate the values of the third approximation of the parameters q_1 and q_2:

$$q_{13} = 0.7 - 0.13 \cdot 1.7 = 0.48,$$

$$q_{23} = 0.95 - 0.39 \cdot 1.7 = 0.28.$$

(10) We determine the third approximation of the criterion:

$$F(0.48, 0.28) = 2.04.$$

(11) The fourth approximation for the parameters and the criterion is calculated analogously:

$$q_{14} = 0.503, \quad q_{24} = 0.252; \quad F(0.503, 0.252) = 2.01.$$

We can terminate the calculations at this point, since the difference between the third and fourth approximations of the criterion $\Delta F = 2.04 - 2.01 = 0.03$ is small.

At this point, the following question arises: With what should we compare the difference $\Delta F = 0.03$? First, it can be compared with the absolute value of the last approximation of the criterion (namely, 2.01) or with the errors in the calculations (in the present case, the errors in the calculations are of the order of 0.01). Comparison of the difference 0.03 with the value of the last approximation of the criterion, namely, 2.01, shows that this difference is approximately one and one half of a percent of the absolute value of the criterion—in short, it is quite small. Comparison of the difference $\Delta F = 0.03$ with the errors in the calculations also indicates that further calculations with the same degree of accuracy are not expedient.

Thus, in the present example, with the values that we have chosen as first approximations of the parameters q_1 and q_2, it proved sufficient to calculate the fourth approximation to obtain satisfactory results. We mention in passing that the example considered in the preceding section enables us to verify the results that we have just obtained. It turns out that the calculations performed in accordance with the method of fastest descent have enabled us to obtain a sufficiently accurate result. In other problems and with a different degree of accuracy in the calculations, a greater number of approximations may be required.

13. DETERMINATION OF THE OPTIMAL WEIGHT FUNCTION OF A SYSTEM WHICH PROVIDES A MINIMUM OF THE SECOND MOMENT OF ERROR ABOUT THE ORIGIN

Above, we considered cases in which the influences on a system were stationary and stationarily connected. In connection with this, we considered a stationary error in the system. The optimal system in such cases also turned out to be stationary. Such cases are encountered in practice, but nonstationary influences are more common. Therefore, we need to consider the more general case in which the input influences are nonstationary. In this case, the optimal system is usually nonstationary as well.

Let us suppose that the useful signal and the noise are nonstationary random functions of a general form. In practice, we often encounter useful signals of the form

$$G(t) = \sum_{i=0}^{m} G_i t^i + G'(t), \tag{3.42}$$

where the G_i are random variables with known distribution laws or else they are unknown quantities that can assume different values and where $G'(t)$ is a random time function with mathematical expectation equal to 0. As a special case, some of the coefficients G_i may be given numbers (that is, random variables with variances equal to 0).

The second initial moment of error is the mathematical expectation of the product of two values of the error $E(t_1)$ $E(t_2)$ (cf. (1.64)). As our criterion, we usually take the value of the second-order initial moment with $t_1 = t_2 = t$; that is,

$$\Gamma_E(t) = M[E^2(t)]. \tag{3.43}$$

In the present case, the error $E(t)$ can be expressed in terms of the weight function of the system as follows:

$$E(t) = \int_0^T \left[\sum_{i=1}^{m} G_i \tau^i + G'(\tau) + Z(\tau) \right] w(t, \tau) d\tau - H(t),$$

where $w(t, \tau)$ is the weight function of the system with regulating time T, where $H(t)$ is the desired output variable (cf. Fig. 2.2), and where the G_i are random variables uncorrelated with each other and with the random functions $G'(t)$ and $Z(t)$. We define $X'(t) = G'(t) + Z(t)$. Then, the second-order initial moment may be written as

$$\Gamma_E(t) = \sum_{i=0}^{m} M[G_i^2] \int_0^T \tau^i w(t, \tau) d\tau \int_0^T \lambda^i w(t, \lambda) d\lambda$$

$$+ \int_0^T \int_0^T M[X'(\tau) X'(\lambda)] w(t, \tau) w(t, \lambda) d\tau d\lambda$$

$$- 2 \int_0^T M[X'(\tau) H(t)] w(t, \tau) d\tau + M[H^2(t)]$$

$$= \sum_{i=0}^{m} \alpha_i \int_0^T \int_0^T \tau^i \lambda^i w(t, \tau) w(t, \lambda) d\tau d\lambda$$

$$+ \int_0^T \int_0^T K_{x'}(\tau, \lambda) w(t, \tau) w(t, \lambda) d\tau d\lambda$$

$$- 2 \int_0^T K_{x'h}(\tau, t) w(t, \tau) d\tau + \Gamma_h(t),$$

where the $\alpha_i = M[G_i^2]$ are the second-order initial moments of the random variables G_i, where $K_{x'}(t_1, t_2)$ is the correlation function of the random function $X'(t)$, where $K_{x'h}(t_1, t_2)$ is the joint correlation function of the random functions $X'(t)$ and $H(t)$, and where $\Gamma_h(t)$ is the second-order initial moment of the random function $H(t)$:

$$\Gamma_h(t) = M[H^2(t)].$$

Let us rewrite the expression for $\Gamma_E(t)$ in the form

$$\Gamma_E(t) = \int_0^T \int_0^T \left\{ \sum_{i=0}^m \alpha_i \tau^i \lambda^i w(t, \tau) w(t, \lambda) \right.$$

$$+ K_{x'}(\tau, \lambda) w(t, \tau) w(t, \lambda) - \frac{1}{T} [K_{x'h}(\tau, t) w(t, \tau)$$

$$\left. + K_{x'h}(\lambda, t) w(t, \lambda)] \right\} d\tau \, d\lambda + \Gamma_h(t). \tag{3.44}$$

The term $\Gamma_h(t)$ is independent of the weight function $w(t, \tau)$. The functional Γ_E of the function $w(t, \tau)$ with fixed t is a special case of the functional (1.139). In the present case, the function Φ is represented by the expression in the braces.

We can use the relation (1.140b) to present a necessary condition that the optimal weight function must satisfy. In the present case, this condition is of the form

$$\int_0^T \left\{ \sum_{i=0}^m \alpha_i \tau^i \lambda^i w(t, \lambda) + K_{x'}(\tau, \lambda) w(t, \lambda) \right.$$

$$\left. - \frac{1}{T} K_{x'h}(\tau, t) \right\} d\lambda = 0, \quad 0 \leqslant \tau \leqslant T.$$

We rewrite this as follows:

$$\int_0^T \left\{ \sum_{i=0}^m \alpha_i \tau^i \lambda^i + K_{x'}(\tau, \lambda) \right\} w(t, \lambda) d\lambda - K_{x'h}(\tau, t) = 0,$$

$$0 \leqslant \tau \leqslant T. \tag{3.45}$$

We need to find the solution of this integral equation for some fixed value of the time t. For fixed t, this equation does not differ in principle from the integral equation (3.6) that we obtained earlier. Both these equations are integral equations of the type

$$\int_0^T K(\tau, \lambda) w(t, \lambda) d\lambda - \phi(\tau, t) = 0, \quad 0 \leqslant \tau \leqslant T, \tag{3.46}$$

where $K(\tau, \lambda)$ is a symmetric kernel and $\phi(\tau, t)$ is the free term of the equation (a given function of the variable τ with parameter t), and $w(t, \tau)$ is the unknown function of the variable τ.

Equation (3.46) is a linear Fredholm integral equation of the first kind. We spoke earlier of ways of solving such equations when we were dealing with the problem of solving equation (3.6). A significant difference in the solution of the problem in this section is the fact that we need to seek a solution of equation (3.45) many times for different values of the variable (time) t. When we seek solutions of equation (3.45), frequency methods are not applicable in the general case. As one can see, the optimal weight function is sought by the same procedure, both in the case of stationary initial conditions (cf. (3.6)) and in the case of nonstationary initial conditions (cf. (3.45)).

It should be noted that it is expedient to search for the set of solutions of equation (3.45), in the general case, on a computing machine.

Let us now look at a somewhat different statement of the problem. Specifically, let us impose some restrictions on the class of admissible automatic-control systems. Let us require that an admissible system reproduce without error an input signal of the type

$$\sum_{i=0}^{m-1} G_i t^i. \tag{3.47}$$

This requirement is equivalent to the requirement that the system possess astaticism of the least mth order.

What are the reasons for this requirement? They may be quite varied. For example, the requirement of astaticism of some order may follow from certain considerations or other. Furthermore, we sometimes know in advance that the random variables $G_0, G_1, \cdots, G_{m-1}$ in the expression for the useful signal $G(t)$ have very high initial second-order moments α_i, considerably exceeding the values of the initial second-order moment of the quantity G_m. In such a case, it is expedient to have a system with small coefficients of error. The limiting (ideal) case is a system in which the first m coefficients of the error are equal to 0, that is, a system with astaticism of order m. In such a case, we get an unbiased estimate of the desired process $H(t)$.

Let us examine in detail the case in which the input signal $X(t)$ is nonstationary but the optimal system is stationary. This interesting case is described by the following initial conditions: The useful signal $G(t)$ is given by the formula

$$G(t) = \sum_{i=1}^{m} G_i t^i + G'(t) = G_h(t) + G'(t),$$

where the G_i are random variables independent of each other, of $G'(t)$, and of the noise $Z(t)$, and where $G'(t)$ is a centralized stationary random function. The noise $Z(t)$ is a stationary random variable. We define $X'(t) = G'(t) + Z(t)$. Thus, the input signal into the system is the sum

$$\sum_{i=1}^{m} G_i t^i + X'(t).$$

The random functions $G'(t)$ and $Z(t)$ are stationarily connected with each other. Consequently, the random function $X'(t)$ is stationary. The correlation function $K_{x'}(\tau)$ is equal to

$$K_{x'}(\tau) = K_{g'}(\tau) + 2K_{g'z}(\tau) + K_z(\tau).$$

Thus, the input signal $X(t) = G_h(t) + G'(t) + Z(t)$ contains a non-stationary component

$$G_h(t) = \sum_{i=0}^{m} G_i t^i.$$

Consequently, the input signal is a nonstationary random function.

Let us make precise the statement of the problem. The block diagram is the same in this case as before (cf. Fig. 1.1). The difference with the preceding case lies in the additional restrictions imposed on the class of admissible weight functions resulting from the requirement of mth-order astaticism of the control system.

Let us describe in greater detail the desired output variable $H(t)$. Just as before, it is the result of applying a linear operator L to the useful signal. Let us suppose that the desired output variable can be represented in the form

$$H(t) = L\{X(t)\} = C_0 G(t) + C_1 G^{(1)}(t) + C_2 G^{(2)}(t) + \cdots \qquad (3.48)$$

We note that not every linear operator can be put in the form (3.48). For example, if

$$H(t) = \int_0^t G(\tau)d\tau,$$

then $H(t)$ cannot be represented by the series (3.48). The following are examples of output variables $H(t)$ that satisfy the condition (3.48):

(a) $H(t) = G(t)$, here $C_0 = 1, \quad C_1 = C_2 = \cdots = 0$;

(b) $H(t) = \dot{G}(t)$, here $C_1 = 1, \quad C_0 = C_2$
$$= C_3 = \cdots = 0;$$

(c) $H(t) = G(t + t_0)$, here $C_0 = 1, \quad C_1 = t_0, \quad C_2 = \dfrac{t_0^2}{2!},$

$$C_3 = \dfrac{t_0^3}{3!}, \cdots$$

Let us write the expression for the error of the system in the case we are considering. We shall assume *a priori* that the control system is stationary and we shall then show that the optimal system in this case is indeed stationary. In writing the expression for the error $E(t)$ of the system, we shall use formulas that are valid for stationary systems:

$$E(t) = Y(t) - H(t)$$
$$= \int_0^T [G_h(t - \tau) + G'(t - \tau) + Z(t - \tau)]w(\tau)d\tau - H(t)$$

$$= \int_0^T G_h(t - \tau)w(\tau)d\tau - \sum_{i=0}^m C_i G_h^{(i)}(t)$$

$$+ \int_0^T X'(t - \tau)w(\tau)d\tau - L\{G'(t)\}.$$

Let us transform the formula that we have obtained. To do this, we expand the function $G_h(t - \tau)$ (which is an mth-degree polynomial) in a series of powers of τ for a fixed value of t:

$$G_h(t - \tau) = G_h(t) - \dot{G}_h(t)\tau + \frac{\ddot{G}_h(t)}{2!}\tau^2 -$$

$$\cdots + (-1)^m \frac{G_h^{(m)}(t)}{m!}\tau^m = \sum_{i=0}^m (-1)^i G_h^{(i)}(t)\frac{\tau^i}{i!}.$$

We denote by $H'(t)$ the result of applying the operator L to the random function $G'(t)$. This $H'(t)$ is the component of the desired output variable $H(t)$ defined by the stationary component $G'(t)$ of the useful signal.

Now, we can rewrite the expression for the error of the system:

$$E(t) = \sum_{i=0}^m (-1)^i \frac{G_h^{(i)}(t)}{i!} \int_0^T \tau^i w(\tau)d\tau - \sum_{i=0}^m G_h^{(i)}(t)C_i$$

$$+ \int_0^T X'(t - \tau)w(\tau)d\tau - H'(t)$$

$$= \sum_{i=0}^{m-1} G_h^{(i)}(t)\left[\frac{(-1)^i}{i!} \int_0^T \tau^i w(\tau)d\tau - C_i \right]$$

$$+ G_h^{(m)}(t)\left[\frac{(-1)^m}{m!} \int_0^T \tau^m w(\tau)d\tau - C_m \right]$$

$$+ \int_0^T X'(t - \tau)w(\tau)d\tau - H'(t).$$

In the foregoing, we imposed the requirement of astaticism of mth-order on the system. This means that, when the input signal is a polynomial in t of degree $(m - 1)$, the error of the system must be equal to 0 (without consideration of initial conditions). Consequently, we must have

$$\frac{(-1)^i}{i!} \int_0^T \tau^i w(\tau)d\tau - C_i = 0, \quad i = 0, 1, 2, \cdots, m - 1. \quad (3.49)$$

These relations can be rewritten as

$$\frac{(-1)^i}{i!}\mu_i - C_i = 0, \quad i = 0, 1, \cdots, m - 1, \quad (3.49a)$$

where $\mu_i = \int_0^T \tau^i w(\tau)d\tau$ is the ith-order moment of the weight function. (Conditions (3.49) and (3.49a) are also called conditions for unbiasedness.)

Thus, the weight function of an admissible system must satisfy conditions (3.49) or, what amounts to the same thing, conditions (3.49a). For an admissible system, the error E is calculated according to the formula

$$E(t) = m! \, G_m \left[\frac{(-1)^m}{m!} \int_0^T \tau^m w(\tau) d\tau - C_m \right]$$
$$+ \int_0^T X'(t - \tau) w(\tau) d\tau - H'(t), \tag{3.50}$$

since $G_h^{(m)}(t) = m! \, G_m$.

The mean square error of the system is equal to

$$\Gamma_E = M[E^2(t)] = (m!)^2 \alpha_m \left[\frac{(-1)^m}{m!} \int_0^T \tau^m w(\tau) d\tau - G_m \right]^2$$
$$+ \int_0^T \int_0^T M[X'(t - \tau) X'(t - \lambda)] w(\tau) w(\lambda) d\tau \, d\lambda$$
$$- 2 \int_0^T M[X'(t - \tau) H'(t)] w(\tau) d\tau + M\{[H'(t)]^2\}$$
$$= \alpha_m \left[(-1)^m \int_0^T \tau^m w(\tau) d\tau - m! C_m \right]^2$$
$$+ \int_0^T \int_0^T K_{x'}(\tau - \lambda) w(\tau) w(\lambda) d\tau \, d\lambda$$
$$- 2 \int_0^T K_{x'h'}(\tau) w(\tau) d\tau + D_{h'}. \tag{3.51}$$

It follows from this formula that the mean square error of the system Γ_E is independent of time. This is a consequence of the fact that, as is obvious from formula (3.50), the error $E(t)$ of the system is a stationary random function. Thus, in the problem that we are considering, despite the fact that the initial conditions are nonstationary (the component of the useful signal $G_h(t)$ is nonstationary), the error of the system is stationary and hence the optimal system also belongs to the class of stationary systems.

The problem of determining the optimal weight function $w_0(\tau)$ reduces to determination of the minimum of the functional (3.51) under the conditions (3.49). This is the problem of determining a conditional extremum, of which we spoke in Chapter 1. To seek a conditional extremum of Γ_E, it is first necessary to determine the conditional extremum of the functional

$$I_E\{w\} = \Gamma_E\{w\} + 2 \sum_{i=0}^{m-1} \gamma_i \mu_i \{w\},$$

and then determine the Lagrange multipliers γ_i from conditions (3.49).

Let us solve the first part of the problem; that is, let us determine the minimum of the functional $I_E\{w\}$. We write the expression for I_E in expanded form:

$$I_E\{w\} = \alpha_m\left[(-1)^m\int_0^T \tau^m w(\tau)\,d\tau - m!\,C_m\right]^2$$

$$+ \int_0^T\int_0^T K_{x'}(\tau - \lambda)w(\tau)w(\lambda)\,d\tau\,d\lambda - 2\int_0^T K_{x'h'}(\tau)w(\tau)\,d\tau$$

$$+ D_{h'} + 2\sum_{i=0}^{m-1}\gamma^i\int_0^T \tau^i w(\tau)\,d\tau. \tag{3.52}$$

The minimum of the quadratic functional (3.52) can be found by the method of fastest descent. If, for some reason or other, this method is not applicable, we can obtain an integral equation determining the optimal weight function and then solve that equation. To do this, we transform the functional I_E to the form (1.139):

$$I_E = \int_0^T\int_0^T \left\{ K_{x'}(\tau - \lambda)w(\tau)w(\lambda) + \alpha_m\tau^m\lambda^m w(\tau)w(\lambda) \right.$$

$$- (-1)^m m!\,C_m\alpha_m\frac{1}{T}[\tau^m w(\tau) + \lambda^m w(\lambda)]$$

$$- \frac{1}{T}[K_{x'h'}(\tau)w(\tau) + K_{x'h'}(\lambda)w(\lambda)]$$

$$+ \frac{1}{T}\sum_{i=0}^{m-1}\gamma_i[\tau^i w(\tau) + \lambda^i w(\lambda)] \left.\right\}d\tau\,d\lambda + D_{h'} + \alpha_m(m!\,C_m)^2. \tag{3.52a}$$

The last two terms are independent of the weight function $w(\tau)$. Therefore, we need not consider them here. In the present case, the function Φ is represented by the expression in the braces constituting the integrand of the iterated integral.

The necessary condition that the optimal weight function must satisfy can be written with the aid of the relation (1.140b). In the present case, it takes the form

$$\int_0^T\left[K_{x'}(\tau - \lambda)w(\lambda) + \alpha_m\tau^m\lambda^m w(\lambda) - \frac{1}{T}(-1)^m m!\,G_m\alpha_m\tau^m \right.$$

$$\left. - \frac{1}{T}K_{x'h'}(\tau) + \frac{1}{T}\sum_{i=0}^{m-1}\gamma_i\tau^i \right]d\lambda = 0, \quad 0 \leqslant \tau \leqslant T,$$

or

$$\int_0^T[K_{x'}(\tau - \lambda) + \alpha_m\tau^m\lambda^m]w(\lambda)\,d\lambda$$

$$- K_{x'h'}(\tau) + \sum_{i=0}^{m-1}\gamma_i\tau^i - (-1)^m m!\,C_m\alpha_m\tau^m = 0, \quad 0 \leqslant \tau \leqslant T. \tag{3.53}$$

This last equation is of the type (3.46). We have already spoken of methods of solving such an equation.

In certain special cases, we can obtain an exact solution of equation (3.53) [Refs. 12, 31, 38, 47, 48]. For example, when $G'(t) = 0$ and $K_z(t)$ is a linear combination of exponential functions:

$$K_z(\tau) = \sum_{s=1}^{l} D_s e^{-d_s |\tau|}$$

(the spectral density $S_z(\omega)$ is a rational function of ω:

$$S_z(\omega) = |\phi(j\omega)|^2 = \frac{A(\omega^2)}{B(\omega^2)}, \quad \text{where} \quad \phi(p) = \frac{e_0 + e_1 p + \cdots + e_k p^k}{c_0 + c_1 p + \cdots + c_l p^l}).$$

The optimal weight function $w_0(\tau)$ is determined in accordance with the formula

$$w_0(\tau) = g_0 + g_1 \tau + \cdots + g_m \tau^m + A_1 e^{-\lambda_1 \tau} + \cdots + A_{2k} e^{-\lambda_{2k} \tau}$$

$$+ \sum_{j=1}^{l-k} [C_{j0} \delta^{(j-1)}(\tau) + C_{jT} \delta^{(j-1)}(\tau - T)], \quad 0 \leqslant \tau \leqslant T, \quad (3.54)$$

$$w_0(\tau) = 0, \quad \tau < 0, \quad \tau > T.$$

Here, $\delta^{(j-1)}(\tau)$ and $\delta^{(j-1)}(\tau - T)$ denote the $(j-1)$st derivatives of the undisplaced and displaced unit δ-functions. The constant coefficients

$$g_0, \cdots, g_m; A_1, \cdots, A_{2k}; \lambda_1, \cdots, \lambda_{2k}; C_{10}, \cdots, C_{l-k,0}; C_{1T}, \cdots, C_{l-k,T}$$

can be determined when we substitute (3.54) into equation (3.53), which then becomes an identity. Here, to determine the $m + 2l + 1$ unknown coefficients, we need to have $m + 2l + 1$ linear algebraic equations, which are obtained by carrying out the integration in (3.53) and setting the coefficients of the $m + 2l + 1$ functions of τ equal to 0:

$$1, t, t^2, \cdots, t^m; e^{-d_1 \tau}, e^{-d_2 \tau}, \cdots, e^{-d_l \tau}; e^{d_1 \tau}, e^{d_2 \tau}, \cdots, e^{d_l \tau}.$$

After we have determined the optimal weight function of the system that satisfies condition (3.53) and conditions (3.49), we can easily determine the minimal mean square error corresponding to this weight function. From equation (3.53), we have

$$\int_0^T [K_{x'}(\tau - \lambda) + \lambda_m \tau^m \lambda^m] w(\lambda) d\lambda$$

$$= K_{x'h'}(\tau) + (-1)^m m! C_m \alpha_m \tau^m - \sum_{i=0}^{m-1} \gamma_i \tau^i. \quad (3.53a)$$

When we substitute (3.53a) into (3.51) we obtain, by virtue of (3.49),

$$\Gamma_{E \min} = \Gamma_E \{w_0(\tau)\} = D_{h'} - \int_0^T K_{x'h'}(\tau) w_0(\tau) d\tau$$

$$- \alpha_m (-1)^m m! C_m \int_0^T \tau^m w_0(\tau) d\tau - \sum_{i=0}^{m-1} \gamma_i (-1)^i i! C_i^i. \quad (3.55)$$

In the general case, calculation of the mean square error of the system (cf. (3.51)) includes evaluation of a double integral. Calculation of the minimal mean square error in accordance with formula (3.55) involves only a simple integration.

EXAMPLE. Suppose that $G(t) = G_0 + G_1 t$ and $K_z(\tau) = \delta(\tau)$. On the weight function $w(\tau)$ we impose the requirement

$$\int_0^T w(\tau)d\tau = 1.$$

The desired output variable $H(t)$ is equal to the useful input signal $G(t)$. The observation time is $T = 1$. Consequently, $G'(t) = 0$, $X'(t) = Z(t)$, $K_{x'}(\tau) = K_z(\tau)$, $m = 1$, $H'(t) = 0$, $K_{x'h'}(\tau) = 0$.

Suppose that G_1 is a given quantity α_1. In the present case, $C_0 = 1$ and $C_1 = 0$. In accordance with formula (3.54), the optimal weight function in this case is of the form

$$w_0(t) = g_0 + g_1 t.$$

To determine the coefficients g_0 and g_1, we substitute $w_0(t)$ into equation (3.53) and regard it as an identity:

$$\int_0^1 [\delta(\tau - \lambda) + \alpha_1 \tau \lambda](g_0 + g_1 \lambda)d\lambda + \gamma_0 \equiv 0, \quad 0 \leqslant \tau \leqslant 1.$$

Let us carry out the integration and write this identity in the following form:

$$g_0 + g_1 \tau + \frac{1}{2}\alpha_1 g_0 \tau + \frac{1}{3}\alpha_1 g_1 \tau + \gamma_0 \equiv 0$$

or

$$g_0 + \gamma_0 + \left(g_1 + \frac{1}{2}\alpha_1 g_0 + \frac{1}{3}\alpha_1 g_1\right)\tau \equiv 0, \quad 0 \leqslant \tau \leqslant 1.$$

For this to hold identically, the coefficients of τ^0 and τ^1 must be equal to 0:

$$g_0 + \gamma_0 = 0, \quad g_1 + \frac{1}{2}\alpha_1 g_0 + \frac{1}{3}\alpha_1 g_1 = 0.$$

We have obtained two equations for determining the unknown parameters. Let us use them and let us express the parameters g_0 and g_1 in terms of γ_0:

$$g_0 = -\gamma_0, \quad g_1 = \frac{\alpha_1 \gamma_0}{2\left(1 + \frac{1}{3}\alpha\right)}.$$

We determine the value of the Lagrange multiplier γ_0 by substituting the weight function

$$w_0(\tau) = -\gamma_0 + \frac{\alpha_1 \gamma_0}{2\left(1 + \frac{1}{3}\alpha_1\right)} \tau$$

into the condition

$$\int_0^T w_0(\tau)d\tau = 1,$$

which means astaticism of first order:

$$\int_0^1 \left[-\gamma_0 + \frac{\alpha_1 \gamma_0 \tau}{2\left(1 + \frac{1}{3}\alpha_1\right)}\right]d\tau = 1.$$

From this we obtain

$$\gamma_0 = \frac{1}{\dfrac{\alpha_1}{4\left(1 + \dfrac{1}{3}\alpha_1\right)} - 1}.$$

If $\alpha_1 = 1$, then

$$\gamma_0 = \frac{16}{13}, \quad g_0 = \frac{16}{13}, \quad g_1 = -\frac{6}{13}, \quad w_0(\tau) = \frac{16}{13} - \frac{6}{13}\tau.$$

Now, by using formula (3.55), we can easily determine the minimum mean square error of the system:

$$\Gamma_{E\min} = -\gamma_0 C_0 = \frac{16}{13} \cdot 1 = \frac{16}{13}.$$

Earlier in this section, we considered the case (frequently encountered in practice) in which the useful signal is represented as the sum of a polynomial in time with random (or unknown) coefficients and a centralized random function $G'(t)$. Sometimes, there is no component of the useful signal in the form of a polynomial in time, and the mathematical expectation of the useful signal has an arbitrary form (not necessarily the form of a polynomial in time). In such cases, it is expedient to pose the following problem:

Suppose that a signal X is applied at the input of the system (Fig. 1.1). Suppose that $X(t)$ is the sum of a useful signal $G(t)$ and a noise $Z(t)$ with arbitrary mathematical expectations $m_x(t)$ and $m_z(t)$ and with joint correlation functions of the useful signal and noise.

Keeping formulas (1.95) and (1.96) and the relation

$$H(t) = \int_0^\infty G(\tau)v(t, \tau)d\tau,$$

in mind, we can write the following expression for the mean square error of the system in the present case:

$$\Gamma_E(t) = m_E^2(t) + D_E(t) = \left[\int_0^T m_x(\tau) w(t, \tau) d\tau - m_h(t) \right]^2$$
$$+ \int_0^T \int_0^T K_x(\tau_1, \tau_2) w(t, \tau_1) w(t, \tau_2) d\tau_1 d\tau_2$$
$$- \int_0^T K_{xh}(\tau_1, t) w(t, \tau_1) d\tau_1 - \int_0^T K_{hx}(\tau_1, t) w(t, \tau_1) d\tau_1 + D_h(t).$$

$$(3.56)$$

Here, the first term represents the square of the mathematical expectation $m_E^2(t)$, and the remaining terms represent the variance of the error $D_E(t)$ at a fixed instant of time t.

The functional (3.56) is a special case of the functional (1.139). Reasoning just as in the preceding cases, we may write the necessary condition (1.140b) for a minimum of the functional in question:

$$\int_0^T [K_x(\tau, \lambda) + m_x(\tau) m_x(\lambda)] w(t, \lambda) d\lambda + m_h(t) m_x(\tau)$$
$$- \frac{1}{2} K_{xh}(\tau, t) - \frac{1}{2} K_{hx}(\tau, t) = 0, \quad 0 \leqslant \tau \leqslant T. \quad (3.57)$$

This integral equation is an equation of the type of equation (3.46). We shall presently speak of methods for solving such equations.

Let us show that the necessary condition (3.57) is also a sufficient one for minimizing the functional (3.56). To do this, let us look at the functional $\Gamma_E\{w(t, \tau)\}$ defined by formula (3.56) for the function $w(t, \tau) = w_0(t, \tau) + v(t, \tau)$, where $w_0(t, \tau)$ is the optimal weight function defined by equation (3.57) and $v(t, \tau)$ is an arbitrary admissible weight function.

Let us write the expression for $\Gamma_E\{w_0(t, \tau) + v(t, \tau)\}$ in expanded form:

$$\Gamma_E\{w_0 + v\} = \left\{ \int_0^T m_x(\tau)[w_0(t, \tau) + v(t, \tau)] d\tau - m_h(t) \right\}^2$$
$$+ \int_0^T \int_0^T K_x(\tau_1, \tau_2)[w_0(t, \tau_1) + v(t, \tau_1)][w_0(t, \tau_2)$$
$$+ v(t, \tau_2)] d\tau_1 d\tau_2 - \int_0^T K_{xh}(\tau_1, t)[w_0(t, \tau_1) + v(t, \tau_1)] d\tau_1$$
$$- \int_0^T K_{hx}(\tau_1, t)[w_0(t, \tau_1) + v(t_1, \tau_1)] d\tau_1 + D_h(t)$$
$$= \Gamma_E\{w_0\} + \int_0^T v(t, \tau) \left\{ \left[\int_0^T K_x(\tau, \lambda) \right. \right.$$
$$+ m_x(\tau) m_x(\lambda) \right] w_0(t, \lambda) d\lambda - m_h(t) m_x(t)$$
$$- \frac{1}{2} K_{xh}(\tau, t) - \frac{1}{2} K_{hx}(\tau, t) \right\} d\tau$$
$$+ \int_0^T \int_0^T [m_x(\tau) m_x(\lambda) + K_x(\tau, \lambda)] v(t, \tau) v(t, \lambda) d\tau d\lambda$$

$$= \Gamma_E\{w_0\} + \int_0^T \int_0^T [m_x(\tau)m_x(\lambda)$$

$$+ K_x(\tau, \lambda)]v(t, \tau)v(t, \lambda)d\tau d\lambda.$$

It follows that

$$\Gamma_E\{w_0 + v\} \geqslant \Gamma_E\{w_0\},$$

since the second term in the last expression for Γ_E is the mean square error at the output of the system with weight function $v(t, \tau)$, which is never negative. This completes the proof of the assertion.

When we have obtained the solution of equation (3.57), we can easily determine the minimum mean square error corresponding to this solution $w_0(t, \tau)$. From (3.56) and (3.57), we have

$$\Gamma_{E\,\min} = \Gamma_E\{w_0\} = D_h(t) + m_h^2(t)$$

$$- \frac{1}{2}\int_0^T K_{xh}(\tau, t)w_0(t, \tau)d\tau - \frac{1}{2}\int_0^T K_{hx}(\tau, t)w_0(t, \tau)d\tau$$

$$- \int_0^T m_h(t)m_x(\tau)w_0(t, \tau)d\tau. \tag{3.58}$$

The minimum mean square error is determined with the aid of a simple integration.

The theory of optimal systems that minimize the mean square error at a given instant of time has been well worked out. Especially profound and far-reaching investigations in this field are expounded by Pugachev [Ref. 47].

14. DETERMINATION OF THE OPTIMAL WEIGHT FUNCTION OF A SYSTEM WHICH PROVIDES AN EXTREMUM OF A QUADRATIC FUNCTIONAL

In the preceding sections of this chapter, we have considered various problems of determining optimal automatic-control systems. These problems differ from each other as regards the form of the criterion, the class of admissible control systems, or the form of the probabilistic characteristics of the influences. Different combinations of all possible criteria, classes of admissible systems, and probabilistic characteristics of the influences constitute a large set of various formulations of problems of choosing optimal systems. Each particular problem has its own peculiarities, which enable us to obtain specific recommendations facilitating the process of obtaining a solution.

The literature on the subject contains developments and recommendations on obtaining solutions in many specific formulations of the problems [Refs. 31, 46, 56, 59]. Together with a description of various specific formulations of the problems, it is convenient to consider the general formulation of the problem, which would include all the special formulations that we have considered and a rather broad class of other formulations, but which would not be essentially different from the problems that we have considered in relation to computational difficulties. Let us suppose that the computational difficulties are the same as in the problems we have considered if the equation determining the optimal system is linear.

As we know [Ref. 36], the problem of finding an extremum of a quadratic functional reduces to the problem of finding a solution of a linear integro-differential equation. Therefore, we may assume that the problem of determining an optimal weight function of a system with respect to a criterion that is a quadratic functional of arbitrary form is a completely solvable problem. In any case, such a problem can be solved by means of the method of fastest descent.

Let us look at some examples of quadratic functionals.

(a) All the criteria previously considered (the variance in the error, the second-order initial moment, a linear combination of the mathematical expectation, and the values of the correlation function of the error) are special cases of a quadratic functional. This is easily shown to be the case. Specifically, all these criteria satisfy the relation

$$I\{w + \Delta \cdot v\} = C_0 + 2\Delta \cdot C_1 + \Delta^2 \cdot C_2^2,$$

where C_0, C_1, and C_2 are independent of the arbitrary number Δ and depend only on the functions $w(\tau)$ and $v(\tau)$.

(b) $$I\{w\} = \int_0^T \int_0^T \sum_{i,j=0}^m K_{ij}(\tau, \lambda) w^{(i)}(t, \tau) w^{(j)}(t, \lambda) d\tau \, d\lambda$$
$$+ 2\int_0^T \sum_{s=0}^n K_s(\tau) w^{(s)}(t, \tau) d\tau + K(t),$$

where $K_{ij}(\tau, \lambda)$, $K_s(\tau)$, and $K(t)$ are given functions of their arguments, $w(t, \tau)$ is the desired function of the argument τ, and t is a fixed value of the parameter. Euler's linear integro-differential equation, determining the optimal weight function from this criterion, can be determined by using the relation (1.136).

The problem leads to such a functional, for example, when we require that the weight function be realizable (see following).

(c) $$I\{w\} = \frac{1}{t_2 - t_1} \int_{t_1}^{t_2} \left\{ \int_0^T \int_0^T \sum_{i,j=0}^m K_{ij}(\tau, \lambda) w^{(i)}(t, \tau) \right.$$
$$\left. \times w^{(j)}(t, \lambda) d\tau \, d\lambda + 2\int_0^T \sum_{s=0}^m K_s(\tau) w^{(s)}(t, \tau) d\tau + K(t) \right\} dt,$$

where $[t_1, t_2]$ is the interval of averaging with respect to the parameter t.

It is convenient to use such a criterion if, for example, instead of the minimum of the variance in the error at a given instant, we find it more convenient to use the minimum of the variance in the error averaged over some interval.

We note that the sum of arbitrary quadratic functionals multiplied by arbitrary real numbers is a quadratic functional.

A quadratic functional is the simplest kind of functional as far as solving the problem of finding an extremum goes. Here, there exists a certain analogue with a second-degree parabola, which is the simplest function with regard to finding its maximum or minimum.

Throughout this chapter, we have not considered cases in which restrictions of the type $a \leq w(\tau) \leq b$ are imposed on the unknown weight function.

Chapter 4

DETERMINATION OF AN OPTIMAL LINEAR AUTOMATIC-CONTROL SYSTEM IN TERMS OF A CRITERION WHICH IS ITSELF A GIVEN FUNCTION OF OTHER CRITERIA

In the present chapter, we shall consider problems in which the choice of an optimal system is made from more complicated criteria. The chapter is primarily devoted to problems in which the criterion chosen is a function of the mathematical expectation of the error, the variances of the different components of the error, or different values of the correlation function of the error. Among such criteria are the following: (1) The probability that the error of the system lies within specified limits at a certain instant. (2) The probability that the error of the system lies within given limits throughout some interval, and so on.

As is obvious, a criterion of this type sufficiently reflects in many cases the purpose of the system. Keeping in mind the practical value of criteria that reflect immediately the purpose of the system and that give an objective quantitative estimate of the error of its solution, we shall expound in detail the methods of choosing optimal systems according to these criteria.

We have previously noted that, at the present time, methods of choosing an optimal system from very simple statistical criteria (such as the variance of the error, the mean square error of the system, and the like) have been well developed. Therefore, in developing methods for choosing optimal systems from more complicated criteria, it is expedient to use the results that we already have and, where possible, to reduce the choice of an optimal system with respect to a complicated criterion to the choice of an optimal system with respect to a simple criterion. This idea will be used a great deal in the present chapter and the two that follow.

15. DETERMINATION OF THE OPTIMAL LINEAR AUTOMATIC-CONTROL SYSTEM WHICH ENSURES THE MAXIMUM PROBABILITY THAT THE ERROR WILL NOT EXCEED ALLOWED LIMITS

1. Analysis of the probability that the error will not exceed allowed limits

Let us analyze the probability that the error will not exceed allowed limits, treating this probability as a functional of the weight function of the system under known initial conditions.

We shall assume that the block diagram is still the one shown in Figure 1.1. Let us first consider the case in which the error is stationary. In this case, in accordance with (3.50), the error of the system is equal to

$$E(t) = m! \, G_m \left[\frac{(-1)^m}{m!} \int_0^T \tau^m w(\tau) d\tau - C_m \right]$$

$$+ \int_0^T X'(t - \tau) w(\tau) d\tau - H'(t).$$

Here, G_m is a random variable. Let us write it in the form

$$G_m = m_0 + G_m^0,$$

where $m_0 = M[G_m]$ is the mathematical expectation of G_m, and G_m^0 is the centralized component of G_m; that is, $M[G_m^0] = 0$. We rewrite the expression for the error in the form

$$E(t) = m_0 \left[(-1)^m \int_0^T \tau^m w(\tau) d\tau - m! \, C_m \right]$$

$$+ G_m^0 \left[(-1)^m \int_0^T \tau^m w(\tau) d\tau - m! \, C_m \right]$$

$$+ \int_0^T X'(t - \tau) w(\tau) d\tau - H'(t). \tag{4.1}$$

The first term in this expression is the mathematical expectation of the error of the system and the other two terms constitute the centralized component of that error. Thus, the mathematical expectation of the error of the system is

$$m_E = m_0 \left[(-1)^m \int_0^T \tau^m w(\tau) d\tau - m! \, C_m \right]. \tag{4.2}$$

The variance of the error of the system can be determined as the difference between the second-order initial moment (3.51) and the square of the mathematical expectation (4.2):

$$D_E = D_m \left[(-1)^m \int_0^T \tau^m w(\tau) d\tau - m! C_m \right]^2$$
$$+ \int_0^T \int_0^T K_{x'}(\tau - \lambda) w(\tau) w(\lambda) d\tau \, d^0\lambda$$
$$- 2 \int_0^T K_{x'h'}(\tau) w(\tau) d\tau + D_h, \tag{4.3}$$

where $D_m = \alpha_m - m_0^2$ is the variance of the random variable G_m.

Consequently, the mathematical expectation and the variance in this case are functionals of the type (1.139); that is, they are double integrals the integrands for which functions Φ of $w(\tau)$ and $w(\lambda)$ are given. We recall that a single integral can be represented as a special case of a double integral.

The functions Φ in the functionals (4.2) and (4.3) always satisfy condition (1.140a); that is, these functions Φ are always symmetric in $w(\tau)$ and $w(\lambda)$.

In the general case in which the system, the initial conditions on the influences, and the error of the system are nonstationary, the mathematical expectation and the variance are determined in accordance with formulas (1.95) and (1.96):

$$m_E(t) = \int_0^\infty m_x(\tau) w(t, \tau) d\tau - \int_0^\infty G(\tau) v(t, \tau) d\tau$$
$$= \int_0^\infty m_x(\tau) w(t, \tau) d\tau - H(t), \tag{4.4}$$
$$D_E(t) = K_E(t, t) = \int_0^\infty \int_0^\infty K_x(\tau_1, \tau_2) w(t, \tau_1) w(t, \tau_2) d\tau_1 d\tau_2$$
$$- 2 \int_0^\infty \int_0^\infty K_{xg}(\tau_1, \tau_2) w(t, \tau_1) v(t, \tau_2) d\tau_1 d\tau_2$$
$$+ \int_0^\infty \int_0^\infty K_g(\tau_1, \tau_2) v(t, \tau_1) v(t, \tau_2) d\tau_1 d\tau_2$$
$$= \int_0^\infty \int_0^\infty K_x(\tau_1, \tau_2) w(t, \tau_1) w(t, \tau_2) d\tau_1 d\tau_2$$
$$- 2 \int_0^\infty K_{xh}(t, \tau_2) w(t, \tau_1) d\tau_1 + D_h(t). \tag{4.5}$$

In making the transformations of the expressions for m_E and D_E, we used the relation that determines the desired output variable of the system $H(t)$:

$$H(t) = \int_0^\infty G(\tau) v(t, \tau) d\tau.$$

If the weight function $w(t, \tau)$ possesses the property that

$$w(t, \tau) = 0 \quad \text{for} \quad \tau - t < 0, \quad \tau - t > T,$$

then, in formulas (4.4) and (4.5), the upper limits of integration with respect to τ_1 and τ_2 can be replaced with T.

The forms of formulas (4.4) and (4.5) bring out the fact that, *for a fixed instant t, the mathematical expectation and the variance in the error of the system are, in the general case, functionals of the type (1.139); that is, they are double integrals in which the integrands are given functions Φ of the weight function w.*

In the present section, we shall assume that the probability that the error will not exceed allowed limits at a fixed instant is determined by only two characteristics of the distribution law of that error; for example, (a) the mathematical expectation and the variance of the error or (b) the variances of two independent components of the error. Such cases are often encountered in practice when one is investigating automatic-control systems. Let us consider a few similar cases.

(1) Suppose that the mathematical expectation of the error of a system is given by formula (4.2) and that the variance of this error is given by formula (4.3). Let us then suppose that the components G_m and G' of the useful signal and noise Z obey a normal law. In this case, the error E also obeys a normal law [Refs. 29, 47]. Consequently, the distribution law is determined by the first two moments of the error (the mathematical expectation m_E and the variance D_E).

We shall assume that the error must fall in the interval $C_1 \leq E \leq C_2$. Usually, $C_1 < 0 < C_2$ and sometimes $C_1 = -C_2$.

As we know [Refs. 18, 46], the probability that the error will not fall outside the allowed limits is expressed in the present case in terms of the mathematical expectation m_E and the variance D_E as follows:

$$P(C_1 \leqslant E \leqslant C_2) = \frac{1}{\sqrt{2\pi D_E}} \int_{-C_1}^{C_2} \exp\left\{-\frac{(m_E - E)^2}{2D_E}\right\} dE. \qquad (4.6)$$

In making mass calculations, it is convenient to use formula (1.34), which, in the given case, is written as

$$P(C_1 \leqslant E \leqslant C_2) = \Phi\left(\frac{C_2 - m_E}{\sqrt{D_E}}\right) - \Phi\left(\frac{C_1 - m_E}{\sqrt{D_E}}\right), \qquad (4.6a)$$

where Φ is Gauss' function.

If $-C_1 = C_2 = C$ and C is small, then the integrand in (4.6) changes only slightly as E varies from $-C$ to $+C$ and we can take it outside the integral sign, writing it simply as $\exp\{-m_E^2/2D_E\}$. In this case, formula (4.6) can be replaced with the following sufficiently accurate approximate formula

$$P(|E| < C) = \frac{2C}{\sqrt{2\pi}} \frac{\exp\left\{-\dfrac{m_E^2}{2D_E}\right\}}{\sqrt{D_E}}. \qquad (4.6b)$$

When we calculate with this formula, we can use the table of the function

$$\Phi'(u) = \frac{1}{\sqrt{2\pi}} \exp\left(-\frac{u^2}{2}\right)$$

(cf. Appendix 2).

(2) Suppose that the mathematical expectation of the error is equal to 0 and that the variance is given by formula (4.3). Suppose that the random variable $G_m = G_m^0$ obeys a law of equal probability between values $-g$ and $+g$; that is, that the probability density of this random variable is

$$P_g = \begin{cases} \dfrac{1}{2g} & \text{if } |G_m| < g, \\ 0 & \text{if } |G_m| > g. \end{cases}$$

We shall assume that the components of the useful signal $G'(t)$ and the noise $Z(t)$ obey a normal distribution law.

In this case, the error E of the system is the sum of two random variables (for fixed time t):

$$E = E_1 + E_2,$$

where

$$E_1 = G_m\left[(-1)^m \int_0^T \tau^m w(\tau)d\tau - m!C_m\right],$$

$$E_2 = \int_0^T X'(t - \tau)w(\tau)d\tau - H'(t).$$

The first component E_1 obeys a law of equal probability in the interval $[-g_1, +g_1]$, where

$$g_1 = g\left[(-1)^m \int_0^T \tau^m w(\tau)d\tau - m!C_m\right]. \tag{4.7}$$

The second component E_2 obeys a normal distribution law with mathematical expectation equal to 0 and with variance equal to

$$D_2 = \int_0^T \int_0^T K_{x'}(\tau - \lambda)w(\tau)w(\lambda)d\tau\, d\lambda$$
$$- 2\int_0^T K_{x'h'}(\tau)w(\tau)d\tau + D_{h'}. \tag{4.8}$$

The variance of the component E_1 is expressed simply in terms of the interval of equal probability:

$$D_1 = \frac{g_1^2}{3} = \frac{g^2}{3}\left[(-1)^m \int_0^T \tau^m w(\tau)d\tau - m!C_m\right]^2$$
$$= D_m\left[(-1)^m \int_0^T \tau^m w(\tau)d\tau - m!C_m\right]^2. \tag{4.9}$$

Thus, the distribution law of the error in the present case is a composite of two distribution laws: A symmetric law of equal probability in the interval $[-g_1, +g_1]$ (with variance $D_1 = g_1^2/3$) and a symmetric distribution law with variance D_2. Consequently, the distribution law of the error of the system is determined in this case by the two variances D_1 and D_2. Both these variances are functionals of the weight function of the system.

The probability that the error will not exceed the allowed limits can, in the present case, be determined from the formula

$$P(C_1 \leqslant E \leqslant C_2) = \frac{1}{2g_1} \int_{-g_1}^{g_1} \frac{1}{\sqrt{2\pi D_2}} \int_{C_1}^{C_2} \exp\left\{-\frac{(E_1 - E_2)^2}{2D_2}\right\} dE_2 dE_1,$$

(4.10)

where g_1 and D_2 are defined by formulas (4.7) and (4.8). This formula can be rewritten in another form if we consider (4.9):

$$P(C_1 \leqslant E \leqslant C_2)$$
$$= \frac{1}{2\sqrt{6\pi D_1 D_2}} \int_{-\sqrt{3D_1}}^{\sqrt{3D_1}} \int_{C_1}^{C_2} \exp\left\{-\frac{(E_1 - E_2)^2}{2D_2}\right\} dE_2 dE_1. \quad (4.10a)$$

If $-C_1 = C_2 = C$ and C is small, then the inner integrand in (4.10) and (4.10a) will vary only slightly as E_2 varies from $-C$ to $+C$ and we can take it outside the inner integral sign, giving it the value

$$\exp\left\{-\frac{E_1^2}{2D_2}\right\}.$$

In this case, formula (4.10) can be replaced with the approximate formula

$$P(|E| < C) = \frac{2C}{g_1\sqrt{2\pi D_2}} \int_0^{g_1} \exp\left\{-\frac{E_1^2}{2D_2}\right\} dE_1, \quad (4.10b)$$

and formula (4.10a) can be replaced with the approximate formula

$$P(|E| < C) = \frac{2C}{\sqrt{6\pi D_1 D_2}} \int_0^{\sqrt{3D_1}} \exp\left\{-\frac{E_1^2}{2D_2}\right\} dE_1. \quad (4.10c)$$

In all these formulas, that is, (4.6), (4.6a), (4.10), (4.10a), (4.10b), and (4.10c), the probability that the error of the system will not exceed allowed limits is represented as a known function of two functionals of the weight function of the system. In (4.6) and (4.6a), these functionals are the mathematical expectation and the variance of the error; in (4.6b), they are the square of the mathematical expectation m_E^2 and the variance in the error; in (4.10) and (4.10b), they are the half-interval g_1 and the variance D_2 of the component E_2; and in (4.10a) and (4.10c), they are the variance D_1 of the first component and the variance D_2 of the second component of the error.

In other similar cases, we can obtain analogous formulas that determine the probability $P(C_1 \leqslant E \leqslant C_2)$ as a function of two parameters characterizing the distribution law of the error.

2. Determination of an optimal weight function from the criterion of probability that the error of the system will not exceed allowed limits

All the foregoing examples of formulas that determine the probability that the error of a system will not exceed allowed limits are included in the following general relationship:

$$I = f(I_1, I_2), \qquad (4.11)$$

where $I_1 = I_1\{w\}$ and $I_2 = I_2\{w\}$ are quadratic functionals of the weight function of the system $w(\tau)$ (in special cases they may be, for example, the mathematical expectation m_E and the variance D_E of the error or the variance D_1 and the variance D_2 of different components of the error), f is a given function of the quantities I_1 and I_2 (in special cases, it may be, for example, the function (4.6) or the function (4.10)). Finally, I is a composite functional of the weight function $w(\tau)$ of the system, which is a given function f of simpler functionals I_1 and I_2 (in special cases, this functional may, for example, be defined by formulas (4.2), (4.3), and (4.6) or (4.4), (4.5), and (4.10)).

Thus, the functional (4.11) includes as special cases the probability that the error of the system will not exceed allowed limits. This functional can have a different interpretation from one problem to another.

On the basis of Theorem 2 of Chapter 1, we conclude that the optimal weight function with respect to the criterion (4.11) must ensure an extremum of the reduced functional

$$I_\theta = \theta I_1 + I_2 \qquad (4.12)$$

for some value of the harmonizing parameter θ (of the harmonizing factor θ).

In all the examples that we have considered, the functionals I_1 and I_2 were quadratic functionals. Consequently, in these examples, the functional I_θ is also a quadratic functional.

Thus, if the functionals I_1 and I_2 in the criterion (4.11) are quadratic functionals, the problem of determining the optimal weight function from the composite criterion I reduces to the considerably simpler problem of finding an extremum of the quadratic functional I_θ and finding the harmonizing factor θ.

Finding the extremum of the functional I_θ is equivalent in difficulty to finding the extremum of the functional $I_1 + I_2$. Finding the necessary value of the harmonizing parameter θ can be done by one of the two methods expounded in Chapter 1. When we have determined the weight function $w_0(\tau, \theta)$ corresponding to the extremum of the functional I_θ for various values of θ, the determination of the harmonizing factor $\theta = \theta_0$ corresponding to an extremum of the functional I is easily done.

We write the expanded expression for the reduced functional I_θ in the general case in which the probabilistic moments of the error of the system are determined by (3.56). In this case, the functional I_1 is either the mathematical expectation of the error $m_E(t)$ or the square of the mathematical expectation of the error $m_E^2(t)$, and the functional I_2 is either the variance of the error or the second-order initial moment of the error. Here, various combinations are possible:

$$I_1 = m_E, \quad I_2 = D_E; \quad I_1 = m_E, \quad I_2 = \Gamma_E;$$
$$I_1 = m_E^2, \quad I_2 = D_E; \quad I_1 = m_E^2, \quad I_2 = \Gamma_E.$$

In each specific case, we need to take that pair of functionals that is most convenient, that is, the one that enables us to organize the calculation of the optimal weight function the most economically. For example, if the function f is determined by the relation (4.6), then $I_1 = m_E$. Here, we cannot take $I_1 = m_E^2$, since the criterion depends not only on the absolute value of the mathematical expectation of the error but also on its sign. For the functional I_2, it is convenient to take the variance of the error D_E, since the criterion is most simply expressed in terms of it. Theoretically, it would be possible to take $I_2 = \Gamma_E = D_E + m_E^2$, but this complicates the computational formulas. On the other hand, if the function f is determined by (4.6b), it is convenient to take for I_1 the square of the mathematical expectation of the error and to take for I_2 the variance of the error D_E. This choice corresponds to the most convenient formulas in the calculations associated with the determination of the optimal weight function. In particular, it is easy to determine the region containing the desired value of the harmonizing parameter θ_0. It must be greater than 1 (see following discussion). In the present case, it is theoretically possible to take for I_1 and I_2 any of the foregoing listed combinations of the functionals m_E, m_E^2, D_E, and Γ_E. However, all other combinations are less convenient than the combination m_E^2, D_E already proposed.

In the case that we are considering, the mean square error Γ_E is determined by formula (3.36), and the mathematical expectation m_E and the variance D_E of the error are determined by the formulas

$$m_E = \int_0^T m_x(\tau) w(t, \tau) d\tau - m_h(t), \tag{4.13}$$

$$D_E = \int_0^T \int_0^T K_x(\tau_1, \tau_2) w(t, \tau_1) w(t, \tau_2) d\tau_1 d\tau_2$$
$$- \int_0^T K_{xh}(\tau_1, t) w(t, \tau_1) d\tau_1 - \int_0^T K_{hx}(\tau_1, t) w(t, \tau_1) d\tau_1 + D_h. \tag{4.14}$$

The reduced functional I_θ is written as follows for various combinations of m_E, D_E, and Γ_E:

(1) $I_\theta = \theta m_E^2 + D_E = \theta \left[\int_0^T m_x(\tau) w(t, \tau) d\tau - m_h(t) \right]^2$

$$+ \int_0^T \int_0^T K_x(\tau_1, \tau_2) w(t, \tau_1) w(t, \tau_2) d\tau_1 d\tau_2$$

$$- \int_0^T K_{xh}(\tau_1, t) w(t, \tau_1) d\tau_1 - \int_0^T K_{hx}(\tau_1, t) w(t, \tau_1) d\tau_1 + D_h;$$

(4.15)

(2) $I_\theta = \theta m_E + D_E = \theta \left[\int_0^T m_x(\tau) w(t, \tau) d\tau - m_h(t) \right]$

$$+ \int_0^T \int_0^T K_x(\tau_1, \tau_2) w(t, \tau_1) w(t, \tau_2) d\tau_1 d\tau_2$$

$$- \int_0^T K_{xh}(\tau_1, t) w(t, \tau_1) d\tau_1 - \int_0^T K_{hx}(\tau_1, t) w(t, \tau_1) d\tau_1 + D_h;$$

(4.16)

(3) $I_\theta = \theta m_E + \Gamma_E;$

(4) $I_\theta = \theta m_E^2 + \Gamma_E.$

In the last two variants, the expressions for the reduced functionals in question are written analogously to the expressions (4.15) and (4.16).

The integral equation that determines the weight function $w_0(t, \tau, \theta)$ and that ensures an extremum of the reduced functional I_θ can be obtained in a manner analogous to the way in which equation (3.57) was obtained. Let us write this equation for the reduced functionals (4.15) and (4.16):

For $I_\theta = \theta m_E^2 + D_E$

$$\int_0^T [K_x(\tau, \lambda) + \theta m_x(\tau) m_x(\lambda)] w_0(t, \lambda, \theta) d\lambda - \theta m_h(t) m_x(\tau)$$

$$- \frac{1}{2} K_{xh}(\tau, t) - \frac{1}{2} K_{hx}(\tau, t) = 0, \quad 0 \leqslant \tau \leqslant T. \qquad (4.17)$$

For $I_\theta = \theta m_E + D_E$

$$\int_0^T K_x(\tau, \lambda) w_0(\tau, \lambda, \theta) d\lambda + \theta m_x(\tau) - \frac{1}{2} K_{xh}(\tau, t)$$

$$- \frac{1}{2} K_{hx}(\tau, t) = 0, \quad 0 \leqslant \tau \leqslant T. \qquad (4.18)$$

Equations (4.17) and (4.18) are integral equations of the type of equation (3.46), and they can be solved for fixed values of time t and the harmonizing factor θ by the methods already shown. When we have found the solution $w_0(t, \tau, \theta)$ for some fixed time and different values of θ, we need to substitute it into the functional (4.11):

$$I = I\{w_0(t, \tau, \theta)\} = \Phi(t, \theta), \qquad (4.19)$$

which then becomes a function of the harmonizing parameter θ. Then, it is easy to determine, graphically for example, the desired maximum or minimum of the criterion I and the corresponding value of the harmonizing parameter θ_0. The desired optimal weight function for a fixed value of time t is

$$w^0(t, \tau) = w_0(t, \tau, \theta_0). \tag{4.20}$$

The result obtained here, expressed by formulas (4.13) through (4.20), deals with the general case of choice of an optimal system ensuring an extremum of the composite functional (4.11). This result applies to various criteria of the type (4.11) and to initial conditions of a given form of the influences on the system or of the admissible systems.

Other less general cases are also of interest. In these more restricted cases, we have succeeded in obtaining deeper and more concrete results.

3. Determination of an optimal weight function with respect to the criterion of probability that the error of the system will not exceed allowed limits $(n = 1)$

Consider the criterion (4.6b), that is, the probability that the error of the system will not exceed small allowed limits at a given instant of time. The initial conditions on the influences and on the admissible systems are assumed the same as in the derivation of equation (3.53) (in Section 13), which determines the optimal weight function of an astatic stationary system with respect to the criterion of minimization of the mean square error. In the present case, we shall again determine the optimal astatic system but with respect to a different criterion; namely, the maximum probability that the error will not exceed allowed limits. In formula (4.6b) defining the criterion chosen, the constant coefficient $2C/\sqrt{2\pi}$ has no effect on the order of calculation of the optimal weight function or on the optimal weight function itself. Therefore, in our subsequent calculations and transformations, it may be dropped.

Thus, an admissible automatic-control system must reproduce without error the $(m - 1)$st-degree polynomial (3.47). Consequently, an admissible weight function of a stationary system $w(\tau)$ must satisfy equations (3.49).

The desired output variable of the system is given by formula (3.48).

The error of the admissible system in this case is determined in accordance with formula (3.50) or formula (4.1):

$$E(t) = m_0\left[(-1)^m \int_0^T \tau^m w(\tau)d\tau - m!\,C_m \right]$$

$$+ G_m^0 \left[(-1)^m \int_0^T \tau^m w(\tau) d\tau - m! C_m \right]$$
$$+ \int_0^T X'(t - \tau) w(\tau) d\tau - H'(t),$$

where m_0 is the mathematical expectation of the random variable G_m, and G_m^0 is the centralized component of this variable. The values of the other quantities and functions in this expression are given in Section 13 of Chapter 3.

The mathematical expectation and the variance of the error of the system are determined in this case in accordance with formulas (4.2) and (4.3). We assume that the error E obeys a normal distribution law.

Let us use (4.6b), (4.2), and (4.3) to express the comparison criterion of systems in terms of the weight function of the system:

$$P(|E| < C) = \frac{2C}{\sqrt{2\pi}\sqrt{D_E}} \exp\left\{ -\frac{m_E^2}{2D_E} \right\} = \frac{2C}{\sqrt{2\pi}\sqrt{D_E}}$$

$$\times \exp\left\{ -\frac{m_0^2 \left[(-1)^m \int_0^T \tau^m w(\tau) d\tau - m! C_m \right]^2}{2\left(D_m \left[(-1)^m \int_0^T \tau^m w(\tau) d\tau - m! C_m \right]^2 + R \right)} \right\},$$

(4.20a)

where

$$R = \int_0^T \int_0^T K_{x'}(\tau - \lambda) w(\tau) w(\lambda) d\tau \, d\lambda$$
$$- 2 \int_0^T K_{x'h'}(\tau) w(\tau) d\tau + D_{h'}.$$

The functional (4.20a) is a special case of the functional (4.11). For the functional I_1 we take the square of the mathematical expectation of the error m_E^2, and for the functional I_2 we take the variance of the error D_E.

In accordance with Theorem 2 of Chapter 1, the problem of finding an extremum of the functional (4.20a) reduces to the problem of finding an extremum of the reduced functional

$$I_\theta = \theta m_E^2 + D_E = \theta m_0^2 \left[(-1)^m \int_0^T \tau^m w(\tau) d\tau - m! C_m \right]^2$$
$$+ D_m \left[(-1)^m \int_0^T \tau^m w(\tau) d\tau - m! C_m \right]^2$$
$$+ \int_0^T \int_0^T K_{x'}(\tau - \lambda) w(\tau) w(\lambda) d\tau \, d\lambda$$
$$- 2 \int_0^T K_{x'h'}(\tau) w(\tau) d\tau + D_{h'}$$

(4.21)

for various values of θ and for the value of the harmonizing parameter $\theta = \theta_0$ corresponding to the maximum of the functional (4.20a).

We need to find an extremum of the functional (4.21) under conditions (3.49). As we know, the problem of finding the conditional extremum of the functional (4.21) reduces to the problem of finding the unconditional extremum of the functional

$$I'_\theta = I_\theta + 2 \sum_{i=0}^{m-1} \gamma_i \int_0^T \tau^i w(\tau) d\tau.$$

The Lagrange multipliers are determined by substituting the found weight function into conditions (3.49). The functional I'_θ in expanded form is written as

$$I'_\theta = \theta m_0^2 \left[(-1)^m \int_0^T \tau^m w(\tau) d\tau - m! C_m \right]^2$$

$$+ D_m \left[(-1)^m \int_0^T \tau^m w(\tau) d\tau - m! C_m \right]^2$$

$$+ \int_0^T \int_0^T K_{x'}(\tau - \lambda) w(\tau) w(\lambda) d\tau d\lambda$$

$$- 2 \int_0^T K_{x'h'}(\tau) w(\tau) d\tau + D_h + 2 \sum_{i=0}^{m-1} \gamma_i \int_0^T \tau^i w(\tau) d\tau. \qquad (4.22)$$

This functional does not differ in any significant way from the functional (3.52). Therefore, the integral equation determining the weight function that ensures an extremum of the functional (4.22) can be obtained in the same way as equation (3.53) was obtained. Let us write this equation:

$$\int_0^T [K_{x'}(\tau - \lambda) + (\theta m_0^2 + D_m) \tau^m \lambda^m] w(\lambda) d\lambda - K_{x'h'}(\tau)$$

$$+ \sum_{i=0}^{m-1} \gamma_i \tau^i - (-1)^m m! C_m (\theta m_0^2 + D_m) \tau^m = 0, \quad 0 \leqslant \tau \leqslant T. \qquad (4.23)$$

Equation (4.23) belongs to the same type as equation (3.46), and for which we have examined a solution.

The weight function w_0 satisfying the integral equation (4.23) depends on $\gamma_0, \gamma_1, \cdots, \gamma_{m-1}$, and θ as parameters:

$$w_0 = w_0(\tau, \gamma_0, \gamma_1, \cdots, \gamma_{m-1}, \theta). \qquad (4.24)$$

The parameters $\gamma_0, \gamma_1, \cdots, \gamma_{m-1}$ are determined for a fixed value of the harmonizing parameter θ by substituting (4.24) into (3.49). In this case, equations (3.49) are linear algebraic equations in the parameters $\gamma_0, \gamma_1, \cdots, \gamma_{m-1}$. If we can obtain the analytic dependence (4.42) of the weight function w_0 on the parameters $\gamma_0, \gamma_1, \cdots, \gamma_{m-1}$, and θ, we can substitute (4.24) into (3.49) and eliminate the parameters $\gamma_0, \gamma_1, \cdots, \gamma_{m-1}$ from (4.24). Then, the weight function w_0 will be represented as a function of the variable τ and a single harmonizing parameter θ:

$$w_0 = w_0(\tau, \theta). \tag{4.25}$$

The value of the harmonizing parameter $\theta = \theta_0$ corresponding to the maximum of the criterion (4.20) can be determined by one of the two methods expounded in Chapter 1.

One of these methods consists in substituting the solution (4.25) into (4.20). In this case, the criterion P becomes a function of the harmonizing parameter θ: $F = F(\theta)$. The value $\theta = \theta_0$ that maximizes the function $F(\theta)$ enables us to determine the optimal weight function

$$w^0(\tau) = w_0(\tau, \theta_0), \tag{4.26}$$

which ensures the maximum probability that the error of the system will not exceed allowed limits.

The value $\theta = \theta_0$ of the harmonizing parameter can be found by a second method, in accordance with equation (1.162) of Chapter 1. In the present case, the equation may be written as

$$\frac{\dfrac{\partial P\{w_0(\tau, \theta_0)\}}{\partial m_E^2}}{\dfrac{\partial P\{w_0(\tau, \theta_0)\}}{\partial D_E}} = \theta_0. \tag{4.27}$$

The left-hand member of this equation should be formed as follows: First, we determine the partial derivatives $\partial P/\partial m_E^2$ and $\partial P/\partial D_E$ by using the dependence (4.20) of the probability P on m_E^2 and D_E. We then write the ratio of the partial derivatives

$$\frac{\partial P}{\partial m_E^2} \bigg/ \frac{\partial P}{\partial D_E}$$

which is a function of m_E^2 and D_E. In this function, we replace m_E^2 with the expression (4.2) and we replace D_E with the expression (4.3), where the weight function is chosen in accordance with formula (4.26). Thus, the left-hand member of equation (4.27) is a function of the harmonizing parameter θ. The solution θ_0 in this equation is the desired value of the harmonizing parameter θ.

Let us find a specific expression for the ratio

$$\frac{\partial P}{\partial m_E^2} \bigg/ \frac{\partial P}{\partial D_E}$$

in terms of the square m_E^2 of the mathematical expectation and the variance D_E of the error of the system. Let us first determine the partial derivatives:

$$\frac{\partial P}{\partial m_E^2} = \frac{2C}{\sqrt{2\pi}\sqrt{D_E}}\left(-\frac{1}{2D_E}\right)\exp\left\{-\frac{m_E^2}{2D_E}\right\},$$

$$\frac{\partial P}{\partial D_E} = \frac{2C}{\sqrt{2\pi}}\left(-\frac{1}{2D_E^{3/2}} + \frac{m_E^2}{2D_E^{5/2}}\right)\exp\left\{-\frac{m_E^2}{2D_E}\right\}.$$

Then, we determine their ratio:

$$\frac{\dfrac{\partial P}{\partial m_E^2}}{\dfrac{\partial P}{\partial D_E}} = \frac{-\dfrac{1}{2D_E^{3/2}}}{\dfrac{m_E^2}{2D_E^{5/2}} - \dfrac{1}{2D_E^{3/2}}} = \frac{-1}{\dfrac{m_E^2}{D_E} - 1}.$$

Consequently, equation (4.27) can be written in the following explicit form

$$\left[1 - \frac{m_E^2(\theta_0)}{D_E(\theta_0)}\right]^{-1} = \theta_0. \tag{4.27a}$$

Depending on the specific form of the solution (4.25), the left-hand member of equation (4.27a) can be the ratio of polynomials in the parameter θ_0 or a transcendental function of that parameter. Accordingly, equation (4.27a) can be either an algebraic or a transcendental equation. If equation (4.27a) is simple, then it is convenient to determine the value of the harmonizing parameter $\theta = \theta_0$ as a solution of this equation. On the other hand, if this equation is very complicated, it will be expedient to determine the desired value of the harmonizing parameter from the condition that the function $F(\theta)$ is maximized. However, even in this case, we can use equation (4.27a) to verify the result obtained.

Perhaps it would be desirable at this point to clarify, with a few examples, the procedure that we have been describing.

EXAMPLE 1. Suppose that an input signal X (see Fig. 1.1) is applied at the input of a linear stationary automatic-control system and that this signal is the sum of a useful signal G and a noise Z. The useful signal is of the form

$$G(t) = G_0 + G_1 t,$$

where G_0 is a random variable with a very high second-order initial moment Γ_{G_0}, G_1 is a given quantity, and t is the time. The noise is a stationary random process obeying a normal distribution law with the following probabilistic characteristics: The mathematical expectation $m_z = M[Z] = 0$ and the correlation function $K_z(\tau) = e^{-\alpha|\tau|}$. The random functions $G(t)$ and $Z(t)$ are uncorrelated. Thus, the input signal is nonstationary (the nonstationariness shows up in the term $G_1(t)$ in the expression for the useful signal).

Let us suppose that the system is designed for extrapolation of the useful signal $G(t)$, that is, for precise determination of the useful signal at an instant $t + T_e$ from the results of measurement of the signal over the interval of time from $T - t$ to t. Consequently, the desired (ideal) output variable of this system is given by the formula

$$H(t) = G(t + T_e) = G_0 + G_1 t + G_1 T_e.$$

Extrapolation problems are often encountered in practice. For example, the problem of arranging for two cosmic bodies, one of them controlled, to collide reduces to an extrapolation problem.

We take as admissible automatic-control systems stationary systems with astaticism of the least first order; that is, systems whose weight functions satisfy the condition

$$\int_0^T w(\tau)d\tau = 1. \tag{a}$$

This condition is a special case of condition (3.49). Here, $m = 1$, $m - 1 = 0$, and $C_0 = 1$. The requirement of at least first-order astaticism, that is, requirement (a), is a natural one here. It follows from the fact that the second-order initial moment of the random variable G_0 is comparatively great. This means that the random variable G_0 can assume very large values (in the limit, infinite values). If condition (a) is not satisfied, then the second-order initial moment of the error of the system $\Gamma_E^{G_0}$ resulting from the random variable G_0 is equal to

$$\Gamma_E^{G_0} = \Gamma_{G_0}\left[\int_0^T w(\tau)d\tau - 1\right]^2. \tag{b}$$

Even for a small value of the difference

$$\int_0^T w(\tau)d\tau - 1$$

the product

$$\Gamma_{G_0}\left[\int_0^T w(\tau)d\tau - 1\right]^2$$

is great if the second-order initial moment Γ_{G_0} of G_0 is sufficiently great. To eliminate the component (b) of the second-order initial moment of the error of the system, it is expedient to impose condition (a). When this condition is satisfied, the value of $\Gamma_E^{G_0}$ is equal to 0 for arbitrary Γ_{G_0}.

As our criterion for the choice of optimal system, we take the probability that the error of the system will not exceed small allowed limits in the interval $[-C, +C]$. This probability is determined from formula (4.6b):

$$P = P(|E| < C) = \frac{2C}{\sqrt{2\pi}} \frac{1}{\sqrt{D_E}} \exp\left\{-\frac{m_E^2}{2D_E}\right\}, \tag{c}$$

where $m_E = M[E]$ and $D_E = M[(E - m_E)^2]$ are the mathematical expectation and the variance of the error of the system, and C is the value of the symmetric tolerability of error.

In accordance with the procedure just expounded, we first need to determine the weight function of the system $w_0(\tau, \theta)$ corresponding to an extremum of the reduced functional for the different values of the harmonizing parameter θ.

We note that, as one can see from the proof of Theorem 2 of Chapter 1, it is immaterial whether we take $I_\theta = \theta I_1 + I_2$ or $I_\theta = I_1 + \theta I_2$; that is, the harmonizing parameter θ can be put either before the functional I_1 or before the functional I_2. In the present problem, it is more convenient to take

$$I_\theta = I_1 + \theta I_2. \tag{d}$$

To determine the value of the harmonizing factor $\theta = \theta_0$ corresponding to the maximum of the criterion (c), we need to use not condition (4.27a) but the condition

$$\frac{\dfrac{\partial P}{\partial D_E}}{\dfrac{\partial P}{\partial m_E^2}}\Bigg|_{\theta = \theta_0} = 1 - \frac{m_E^2(\theta_0)}{D_E(\theta_0)} = \theta_0. \tag{e}$$

Obviously, in the present case, we need to find the optimal weight function $w_0(\tau, \theta)$ corresponding to the minimum of the reduced functional I_θ. The mathematical expectation of the error can be determined in accordance with formula (4.2). Since $m = 1$, $m_0 = G_1$, and $C_m = T_e$, we have

$$m_E = -G_1\left[\int_0^T \tau w(\tau)d\tau + T_e\right],$$

$$m_E^2 = G_1^2\left[\int_0^T \tau w(\tau)d\tau + T_e\right]^2. \tag{f}$$

The variance of the error of the system is determined in accordance with formula (4.3). In the present case,

$$D_m = 0, \quad K_{x'}(\tau) = K_z(\tau), \quad K_{x'h'}(\tau) = D_{h'} = 0. \tag{g}$$

Consequently,

$$D_E = \int_0^T\int_0^T K_z(\tau - \lambda)w(\tau)w(\lambda)d\tau\, d\lambda. \tag{h}$$

If we substitute (f) and (h) into (d), we obtain

$$I_\theta = G_1^2\left[\int_0^T \tau w(\tau)d\tau + T_e\right]^2 + \theta\int_0^T\int_0^T K_z(\tau - \lambda)w(\tau)w(\lambda)d\tau\, d\lambda. \tag{i}$$

We need to seek the minimum of the functional (i) subject to condition (a). To do this, we first need to find the weight function w_0 that provides the unconditional minimum of the functional (4.22):

$$I_\theta' = I_\theta + 2\gamma\int_0^T w(\tau)d\tau = G_1^2\left[\int_0^T \tau w(\tau)d\tau + T_e\right]^2$$

$$+ \theta\int_0^T\int_0^T K_z(\tau - \lambda)w(\tau)w(\lambda)d\tau\, d\lambda + 2\gamma_0\int_0^T w(\tau)d\tau, \tag{j}$$

where γ_0 is the Lagrange multiplier.

A necessary condition for the weight function $w_0(\tau, \theta)$ to minimize the quadratic functional (j) is that the integral equation

$$\theta \int_0^T K_z(\tau - \lambda) w(\lambda) d\lambda + G_1^2 \tau \int_0^T \lambda w(\lambda) d\lambda + G_1^2 T_e \tau + \gamma_0 = 0, \qquad (k)$$

which is a special case of equation (4.23), be satisfied.

Remembering that, in the present problem, $K_z(\tau) = e^{-\alpha|\tau|}$ such that the spectral density of the noise

$$S_z(\omega) = \frac{2\alpha}{\omega^2 + \alpha^2}, \qquad (l)$$

we can, in accordance with (3.54), write the formula for determining the solution of equation (k):

$$w_0(\tau, \theta) = g_0 + g_1\tau + C_{10}\delta(\tau) + C_{1T}\delta(\tau - T). \qquad (m)$$

We determine the coefficients g_0, g_1, C_{10}, and C_{1T} by substituting (m) into (k), carrying out the integration, and setting the coefficients of the functions $1 = t^0$, t, $e^{-\alpha\tau}$, and $e^{\alpha\tau}$ equal to 0:

$$\theta \int_0^T e^{-\alpha|\tau - \lambda|} [g_0 + g_1\lambda + C_{10}\delta(\lambda) + C_{1T}\delta(\lambda - T)] d\lambda$$

$$+ G_1^2\tau \int_0^T \lambda [g_0 + g_1\lambda + C_{10}\delta(\lambda) + C_{1T}\delta(\lambda - T)] d\lambda + G_1^2 T_e\tau + \gamma_0 = 0.$$

When we carry out the integration in this equation and set the coefficients of these four functions equal to 0, we obtain the four equations

$$\frac{2\theta}{\alpha} g_0 + \gamma_0 = 0,$$

$$\frac{T^2}{2} g_0 + \left(\frac{T^3}{3} + \frac{2\theta}{\alpha G_1^2} \right) g_1 + TC_{1T} - T_e = 0,$$

$$\alpha g_0 + (\alpha T + 1) g_1 - \alpha^2 C_{1T} = 0,$$

$$\alpha g_0 - g_1 - \alpha^2 C_{10} = 0.$$

When we substitute (m) into (a) and carry out the integration, we obtain another equation

$$T g_0 + \frac{T^2}{2} g_1 + C_{10} + C_{1T} = 1.$$

Solution of the system of five linear algebraic equations in five unknowns enables us to determine all five unknowns g_0, g_1, C_{10}, C_{1T}, and γ_0:

$$g_0 = \frac{\alpha^2}{D_0} \left[(\alpha T + 1) T + \left(\frac{T^3}{3} + \frac{2\theta}{\alpha G_1^2} \right) \alpha + \left(\alpha T + \frac{\alpha^2 T^2}{2} \right) T_e \right],$$

$$g_1 = -\frac{\alpha}{D_0} \left[\alpha T + \frac{\alpha^2 T^2}{2} + \alpha T_e(\alpha T + 2) \right],$$

$$C_{10} = -\frac{\alpha^2\left[\alpha\left(\dfrac{T^3}{3}+\dfrac{20}{\alpha G_1^2}\right)+\dfrac{T^2}{2}+T_e T\left(\dfrac{\alpha T}{2}+1\right)\right]+\alpha(2+\alpha T)(T+T_e)}{D_0},$$

$$C_{1T} = \frac{\alpha^2}{D_0}\left[T(\alpha T+1)\left(\frac{T}{2}+T_e\right)-\alpha T^2\left(\frac{T}{3}+\frac{T_e}{2}\right)-\frac{20}{G_1^2}\right],$$

$$\gamma_0 = -\frac{20}{\alpha}g_0,$$

where

$$D_0 = 4\frac{\theta\alpha^2}{G_1^2}+2\alpha T\left(\theta\frac{\alpha^2}{G_1^2}+1\right)+2\alpha^2 T^2+\frac{2}{3}\alpha^3 T^3+\frac{\alpha^4 T^4}{12}.$$

Thus, the weight function $w_0(\tau, \theta)$ is determined. It depends on the harmonizing parameter θ. We need to determine the value of this parameter $\theta = \theta_0$ corresponding to a maximum of the probability P.

To do this, we express the square of the mathematical expectation m_E^2 and the variance D_E of the error in terms of the harmonizing parameter. As a preliminary, let us find the first moment of the weight function $w_0(\tau, \theta)$:

$$\mu_1 = \int_0^T \tau w_0(\tau, \theta)d\tau. \tag{n}$$

Evaluation of this integral yields the result

$$\mu_1 = -\frac{20}{\alpha G_1^2}g_1 - T_e. \tag{o}$$

Now, if we substitute (o) into (f) and use the expression for the coefficient g_1 in terms of the initial conditions, we can write

$$m_E^2(\theta) = G_1^2[\mu_1 + T_e]^2 = G_1^2\left(\frac{20}{\alpha G_1^2}g_1\right)^2$$

$$= 4\frac{\alpha^2}{G_1^2}\theta^2\frac{(\alpha T+2)^2\left(\dfrac{\alpha T}{2}+\alpha T_e\right)^2}{D_\theta^2}. \tag{p}$$

When we substitute (m) into (h) and use (o) and the expressions for g_0, g_1, C_{10}, C_{1T}, and γ_0 in terms of the initial conditions, we obtain

$$D_E(\theta) = -\frac{\gamma_0}{\theta}-\frac{G_1^2}{\theta}(T_e-\mu_1)\mu_1 = \frac{2}{\alpha}g_0-\frac{2}{\alpha}g_1\left(\frac{20}{\alpha G_1^2}A_1+T_e\right)$$

$$= \frac{2\alpha}{D_0}\left[(\alpha T+1)T+\alpha^2\left(\frac{T^3}{3}+\frac{20}{\alpha G_1^2}\right)+\alpha T\left(1+\frac{\alpha T}{2}\right)T_e\right]$$

$$+\frac{2\alpha^2\left[T\left(1+\dfrac{\alpha T}{2}\right)+(\alpha T+2)T_e\right]}{D_0}$$

$$\times\left[\, 2\alpha\frac{\theta}{G_1^2}\frac{-\alpha T\left(1 + \dfrac{\alpha T}{2}\right) - \alpha(\alpha T + 2)\,T_e}{D_0} + T_e\,\right].$$

We introduce the notations of the dimensionless quantities:

$$\kappa = \alpha T, \quad \kappa_e = \alpha T_e, \quad \gamma^2 = \frac{\alpha^2}{G_1^2}.$$

Using this notation and somewhat transforming the expressions for m_E^2 and D_E, we write them in the following form:

$$m_E^2(\theta) = 4\gamma^2\frac{(\kappa + 2)^2\left(\dfrac{\kappa}{2} + \kappa_e\right)^2}{D_0^2}\theta^2,$$

$$D_E(\theta) = \frac{2}{D_0^2}\left\{ 40^2(2 + \kappa)\gamma^4 + 4\left(2 + 2\kappa + \frac{2}{3}\kappa^2 + \frac{1}{12}\kappa^3\right)\kappa\gamma^2\theta \right.$$

$$+ \kappa\left(2 + 2\kappa + \frac{2}{3}\kappa^2 + \frac{1}{12}\kappa^3\right)\left[\kappa\left(1 + \kappa + \frac{\kappa^2}{3}\right)\right.$$

$$\left.\left. + (2 + \kappa)\kappa_e(\kappa_e + \kappa)\right]\right\},$$

where

$$D_0 = 2\gamma^2(2 + \kappa)\theta + 2\kappa + 2\kappa^2 + \frac{2}{3}\kappa^3 + \frac{\kappa^4}{12}.$$

We now set

$$\kappa = 3, \quad \kappa_e = 6, \quad \gamma^2 = 20.$$

With these particular numerical values of the initial data, the square of the mathematical expectation m_E^2 and the variance D_E of the error of the system, which are what we are interested in, are expressed in terms of the harmonizing parameter θ as follows:

$$m_E^2(\theta) = \frac{2.80\theta^2}{(\theta + 0.24)^2}, \quad D_E(\theta) = \frac{0.40\theta^2 + 0.39\theta + 0.65}{(\theta + 0.24)^2}. \tag{q}$$

To find the value of the harmonizing parameter $\theta = \theta_0$ maximizing the criterion P, we use the first method. Let us substitute the expression for the square of the mathematical expectation $m_E^2(\theta)$ and the variance $D_E(\theta)$ of the error into formula (4.6b) and let us calculate the value of P for several values of the harmonizing parameter θ. Here, the following question arises: In what region should we take the values of the parameter θ in making these calculations? In the particular case in which we take for our criterion the expression (4.6b), we need to take the values of the multiplier θ (for D_E) as less than unity (the multiplier for m_E^2 must be taken as greater than unity).

We amplify this remark with the following considerations: The harmonizing parameter θ has the geometric interpretation of the tangent of the angle α (up to an arbitrary factor k_m depending on the scales used for the I_1- and I_2-axes) formed by the straight line a and the ordinate in Figure 1.3 or by the straight line N and the abscissa in Figure 1.4. Consequently, the ratio $I_2/I_1 = k_m \tan \alpha = \theta$. In the present case, $I_1 = D_E$ and $I_2 = m_E^2$. Consequently, the square of the mathematical expectation m_E^2 and the variance D_E of the error which correspond to the weight function $w_0(\tau, \theta)$ satisfy the condition

$$\frac{m_E^2(\theta)}{D_E(\theta)} = \theta.$$

This means that the greater the harmonizing parameter θ, the greater will be the ratio m_E^2/D_E and, conversely, the smaller the value of θ, the smaller will be this ratio. We raise the following question: How can we increase the probability P defined by formula (4.6b)? When we shift from the weight function $w_0(\tau, 1)$ to the weight function $m_0(\tau, \theta)$, where $\theta \neq 1$, the mean square error can only increase; that is,

$$m_E^2(1) + D_E(1) \leqslant m_E^2(\theta) + D_E(\theta). \tag{4.28}$$

We know that, for a constant mean square error, the criterion (4.6b) decreases with increasing m_E^2. Consequently, in the present case (with condition (4.28) holding), the criterion (4.6b) can increase only when m_E^2 decreases, and this can happen only when $\theta < 1$. Thus, we need to consider only the values of the harmonizing factor θ less than unity.

By using formulas (c) and (4.6b), let us calculate the values of the square of the mathematical expectation $m_E^2(\theta)$ and the variance $D_E(\theta)$ of the error and the values of the probability P for various values of the factor θ, and let us draw up a table for P:

Table 1.

θ	1.00	0.80	0.60	0.50	0.42	0.40	0.30	0.20	0.00
$P(\theta)$	0.395	0.458	0.508	0.534	0.542	0.540	0.521	0.480	0.315
$\dfrac{P(\theta)}{P(1)}$	1.00	1.16	1.29	1.35	1.38	1.38	1.32	1.22	0.85

The probability P was calculated for $C = 1/2$. Also, for convenience in constructing graphs, we have displayed in the third row of the table the values of the normalized probability that represent the ratio of the variable probability $P(\theta)$ to the probability $P(1)$. This ratio corresponds to the weight function $w_0(\tau, 1)$ determined in accordance with the criterion of minimization of the mean square error of the system. The

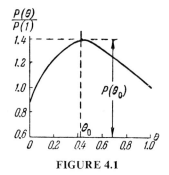

FIGURE 4.1

values of $P(\theta)$ have been calculated to the nearest thousandth, those of $P(\theta)/P(1)$ to the nearest hundredth. In the interval $0.35 \leqslant \theta \leqslant 0.45$, the function $P(\theta)$ changes only slightly and hence the value of $\theta = \theta_0$ is difficult to determine. From a practical point of view, we can allow certain errors, since the significant deviation of the optimal value of the harmonizing parameter $\theta = \theta_0$ (for example, a deviation by a tenth of a unit) causes only insignificant deviations in the criterion P from its maximum value (approximately two hundredths of a unit). The graph of the normalized probability $P(\theta)/P(1)$ is constructed from the calculated results depending on the parameter θ (see Fig. 4.1). From this graph, we can determine the value of the harmonizing parameter θ_0 and the corresponding value of the maximum normalized probability:

$$\frac{P(\theta_0)}{P(1)} \simeq 1.38 \quad \text{for} \quad \theta_0 \simeq 0.42.$$

Thus, the shift from the criterion of minimization of the mean square error to the criterion of maximum probability that the error will not exceed allowed limits has enabled us to obtain a gain of 38% in this probability.

When we have determined the value of the parameter $\theta_0 = 0.42$, we can consider the problem of determining the optimal weight function solved. It is equal to $w^0(\tau) = w_0(\tau, 0.42)$. Furthermore, we can indicate the permissible deviation of the parameter θ from the value θ_0 in order for the deviation of the criterion P from its maximum value to be admissible.

Let us also use the second way of determining the harmonizing parameter $\theta = \theta_0$. We substitute the expression (q) into equation (e) and we obtain

$$\frac{2.8\theta^2}{0.40\theta^2 + 0.39\theta + 0.65} = 1 - \theta.$$

This equation in the parameter θ can be transformed to the form

$$\theta^3 + 7\theta^2 + 0.66\theta - 1.63 = 0. \tag{r}$$

It follows from Descartes' theorem [Ref. 28] that the algebraic equation (r) has one positive root and two negative roots. We disregard the negative roots, since one can show that, for negative values of the harmonizing parameter θ, the sufficient condition for minimization of the reduced functional I_θ (or I'_θ) is not satisfied and the maximum of the probability P is not attained. In the foregoing, we showed that $\theta_0 \leq 1$. Consequently, we need to seek the root of the equation between 0 and 1. Correct to two decimal places, this root is 0.42, which substantiates the validity of the calculations for determining the parameter $\theta = \theta_0$ by the first method.

Suppose that, instead of the criterion P defined by formula (4.6b), we take the criterion P^2. Then, all the calculations remain essentially unchanged. It is easy to see that θ_0 is still equal to 0.42, but the gain in the value of the criterion when we shift from the weight function $w_0(\tau, 1)$ to the weight function $w_0(\tau, 0.42)$ amounts to 90%. The functional P^2 was not chosen randomly. It has a definite physical meaning. With the aid of the functional

$$P^2 = \frac{4C^2}{2\pi D_E} \exp\left\{-\frac{m_E^2}{D_E}\right\} \tag{4.29}$$

we can calculate approximately (and with a sufficiently high degree of accuracy) the probability that the errors of two analogous automatic-control systems displacing the control object in two mutually perpendicular directions will not exceed small allowed limits, provided that uncorrelated signals with identical probabilistic characteristics are applied at the inputs of these systems.

Let us verify that the sufficient conditions for maximization of the criterion P^2 are satisfied in this example. These sufficient conditions are listed in (a), (b), and (c) of Section 5 of Chapter 1. Condition (a) requires that the sufficient conditions for an extremum of the reduced functional I_θ be satisfied for $|\theta - \theta_0| < \varepsilon$, where ε is a small positive number. Let us show that this condition is satisfied in the present example. To do this, we write the expression for $I_\theta\{w^0 + v\}$, where $v(\tau)$ is an arbitrary admissible weight function:

$$I_\theta\{w^0 + v\} = G_1^2 \left\{ \int_0^T \tau[w^0(\tau) + v(\tau)]d\tau + T_e \right\}^2$$

$$+ \theta \int_0^T \int_0^T K_z(\tau - \lambda)[w^0(\tau) + v(\tau)][w^0(\lambda) + v(\lambda)]d\tau d\lambda$$

$$= I_\theta\{w^0\} + 2\int_0^T v(\tau)\left\{ \int_0^T [G_1^2\tau\lambda + K_z(\tau - \lambda)]w(\lambda)d\lambda + G_1^2 T_e\tau \right\}d\tau$$

$$+ \int_0^T \int_0^T K_z(\tau - \lambda)v(\tau)v(\lambda)d\tau d\lambda + C_1^2 T_e^2.$$

Using the relation (i), we rewrite this last relation as

$$I_\theta\{w^0 + v\} = I_0\{w^0\} - 2\gamma_0 \int_0^T v(\tau)d\tau$$
$$+ \int_0^T \int_0^T K_z(\tau - \lambda)v(\tau)v(\lambda)d\tau\,d\lambda.$$

It follows from condition (a) that

$$\int_0^T v(\tau)d\tau = 0.$$

Remembering this and the fact that

$$\int_0^T \int_0^T K_z(\tau - \lambda)v(\tau)v(\lambda)d\tau\,d\lambda,$$

for an arbitrary function $v(\tau)$ is positive, we may write the following:

$$I_\theta\{w^0 + v\} \geqslant I_0\{w^0\}.$$

From this it follows that, for $w = w^0$, the sufficient conditions for minimization of the reduced functional I_θ are satisfied.

Satisfaction of (b) follows from the first method of determining the desired value of the harmonizing parameter $\theta = \theta_0 = 0.42$.

Let us verify that (c) is satisfied. To do this, we first obtain the function $\varphi(\alpha)$ (cf. (1.176a)). To do this, let us determine $m_E^2(0.42)$, $D_E(0.42)$, and the derivatives

$$\frac{\partial m_E^2(\theta)}{\partial \theta}, \quad \frac{\partial D_E(\theta)}{\partial \theta}$$

evaluated at $\theta = 0.42$. Using formula (q), we obtain

$$m_E^2(0.42) = \frac{2.80 \cdot 0.42^2}{(0.42 + 0.24)^2} = 1.1,$$

$$D_E(0.42) = \frac{0.40 \cdot 0.42^2 + 0.39 \cdot 0.42 + 0.65}{(0.42 + 0.24)^2} = 3.5,$$

$$\frac{\partial m_E^2(\theta)}{\partial \theta}\bigg|_{\theta = 0.42}$$

$$= \frac{2.28 \cdot 0.42(0.42 + 0.24)^2 - 2(0.42 + 0.24) \cdot 2.8 \cdot 0.42^2}{(0.42 + 0.24)^4} = 1.8,$$

$$\frac{\partial D_E(\theta)}{\partial \theta}\bigg|_{\theta = 0.42} = \frac{1}{(0.42 + 0.24)^4}$$
$$\times [(2 \cdot 0.40 \cdot 0.42 + 0.39)(0.42 + 0.24)^2$$
$$- 2(0.42 + 0.24)(0.4 \cdot 0.42 + 0.39 \cdot 0.42 + 0.65)] = 4.4.$$

Now, the function $\varphi(\alpha)$ can, in accordance with (1.176a) be determined from the criterion P^2:

$$\varphi(\alpha) = \frac{4C^2}{2\pi} \frac{\exp\left\{-\dfrac{1.1 + \dfrac{\alpha}{4.4}}{3.5 + \dfrac{\alpha}{1.8}}\right\}}{3.5 + \dfrac{\alpha}{1.8}}.$$

Corresponding to the motion from the point on the boundary L with coordinates $m_E^2(\theta_0)$ and $D_E(\theta_0)$ inside the region G (see Fig. 1.3) is the change of the parameter α on the side of positive values (that is, increase in the parameter α from 0). Consequently, to show that the criterion P^2 decreases as we move along the normal from the point $(m_E^2(\theta_0), D_E(\theta_0))$ inside the region G, we need to show that the function $\varphi(\alpha)$ has a negative derivative at $\alpha = 0$. The evaluation of the derivative $d\varphi(\alpha)/d\alpha|_{\alpha=0}$ yields the result

$$\frac{d\varphi(\alpha)}{d\alpha}\bigg|_{\alpha=0} = \frac{2C^2}{\pi}(-0.61) < 0.$$

Thus, the sufficient conditions for maximizing the criterion P^2 with weight function w^0 are satisfied in this example.

EXAMPLE 2. Suppose that a signal X representing the sum of a useful signal $G(t)$ and a noise $Z(t)$ is applied at the input of a linear stationary system (see Fig. 1.1). The useful signal is of the form

$$G(t) = G_0 + G_1 t,$$

where G_0 is a random variable with a very large second-order initial moment and G_1 is a random variable distributed according to an equal-probability law in the interval from $-q$ to $+q$. The random variables G_0 and G_1 and the random function $Z(t)$ are mutually uncorrelated. The noise is a stationary random process obeying a normal distribution law with the following characteristics: The mathematical expectation $m_z = M[Z] = 0$ and the correlation function $K_z(\tau) = e^{-\alpha|\tau|}$.

The system is designed for extrapolation of a useful signal $G(t)$. Consequently, the desired output variable of this system is determined by the formula $H(t) = G(t + T_e)$.

For admissible automatic-control systems, we take, just as in Example 1, stationary systems with astaticism of at least first order, that is, systems satisfying condition (a) of the preceding example. As a criterion for choosing the optimal system, we take the probability that the error of the system will not fall outside the interval $[-C, +C]$. In the present case, this probability is given by formula (4.10c):

$$P = P(|E| < C) = \frac{2C}{\sqrt{6\pi D_{E_1} D_{E_2}}} \int_0^{\sqrt{3D_{E_1}}} \exp\left\{-\frac{E_1^2}{2D_{E_2}}\right\} dE_1,$$

where D_E is the variance of that component E_1 of the error of the system that is due to the random component $G_1 t$ of the useful signal, and D_{E_2} is the variance of the component of the error E_2 of the system that is caused by the noise $Z(t)$. The variance D_{E_1} is the first term in formula (4.3). Remembering that, in this case, $m = 1$ and $C_1 = T_e$, we can write the following formula for determining D_{E_1}:

$$D_{E_1} = D_1 \left[\int_0^T \tau w(\tau) d\tau + T_e \right]^2,$$

which is analogous to formula (f) of the preceding example. In the present example, D_1 is the variance of the random variable G_1. It is equal to $g_1^2/3$.

The variance D_{E_2} is determined, just as in the first example, in accordance with the formula (g).

It is convenient to use the substitution $y = E_1/\sqrt{D_{E_2}}$ to determine the probability P. When we do this, we obtain

$$P = P(|E| < C) = \frac{2C}{\sqrt{3 D_{E_1}}} \frac{1}{\sqrt{2\pi}} \int_0^{\sqrt{\frac{3 D_{E_1}}{D_{E_2}}}} \exp \left\{ -\frac{y^2}{2} \right\} dy.$$

This formula is more convenient for computation, since the second factor is a tabulated function (cf. Appendix 1). Now, just as in the first example, we write the expression for the reduced functional I_θ'. It differs from (j) only in that it has D_{E_1} in place of G_1^2. Consequently, the remainder of the solution coincides with the solution of the first example except that the dimensionless parameter γ^2 should be determined by use of the formula

$$\gamma^2 = \frac{\alpha^2}{D_{E_1}^2} = \sqrt{3} \frac{\alpha^2}{g_1^2}.$$

When we give the dimensionless parameters the values $\kappa = 3$, $\kappa_e = 6$, and $\gamma^2 = 20$, the variances $D_{E_1}(\theta)$ and $D_{E_2}(\theta)$, an functions of the harmonizing parameter θ, are determined in accordance with formula (q) of the first example:

$$D_{E_1}(\theta) = \frac{2.80\theta^2}{(\theta + 0.24)^2}, \quad D_{E_2}(\theta) = \frac{0.40\theta^2 + 0.39\theta + 0.65}{(\theta + 0.24)^2}.$$

We substitute these expressions for the variances into the formula for determining the probability P and we find the maximum value of the probability $P = P(\theta)$ as a function of the parameter θ. Calculations show that, in this case, the value of the parameter $\theta = \theta_0$ corresponding to the maximum of the function $F(\theta) = P(\theta)$ is equal to 0.43. The relative gains in the probabilities P and P^2 when we shift from the weight function $w_0(\tau, 1)$ to the weight function $w_0(\tau, 0.43)$ are respectively

$$\frac{P(0.43) - P(1)}{P(1)} \equiv 0.09, \qquad \frac{P^2(0.43) - P^2(1)}{P^2(1)} \equiv 0.18.$$

In these two examples, the shift from the weight function $w_0(\tau, 1)$ to the weight function $w_0(\tau, 0.42)$ made possible a great gain in the value of the criteria P and P^2. Therefore, it is convenient here to use the criterion P or the criterion P^2. However, cases are possible in which the shift from the criterion of the minimum mean square error to the criterion of maximum probability that the error will not exceed given small limits does not yield a significant gain in this probability. Therefore, it is desirable to have an estimate for the gain in the probability P or P^2 when we shift from the weight function $w_0(\tau, 1)$ to the weight function $w_0(\tau, \theta_0)$. This estimate (if it is expressed by a simple formula) enables us to avoid the more complicated calculations of $w_0(\tau, \theta_0)$ and to confine ourselves to the calculations of $w_0(\tau, 1)$ when the gain in the probability P as we shift from $w_0(\tau, 1)$ to $w_0(\tau, \theta_0)$ is negligibly small.

It is desirable to have estimates in the gain both from below and from above. Let us obtain these estimates as applied to the criterion P^2 determined by formula (4.29).

4. Estimate of the gain, when we shift from $w_0(\tau, 1)$ to $w_0(\tau, \theta_0)$, in the probability that the error of the system will not exceed small allowed limits

Let us formulate the statement of the problem. Suppose that, under given initial conditions, the weight function $w_0(\tau, 1)$ of the system minimizing the mean square error $\Gamma_{E\,min}$ is known. Here, the square of the mathematical expectation of the error is equal to $m_E^2(1)$ and the variance of the error is equal to $D_E(1)$. Of course, under these conditions,

$$\Gamma_{E\,min} = m_E^2(1) + D_E(1).$$

Suppose that we are required, without seeking a solution with respect to the criterion of the probability P^2, to give an estimate from above and from below of the gain in the criterion P^2 that could be obtained in shifting to the control system with weight function $w_0(\tau, \theta_0)$, that is, the weight function corresponding to the maximum of the criterion P^2.

Since the square of the mathematical expectation $m_E^2(\theta_0)$ and the variance $D_E(\theta_0)$ correspond to the weight function $w_0(\tau, \theta_0)$, the relative gain in the criterion P^2 can be written in the form

$$\frac{P^2(\theta_0) - P^2(1)}{P^2(1)} = \frac{\dfrac{\exp\left\{-\dfrac{m_E^2(\theta_0)}{D_E(\theta_0)}\right\}}{D_E(\theta_0)} - \dfrac{\exp\left\{-\dfrac{m_E^2(1)}{D_E(1)}\right\}}{D_E(1)}}{\dfrac{\exp\left\{-\dfrac{m_E^2(1)}{D_E(1)}\right\}}{D_E(1)}}. \tag{4.30}$$

We have already pointed out that, for an arbitrary value of the parameter θ,

$$m_E^2(1) + D_E(1) \leqslant m_E^2(\theta) + D_E(\theta). \tag{4.31}$$

Consequently, this inequality holds for $\theta = \theta_0$. Let us replace the unknown maximum value of the criterion $P^2(\theta_0)$ with a quantity that we know is greater than this. We determine this latter quantity as follows: Instead of the maximum value of the criterion $P^2(\theta_0)$, which is defined on the class of admissible linear systems, we take the maximum value of the probability P^2 on the set of all possible values of m_E^2 and D_E satisfying the condition

$$m_E^2 + D_E = \Gamma_{E \min} = m_E^2(1) + D_E(1). \tag{4.32}$$

It is easy to see that

$$P_{\max}^2 \geqslant P^2(\theta_0). \tag{4.33}$$

Let us determine the quantity $P_{\max}^2$:

$$P_{\max}^2 = \max_{D_E} \left[\frac{4C^2}{2\pi} \frac{\exp\left\{ -\dfrac{m_E^2}{D_E} \right\}}{D_E} \right]$$

under the condition

$$m_E^2 + D_E = \Gamma_{E \min}.$$

Elementary investigation of the function in the square brackets under the condition indicated shows that this function increases monotonically from D_E and attains its maximum at $D_E = \Gamma_{E \min}$ (and hence $m_E^2 = 0$ at that value). This means that

$$P_{\max}^2 = \frac{4C^2}{2\pi \Gamma_{E \min}} = \frac{4C^2}{2\pi [m_E^2(1) + D_E(1)]}. \tag{4.34}$$

From (4.30), (4.33), and (4.34), we obtain

$$\frac{P^2(\theta_0) - P^2(1)}{P^2(1)} \leqslant \frac{\dfrac{1}{m_E^2(1) + D_E(1)} - \dfrac{\exp\left\{ -\dfrac{m_E^2(1)}{D_E(1)} \right\}}{D_E(1)}}{\dfrac{\exp\left\{ -\dfrac{m_E^2(1)}{D_E(1)} \right\}}{D_E(1)}}$$

$$= \frac{\exp\left\{ \dfrac{m_E^2(1)}{D_E(1)} \right\}}{\dfrac{m_E^2(1)}{D_E(1)} + 1} - 1. \tag{4.35}$$

From this it follows that the greater the ratio $m_E^2(1)/D_E(1)$, the greater will be the relative increase in the criterion P^2. If the ratio $m_E^2(1)/D_E(1)$

is small, it makes no sense to shift from the criterion of the minimum mean square error to the more complicated criterion of the maximum probability that the error will not exceed allowed limits. For example, if the ratio $m_E^2(1)/D_E(1) = 0.125$, then, in accordance with formula (4.35), we have

$$\frac{P^2(\theta_0) - P^2(1)}{P^2(1)} \leqslant \frac{\exp{(0.125)}}{0.125 + 1} - 1 < 0.005.$$

Let us also give an estimate of the increment in the criterion P^2 from below, which we shall do under the condition that $m_E^2(1) > D_E(1)$. In this case, we replace the maximum value of the criterion $P^2(\theta_0)$ with the value of the criterion P_0^2 (which we know to be smaller):

$$P_0^2 = \frac{4C^2 \exp{(-1)}}{2\pi m_E^2(1)},$$

calculated for $D_E = m_E^2(1)$ and $m_E^2 = m_E^2(1)$. Let us show that P_0^2 does not exceed $P^2(\theta_0)$. We shall reason as follows: As the harmonizing parameter θ decreases from 1 to 0, the square of the mathematical expectation $m_E^2(\theta)$ of the error decreases and the variance $D_E(\theta)$ of this error increases. The criterion P^2 attains its maximum at some value of the parameter $\theta = \theta_0$. Let us consider another law of variation of the quantities m_E^2 and D_E. Specifically, let us assume that m_E^2 is constant and that D_E increases. Let us determine the maximum value of the probability P^2 in this case. Obviously, it does not exceed $P^2(\theta_0)$. We know that the maximum value of the probability P^2 with constant mathematical expectation is attained when $D_E = m_E^2$ (as is easily verified by setting the derivative of P^2 with respect to D_E equal to 0 and solving the resulting equation for D_E):

$$P^2 = P_0^2.$$

Consequently, we may write

$$\frac{P^2(\theta_0) - P^2(1)}{P^2(1)} \geqslant \frac{\dfrac{1}{em_E^2(1)} - \dfrac{\exp\left\{-\dfrac{m_E^2(1)}{D_E(1)}\right\}}{D_E(1)}}{\dfrac{\exp\left\{-\dfrac{m_E^2(1)}{D_E(1)}\right\}}{D_E(1)}}$$

$$= \frac{D_E(1)}{m_E^2(1)} \exp\left\{\frac{m_E^2(1)}{D_E(1)} - 1\right\} - 1, \qquad (4.36)$$

$$D_E(1) > m_E^2(1).$$

These estimates regarding the increment in the criterion P^2 as we shift from $w_0(\tau, 1)$ to $w_0(\tau, \theta_0)$ enable us to draw the following conclusions with regard to Example 1. For fixed finite values of κ_e and γ, the ratio $m_E^2(1)/D_E(1)$ approaches 0 as $\kappa \to \infty$. Consequently, under these conditions, it is not expedient to shift to the criterion P^2, since this criterion does not yield an appreciable increase in the value of that criterion. For fixed γ^2, the ratio $m_E^2(1)/D_E(1)$ approaches ∞ as $\gamma_e \to \infty$ and $\kappa \to 0$. Consequently, for large values of κ_e and small values of κ, the shift to the criterion P^2 is expedient, since it effects a considerable gain in P^2 (or P).

The conclusions, formulated in connection with Example 1, regarding the estimate of the increments in the criteria P and P^2 when one shifts from the weight function $w_0(\tau, 1)$ to the weight function $w_0(\tau, \theta_0)$ remain valid in a qualitative sort of way for Example 2.

16. DETERMINATION OF AN OPTIMAL SYSTEM WITH RESPECT TO A CRITERION WHICH IS ITSELF AN ARBITRARY GIVEN FUNCTION OF OTHER, SIMPLER CRITERIA

The exposition in the present section is based on Theorem 2a of Chapter 1. This theorem is valid for arbitrary functionals $I_1, \cdots, I_{n+1}$. Here, we assume that the functionals $I_1, \cdots, I_{n+1}$ are quadratic functionals of the weight function of the system. Thus, the problem of the present section is that of developing a method of determining the weight function $w^0(t, \tau)$ of an automatic-control system ensuring an extremum of the criterion I, which is a given function f of the quadratic functionals $I_1, \cdots, I_{n+1}$. All these quadratic functionals of the weight function $w(t, \tau)$ in each particular problem have some specific form or other. In particular, they may be double integrals with respect to the variables τ and λ of expressions of the form

$$K_i(\tau, \lambda)w(\tau)w(\lambda),$$

where the $K_i(\tau, \lambda)$ are, for $i = 1, \cdots, n+1$, known functions of their arguments.

Let us first consider the problem of determining the optimal weight function of a system from a criterion of a general form and then let us look at certain particular cases of this problem.

1. Determination of an optimal automatic-control system with respect to a criterion that is an arbitrary given function f of criteria $I_1, \cdots, I_{n+1}$ that are quadratic functionals of the weight function of the system

The block diagram is outlined in Figure 2.2. All the required probabilistic characteristics of the influences are given. The desired output variable $H(t)$ is determined: $H(t) = L\{G(t)\}$. The criterion for comparison of two systems is the functional I of the weight function of the system $w(t, \tau)$:

$$I\{w\} = f(I_1\{w\}, I_2\{w\}, \cdots, I_{n+1}\{w\}), \qquad (4.37)$$

where f is an arbitrary given function of the variables $I_1, I_2, \cdots, I_{n+1}$, where $I_i\{w\}$ is a quadratic functional of the weight function $w(t, \tau)$ of the system, and where t is a fixed instant of time for which the criterion I is determined. The criterion I depends on t as a parameter.

In accordance with Theorem 2a of Chapter 1, the search for the optimal weight function w^0 with respect to the criterion (4.37) can be broken into two stages. The first stage consists in determining the weight function $w_0(t, \tau, \theta_1, \cdots, \theta_n)$ corresponding to an extremum of the reduced functional

$$I_\theta = \theta_1 I_1 + \theta_2 I_2 + \cdots + \theta_n I_n + I_{n+1}. \qquad (4.38)$$

Of course, this function is also a quadratic functional. The weight function $w_0(t, \tau, \theta_1, \cdots, \theta_n)$ must be determined for various values of the harmonizing parameters $\theta_1, \cdots, \theta_n$. The region Θ in which the parameters $\theta_1, \cdots, \theta_n$ must be assigned can be made precise by considering the peculiarities of a particular problem. For example, in the problems of the preceding section, the parameter θ (in both problems, $n = 1$) must vary from 0 to 1. This means that the region Θ in those problems is the segment of the θ-axis extending from 0 to 1.

We have examined (for example, in Chapter 1) the ways of finding the extrema of quadratic functionals. Let us suppose that we have obtained by some means or other a solution of the first stage of the problem; that is, that we have obtained the dependence

$$w_0 = w_0(t, \tau, \theta_1, \cdots, \theta_n). \qquad (4.39)$$

The second stage is the determination of the values of the harmonizing parameters $\theta_1 = \theta_{10}, \cdots, \theta_n = \theta_{n0}$ corresponding to the extremum of the criterion I. We have two ways of solving this problem.

First method. It follows from what was said in Chapter 1 that the optimal function can be obtained from (4.39) for certain values of the harmonizing parameters θ_i. These values of the parameters θ_i can be determined by substituting (4.39) into (4.37). When we make this substitution, we obtain

$$\begin{aligned} I\{w_0\} &= f[I_0\{w_0(t, \tau, \theta_1, \cdots, \theta_n)\}, \cdots, I_{n+1}\{w_0(t, \tau, \theta_1, \cdots, \theta_n)\}] \\ &= \Phi(t, \theta_1, \cdots, \theta_n), \end{aligned}$$

where

$$\Phi(t, \theta_1, \cdots, \theta_n) \qquad (4.40)$$

is a known function.

An extremum of the functional I coincides with one of the extrema of the function Φ. Consequently, the problem is now reduced to determining an extremum of a function of several variables. Here, we can use the method of fastest descent (see Section 12, Chapter 3).

Second method. The desired values of the harmonizing parameters $\theta_i = \theta_{i0}$ can be determined from equations (1.167), which in the present case become

$$\frac{\dfrac{\partial f(I_1, \cdots, I_n)}{\partial I_i}}{\dfrac{\partial f(I_1, \cdots, I_n)}{\partial I_{n+1}}} = \theta_{i0}, \quad i = 1, \cdots, n. \qquad (4.41)$$

Here, the partial derivatives $\partial f/\partial I_j$, for $j = 1, \cdots, n+1$, are functions of the functionals $I_k = I_k\{w\}$. We need to substitute for functions $w_0(t, \tau, \theta_{10}, \cdots, \theta_{n0})$ into the functionals. Then, the ratios of the partial derivatives in the left-hand members of equations (4.41) will be known functions F of the harmonizing parameters θ_i. Therefore, equations (4.41) can be represented in the form

$$F_i(\theta_{10}, \cdots, \theta_{n0}) = \theta_{i0}, \quad i = 1, \cdots, n. \qquad (4.41a)$$

One of the solutions of these equations provides the desired values of the parameters θ_i.

In the general case, the system (4.41) has more than one solution. Out of the set of solutions of this system, we need to choose the one that corresponds to the greatest of the maxima or the smallest of the minima of the criterion I. Equations (4.41) or (4.41a) are usually nonlinear algebraic or transcendental equations. The problem of finding the solutions of these equations is a complicated one.

The second method of finding the values of the harmonizing parameters $\theta_i = \theta_{i0}$ is less convenient than the first in practical computations. However, it can be used to find the values of $\theta_i = \theta_{i0}$ in those cases when the system (4.41) is simple, and it can also be used to verify the validity of a solution obtained by the first method (in all cases).

The weight function $w^0(t, \tau) = w_0(t, \tau, \theta_{10}, \cdots, \theta_{n0})$, obtained by the method previously indicated satisfies the necessary condition for an extremum of the criterion I. To show that this weight function actually does represent an extremum of the functional I, we need to verify that sufficient conditions for an extremum of this criterion are satisfied. In the general form, such conditions are formulated in Section 5 of Chapter 1. They include (a), (b), and (c) on page 53. In the present case, (a) is always satisfied, since in this case the reduced functional I_θ is quadratic and a quadratic functional possesses the property that the necessary conditions for an extremum of it coincide with the sufficient ones (it remains only to show what kind of extremum it is, maximum or minimum). Requirement (b) is verified automatically when we seek the values of the harmonizing factors $\theta = \theta_{i0}$ by the first method. Requirement (c) needs some extra verification if its satisfaction does not follow from other considerations (for example, from the physical nature of the solution of the problem). This verification can be made by studying the behavior of the function (1.176) in a neighborhood of the value $\alpha = 0$.

2. Determination of an optimal automatic-control system from the maximum probability that the error of the system will not exceed given small allowed limits $(n > 1)$

Here, we shall examine a procedure for determining the optimal weight function from two different criteria, which are special cases of the criterion (4.37). These criteria are of practical value, and for this reason it will be expedient to look at them separately.

Both these criteria are probabilities of an event. In the first case, the criterion is the probability that the error of the system will not exceed small allowed limits if the error of the system consists of two components which obey different distribution laws and if it has nonzero mathematical expectation. In the second case, the criterion is the probability that the error of the system will not exceed given allowed limits at fixed instants of time.

Let us consider the first case, and formulate the statement of the problem. We shall assume that the block diagram of the system is represented in Figure 2.2. Suppose that the useful signal $G(t)$ is of the form

$$G(t) = \sum_{i=0}^{m} G_i t^i + G'(t), \qquad (4.42)$$

where the G_i are random variables (the distribution law G_m being known) and $G(t)$ is a stationary random function. The noise $Z(t)$ is also a stationary random function. The correlation functions $K_g(\tau)$ and $K_z(\tau)$ and the joint correlation function $K_{xz}(\tau)$ are known. Without loss of generality, we may assume that the mathematical expectations of the random functions $G'(t)$ and $Z(t)$ are zero:

$$m_{g'} = M[G'(t)] = m_z = M[Z(t)] = 0.$$

The desired output variable of the system is given:

$$H(t) = L\{G(t)\} = C_0 G(t) + C_1 \dot{G}(t) + C_2 \ddot{G}(t) = \cdots$$

We are required to determine the optimal weight function of the system from the criterion of maximum probability P that the error will not exceed allowed limits at a certain instant of time. For admissible systems, we take systems possessing astaticism of order m, that is, systems whose weight functions satisfy conditions (3.49).

To write the formula determining the probability P, we need to know the distribution law of the error of the system. Let us consider in greater detail the different components of this error. In accordance with formula (3.50), this error is given by

$$E(t) = G_m \left[(-1)^m \int_0^T \tau^m w(\tau) d\tau - m! C_m \right] + \int_0^T X'(t - \tau) w(\tau) d\tau - H'(t),$$

where

$$H'(t) = L\{G'(t)\}, \quad X'(t) = G'(t) + Z(t).$$

Since the probability P is chosen as a criterion, the first two moments of the input influences are insufficient. We need to know the distribution laws of these influences. In the present case, we shall assume that the random variable G_m can be represented in the form of a sum $m_0 + G_m^0$, where m_0 is the mathematical expectation, and G_m^0 is a centralized random variable obeying a law of equal probability in the interval from $-g_m$ to $+g_m$. We shall also assume that the random function $X'(t)$ obeys a normal distribution law. Hence, the component of the error of the system depending on $G'(t)$ and $Z(t)$

$$E_2(t) = \int_0^T X'(t - \tau) w(\tau) d\tau - H'(t),$$

also obeys a normal distribution law. It is now expedient to represent the error E of the system in the form

$$E(t) = m_E + E_1 + E_2 = m_0 \left[(-1)^m \int_0^T \tau^m w(\tau) d\tau - m! C_m \right]$$
$$+ G_m^0 \left[(-1)^m \int_0^T \tau^m w(\tau) d\tau - m! C_m \right]$$
$$+ \left[\int_0^T X'(t - \tau) w(\tau) d\tau - H'(t) \right]. \tag{4.43}$$

Here, the first term is the mathematical expectation of the error, the second term is that component of the error that obeys a law of equal probability, and the third term is that component that obeys a normal distribution law.

In the present case, the distribution law of the error E is a complicated function. We shall not seek an analytic expression for this law but shall find the required exhaustive characteristics of the distribution laws of the components E_1 and E_2 instead. We shall then express the criterion that we have chosen in terms of the mathematical expectation of the error and the characteristics of the components E_1 and E_2. The exhaustive characteristics of the components E_1 and E_2 are their variances (we assume that E_1 and E_2 are uncorrelated). Thus, to determine the criterion P, it is necessary to know

(1)   the mathematical expectation of the error m_E,
(2)   the variance of the component E_1,
(3)   the variance of the component E_2.

By virtue of (4.43), we can write the following formulas for determining these characteristics:

$$m_E = m_0\left[(-1)^m\int_0^T \tau^m w(\tau)d\tau - m!\,C_m\right],$$

$$D_{E_1} = D_m\left[(-1)^m\int_0^T \tau^m w(\tau)d\tau - m!\,C_m\right]^2, \qquad (4.44)$$

where

$$D_m = M[G_m^0] = \frac{g_m^2}{3},$$

$$D_{E_2} = \int_0^T\int_0^T K_{x'}(\tau - \lambda)w(\tau)w(\lambda)d\tau\,d\lambda$$
$$- 2\int_0^T K_{x'h'}(\tau)w(\tau)d\tau + D_{h'}.$$

Here, $K_{x'}(\tau)$ is the correlation function of the random function $X'(t)$, the function $K_{x'h'}(\tau)$ is the joint correlation function of $X'(t)$ and $H'(t)$, and $D_{h'}$ is the variance of the random function $H'(t)$.

The probability that the error will not exceed small allowed limits, that is, that it will fall in the interval $[-C, +C]$, can be expressed in terms of m_{E_1}, D_{E_1}, and D_{E_2} as follows:

$$P = P(|E| < C)$$

$$\simeq \frac{2C}{\sqrt{2\pi}\cdot 2\sqrt{3D_{E_1}}}\int_{-\sqrt{3D_{E_1}}}^{\sqrt{3D_{E_1}}}\frac{\exp\left\{-\dfrac{(m_E + E_1)^2}{2D_{E_2}}\right\}}{\sqrt{D_{E_2}}}dE_1. \qquad (4.45)$$

By making the change of variable $E_1 = \sqrt{D_{E_2}}\,y - m_E$, we rewrite the formula for the probability P as follows:

$$P = \frac{C}{\sqrt{3D_{E_1}}}\frac{1}{\sqrt{2\pi}}\int_{m'-\sqrt{3}\sigma_0}^{m'+\sqrt{3}\sigma_0}\exp\left\{-\frac{y^2}{2}\right\}dy, \qquad (4.45a)$$

where

$$m' = \frac{m_E}{\sqrt{D_{E_2}}}, \qquad \sigma_0 = \sqrt{\frac{D_{E_1}}{D_{E_2}}}.$$

Calculations of the probability P in accordance with formula (4.45a) can be made with the aid of tables of Gauss' function (see Appendix 1).

In the present case, the criterion P is a function of the three functionals m_E, D_{E_1}, and D_{E_2} of the weight function that are determined by formulas (4.44):

$$P = P(m_E, D_{E_1}, D_{E_2}). \qquad (4.46)$$

In accordance with the general procedure expounded in Subsection 1 of the present section, to find the optimal weight function corresponding to the maximum of the criterion (4.46), we need first to find the weight function $w_0(\tau, \theta_1, \theta_2)$ corresponding to the extremum of the reduced functional

$$I_\theta = \theta_1 D_{E_1} + \theta_2 D_{E_2} + m_E, \tag{4.47}$$

for different values of the harmonizing parameters θ_1 and θ_2.

When we substitute (4.44) into (4.47), we obtain

$$
\begin{aligned}
I_\theta = \theta_1 D_m & \left[(-1)^m \int_0^T \tau^m w(\tau) \, d\tau - m! \, C_m \right]^2 \\
& + \theta_2 \left[\int_0^T \int_0^T K_{x'}(\tau - \lambda) w(\tau) w(\lambda) \, d\tau \, d\lambda \right. \\
& \left. - 2 \int_0^T K_{x'h'}(\tau) w(\tau) \, d\tau + D_{h'} \right] \\
& + m_0 \left[(-1)^m \int_0^T \tau^m w(\tau) \, d\tau - m! \, C_m \right].
\end{aligned}
\tag{4.48}
$$

The desired weight function $w_0(\tau, \theta_1, \theta_2)$ must ensure an extremum of the functional (4.48) under conditions (3.49). As we know, solution of this problem amounts to finding the function

$$w_0(\tau, \theta_1, \theta_2, \gamma_0, \cdots, \gamma_{m-1}),$$

ensuring an unconditional extremum of the functional

$$I' = I_\theta + 2 \sum_{i=0}^{m-1} \gamma_i \int_0^T \tau_i w(\tau) \, d\tau. \tag{4.49}$$

A necessary condition that the function

$$w_0(\tau, \theta_1, \theta_2, \gamma_0, \gamma_1, \cdots, \gamma_{m-1}),$$

corresponding to the extremum of the functional (4.49), must satisfy is easily obtained from the procedure previously described (see Chapter 1, equation (1.140b)). In the present case, it takes the form

$$
\theta_1 D_m \int_0^T \tau^m \lambda^m w(\lambda) \, d\lambda + \theta_2 \int_0^T K_{x'}(\tau - \lambda) w(\lambda) \, d\lambda
$$
$$
- \theta_1 D_m (-1)^m m! \, C_m \tau^m - \theta_2 K_{x'h'}(\tau) + \frac{m_0}{2} (-1)^m \tau^m
$$
$$
+ \sum_{i=0}^{m-1} \gamma_i \tau^i = 0, \quad 0 \leqslant \tau \leqslant T. \tag{4.50}
$$

We have obtained an integral equation of the type (3.46). The solution w_0 of this equation depends on the m Lagrange multipliers γ_i and on the two harmonizing parameters θ_1 and θ_2. The values of the multipliers γ_i are determined from conditions (3.49) and then the solution is represented as a function of τ and the two parameters θ_1 and θ_2:

$$w_0 = w_0(\tau, \theta_1, \theta_2).$$

The values of the harmonizing parameters $\theta_1 = \theta_{10}$, $\theta_2 = \theta_{20}$ corresponding to the maximum of the criterion (4.45) are determined as follows: After the Lagrange multipliers are determined, the solution $w_0(\tau, \theta_1, \theta_2)$ of equation (4.50) is substituted into the expression (4.45) for the criterion P. In this case, the criterion P is a function of the two variables θ_1 and θ_2. The values $\theta_1 = \theta_{10}$ and $\theta_2 = \theta_{20}$ corresponding to the maximum of P can be found, for example, by the method of fastest descent (as expounded in Chapter 3). These values θ_{10} and θ_{20} of the harmonizing parameters can also be determined from equations (4.41), which, in the present case, can be written as follows:

$$
\left.
\begin{aligned}
\frac{-\dfrac{1}{2D_{E_1}}\displaystyle\int_{-\sqrt{3D_{E_1}}}^{\sqrt{3D_{E_1}}} N_1\,dE_1 + N_2}{-\dfrac{m_E}{D_{E_2}}\displaystyle\int_{-\sqrt{3D_{E_1}}}^{\sqrt{3D_{E_1}}} N_1\,dE_1 + N_2} &= \theta_{10}, \\[3em]
\frac{\dfrac{1}{2D_{E_2}}\displaystyle\int_{-\sqrt{3D_{E_1}}}^{\sqrt{3D_{E_1}}} N_1\,dE_1 + \dfrac{1}{2D_{E_2}^2}\displaystyle\int_{-\sqrt{3D_{E_1}}}^{\sqrt{3D_{E_1}}} N_1(m_E + E_1)^2\,dE_1}{-\dfrac{m_E}{D_{E_2}}\displaystyle\int_{-\sqrt{3D_{E_1}}}^{\sqrt{3D_{E_1}}} N_1\,dE_1 + N_2} &= \theta_{20},
\end{aligned}
\right\}
\qquad (4.51)
$$

where

$$N_1 = \exp\left\{-\frac{(m_E + E_1)^2}{2D_{E_2}}\right\},$$

$$N_2 = \exp\left\{-\frac{(m_E + \sqrt{3D_{E_1}})^2}{2D_{E_2}}\right\} - \exp\left\{-\frac{(m_E - \sqrt{3D_{E_1}})^2}{2D_{E_2}}\right\}.$$

The left hand members of equations (4.51) are functions of θ_{10} and θ_{20}, which are obtained by substituting the function $w_0(\tau, \theta_{10}, \theta_{20})$ into the functionals m_E, D_{E_1}, and D_{E_2}. The solution of the transcendental equations (4.51) provide the values of the harmonizing parameters θ_{10} and θ_{20}. In the general case, these equations are complicated and it is not convenient to use them to determine the parameters θ_{10} and θ_{20}. However, they can be used successfully to verify the validity of the solution θ_{10}, θ_{20} obtained by the first (approximate) method.

Let us now look at the second case, and formulate the statement of the problem. Let us assume that the block diagram of the system is as shown in Figure 2.2. The useful signal $G(t)$ and the noise obey normal distribution laws. The mathematical expectation $m_g(t)$ and the correlation function $K_g(t_1, t_2)$ of the useful signal are known. We also know the mathematical expectation $m_z(t)$ and the correlation function of the noise $K_z(t_1, t_2)$ and the joint correlation function $K_{gz}(t_1, t_2)$ between the useful signal and the noise. Consequently, we also know the correlation function of the input signal $X(t) = G(t) + Z(t)$. We denote it by $K_x(t_1$,

t_2). The desired output variable of the system $H(t)$ is the result of application of an arbitrary linear operator L: $H(t) = L\{G(t)\}$ to the useful signal.

We are required to determine the optimal weight function of the linear system with respect to the criterion of maximal probability that the error of the system will not exceed given allowed limits at fixed instants of time. The probability density of a multidimensional normal distribution of the error vector $E(t_1)$, $E(t_2)$, $\cdots$, $E(t_m)$ can be determined from formula (1.54), which in the present case takes the form

$$f(E_1, \cdots, E_m) = \frac{1}{\sqrt{2^m \pi^m |K|}} \exp \left\{ -\frac{1}{2|K|} \right.$$

$$\left. \times \sum_{\nu,\mu=1}^{m} k_{\nu\mu}(E_\nu - m_{E_\nu})(E_\mu - m_{E_\mu}) \right\}, \qquad (4.52)$$

where K is the matrix (1.53) with elements $K_{\nu\mu}$ that are values of the correlation function of the error $E(t)$ of the system at the instants t_ν and t_μ:

$$K_{\nu\mu} = K_E(t_\nu, t_\mu) = M[\overset{0}{E}(t_\nu)\overset{0}{E}(t_\mu)];$$

$|K|$ is the determinant of the matrix K; $k_{\nu\mu}$ is the cofactor of the element $K_{\nu\mu}$ in the determinant $|K|$; t_ν and t_μ are fixed instants of time for ν, $\mu = 1, \cdots, m$.

The probability that the error of the system will not exceed allowed limits $C_{1i} \leq E(t_i) \leq C_{2i}$ can be determined from the formula

$$P(C_{11} \leq E(t_1) \leq C_{21}, \cdots, C_{1p} \leq E(t_m) \leq C_{2m})$$

$$= \frac{1}{\sqrt{2^m \pi^m |K|}} \int_{C_{11}}^{C_{21}} \cdots \int_{C_{1k}}^{C_{2k}} \exp \left\{ -\frac{1}{2|K|} \right.$$

$$\left. \times \sum_{\nu,\mu=1}^{m} k_{\nu\mu}(E_\nu - m_{E_\nu})(E_\mu - m_{E_\mu}) \right\} dE \cdots dE_m. \qquad (4.53)$$

In the case in which the allowed limits are low, that is, when $-C_{1i} = C_{2i} = C \ll 1$ for $i = 1, \cdots, m$, formula (4.53) can be replaced with the following approximate formula:

$$P\{C \leqslant E(t_1) \leqslant C\}$$

$$= \frac{C^m 2^{\frac{m}{2}}}{\sqrt{\pi^m |K|}} \exp \left\{ -\frac{1}{2|K|} \sum_{\nu,\mu=1}^{m} k_{\nu\mu} m_{E_\nu} m_{E_\mu} \right\}. \qquad (4.54)$$

In both cases, the criterion P is a function of m mathematical expectations and $m(m+1)/2$ values of the correlation function $K_E(t_\nu, t_\mu)$ of the error of the system (remember that $K_{\nu\mu} = K_{\mu\nu}$).

The criterion P determined by formula (4.53) or (4.54) is a special case of the functional (4.37). In the present case, $n + 1 = m(m+3)/2$ and the reduced functional (4.38) is of the form

$$I_\theta = \sum_{\substack{\nu = 1 \\ \mu \geqslant \nu}}^{m} \theta_{\nu\mu} K_E(t_\nu, t_\mu) + \sum_{i=1}^{m-1} \theta_i m_E(t_i) + m_E(t_m).\qquad (4.55)$$

In view of formulas (1.95) and (1.96) and the relation

$$H(t) = \int_0^\infty G(\tau)v(t, \tau)d\tau,$$

we can write the following expressions for the mathematical expectation of the error:

$$m_E(t_i) = \int_0^\infty m_x(\tau)w(t_i, \tau)d\tau - m_h(t_i), \quad i = 1, \cdots, m, \qquad (4.56)$$

and for the correlation function of the error:

$$K_E(t_\nu, t_\mu) = \int_0^\infty \int_0^\infty K_x(\tau, \lambda)w(t_\nu, \tau)w(t_\mu, \lambda)d\tau d\lambda$$
$$- \int_0^\infty K_{xh}(t_\nu, \tau)w(t_\mu, \tau)d\tau - \int_0^\infty K_{hx}(t_\mu, \tau)w(t_\theta, \tau)d\tau$$
$$+ K_h(t_\nu, t_\mu), \quad \nu = 1, \cdots, m, \ \mu \geqslant \nu, \qquad (4.57)$$

where $K_{xh}(\tau, \lambda)$ and $K_{hx}(\tau, \lambda)$ are the joint correlation functions of the random functions $X(t)$ and $H(t)$.

For stationary influences and a stationary automatic-control system, formulas (4.54) through (4.57) take the simpler form

$$P\{-C \leqslant E(t_i) \leqslant C\}$$
$$= \frac{2^{\frac{m}{2}}C^m}{\sqrt{\pi^m|K|}} \exp\left\{-\frac{1}{2|K|} \sum_{\nu, \mu = 1}^{m} k_{\nu\mu}m_{E_0}^2\right\}. \qquad (4.54a)$$

Here, m_{E_0} is the constant mathematical expectation of the error and K is the matrix of the corresponding correlation function $K_E(t_2 - t_1)$:

$$I_\theta = \sum_{\nu=1}^{m} \theta_{m-\nu} K_E(t_m - t_\nu) + m_{E_0}^2, \qquad (4.55a)$$

$$m_{E_0} = m_{x_0} \int_0^\infty w(\tau)d\tau - m_{h_0}, \qquad (4.56a)$$

$$K_E(t_m - t_\nu) = \int_0^\infty \int_0^\infty K_x(t_m - t_\nu + \tau - \lambda)w(\tau)w(\lambda)d\tau d\lambda$$
$$- 2\int_0^\infty K_{xh}(t_m - t_\nu + \tau)w(\tau)d\tau + D_h. \qquad (4.57a)$$

When we substitute (4.56a) and (4.57a) into (4.55a), we obtain a functional of the type (1.139). In the present case the integrand Φ in it satisfies condition (1.140a). Consequently, the integral equation (1.140b), which enables us to determine the weight function $w_0(\tau, \theta_1, \cdots, \theta_m)$ corresponding to an extremum of the reduced functional (4.55a), takes the form

$$\int_0^\infty \sum_{\nu=1}^m \theta_{m-\nu} K_x(t_m - t_\nu + \tau - \lambda) w_0(\lambda, \theta_1, \cdots, \theta_m) d\lambda$$

$$- \sum_{\nu=1}^m \theta_{m-\nu} K_{xh}(t_m - t_\nu + \tau) + m_{x_0}^2 \int_0^\infty w_0(\lambda, \theta_1, \cdots, \theta_m) d\lambda$$

$$- m_{x_0} m_{h_0} = 0, \quad 0 \leqslant \tau \leqslant \infty. \tag{4.58}$$

If the fixed instants of time in which we are interested are evenly spaced, that is, if $t_{i+1} - t_i = \Delta$, then equation (4.58) takes the simpler form

$$\int_0^\infty \sum_{\nu=1}^m \theta_\nu K_x(\nu\Delta + \tau - \lambda) w_0(\lambda, \theta_1, \cdots, \theta_m) d\lambda$$

$$- \sum_{\nu=1}^m \theta_\nu K_{xh}(\nu\Delta + \tau) + m_{x_0}^2 \int_0^\infty w_0(\lambda, \theta_1, \cdots, \theta_m) d\lambda$$

$$- m_{x_0} m_{h_0} = 0, \quad 0 \leqslant \tau \leqslant \infty. \tag{4.58a}$$

Let us write equations (4.54a) through (4.58a) for the case in which $t_{i+1} - t_i = \Delta$, $m = 3$, and $m_x = m_h = 0$. Let us begin with the criterion P. First, we write the matrix K:

$$K = \begin{Vmatrix} K_E(0) & K_E(\Delta) & K_E(2\Delta) \\ K_E(\Delta) & K_E(0) & K_E(\Delta) \\ K_E(2\Delta) & K_E(\Delta) & K_E(0) \end{Vmatrix}.$$

The determinant of this matrix is

$$|K| = K_E^3(0) + 2K_E^2(\Delta) K_E(2\Delta)$$
$$- 2K_E^2(\Delta) K_E(0) - K_E(0) K_E^2(2\Delta). \tag{4.59}$$

Now, we can write a formula determining the criterion (4.54a):

$$P\{-C \leqslant E(t_1) \leqslant C\}$$

$$= \frac{2^{\frac{3}{2}} C^3}{\sqrt{\pi^3} \sqrt{K_E^3(0) + 2K_E^2(\Delta) K_E(2\Delta) - 2K_E^2(\Delta) K_E(0) - K_E(0) K_E^2(2\Delta)}}. \tag{4.60}$$

The maximum of this criterion corresponds to the minimum of the functional (4.59). Consequently, in the present case, the optimal weight function w^0 must ensure a minimum of the determinant $|K|$. This determinant is an algebraic function of the values of the correlation function of the error

$$K_E(0), \quad K_E(\Delta), \quad K_E(2\Delta).$$

Thus, the reduced functional I_θ is of the form

$$I_\theta = K_E(0) + \theta_1 K_E(\Delta) + \theta_2 K_E(2\Delta), \tag{4.61}$$

where

$$
\begin{aligned}
K_E(0) = D_E &= \int_0^\infty \int_0^\infty K_x(\tau - \lambda) w(\tau) w(\lambda) d\tau d\lambda \\
&\quad - 2 \int_0^\infty K_{xh}(\tau) w(\tau) d\tau + D_h,
\end{aligned}
$$

$$
\begin{aligned}
K_E(\Delta) &= \int_0^\infty \int_0^\infty K_x(\Delta + \tau - \lambda) w(\tau) w(\lambda) d\tau d\lambda \\
&\quad - 2 \int_0^\infty K_{xh}(\Delta + \tau) w(\tau) d\tau + D_h,
\end{aligned}
$$

$$
\begin{aligned}
K_E(2\Delta) &= \int_0^\infty \int_0^\infty K_x(2\Delta + \tau - \lambda) w(\tau) w(\lambda) d\tau d\lambda \\
&\quad - 2 \int_0^\infty K_{xh}(2\Delta + \tau) w(\tau) d\tau + D_h.
\end{aligned}
$$

$$(4.62)$$

The integral equation (4.58) in this case may be written as

$$
\begin{aligned}
\int_0^\infty [K_x(\tau - \lambda) &+ \theta_1 K_x(\Delta + \tau - \lambda) + \theta_2 K_x(2\Delta + \tau - \lambda)] \\
&\times w_0(\lambda, \theta_1, \theta_2) d\lambda - K_{xh}(\tau) - \theta_1 K_{xh}(\Delta + \tau) \\
&- \theta_2 K_{xh}(2\Delta + \tau) = 0, \quad 0 \leqslant \tau \leqslant \infty.
\end{aligned}
$$

$$(4.63)$$

If for admissible systems we take systems for which $w(\tau) = 0$ whenever $\tau > T$, we need to replace ∞ everywhere as the upper limits of integration in (4.62) and (4.63) with a finite time T. In this case, the integral equation (4.63) must be satisfied in the interval $0 \leqslant \tau \leqslant T$.

Equation (4.63) is an equation of the type (3.46). We need to find a solution $w_0(\tau, \theta_1, \theta_2)$ of this equation for different values of the harmonizing parameters θ_1 and θ_2 and then determine the values of the harmonizing parameters $\theta_1 = \theta_{10}$ and $\theta_2 = \theta_{20}$ that correspond to the minimum of the determinant $|K|$. These values θ_{10} and θ_{20} can be determined as follows: We substitute the solution $w_0(\tau, \theta_1, \theta_2)$ into (4.63) and we substitute (4.63) into (4.59). Thus, we obtain the determinant $|K|$ as a function of the parameters θ_1 and θ_2. The minimum of this function and the values of the harmonizing parameters $\theta_1 = \theta_{10}$ and $\theta_2 = \theta_{20}$ corresponding to it are obtained by the method of fastest descent.

The values of the harmonizing parameters can also be found by another procedure, which consists in solving the two equations

$$
\left.
\begin{aligned}
\frac{\dfrac{\partial}{\partial K_E(\Delta)} |K|}{\dfrac{\partial}{\partial K(0)} |K|} &= \frac{4 K_E(\Delta) [K_E(2\Delta) - K_E(\Delta)]}{3 K_E^2(0) - 2 K_E^2(\Delta) - K_E^2(2\Delta)} = \theta_{10}, \\[2em]
\frac{\dfrac{\partial}{\partial K_E(2\Delta)} |K|}{\dfrac{\partial}{\partial K_E(0)} |K|} &= \frac{2 [K_E^2(\Delta) - K_E(0) K_E(2\Delta)]}{3 K_E^2(0) - 2 K_E^2(\Delta) - K_E^2(2\Delta)} = \theta_{20}
\end{aligned}
\right\}
$$

$$(4.64)$$

in the two unknowns θ_{10} and θ_{20}.

If these equations are very complicated, the first method is the more appropriate one, but equations (4.64) should be used to check the solution obtained by the method of fastest descent.

3. Determination of an optimal system of given structure from a criterion of general form

The following statement of the problem is of interest from a practical point of view. Suppose that the block diagram of the system is given. This means that the transfer function (or the weight function) is determined up to several parameters $q_1, \cdots, q_n$:

$$W = W(p, q_1, \cdots, q_n) \quad (\text{or } w = w(\tau, q_1, \cdots, q_n)).$$

The useful signal $G(t)$ and the noise $Z(t)$ (see Fig. 3.6) act on the system. Suppose that the useful signal and the noise are stationary and stationarily connected. As criterion we take the criterion I, which is a given function of the mathematical expectation m_E and variance D_E of the error of the system:

$$I = f(m_E, D_E).$$

The mathematical expectation and the variance can be expressed in terms of the parameters of the system $q_1, \cdots, q_n$:

$$m_E = m_E(q_1, \cdots, q_n), \quad D_E = D_E(q_1, \cdots, q_n).$$

Consequently, the criterion I can also be represented as a function of these parameters:

$$I = f[m_E(q_1, \cdots, q_n), D_E(q_1, \cdots, q_n)] = F(q_1, \cdots, q_n). \quad (4.65)$$

The optimal parameters $q_{10}, \cdots, q_{n0}$ must ensure an extremum of the function F. These optimal parameters can be found by the method of fastest descent (see Section 12).

If the function $F = F(q_1, \cdots, q_n)$ is a very complicated function of $q_1, \cdots, q_n$, there is another procedure for solving the problem. Reasoning just as in the proof of Theorem 2 of Chapter 1, we can show that the solution of the problem of finding the optimal parameters that ensure an extremum of the criterion (4.65) can be broken into two stages. In the first stage, we need to find the parameters ensuring an extremum of the reduced function of the parameters $q_1, \cdots, q_n$:

$$f_\theta = m_E(q_1, \cdots, q_n) + \theta D_E(q_1, \cdots, q_n) \quad (4.66)$$

for different values of the harmonizing factor θ. These values of the parameters

$$q_{10} = q_{10}(\theta), \cdots, q_{n0} = q_{n0}(\theta)$$

depend on the harmonizing parameter θ. In the second stage, we need to determine the value of the harmonizing factor $\theta = \theta_0$ corresponding to an extremum of the criterion I, that is, to an extremum of the function

$$F = F[q_{10}(0, \cdots, q_{n0}(\theta)] = \varphi(\theta).$$

The value $\theta = \theta_0$ corresponds to an extremum of the function $\varphi(\theta)$. The determination of $\theta = \theta_0$ in this case presents no difficulty. The values of the parameters

$$q_1^0 = q_{10}(\theta_0), \cdots, q_n^0 = q_{n0}(\theta_0)$$

are optimal. If the reduced function f_θ is considerably simpler than the function F, the switch to the former leads to a shortening and simplification of the computational procedure.

If the criterion I is a function of several characteristics

$$I = f(I_1, \cdots, I_{n+1}),$$

where the I_i are characteristics of the error (mathematical expectation, value of the correlation function for different values of the time, and so on), the problem is solved in an analogous way. If one uses the second method, the reduced function will contain not one but n harmonizing parameters $\theta_1, \cdots, \theta_n$. If n is great, this method is usually inconvenient in such cases: It does not simplify the calculation as compared with the first method of finding the extremum of the original function $F(q_1, \cdots, q_n)$.

The method described here can also be used to choose optimal parameters of a system with variable parameters with respect to a criterion characterizing the error at a given instant of time.

In all the block diagrams that we have considered (see Figs. 1.1, 2.2, and 3.6), the influences were applied to a single point of the system. In practice, we often encounter cases in which different influences are applied at different points of the system. In such a case, how can we choose the optimal automatic-control system? In such a case, we need to know the block diagram of the system, the points at which the influences are applied, the probabilistic characteristics of the influences, and the transfer functions of the components separating the influences. One component remains unknown, namely, the correcting device. We need to determine the weight function (or transfer function) of this correcting device. Such a problem of choosing the optimal correcting device in accordance with the minimum mean square error of the system has been solved [Refs. 38, 47, 52]. The results obtained in the references indicated can be generalized without difficulty to the case in which the comparison criterion is a criterion of the general form (4.37).

Chapter 5

DETERMINATION OF AN OPTIMAL LINEAR DISCRETE AUTOMATIC-CONTROL SYSTEM IN TERMS OF STATISTICAL CRITERIA

In this chapter, we shall consider discrete linear automatic-control systems. In essence, what we shall study are sampled-data systems with amplitude modulation. These systems are investigated by methods analogous to those expounded in the preceding chapters. A difference consists in the fact that instead of the operation of "finding a derivative," we need to use the operation of "finding a finite difference," and instead of "integration," we use "summation." However, the transition from continuous systems to discrete ones involves the use of a somewhat different mathematical apparatus. Therefore, it will be expedient to study discrete systems independently, using the ideas and principal aspects described in the preceding chapters of the book.

17. PRECISION ANALYSIS OF DISCRETE AUTOMATIC-CONTROL SYSTEMS

1. Probabilistic characteristics of discrete random processes

In the general case, to study the precision of an automatic-control system, we need to know the probabilistic distribution laws of the input influences. However, in many cases that are important in practice, it is sufficient to know the first two probabilistic moments of these influences. For example, if the input influences obey a normal distribution law, the first two probabilistic moments, namely, the mathematical expectation and the correlation function, completely determine the influences from a probabilistic point of view. In such a case, if the system is a linear system, the output variables also obey a normal distribution law [Ref. 29]. Consequently, the output variables are completely characterized by the first two probabilistic moments. If the input or the output process obeys some other distribution law or an unknown distribution law, the first and second probabilistic moments of the process yield some sort of representation of the process. Thus, we shall concern ourselves with determining the mathematical expectations and the correlation functions of the input and output variables of the system.

Let us consider a discrete system with constant period T of alternation of impulses. In this case, it is convenient to represent the time t as an independent variable, in the form $t = nT + \Delta T$, where n is the number of periods of alternation and ΔT is an interval of time less than the period of alternation: $0 \leqslant \Delta T < T$. For convenience in writing, we shift to the relative time $t/T = n + \varepsilon$, where $\varepsilon = \Delta T/T$. Thus, we shall represent the relative time (as argument of the random functions, that is, the input and output of the system) in what follows in the form $n + \varepsilon$, where n denotes the number of entire periods of alternation T and ε denotes a portion of a single period of alternation $(0 \leqslant \varepsilon < 1)$. Our denoting the argument (the relative time) in the form $n + \varepsilon$ is essentially equivalent to denoting it by (n, ε) (cf. [Ref. 39, 53]), since the numbers $n + \varepsilon$ and the pairs of numbers (n, ε) can be put in a one-to-one correspondence.

Let $X = X(n + \varepsilon)$ denote a random function. If this function is defined at the input of an impulse element, the only things that will be significant are its values at the instants at which the impulses are applied, that is, the values of the function at $\varepsilon = 0$. On the other hand, if this function is the output variable of the system taken from the output of a continuous component, it will be a continuous function whose value will be significant for an arbitrary value of the argument. However, sometimes, when we are investigating a discrete system, we confine ourselves to the study of the values of the output variable at the instant n (for $\varepsilon = 0$), since obtaining the probabilistic characteritics of the output variable of a discrete system at instants of operation of an impulse element can sometimes be done in a relatively easy manner and, in addition, in some cases we need only know the characteristics of the output variable at these discrete instants of time. This is one of the distinctive features of the study of discrete systems.

The mathematical expectation $m_x(n + \varepsilon)$ of a random function $X(n + \varepsilon)$ can be determined in accordance with formula (1.56) where in place of t we have $n + \varepsilon$:

$$m_x(n + \varepsilon) = M[X(n + \varepsilon)] = \int_{-\infty}^{\infty} x f_1(x, n + \varepsilon)dx, \qquad (5.1)$$

where $f_1(x, n + \varepsilon)$ is a one-dimensional probability density of the function $X(n + \varepsilon)$.

From experimental results $X_i(n + \varepsilon)$, for $i = 1, \cdots, m$, we can determine the mathematical expectation of a random function $X(n + \varepsilon)$ as the arithmetic mean of the set of sample functions

$$m_x(n + \varepsilon) = \frac{1}{m} \sum_{i=1}^{m} X_i(n + \varepsilon). \tag{5.1a}$$

The greater the number m of experiments, the more accurate is this approximation formula.

In the special case of random processes that satisfy an ergodic hypothesis, we have the following formula:

$$m_x(n + \varepsilon) = \lim_{m \to \infty} \frac{1}{2m} \sum_{n=-m}^{m} X_i(n + \varepsilon) = m_x ,$$

which enables us to determine the mathematical expectation just from the ith sample function $X_i(n + \varepsilon)$. The correlation function $K_x(n_1 + \varepsilon_1, n_2 + \varepsilon_2)$ of the random function $X(n + \varepsilon)$ is determined from formulas (1.57) and (1.58). In the present case, these two formulas can be written as

$$K_x(n_1 + \varepsilon_1, n_2 + \varepsilon_2)$$
$$= M[\{X(n_1 + \varepsilon_1) - m_x(n_1 + \varepsilon_1)\}\{X(n_2 + \varepsilon_2) - m_x(n_2 + \varepsilon_2)\}]$$
$$= \int_{-\infty}^{\infty}\int_{-\infty}^{\infty} [x_1 - m_x(n_1 + \varepsilon_1)][x_2 - m_x(n_2 + \varepsilon_2)]$$
$$\times f_2(x_1, x_2; n_1 + \varepsilon_1, n_2 + \varepsilon_2)dx_1dx_2, \tag{5.2}$$

where $f_2(x_1, x_2; n_1 + \varepsilon_1, n_2 + \varepsilon_2)$ is the two-dimensional probability density of the random function $X(n + \varepsilon)$.

The correlation function can be determined from the experimental results in accordance with the formula

$$K_x(n_1 + \varepsilon_1, n_2 + \varepsilon_2) = \frac{1}{m} \sum_{i=1}^{m} [X_i(n_1 + \varepsilon_1) - m_x(n_1 + \varepsilon_1)]$$
$$\times [X_i(n_2 + \varepsilon_2) - m_x(n_2 + \varepsilon_2)], \tag{5.2a}$$

where m is the number of experiments.

The variance of the random function $X(n + \varepsilon)$ is the value of the correlation function K_x, where $n_1 + \varepsilon_1 = n_2 + \varepsilon_2 = n + \varepsilon$:

$$D_x(n + \varepsilon) = K_x(n + \varepsilon, n + \varepsilon) = \int_{-\infty}^{\infty} [x - m_x(n + \varepsilon)]^2 f_1(x, t)dx. \tag{5.3}$$

If the random function $X(n + \varepsilon)$ is stationary, the correlation function K_x depends on the difference between the arguments:

$$K_x = K_x(n_2 - n_1 + \varepsilon_2 - \varepsilon_1).$$

The joint correlation function K_{xy} of two random functions $X(n + \varepsilon)$ and $Y(n + \varepsilon)$ is determined in accordance with formula (1.67), which, in the present case, takes the form

$$K_{xy}(n_1 + \varepsilon_1, n_2 + \varepsilon_2) = M[\overset{0}{X}(n_1 + \varepsilon_1)\overset{0}{Y}(n_2 + \varepsilon_2)]$$
$$= \int_{-\infty}^{\infty}\int_{-\infty}^{\infty} [x - m_x(n_1 + \varepsilon_1)][y - m_y(n_2 + \varepsilon_2)]$$
$$\times f_2(x, y; n_1 + \varepsilon_1, n_2 + \varepsilon_2)dxdy. \tag{5.4}$$

Let us find the relationship between the probabilistic characteristics of the input and output variables of a discrete system with weight function w. The weight function of a discrete system with variable parameters depends on two arguments: $w = w(n + \varepsilon, m)$. Here, $n + \varepsilon$ is the value of the time (variable) at which the reaction of the system to a unit impulse is measured and m is the instant at which a unit impulse is applied.

The mathematical expectation of a random function is a nonrandom function. Hence, it can be represented by a linear discrete system in accordance with the familiar formula [Refs. 14, 26, 39]

$$m_y(n + \varepsilon) = M[Y(n + \varepsilon)] = M\left[\sum_{m=0}^{n} X(m)w(n + \varepsilon, m)\right]$$

$$= \sum_{m=0}^{n} m_x(m)w(n + \varepsilon, m), \tag{5.5}$$

where $w(n + \varepsilon, m)$ is the weight function of a nonstationary linear discrete system, $Y(n + \varepsilon)$ is the output variable of the system at the instant $n + \varepsilon$, and $X(m)$ is the input variable of the system. (If X is a discrete function, then $X(m)$ denotes the limit $\lim_{\varepsilon \to 1} X(m - 1 + \varepsilon)$.) Let us find the relationship between the correlation function K_x of the input variable X and the correlation function K_y of the output variable Y of a discrete system:

$$K_y(n_1 + \varepsilon_1, n_2 + \varepsilon_2) = M[\overset{0}{Y}(n_1 + \varepsilon_1)\overset{0}{Y}(n_2 + \varepsilon_2)]$$
$$= M\left[\sum_{i=0}^{n_1} \overset{0}{X}(i)w(n_1 + \varepsilon_1, i) \sum_{l=0}^{n_2} \overset{0}{X}(l)w(n_2 + \varepsilon_2, l)\right]$$
$$= M\left[\sum_{i=0}^{n_1}\sum_{l=0}^{n_2} \overset{0}{X}(i)\overset{0}{X}(l)w(n_1 + \varepsilon_1, i)w(n_2 + \varepsilon_2, l)\right],$$

where $\overset{0}{X}(i)$ is a centralized random function.

Remembering that the operation of taking the mathematical expectation commutes with the operation of summation, we can rewrite this last expression for the correlation function in the form

$$K_y(n_1 + \varepsilon_1, n_2 + \varepsilon_2) = \sum_{i=0}^{n_1} \sum_{l=0}^{n_2} K_x(i, l) w(n_1 + \varepsilon_1, i) w(n_2 + \varepsilon_2, l). \quad (5.6)$$

Here, $w(n+\varepsilon, i)$ is the weight function of a nonstationary discrete system.

In the particular case in which the input influence X and the sampled-data system are stationary and we can neglect the initial conditions (that is, if n is sufficiently great), for $\varepsilon_1 = \varepsilon_2 = \varepsilon$ formula (5.6) can be transformed. In this case, the weight function depends on the difference in the arguments $n + \varepsilon - l$ (or $n + \varepsilon - i$):

$$w = w(n + \varepsilon - l).$$

Consequently, the output variable can be expressed in terms of the input variable and the weight function:

$$\overset{0}{Y}(n + \varepsilon) = \sum_{l=0}^{n} \overset{0}{X}(l) w(n + \varepsilon - l) = \sum_{i=0}^{n} \overset{0}{X}(n - i) w(i + \varepsilon). \quad (5.7)$$

The correlation function of the output variable Y is now easily obtained.

$$
\begin{aligned}
K_y &= \lim_{n_1, n_2 \to \infty} \left\{ M\left[\sum_{i=0}^{n_1} \overset{0}{X}(n_1 - i) w(i + \varepsilon) \times \sum_{l=0}^{n_2} \overset{0}{X}(n_2 - l) w(l + \varepsilon) \right] \right\} \\
&= \lim_{n_1, n_2 \to \infty} \left\{ M\left[\sum_{i=0}^{n_1} \sum_{l=0}^{n_2} \overset{0}{X}(n_1 - i) \overset{0}{X}(n_2 - l) \times w(i + \varepsilon) w(l + \varepsilon) \right] \right\}.
\end{aligned}
$$

By virtue of the stationariness of the random function X and the commutativity of the mathematical-expectation and summation operators, this last equation can be converted to the form

$$K_y(m + \varepsilon) = \sum_{i=0}^{\infty} \sum_{l=0}^{\infty} K_x(m + i - l) w(i + \varepsilon) w(l + \varepsilon). \quad (5.8)$$

where $m = n_2 - n_1$.

The variance D_y of an output variable Y of a system is determined in accordance with formula (5.6), where $n_1 + \varepsilon_1 = n_2 + \varepsilon_2 = n + \varepsilon$:

$$D_y(n + \varepsilon) = \sum_{i=1}^{n} \sum_{l=1}^{n} K_x(i, l) w(n + \varepsilon, i) w(n + \varepsilon, l). \quad (5.9)$$

The variance of the output variable in the case of a stationary input variable and a stationary system is determined in accordance with formula (5.8) with $m = 0$:

$$D_y(\varepsilon) = \sum_{i=0}^{\infty} \sum_{l=0}^{\infty} K_x(i - l) w(i + \varepsilon) w(l + \varepsilon). \quad (5.10)$$

The variance of the output variable is a periodic function of the time with unit period (in dimensional time, with period T). Here, the nonstationariness is introduced by an impulse element, which we may regard as an element with variable parameters.

When we study automatic-control systems, it is sometimes necessary to know the joint correlation function

$$K_{x_1 x_2}(n_1 + \varepsilon_1, n_2 + \varepsilon_2)$$

between two random functions $X_1(t)$ and $X_2(t)$. It is defined as follows:

$$K_{x_1 x_2}(n_1 + \varepsilon_1, n_2 + \varepsilon_2) = M[\overset{0}{X_1}(n_1 + \varepsilon_1) \overset{0}{X_2}(n_2 + \varepsilon_2)]. \qquad (5.11)$$

If the random functions $X_1(t)$ and $X_2(t)$ are stationary and stationarily connected, then

$$K_{x_1 x_2}(n_1 + \varepsilon_1, n_2 + \varepsilon_2) = K_{x_1 x_2}(n_1 + \varepsilon_1 - n_2 - \varepsilon_2). \qquad (5.12)$$

As an example, we can determine the joint correlation function of the input and output variables of the system:

$$K_{xy}(n_1 + \varepsilon_1, n_2 + \varepsilon_2) = M[\overset{0}{X}(n_1 + \varepsilon_1) \overset{0}{Y}(n_2 + \varepsilon_2]$$

$$= M\left[\overset{0}{X}(n_1 + \varepsilon_1) \sum_{i=0}^{n_2} \overset{0}{X}(i) w(n_2 + \varepsilon_2, i) \right]$$

$$= M\left[\sum_{i=0}^{n_2} \overset{0}{X}(n_1 + \varepsilon_1) \overset{0}{X}(i) w(n_2 + \varepsilon_2, i) \right]$$

$$= \sum_{i=0}^{n_2} K_x(n_1 + \varepsilon, i) w(n_2 + \varepsilon_2, i). \qquad (5.13)$$

If the random function $X(t)$ and the system are stationary and if $\varepsilon_1 = \varepsilon_2 = 0$, then the joint correlation function K_{xy} of the input and output variables of the system is determined as follows:

$$K_{xy}(m) = \lim_{n_1, n_2 \to \infty} \{M[\overset{0}{X}(n_1) \overset{0}{Y}(n_2)]\}$$

$$= \lim_{n_1, n_2 \to \infty} \left\{ M\left[\overset{0}{X}(n_1) \sum_{l=0}^{n_2} \overset{0}{X}(n_2 - l) w(l) \right] \right\}$$

$$= \lim_{n_1, n_2 \to \infty} \left\{ M\left[\sum_{l=0}^{n_2} \overset{0}{X}(n_1) \overset{0}{X}(n_2 - l) w(l) \right] \right\}$$

$$= \sum_{l=0}^{\infty} K_x(m - l) w(l), \qquad (5.14)$$

where $m = n_2 - n_1$.

If $\varepsilon_1 = \varepsilon_2 = \varepsilon > 0$, we can obtain the formula for determining K_{xy} in an analogous manner:

$$K_{xy}(m + \varepsilon) = \sum_{l=0}^{\infty} K_x(m - \varepsilon - l) w(l + \varepsilon). \qquad (5.15)$$

If the joint correlation function of the functions X and Y is equal to zero $(K_{xy} = K_{yx} = 0)$, we say that these two random functions are uncorrelated,

In all that follows, unless the contrary is explicity stated, we shall always assume that $\varepsilon_1 = \varepsilon_2 = \varepsilon$.

When we study stationary systems subject to stationary influences, it is sometimes expedient to use frequency methods. In this connection, we introduce the concept of the spectral density $S(\omega, \varepsilon)$ of a stationary discrete process $X(n + \varepsilon)$:

$$S(\omega, \varepsilon) = \sum_{m=-\infty}^{\infty} K_x(m + \varepsilon)e^{-j\omega m}. \tag{5.16}$$

We define analogously the joint spectral density $S_{x_1 x_2}(\omega, \varepsilon)$ of stationary and stationarily connected processes of the random variables $X_1(n + \varepsilon)$ and $X_2(n + \varepsilon)$:

$$S_{x_1 x_2}(\omega, \varepsilon) = \sum_{m=-\infty}^{\infty} K_{x_1 x_2}(m, \varepsilon)e^{-j\omega m}. \tag{5.17}$$

In certain cases, a shift to a complex region simplifies the study of sampled-data systems. For example, the spectral density of the output variable of a sampled-data system can be expressed very simply in terms of its frequency characteristic and the spectral density of the input variable:

$$S_y(\omega, \varepsilon) = |W(j\omega, \varepsilon)|^2 S_x(\omega, \varepsilon), \tag{5.18}$$

where $W(p, \varepsilon)$ is the operator transfer function of a sampled-data system, so that $|W(j\omega, \varepsilon)|^2$ is the square of the amplitude frequency characteristic of that system.

Let us prove (5.18). We write the expression for the spectral density corresponding to the correlation function (5.8):

$$S_y(\omega, \varepsilon) = \sum_{m=-\infty}^{\infty} K_y(m, \varepsilon)^{-j\omega m}$$

$$= \sum_{m=-\infty}^{\infty} \left\{ \sum_{i=0}^{\infty} \sum_{l=0}^{\infty} K_x(m + i - l)\omega(i + \varepsilon)\omega(l + \varepsilon) \right\} e^{-j\omega m}.$$

Let us suppose that the series in the braces converge and that the order of summation can be reversed. In practical problems, this is usually the case. Therefore, we can write the expression for S_y in the form

$$S_y(\omega, \varepsilon) = \sum_{i=0}^{\infty} \left\{ \sum_{m=-\infty}^{\infty} \sum_{i=0}^{\infty} K_x(m + i - l)w(i + \varepsilon)w(l + \varepsilon) \right.$$

$$\times e^{-j\omega(m + i - l)}e^{-j\omega(l - i)} \left. \right\} = \sum_{l=0}^{\infty} w(l + \varepsilon)e^{-j\omega l}$$

$$\times \left\{ \sum_{i=0}^{\infty} w(i + \varepsilon)e^{j\omega i} \sum_{m=-\infty}^{\infty} K_x(m + i - l)e^{-j\omega(m + i - l)} \right\}.$$

For arbitrary fixed values of i and l, in the summation with respect to m we can make the change of variable $\eta = m + i - l$. Then, this summation takes the form

$$\sum_{m=-\infty}^{\infty} K_x(m + i - l)e^{-j\lambda(m+i-l)} = \sum_{\eta=-\infty}^{\infty} K_x(\eta)e^{-j\omega\eta} = S_x(\omega, \varepsilon).$$

Consequently, the expression for $S_y(\omega, \varepsilon)$ can be rewritten as

$$S_y(\omega, \varepsilon) = \sum_{l=0}^{\infty} w(l + \varepsilon)e^{-j\omega l} \sum_{i=0}^{\infty} w(i + \varepsilon)e^{j\omega l}S_x(\omega, \varepsilon)$$
$$= W(j\omega)W(-j\omega)S_x(\omega, \varepsilon) = |W(j\omega, \varepsilon)|^2 S_x(\omega, \varepsilon)$$

which completes the proof of formula (5.18).

The transition from spectral densities to the corresponding correlational functions of stationary random processes is made with the aid of the formulas for the inverse transformation:

$$K_x(m, \varepsilon) = \frac{1}{2\pi} \int_{-\pi}^{\pi} S_x(\omega, \varepsilon)e^{j\omega m}d\omega = \frac{1}{\pi} \int_0^{\pi} S_x(\omega, \varepsilon) \cos \omega m \, d\omega, \quad \textbf{(5.19)}$$

$$K_{x_1x_2}(m, \varepsilon) = \frac{1}{2\pi} \int_{-\pi}^{\pi} S_{x_1x_2}(\omega, \varepsilon)e^{j\omega m}d\omega. \quad \textbf{(5.20)}$$

By using formulas (5.18) and (5.19), we can write the expression for the variance of the output variable of a sampled-data stationary system when the input variable is stationary:

$$D_y(\varepsilon) = K_y(0, \varepsilon) = \frac{1}{\pi} \int_0^{\pi} |W(j\omega, \varepsilon)|^2 S_x(\omega, \varepsilon)d\omega. \quad \textbf{(5.21)}$$

This formula enables us to obtain easily the variance of the output variable from the spectral density of the input variable and the operator transfer function of the system (from the amplitude frequency characteristic of the system).

2. Characteristics of the error of a system

The instantaneous value of the error of the system $E(n + \varepsilon)$ is defined as the difference between the instantaneous value of the actual output variable $Y(n + \varepsilon)$ of a sampled-data system and the instantaneous value of the desired output variable $H(n + \varepsilon)$:

$$E(n + \varepsilon) = Y(n + \varepsilon) - H(n + \varepsilon). \quad \textbf{(5.22)}$$

Let us assume that the desired output variable $H(n + \varepsilon)$ is the result of application of a linear operator L to the useful signal $G(n + \varepsilon)$:

$$H(n + \varepsilon) = L\{G(n + \varepsilon)\}. \quad \textbf{(5.23)}$$

Examples of what might be the desired output variable H are

(a) $$H(n + \varepsilon) = G(n + \varepsilon),$$
(b) $$H(n + \varepsilon) = G(n + \varepsilon + n_e),$$

where n_e is the extrapolation time.

The block diagram for this case is shown in Figure 5.1. At the input of the system a random function $X(n + \varepsilon)$ is applied, which is the sum of the useful signal $G(n + \varepsilon)$ and a noise $Z(n + \varepsilon)$ with known probabilistic characteristics. Let us suppose that the time of the transitional process of the impulse signal is N. In this case, formula (5.22), giving the instantaneous value of the error of the system at the instant $n + \varepsilon$, takes the form

$$E(n + \varepsilon) = \sum_{l=0}^{N} [G(l) + Z(l)]w(n + \varepsilon, l) - H(n + \varepsilon). \tag{5.24}$$

The mathematical expectation m_E of the error of the system is, in accordance with formula (5.24), equal to

$$m_E(n + \varepsilon) = \sum_{l=0}^{N} [m_g(l) + m_z(l)]w(n + \varepsilon, l) - L\{m_g(n + \varepsilon)\}$$

$$= \sum_{l=0}^{N} m_x(l)w(n + \varepsilon, l) - m_h(n + \varepsilon), \tag{5.25}$$

where m_g, m_z, m_x, and m_h are the mathematical expectations of the useful signal, the noise, the input variable, and the desired output variable of the system.

The correlation function $K_E(n_1 + \varepsilon_1, n_2 + \varepsilon_2)$ of the error of the sampled-data system is, by definition, equal to

$$K_E(n_1 + \varepsilon_1, n_2 + \varepsilon_2) = M[\overset{0}{E}(n_1 + \varepsilon_1)\overset{0}{E}(n_2 + \varepsilon_2)]$$

$$= M\Bigg\{ \Bigg[\sum_{i=0}^{N} \overset{0}{X}(l)w(n_1 + \varepsilon_1, l) - H(n_1 + \varepsilon_1) \Bigg]$$

$$\times \Bigg[\sum_{i=0}^{N} \overset{0}{X}(l)w(n_2 + \varepsilon_2, i) - H(n_2 + \varepsilon_2) \Bigg] \Bigg\}.$$

By using the commutativity of the mathematical-expectation and summation operators, we can transform this expression for the correlation function of the error to the form

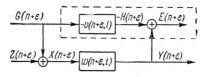

FIGURE 5.1.

$$K_E(n_1 + \varepsilon_1, n_2 + \varepsilon_2) = \sum_{l=0}^{N} \sum_{i=0}^{N} K_x(l, i) w(n_1 + \varepsilon_1, l) w(n_2 + \varepsilon_2, i)$$

$$- \sum_{l=0}^{N} K_{xh}(l, n_2 + \varepsilon_2) w(n_1 + \varepsilon_1, l)$$

$$- \sum_{i=0}^{N} K_{xh}(l, n_1 + \varepsilon_1) w(n_2 + \varepsilon_2, l)$$

$$+ K_h(n_1 + \varepsilon_1, n_2 + \varepsilon_2), \qquad (5.26)$$

where K_x and K_h are the correlation functions of the input signal and the desired output variable of the system, and K_{xh} is the joint correlation function of the input signal and the desired output variable.

The variance of the error of the system is the value of the correlation function (5.26) for $n_1 = n_2 = n$, $\varepsilon_1 = \varepsilon_2 = \varepsilon$ and it is given by the formula

$$D_E(n + \varepsilon) = \sum_{l=0}^{N} \sum_{i=0}^{N} K_x(l, i) w(n + \varepsilon, l) w(n + \varepsilon, i)$$

$$- 2 \sum_{l=0}^{N} K_{xh}(l, n + \varepsilon) w(n + \varepsilon, l) + D_h(n + \varepsilon). \qquad (5.27)$$

If the centralized random functions $\overset{0}{G}$ and $\overset{0}{Z}$ are stationary and stationarily connected and if the sampled-data system is also stationary (if the continuous equivalent part of the sampled-data system is stationary), then the expressions for the correlation function (5.26) and the variance (5.27) of the error take the simpler forms (remember that we are always assuming that $\varepsilon_1 = \varepsilon_2 = \varepsilon$)

$$K_E(m + \varepsilon) = M[\overset{0}{E}(n_1 + \varepsilon) \overset{0}{E}(n_2 + \varepsilon)]$$

$$= M\left\{ \left[\sum_{i=0}^{N} \overset{0}{X}(n_1 - l) w(l + \varepsilon) - H(n_1 + \varepsilon) \right] \right.$$

$$\left. \times \left[\sum_{l=0}^{N} \overset{0}{X}(n_2 - i) w(l + \varepsilon) - H(n_2 + \varepsilon) \right] \right\}$$

$$= \sum_{l=0}^{N} \sum_{i=0}^{N} K_x(m + l - i) w(l + \varepsilon) w(i + \varepsilon)$$

$$- \sum_{l=0}^{N} K_{xh}(m + l + \varepsilon) w(l + \varepsilon)$$

$$- \sum_{i=0}^{N} K_{xh}(m - i - \varepsilon) w(i + \varepsilon) + K_h(m). \qquad (5.28)$$

where $m = n_2 - n_1$.

In this case, the variance in the error is determined from the following simple formula, which is convenient for calculations:

$$D_E(\varepsilon) = \sum_{l=0}^{N} \sum_{i=0}^{N} K_x(l-i)w(l+\varepsilon)w(i+\varepsilon)$$

$$- 2 \sum_{l=0}^{N} K_{xh}(l+\varepsilon)w(l+\varepsilon) + D_h. \tag{5.29}$$

The mathematical expectation of the error of a stationary system can be determined from formula (5.25) or from the formula

$$m_E(n+\varepsilon) = \sum_{i=0}^{N} m_x(n-i)w(i+\varepsilon) - m_n(n+\varepsilon). \tag{5.30}$$

which is determined from (5.25) by making the substitution $n + \varepsilon - l = i + \varepsilon$ and using the property of the weight function of a stationary system

$$w = w(n+\varepsilon, l) = w(n+\varepsilon-l).$$

In this case, the mean square error is determined from the formula

$$\Gamma_E(n+\varepsilon) = m_E^2(n+\varepsilon) + D_E(\varepsilon)$$

$$= \left[\sum_{i=0}^{N} m_x(n-i)w(i+\varepsilon) - m_h(n+\varepsilon) \right]^2$$

$$+ \sum_{l=0}^{N} \sum_{i=0}^{N} K_x(l-i)w(l+\varepsilon)w(i+\varepsilon)$$

$$- \sum_{i=0}^{N} K_{xh}(l+\varepsilon)w(l+\varepsilon) - \sum_{i=0}^{N} K_{xh}(i+\varepsilon)w(i+\varepsilon) + D_h. \tag{5.31}$$

Let us study in greater detail the methods of calculating the second component of the mean square error, that is, the variance of the error of the system.

Let us look at the case (frequently encountered) when the useful signal $G(n+\varepsilon)$ can be represented in the form of a sum

$$G(n+\varepsilon) = G_1(n+\varepsilon) + G_2(n+\varepsilon), \tag{5.32}$$

where $G_1(n+\varepsilon)$ is a polynomial in the time:

$$G_1(n-l+\varepsilon) = G_1(n+\varepsilon) - \dot{G}_1(n+\varepsilon)l + \frac{1}{2!}\ddot{G}_1(n+\varepsilon)l^2$$

$$- \cdots + G_1^{(r)}(n+\varepsilon)\frac{(-l)^r}{r!}, \tag{5.33}$$

and $G_2(n+\varepsilon)$ is a stationary random function.

Let us also assume that the noise $Z(n+\varepsilon)$ can also be represented as a sum of the form

$$Z(n+\varepsilon) = Z_1(n+\varepsilon) + Z_2(n+\varepsilon), \tag{5.34}$$

where $Z_1(n + \varepsilon)$ is a polynomial in the time:

$$Z_1(n - l + \varepsilon) = Z_1(n + \varepsilon) - \dot{Z}_1(n + \varepsilon)l + \ddot{Z}_1(n + \varepsilon)\frac{l^2}{2!}$$

$$- \cdots + Z_1^{(r)}(n + \varepsilon)\frac{(-l)^r}{r!}, \qquad (5.35)$$

and $Z_2(n + \varepsilon)$ is a stationary random function.

To simplify our notation, let us suppose that $G_1, G_2, Z_1,$ and Z_2 are mutually uncorrelated.

Let us determine the variance of the error of the stationary system by using formula (5.29), keeping (5.32) through (5.35) in mind, and assuming that the desired output variable H can be represented in the form

$$H(n + \varepsilon) = C_0 G(n + \varepsilon) + C_1 \dot{G}(n + \varepsilon) + \cdots + C_s G^{(s)}(n + \varepsilon) + \cdots \qquad (5.36)$$

In this case, the variance in the error of the system can be represented as follows:

$$D_E(n + \varepsilon)$$

$$= \sum_{l=0}^{N} \sum_{i=0}^{N} \left[\sum_{k=0}^{r} \sum_{j=0}^{r} \frac{(-l)^k(-i)^j}{k!\,j!} (\mu_{gkj} + \mu_{zkj}) \right] w(l + \varepsilon) w(i + \varepsilon)$$

$$+ \sum_{l=0}^{N} \sum_{i=0}^{N} [K_{g_2}(l - i) + K_{z_2}(l - i)] w(l + \varepsilon) w(i + \varepsilon)$$

$$- 2 \sum_{l=0}^{N} \left[\sum_{k=0}^{r} \sum_{j=0}^{r} \frac{(-l)^k C_j}{k!} \mu'_{gkj} \right] w(l + \varepsilon)$$

$$+ \sum_{k=0}^{r} \sum_{j=0}^{r} C_k C_j \mu''_{gkj} + D_{h_2}(\varepsilon),$$

where

$$\mu_{gkj} = M[\overset{0}{G_1^{(k)}}(n)\overset{0}{G_1^{(j)}}(n)],$$

$$\mu_{zkj} = M[\overset{0}{Z_1^{(k)}}(n)\overset{0}{Z_1^{(j)}}(n)],$$

$$\mu'_{gkj} = M[\overset{0}{G_1^{(k)}}(n + \varepsilon)\overset{0}{G_1^{(j)}}(n)],$$

$$\mu''_{gkj} = M[\overset{0}{G_1^{(k)}}(n + \varepsilon)\overset{0}{G_1^{(j)}}(n + \varepsilon)];$$

$$H_2(n + \varepsilon) = L\{G_2(n + \varepsilon)\}.$$

As we know, the expression

$$\mu_i = \sum_{j=0}^{N} l^i \omega(n + \varepsilon) \qquad (5.38)$$

is the ith-order moment of the weight function of the sampled-data system. When we use notation, we can rewrite formula (5.37) in another form:

$$D_E(n + \varepsilon) = \sum_{k=0}^{r} \sum_{j=0}^{r} \frac{(-1)^{k+j}}{k_j!} (\mu_{gkj} + \mu_{zkj}) \mu_k \mu_j$$

$$+ \sum_{l=0}^{N} \sum_{i=0}^{N} [K_{gz}(l - i) + K_{z_2}(l - i)] w(l + \varepsilon) w(i + \varepsilon)$$

$$- 2 \sum_{k=0}^{r} \sum_{j=0}^{r} \frac{(-1)^k}{k!} C_j \mu'_{gkj} \mu_k + \sum_{k=0}^{r} \sum_{j=0}^{r} C_k C_j \mu''_{gkj} + D_h(\varepsilon).$$

$$(5.37a)$$

In the particular case in which $G_2(n+\varepsilon) \equiv 0$, $Z_1(n+\varepsilon) \equiv 0$, and $\mu_{gkj} = 0$ for $k \neq j$, the formula for the variance of the error of the sampled-data system assumes the form

$$D_E(n + \varepsilon) = \sum_{k=0}^{r} \left[\frac{(-1)^k}{k!} \mu_k - C_k \right]^2 \mu_{kk}$$

$$+ \sum_{l=0}^{N} \sum_{i=0}^{N} K_z(l - i) w(l + \varepsilon) w(l + \varepsilon). \qquad (5.39)$$

The moments of the weight function μ_k are easily determined if we know the transfer function of the sampled-data system [Refs. 14, 39]. The formulas that we have obtained are analogous to the corresponding formulas for determining the probabilistic characteristic of the error of a linear continuous system. Other formulas can be obtained by an analogous procedure.

18. DETERMINATION OF THE OPTIMAL SAMPLED-DATA SYSTEM THAT ENSURES A MINIMUM MEAN SQUARE ERROR

In the present section, we shall consider several statements of problems of determining an optimal sampled-data system. Throughout, we shall take as our criterion the mean square error of the system. The material of the section is necessary for an exposition of the procedure for choosing an optimal sampled-data system with respect to more complicated criteria.

1. Determination of an optimal sampled-data system minimizing the variance of the error for given coefficients of the error and given duration of the transition process

In studying sampled-data systems, just as in studying continuous systems, there are various possible statements of problems of determining optimal systems. These problems differ from each other by the criterion for comparing two systems, the class of admissible systems, and the initial data on the influences. In the present subsection, we take as our criterion the variance for given coefficients of error of the system. This criterion is not always closely connected with the purpose of the system but its use is sometimes expedient. For small values of the coefficients of error, it usually enables us to choose a system close to the optimal one with respect to the probability that the error will not exceed given allowed limits. The minimum-variance criterion is the simplest of the probabilistic criteria. The choice of optimal system with respect to this criterion is the simplest problem. The procedure of choosing the optimal system with respect to minimum variance of error for given coefficients of error can be used to carry out one stage of the solution of the problem of choosing the optimal system with respect to more complicated criteria.

Let us formulate a statement of the problem. Suppose that the block diagram of the system has the form shown in Figure 5.1. A random function $X(n + \varepsilon)$, which is the sum of a useful signal $G(n + \varepsilon)$ and a noise $Z(n + \varepsilon)$, is applied to the input of the system. The useful signal is a polynomial in time (cf. (5.33)) with given coefficients, and the noise is a centralized stationary random function with correlation function $K_{z(m)}$, where $m = n_2 - n_1$, and where in turn n_2 and n_1 are the instants at which the value of the correlation function K_z is being considered. The desired output variable of the system $H(n + \varepsilon)$ is the result of a linear transformation of the useful signal $G(n + \varepsilon)$ and can be expressed by formula (5.36). The coefficients C_i are known. For example, if $H(n + \varepsilon) = G(n + \varepsilon)$, then $C_0 = 1, C_1 = \varepsilon, \cdots, C_k = \varepsilon^k/k!$. If $H(n + \varepsilon) = G(n + \varepsilon + n_e)$, then $C_0 = 1, C_1 = n_e + \varepsilon, \cdots, C_i = (n_e + \varepsilon)^{i}/i!$.

The class of admissible sampled-data systems on which the optimal system is determined consists of all linear sampled-data systems for which the duration of the transition process is N and the coefficients of the errors are $D_0, D_1 \cdots, D_r$. The coefficients of the error are expressed in terms of the initial conditions as follows:

$$D_s = \frac{(-1)^s \mu_s}{s!} - C_{s'}, \quad s = 0, 1, \cdots, r, \tag{5.40}$$

where

$$\mu_s = \sum_{s=0}^{N} l^s \omega (l + \varepsilon)$$

is the sth-order moment of the weight function of the sampled-data system.

If the coefficients of the error are small, then the component of the error that depends on the useful signal $G(n + \varepsilon)$ is also small. Occasionally, it is expedient for some reason or other to require that this component of the error be bounded. We can arrange for this to be the case by supplying the coefficients of the error D_s. In the special case in which the coefficients of the error are equal to 0, that is, when $D_s = 0$ for $s = 0, 1, \cdots, r$, the component of the error due to the useful signal is equal to 0. In this case, the variance in the error coincides with the mean square error, since the mathematical expectation due to the useful signal $G(n + \varepsilon)$ is then 0.

The variance in the error of the system is determined in this case by formula (5.39), where $\mu_{gkk} = 0$ for $k = 0, 1, \cdots, r$. Consequently, we may write

$$D_E(\varepsilon) = \sum_{l=0}^{N} \sum_{i=0}^{N} K_z(l - i) w(l + \varepsilon) w(i + \varepsilon). \qquad (5.41)$$

We need to determine the weight function $w_0(l + \varepsilon)$ that minimizes the variance D_E under conditions (5.40). This is a typical problem involving a conditional extremum. The variance $D_E(\varepsilon)$ is by its nature a function of $N + 1$ values of the weight function $w(\varepsilon), w(1 + \varepsilon), \cdots, w(n + \varepsilon)$. We need to determine the minimum of this function of $N + 1$ variables under conditions (5.40). As we know, finding such a conditional minimum reduces to the problem of finding the unconditional minimum of the function I:

$$I(\varepsilon) = D_E + 2 \sum_{s=0}^{r} \gamma_s \mu_s = \sum_{l=0}^{N} \sum_{i=0}^{N} K_z(l - i) w(l + \varepsilon) w(i + \varepsilon)$$

$$+ 2 \sum_{s=0}^{r} \gamma_s \left[\sum_{s=0}^{N} l^s w(l + \varepsilon) \right], \qquad (5.42)$$

where the undetermined multipliers γ_s can be determined from conditions (5.40).

The extremum of the function (5.42) can be found by the usual method of finding an extremum of a function of several variables, as expounded in mathematical analysis courses. However, for fixed ε, the quantity I can also be regarded as a functional of the function $w(l + \varepsilon)$ defined on a finite set of values of the argument $l + \varepsilon$. To begin with, let us use just this interpretation of the quantity I in order to obtain a procedure completely analogous to the procedure expounded in the preceding chapters. Specifically, the functional (5.42) is analogous to the functional (3.52). The only difference is that the integration over an infinite set of values of the continuous argument t is replaced with summation over a finite set of values of the argument $n + \varepsilon$.

To find a minimum of the functional I (for a fixed value of ε), we use (1.140b), since the functional (5.42) is a special case of the functional (1.139). In the present case, the integrand Φ (or the function under the summation sign) is of the form

$$K_z(l - i)w(l + \varepsilon)w(i + \varepsilon) + \frac{1}{N+1}\sum_{s=0}^{r}\gamma_s([l^s w(l + \varepsilon) + i^s w(i + \varepsilon)].$$

Use of formula (1.140b) enables us in this case to write the equation

$$\sum_{i=0}^{N} K_z(l - i)\omega_0(i + \varepsilon) + \sum_{s=0}^{r}\gamma_s l^s = 0, \quad 0 \leqslant l \leqslant N. \qquad \textbf{(5.43)}$$

This equation is analogous to equation (3.53). Its satisfaction is a necessary condition for the weight function $w_0(n + \varepsilon)$ to minimize the functional I. It is essentially a system of $N + 1$ equations for determining the $N + 1$ unknowns $w(i + \varepsilon)$, for $i = 0, 1, \cdots, N$. Equations (5.43) are all linear algebraic equations in $w_0(i + \varepsilon)$. A solution of this system, however obtained, is a linear function of the parameters $\gamma_0, \gamma_1, \cdots, \gamma_r$. When we substitute the function

$$w_0(l + \varepsilon, \gamma_0, \gamma_1, \cdots, \gamma_r)$$

into condition (5.40), we obtain $r + 1$ linear algebraic equations in the unknowns γ_i:

$$\sum_{l=0}^{N} l^s w_0(l + \varepsilon, \gamma_0, \gamma_1, \cdots, \gamma_r) = s!(-1)^s(D_s + C_s),$$

$$s = 0, 1, \cdots, r. \qquad \textbf{(5.44)}$$

Thus, the problem of finding the optimal weight function w_0 reduces in this case to solving a system of $N + r + 2$ linear algebraic equations.

We have stated that condition (5.43) is necessary for minimization of the functional I. Let us show that it is also sufficient. To do this, we obtain an expression for the functional $I\{w_0 + v\}$, where v is an arbitrary weight function in the class of admissible weight functions.

$$I\{w_0 + v\}$$

$$= \sum_{l=0}^{N}\sum_{i=0}^{N} K_z(l - i)[w_0(l + \varepsilon) + v(l + \varepsilon)][w_0(i + \varepsilon) + v(i + \varepsilon)]$$

$$+ 2\sum_{s=0}^{r}\gamma_s\left\{\sum_{l=0}^{N} l^s[w_0(l + \varepsilon) + v(l + \varepsilon)]\right\} = I\{w_0\}$$

$$+ 2\sum_{l=0}^{N} v(l + \varepsilon)\left[\sum_{i=0}^{N} K_z(l - i)w_0(i + \varepsilon) + \sum_{s=0}^{r}\gamma_s l^s\right]$$

$$+ \sum_{i=0}^{N}\sum_{i=0}^{N} K_z(l - i)v(l + \varepsilon)v(i + \varepsilon). \qquad \textbf{(5.45)}$$

From (5.43) and (5.45), we get the following relationship between $I\{w_0 + v\}$ and $I\{w_0\}$:

$$I\{w_0 + v\} = I\{w_0\} + D_z.$$

Here, the quantity

$$D_2 = \sum_{l=0}^{N} \sum_{i=0}^{N} K_z(l - i)v(l + \varepsilon)v(i + \varepsilon)$$

is always nonnegative. One can easily see this, since D_2 is the variance of the output variable of the system with weight function $v(n + \varepsilon)$ at the input of which the random function $Z(n + \varepsilon)$ is applied. Thus, we have proved the inequality

$$I\{w_0 + v\} \geqslant I\{w_0\}$$

for an arbitrary admissible weight function $v(n +\varepsilon)$. This completes the proof of the sufficiency of condition (5.43).

Let us determine the minimum variance $D_{E\,min}$ of the error corresponding to the optimal weight function $w_0(n + \varepsilon, \gamma_{00}, \gamma_{10}, \cdots \gamma_{r0})$. To do this, we substitute the relations

$$\sum_{i=0}^{N} K_z(l - i)w_0(i + \varepsilon, \gamma_{00}, \gamma_{10}, \gamma_{r0}) = -\sum_{s=0}^{r} \gamma_s l^s;$$

obtained from equations (5.43) into equation (5.41). We obtain

$$D_E\{w_0\} = D_{E\,min} = -\sum_{s=0}^{r} \gamma_s \sum_{l=0}^{N} l^s w_0(l + \varepsilon, \gamma_{00}, \gamma_{10}, \cdots, \gamma_{r0}).$$

Substituting (5.44) into this formula, we obtain

$$D_{E\,min} = -\sum_{s=0}^{r} \gamma_s(-1)^s s!(D_s + C_s). \tag{5.46}$$

EXAMPLE. Suppose that the signal that is the sum of a useful signal and a noise is applied to the input of a reproducing sampled-data system. The useful signal is a second-degree polynomial in time. The noise is a stationary random function with correlation function

$$K_z(m, \varepsilon) = \begin{cases} K_0^2 & \text{for } m = 0, \\ 0 & \text{for } m \neq 0. \end{cases}$$

The problem is to find the weight function of a sampled-data system for which the duration of the transition process is equal to two periods of alternation ($N = 2$) and which minimizes the variance of the output variable for the following values of the coefficients of error: $D_0 = D_1 = D_2 = 0$. An exact reproduction of the useful signal is required.

In the present example, $H(n + \varepsilon) = G(n + \varepsilon)$. Consequently, $C_0 = 1$, $C_1 = \varepsilon$, and $C_2 = \varepsilon^2/2$. The variance coincides with the mean square error (the mathematical expectation is 0).

We begin our solution by setting up equations (5.43). In the present case, these equations are

$$K_0^2 w_0(0 + \varepsilon) + \gamma_0 = 0,$$
$$K_0^2 w_0(1 + \varepsilon) + \gamma_0 + \gamma_1 + \gamma_2 = 0,$$
$$K_0^2 w_0(2 + \varepsilon) + \gamma_0 + 2\gamma_1 + 4\gamma_2 = 0.$$

This system of three linear algebraic equations in three unknowns is easily solved:

$$w_0(0 + \varepsilon) = - \frac{\gamma_0}{K_0^2},$$

$$w_0(1 + \varepsilon) = - \frac{\gamma_0 + \gamma_1 + \gamma_2}{K_2^0},$$

$$w_0(2 + \varepsilon) = - \frac{\gamma_0 + 2\gamma_1 + 4\gamma_2}{K_0^2}.$$

Thus, we have expressions for the optimal weight function in terms of the undetermined multipliers γ_0, γ_1, and γ_2. As one can see, these values of the weight function w_0 depend on γ_0, γ_1, and γ_2 linearly. Let us substitute the values for $w_0(0 + \varepsilon)$, $w_0(1 + \varepsilon)$, and $w_0(2 + \varepsilon)$ into (5.44), remembering that $D_0 = D_1 = D_2 = 0$, $C_0 = 1$, $C_1 = \varepsilon$, and $C_2 = \varepsilon^2/2$. We obtain

$$\frac{\gamma_0}{K_0^2} - \frac{\gamma_0 + \gamma_1 + \gamma_2}{K_0^2} - \frac{\gamma_0 + 2\gamma_1 + 4\gamma_2}{K_0^2} = 1,$$

$$\frac{\gamma_0 + \gamma_1 + \gamma_2}{K_0^2} - 2\frac{\gamma_0 + 2\gamma_1 + 4\gamma_2}{K_0^2} = -\varepsilon,$$

$$\frac{\gamma_0 + \gamma_1 + \gamma_2}{K_0^2} - 4\frac{\gamma_0 + 2\gamma_1 + 4\gamma_2}{K_0^2} = \varepsilon^2.$$

The solution of this system of linear algebraic equations may be written as

$$\gamma_{00} = - (1.0 + 1.5\varepsilon + \varepsilon^2) K_0^2,$$
$$\gamma_{10} = (1.5 + 6.5\varepsilon + 6.0\varepsilon^2) K_0^2,$$
$$\gamma_{20} = - (0.5 + 3.0\varepsilon + 3.0\varepsilon^2) K_0^2.$$

When we substitute the values of the factors γ_{00}, γ_{10}, and γ_{20} into the weight function, we obtain (see Fig. 5.2)

$$w_0(0 + \varepsilon) = 1.0 + 1.5\varepsilon + \varepsilon^2,$$
$$w_0(1 + \varepsilon) = - 2\varepsilon - 2\varepsilon^2,$$
$$w_0(2 + \varepsilon) = 0.5\varepsilon + \varepsilon^2,$$
$$\cdots \cdots \cdots \cdots \cdots \cdots$$
$$w_0(n + \varepsilon) = 0 \quad \text{for} \quad n > 2.$$

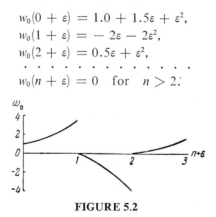

FIGURE 5.2

We determine the variance of the error of the optimal system from formula (5.46):

$$D_{E \min} = [(1.0 + 1.5\varepsilon + \varepsilon^2) + (1.5 + 6.5\varepsilon + 6.0\varepsilon^2)\varepsilon$$
$$+ 2(0.5 + 3.0\varepsilon + 3.0\varepsilon^2)\varepsilon^2]K_0^2$$
$$= (1.0 + 3\varepsilon + 8.5\varepsilon^2 + 12\varepsilon^3 + 6\varepsilon^4)K_0^2.$$

All the above derivations were based on the interpretation of the quantities D_E and I as functionals of the weight function w of a sample-data system. Let us derive the basic equation (5.43) that interprets these two quantities as functions of the $N + 1$ variables $w(0 + \varepsilon)$, $w(1 + \varepsilon), \cdots, w(N + \varepsilon)$. Thus, let us look at $D_E(\varepsilon)$ and $I = I(\varepsilon)$ as functions of $w(0 + \varepsilon)$, $w(1 + \varepsilon), \cdots, w(N + \varepsilon)$. We need to find a combination of the variables $w_0(0 + \varepsilon)$, $w_0(1 + \varepsilon), \cdots, w_0(N + \varepsilon)$ corresponding to the minimum of the variance $D_E(\varepsilon)$ under condition (5.40). As we know, the problem of finding the minimum of the function D_E of several variables under condition (5.40) reduces to the problem of finding an extremum of the function I, which is the sum

$$D_E + 2\sum_{s=0}^{r} \gamma_s \mu_s$$

(cf. (5.42)).

Let us find the necessary conditions for an extremum of the function I of several variables. To do this, we need to set the partial derivatives of I with respect to the variables $w(v + \varepsilon)$, for $v = 0, 1, \cdots, N$, equal to 0. The partial derivative of

$$2\sum_{s=0}^{r} \gamma_s \left[\sum_{l=0}^{N} l^s w(l + \varepsilon) \right]$$

with respect to $w(v + \varepsilon)$ is easily found. It is

$$2\sum_{s=0}^{r} \gamma_s v^s. \tag{a}$$

Let us find the partial derivative of the double summation

$$\sum_{l=0}^{N} \sum_{i=0}^{N} K_z(l - i)w(l + \varepsilon)w(i + \varepsilon)$$

with respect to $w(v + \varepsilon)$ for $0 \le v \le N$. To do this, let us consider only those terms in the double summation that contain at least one factor of the form $w(v + \varepsilon)$:

$$K_z(0)w(v + \varepsilon)w(v + \varepsilon) + \sum_{i \ne v} K_z(v - i)w(v + \varepsilon)w(i + \varepsilon)$$
$$+ \sum_{l \ne v} K_z(l - v)w(l + \varepsilon)w(v + \varepsilon).$$

In the first sum, the index i ranges over all integral values from 0 to N

with the exception of v; in the second summation, the index l ranges over all values from 0 to N with the exception of v. The second summation is equal to the first one and hence we can write the sum of terms containing at least one factor of the form $w(v + \varepsilon)$ as follows:

$$K_z(0)w(v + \varepsilon)w(v + \varepsilon) + 2 \sum_{i \neq v} K_z(v - i)w(v + \varepsilon)w(i + \varepsilon).$$

The derivative of this sum with respect to $w(v + \varepsilon)$ is equal to

$$2K_z(0)w(v + \varepsilon) + 2 \sum_{i \neq v} K_z(v - i)w(i + \varepsilon)$$

$$= 2 \sum_{i=0}^{N} K_z(v - i)w(i + \varepsilon). \qquad \text{(b)}$$

Thus, the partial derivative of the function I with respect to $w(v + \varepsilon)$ is equal to (a) + (b). This means that

$$2 \sum_{i=0}^{N} K_z(v - i)w(i + \varepsilon) + 2 \sum_{s=0}^{r} r_s v^s = 0, \quad v = 0, 1, \cdots, N.$$

We have obtained the necessary conditions (5.43) by a different procedure. Sometimes, such an approach to the problem of determining an optimal sampled-data system can be fruitful and convenient.

Let us pause briefly to look at the question as to what considerations might influence our choice of the quantities r_s, N, D_0, D_1, $\cdots$, D_r, which constitute the initial data for determining the optimal weight function of a sampled-data system. In choosing the degree of the polynomial r, we need to keep the following in mind: Ordinarily, the polynomial $G(t)$ is an approximate representation of the useful signal. The lower the degree r of this polynomial, the simpler will be the procedure for determining the optimal weight function of the system (that is, the fewer equations there will be in the system (5.44)). However, the greater the degree r of the polynomial $G(t)$, the more accurate will the approximate representation of the useful signal be. In practice, we need to choose the number r so that the polynomial $G(t)$ reproduces in an essentially accurate way the useful signal.

The duration of the transition process of the optimal sampled-data system, which we denote by N, is also determined by contradictory considerations. On the one hand, it is desirable to have N as great as possible because the greater the value of N the less will be the variance provided by the optimal system. However, increasing N is not always possible, since for large N the representation of the useful signal as a polynomial of degree r becomes unacceptable (the greater the value of N, the greater must be the degree of the polynomial r for the same accuracy of approximation). The value of N needs to be restricted for another, no less important, reason. The duration of the transition process N is itself an important characteristic of the quality of the system. Usually, it is desirable for N to be small. Consequently, even in choosing N, we run into a situation where for one reason it is desirable to have N as large as possible and for another reason it is desirable to have it as small as possible. Apart from these considerations, it is necessary when choosing N to keep in mind that the duration of the transition process of a sampled-data system must be no less than the number of derivatives of the useful signal G that we are considering; that is, we need to have $N > r$. This is explained by the fact that, for operation of the system with r derivatives of the useful signal taken into account, the system must determine the first r finite differences of the signal. For this, we need to consider no fewer than $r + 1$ values of the input variable that correspond to discrete instants of time preceding the current instant. This last consideration is possible provided $N \geqslant r$. The most suitable duration of the transition process of an optimal sampled-data system can be chosen only when we take all these factors into consideration.

The values of the coefficients of the error $D_0, D_1, \cdots, D_r$ are sometimes taken equal to 0. This is the most expedient procedure if, for example, $G(n), \dot{G}(n), \cdots, G^{(r)}(n)$ are very great or if they are unknown but may assume very high values. In other words, it is expedient to take the coefficients of error equal to 0 if the coefficients in the polynomial $G(n)$ either are very great or may assume very high values. On the other hand, if any of the coefficients in this polynomial are bounded, it is difficult to set the values of the coefficients of the error intelligently. Therefore, we must consider that fixing the coefficients of the error of the system is a weak spot in determining the class of admissible weight functions in the case being considered. We cannot always intelligently set the values of these coefficients in advance. Therefore, another formulation of the problem of determining the optimal-data system is expedient. In this formulation of the problem, we state certain coefficients of error, and the other coefficients of error are determined in the process of finding the optimal system.

Special cases in this formulation of the problem are (a) the case in which all the coefficients of the error are given, and (b) the case in which none of these coefficients are given.

2. Determination of the optimal sampled-data system minimizing the mean square error for given time N of the transition process of the system

Let us consider the following formulation of the problem. Suppose that the block diagram of the system corresponds to Figure 5.1. The input signal $X(n + \varepsilon)$ is the sum of a useful signal $G(n + \varepsilon)$ and a noise $Z(n + \varepsilon)$. The useful signal is an rth-degree polynomial in time and the noise is a stationary random function with mathematical expectation equal to 0. In the general case, the coefficients of the polynomial $G(n+\varepsilon)$ are random variables with nonzero mathematical expectations. The desired output variables $H(n + \varepsilon)$ can be represented in the form (5.36). The coefficients of error of the system $D_0 = \cdots = D_{r-1} = 0$. No restrictions are imposed on the coefficient of error D_r.

We need to determine the optimal weight function of a sampled-data system minimizing the mean square error. In this case, the mathematical expectation of the error is

$$m_E = \left[\frac{(-1)^r}{r!}\mu_r - C_r\right]M[G^{(r)}] = \left[\frac{(-1)^r}{r!}\mu_r - C_r\right]r!\, m_{g_r}, \qquad (5.47)$$

where

$$\mu_r = \sum_{l=0}^{N} l^r w(l + \varepsilon)$$

is the rth-order moment of the weight function of the sampled-data system,

$$r!\, m_{g_r} = M[G^{(r)}]$$

is the mathematical expectation of the rth-derivative of the useful signal with respect to time, and m_{g_r} is the mathematical expectation of the coefficient of the leading term of the polynomial $G(n + \varepsilon)$. The variance in the error of the system is determined in accordance with formula (5.39):

$$D_E = \left[\frac{(-1)^r}{r!}\mu_r - C_r\right]^2 (r!)^2 D_{g_r}$$

$$+ \sum_{l=0}^{N}\sum_{i=0}^{N} K_z(l - i)w(l + \varepsilon)w(i + \varepsilon), \qquad (5.48)$$

where $(r!)^2 D_{g_r}$ is the variance of the rth derivative of the useful signal with respect to time, D_{g_r} is the variance of the coefficient of the leading term of the polynomial $G(n + \varepsilon)$, and $K_z(m)$ is the correlation function of the noise. When we write formulas (5.47) and (5.48), we keep in mind the fact that the first r coefficients of the error are equal to 0.

The mean square error of the system is equal to the sum of the square of the mathematical expectation and the variance of the error:

$$\Gamma_E = \left[\frac{(-1)^r}{r!}\mu_r - C_r\right]^2 (r!\, m_{g_r})^2 + \left[\frac{(-1)^r}{r!}\mu_r - C_r\right]^2 (r!) D_{g_r}$$

$$+ \sum_{l=0}^{N}\sum_{i=0}^{N} K_z(l - i)w(l + \varepsilon)w(i + \varepsilon). \qquad (5.48a)$$

We need to determine the minimum of the mean square error (5.48a) under the conditions

$$\frac{(-1)^k}{k!}\mu_k - C_k = 0, \quad k = 0, 1, \cdots, r - 1, \tag{5.49}$$

which reflect the fact that the first r coefficients of the error are equal to 0. The problem of minimizing Γ_E under condition (5.49) reduces to the problem of finding the unconditional minimum of the functional

$$I' = \Gamma_E + 2\sum_{k=0}^{r-1}\gamma_k\mu_k = \sum_{l=0}^{N}\sum_{i=0}^{N}K_z(l-i)w(l+\varepsilon)w(i+\varepsilon)$$

$$+ \left[\frac{(-1)^r}{r!}\mu_r - C_r\right]^2 (r!)^2 m_{g_r}^2$$

$$+ \left[\frac{(-1)^r}{r!}\mu_r - C_r\right]^2 (r!)^2 D_{g_r} + 2\sum_{k=0}^{r-1}\gamma_k\mu_k. \tag{5.50}$$

The quantity I' can be regarded as a quadratic functional of the weight function $w(n + \varepsilon)$ or as a bilinear form of the values of the weight function $w(0 + \varepsilon), w(1 + \varepsilon), \cdots, w(N + \varepsilon)$. The functional (respectively function) (5.50) does not differ in principle from the functional (respectively function) (5.42). The minimum of this functional can be found, for example, by the method of fastest descent. By using the methods expounded in the preceding subsection, we can obtain a system of linear algebraic equations defining the optimum weight function of the sampled-data system:

$$\sum_{i=0}^{N}[K_z(l-i) + (m_{g_r}^2 + D_{g_r})l^r i^r]w_0(i+\varepsilon)$$

$$+ \sum_{k=0}^{r-1}\gamma_k l^k - (-1)^r r!(m_{g_r}^2 + D_{g_r})C_r l^r = 0, \quad l = 0, 1, \cdots, N. \tag{5.51}$$

The $N + 1$ equations (5.51) enable us to determine $w_0(0 + \varepsilon), w_0(1 + \varepsilon), \cdots, w_0(N + \varepsilon)$ as functions of the unknown parameters $\gamma_0, \gamma_1, \cdots, \gamma_{r-1}$. To determine these parameters, we can use equations (5.49). All these equations are linear in the unknowns. The sufficiency of condition (5.51) for minimization of (5.50) can be proved in the same way as the sufficiency of condition (5.43) was proved for minimization of (5.42).

We obtain a formula for minimizing the mean square error $\Gamma_{E\,min}$ corresponding to the minimal weight function $w_0(n + \varepsilon)$. To do this, we substitute the expression

$$\sum_{l=0}^{N}[K_z(l-i) + (m_{g_r}^2 + D_{g_r})l^r i^r]w_0(i+\varepsilon)$$

$$= -\sum_{k=0}^{r-1}\gamma_k l^k + (-1)^r r!(m_{g_r}^2 + D_{g_r})C_r l^r, \quad l = 0, 1 \cdots, N,$$

obtained from (5.51) into (5.50). As a result, we obtain

$$\Gamma_{E\min} = (-1)^r r! (m_{g_r}^2 + D_{g_r}) C_r \mu_r - \sum_{k=0}^{r-1} \gamma_k \gamma_k, \qquad (5.52)$$

where

$$\mu_k = \sum_{k=0}^{k} l^k w_0 (l + \varepsilon)$$

for $k = 0, 1, \cdots, r$, are the moments of the weight function that are calculated for the optimal weight function, and where the γ_k, for $k = 0, 1, \cdots, r - 1$ are the parameters determined from conditions (5.49).

In an analogous manner, we can consider other formulations of problems of determining the optimal weight function of a sampled-data system minimizing the mean square error. In cases in which the system and the initial data regarding the influences on it are nonstationary, the mean square error depends not only on ε, but also on n. In such cases, the optimal weight function depends on the two variables $n + \varepsilon$ and l. The systems of equations determining the optimal nonstationary weight function are essentially the same. However, the problem of obtaining the solution of these equations is usually more complicated. In this case, we need to obtain the solution for several instants $n + \varepsilon$ (for various values of n). The methods previously expounded enable us to solve analogous problems for the determination of optimal sampled-data linear systems under given initial conditions on the influences and on the class of admissible systems.

EXAMPLE. The block diagram of the system is shown in Figure 5.1. The useful signal is a second-degree polynomial in time:

$$G(n + \varepsilon) = G_0 + G_1 (n + \varepsilon) G_2 (n + \varepsilon)^2,$$

where the coefficients G_0 and G_1 may assume very large values. The coefficient G_2 is a random variable with given second-order initial moment

$$\mu_2 = m_{g_r}^2 + D_{g_r}.$$

The noise is a stationary random function with mathematical expectation equal to 0 and with correlation function of the form

$$K_z(m) = \begin{cases} K_0^2 & \text{for } m = 0, \\ 0 & \text{for } m \neq 0. \end{cases}$$

We assume that $M[ZG_2] = 0$. The desired output variable $H(n + \varepsilon)$ is equal to the useful signal $G(n + \varepsilon)$; that is, it is a reproducing system. In this case, as we know, $C_0 = 1$, $C_1 = \varepsilon$, and $C_2 = \varepsilon^2/2$. We consider systems with coefficients of error $D_0 = D_1 = 0$ admissible.

We are required to determine the weight function of the sampled-data system minimizing the mean square error under these initial conditions. To do this, we write the system of equations (5.51), taking into account the specific initial conditions in the following manner:

$$K_0^2 w_0(0 + \varepsilon) + \gamma_0 = 0,$$
$$K_0^2 w_0(1 + \varepsilon) + \gamma_0 + \gamma_1 - \varepsilon(\varepsilon + 1)\mu_2 = 0,$$
$$K_0^2 w_0(2 + \varepsilon) + 4\mu_2[w_0(0 + \varepsilon) + w_0(1 + \varepsilon) + 4w_0(2 + \varepsilon)$$
$$+ \gamma_0 + 2\gamma_1 - 4\varepsilon^2\mu_2 = 0.$$

This system of equations enables us to determine the desired values of the optimal weight function:

$$
\left.
\begin{aligned}
& w_0(0 + \varepsilon) = -\frac{\gamma_0}{K_0^2}, \\[2mm]
& w_0(1 + \varepsilon) = \frac{-\gamma_0 - \gamma_1 + \varepsilon(1 + \varepsilon)\mu_2}{K_0^2}, \\[2mm]
& w_0(2 + \varepsilon) \\
& \quad = \frac{(8\mu_2 - K_0^2)\gamma_0 + 2(2\mu_2 - K_0^2)\gamma_1 + 4\varepsilon[\varepsilon K_0^2 + \mu_2(1 + \varepsilon)]\mu_2}{K_0^2(K_0^2 + 16\mu_2)}.
\end{aligned}
\right\} \quad \text{(a)}
$$

Conditions (5.49) yield two other equations for determining the parameters γ_0 and γ_1:

$$
\left.
\begin{aligned}
& -\frac{\gamma_2}{K_0^2} + \frac{\varepsilon(1 + \varepsilon)\mu - \gamma_0 - \gamma_1}{K_0^2} \\
& + \frac{(8\mu_2 - K_0^2)\gamma_0 + 2(2\mu_2 - K_0^2)\gamma_1 + 4\varepsilon[\varepsilon K_0^2 + \mu_2(1 + \varepsilon)]\mu_2}{K_0^2(K_0^2 + 16\mu_2)} = 1, \\[2mm]
& -\frac{\gamma_0}{K_0^2} + \frac{\varepsilon(1 + \varepsilon)\mu_2 - \gamma_0 - \gamma_1}{K_0^2} \\
& + 2\frac{(8\mu_2 - K_0^2)\gamma_0 + 2(2\mu_2 - K_0^2)\gamma_1 + 4\varepsilon[\varepsilon K_0^2 + \mu_2(1 + \varepsilon)]\mu_2}{K_0^2(K_0^2 + 16\mu_2)} = -\varepsilon.
\end{aligned}
\right\}
$$

$$\text{(b)}$$

The three equations (a) and the two equations (b) enable us to determine the five unknowns

$$w_0(0 + \varepsilon), \ w_0(1 + \varepsilon), \ w_0(2 + \varepsilon), \ \gamma_0, \text{ and } \gamma_1.$$

We have mentioned that the criterion of mean square error does not always reflect the purpose of the system and hence it may not be a good criterion for comparing systems. Frequently, the probability that the error of the system does not exceed given allowed limits is a more suitable criterion. In connection with this, in the following section we shall expound the method of determining the optimal sampled-data system maximizing the probability that the error of the system will not exceed given limits.

In the general case of nonstationary initial conditions, the mathematical expectation m_E and the variance D_E of the error of the system are given by formulas (5.25) and (5.27). The mean square error in this case is

$$\Gamma_E = \left[\sum_{l=0}^{N} m_x(l) w(n + \varepsilon, l) - m_h n\, (+\, \varepsilon) \right]^2$$

$$+ \sum_{l=0}^{N} \sum_{i=0}^{N} K_x(l, i) w(n + \varepsilon, l) w(n + \varepsilon, i)$$

$$- 2 \sum_{l=0}^{N} K_{xh}(l, n + \varepsilon) w(n + \varepsilon, l) + D_h(n + \varepsilon). \qquad (5.53)$$

The optimal weight function of the sampled-data system corresponds to the minimum of the mean square error determined in accordance with formula (5.53). The functional (5.53) is similar to the functionals (5.49) and (5.50) which we previously considered. In a manner analogous to the way we obtained the systems of equations (5.43) and (5.51), we can obtain a system of equations determining the optimal weight function corresponding to the minimum of the mean square error (5.53):

$$\sum_{i=0}^{N} [K_x(l, i) + m_x(l) m_x(i)] w_0(n + \varepsilon, i)$$

$$- K_{xh}(l, n + \varepsilon) - m_x(l) m_h(n + \varepsilon) = 0, \quad 0 \leqslant l = N. \qquad (5.54)$$

19. DETERMINATION OF THE OPTIMAL LINEAR SAMPLED-DATA SYSTEM THAT ENSURES THE MAXIMUM PROBABILITY THAT THE SYSTEM ERROR WILL NOT EXCEED ALLOWED LIMITS $(n = 1)$

In Chapter 4, we showed that, in many cases, the probability P that the error will not exceed allowed limits can be represented as a function of two functionals:

$$P = I = f(I_1, I_2), \qquad (5.55)$$

where $I_1 = I_1\{w\}$ and $I_2 = I_2\{w\}$ are quadratic functionals of the weight function. Examples of the functionals I_1 and I_2 are the mathematical expectation and the variance of the error of the system or the variance of different components of the error of the system that obey different distribution laws. The function f is a known function of I_1 and I_2. Examples of the function f are (4.6) and (4.10).

On the basis of Theorem 2 of Chapter 1, we conclude that the optimal weight function of the sampled-data system with respect to the criterion (5.53) must ensure an extremum of the reduced criterion

$$I_\theta = \theta I_1 + I_2 \qquad (5.56)$$

for some value of the harmonizing parameter θ. Theorem 2 was proved for weight functions of continuous systems. However, it follows from the way that Theorem 2 was proved that it also remains valid when the class of admissible systems is the class of linear sampled-data systems [Refs. 6, 7].

Determination of the weight function of a sampled-data system ensuring an extremum of the reduced functional I_θ is a considerably easier problem than that of determining an extremum of the functional (5.55).

We can use one of the methods expounded in Chapter 1 to find the necessary value of the harmonizing parameter θ.

1. Initial data of a general form

Let us write out the expanded expression for the reduced functional I_θ for the general case in which the probabilistic moments of the error of the system are determined by the relations (5.25) and (5.27).

The functionals I_1 and I_2 have analogous roles in the reduced functional (5.56). The harmonizing factor θ can be put in front of either of these functionals. For the functional I_1 (or I_2) we can take either the mathematical expectation of the error (if the probability P is determined in accordance with formula (4.46)) or the square of the mathematical expectation of the error (if the probability P is determined by formula (4.6b)). In such cases, it is convenient to take the variance of the error of the system as the functional I_2.

Thus, if we take as a criterion for comparing sampled-data systems the probability that the error will not exceed allowed limits, which is determined in accordance with formula (4.6), it is convenient to take for the reduced functional I_θ

$$I_\theta = \theta m_E + D_E = \theta \left[\sum_{l=0}^{N} m_x(l) w(n + \varepsilon, l) - m_n(n + \varepsilon) \right]$$

$$+ \sum_{l=0}^{N} \sum_{i=0}^{N} K_x(l, i) w(n + \varepsilon, l) w(n + \varepsilon, l)$$

$$- 2 \sum_{l=0}^{N} K_{xh}(l, n + \varepsilon) w(n + \varepsilon, l) + D_h(n + \varepsilon). \qquad (5.57)$$

Here, the mathematical expectation m_E and the variance D_E of the error are determined in accordance with formulas (5.25) and (5.27), which are valid in the general case when the initial data and the sampled-data system are nonstationary. In this case, the reduced functional I_θ depends on n and ε as parameters. The optimal weight function is to be found for fixed values of these parameters, that is, for a fixed value of the time $n + \varepsilon$.

If the sampled-data system and the initial data on the influences are stationary, we can use the simpler formulas (5.29) and (5.30) to determine the mathematical expectation m_E and the variance D_E. In this case, the reduced functional I_θ assumes the form

$$I_\theta = \theta m_E + D_E = \theta \left[\sum_{i=0}^{N} m_x(n - i) w(i + \varepsilon) - m_h(n + \varepsilon) \right]$$

$$+ \sum_{l=0}^{N} \sum_{i=0}^{N} K_x(l - i) w(l + \varepsilon) w(i + \varepsilon)$$

$$- 2 \sum_{l=0}^{N} K_{xh}(l + \varepsilon) w(l + \varepsilon) + D_h. \qquad (5.58)$$

Here, the mathematical expectation m_E and the variance D_E of the error depend only on ε and hence the reduced functional depends only on ε (and, of course, the harmonizing parameter θ). We seek the optimal weight function for a fixed value of ε.

If for a comparison criterion we take the probability that the error will not exceed small allowed limits, as determined by formula (4.6b), we may take for the reduced functional I_θ the functional (5.57), or the functional (5.56), or the functional

$$I_\theta = \theta m_E^2 + D_E = \theta \left[\sum_{l=0}^{N} m_x(l) w(n + \varepsilon, l) - m_h(n + \varepsilon) \right]^2$$

$$+ \sum_{l=0}^{N} \sum_{i=0}^{N} K_x(l, i) w(n + \varepsilon, l) w(n + \varepsilon, i)$$

$$- 2 \sum_{i=0}^{N} K_{xh}(l, n + \varepsilon) w(n + \varepsilon, l) + D_h(n + \varepsilon) \qquad (5.59)$$

in the case of nonstationary influences and a nonstationary system. We may take the functional

$$I_\theta = \theta m_E^2 + D_E = \theta \left[\sum_{i=0}^{N} m_x(n - i) w(i + \varepsilon) - m_h(n + \varepsilon) \right]^2$$

$$+ \sum_{l=0}^{N} \sum_{i=0}^{N} K_x(l - i) w(l + \varepsilon) w(i + \varepsilon)$$

$$- 2 \sum_{l=0}^{N} K_{xh}(l + \varepsilon) w(l + \varepsilon) + D_h \qquad (5.60)$$

in the case of stationary influences but a nonstationary system.

In this case, we can also use either of the reduced functionals (5.57) or (5.58). In accordance with the procedure previously expounded, we need to find the weight function w_0 of a sampled-data system that ensures an extremum of the corresponding functional, that is, one of the functionals (5.57) through (5.60). To determine this weight function w_0, we need, in each of these cases, to obtain a system of linear algebraic equations analogous to the systems (5.43), (5.51), and (5.54).

Let us write these systems of equations:
(a) for the functional (5.57),

$$\sum_{i=0}^{N} K_x(l, i) w_0(n + \varepsilon, i) - K_{xh}(l, n + \varepsilon) + \frac{1}{2} \theta m_x(l) = 0; \qquad (5.61)$$

(b) for the functional (5.58),

$$\sum_{i=0}^{N} K_x(l - i) w_0(i + \varepsilon) - K_{xh}(l + \varepsilon) + \frac{1}{2} \theta m_{x_0} = 0, \quad 0 \leqslant l \leqslant N,$$

$$(5.62)$$

where $m_{x_0} = m_x(n - l)$ is a constant;
(c) for the functional (5.59),

$$\sum_{i=0}^{N} [K_x(l, i) + \theta m_x(l) m_x(i)] w_0(n + \varepsilon, i) - K_{xh}(l, n + \varepsilon)$$

$$- \theta m_x(l) m_h(n + \varepsilon) = 0, \quad 0 \leqslant l \leqslant N; \qquad (5.63)$$

(d) for the functional (5.60),

$$\sum_{i=0}^{N} [K_x(l - i) + \theta m_{x_0}^2] w_0(i + \varepsilon) - K_{xh}(l + \varepsilon) - \theta m_{x_0} m_{h_0} = 0, \qquad (5.64)$$

where m_{x_0} and m_{h_0} are constants.

All these systems of equations are linear algebraic systems of equations and can be solved by the methods used in algebra. The solution $w_0(n + \varepsilon, l, \theta)$ in the nonstationary case or the solution $w_0(i + \varepsilon, \theta)$ in the stationary case is substituted into the expression for the criterion (4.6) or (4.6b). In this case, the corresponding criterion is a function of the parameter θ (for fixed time $n + \varepsilon$). The value of the corresponding parameter $\theta = \theta_0$ corresponding to the maximum of the probability P is determined by one the methods expounded in Chapter 1.

We have just considered the case in which the initial conditions on the influences were of a general nature. Let us now consider a more special case.

2. **Determination of an optimal stationary sampled-data system when the useful signal is a polynomial in time**

Suppose that the block diagram of the system corresponds to Figure 5.1. The input signal X is the sum of the useful signal G and the noise Z. The useful signal G is an rth-degree polynomial in time. The coefficients of the polynomial are random variables. The noise is a centralized stationary random function of time with given correlation function K_z. The desired output variable H is determined by equation (5.36). For admissible weight functions we take weight functions that satisfy conditions (5.49); that is, weight functions of sampled-data systems possessing astaticism of at least $(r + 1)$st order.

We are required to determine the optimal weight function maximizing the probability that the error will not exceed given limits. Let us suppose that the probability P is determined in accordance with formula (4.6).

Here, we need to take as our reduced functional

$$I_\theta = \theta m_E + D_E.$$

The mathematical expectation m_E and the variance D_E of the error of the system are determined in this case in accordance with formulas (5.47) and (5.48). Let us suppose that the noise Z and the coefficient of the leading term in the polynomial G obey a normal distribution law and that they are uncorrelated with each other. Under these assumptions, the probability that the error of the system will not exceed given limits $P(C_1 \leqslant E \leqslant C_2)$ is determined by formula (4.6). Let us write in expanded form the expression for the reduced functional I_θ in the given case:

$$
\begin{aligned}
I_\theta = \theta &\left[(-1)^r \sum_{l=0}^{N} l^r w(l + \varepsilon) - r!\, C_r \right] m_{gr} \\
&+ \left[(-1)^r \sum_{l=0}^{N} l^r w(l + \varepsilon) - r!\, C_r \right] D_{gr} \\
&+ \sum_{l=0}^{N} \sum_{i=0}^{N} K_z(l - i) w(l + \varepsilon) w(i + \varepsilon),
\end{aligned}
\tag{5.65}
$$

where m_{gr} is the mathematical expectation of the coefficient of the leading term of the polynomial G, and D_{gr} is the variance of that coefficient. We now need to determine the weight function w_0 minimizing the reduced functional (5.65) under conditions (5.49). The problem of minimizing the functional (5.65) under conditions (5.49) reduces to the problem of finding the unconditional minimum of the functional

$$
\begin{aligned}
I' = I_\theta + \sum_{k=0}^{r-1} \gamma_k \mu_k = \theta &\left[(-1)^r \sum_{l=0}^{N} l^r w(l + \varepsilon) - r!\, C_r \right] m_{gr} \\
&+ \left[(-1)^r \sum_{l=0}^{N} l^r w(l + \varepsilon) - r!\, C_r \right]^2 D_{gr} \\
&+ \sum_{l=0}^{N} \sum_{i=0}^{N} K_z(l - i) w(l + \varepsilon) w(i + \varepsilon) + 2 \sum_{k=0}^{r=0} \gamma_k \sum_{i=0}^{\infty} i^r w(i + \varepsilon),
\end{aligned}
\tag{5.66}
$$

where the γ_k are undetermined multipliers.

The quadratic functional (5.66) is not essentially different from the quadratic functional (5.50). The system of equations determining the weight function w_0 corresponding to the minimum of the functional (5.66) can be obtained in a manner analogous to the way we obtained the systems of equations (5.43) and (5.51):

$$\sum_{i=0}^{N} [K_z(l - i) + D_{g_r}l^r i^r] w_0 (i + \varepsilon)$$

$$+ \sum_{k=0}^{r-1} \gamma_k l^k - (-1)^r r! \, C_r D_{g_r} l^r + \theta(-1)^r m_{g_r} l^r = 0, \quad 0 \leqslant l \leqslant N.$$

$$(5.67)$$

The $N + 1$ equations (5.67) enable us to determine the values

$$w_0(l + \varepsilon, \gamma_0, \gamma_1, \cdots, \gamma_{r-1}),$$

for $l = 0, 1, \cdots, N$, of the desired weight function. The values of the coefficients

$$\gamma_0 = \gamma_{00}, \cdots, \gamma_{r-1, 0}$$

can be determined from the system of equations (5.49). When we have determined the values of the parameters

$$\gamma_{00}, \gamma_{10}, \cdots, \gamma_{r-1, 0},$$

we need to substitute the weight function

$$\omega_0(l + \varepsilon, 0, \gamma_{00}, \gamma_{10}, \cdots, \gamma_{r-1, 0})$$

into formulas (5.47) and (5.48). In this case, the mathematical expectation m_E and the variance D_E of the error of the system will be known functions of the parameter θ. Consequently, the criterion (4.6) will also be a known function of the parameter θ:

$$P = \varphi(\theta).$$

The value of the harmonizing parameter $\theta = \theta_0$ that maximizes the function $\varphi(\theta)$ is the desired value determining the optimal weight function w^0 of the sampled-data system:

$$w^0 = w^0(l + \varepsilon, \theta_0, \gamma_{00}, \gamma_{10}, \cdots, \gamma_{r-1, 0}).$$

This weight function w^0 represents the maximum of the criterion (4.6).

If we take for our criterion the criterion (4.6b), then, instead of the reduced functional $I_\theta = \theta m_E + D_E$, we can take

$$I_\theta = \theta m_E^2 + D_E.$$

If we substitute into this expression the values for m_E and D_E given by formulas (5.47) and (5.48), we obtain the following expression for I_θ:

$$I_\theta = \left[(-1)^r \sum_{l=0}^{N} l^r w(l + \varepsilon) - r! \, C_r \right]^2 (m_{g_r}^2 \theta + D_{g_r})$$

$$+ \sum_{l=0}^{N} \sum_{i=0}^{N} K_z(l - i) w(l + \varepsilon) w(i + \varepsilon). \qquad (5.68)$$

In the present case, the functional I' is determined not by (5.66) but by the formula

$$I' = \left[(-1)^r \sum_{l=0}^{N} l^r w(l + \varepsilon) - r! \, C_r \right]^2 (m_{g_r}^2 \theta + D_{g_r})$$

$$+ \sum_{l=0}^{N} \sum_{i=0}^{N} K_z(l - i) w(l + \varepsilon) w(i + \varepsilon) + 2 \sum_{k=0}^{r-1} \gamma_k \sum_{i=0}^{\infty} l^r w(i + \varepsilon).$$

$$(5.69)$$

This quadratic functional is more convenient, since it does not differ in any significant way from the functional (5.50), which is used to determine the optimal system minimizing the mean square error. We have noted that, before we set about determining the optimal system with respect to the criterion (4.6) or the criterion (4.6b), it is expedient to determine the optimal system with respect to the criterion of the minimum of the mean square error and to judge whether the probability P may increase when we shift from the weight function w_0 to the weight function w^0. If the possible gain in the probability P is significant, we choose the optimal weight function with respect to the criterion (4.6b). In this case, the functional (5.69) is more convenient than the functional (5.66), since, by virtue of its structure, it coincides exactly with the functional (5.50). Here, the computational formulas remain as before up to a factor. Furthermore, when we are determining the value of the harmonizing parameter $\theta = \theta_0$, the use of the functionals (5.68) and (5.69) determines uniquely the region in which the desired value θ_0 is to be found. As was shown in Chapter 4, the value θ_0 must be greater than unity.

In the present case, a system of equations enabling us to determine the weight function w_0 minimizing the functional (5.69) can be obtained from the system (5.51) by substituting m_{g_r} for $\theta m_{g_r}^2$:

$$\sum_{i=0}^{N} [K_z(l - i) + (\theta m_{g_r}^2 + D_{g_r}) l^r i^r] w_0(i + \varepsilon)$$

$$+ \sum_{k=0}^{r-1} \gamma_k l^k - (-1)^r r! \, (\theta m_{g_r}^2 + D_{g_r}) C_r l^r = 0, \quad l = 0, 1, \cdots, N.$$

$$(5.70)$$

A solution of the system of equations (5.70) can be obtained automatically from the solution of equation (5.51) by replacing $m_{g_r}^2$ with $\theta m_{g_r}^2$ in the latter equation.

The values of the parameters

$$\gamma_0 = \gamma_{00}, \gamma_1 = \gamma_{10}, \cdots, \gamma_{r-1} = \gamma_{r-1, 0}$$

and of the harmonizing parameter $\theta = \theta_0$ are determined just as in the preceding case.

The following problem is also of interest: Suppose that the block diagram corresponds to Figure 5.1. The useful signal is expressed by an

rth-degree polynomial in time and the noise Z is expressed by a centralized stationary random function. The desired output variable H is given by equation (5.36). For admissible systems, we take systems satisfying conditions (5.49). The coefficient G_r of the leading term in the polynomial $G(n + \varepsilon)$ is a random variable which obeys a law of equal probability in the interval $[-g_r, +g_r]$. Hence, its mathematical expectation is zero. The noise Z obeys a normal distributions law and is uncorrelated with the coefficient G_r.

For a criterion for comparing systems, we take the probability that the error will not exceed given limits. In this case, this probability is given by formula (4.10). In accordance with the method previously expounded, we first need to write the expression for reduced functional I_θ:

$$I_\theta = \theta D_{E_1} + D_{E_2} = \theta \left[(-1)^r \sum_{l=0}^{N} l^r w(l + \varepsilon) - r! \, C_r \right]^2 D_{g_r}$$

$$+ \sum_{l=0}^{N} \sum_{i=0}^{N} K_z(l - i) w(l + \varepsilon) w(i + \varepsilon), \tag{5.71}$$

where D_{E_1} is the variance of the first component E_1 of the error of the system, which depends on the coefficient G_r of the polynomial G and where D_{E_2} is the variance of the second component E_2 of the system, which depends on the noise Z. The component E_1 obeys an equal-probability law, the component E_2 a normal distribution law.

The problem of minimizing the functional (5.71) under condition (5.49) reduces to the problem of finding the unconditional minimum of the functional I':

$$I' = I_\theta + 2 \sum_{k=0}^{r-1} \gamma_k \mu_k = \theta \left[(-1)^r \sum_{l=0}^{N} l^r w(l + \varepsilon) - r! \, C_r \right]^2 D_{g_r}$$

$$+ \sum_{l=0}^{N} \sum_{i=0}^{N} K_z(l - i) w(l + \varepsilon) w(i + \varepsilon) + 2 \sum_{k=0}^{r} \gamma_k \sum_{l=0}^{N} l^k w(l + \varepsilon).$$

$$\tag{5.72}$$

By the method previously expounded, we can obtain a system of equations determining the weight function w_0 corresponding to the minimum of the functional (5.72):

$$\sum_{i=0}^{N} [K_z(l - i) + \theta D_{g_r} l^r l_r] w_0(i + \varepsilon)$$

$$+ \sum_{k=0}^{r-1} \gamma_k l^k - (-1)^r r! \, \theta D_{g_r} C_r l^r = 0, \quad 0 \leqslant l \leqslant N. \tag{5.73}$$

The solution $w_0(l + \varepsilon, \theta, \gamma_0, \gamma_1, \cdots, \gamma_{r-1})$ of the system (5.73) of algebraic equations is found just as in the preceding cases. Substitution of the solution obtained into (5.49) enable us to determine the needed values of the undetermined multipliers $\gamma_0, \gamma_1, \cdots, \gamma_{r-1}$. The value of the harmonizing parameter $\theta = \theta_0$ corresponding to the maximum of the criterion (4.10) is easily determined when we substitute the function

$$w_0(l + \varepsilon, \theta, \gamma_{00}, \gamma_{10}, \cdots, \gamma_{r-0,0})$$

into (4.10).

EXAMPLE. The block diagram of the system corresponds to Figure 5.1. The useful signal G is second-degree polynomial in time. The coefficient of $(n + \varepsilon)^2$ is a known quantity $G_2 = m_{g_r}$. The noise Z is expressed by a centralized stationary random function subject to a normal distribution law. The correlation function for this random function is of the form

$$K_z(m) = \begin{cases} K_3^2 & \text{for} \quad m = 0, \\ 0 & \text{for} \quad m \neq 0. \end{cases}$$

The desired output variable H coincides with the useful signal; that is, $H(n + \varepsilon) = G(n + \varepsilon)$. Admissible systems are linear sampled-data systems possessing astaticism of at least second order $(D_0 = D_1 = 0)$ for which the time of the transition process does not exceed 2; that is, systems with $N = 2$. As criterion for comparing systems, we take the probability given by formula (4.6b) that the error of the system will not exceed small allowed limits.

Determine the optimal weight function of a linear sampled-data system maximizing the chosen criterion (4.6b).

In the present case, the error has nonzero mathematical expectation m_E and it has a centralized component $\overset{0}{E}$, obeying a normal distribution law. The criterion (4.6b) depends on the square of the mathematical expectation m_E^2 and on the variance D_E of the error. Consequently, the reduced functional I_θ can be represented in the form

$$I_\theta = \theta m_E^2 + D_E,$$

where θ is a harmonizing parameter. (Of course, we might have taken

$$I_\theta = m_E^2 + \theta D_E$$

instead, and the procedure would be essentially the same in both cases.) In the present case, the mathematical expectation of the error is determined by formula (5.47), where we need to take $r = 2$, $C_r = \varepsilon^2/2$, and the variance is determined by formula (5.48), where we need to set $D_{g_r} = 0$. Consequently, we may write

$$\left.\begin{aligned} m_E^2 &= \left[\sum_{l=0}^{2} l^2 w(l + \varepsilon) - \varepsilon^2 \right]^2 m_{g_2}^2, \\[2mm] D_E &= \sum_{l=0}^{2} \sum_{i=0}^{2} K_z(l - i) w(l + \varepsilon) w(i + \varepsilon) = K_0^2 \sum_{l=0}^{2} w^2(l + \varepsilon). \end{aligned}\right\} \quad \text{(a)}$$

The reduced functional I_θ is written in the following form:

$$I_\theta = \theta \left[\sum_{l=0}^{2} l^2 w(l + \varepsilon) - \varepsilon^2 \right]^2 m_{g_2}^2 + K_2^0 \sum_{l=0}^{2} w^2(l + \varepsilon).$$

We are required to determine the weight function minimizing this functional I_θ under conditions (5.49), which, in the present case, take the following specific forms:

$$\sum_{l=0}^{2} w(l + \varepsilon) - 1 = 0,$$

$$- \sum_{l=0}^{2} lw(l + \varepsilon) - \varepsilon = 0.$$

(b)

Determination of the conditional minimum of the reduced functional I_θ leads to determination of the unconditional minimum of the functional I':

$$I' = + 2 \sum_{k=0}^{1} \gamma_k \mu_k = \theta \left[\sum_{l=0}^{2} l^2 w(l + \varepsilon) - \varepsilon^2 \right] m_{g_2}^2$$

$$+ K_0^2 \sum_{k=0}^{2} w^2(l + \varepsilon) + 2 \sum_{k=0}^{1} \gamma_k l^k w(l + \varepsilon).$$

In the present case, the system of equations (5.70) becomes

$$K_0^2 w_0(0 + \varepsilon) + \gamma_0 = 0,$$
$$K_0^2 w_0(1 + \varepsilon) + \gamma_0 + \gamma_1 - \varepsilon(\varepsilon + 1)\theta m_{g_2}^2 = 0,$$
$$K_0^2 w_0(2 + \varepsilon) + 40 m_{g_2}^2 [w_0(0 + \varepsilon) + w_0(1 + \varepsilon) + 4w_0(2 + \varepsilon)]$$
$$- \gamma_0 + 2\gamma_1 - 4\varepsilon^2 \theta m_{g_2}^2 = 0.$$

(c)

Conditions (5.49) yield two more equations:

$$- \frac{\gamma_0}{K_0^2} + \frac{\varepsilon(1 + \varepsilon) m_{g_2}^2 \theta - \gamma_0 - \gamma_1}{K_0^2}$$
$$+ \frac{(8m_{g_2}^2 \theta - K_0^2)\gamma_0 + 2(2m_{g_2}^2 \theta - K_0^2)\gamma_1 + R}{K_0^2(K_0^2 + 16m_{g_2}^2 \theta)} = 1,$$

$$- \frac{\gamma_0}{K_0^2} + \frac{\varepsilon(1 + \varepsilon) m_{g_2}^2 \theta - \gamma_0 - \gamma_1}{K_0^2}$$
$$+ 2 \frac{(8m_{g_2}^2 \theta - K_0^2)\gamma_0 + 2(2m_{g_2}^2 \theta - K_0^2)\gamma_1 + R}{K_0^2(K_0^2 + 16m_{g_2}^2 \theta)} = - \varepsilon,$$

(d)

where

$$R = 4\varepsilon[\varepsilon K_0^2 + m_{g_2}^2 \theta(1 + \varepsilon)] m_{g_2}^2 \theta.$$

The system (c)-(d) enables us to express the coefficients γ_0 and γ_1, the values of the weight function w_0, in terms of the harmonizing parameter θ and the initial data of the example $(m_{g_2}^2, K_0^2)$. When we substitute the values

$$w_0(0 + \varepsilon, \theta), \quad w_0(1 + \varepsilon, \theta), \quad w_0(2 + \varepsilon, \theta),$$

into (a), we obtain the square of the mathematical expectation m_E^2 and the variance D_E of the error of the system as known functions of the parameter θ. Then, by substituting $m_E^2 = m_E^2(\theta)$ and $D_E = D_E(\theta)$ into the criterion (4.6b), we obtain this criterion as a function of the parameter θ; $P = \varphi(\theta)$. The value of the parameter $\theta = \theta_0$ corresponding to the maximal probability $P_{\max}$ that the error will not exceed allowed limits can be determined in a manner analogous to what was done in Section 15 of Chapter 4.

The present problem has the peculiarity that the probability P was investigated for some fixed value of ε. Therefore, the optimal weight function found maximizes the probability P for fixed ε. For a different value of ε, this weight function will no longer be optimal. If the optimal weight function w^0 is only slightly dependent on the time ε, we can make our choice at any value of ε; for example, at the value $\varepsilon = 1/2$. On the other hand, if the weight function w^0 changes sharply when ε changes, then, for given initial conditions, we need to shift from the stationary continuous portion of the sampled-data system to the nonstationary portion. In this case, it is also possible to remain in the class of stationary systems if we take as our criterion not the criterion (4.6b) for some ε but the averaged criterion (4.6b):

$$\bar{P} = \int_0^1 D(\varepsilon)\,d\varepsilon, \qquad (5.74)$$

where $P(\varepsilon)$ is the probability that the error of the system will not exceed small allowed limits, which is given by formula (4.6b) for every value of ε.

An estimate of the possible gain in the criterion (4.6b) when we shift from the weight function w_0 to the weight function w^0 can be obtained in the same way as was done in Section 15 of Chapter 4 when we were investigating continuous systems.

20. DETERMINATION OF THE OPTIMAL LINEAR SAMPLED-DATA SYSTEM THAT ENSURES THE MAXIMUM PROBABILITY THAT THE SYSTEM ERROR WILL NOT EXCEED ALLOWED LIMITS (FOR $n > 1$)

1. The general case

In many cases, the probability P that the error of the system will not exceed allowed limits is a function f of the quadratic functionals $I_1, \cdots, I_{n+1}$ of the weight function of the system (see Section 16 of Chapter 4, formula (4.37)). In accordance with Theorem 2a of Chapter 1, the search for the weight function w^0 in accordance with the criterion (4.37) can be broken into two stages. The first stage consists in determining the weight function $w_0(n + \varepsilon, l, \theta_1, \cdots, \theta_n)$ corresponding to an extremum of the reduced functional

$$I_\theta = \theta_1 I_1 + \cdots + \theta_n I_n + I_{n+1}. \tag{5.75}$$

This functional is also a quadratic functional. The weight function $w_0(n + \varepsilon, l, \theta_1, \cdots, \theta_n)$ must be determined by one of the methods previously expounded for different values of the parameters $\theta_1, \cdots, \theta_n$.

The second stage consists in determining the harmonizing parameters

$$\theta_1 = \theta_{10}, \cdots, \theta_n = \theta_{n0},$$

corresponding to an extremum of the criterion (4.37). Two ways of determining these values of parameters are described in Section 16 of Chapter 4.

We shall consider two typical cases illustrating the choice of optimal systems with respect to the criterion of probability that the error will not exceed allowed limits. In the first case, the error of the system is the sum of several errors each of which obeys its own distribution law. The criterion for comparing systems is the probability that the error of the system will not exceed allowed limits at a fixed instant $n + \varepsilon$. In the second case, the error of the system obeys a normal distribution law. The criterion for comparing systems is the probability that the error of the system at fixed instants $n_1 + \varepsilon_1, \cdots, n_k + \varepsilon_k$ will not exceed allowed limits.

2. Determination of an optimal linear sampled-data system when the components of the system obey different distribution laws

The block diagram of the system is shown in Figure 5.1. The useful signal $G(n + \varepsilon)$ is of the form

$$G(n + \varepsilon) = \sum_{i=0}^{r} G_i(n + \varepsilon)^i + G'(n + \varepsilon), \tag{5.76}$$

where the G_i are random variables and $G'(n + \varepsilon)$ is a centralized stationary random function. Its correlation function $K_{g'}$ is known. The noise Z is also a centralized stationary random function. The desired output variable $H = L\{G(n + \varepsilon)\}$ of the system is determined in accordance with formula (5.36), in which all the coefficients $C_0, C_1, \cdots, C_r$ are given quantities. The random variables G_1 are uncorrelated with the random functions G' and Z. We are given correlation functions $K_{x'}$ and $K_{x'h'}$, where

$$X'(n + \varepsilon) = G'(n + \varepsilon) + Z(n + \varepsilon)$$

and

$$H'(n + \varepsilon) = L\{G'(n + \varepsilon)\},$$

as well as the mathematical expectation m_{g_r} and the variance D_{g_r} of the coefficient of the leading term of the polynomial

$$\sum_{i=0}^{r} G_i (n + \varepsilon)^i.$$

We are required to determine the optimal weight function of the system with respect to the criterion of maximization of the probability P that the error of the system will not exceed allowed limits. For admissible systems, we take sampled-data systems whose weight functions satisfy conditions (5.49).

To determine the probability that the error of the system will not exceed allowed limits, we need to know the distribution law of that error. Ordinarily, the error E of a linear system can be broken into several components; for example, into two components E_1 and E_2. In such a case, we usually know in advance the forms of the distribution laws of these components. For example, we may know that one component obeys a law of equal probability and that the other obeys a normal distribution law. We may also consider the mathematical expectation of the error separately. In such cases, only the parameters of the known distribution laws, namely, the mathematical expectation (which may be applied to any component and considered separately) and the variance of the components of the error are dependent on the weight function of the system. In studying a system, it is necessary to ascertain exactly how the parameters of the distribution laws of the components of the error depend on the weight function of the system.

Let us look at the individual components of the error of the system in the present case and let us determine the rules of dependence of the parameters of the distribution laws of these components on the weight function of the discrete system. The mathematical expectation of a stationary system is determined in the general case in accordance with formula (5.30), which assumes, under conditions (5.49), the form

$$m_E = [(-1)^r \mu_r - r!\, C_r] m_{g_r}, \tag{5.77}$$

where m_{g_r} is the mathemetical expectation of the coefficient of $(n + \varepsilon)^r$.

In the present case, the centralized component of the error $\overset{0}{E}$ of the system is

$$\overset{0}{E} = \overset{0}{E_1} + \overset{0}{E_2} = \overset{0}{Y} - \overset{0}{H} = \sum_{l=0}^{N} \overset{0}{X}(n - l) w(l + \varepsilon) - \overset{0}{H}(n + \varepsilon)$$

$$= [(-1)^r \mu_r - r!\, C_r] \overset{0}{G_r} + \sum_{l=0}^{N} \overset{0}{X'}(n + l) w(l + \varepsilon) - \overset{0}{H'}(n + \varepsilon),$$

where $\overset{0}{G_r}$ is the centralized component of the coefficient G_r. Here

$$\overset{0}{E}_1 = [(-1)^r \mu_r - r! \, C_r] \overset{0}{G}_r,$$

$$\overset{0}{E}_2 = \sum_{l=0}^{N} \overset{0}{X'}(n - l) w(l + \varepsilon) - H'(n + \varepsilon).$$

In the present case, the variance of the error is determined in accordance with formula (5.29), which may be written as

$$D_E = [(-1)^r \mu_r - r! C_r]^2 D_{g_r}$$

$$+ \sum_{l=0}^{N} \sum_{i=0}^{N} K_x (l - i) \, w(l + \varepsilon) \, w(i + \varepsilon)$$

$$- 2 \sum_{l=0}^{N} K_{x'h'}(l + \varepsilon) \, w(l + \varepsilon) + D_{h'}(\varepsilon).$$

Here, the first term is the variance of the component E_1 of the error of the system. It is determined by the coefficient G_r of the polynomial appearing in the composition of the useful signal. Let us assume that the coefficient G_r is distributed according to an equal-probability law, and hence the random variable E_1 is distributed according to an equal-probability law and the variance of this random variable is equal to

$$D_{E_1} = [(-1)^r \mu_r - r! C_r]^2 D_{g_r}. \qquad (5.78)$$

The remaining three terms constitute the variance of the second component E_2 of the error. Consequently, we may write

$$D_{E_2} = \sum_{l=0}^{N} \sum_{i=0}^{N} K_{x'}(l - i) \, w(l + \varepsilon)$$

$$- 2 \sum_{l=0}^{N} K_{x'h'}(l + \varepsilon) \, w(l + \varepsilon) + D_{h'}(\varepsilon). \qquad (5.79)$$

Let us suppose that the random function X' obeys a normal distribution law. Consequently, the component E_1 the the error of the system also obeys a normal distribution law. Thus, the error of the system has a mathematical expectation m_E given by formula (5.77), a centralized component E_1 distributed according to an equal-probability law and possessing a variance D_{E_1} given by formula (5.78), and a second centralized component E_2 obeying a normal distribution law with variance D_{E_2} given by formula (5.79). For given initial conditions and a fixed value of ε, all three characteristics m_E, D_{E_1}, and D_{E_2} are functionals of the weight function of the sampled-data system.

It follows from formula (4.45) that the probability that the error of the system will not exceed allowed limits is, in the present case, a known function of these characteristics m_E, D_{E_1}, and D_{E_2}:

$$P = P(m_E, D_{E_1}, D_{E_2}). \qquad (5.80)$$

In accordance with the general procedure expounded in Chapter

4 and in the present section, to find the optimal weight function maximizing the criterion (5.80), we begin by finding the weight function $w_0(l + \varepsilon, \theta_1, \theta_2)$ corresponding to an extremum of the reduced functional I_θ:

$$I_\theta = \theta_1 D_{E_1} + \theta_2 D_{E_2} + m_E \tag{5.81}$$

for different values of the harmonizing parameters θ_1 and θ_2.

When we substitute (5.77) through (5.79) into (5.81), we obtain

$$I_\theta = \theta_1 D_{g_r} \left[(-1)^r \sum_{l=0}^{N} l^r w(l + \varepsilon) - r! C_r \right]^2$$

$$+ \theta_2 \left[\sum_{l=0}^{N} \sum_{i=0}^{N} K_{x'}(l - i) \, w(l + \varepsilon) \, w(i + \varepsilon) \right.$$

$$\left. - 2 \sum_{l=0}^{N} K_{x'h'}(l + \varepsilon) \, w(l + \varepsilon) + D_{h'}(\varepsilon) \right]$$

$$+ m_{g_r} \left[(-1)^r \sum_{l=0}^{N} l^r w(l + \varepsilon) - r! C_r \right]. \tag{5.82}$$

The weight function $w_0(l + \varepsilon, \theta_1, \theta_2)$ that we are seeking must ensure an extremum of the functional (5.82) under conditions (5.49). As we know, solution of this problem reduces to finding the function

$$w_0(l + \varepsilon, \theta_1, \theta_2, \gamma_0, \cdots, \gamma_{r-1}),$$

that provides an unconditional extremum of the functional

$$I' = I_\theta + 2 \sum_{i=0}^{r-1} \gamma_i \sum_{l=0}^{N} l^i w(l + \varepsilon). \tag{5.83}$$

A necessary condition that the function

$$w_0(l + \varepsilon, \theta_1, \theta_2, \gamma_0, \cdots, \gamma_{r-1})$$

must satisfy is easily obtained by the foregoing method. In the present case, it is the following system of linear algebraic equations:

$$\theta_1 D_{g_r} \sum_{i=0}^{N} l^r i^r w(i + \varepsilon) + \theta_2 \sum_{i=0}^{N} K_{x'}(l - i) \, w(i + \varepsilon)$$

$$- \theta_1 D_{g_r}(-1)^r r! C_r l^r - \theta_2 K_{x'h'}(l + \varepsilon)$$

$$+ \frac{m_{g_r}}{2}(-1)^r l^r + \sum_{i=1}^{r-1} \gamma_i l^i = 0, \quad 0 \leqslant l \leqslant N. \tag{5.84}$$

The solution w_0 of this system of linear algebraic equations is a function of the r parameters γ_i and the two harmonizing parameters θ_1 and θ_2. The values of the parameters γ_i are determined from conditions (5.49). Then, the solution w_0 is represented as a function of two unknown parameters θ_1 and θ_2: $w_0(l + \varepsilon, \theta_1, \theta_2)$.

The values of the harmonizing parameters $\theta_1 = \theta_{10}$ and $\theta_2 = \theta_{20}$ corresponding to the maximum of the criterion (4.45) are determined as follows: The solution $w_0(l + \varepsilon, \theta_1, \theta_2)$ of equation (5.84) is substituted into the expression for the criterion (4.45). Then, this criterion P is a function of the two variables θ_1 and θ_2. The values $\theta_1 = \theta_{10}$ and $\theta_2 = \theta_{20}$ corresponding to the maximum P are easily determined, for example, by the method of fastest descent. These values of the harmonizing parameters can also be determined from equations (4.51).

3. Determination of an optimal linear impulse system whose error obeys a normal distribution law

In the present case, the block diagram remains as before. The useful signal $G(n + \varepsilon)$ and the noise $Z(n + \varepsilon)$ obey a normal distribution law with given characteristics. The mathematical expections m_g and m_z and the correlation functions K_g and K_z of the useful signal and the noise and the joint correlation function K_{gz} of the useful signal and the noise are known. Consequently, we also know the correlation function K_x of the input signal $X = G + Z$. The desired output variable H of the system is the result of applying an arbitrary given linear operator L to the useful signal G:

$$H(n + \varepsilon) = L\{G(n + \varepsilon)\}.$$

Consequently, the joint correlation function K_{xh} of the input variable X and the desired output variable H can be determined.

We are required to determine the optimal weight function of a linear sampled-data system with respect to the criterion of maximum probability that the error of the system will not exceed allowed limits at fixed instants of time.

The error of the system $E(n + \varepsilon)$ at m fixed instants of time $n_1 + \varepsilon$, $n_2 + \varepsilon$, $\cdots$, $n_m + \varepsilon$ can be represented as an m-dimensional vector with components along the axes $E(n_1 + \varepsilon)$, $E(n_2 + \varepsilon)$, $\cdots$, $E(n_m + \varepsilon)$ that obeys a normal distribution law. The characteristics (mathematical expectations and correlation functions) of the components $E(n_1 + \varepsilon)$, $\cdots$, $E(n_m + \varepsilon)$ are determined by the initial conditions on the influences and the desired output variable (that is, on the purpose of the system) and by the weight function of the sampled-data system.

Suppose that we are given the following limits on the error of the system:

$$C_{1i} \leqslant E(n_i + \varepsilon) \leqslant C_{2i}, \qquad i = 1, 2, \cdots, m.$$

In this case, the probability P that the error of the system will not exceed the given limits is determined in accordance with formula (4.53) or formula (4.54). In both cases, the criterion P is a function of the m mathematical expectations

$$m_{E_1} = m_E(n_1 + \varepsilon), \cdots, m_{E_m} = m_E(n_m + \varepsilon)$$

and $m(m + 1)/2$ values of the correlation function

$$K_{\nu\mu} = K(n_\nu + \varepsilon, n_\mu + \varepsilon)$$

of the error of the system. The criterion P, given by formula (4.53) or formula (4.54), is a special case of the functional (4.37). In the present case, $n + 1 = m(m + 3)/2$ and the reduced functional (5.75) is of the form

$$I_\theta = \sum_{\substack{\nu=1 \\ \mu \geqslant \nu}}^{m} \theta_{\nu\mu} K_E(n_\nu + \varepsilon, n_\mu + \varepsilon)$$

$$+ \sum_{i=1}^{m-1} \theta_i m_E(n_i + \varepsilon) + m_E(n_E + \varepsilon). \qquad (5.85)$$

In view of formulas (5.25) and (5.26) for the mathematical expectation and the correlation function of the error of the sampled-data system, we can, in the general case, write an expression for the reduced functional I_θ of the weight function $w(n + \varepsilon, l)$ of the sampled-data system.

For stationary influences and a stationary sampled-data system, formula (4.54) takes the simpler form (4.54a). Formula (5.85) also becomes simpler and more convenient for calculations:

$$I_\theta = \sum_{\substack{\nu=1 \\ \mu \geqslant \nu}}^{m} \theta_{\mu-\nu} K_E(n_\nu - n_\mu, \varepsilon) + m_{E_0}^0. \qquad (5.85a)$$

Here,

$$m_{E_0} = \sum_{l=0}^{N} w(l + \varepsilon) \cdot m_{x_0} - m_{h_0}. \qquad (5.86)$$

where m_{x_0}, m_{h_0}, and m_{E_0} are the constant mathematical expectations of the stationary random functions X, H, and E respectively. The values of the correlation function

$$K_{\nu\mu} = E_E(n_\nu - n_\mu, \varepsilon)$$

are determined from the simpler formula (5.28). By substituting into (5.85a), the expression (5.86) and the values of $K_E(n_\nu - n_\mu, \varepsilon)$ given by formula (5.28), we obtain a quadratic functional of the weight function w of the sampled-data system. The system of equations enabling us to determine the weight function $w_0(l + \varepsilon, \theta_1, \cdots, \theta_m)$ corresponding to an extremum of the reduced functional (5.85a) can, in the present case, be obtained by the methods previously expounded. It takes the form

$$\sum_{i=0}^{N} \sum_{\substack{\nu=1 \\ \mu \geqslant \nu}}^{m} \theta_{\mu-\nu} K_x(n_\mu - n_\nu + l - i) w_0(i + \varepsilon, \theta_1, \cdots, \theta_m)$$

$$- \frac{1}{2} \sum_{\substack{\nu=1 \\ \mu \geqslant \nu}}^{m} \theta_{\mu-\nu} [K_{xh}(n_\mu - n_\nu + l + \varepsilon) + K_{xh}(n_\mu - n_\nu + l - \varepsilon)]$$

$$+ m_{x_0}^2 \sum_{i=0}^{N} w_0(i + \varepsilon, \theta_1, \cdots, \theta_m) - m_{x_0} m_{h_0} = 0, \quad 0 \leqslant l \leqslant N. \quad (5.87)$$

If the fixed instants $n_i + \varepsilon$ are evenly spaced, that is, if $n_{i+1} - n_i = \Delta$ for every i and if $\varepsilon = 0$, then the system (5.87) takes the simpler form

$$\sum_{i=0}^{N} \left[\sum_{\nu=1}^{m} \theta_\nu K_x(\nu\Delta + l - i) + m_{x0}^2 \right] w_0(i, \theta_1, \cdots, \theta_m)$$

$$- \sum_{\nu=1}^{m} \theta_\nu K_{xh}(\nu\Delta + l) - m_{x_0} m_{h_0} = 0,$$

$$0 \leqslant l \leqslant N. \tag{5.87a}$$

In practice, we frequently encounter the case in which the mathematical expectation m_x of the input variable is equal to 0 and hence the mathematical expectation of the desired output variable and the mathematical expectation of the error are equal to 0. All our computational formulas then become considerably simplified. Let us illustrate this with an example. Suppose that the number m of fixed instants of time is 3. In this special case, the probability that the error of the sampled-data system at the instant $n_1 = 0$, $n_2 = \Delta$, and $n_3 = 2\Delta$ (where Δ is an integer) will not exceed small allowed errors is given by formula (4.60). It follows that the optimal impulse system must minimize the determinant $|K|$ in (4.59). This determinant is a third-degree polynomial in the values $K_E(0)$, $K_E(\Delta)$, and $K_E(2\Delta)$ of the correlation function of the error of the system. In this example, the reduced functional I_θ has the relatively simple form

$$I_\theta = K_E(0) + \theta_1 K_E(\Delta) + \theta_2 K_E(2\Delta)$$

$$= \sum_{l=0}^{N} \sum_{i=0}^{N} [K_x(l - i) + \theta_1 K_x(\Delta + l - i) + \theta_2 K_x(2\Delta + l - i)]$$

$$\times w(l) \, w(i) - 2 \sum_{l=0}^{N} [K_{xh}(l) + \theta_1 K_{xh}(\Delta + l) + \theta_2 K_{xh}(2\Delta + l)]$$

$$\times w(l) + (1 + \theta_1 + \theta_2) D_h. \tag{5.88}$$

Of course, the last term in this expression has no influence on the choice of optimal weight function.

The system of equations determining the weight function $w_0(l, \theta_1, \theta_2)$ minimizing the reduced functional (5.88) for certain values of the harmonizing parameters θ_1 and θ_2 is written this case as

$$\sum_{i=0}^{N} [K_x(l - i) + \theta_1 K_x(\Delta + l - i)$$

$$+ \theta_2 K_x(2\Delta + l - i)] w_0(l, \theta_1, \theta_2) - K_{xh}(l)$$

$$- \theta K_{xh}(\Delta + l) - \theta_2 K_{xh}(2\Delta + l) = 0,$$

$$0 \leqslant l \leqslant N. \tag{5.89}$$

When we have found the solution $w_0(l, \theta_1, \theta_2)$ of the linear algebraic equations (5.89) for different values of the harmonizing parameters θ_1 and θ, we need to substitute it into (4.60). The determinant $|K|$ then becomes a known function of the parameters θ_1 and θ_2:

$$|K| = \Phi(\theta_1, \theta_2). \tag{5.90}$$

When, by some method or other (for example, the method of fastest descent), we know the values of the parameters $\theta_1 = \theta_{10}$ and $\theta_2 = \theta_{20}$ minimizing the function (5.90), we need to substitute them into the function $w_0(l, \theta_1, \theta_2)$. The completely defined function of l that we then obtain

$$l\,w^0 = w^0(l) = w_0(l, \theta_{10}, \theta_{20})$$

is the optimal weight function minimizing the determinant $|K|$ and maximizing the criterion (4.60).

To find the values of the harmonizing parameters $\theta_1 = \theta_{10}$ and $\theta_2 = \theta_{20}$ or to verify the solution $\theta_1 = \theta_{10}$, $\theta_2 = \theta_{20}$ obtained by the method of fastest descent, we can use the two-equation system (4.64).

In all the cases examined in this section, the criterion P depends on the value of ε; that is, on the position of the fixed instant (or instants) in the interval of discreteness T. If the dependence of the criterion on the value of ε is insignificant with an optimal weight function w^0, we can take for the realization of the optimal weight function $w^0(l + \varepsilon_0)$, where ε_0 is some mean value $0 \leq \varepsilon_0 \leq 1$.

On the other hand, if there is a strong dependence of the criterion on ε, we need either to make the choice of optimal weight functions for several values of ε and determine the dependence of w^0 on ε or else to make the choice of optimal sampled-data weight function w^0 from the averaged criterion

$$\bar{P} = \int_0^1 P(\varepsilon)d\varepsilon,$$

where $P(\varepsilon)$ is the probability that the error of the system will not exceed allowed limits at a fixed instant of time (that is for fixed ε).

Determination of the parameters of an optimal sampled-data system, with a given block diagram, by using any of the criteria that we have been considering can be carried out exactly as described in Chapters 3 and 4 in connection with the choice of the parameters of a continuous system.

Chapter 6

REALIZATION OF LINEAR SYSTEMS
THAT ARE NEARLY OPTIMAL

We have examined methods for determining optimal systems that operate under conditions of random influences. Our main attention was directed to methods enabling us to determine the optimal weight function of a system. We also showed how one can determine the optimal combination of parameters of a system with a given structure. In the latter case, the very formulation of the problem assumed the realizability of the block diagram and the optimal parameters in question. Herein lies the great value of the given formulation of the problem. A defect in it is the fact that the range of admissible systems is artificially restricted in advance by the block diagram (or combinations of block diagrams). This keeps us from considering other block diagrams, some of which may prove better than the one or ones we are considering.

Another formulation of the problem whose purpose is to choose an optimal weight function has the advantage that the class of admissible systems is not restricted artificially by one or several block diagrams. With this formulation of the problem, we can obtain a higher value of the criterion chosen. However, even here, there is a defect: It is usually impossible to realize exactly the weight function obtained as a result of solving the problem. The impossibility of exact realization of a system having optimal weight function w_0 is due to the fact that the optimal weight function often contains components corresponding to unreal elements, such as an ideal amplifying component, an ideal retarding component, an ideal differentiating component and so on. Furthermore, the real elements of the systems at the disposal of the designer do not always enable him to realize exactly even a theoretically realizable weight function. Additional difficulties stem from the fact that a portion of the block diagram of the system is always given in advance. It is determined by the control object (governing device) and the other elements, which are usually given before the system is planned. Of what value are the methods of determining optimal weight functions that we have been considering if it is impossible to realize them exactly ? The value of these methods and the results obtained by their use consist in the following: (1) They enable us to obtain the ideal for which we must strive in constructing actual systems; (2) they point out the way to realize systems close to the ideal optimal ones; (3) they enable us to justify practical-technical requirements on newly constructed systems; (4) they enable us to estimate the degree of technological perfection of existing systems.

Let us consider in greater detail the second point, namely, the realization of systems which are nearly optimal. By **realization** or **synthesis** of a system, we mean the determination of the block diagram and the parameters of the system from the condition that the dynamical characteristics of the projected system are nearly optimal. A typical dynamical characteristic of a system is its weight function. For a stationary system, we could also take the frequency response. Consequently, the problem of obtaining the block diagram of a system and its parameters in such a way that the weight function or the frequency response or the transfer function will be close to the corresponding dynamical characteristics of the optimal system is a problem of synthesis. At the present time, we still have no general methods of synthesis of automatic control systems. In the case of a stationary optimal linear system, synthesis problems can be solved more simply.

21. SYNTHESIS OF AN OPTIMAL STATIONARY LINEAR SYSTEM BY THE METHOD OF FREQUENCY RESPONSE

We shall assume that the optimal weight function $w_0\,(\tau)$ is determined. From the weight function one can always determine the transfer function $W_0(p)$ of the system (by using the Laplace transformation), and from the transfer function one can determine the amplitude and phase frequency responses ($A_0(\omega)$ and $\varphi_0(\omega)$ respectively) of the optimal system. Thus, before the synthesis of an optimal system, we know all the characteristics of the optimal system that we have enumerated. We also know the analogous characteristics of components not depending on the designer (the control object, the governing device, and the like). We need to find the transfer function (frequency response) of the portion of the system being modified in such a way that the general transfer function (frequency response) of the system will differ only slightly from the optimal transfer function or frequency response. In this case, the portion of the system being modified is called the **correcting circuit**. Various ways of connecting the correcting circuit to the unmodified

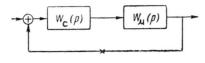

FIGURE 6.1

(previously determined) portion of the system are possible. We note that one can construct both a closed and an open loop linear system from the optimal transfer function. We shall keep in mind the fact that we are constructing a closed system, since a closed system is less sensitive to other external and internal noises not taken into account.

Let us look at various possible ways of putting a correcting circuit in the overall diagram of the system and let us show how one then determines the transfer function of the correcting circuit in terms of the transfer function of the unmodified portion of the diagram and in terms of the optimal transfer function.

1. Series connection of the correcting circuit (see Fig. 6.1). The transfer function of a closed system must coincide with the optimal transfer function $W_0(p)$. Consequently, the transfer function of an open system must be determined in this case from the relation [Ref. 49]

$$W_{0p}(p) = \frac{W_0(p)}{1 - W_0(p)}.$$

This means that the transfer function $W_c(p)$ of a correcting circuit connected in series must be determined by the formula

$$W_c(p) = \frac{W_0(p)}{W_u(p)[1 - W_0(p)]}, \tag{6.1}$$

where $W_u(p)$ is the transfer function of the unmodified portion of the system.

2. Correcting network in main feedback loop (see Fig. 6.2). In this case, the dependence of the transfer of the correcting network on the optimal transfer function and the transfer function of the unmodified portion of the system is also easily obtained [Ref. 49]:

$$W_c(p) = \frac{W_u(p) - W_0(p)}{W_u(p) W_0(p)}. \tag{6.2}$$

Sometimes, it is expedient to connect the correcting network in parallel with certain components in the unmodified portion of the system. In such a case, we can use both a direct and a feedback parallel connecting network.

3. A correcting network in a direct parallel loop (see Fig. 6.3). We denote by $W_{u1}(p)$ the transfer function of that portion of the components included in the parallel correcting network. We denote by $W_{u2}(p)$ the transfer function of the remaining components in the un-

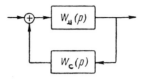

FIGURE 6.2

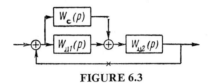

FIGURE 6.3

modified portion of the system. As before, we denote by $W_c(p)$ the transfer function of the correcting network. It can be determined from the formula

$$W_c(p) = \frac{W_{u1}(p) \, W_{u2}(p)[1 - W_0(p)] - W_0(p)}{W_{u2}(p)[W_0(p) - 1]}. \tag{6.3}$$

4. Correcting network in an interior feedback loop (see Fig. 6.4). By means of simple transformations, one can easily obtain a formula for determining the correcting network in this case as well:

$$W_c(p) = \frac{W_{u1}(p) \, W_{u2}(p)[1 - W_0(p)] - W_0(p)}{W_{u1}(p) \, W_0(p)}. \tag{6.4}$$

Other types of connection of correcting networks are possible. In all similar cases, one can easily express the optimal transfer function $W_c(p)$ of the correcting network in terms of the optimal transfer function $W_0(p)$ of a system and the transfer functions $W_{u1}(p)$, $W_{u2}(p)$, $\cdots$, $W_{uk}(p)$ of the unmodified components in the system.

The optimal transfer function $W_0(p)$ can be either a rational or a transcendental function of the statistical characteristics of the useful signal, the noise, and the interval of observation T. If the optimal transfer function is a rational function of these quantities, it corresponds to the optimal weight function $w_0(\tau)$, which is a sum of exponential functions of $|\tau|$. If it is a transcendental function, it corresponds to the optimal weight function $w_0(\tau)$, containing in its composition mixed delta functions of the type $D_i \delta^{(i)}(\tau - T)$. The transfer functions $W_u(p)$,

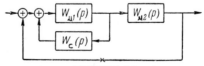

FIGURE 6.4

$W_{u1}(p)$ and $W_{u2}(p)$ of the unmodified actual components of the system are usually rational functions of p. As one can easily see from formulas (6.1) through (6.4), the transfer function of the optimal correcting network $W_c(p)$ is a rational function if the optimal transfer function $W_0(p)$ is a rational function. The transfer function $W_c(p)$ is transcendental if the transfer function $W_0(p)$ is transcendental. In the latter case, it is impossible to realize the optimal transfer function of the correcting network with the aid of elementary real components. For approximate realization of the transfer function of the correcting network, we need to approximate it with a rational function that is acceptable from the point of view of its complexity. Here, we can use the method of logarithmic frequency responses.

In this case, to get an approximate representaion of the optimal transfer function of the correcting network by means of a rational function, we need to construct its amplitude and phase logarithmic frequency responses from the value found for the transfer function of the optimal system. In the case of a correcting network in series, we need to determine the logarithmic frequency response of the closed system. This can easily be done with the aid of a Φ-nomogram connecting the logarithmic frequency characteristics of open and closed (with unit negative feedback loop) systems (see Appendix 4). If we subtract from the frequency response of an open system the corresponding logarithmic frequency response of the unmodified portion of the system, we obtain the logarithmic frequency response of the optimal correcting network. In the case in which the correcting network consists of a main feedback loop, the block diagram shown in Figure 6.2 is transformed according to known rules [Refs. 46, 49] into the diagram shown in Figure 6.5. Then, the logarithmic frequency response of the unmodified portion of the system which corresponds to the transfer function $W_0(p)$ is subtracted from the corresponding frequency response of the optimal system. Thus, we determine the frequency response of the closed system shown in Figure 6.5. Then, by using the nomogram just mentioned, we find the logarithmic frequency response of the closed system, that is, the frequency response corresponding to the transfer function $1/(W_c(p)\,W_u(p))$. We need to add the frequency response of the unmodified portion of the system to this frequency response and change the signs of the sums. This yields the logarithmic frequency response of the optimal correcting network. The amplitude frequency response obtained in this manner for the correcting network is approximated by segments of straight lines. As a result, the types of elementary components in the composition of the correcting network and their parameters are determined. At the same time, we need to construct the phase characteristic of the correcting network obtained and make sure that it is close to the optimal one.

When the correcting network is included in parallel with certain

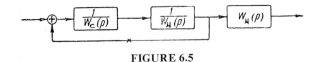

FIGURE 6.5

components of the unmodified portion of the system (see Fig. 6.3), we can find the logarithmic frequency response of an open system with transfer function $W_{op}(p) = W_0(p)/[1 - W_0(p)]$ from the nomogram. By subtracting from this frequency response the logarithmic frequency response corresponding to the transfer function $W_{u2}(p)$, we can obtain the logarithmic frequency characteristics of the composite component with transfer function $W_c(p) + W_{u1}(p)$. From the logarithmic amplitude and phase responses of a composite component, we can obtain the real and imaginary frequency responses of that component by using the P, Q nomogram shown in Appendix 5. Then, by subtracting from these frequency responses the frequency responses corresponding to the transfer function $W_{u1}(p)$, we can obtain the real and imaginary frequency responses of the optimal correcting network in the present case. Then, it will be expedient to determine from this same P, Q nomogram the logarithmic amplitude and phase frequency characteristics of the correcting network. After that, the amplitude characteristic of the optimal correcting network is approximated by segments of straight lines. As a result of this approximation, the types of elementary components in the correcting network and their parameters are determined. Simultaneously, we construct the phase frequency response of the correcting network obtained and see that it is close to the optimal one.

In the case in which the correcting network is included in a feedback loop containing the component with the transfer function $W_{u1}(p)$ (see Fig. 6.4), we find from the nomogram the logarithmic frequency response of the closed system. Then, from these characteristics we subtract the logarithmic frequency response corresponding to the component with transfer function $W_{u2}(p)$. As a result of these operations, we determine the logarithmic frequency response of the composite component with transfer function

$$\frac{W_{u1}(p)}{1 + W_{u1}(p) W_c(p)}.$$

Then, we need to subtract from the frequency response obtained the logarithmic frequency response of the component with transfer function $W_{u1}(p)$ and thus obtain the frequency responses corresponding to the transfer function

$$\frac{1}{1 + W_{u1}(p) W_c(p)}.$$

From this response, by using the same nomogram, we can easily obtain the logarithmic frequency response corresponding to the transfer function $W'(p) = W_{u1}W_c(p)$. By subtracting from the response obtained the logarithmic frequency response corresponding to the transfer function $W_{u1}(p)$, we can obtain the logarithmic frequency response of the optimal correcting network. We then need to carry out the approximation of the response obtained by the method shown in the previous examples and to obtain the types and parameters of the components of the correcting network.

The transfer functions of the correcting networks $W_c(p)$ determined by the method shown are rational functions. However, the degree of the numerator of these functions may be greater than the degree of the denominator. Such transfer functions, like transcendental functions, cannot be realized in practice. To avoid such transfer functions of the correcting networks, we need to restrict the class of admissible linear systems in which we are seeking the optimal system. This extra restriction may consist, for example, in the requirement that, under the application of a white noise at the input, the derivatives of the output variable of the optimal system up to a certain order have finite variances [Refs. 10, 27].

22. DETERMINATION OF THE OPTIMAL WEIGHT FUNCTION OF AN AUTOMATIC-CONTROL SYSTEM WITH REGARD TO THE NECESSITY OF SYNTHESIS OF THIS SYSTEM

We have noted that the optimal weight function, with respect to the criterion of minimum of the mean square error or some other analogous criterion, cannot always be realized in practice. One of the reasons for this is the presence of delta functions in the optimal weight function. Even in the process of determining the optimal weight function, we need to consider the necessity of synthesis of the weight function obtained and, to do this, we need to impose on the admissible weight functions additional restrictions that exclude unrealizable weight functions. However, we need to make sure that these additional restrictions do not exclude a portion of the realizable weight functions as well. If these additional restrictions rule out only those realizable functions that have no effect on the extremum of the criterion, these restrictions can be considered acceptable. Consequently, the extra restrictions on admissible weight functions of the system that lead to realizable optimal systems can be chosen in more than one way. Here, the basic principle must be that the additional restrictions must not decrease (respectively increase) the maximum (respectively minimum) value of the criterion corresponding to the optimal system.

It is possible and expedient to introduce additional restrictions on the admissible systems even when we can obtain a realizable optimal weight function without them if our purpose is to obtain a realizable weight function in a simpler manner; that is, if we wish a cheaper system. This direction in synthesis of optimal systems has not yet been sufficiently worked out and clarified in the literature. Let us look at one of the variations of additional restrictions that enable us to obtain a realizable weight function in a number of cases.

Almost all the problems that we have considered on the determination of an optimal weight function of a linear system reduced to finding the minimum of a quadratic functional of the form

$$I = \int_{t_0}^{t_1} \int_{t_0}^{t_1} K_2(\tau,\, s) w(t_1,\, \tau) w(t_1,\, s) d\tau ds$$
$$- 2 \int_{t_0}^{t_1} K_1(t_1,\, \tau) w(t_1,\, \tau) d\tau + D(t_1), \qquad (6.5)$$

where t_0 and t_1 are the lower and upper end-points of the interval of observation, $w(t_1,\, \tau)$ is the weight function of a nonstationary (in the general case) linear system, and $K_2(\tau,\, s)$ is usually a symmetric function of the variables τ and s. In the different cases, it is either the correlation function K_x of the input signal of the system or the sum of the correlation function K_x and other symmetric functions of the variables τ and s that involve the conditions under which we are seeking the minimum of the criterion. $K_1(t_1,\, \tau)$ is a function of the variable τ, which depends on the time t_1 as a parameter. This is either the joint correlation function K_{xh} between the input variable and the desired output variable of the system or the sum of this joint correlation function K_{xh} and other functions of the variable τ that involve the conditions under which we seek the minimum of the criterion (for example, condition (5.49) that the system be astatic of at least order r). The term $D(t_1)$ has no influence on the process of finding the optimal system.

The functions $K_2(\tau,\, s)$ and $K_1(t_1,\, \tau)$ are usually bounded functions in the interval $[t_0,\, t_1]$. Certain restrictions, varying according to the formulation of the problem (see Chapters 3 and 4) are imposed on the weight function $w(t_1,\, \tau)$.

In addition to restrictions of the type (5.49), we impose on the weight function $w(t_1,\, \tau)$ other restrictions not associated with the initial conditions on the influences or the form of the criterion but caused by our desire to obtain an optimal weight function that is more easily realized. We take for these additional restrictions the inequalities

$$\int_{t_0}^{t_1} [w^{(i)}(t_1,\, \tau)]^2 d\tau < \infty, \qquad l = 0,\, 1,\, \cdots,\, m, \qquad (6.6)$$

where the superscript (i) denotes the ith derivative of the weight function with respect to τ. Inequalities (6.6) mean that the optimal weight function and its first m derivatives are required to be square-integrable functions. It is possible to give another interpretation of inequalities (6.6), one associated with the physical properties of the processes taking place in the systems. For $m = 0$, condition (6.6) is equivalent to the requirement that the variance of the output variable of the system with weight function $w(t_1, \tau)$ be bounded if a white noise is applied at the input of that system. For $m > 0$, this condition is equivalent to the condition that the variance of the output variable of the system with weight function $w(t_1, \tau)$ and its first m derivatives be bounded if a white noise is applied at the input of that system.

Inequalities (6.6) cannot be used directly in the derivation of necessary and sufficient conditions that the optimal weight function $w_0(t_1, \tau)$ minimizing the criterion (6.5) must satisfy. Therefore, instead of inequalities (6.6), in what follows we shall use the equalities

$$\int_{t_0}^{t_1} [w^{(i)}(t_1, \tau)]^2 d\tau = C_i, \quad i = 0, 1, \cdots, m, \tag{6.7}$$

where the constants C_i may assume arbitrary finite values.

We need to show in detail the possibility and desirability of shifting from conditions (6.6) to conditions (6.7). First of all, we note that, by assigning different values of the constants C_i in the interval $[0, \infty]$ and determining the optimal weight function for these values of the constants C_i, we can obtain a set of optimal weight functions $w_0(C_0, C_1, \cdots, C_m)$ that depends on $C_0, C_1, \cdots, C_m$ as parameters. Then, we can determine the criterion I on this set of the optimal weight functions determined under conditions (6.7). The criterion I is a function of the parameters $C_0, C_1, \cdots, C_m$:

$$I = I(C_0, C_1, \cdots, C_m) = \varphi(C_0, \cdots, C_m),$$
$$0 \leqslant C_i \leqslant C < \infty, \quad i = 0, 1, \cdots, m.$$

We can then find the minimum of the function $\varphi(C_0, C_1, \cdots, C_m)$, which is a function of $m+1$ variables. If this minimum exists, the values of the constants $C_0 = C_{00}, C_1 = C_{10}, \cdots, C_m = C_{m0}$ at which this minimum is attained correspond to the optimal weight function minimizing the criterion I under conditions (6.6).

Here, two cases are possible. In the first case, the minimum of the function $\varphi(C_0, C_1, \cdots, C_m)$ is attained at $C_0 = C_{00} < \infty, C_1 = C_{10} < \infty, \cdots, C_m = C_{m0} < \infty$. Here, for optimal weight function we take the weight function

$$w_0(t_1, \tau, C_{00}, C_{10}, \cdots, C_{m0}).$$

In the second case, the minimum of the function $\varphi(C_0, \cdots, C_m)$ is not attained at finite values of the parameters $C_0, C_1, \cdots, C_m$. When these parameters are increased and allowed to approach infinity, the function φ decreases monotonically, approaching asymptotically the value of the criterion I corresponding to the optimal weight function determined without the additional restrictions (6.6) or (6.7). In this case, the constants C_i need to be determined from other requirements, for example, from the requirement that the value of the criterion I^c_{min} corresponding to the optimal weight function

$$w_0(t_1, \tau, C_0, C_1, \cdots, C_m),$$

determined under conditions (6.7) exceed by no more than Δ the minimal value of this criterion I_{min} determined without the restrictions (6.7):

$$I^c_{min} - I_{min} \leqslant \Delta, \qquad (6.8)$$

where Δ is a small positive number characterizing the allowed deviations of the criterion I from its minimal value I_{min}.

Thus, in the second (and more probable) case, the supplementary restrictions (6.7) enable us to obtain more conveniently a realizable optimal weight function of the system, though at the cost of quality; that is, at the cost of increasing (or decreasing) the value of the criterion I. Here, the following question naturally arises: Is it not better to perform the shift from the ideal optimal weight function determined without supplementary restrictions (6.7) in the process of realization of an optimal system ? The method that we have proposed here for choosing the optimal weight function by using the supplementary restrictions (6.7) is better in that it leads more quickly to our goal and in addition is a regular method. Here, it is clear in what direction we need to change the restrictions (the values of the parameters $C_0, C_1, \cdots, C_m$) to obtain a weight function close to the ideal optimal weight function.

Of course, this method does not replace or exclude other methods and procedures for obtaining realizable weight functions close to the optimal ones. It supplements these methods.

Let us now see how to determine the minimum of the criterion I under conditions (6.7). As we know, the problem of finding a conditional minimum of the functional I reduces to the problem of finding the unconditional minimum of the functional I':

$$I' = I + \sum_{i=0}^{m} \lambda_i \int_{t_0}^{t_1} [w^{(i)}(t_1, \tau)]^2 d\tau = \int_{t_0}^{t_1}\int_{t_0}^{t_1} K_2(\tau, s)w(t_1, \tau)w(t_1, s)d\tau ds$$

$$- 2\int_{t_0}^{t_1} K_1(t_1, \tau)w(t_1, \tau)d\tau + D(t_1) + \sum_{i=0}^{m} \lambda_i \int_{t_0}^{t_1} [w^{(i)}(t_1, \tau)]^2 d\tau, \quad (6.9)$$

where the λ_i are undetermined multipliers that can be evaluated from conditions (6.7).

The functional I' is a special case of the functional (1.139). In the present case, the integrand Φ is of the following form:

$$\Phi = K_2(\tau,\, s)\, w(t_1,\, s)\, w(t_1,\, \tau) - \frac{1}{t_1 - t_0}\, [K_1(t_1,\, \tau)\, w(t_1,\, \tau)$$

$$+ K_1(t_1,\, s)\, w(t_1,\, s)] + \frac{1}{(t_1 - t_0)^2}\, D(t_1)$$

$$+ \frac{1}{t_1 - t_0} \sum_{i=0}^{m} \lambda_i \{[w^{(i)}(t_1,\, \tau)]^2 + [w^{(i)}(t_1,\, s)]^2\},\qquad (6.10)$$

where $w^{(i)}(t_1,\, s)$ is the ith derivative of $w(t_1,\, s)$ with respect to s.

On the basis of Theorem 1 of Chapter 1, we conclude that the necessary condition for minimization of the functional I' is satisfaction of equation (1.136). Before writing down this equation for a given particular functional I', we note that the function (6.10) is symmetric in $w^{(i)}(t_1,\, \tau)$ and $w^{(i)}(t_1,\, s)$. In this special case, equation (1.136) assumes the simpler form

$$\int_{t_0}^{t_1} \left[\frac{\partial \Phi}{\partial w_\tau} - \frac{d}{d\tau}\left(\frac{\partial \Phi}{\partial w_\tau}\right) + \cdots + (-1)^m \frac{d^m}{d\tau^m}\left(\frac{\partial \Phi}{\partial w_\tau^{(m)}}\right) \right] ds = 0.$$

$$t_0 \leqslant \tau \leqslant t_1. \qquad (6.11)$$

Let us substitute (6.10) into (6.11) and let us obtain a necessary condition that the optimal weight function w must satisfy;

$$\int_{t_0}^{t_1} K_2(\tau,\, s)\, w_0(t_1,\, s)\, ds - K_1(t_1,\, \tau)$$

$$+ \sum_{i=0}^{m} \lambda_i (-1)^i w_0^{(2i)}(t_1,\, \tau) = 0,\quad t_0 \leqslant \tau \leqslant t_1. \qquad (6.12)$$

Theorem 1 is valid if the admissibile functions $w(t_1,\, \tau)$ belong to the class C^m (that is, the class of m times continuously differentiable functions) and satisfy the following conditions at the end-points:

$$w^{(i)}(t_1,\, t_0) = w^{0(i)},\; w^{(i)}(t_1,\, t_1) = w^{1(i)},$$

$$i = 0,\, 1,\, \cdots,\, m - 1; \qquad (6.13)$$

that is, if they assume given values at the end-points of the interval of integration $[t_0,\, t_1]$. Here, we encounter condition (6.13) which does not follow from the statement of the problem but is a peculiarity of the method of investigation. However, we can easily get rid of this condition. To do this, we need to determine the solution of equation (6.12). It depends on $2m$ constants $w^{0(i)}$, $w^{1(i)}$, for $i = 0,\, 1,\, \cdots,\, m - 1$:

$$w_0 = w_0(t_1,\, \tau,\, w^{0(i)},\, w^{1(i)}). \qquad (6.14)$$

We impose no restrictions on the value of $w^{0(i)}$ and $w^{1(i)}$. We substitute the solution (6.14) of equation (6.12) into the criterion I. This criterion is a function of the $2m$ parameters $w^{0(i)}$, $w^{1(i)}$:

$$I\{w_0(t_1,\, \tau,\, w^{0(i)},\, w^{1(i)})\} = \chi(w^{0(i)},\, w^{1(i)}). \qquad (6.15)$$

Then, we need to find the minimum of the function $\chi(w^{0(i)}, w^{1(i)})$ and the corresponding values of the parameters $w_0^{0(i)}$ and $w_0^{1(i)}$. The weight function

$$w^0(t_1, \tau) = w_0(t_1, \tau, w_0^{0(i)}, w_0^{1(i)}) \tag{6.16}$$

minimizes the criterion I without the artificial conditions (6.13).

Let us make clear just when the necessary conditions (6.12) and (6.13) are also sufficient for minimization of the functional I'. To do this, we write out the expression for the value of the functional I' corresponding to an arbitrary admissible function

$$w(t_1, \tau) = w_0(t_1, \tau) + v(t_1, \tau),$$

where $w_0(t_1, \tau)$ is a weight function satisfying conditions (6.12) and (6.13) for certain values $w^{0(i)}$ and $w^{1(i)}$ and where $v(t_1, \tau)$ is an arbitrary admissible weight function satisfying the conditions

$$v^{(i)}(t_1, t_0) = v^{(i)}(t_1, t_1) = 0, \ i = 0, 1, \cdots, m - 1. \tag{6.17}$$

We shall then show that

$$I'\{w_0(t_1, \tau) + v(t_1, \tau)\} \geqslant I\{w_0(t_1, \tau)\}. \tag{6.18}$$

One can easily see that

$$I'\{w_0 + v\} = E_0 + E_1 + E_2, \tag{6.19}$$

where

$$
\begin{aligned}
E_0 &= \int_{t_0}^{t_1}\int_{t_0}^{t_1} K_2(\tau, s)\, w_0(t_1, \tau)\, w_0(t_1, s)\, d\tau ds \\
&\quad - 2\int_{t_0}^{t_1} K_1(t_1, \tau)\, w_0(t_1, \tau)\, d\tau \\
&\quad + \sum_{i=0}^{m} \lambda_i \int_{t_0}^{t_1} [w_0^{(i)}(t_1, \tau)]^2 d\tau + D_1(t_1), \\
E_1 &= 2\left[\int_{t_0}^{t_1}\int_{t_0}^{t_1} K_2(\tau, s)\, w_0(t_1, s)\, v(t_1, \tau)\, d\tau ds \right. \\
&\quad - \int_{t_0}^{t_1} K_1(t_1, \tau)\, v(t_1, \tau)\, d\tau \\
&\quad \left. + \sum_{i=0}^{m} \lambda_i \int_{t_0}^{t_1} w_0^{(i)}(t_1, \tau)\, v^{(i)}(t_1, \tau)\, d\tau \right], \\
E_2 &= \int_{t_0}^{t_1}\int_{t_0}^{t_1} K_2(\tau, s)\, v(t_1, \tau)\, v(t_1, s)\, d\tau ds \\
&\quad + \sum_{i=0}^{m} \lambda_i \int_{t_0}^{t_1} [v^{(i)}(t_1, \tau)]^2 d\tau.
\end{aligned}
\tag{6.19a}
$$

Here, E_0 is the value of the functional I' for $w = w_0$: $E_0 = I'\{w_0\}$. Let us show that $E_1 = 0$. To do this, we make a substitution in accordance with the equations

$$\int_{t_0}^{t_1} w_0^{(i)}(t_1, \tau) v^{(i)}(t_1, \tau) d\tau = (-1)^i \int_{t_0}^{t_1} w_0^{(2i)}(t_1, \tau) v(t_1, \tau) d\tau. \qquad (6.20)$$

These equations are obtained by repeated integration by parts in the left-hand members of (6.20), taking the relations (6.17) into account. In view of (6.20), we can write the terms E_1 in the form

$$E_1 = 2 \int_{t_0}^{t_1} v(t_1, \tau) \left[\int_{t_0}^{t_1} K_2(\tau, s) w_0(t_1, s) ds - K_1(t_1, \tau) \right.$$
$$\left. + \sum_{i=0}^{m} \lambda_i (-1)^i w_0^{(2i)}(t_1, \tau) \right] d\tau.$$

It follows from condition (6.12) that the expression in the square brackets vanishes for $t_0 \leq \tau \leq t_1$. Consequently, the quantity E_1 is equal to zero. Thus, we may write

$$I'\{w_0 + v\} = I'\{w_0\} + E_2.$$

One can easily see that, if each λ_i for $i = 0, 1, \cdots, m$ is positive, the quantity E_2 is nonnegative for an arbitrary weight function $v(t_1, \tau)$. This means that inequality (6.18) is valid for an arbitrary weight function $v(t_1, \tau)$ satisfying conditions (6.17).

Equation (6.12), determining the weight function w_0, is in the general case a linear integro-differential equation. For $m = 0$, this equation is a nonhomogeneous Fredholm integral equation of the *second* kind:

$$w_0(t_1, \tau) + \frac{1}{\lambda_0} \int_{t_0}^{t_1} K_2(\tau, s) w_0(t_1, s) ds = -\frac{1}{\lambda_0} K_1(t_1, \tau). \qquad (6.21)$$

Methods for obtaining continuous solutions of Fredholm equations of the second kind are well-developed [Refs. 41, 50].

We note that there is an essential difference between equation (6.21) and equation (3.46) or others like it. Specifically, the unknown function w_0 appears both under the integral sign and outside it, whereas this function appears only under the integral sign in (3.46). Therefore, for continuous functions $K(t, \tau)$ and $\Psi(t, \tau)$, solutions of equation (3.46) containing delta functions are possible. The integration "smooths" these delta-functions. For continuous functions $K_2(\tau, s)$ and $K_1(t_1, \tau)$, equation (6.21) cannot have discontinuous solutions in the form of delta functions, since the integral of the product of a delta function and a continuous function is a continuous function.

We can determine the minimum of the functional (6.5) without resorting to the derivaton of equation (6.12). This minimum of the quadratic functional I can be determined, for example, by the method of fastest descent. Let us outline this method as applied to the present problem. As was stated in Chapters 1 and 3, the method of fastest descent is a method of successive approximations. Let $w(t_1, \tau) = w_1(t_1, \tau)$ denote the first approximation (chosen on some basis or other) of the weight function. Then, following the usual procedure, we determine the direction of the gradient in the normed space of the function w, that is, the direction in which the functional (6.9) decreases the most rapidly. For the norm it is natural to take

$$||w(t_1, \tau)|| = \int_{t_0}^{t_1} [w(t_1, \tau)]^2 d\tau \qquad (6.22)$$

The function $v_1(t_1, \tau)$ corresponding to the direction of the gradient must minimize (maximize in absolute value) the quantity

$$\frac{dI'\{w_1 + \Delta v_1\}}{d\Delta}\bigg|_{\Delta = 0} \qquad (6.23)$$

under the condition

$$\int_{t_0}^{t_1} [v_1(t_1, \tau)]^2 d\tau = 1. \qquad (6.24)$$

The problem of minimizing the functional (6.23) with condition (6.24) reduces, as we know, to the problem of finding the unconditional minimum of the functional

$$I'' = \frac{dI'\{w_1 + \Delta v_1\}}{d\Delta}\bigg|_{\Delta = 0} + \mu \int_0^T [v_1(t_1, \tau)]^2 d\tau, \qquad (6.25)$$

where μ is a multiplier to be determined from condition (6.24). In the present problem, this multiplier is insignificant and it cannot be determined from condition (6.24). Keeping (6.9) and (6.19) in mind, we may write

$$I'\{w_1 + \Delta v_1\} = E_0 + \Delta E_1 + \Delta^2 E_2, \qquad (6.26)$$

where E_0, E_1, and E_2 are defined by equations (6.19a) except that we must replace w_0 and v with w_1 and v_1 respectively. In view of equations (6.26) and (6.20), we have the following expression for the functional I'':

$$\begin{aligned}
I'' &= E_1 + \mu \int_{t_0}^{t_1} [v_1(t_1, \tau)]^2 d\tau \\
&= 2 \int_{t_0}^{t_1} \int_{t_0}^{t_1} K_2(\tau, s) w_1(t_1, \tau) v_1(t_1, s) d\tau \, ds \\
&\quad - 2 \int_{t_0}^{t_1} K_1(t_1, \tau) v_1(t_1, \tau) d\tau \\
&\quad + 2 \sum_{i=0}^{m} \lambda_i (-1)^i \int_{t_0}^{t_1} w_1^{(2i)}(t_1, \tau) v_1(t_1, \tau) d\tau \\
&\quad + \mu \int_{t_0}^{t_1} [v_1(t_1, \tau)]^2 d\tau.
\end{aligned} \qquad (6.27)$$

This functional (6.27) of the function $v_1(t_1, \tau)$ is a special case of the functional (1.139).

As shown in Chapter 1, a necessary condition for minimization of the functional I'' is given by equation (1.140b). In the present case, this condition is

$$\int_{t_0}^{t_1} K_2(\tau, s) w_1(t_1, s) ds - K_1(t_1, \tau) + \sum_{i=0}^{m} \lambda_i(-1)^i w_1^{(2i)}(t_1, \tau)$$

$$+ \mu v_1(t_1, \tau) = 0, \quad t_0 \leqslant \tau \leqslant t_1. \tag{6.28}$$

Therefore, the function $v_1(t_1, \tau)$ is determined up to a constant factor:

$$v_1(t_1, \tau) = \int_{t_0}^{t_1} K_2(\tau, s) w_1(t_1, s) ds - K_1(t_1, \tau)$$

$$+ \sum_{i=0}^{m} \lambda_i(-1)^i w_1^{(2i)}(t_1, \tau). \tag{6.29}$$

As our second approximation of the function w, we take

$$w_2(t_1, \tau) = w_1(t_1, \tau) + \varepsilon_1 v_1(t_1, \tau), \tag{6.30}$$

where the factor ε_1 is determined from the condition of minimization of the functional

$$I' = I'\{w_1 + \varepsilon v_1\} = \chi(\varepsilon),$$

considered as a function of the parameter ε. It follows from (6.26) that the minimum of the function $\chi(\varepsilon)$ is attained at $\varepsilon = \varepsilon_1$, which satisfies the condition

$$\varepsilon_1 = \frac{-E_1}{2E_2}.$$

In view of the expressions for E_1 and E_2 and equation (6.29), we may write

$$\varepsilon_1 = \cfrac{-\int_{t_0}^{t_1} [v_1(t_1, \tau)]^2 d\tau}{\int_{t_0}^{t_1}\int_{t_0}^{t_1} K_2(\tau, s) v_1(t_1, \tau) v_1(t_1, s) d\tau ds + \sum_{i=0}^{m} \lambda_i \int_{t_0}^{t_1} [v_1^{(i)}(t_1, \tau)]^2 d\tau}. \tag{6.31}$$

The third and subsequent approximations are chosen analogously. It is easy to program the calculation of the successive approximations on a high-speed digital computer. All the calculations are considerably simplified in the special case of $m = 0$, as one can see from formulas (6.9), (6.12), (6.29) through (6.31).

When we have determined the optimal weight function w^0 minimizing the criterion (6.5), we can easily determine the minimum value of that criterion. To do this, we use the relationship

$$\int_{t_0}^{t_1} K_2(\tau, s) w^0(t_1, s) ds = K_1(t_1, \tau) - \sum_{i=0}^{m} (-1)^i \lambda_i w^{0(2i)}(t_1, \tau),$$

$$t_0 \leqslant \tau \leqslant t_1,$$

obtained from equation (6.12), and we evaluate the double integral

$$
\int_{t_0}^{t_1}\int_{t_0}^{t_1} K_2(\tau,\ s)\ w^0(t_1,\ \tau)\ w^0(t_1,\ s)d\tau\ ds
$$

$$
= \int_{t_0}^{t_1} K_1(t_1,\ \tau)\ w^0(t_1,\ \tau)d\tau
$$

$$
- \sum_{i=0}^{m} (-1)^i\ \lambda_i \int_{t_0}^{t_1} w^{0\,(2i)}(t_1,\ \tau)w^0(t_1,\ \tau)d\tau. \qquad \textbf{(6.32)}
$$

Substituting (6.32) into (6.5), we obtain

$$
I_{\min} = I\{w^0\} = -\int_{t_0}^{t_1} K_1(t_1,\ \tau)\ w^0(t_1,\ \tau)d\tau + D(t_1)
$$

$$
- \sum_{i=0}^{m} (-1)^i\ \lambda_i \int_{t_0}^{t_1} w^{0\,(2i)}(t_1,\ \tau)\ w^0(t_1,\ \tau)d\tau. \qquad \textbf{(6.33)}
$$

All the calculations in this section can be carried out under more general restrictions imposed on the weight function. Instead of the restrictions (6.6), we might take the following:

$$
\int_{t_0}^{t_1} w^{(i)}(t_1,\ \tau)\ w^{(j)}(t_1,\ \tau)d\tau < \infty,\quad i,\ j = 0,\ 1,\ \cdots,\ m. \qquad \textbf{(6.6a)}
$$

All the transformations and calculations of this section remain the same as far as the theory is concerned, though they would become more laborious.

In this section, we have examined a method of choosing an optimal nonstationary system with weight function depending on two parameters t_1 and τ. In the special case in which we are determining the stationary optimal system under stationary initial conditions on the influences, all the formulas and relationships become simplified.

Let us write the basic relationships for this case. They take the following forms:

$$
I = \int_{t_0}^{t_1}\int_{t_0}^{t_1} K_2(\tau,\ s)\ w(t_1,\ \tau)\ w(t_1,\ s)d\tau\ ds
$$

$$
- 2 \int_{t_0}^{t_1} K_1(t_1,\ \tau)\ w(t_1,\ \tau)d\tau + D, \qquad \textbf{(6.5a)}
$$

$$
I' = I + \sum_{i,j=0}^{m} \lambda_{i,j} \int_{t_0}^{t_1} w^{(i)}(t_1,\ \tau)\ w^{(j)}(t_1,\ \tau)d\tau, \qquad \textbf{(6.9a)}
$$

$$
\int_{t_0}^{t_1} K_2(\tau,\ s)\ w_0(t_1,\ s)ds - K_1(t_1,\ \tau) + \frac{1}{2}\sum_{i,j=0}^{m} [(-1)^i
$$

$$
+ (-1)^j]\lambda_{ij}w_0^{(i+j)}(t_1,\ \tau),\quad t_0 \leqslant \tau \leqslant t_1, \qquad \textbf{(6.12a)}
$$

$$
I_{\min} = I\{w_0\} = -\int_{t_0}^{t_1} K_1(t_1,\ \tau)\ w_0(t_1,\ \tau)d\tau
$$

$$+ D - \frac{1}{2} \sum_{i,j=0}^{m} [(-1)^i + (-1)^j] \lambda_{ij} \int_{t_0}^{t_1} w_0^{(i+j)}(t_1, \tau) w_0(t_1, \tau) d\tau.$$

(6.33a)

In the general case, equation (6.12a) is an integro-differential equation. For $m = 0$, this equation is a Fredholm integral equation of the second kind:

$$\int_{t_0}^{t_1} K_2(\tau, s) w_0(t_1, s) ds + \lambda_0 w_0(t_1, \tau) = K_1(t_1, \tau), \quad t_0 \leqslant \tau \leqslant t_1. \quad (6.12b)$$

An extensive literature [Refs. 41, 47, 50, and the like] is devoted to the solution of equations of this kind.

EXAMPLE. The block diagram of the system is shown in Figure 1.1. The useful signal $G(t)$ is a first-degree polynomial in time. The noise is a centralized stationary random function and the correlation function of the noise is an exponential function of $|\tau|$:

$$K_z(\tau) = e^{-\alpha|\tau|}.$$

Corresponding to this correlation function is the spectral density

$$S_z(\omega) = \frac{2\alpha}{\alpha^2 + \omega^2}.$$

The noise and the useful signal are uncorrelated. The desired output variable of the system $H(t)$ is equal to the useful signal: $H(t) = G(t)$. Determine the optimal weight function $w(\tau)$ of the stationary system minimizing the variance of the error.

For admissible systems, we take systems with regulating time T and having astaticism of at least second order. Consequently, the weight function of an admissible system must satisfy the conditions

$$\int_0^T w(\tau) d\tau = 1, \quad \int_0^T \tau w(\tau) d\tau = 0. \quad (a)$$

We need to determine the optimal weight function of the system without supplementary restrictions of the type (6.7) and then we need to do this with these restrictions. The error of the system in this case is equal to

$$E(t) = \int_0^T Z(t - \tau) \, w(\tau) d\tau.$$

Consequently, the variance of the error is determined according to the formula

$$D_E = \int_0^T \int_0^T K_z(\tau - s) \, w(\tau) \, w(s) d\tau \, ds$$

$$= \int_0^T \int_0^T e^{-\alpha|\tau-s|} \, w(\tau) \, w(s) d\tau \, ds. \quad (b)$$

In this case, the search for the optimal weight function of the system reduces to finding the extremum of the functional I (cf. Section 13):

$$I = D_E + 2\gamma_0 \int_0^T w(\tau)d\tau + 2\gamma_1 \int_0^T \tau w(\tau)d\tau$$

$$= \int_0^T \int_0^T e^{-\alpha|\tau-s|} w(\tau) w(s)d\tau\,ds + \gamma_0 \int_0^T w(\tau)d\tau + \gamma_1 \int_0^T \tau w(\tau)d\tau. \quad \text{(c)}$$

When we have found the function $w_0 = w_0(\tau, \gamma_0, \gamma_1)$, corresponding to an extremum of the functional (c) and have determined the values of the parameters γ_0 and γ_1 from conditions (a), we obtain the optimal weight function $w_0(\tau, \gamma_{00}, \gamma_{10})$, minimizing the variance of the error.

It follows from formula (3.54) that the optimal weight function w_0 in the present case is of the form

$$\omega_0(\tau) = g_0 + g_1\tau + C_{10}\delta(\tau) + C_{1T}\delta(\tau - T). \quad \text{(d)}$$

The coefficients g_0, g_1, C_{10}, and C_{1T} can be determined by substituting (d) into the integral equation (3.53), which in the present case takes the form

$$\int_0^T e^{-\alpha|\tau-s|} w_0(s)ds + \gamma_0 + \gamma_1\tau \equiv 0, \quad 0 \leqslant \tau \leqslant T. \quad \text{(e)}$$

Setting the coefficients of the functions 1, τ, $e^{-\alpha\tau}$, $e^{+\alpha\tau}$ in this identity equal to zero enables us to obtain four equations for determining the four unknowns g_0, g_1, C_{10}, and C_{1T}. In this case, the minimum variance is equal to

$$D_{E\,\text{min}} = -\gamma_0.$$

We shall not determine these coefficients at this time, since our problem consists not in obtaining specific numbers but in comparing two optimal weight functions from a qualitative point of view and showing that the introduction of supplementary restrictions of the type (6.7) leads to vanishing of the delta functions from the composition of the optimal weight function. Having this in mind, let us determine the optimal weight function w_0 in the present example with the supplementary condition

$$\int_0^T [w(\tau)]^2 d\tau = C_0, \quad \text{(f)}$$

imposed on the admissible weight functions.

In the present case, the optimal weight function must minimize the functional (6.9), which in this example takes the form

$$I' = I + \lambda_0 \int_0^T [w(\tau)]^2 d\tau = \int_0^T \int_0^T e^{-\alpha|\tau-s|} w(\tau)w(s)d\tau\,ds$$

$$+ \gamma_0 \int_0^T w(\tau)d\tau + \gamma_1 \int_0^T \tau w(\tau)d\tau + \lambda_0 \int_0^T [w(\tau)]^2 d\tau. \quad \text{(g)}$$

Equation (6.12) determining the weight function w_0 becomes

$$\int_0^T e^{-\alpha|\tau-s|} w_0(s)\, ds + \gamma_0 + \gamma_1 \tau + \lambda_0 \omega_0(\tau) = 0 \tag{h}$$

or

$$\int_0^T [e^{-\alpha|\tau-s|} + \lambda_0 \delta(s - \tau)]\, w_0(s)\, ds + \gamma_0 + \gamma_1 \tau = 0, \quad 0 \leqslant \tau \leqslant T. \tag{i}$$

The integral equation (i) differs from the integral equation (e) only in that we have under the integral sign not the correlation function $e^{-\alpha|\tau-s|}$ but the function

$$[e^{-\alpha|\tau-s|} + \lambda_0 \delta(s - \tau)].$$

This function can be considered as the correlation function of some other process (e.g., noise). The spectral density corresponding to this new correlation function is equal to

$$\frac{2\alpha}{\alpha^2 + \omega^2} + \lambda_0 = \frac{\lambda_0 \omega^2 + \lambda_0 \alpha^2 + 2\alpha}{\omega^2 + \alpha^2}.$$

It follows from formula (3.54) that, in the present case, the optimal weight function takes the form

$$w_0(\tau) = B_0 + B_1 \tau + B_2 e^{b\tau} + B_3 e^{-b\tau}, \tag{j}$$

where

$$b = \sqrt{\frac{2\alpha}{\lambda_0} + \alpha_2}.$$

The coefficients B_0, B_1, B_2, and B_3 can be determined by substituting (j) into (i), carrying out the integration, and setting the coefficients of the functions 1, τ, $e^{-\alpha\tau}$, $e^{\alpha\tau}$ equal to 0. We then obtain four linear algebraic equations for determining four unknowns. To determine the coefficients γ_0 and γ_1, we can use equation (a).

The minimum variance of the error is determined from formula (6.33a), which in the present case takes the form

$$D_{E\min} = -\gamma_0 - \lambda_0 \int_0^T (B_0 + B_1 \tau + B_2 e^{b\tau} + B_3 e^{-b\tau})\, d\tau.$$

The closer λ_0 is to zero, the closer the weight function (j) will be to the weight function (d) and the less will the variance corresponding to the weight function (j) exceed the variance corresponding to the weight function (d). With increasing λ_0, the coefficient b increases and the terms $B_2 e^{-b\tau}$ and $B_3 e^{b\tau}$ approach the delta functions $C_{10}\delta(\tau)$ and $C_{1T}\delta(\tau - T)$. The coefficient λ_0 should be chosen in such a way that increase in the variance as we shift to the weight function (j) will be small and at the same time it will be possible to realize a system corresponding to this weight function.

If we replace the supplementary requirement (f) with the stronger requirement

$$\int_0^T [w(\tau)]^2 d\tau = C_0, \quad \int_0^T \left[\frac{dw(\tau)}{d\tau} \right]^2 d\tau = C_1,$$

then equation (6.12) takes the form

$$\int_0^T [e^{-\alpha|\tau-s|} + \lambda_0 \delta(s-\tau) - \lambda_1 \delta_3(s-\tau)] w_0(s) ds + \gamma_0 + \gamma_1 \tau = 0,$$
$$0 \leqslant \tau \leqslant T,$$

where $\delta_3(\tau)$ is a third-order delta function equal to the second derivative of a first-order delta-function, that is, of $\delta(\tau)$. In accordance with (3.54), a solution of this equation is the weight function

$$w_0(\tau) = B_0 + B_1 \tau + B_2 e^{b_1 \tau} + B_3 e^{-b_1 \tau} + B_4 e^{b_2 \tau} + B_5 e^{-b_2 \tau}.$$

The coefficients $b_1, b_2, -b_1, -b_2$ are the roots of the biquadratic equation

$$2\alpha + \lambda_0(-x^2 + \alpha^2) + \lambda_1 x^2(-x^2 + \alpha^2) = 0.$$

To determine the coefficients $B_0, B_1, B_2, B_3, B_4, B_5, \gamma_0, \gamma_1$ we have the two equations (a) and the four equations obtained by substituting the solution w_0 into the integral equation and setting the coefficients of the functions $1, \tau, e^{-a\tau}, e^{a\tau}$, equal to zero. For the system of equation to be closed, we use the conditions on the end-points of the interval $[0, T]$:

$$w_0(0) = w^{00}, \quad w_0(T) = w^{0T}.$$

23. THE REALIZATION OF SAMPLED-DATA SYSTEMS THAT ARE NEARLY OPTIMAL [Refs. 14, 39]

The problem of the synthesis of optimal sampled-data systems, like the problem of synthesis of optimal continuous systems, is a complex technological problem. As a rule, we determine from known characteristics of an optimal sampled-data system the transfer function of its equivalent continuous portion. Then, we realize in practice a sampled-data element and the continuous portion of the sampled-data system in such a way that the product of their transfer functions $W_d(p)$ and $W_c(p)$ is equal to the value found for the transfer function $W_e(p)$ of the equivalent continuous portion of the system. Thus, the problem reduces to realization of a continuous system on the basis of a known transfer function. Usually, in the synthesis of a sampled-data system, just as in the synthesis of a continuous system, we do not try to choose a sampled-data element and a continuous portion of the sampled-data system that realize precisely the optimal transfer function $W_e(p)$ of the equivalent continuous portion; instead, we use the optimal characteristics found for the sampled-data system to find a transfer function of its equivalent continuous portion that is easily realized and that ensures properties of a sampled-data system that are nearly optimal. We shall call such a transfer function of the equivalent continuous portion the desired transfer function $W_*(p)$ [Ref. 39] and we shall call the weight function corresponding to it the desired weight function $w_*(n + \varepsilon)$ of the equivalent continuous portion of the sampled-data system.

Let us pause to look at the general methods of determining the desired transfer function of the equivalent continuous portion of the system.

To every realizable transfer or weight function there corresponds an open and a closed sampled-data system. Of course, the structures of these systems are considerably different. Therefore, the method of realizing the desired system depends in a very real way on whether we are required to realize the desired system with a closed or an open system.

Let us first look briefly at the question of realizing the desired sampled-data system with the aid of open sampled-data systems.

It follows from the equations previously obtained for determining the weight function that this function, in its general form, can be written as

$$w(n + \varepsilon) = w_0(n) + w_1(n)\varepsilon + \cdots + w_r(n)\varepsilon^r,$$
$$n = 0, 1, \cdots, N. \tag{6.34}$$

The corresponding transfer function of the sampled-data system can be represented by the expression

$$W^*(p, \varepsilon) = D\{w(n + \varepsilon)\} = \sum_{n=0}^{N} w(n + \varepsilon)e^{-pn}$$

$$= \sum_{n=0}^{N} [w_0(n) + w_1(n)\varepsilon + \cdots + w_r(n)\varepsilon^r]e^{-pn}. \tag{6.35}$$

Of practical interest is the special case when $r = 2$. Formula (6.35) then takes the form

$$W^*(p, \varepsilon) = \sum_{n=0}^{N} [w_0(n) + w_1(n)\varepsilon + w_2(n)\varepsilon^2]e^{-pn}. \tag{6.36}$$

The tranfer function $W_e(p)$ of the equivalent continuous portion, which corresponds to the transfer function of the sampled-data system (3.36), is determined from the formula

$$W_e(p) = \int_0^1 W^*(p, \varepsilon)e^{-p\varepsilon}d\varepsilon = \frac{1 - e^{-p}}{p} \sum_{n=0}^{N} w_0(n)e^{-pn}$$

$$+ \left(\frac{1 - e^{-p}}{p^2} - \frac{e^{-p}}{p} \right) \sum_{n=0}^{N} w_1(n)e^{-pn}$$

$$+ \left(2\frac{1 - e^{-p}}{p^2} - \frac{2e^{-p}}{p^2} - \frac{e^{-p}}{p} \right) \sum_{n=0}^{N} w_2(n)e^{-pn}. \qquad (6.37)$$

As one can see from this formula, the equivalent continuous portion of the sampled-data system must contain retarding components and integrating components. In the present case, the realization of the system reduces to constructing a sampled-data element with spacing close to zero and a continuous portion consisting of a combination of the integrating and retarding links in accordance with formula (6.37). Here, we may run into technological difficulties: Sometimes it is difficult to realize the required retarding components and the necessary number of integrating components.

Let us turn to the question of realizing optimal characteristics with the aid of closed sampled-data systems. Here, the main problem is to determine the desired transfer or weight function of the equivalent continuous portion of the closed system.

Suppose that we know the weight (or transfer) function of an optimal closed sampled-data system $w_{cl}(n + \varepsilon)$ and that we are required to determine the desired transfer function of its equivalent continuous portion. From the weight function, we determine the weight function of the corresponding open system $w_{op}(n + \varepsilon)$, which, as we know, coincides with the weight function of the equivalent continuous portion of that system:

$$w_{op}(n + \varepsilon) = w_e(n + \varepsilon).$$

Usually, the exact realization of the weight function $w_e(n + \varepsilon)$ that we have obtained is a difficult problem in practice. Therefore, we replace it with the desired weight function $w_*(n + \varepsilon)$, which is easy to realize with the aid of typical components. Having found the desired weight function, we then need to find the desired transfer function of the equivalent continuous portion:

$$W_*(p) = \int_0^{\infty} w_*(t)e^{-tp}dt.$$

Then, we need to choose the transfer functions of the continuous portion $W_c(p)$ and the sampled-data element $W_s(p)$ that will satisfy the equation

$$W_c(p)\,W_s(p) = W_*(p).$$

To determine the desired transfer function of an equivalent stationary continuous portion, we can also use the frequency-response method.

When we have determined the desired transfer function of the equivalent continuous portion, we need to see what properties it ensures in the sampled-data system. Here, we need to calculate the value of the criterion and to compare this value of the criterion with the value ensured by the optimal system.

Furthermore, it is convenient to determine other indices of the quality of the system that are not taken into account by the criterion chosen (for example, the crudeness of the system, the maximum loads, and the like).

In conclusion, it should be noted that the synthesis of an optimal linear system maximizing the probability that the error will not exceed allowed limits at a fixed instant of time is in no essential way different from the synthesis of an optimal linear system minimizing the mean square error. The block diagram of the optimal system is the same in both cases. The only difference is that the parameters are different for the two systems. The synthesis of an optimal system with respect to probability that the error will not exceed allowed limits at fixed instants of time is not essentially different from the synthesis of an optimal system minimizing the sum of the values of the correlation function for different values of time t_1 and t_2.

In the general case, a switch from the criterion representing the sum of the quadratic functionals $I_1, \cdots, I_{n+1}$ to the criterion representing an arbitrary function of these parameters does not cause a change in the block diagram of the optimal system but merely necessitates change of the parameters of that system. Consequently, the procedure and technology of the synthesis can remain as before. This fact should be recognized as an advantageous property of the methods previously expounded for determining optimal systems with respect to a criterion of general form.

Chapter 7

DETERMINATION OF OPTIMAL NONLINEAR AUTOMATIC-CONTROL SYSTEMS

24. DETERMINATION OF THE OPTIMAL NONLINEAR SYSTEM IN TERMS OF THE MINIMUM MEAN SQUARE ERROR

The methods we have considered for determining optimal linear systems with respect to various criteria enable us to solve a large number of practical problems. However, an optimal linear system does not always provide the best solution of a problem. In a number of cases, the shift from the class of linear systems to the broader class of nonlinear systems enables us to obtain a lower value for the mean square error and, in general, a system of higher quality with respect to some criterion or other. Therefore, it is convenient to consider the problem of determining an optimal nonlinear system with respect to different criteria. Of course, it is natural to expect this problem to be considerably more complicated than the problem of determining the optimal linear system with respect to an analogous criterion. Important results in this field have been obtained by Pugachev [Refs. 42, 44–45, 47].

1. Determination of the optimal nonlinear system when the noise obeys a normal distribution law

In the present subsection, we shall, following Pugachev, consider the problem of determining the optimal nonlinear system minimizing the mean square error for the important special case in which the noise $Z(t)$ obeys a normal distribution law. This case is often encountered in practice when one is investigating automatic-control systems. Let us suppose that a signal $X(t)$ consisting of a useful signal $G(t)$ and a noise $Z(t)$ is applied at the input of a system. Without loss of generality, we may assume that the mathematical expectation of the noise is identically zero. The useful signal is a known function of the time t and several unknown parameters $V_1, \cdots, V_n$, which are random variables. (If any of these parameters are unknown quantities, we may assume that they are random variables with infinite variances.) For brevity in writing, we shall denote all these parameters by the single letter V, which is essentially a vector-valued random variable with components $V_1, \cdots, V_n$. Then the useful signal is expressed by the formula

$$G(t) = \varphi(t, V). \tag{7.1}$$

The following are examples of such a function φ:

$$\varphi(t, V) = \varphi(t, V_1, \cdots, V_n) = \varphi_1(t) V_1 + \cdots + \varphi_n(t) V_n, \tag{a}$$

where $\varphi_1(t), \cdots, \varphi_n(t)$ are given functions of time;

$$\varphi(t, V) = \varphi(t, V_1, \cdots, V_n) = \varphi_1(t) e^{V_1 t} + \cdots + \varphi_n(t) e^{V_n t}; \tag{b}$$

$$\varphi(t, V) = \varphi(t, V_1, \cdots, V_n) = \sum_{i, j=1}^{N} \varphi_{ij}(t) V_i V_j, \tag{c}$$

where the $\varphi_{ij}(t)$ are given functions of time.

In accordance with our assumption, the noise $Z(t)$ obeys a normal distribution law and is independent of V. The desired output variable of the system $H(t)$ is determined in accordance with the formula

$$H(t) = \chi(t, V) = P_t \varphi(t, V), \tag{7.2}$$

where P_t is an operator—in the general case, nonlinear. Examples of the desired output variable might be

$$H(t) = G(t) = \varphi(t, V), \tag{a}$$

$$H(t) = \int_0^t \nu(t, \tau) G^2(\tau) d\tau = \int_0^t \nu(t, \tau) \varphi^2(\tau, V) d\tau. \tag{b}$$

We are required to determine the optimal system minimizing the mean square error at a fixed instant of time t. In this case, the mean square error is determined as follows:

$$\Gamma_E(t) = M[E^2(t)] = M[\{Y(t) - H(t)\}^2], \tag{7.3}$$

where $Y(t)$ is the output variable of the system.

For admissible systems, we take all possible systems, linear and nonlinear. Such a formulation of the problem enables us to find systems ensuring the absolute minimum of the mean square error of the system, this minimum determining the limiting theoretical exactness of the system under the given conditions.

Let us determine the law of formation of the output variable of the system $Y(t)$ corresponding to the minimum of this criterion.

The mean square error (7.3) can be obtained in two steps: First we average the square of the error of system over all possible values of the signal $Y(t)$ for a given fixed sample function of the random function $X(t)$, and then we average the result obtained over all sample functions of the random function $X(t)$. As a result of these two averagings, we obtain the unconditional mathematical expectation of the square of the error of the system, that is, the mean square error of the system:

$$\Gamma_E = M[E^2] = M[(Y - H)^2] = M_x[M_y(Y - H)^2/x]. \qquad (7.4)$$

One can easily see that, if we find a system minimizing the conditional mean square error for every sample function x of the random function X:

$$M_y[(Y - H)^2/x] = \min, \qquad (7.5)$$

then this system will also give the absolute minimum of the unconditional mean square error; that is, it will be the desired optimal system out of all possible systems.

To find the conditional mathematical expectation (7.5), it is first necessary to find the conditional probability density of the signal Y or, what amounts to the same thing, of the parameters V defining this signal relative to the input random function X. For this, let us suppose that we are interested in the error of the system at the instant t and that the output variable Y of the system is determined from observations of the input variable X during the interval $[t - T, t]$. Let us represent the noise $Z(t)$ in this interval by some sort of canonical decomposition:

$$Z(\tau) = \sum_{\nu=0}^{\infty} V_\nu z_\nu(\tau), \quad t - T \leqslant \tau \leqslant t, \qquad (7.6)$$

where $V_1, V_2, \cdots$ are uncorrelated random variables whose mathematical expectations are equal to zero and where $z_1(\tau), z_2(\tau), \cdots$ are coordinate functions. The random variables V_ν are expressed in terms of the random function $Z(\tau)$ as follows:

$$V_\nu = \int_{t-T}^{t} a_\nu(\tau) Z(\tau) d\tau, \quad \nu = 1, 2, \cdots, \qquad (7.7)$$

where $a_1(\tau), a_2(\tau), \cdots$ are functions satisfying, along with the coordinate functions $z_\nu(\tau)$, the biorthogonality condition

$$\int_{t-T}^{t} a_\mu(\tau) z_\nu(\tau) d\tau = \begin{cases} 1 \text{ if } \mu = \nu, \\ 0 \text{ if } \mu \neq \nu. \end{cases} \qquad (7.8)$$

Since the noise $Z(t)$ has a normal distribution and the random variables V_ν result from the linear transformation (7.7) of the random function $Z(\tau)$, the random variables V_ν have a normal distribution. We know that uncorrelated random variables obeying a normal distribution law are independent. Therefore, the joint probability density of the random variables $V_1, \cdots, V_n$ is expressed for arbitrary n by the formula

$$f_V(V_1, \cdots, V_n) = \frac{1}{\sqrt{(2\pi)^n D_1, \cdots, D_n}} \exp\left\{-\frac{1}{2} \sum_{\nu=1}^{n} \frac{V_\nu^2}{D_\nu}\right\}, \quad (7.9)$$

where $D_1, D_2, \cdots$ are the variances of the random variables $V_1, V_2, \cdots$.
Let us now look at the random variables

$$X_\nu = \int_{t-T}^{t} a_\nu(\tau) X(\tau) d\tau, \quad \nu = 1, 2, \cdots . \quad (7.10)$$

The random input function X is the sum of a useful signal and a noise:

$$X(\tau) = \varphi(\tau, V) + Z(\tau). \quad (7.11)$$

Substituting this expression into (7.10) and keeping (7.7) in mind, we obtain

$$X_\nu = \int_{t-T}^{t} a_\nu(\tau) \varphi(\tau, V) d\tau + V_\nu. \quad (7.12)$$

By introducing the notation

$$\alpha_\nu(U) = \frac{1}{D_\nu} \int_{t-T}^{t} a_\nu(\tau) \varphi(\tau, U) d\tau, \quad \nu = 1, 2, \cdots, \quad (7.13)$$

we can rewrite formula (7.12) in the form

$$X_\nu = D_\nu \alpha_\nu(U) + V_\nu, \quad \nu = 1, 2, \cdots \quad (7.14)$$

The random variables X_ν are functions of the random parameters U and the corresponding random variables V_ν. On the basis of (7.6) and (7.14), we can write

$$\sum_{\nu=1}^{\infty} X_\nu z_\nu(\tau) = \sum_{\nu=1}^{\infty} D_\nu \alpha_\nu(U) z_\nu(\tau) + Z(\tau), \quad t - T \leqslant \tau \leqslant t. \quad (7.15)$$

Let us suppose in addition that the function $\varphi(\tau, U)$ can be represented in the interval of observation by an expansion in the coordinate functions $z_\nu(\tau)$:

$$\varphi(\tau, U) = \sum_{\nu=1}^{\infty} D_\nu \alpha_\nu(U) z_\nu(\tau), \quad t - T \leqslant \tau \leqslant t. \quad (7.16)$$

Now, it follows from (7.11), (7.15), and (7.16) that

$$X(\tau) = \sum_{\nu=1}^{\infty} X_\nu z_\nu(\tau), \quad t - T \leqslant \tau \leqslant t. \quad (7.17)$$

Formulas (7.10) and (7.17) define a one-to-one correspondence between the random function $X(\tau)$ and the set of random variables $X_1, X_2, \cdots$. Therefore, the conditional distribution law of the random parameters U_i with respect to the random function $X(\tau)$ coincides identically with the conditional distribution law of the random parameters U with respect to the set of random variables $X_1, X_2, \cdots$.

On the basis of familiar formulas from probability theory, we can write the expression of the conditional probability density $f_1(u/x_1, \cdots, x_n)$ of the parameters U with respect to a finite number n of random variables $X_1, \cdots, X_n$:

$$f_1(u/x_1, \cdots, x_n) = \frac{f(u)f_2(x_1, \cdots, x_n/u)}{\displaystyle\int_{-\infty}^{\infty} f(u)f_2(x_1, \cdots, x_n/u)\,du}, \qquad (7.18)$$

where $f(u)$ is the unconditional (*a priori*) probability density of the parameters U, which we assume known, and where $f_2(x_1, \cdots, x_n/u)$ is the conditional probability density of the random variables $X_1, \cdots, X_n$ with respect to the random parameters U. To determine the conditional probability density of the random variables $X_1, \cdots, X_n$ with respect to the random variables U, we need to replace the random variables in (7.14) with their possible values u. Then, the random variables X_ν are linear functions of the corresponding random variables:

$$X_\nu = D_\nu \alpha_\nu(u) + V_\nu.$$

Now, in accordance with (7.9), we may write

$$f_2(x_1, \cdots, x_n/u)$$

$$= \frac{1}{\sqrt{(2\pi)^n D_1, \cdots, D_n}} \exp\left\{ -\frac{1}{2} \sum_{\nu=1}^{n} \frac{1}{D_\nu} [x_\nu - D_\nu \alpha_\nu(u)]^2 \right\}$$

$$= \frac{1}{\sqrt{(2\pi)^n D_1, \cdots, D_n}} \exp\left\{ -\sum_{\nu=1}^{n} \frac{x_\nu^2}{2D_\nu} + \sum_{\nu=1}^{n} \alpha_\nu(u) x_\nu \right.$$

$$\left. -\frac{1}{2} \sum_{\nu=1}^{n} D_\nu \alpha_\nu^2(u) \right\}. \qquad (7.19)$$

When we substitute this expression into (7.18) and cancel out the constant factors, we obtain the conditional probability density of the random variables U with respect to the random variables $X_1, \cdots, X_n$:

$$f_1(u/x_1, \cdots, x_n) = \frac{f(u)\exp\left\{ \displaystyle\sum_{\nu=1}^{n} \alpha_\nu(u) x_\nu - \frac{1}{2} \sum_{\nu=1}^{n} D_\nu \alpha_\nu^2(u) \right\}}{\displaystyle\int_{-\infty}^{\infty} f(u)\exp\left\{ \sum_{\nu=1}^{n} \alpha_\nu(u) x_\nu - \frac{1}{2} \sum_{\nu=1}^{n} D_\nu \alpha_\nu^2(u) \right\} du}.$$

$$(7.20)$$

If we take the limit in this formula as $n \to \infty$, we find the conditional probability density of the random variables U with respect to the set of all random functions X_ν:

$$f_1(u/x_1, x_2, \cdots) = \frac{f(u) \exp\left\{\sum_{\nu=1}^{\infty} \alpha_\nu(u) x_\nu - \frac{1}{2} \sum_{\nu=1}^{\infty} D_\nu \alpha_\nu^2(u)\right\}}{\int_{-\infty}^{\infty} f(u) \exp\left\{\sum_{\nu=1}^{\infty} \alpha_\nu(u) x_\nu - \frac{1}{2} \sum_{\nu=1}^{\infty} D_\nu \alpha_\nu^2(u)\right\} du}.$$

(7.21)

On the basis of (7.10), we may write

$$\sum_{\nu=1}^{\infty} \alpha_\nu(u) X_\nu = \int_{t-T}^{t} \sum_{\nu=1}^{\infty} \alpha_\nu(u) a_\nu(\tau) X(\tau) d\tau = \int_{t-T}^{t} A(t, \tau, u) X(\tau) d\tau,$$

(7.22)

where

$$A(t, \tau, u) = \sum_{\nu=1}^{\infty} \alpha_\nu(u) a_\nu(\tau).$$

(7.23)

The function A depends not only on u and τ but also on t, as is obvious from formulas (7.8) and (7.13).

We introduce the function

$$\beta(u) = \sum_{\nu=1}^{\infty} D_\nu \alpha_\nu^2(u)$$

(7.24)

and note that the set of numbers $x_1, x_2, \cdots$, which are fixed values of the random variables $X_1, X_2, \cdots$, is equivalent to the function $x(\tau)$, which is a sample function of the random function $X(\tau)$. This enables us to write

$$f_1(u/x) = \kappa(x) f(u) \exp\left\{\int_{t-T}^{t} A(t, \tau, u) x(\tau) d\tau - \frac{1}{2} \beta(u)\right\}, \quad (7.25)$$

where

$$\kappa(x) = \left[\int_{-\infty}^{\infty} f(u) \exp\left\{\int_{t-T}^{t} A(t, \tau, u) x(\tau) d\tau - \frac{1}{2} \beta(u)\right\} du\right]^{-1} \quad (7.26)$$

is a constant (with respect to u) normalizing factor dependent on the sample function x of the random function X.

On the basis of (7.13) and (7.23), formula (7.24) for the function $\beta(u)$ can be rewritten as

$$\beta(u) = \int_{t-T}^{t} A(t, \tau, u) \varphi(\tau, u) d\tau.$$

(7.27)

Formula (7.25) gives the conditional probability density of the random parameters U with respect to the input random function of the system X, that is, the *a posteriori* probability density of the parameters U. This probability density is determined from observation when we known the sample function x of the random function X. When we know the *a posteriori* probability density $f(u)$ of the parameters U, we can calculate the *a posteriori* mathematical expectation (the conditional mathematical expectation with respect to the input function X) of the square of the error of the system:

$$\Gamma_{EX} = M_Y[(Y-H)^2/X] = \kappa(x) \int_{-\infty}^{\infty} [Y-\chi(t,u)]^2 f(u)$$

$$\times \exp\left\{\int_{t-T}^{t} A(t,\tau,u)x(\tau)d\tau - \frac{1}{2}\beta(u)\right\}du. \qquad (7.28)$$

Now, for each fixed value of the time t it is possible to determine the output variable of the system $Y(t)$ from the condition that the integral in (7.28) is minimized. To find the minimum of this integral, we set its derivative with respect to Y equal to zero and we obtain

$$\int_{-\infty}^{\infty} [Y-\chi(t,u)]f(u) \exp\left\{\int_{t-T}^{t} A(t,\tau,u)x(\tau)d\tau - \frac{1}{2}\beta(u)\right\}du = 0.$$

$$(7.29)$$

The solution of this equation is easily found:

$$Y(t) = \frac{\int_{-\infty}^{\infty} \chi(t,u)f(u) \exp\left\{\int_{t-T}^{t} A(t,\tau,u)x(\tau)d\tau - \frac{1}{2}\beta(u)\right\}du}{\int_{-\infty}^{\infty} f(u) \exp\left\{\int_{t-T}^{t} A(t,\tau,u)x(\tau)d\tau - \frac{1}{2}\beta(u)\right\}du}. \qquad (7.30)$$

By virtue of (7.25) and (7.26), the right hand number of this formula is the conditional mathematical expectation of the function $\chi(t,u)$ with respect to the input random function $X(t)$; that is, the conditional mathematical expectation of the desired output variable $H(t)$ with respect to the input random function $X(t)$. Consequently, formula (7.30) can be rewritten as

$$Y(t) = M[H(t)/X]. \qquad (7.31)$$

Thus, *in the present case, the optimal system out of all possible systems is the system that yields at the output the conditional mathematical expectation of the desired output variable H with respect to the input function X, that is, the a posteriori mathematical expectation of the desired output variable.* For each specific sample function $x(t)$ of the input signal $X(t)$, the calculation of this *a posteriori* mathematical expectation is carried out in accordance with formula (7.30).

Consequently, in the present case the optimal operator of the system is the set consisting of the following mathematical operators:

(1)   Determination of the function $A(t,\tau,u)$ in accordance with formula (7.23),

(2)   calculation of the function $\beta(u)$ (which also depends on the time t) in accordance with formula (7.27),

(3)   determination of the value of the output function Y at each given instant t in accordance with formula (7.30).

The function $A(t, \tau, u)$ can be determined in another way. Let us substitute the expression (7.13) for the function $\alpha_\nu(u)$ into formula (7.23). This yields

$$A(t, \tau, u) = \sum_{\nu=1}^{\infty} \frac{a_\nu(\tau)}{D_\nu} \int_{t-T}^{t} \alpha_\nu(\lambda)\varphi(\lambda, u)d\lambda. \qquad (7.32)$$

We know [Refs. 46, 47] that the function $A(t, \tau, u)$ defined by formula (7.32) is a solution of the integral equation

$$\int_{t-T}^{t} K_z(\tau, \lambda) A(t, \tau, u)d\tau = \varphi(\lambda, u), \quad t - T \leqslant \lambda \leqslant t, \qquad (7.33)$$

where $K_z(\tau, \lambda)$ is a correlation function of the noise $Z(t)$. Formulas (7.13) and (7.23), which are equivalent to formula (7.32), yield a solution of the integral equation (7.33) in the form of an infinite series.

We have described mathematical operations enabling us to determine the function $A(t, \tau, u)$ from formulas (7.13) and (7.23). However, it is sometimes more convenient to determine the function $A(t, \tau, u)$ not from formulas (7.13) and (7.23) but by solving equation (7.33) directly. Then, the operator of the optimal system is the following sequence of mathematical operations:

(1)   Determination of the function $A(t, \tau, u)$ by solving the integral equation (7.33),

(2)   calculation of the function $\beta(u)$ by using formula (7.27),

(3)   determination of the value of the output function Y at each value of the time t on the basis of formula (7.30).

The problem of finding the optimal operator is considerably simplified when the useful signal $G(t)$ is linearly dependent on the parameters $U_1, \cdots, U_N$:

$$\varphi(t, U) = \sum_{i=1}^{N} U_i\varphi_i(t). \qquad (7.34)$$

In this case, the solution of the integral equation (7.33) also depends linearly on the parameters $U_1, \cdots, U_N$:

$$A(t, \tau, u) = \sum_{i=1}^{N} u_i A_i(t, \tau), \qquad (7.35)$$

where the $A_i(t, \tau)$ are weight functions determined by the integral equations

$$\int_{t-T}^{t} K_z(\tau, \lambda) A_i(t, \tau)d\tau = \varphi_i(\lambda), \quad t - T \leqslant \lambda \leqslant t, \quad i = 1, \cdots, N. \qquad (7.36)$$

Equation (7.36) is considerably simpler than equation (7.30). If we substitute the expression (7.34) (with the U_i replaced by their possible values u_i) and the expression (7.35) into formula (7.27), we obtain

$$\beta(u) = \sum_{p,\,q=1}^{N} b_{pq} u_p u_q, \tag{7.37}$$

where

$$b_{pq} = \int_{t-T}^{t} A_q(t,\tau)\varphi_p(\tau)d\tau, \quad p, q = 1, \cdots, N. \tag{7.38}$$

If we substitute (7.35) and (7.37) into (7.30), we obtain

$$Y(t) = \frac{\displaystyle\int_{-\infty}^{\infty} \chi(t,u)S(u)du_1, \cdots, du_N}{\displaystyle\int_{-\infty}^{\infty} S(u)du_1, \cdots, du_N}, \tag{7.39}$$

where

$$S(u) = f(u)\exp\left\{\sum_{i=1}^{N} u_i \int_{t-T}^{t} A_i(t,\tau)x(\tau)d\tau - \frac{1}{2}\sum_{p,\,q=1}^{N} b_{pq} u_p u_q\right\}.$$

If the desired output variable $H(t)$ is a linear function of the parameters $U_1, \cdots, U_N$:

$$H(t) = \chi(t,U) = \sum_{i=1}^{N} U_i \chi_i(t), \tag{7.40}$$

then formula (7.31) takes the form

$$Y(t) = \sum_{i=1}^{N} M[U_i/X]\chi_i(t). \tag{7.41}$$

Here, the quantities $M[U_i/X]$ are the optimal estimates of the parameters $U_1, \cdots, U_N$ with respect to the criterion of minimization of the mean square error (cf. formula (7.31)). Consequently, to estimate the signal $H(t)$, which is a linear function of the parameters $U_1, \cdots, U_N$ with respect to the criterion of minimization of the mean square error, we need only find estimates $M[U_i/X]$ of the parameters $U_1, \cdots, U_N$ and replace the parameters $U_1, \cdots, U_N$ in the expression (7.40) with these estimates.

Pugachev has shown [Refs. 45–47] that if the input signal X and the desired output variable H depend linearly on the parameters $U_1, \cdots, U_N$ and if the parameters $U_1, \cdots, U_N$ and the noise $Z(t)$ have normal distributions, the optimal system out of all possible systems is linear. This theoretical result is of great significance for practical applications. It ensures the expediency of using the methods (thoroughly worked out and widely used) of determining the optimal systems with respect to statistical criteria. Pugachev also showed that, for such initial conditions and for criteria I of the more general form

$$I = M[l(Y - H)], \tag{7.42}$$

where $l(Y - H)$ is an arbitrary function of the error of the system, the optimal system out of all possible systems is a linear system.

EXAMPLE. Suppose that the useful signal $G(t)$ is a random variable U that can assume three values $+c$, 0, and $-c$ with equal probabilities. Consequently,

$$f(u) = \frac{1}{3}[\delta(u - c) + \delta(u) + \delta(u + c)].$$ (a)

The noise $Z(t)$ is a stationary random function. It has the correlation function

$$K_z(\tau) = D_z e^{-\alpha|\tau|},$$ (b)

where D_z is the variance of the noise (a given number) and α is a given (positive) coefficient. The time of observation is T. The desired output variable is

$$H(t) = \chi(t, U) = kG(t) = kU_1,$$ (c)

where k is a constant coefficient.

Suppose that we are required to determine the optimal operator in the class of all possible operators. We begin by determining the function $A_1(t, \tau)$. In the present case, this function depends on the single parameter τ, since the initial data are stationary. To determine the function $A_1(\tau)$, we use the integral equation (7.36), which, in the special case that we are considering, can be written as

$$\int_0^T D_z e^{-\alpha|\tau - \lambda|} A_1(\lambda)d\lambda = 1, \quad 0 \leqslant \tau \leqslant T.$$ (d)

In accordance with (3.54), the solution of this equation is of the form

$$A_1(\tau) = a_0 + a_1\delta(\tau) + a_2\delta(\tau - T).$$ (e)

The coefficients a_0, a_1, and a_2 can be determined by substituting (e) into equation (d), integrating from 0 to T, and setting the coefficients of the functions l, $e^{-\alpha\tau}$, and $e^{\alpha\tau}$ identically equal to zero. We omit the details of these elementary calculations and simply write the expressions for the coefficients sought:

$$a_0 = \frac{a}{2D_z}, \quad a_1 = a_2 = \frac{1 - e^{\alpha T}}{1 - e^{2\alpha T}}\frac{1}{2D_z}.$$ (f)

We now need to obtain an expression for the integral of the product of the function $A_1(\tau)$ and the sample function $x(\tau)$:

$$\int_0^T A_1(\tau)x(\tau)d\tau = \int_0^T [a_0 + a_1\delta(\tau) + a_2\delta(\tau - T)]x(\tau)d\tau$$
$$= a_0 \int_0^T x(\tau)d\tau + a_1x(0) + a_2x(T).$$ (g)

Now, we need to determine the coefficient b_{11} in accordance with formula (7.38), setting $p = q = 1$:

$$b_{11} = \int_0^T A_1(\tau)\varphi_1(\tau)d\tau = \int_0^T [a_0 + a_1\delta(\tau) + a_2\delta(\tau - T)]\cdot 1 \cdot d\tau$$
$$= Ta_0 + a_1 + a_2 = Ta_0 + 2a_1. \qquad (h)$$

When we substitute the expressions for (a), (c), (g), and (h) into formula (7.39), we obtain

$$Y = \frac{\displaystyle\int_{-\infty}^{\infty} ku_1 Q(u_1)\,du_1}{\displaystyle\int_{-\infty}^{\infty} Q(u_1)\,du_1} = ck\frac{V(T)}{V(T) + 1}, \qquad (i)$$

where

$$Q(u_1) = \frac{1}{3}[\delta(u_1 - c) + \delta(u_1) + \delta(u_1 + c)]$$

$$\times \exp\left\{u_1\left[a_0\int_0^T x(\tau)d\tau + a_1 x(0) + a_2 x(T)\right]\frac{1}{2}(Ta_0 + 2a_1)u_1^2\right\},$$

$$V(T) = \exp\left\{c\left[a_0\int_0^T x(\tau)d\tau + a_1 x(0) + a_2 x(T)\right] - \frac{1}{2}(Ta_0 + 2a_1)c^2\right\}$$

$$- \exp\left\{-c\left[a_0\int_0^T x(\tau)d\tau + a_1 x(0) + a_2 x(T)\right] - \frac{1}{2}(Ta_0 + 2a_1)c^2\right\}.$$

This formula can be rewritten in the following form:

$$Y = \frac{ckM}{M + \exp\left\{\frac{1}{2}(Ta_0 + 2a_1)c^2\right\}}, \qquad (j)$$

where

$$M = \exp\left\{c\left[a_0\int_0^T x(\tau)d\tau + a_1 x(0) + a_2 x(T)\right]\right\}$$

$$- \exp\left\{-c\left[a_0\int_0^T x(\tau)d\tau + a_1 x(0) + a_2 x(T)\right]\right\}.$$

We note that for initial conditions of this example, the optimal weight function $w_0(\tau)$ of the linear system possessing astaticism of the first order could have been determined as the solution of the linear integral equation

$$\int_0^T D_z e^{-\alpha|\tau - \lambda|}w_0(\lambda)d\lambda = \gamma_0.$$

The undetermined coefficient could then have been determined from the condition

$$\int_0^T w_0(\tau)d\tau = 1.$$

From this it follows that, up to a constant factor, the optimal weight function $w_0(\tau)$ coincides with the function $A_1(\tau)$. The output variable of the optimal linear system Y_l is determined from the formula

$$Y_\pi = \int_0^T w_0(\tau) x(\tau) d\tau. \tag{k}$$

Comparison of formulas (j) and (k) gives us an idea of how much more complicated the algorithm for calculating the output variable of an optimal nonlinear system is than the algorithm for calculating the optimal output variable of a linear system.

2.   A general condition for the minimum of the mean square error

In the present subsection, we shall consider the general case in which the automatic-control system (operator) can be arbitrary. Moreover, we impose no restrictions on the influences. Under the general conditions, we shall derive a condition determining the optimal system (the optimal operator) out of the class of all possible systems. Let us formulate the statement of the problem. Suppose that a random function $X(t)$ acts on the input of a system and that we wish to have a random function $H(t)$ at the output of the system. The operator A characterizing the system and determining the output function of the system $Y(t)$:

$$Y(t) = AX(t). \tag{7.43}$$

belongs to some set of operators R, which is a linear space. We recall that a linear space R is defined as a set of elements A with the property that, for any elements A_1 and A_2 belonging to the set R, the element $k_1 A_1 + k_2 A_2$ also belongs to R:

$$\left.\begin{array}{c} A_1 \in R \\ A_2 \in R \end{array}\right\} \Longrightarrow k_1 A_1 + k_2 A_2 \in R.$$

Here, k_1 and k_2 are arbitary real numbers. Examples of linear spaces are (a) all nonlinear operators (systems), (b) all linear operators (systems), (c) all asymptotically stable systems.

It follows from our assumption that if the systems characterized by the operators A_1 and A_2 are admissible, so is the system characterized by the operator $k_1 A_1 + k_2 A_2$; that is, the system obtained from the two original systems by hooking them onto the outputs of ideal amplifiers and connecting the composite systems in parallel.

We make no further restrictions on the class of admissible systems (operators A). Consequently, the problem is posed under general assumptions regarding admissible systems, i.e., under weak restrictions imposed on them. We make no restrictions at all on the initial data concerning the influences. We assume only that their probabilistic characteristics can be obtained.

For our criterion, we take the mean square error of the system at a fixed instant of time. It can be determined for an arbitary admissible operator A in accordance with the formula

$$\Gamma_E = M[(Y - H)^2] = M\{[AX(t) - H(t)]^2\}. \tag{7.44}$$

Let us transform this formula to the following form:

$$\begin{aligned}
\Gamma_E &= M\{[AX(t) - A_0X(t) + A_0X(t) - H(t)]^2\} \\
&= M[AX(t) - A_0X(t)]^2 + 2M\{[AX(t) - A_0X(t)] \\
&\quad \times [A_0X(t) - H(t)]\} + M\{[A_0X(t) - H(t)]^2\},
\end{aligned} \tag{7.45}$$

where A_0 is the optimal operator in the class R.

Suppose that there exists an operator A_0 such that, for all operators $A \in R$,

$$M\{[AX(t) - A_0X(t)][A_0X(t) - H(t)]\} = 0. \tag{7.46}$$

Then, for an arbitrary operator $A \in R$, equation (7.45) takes the form

$$\begin{aligned}
\Gamma_E &= M\{[AX(t) - H(t)]^2\} \\
&= M\{[AX(t) - A_0X(t)]^2\} + M\{[A_0X(t) - H(t)]^2\}.
\end{aligned} \tag{7.47}$$

Consequently, when condition (7.46) is satisfied, we have

$$M\{[AX(t) - H(t)]^2\} \geqslant M\{[A_0X(t) - H(t)]^2\}. \tag{7.48}$$

Thus, equation (7.46) is a sufficient condition for the operator A_0 to minimize the mean square error of the system in the present case. Let us show that condition (7.46) is also necessary for the operator A_0 to minimize the mean square error of the system (7.44); that is, for inequality (7.48) to be satisfied for all $A \in R$. To do this, let us suppose that, for some $A_1 \in R$, condition (7.46) is not satisfied; that is, that

$$M\{[A_1X(t) - A_0X(t)][A_0X(t) - H(t)]\} \neq 0. \tag{7.49}$$

We define

$$A_\alpha = A_0 + \alpha(A_1 - A_0), \tag{7.50}$$

where α is an arbitrary number. The operator A_α belongs to the class R, since the class R is a linear space. For the operator A_α, we can write

$$M\{[A_0X(t) - A_\alpha X(t)]^2\} = \alpha^2 M\{[A_1X(t) - A_0X(t)]^2\}. \tag{7.51}$$

Now, we can write the following equation, analogous to equation (7.45):

$$\begin{aligned}
M\{[A_\alpha X(t) - H(t)]^2\} &= M[\{[A_0X(t) - H(t)] + \alpha[A_1X(t) - A_0X(t)]\}^2] \\
&= M\{[A_0X(t) - H(t)]^2\} + 2\alpha M\{[A_0X(t) - H(t)][A_1X(t) - A_0X(t)]\} \\
&\quad + \alpha^2 M\{[A_1X(t) - A_0X(t)]^2\}.
\end{aligned} \tag{7.52}$$

From this it is clear that if we take α sufficiently small in absolute value and opposite in sign to the quantity

$$M\{[A_0X(t) - H(t)][A_1X(t) - A_0X(t)]\},$$

then the following inequality will hold:

$$M\{[A_\alpha X(t) - H(t)]^2\} < M\{[A_0X(t) - H(t)]^2\}.$$

This means that if condition (7.49) is satisfied f)r at least one operator A_1, then the operator A_0 cannot be optimal. Thi; completes the proof of the necessity of condition (7.46).

Thus, condition (7.46) is a necessary and sufficient condition for the operator A_0 to minimize the mean square error in the general case that we are considering.

Remembering that the operator A is an arbitary member of the class R, we can replace the sum of the operators $A + A_0$ with the operator A. Then, condition (7.46) can be rewritten as

$$M\{AX(t)[A_0X(t) - H(t)]\} = 0 \qquad (7.53)$$

for an arbitrary operator $A \in R$.

Pugachev's condition is a necessary and sufficient condition for minimization of the mean square error attained in the class of operators A belonging to the class R. This equation has a very broad field of application. By using it, we can obtain conditions determining optimal systems in various specific cases. In what follows, we shall encounter examples of the use of this equation.

3. The case in which the admissible operators are all nonlinear integral operators

Let us consider the case when the class R of admissible operators A consists of all nonlinear integral operators:

$$AX(t) = \int_T \varphi[X(t), t, s]dt, \qquad (7.54)$$

where $\varphi(x, t, s)$ is an arbitrary function of the variables x, t, and s and T is a fixed interval of integration with respect to time t. The output variable of the system $Y(s) = AX(t)$ is also usually a function of time, but this time is sometimes measured in another region (not the region T). In what follows, we shall find it convenient to denote it by a different letter; for example, s. In special cases, the time s coincides with the time t. Formula (7.54) is similar to the formula connecting the output variable with the input variable of a linear system. The difference consists in the fact that, here, the function φ depends in an arbitrary manner on the input variable X, whereas, in the case of a linear system, the integrand is a linear function of X. The class of nonlinear systems with operators of the type (7.54) includes the class of all linear systems.

One can easily see that the class R of operators of the type (7.54) is a linear space. Suppose that the desired output variable of the system is of the form

$$H(s) = \int_Q h[G(t), t, s]dt, \qquad (7.55)$$

where $h(z, t, s)$ is a given function of its variables, Q is a fixed interval of integration, and s is time.

In all our subsequent investigations, the instant of time s will be arbitrary but fixed. Consequently, the operators $Y(s)$ and $H(s)$ can be regarded as functionals (with s fixed).

To obtain an equation determining an optimal operator of the type (7.54), we use Pugachev's equation (7.53), which may be written as

$$M\left(\int_T \varphi[X(u), u, s]du \left\{ \int_T \varphi_0[X(t), t, s]dt - \int_Q h[G(t), t, s]dt \right\} \right) = 0,$$

$$(7.56)$$

where $\varphi_0(x, t, s)$ is the optimal characteristic function and $\varphi(x, u, s)$ is an arbitrary function of its parameters. We note that the variable of integration has no effect on the value of the integral. Therefore, in the first integral we may replace the variable t with the variable u. We make this change for convenience in the presentation of subsequent double integrals.

Equation (7.56) must be satisfied for an arbitrary operator A of the type (7.54), that is, for an arbitrary function $\varphi(x, u, s)$.

Let us rewrite equation (7.56) in another form, replacing the products of ordinary integrals with double integrals:

$$M\left\{ \int_T \int_T \varphi[X(u), u, s]\varphi_0[X(t), t, s]dtdu \right.$$

$$\left. - \int_T \int_Q \varphi[X(u), u, s]h[G(t), t, s]dtdu \right\} = 0. \qquad (7.57)$$

Suppose that we know the quantities $f_{xx}(x, x', t, t')$ (that is, the two-dimensional probability density of the random function $X(t)$) and $f_{xg}(x, g, t, t')$ (that is, the two-dimensional joint probability density of the random functions $X(t)$ and $G(t)$). Then, remembering that the operations of taking the mathematical expectation and integration are commutative, we can rewrite equation (7.57) in the following form:

$$\int_T \int_T dt\,du \int_{-\infty}^{\infty} \int_{-\infty}^{\infty} \varphi(x, u, s)\varphi_0(x', t, s)f_{xx}(x, x', u, t)dx\,dx'$$

$$- \int_T \int_Q dt\,du \int_{-\infty}^{\infty} \int_{-\infty}^{\infty} \varphi(x, u, s)h(g, t, s)f_{xg}(x, g, u, t)dx\,dg = 0$$

$$(7.58)$$

or

$$\int_T du \int_{-\infty}^{\infty} \left\{ \int_T dt \int_{-\infty}^{\infty} \varphi_0(x', t, s) f_{xx}(x, x', u, t) dx' \right.$$
$$\left. - \int_Q dt \int_{-\infty}^{\infty} h(g, t, s) f_{xg}(x, g, u, t) dg \right\} \varphi(x, u, s) dx = 0. \quad (7.59)$$

This equation must be satisfied for an arbitrary function φ, which is possible only when the expression in the brace vanishes for arbitrary x and arbitrary $u \in T$. This means that the function φ_0 must satisfy the equation

$$\int_T dt \int_{-\infty}^{\infty} \varphi_0(x', t, s) f_{xx}(x, x', u, t) dx'$$
$$- \int_Q dt \int_{-\infty}^{\infty} h(g, t, s) f_{xg}(x, g, u, t) dg = 0,$$
$$u \in T, \quad -\infty < x < \infty. \quad (7.60)$$

Equation (7.60) is a necessary condition for optimality of the characteristic function φ_0 and hence of the operator

$$A_0 X(t) = \int_T \varphi_0[X(t), t, s] dt.$$

This equation was first obtained by Zadeh.

In the particular case in which the desired output variable is equal to the useful signal, that is, when $H(s) = G(s)$, the function h in (7.55) is given by the formula

$$h(g, t, s) = g\delta(s - t). \quad (7.61)$$

Let us substitute this expression into equation (7.60) and let us obtain a necessary condition determining the optimal function φ_0 in this case:

$$\int_T dt \int_{-\infty}^{\infty} \varphi_0(x', t, s) f_{xx}(x, x', u, t) dx' = \int_{-\infty}^{\infty} g f_{xg}(x, g, u, s) dg,$$
$$u \in T, \quad -\infty < x < \infty. \quad (7.62)$$

This equation and equation (7.60) can be solved by various approximation methods. In the general case, the problem of solving these two equations is quite difficult.

The material of the present section enables us to conclude that determination of the optimal nonlinear operator when the criterion is minimization of the mean square error is a problem incomparably more difficult than the problem of determining the optimal linear operator (the weight function of the system). We might expect this to be the case. We know that the analysis of precision of nonlinear systems is incomparably more complex than the analysis of precision of linear systems. Synthesis of systems and a component of it, the determination of optimal systems, rests on formulas and relationships obtained in the analysis of these systems. Therefore, systems requiring a more complex apparatus in their analysis will also require a more complex apparatus in their synthesis. In the general case, both in the analysis and the synthesis of nonlinear systems, we have succeeded in obtaining quite complex relationships from which it is difficult to arrive at the final result. Obviously, in the synthesis of nonlinear systems, just as in the analysis of these systems, it is expedient to develop approximate methods of investigation that can be applied under specific restrictions imposed on the class of admissible systems and on the influences. Obviously, the search for optimal parameters of a nonlinear system when we have a given structure and a given type of nonlinear components included in the system can also be fruitful. In such a formulation of the problem, we can use the method of fastest descent. Here, we need to calculate the criterion repeatedly with different values of the parameters. It is difficult to carry out this operation analytically. Therefore, to determine the criterion, it is expedient to use a model. A number of experiments on models involving analytical calculations in accordance with the method of fastest descent enable us to find in a limited period of time the optimal combinations of parameters of a nonlinear system with given characteristics of random influences.

25. DETERMINATION OF THE OPTIMAL NONLINEAR SYSTEM IN TERMS OF CRITERIA OF A GENERAL FORM

1. Determination of the optimal nonlinear operator when the criterion is a given function of other criteria

In the preceding chapters, we mentioned that the mean square error does not always reflect the purpose of a linear system. This very simple probabilistic criterion does not always reflect the purpose even of a nonlinear system. The error of a nonlinear system usually obeys a complicated distribution law, which we do not know in advance. Therefore, a natural criterion, such as the probability that the error of a nonlinear system will not exceed given allowed limits cannot be expressed in the general case in terms of the characteristics of the system. We find ourselves in the following position: To determine the optimal nonlinear system, we need to express the criterion in terms of the characteristics of the system, and to express the criterion in the terms of the characteristics of the system, we need to know the optimal system (and the distribution law of its error). As usual, in such cases, we can recommend the following way out of the difficulty. We can assign, by some method or other, the form of the distribution law of the error of the system, let us say, a normal distribution law of the error with undetermined variance and mathematical expectation or a law of equal probability with undetermined variance and mathematical expectation or a triangular distribution law with three undetermined parameters, and so on. After we have specified the form of the distribution law, we can express the probability that the error of the system will not exceed given allowed limits in terms of the parameters of that distribution law; for example, in terms of the mathematical expectation and the variance. We then need to express the parameters of the distribution law in terms of the characteristics of the nonlinear system. Then, the criterion itself will be expressed in terms of the characteristics of the nonlinear system. After that, we need to find the optimal characteristics of the system (maximizing the criterion). If the parameters of the distribution law are denoted by $I_1, I_2, \cdots, I_{n+1}$ and the dependence of the criterion on these parameters by f, we can write

$$P(c_1 < E < c_2) = f(I_1, \cdots, I_{n+1}), \tag{7.63}$$

where the parameters I_i depend on the characteristics of the nonlinear system (on the nonlinear operator A).

We then need to find the nonlinear system (its dynamic characteristics) that maximizes the criterion (7.63) and to determine the distribution law of the error of the system. If it turns out to be close to the distribution law previously chosen, we can consider the problem solved. However, we cannot count on such a result in the general case. It is natural to assume that, after we have found the optimal system of the first approximation, it will turn out that the distribution law of the error of the system will differ considerably from the law with which we started. In such a typical case, we need to assign a form of the distribution law of the error of the system that is close to the one obtained. (We shall call it the distribution law of the second approximation.)

Now, we repeat all our calculations. This process of successive approximations should be terminated when two successive approximations of the distribution law of the error of the system are close to each other. We can say nothing about the speed of convergence of the process of calculating the successive approximations. In this process, the problem of finding the nonlinear system maximizing the complicated criterion (7.63) is a very complicated problem. Therefore, it is desirable to reduce the choice of the optimal system in accordance with the criterion (7.63) to a simpler problem. This can be done. Theorem 2a of Chapter 1, formulated for the functionals $I_1, \cdots, I_{n+1}$ of a definite type can, without difficulty, be carried over to the present more general case. We restate the theorem as it applies to this case.

THEOREM 2b. *For a nonlinear operator (nonlinear system) to correspond to an extremum of a criterion of the type (7.63), it is necessary that this operator correspond to an extremum of the reduced criterion*

$$I_\theta = \theta_1 I_1 + \cdots + \theta_n I_n + I_{n+1} \tag{7.64}$$

for certain values of the harmonizing parameters

$$\theta_1 = \theta_{10}, \cdots, \theta_n = \theta_{n0}.$$

Determination of the nonlinear operator $A_0(\theta_1, \cdots, \theta_n)$, corresponding to an extremum of the reduced criterion I_θ is usually easier to do than is the determination of the nonlinear operator A_0 corresponding to an extremum of the criterion (7.63). When we have determined the operator $A_0(\theta_1, \cdots, \theta_n)$, we can determine the values of the parameters

$$\theta_1 = \theta_{10}, \cdots, \theta_n = \theta_{n0}$$

corresponding to an extremum of the criterion (7.63) in the following manner: The operator $A_0(\theta_1, \cdots, \theta_n)$ is substituted into the criterion (7.63). Then, the criterion (7.63) becomes a known function $\Phi(\theta_1, \cdots, \theta_n)$ of the parameters $\theta_1, \cdots, \theta_n$. We then need to find the parameters

$$\theta_1 = \theta_{10}, \cdots, \theta_n = \theta_{n0}$$

corresponding to an extremum of the function Φ. The parameters $\theta_{10}, \cdots, \theta_{n0}$ are unknown values of the harmonizing parameters. The operator

$$A^0 = A_0(\theta_{10}, \cdots, \theta_{n0})$$

is the desired optimal nonlinear operator ensuring an extremum of the criterion (7.63). Let us look at the application of this procedure in certain particular cases.

2. Determination of the optimal nonlinear operator with respect to a criterion that is a given function $f(m_E, \Gamma_E)$ of the mathematical expectation and the mean square error (the noise obeying a normal distribution law)

Consider the following formulation of the problem. Suppose that a signal $X(t)$, which is the sum of the useful signal $G(t)$ and the noise $Z(t)$, is applied at the input of the system. The useful signal is a known function of the time and the random variables $U_1, \cdots, U_N$. For brevity, we denote these random variables by U. The useful signal can then be described by formula (7.1). The noise $Z(t)$ is a centralized random function obeying a normal distribution law and is uncorrelated with the random variables U_i.

The desired output variable $H(t)$ of the system is determined in accordance with formula (7.2). For admissible systems, we take all possible systems (linear and nonlinear).

We need to determine the optimal system ensuring an extremum of the given function f of the mathematical expectation m_E and the mean square error Γ_E of the system at some fixed instant of time. Consequently, in the present problem, for the criterion I we take the following probabilistic characteristic of the error of the system.

$$I = f(m_E, \Gamma_E). \qquad (7.65)$$

When we were studying linear systems, we took as criterion a function of the mathematical expectation m_E and the variance D_E of the error of the system. Here, we took as our criterion a function of the mathematical expectation m_E and the mean square error Γ_E of the system. These two criteria do not differ significantly from each other. The mean square error, the variance, and the mathematical expectation of the error of the system are related by the familiar equation

$$\Gamma_E = D_E + m_E^2.$$

Therefore, from a theoretical standpoint it is immaterial whether we take $f(m_E, \Gamma_E)$ or $f(m_E, D_E)$ as our criterion. It is expedient to take whichever one of these is more convenient for our calculations and transformations. In studying linear systems, we take as our criterion a function of the mathematical expectation and variance of the error, since specific criteria for comparing systems (the probabilities that the error in the systems will not exceed given limits) are most conveniently and simply expressed in terms of these probabilistic characteristics. In studying nonlinear systems, it is expedient to take as our comparison criterion a function of the mathematical expectation and mean square error of the system, since, in this case, the reduced criterion (7.64) is most simply expressed in terms of the operator of the nonlinear system.

Let us compare the formulation of the problem in the subsection with the formulation of the problem in the first subsection of the preceding section. The two formulations are similar in every way except as regards the criterion for comparing systems. Whereas we took the mean square error as our criterion in the problem of the first subsection of the preceding section, we take the criterion (7.65) in the present problem.

Let us proceed to solve the problem posed. In accordance with Theorem 2b, we conclude that the nonlinear operator that is optimal with respect to the criterion (7.65) must ensure an extremum of the reduced criterion

$$I_\theta = \theta m_E + \Gamma_E \qquad (7.66)$$

for some value of the harmonizing parameter $\theta = \theta_0$. Thus, we can solve the problem in two stages. In the first stage, we need to determine the nonlinear operator $A_0(\theta)$ that ensures an extremum of the reduced functional (7.66) for different values of the harmonizing parameter θ. In the second stage, we need to substitute the operator $A_0(\theta)$ into the criterion (7.65), after which it becomes a function $\Phi(\theta)$ of the parameter θ. We need to find, by some method or other, the extremum of the function $\Phi(\theta)$ and the value, corresponding to this extremum, of the harmonizing parameter $\theta = \theta_0$. When we have completed these two stages, we shall have determined the optimal nonlinear operator $A^0 = A_0(\theta_0)$ ensuring an extremum of the criterion (7.65).

Of course, it may turn out that the function $\Phi(\theta)$ whose extremum we are seeking has several extrema. In such a case, we need to choose out of these extrema that one that we are most interested in (the *maximum maximorum* or the *minimum minimorum*).

The more complicated of these two stages is in general the first, that of determining the nonlinear operator $A_0(\theta)$. Let us examine this stage in the solution of the problem that we have posed.

The reduced criterion (7.66) can be written as follows:

$$I_\theta = \theta M[E(t)] + M[E^2(t)] = \theta M[Y(t) - H(t)] + M[\{Y(t) - H(t)\}^2],$$

where $E(t) = Y(t) - H(t)$ is the error of the system at a fixed instant of time, $Y(t)$ is the actual output variable of the nonlinear system, and $H(t)$ is the desired output variable of that sytem. For subsequent investigations, it is convenient to represent the reduced criterion in the form

$$I_\theta = M[\{Y(t) - H(t)\}^2 + \theta\{Y(t) - H(t)\}]. \tag{7.67}$$

The reduced criterion (7.67), like the criterion (7.3), can be obtained in two steps: First, we take the average of the quantity

$$\{Y(t) - H(t)\}^2 + \theta\{Y(t) - H(t)\}$$

over all possible values of the signal $Y(t)$ for a given fixed sample function of the random function $X(t)$, and then we average this result over all sample functions of the random function $X(t)$. As a result of these successive averagings, we obtain the reduced criterion

$$I_\theta = M_x[M_y\{(Y - H)^2 + \theta(Y - H)/x\}]. \tag{7.68}$$

One can easily see that the system ensuring an extremum of the conditional mathematical expectation of the quantity $(Y - H)^2 + \theta(Y - H)$ for each sample function x of the random function X ensures an unconditional extremum of that quantity; that is, it is the system that we are seeking. Consequently, we need to find the system ensuring an extremum of the quantity

$$I_{\theta x} = M_y[\{(Y - H)^2 + \theta(Y - H)\}/x] \tag{7.69}$$

for each realization x of the random function X. To find the conditional mathematical expectation (7.69), we first need to find the conditional probability density of the signal Y or of the parameters U determining that signal relative to the input random function X. This conditional probability density $f_1(u/x)$ is determined in just the same way as in the first subsection of the preceding section and is given by formulas (7.25) and (7.26).

The conditional (*a posteriori*) mathematical expectation (7.69) of the quantity $(Y - H)^2 + \theta(Y - H)$ can be calculated from formula (7.28), in which we replace $[Y - \chi(t, u)]^2$ with

$$\{Y - \chi(t, u)\}^2 + \theta\{Y - \chi(t, u)\}.$$

We obtain

$$I_{\theta x} = \kappa(x) \int_{-\infty}^{\infty} [\{Y - \chi(t, u)\}^2 + \theta\{Y - \chi(t, u)\}] f(u)$$

$$\times \exp\left\{\int_{t-T}^{t} A(t, \tau, u) x(\tau) d\tau - \frac{1}{2} \beta(u)\right\} du, \qquad (7.70)$$

where the functions $\kappa(x)$, and $\beta(u)$ and the operator $A(t, \tau, u)$ are determined from the corresponding formulas of the first subsection of the preceding section and where $f(u)$ is a given distribution density of the parameters $U_1, \cdots, U_n$. Now, for each fixed value of t, we can easily determine the output variable of the system $Y(t)$ from the condition that the integral in (7.70) is maximized or minimized. To do this, we set equal to 0 the derivative of this integral with respect to Y and we get the following equation:

$$\int_{-\infty}^{\infty} \left[Y - \chi(t, u) + \frac{1}{2} \theta \right]$$

$$\times f(u) \exp\left\{\int_{t-T}^{t} A(t, \tau, u) x(\tau) d\tau - \frac{1}{2} \beta(u)\right\} du = 0. \qquad (7.71)$$

The solution of this equation is easily found:

$$Y(t, \theta) = -\frac{1}{2} \theta$$

$$+ \frac{\int_{-\infty}^{\infty} \chi(t, u) f(u) \exp\left\{\int_{t-T}^{t} A(t, \tau, u) x(\tau) d\tau - \frac{1}{2} \beta(u)\right\} du}{\int_{-\infty}^{\infty} f(u) \exp\left\{\int_{t-T}^{t} A(t, \tau, u) x(\tau) d\tau - \frac{1}{2} \beta(u)\right\} du}. \qquad (7.72)$$

The fraction on the right is the conditional mathematical expectation of the function $\chi(t, u)$ with respect to the input random variable $X(t)$; that is, the conditional mathematical expectation of the desired output variable

$$H(t) = \chi(t, u)$$

with respect to the random function $X(t)$. Consequently, formula (7.72) can be rewritten as follows:

$$Y(t, \theta) = M[H(t)/X] \frac{1}{2} \theta. \qquad (7.73)$$

Thus, *in the present case, the system we are seeking is the system that produces at the output the conditional mathematical expectation of the desired output variable X with respect to the input function X(t) displaced by an amount* $-\theta/2$; *that is, the a posteriori mathematical expectation of the desired output variable displaced by an amount* $-\theta/2$.

Formulas (7.72) and (7.73) differ from formulas (7.30) and (7.31) only by the term $-\theta/2$. This means that determining the output variable $Y(t, \theta)$ differs from determining the output variable $Y(t)$ in the problem of the first subsection of the preceding section only by our addition of the term $-\theta/2$ to the quantity $Y(t)$. This in turn means that the problem of finding the optimal system with respect to the reduced criterion (7.66) is essentially no different from the problem of finding the optimal system with respect to the minimum of the mean square error. All our suggestions regarding the calculation of the functions $A(t, \tau, u)$ and $\beta(u)$ in that subsection remain valid in the present case.

After we have solved the problem constituting the first stage, that is, after we have obtained an expression for the output variable $Y = Y(t, \theta)$, we need to substitute this quantity into the criterion (7.65), which, in the present case, can be written as

$$I = f(M[Y(t, \theta) - H(t)], \quad M\{Y(t, \theta) - H(t)\}^2) = \Phi(\theta). \quad (7.74)$$

For a fixed value of t, the criterion I becomes a known function $\Phi(\theta)$ of the harmonizing parameter θ. Now, we can easily determine the value of the harmonizing parameter $\theta = \theta_0$ corresponding to the desired extremum of the criterion I. The output variable Y of the system, which is determined from formula (7.72) with $\theta = \theta_0$, is the optimal output variable ensuring an extremum of the criterion (7.63). The optimal operator in the present case, as one can see from formula (7.72), is a nonlinear operator.

3. A general condition for an extremum of a criterion that is a given function of the mathematical expectation and mean square error of a system

Here, we shall consider the problem of determining the optimal nonlinear operator of a system, ensuring an extremum of the criterion (7.65), which is a given function of the mathematical expectation and the mean square error of the system at a fixed instant of time. For admissible systems, we take systems whose operators A belong to some linear space R (cf. Subsection 2 of the preceding section). We impose no restrictions on the initial data regarding the influences. We assume only that their probabilistic characteristics are known.

On the basis of Theorem 2b of the present chapter, we conclude that this problem can be solved in two stages. In the first stage, we need to find the operator A_0 ensuring an extremum of the reduced criterion (7.66) for various values of the harmonizing parameter θ. Let us find a condition that the operator A_0 corresponding to an extremum of the criterion (7.66) must satisfy. To do this, we write the formula determining the criterion for an arbitrary admissible operator A:

$$
\begin{aligned}
I_\theta &= \theta M[E(t)] + M[E^2(t)] \\
&= \theta M[Y(t) - H(t)] + M[\{Y(t) - H(t)\}^2] \\
&= \theta M[AX(t) - H(t)] + M[\{AX(t) - H(t)\}^2].
\end{aligned}
$$

Let us transform this formula as follows:

$$
\begin{aligned}
I_\theta\{A\} &= \theta M[AX(t) - A_0X(t) + A_0X(t) - H(t)] \\
&\quad + M[\{AX(t) - A_0X(t) + A_0X(t) - H(t)\}^2] \\
&= \theta M[A_0X(t) - H(t)] + M[\{A_0X(t) - H(t)\}^2] \\
&\quad + M[\{AX(t) - A_0X(t)\}^2] + \theta M[AX(t) - A_0X(t)] \\
&\quad + 2M[\{AX(t) - A_0X(t)\}\{A_0X(t) - H(t)\}], \tag{7.75}
\end{aligned}
$$

where A_0 is the operator that we are seeking in the class R (minimizing the reduced criterion (7.66)).

Suppose that the operator A_0 has the property that, for all operators $A \in R$,

$$
2M[\{AX(t) - A_0X(t)\}\{A_0X(t) - H(t)\}] + \theta M[AX(t) - A_0X(t)] = 0. \tag{7.76}
$$

Then, for an arbitrary operator $A \in R$, formula (7.75) takes the following form:

$$
\begin{aligned}
I_\delta &= \theta M[AX(t) + H(t)] + M[\{AX(t) - H(t)\}^2] \\
&= \theta M[A_0X(t) - H(t)] + M[\{A_0X(t) - H(t)\}^2] \\
&\quad + M[\{AX(t) - A_0X(t)\}^2]. \tag{7.77}
\end{aligned}
$$

Consequently, when condition (7.76) is satisfied, we have the inequality

$$
\begin{aligned}
&\theta M[AX(t) - H(t)] + M[\{AX(t) - H(t)\}^2] \\
&\quad \geqslant \theta M[A_0X(t) - H(t)] + M[\{A_0X(t) - H(t)\}^2] \tag{7.78}
\end{aligned}
$$

for an arbitrary operator A in the class R. This inequality can be briefly written as

$$
I_\theta(A) \geqslant I_\theta(A_0). \tag{7.79}
$$

It follows from inequality (7.78) or (7.79) that equation (7.76) is a sufficient condition for the operator A_0 to minimize the reduced criterion I_θ in the present case.

Let us prove that condition (7.76) is a necessary condition for the operator A_0 to minimize the reduced criterion I_θ, that is, for inequality (7.78) (or inequality (7.79), which amounts to the same thing) to be satisfied for all $A \in R$. To do this, we assume that condition (7.76) is not satisfied for some $A_1 \in R$; that is, we assume that, for this $A_1 \in R$,

$$2M[\{A_1X(t) - A_0X(t)\}\{A_0X(t) - H(t)\}]$$
$$+ \theta M[A_1X(t) - A_0X(t)] \neq 0. \qquad (7.80)$$

Consider the operator

$$A_\alpha = A_0 + \alpha(A_1 - A_0), \qquad (7.81)$$

where α is an arbitrary number. This operator belongs to the class R, since R is a linear space. In view of the easily obtained relationship

$$A_\alpha X(t) - A_0 X(t) = \alpha[A_1 X(t) - A_0 X(t)], \qquad (7.82)$$

we can obtain the following equation, which is analogous to equation (7.75):

$$\begin{aligned}
I_\theta(A_\alpha) &= \theta M[A_\alpha X(t) - H(t)] + M\{A_\alpha X(t) - H(t)\}^2] \\
&= \theta M[A_0 X(t) - H(t)] + M[\{A_0 X(t) - H(t)\}^2] \\
&\quad + \alpha^2 M[\{A_1 X(t) - A_0 X(t)\}^2] + \theta \alpha M[A_1 X(t) - A_0 X(t)] \\
&\quad + 2\alpha M[\{A_1 X(t) - A_0 X(t)\}\{A_0 X(t) - H(t)\}].
\end{aligned} \qquad (7.83)$$

From this it is obvious that, if we take α sufficiently small in absolute value and opposite in sign to the quantity

$$\theta M[A_1 X(t) - A_0 X(t)] + 2M[\{A_1 X(t) - A_0 X(t)\}\{A_0 X(t) - H(t)\}],$$

then the inequality

$$I_\theta\{A_\alpha\} < I_\theta\{A_0\}$$

will hold. This means that if condition (7.80) holds for at least one operator A_1, the operator A_0 cannot be optimal. This completes the proof of the necessity of condition (7.76). Thus, equation (7.76) is a necessary and sufficient condition for the operator A_0 to minimize the reduced criterion I_θ in the general case that we are considering. Remembering that the operator A is an arbitrary operator in the class R, we can replace the difference $A - A_0$ with the operator A and then rewrite the condition (7.76) in the form

$$2M[AX(t)\{A_0X(t) - H(t)\}] + \theta M[AX(t)] = 0, \quad A \in R,$$

or

$$M\left[AX(t)\left\{A_0X(t) - H(t) + \frac{1}{2}\theta\right\}\right] = 0, \quad A \in R. \qquad (7.84)$$

This is the final form of our necessary and sufficient condition for minimization of the reduced criterion I_θ. The coefficient $1/2$ in front of the θ is not significant here. The solution of this equation, the operator A_0, depends on the harmonizing parameter θ:

$$A_0 = A_0(\theta).$$

The value of the parameter $\theta = \theta_0$, corresponding to an extreme of the criterion (7.65), can be found by the method expounded in the preceding subsection of the present section.

4. An equation determining the optimal nonlinear integral operator with respect to the criterion $f(m_E, \Gamma_E)$

In the present subsection, we shall consider the special case when the class R of admissible operators A consists of all nonlinear integral operators:

$$AX(t) = \int_T \varphi[X(t), t, s]dt, \qquad (7.85)$$

where $\varphi(x, t, s)$ is an arbitrary function of x, t, and s and where T is a fixed interval of integration with respect to time t. Usually, the output variable of the system $Y(s) = AX(t)$ is, like the input variable, a function of time, but this time is sometimes measured in a different interval (not in the interval T). In what follows, we shall find it convenient to denote this latter quantity by a different letter; for example, the letter s. In special cases, the time s coincides with the time t. It is easy to see that the class R of operators of the type (7.85) is a linear space. Let us suppose that the desired output variable of the system (also a function of s) can be represented by the formula

$$H(s) = \int_Q h[G(t), t, s]dt, \qquad (7.86)$$

where $h(z, t, s)$ is a given function of its arguments, Q is a fixed interval of integration, and s denotes time.

In all our subsequent investigations, we shall assume the instant of time s to be arbitrary but fixed. Consequently, the operators $Y(s)$ and $H(s)$ can be regarded as functionals in this case. We take for our criterion for comparing systems the criterion (7.65); that is, a given function of the mathematical expectation and the mean square error of the system. On the basis of Theorem 2b of the present chapter, we conclude that the nonlinear operator that is optimal with respect to the criterion (7.65) must minimize the reduced functional I_θ determined by formula (7.66) for some value of the harmonizing parameter $\theta = \theta_0$. In accordance with the procedure previously described, we first find the condition determining the operator A_0 that corresponds to a minimum of the reduced criterion (7.66). In the present particular case, equation (7.84) can be written as

$$M\left[\int_T \varphi(X(u), u, s)du\left\{\int_T \varphi_0(X(t), t, s)dt - \int_Q h(G(t), t, s)dt + \theta\right\}\right] = 0,$$

$$(7.87)$$

where $\varphi_0(x, t, s)$ is the optimal characteristic function and $\varphi(x, u, s)$ is an arbitrary function. Each of these functions determines the corresponding operator (7.85). Instead of the term $\theta/2$ in equation (7.84) we have put the term θ in order to simplify the writing. This change does not affect the principles involved, since the parameter θ is still undetermined. In order to make subsequent transformations easier, we have replaced the variable t in the first integral with u.

Equation (7.87) must be satisfied for an arbitrary operator A of the type (7.85), that is, for an arbitrary function $\varphi(x, u, s)$. To transform equation (7.87) to a more convenient form, let us rewrite it, replacing the product of two integrals with double integrals:

$$M\left[\int_T \int_T \varphi(X(u), u, s)\varphi_0(X(t), t, s)\,dt\,du \right.$$
$$- \int_T \int_Q \varphi(X(u), u, s)h(G(t), t, s)\,dt\,du$$
$$\left. + \theta \int_T \varphi(X(u), u, s)\,du \right] = 0. \qquad (7.88)$$

Let $f_{xx}(x, x', t, t')$ denote the two-dimensional probability density of the random function $X(t)$, let $f_{xg}(x, g, t, t')$ denote the two-dimensional joint probability density of the random functions $X(t)$ and $G(t')$, and let $f_x(x, t)$ denote the one-dimensional probability density of the random function $X(t)$. Suppose that we know these quantities. We assume that, in equation (7.88), we can reverse the order of the operations of integration by taking the mathematical expectation (in practice, we can almost always reverse the order of these two linear operations). Then, let us rewrite equation (7.88) in the following form:

$$\int_T \int_T dt\,du \int_{-\infty}^{\infty} \int_{-\infty}^{\infty} \varphi(x, u, s)\varphi_0(x', t, s)f_{xx}(x, x', u, t)\,dx\,dx'$$
$$- \int_T \int_Q dt\,du \int_{-\infty}^{\infty} \int_{-\infty}^{\infty} \varphi(x, u, s)h(g, t, s)f_{xg}(x, g, u, t)\,dx\,dg$$
$$+ \theta \int_T du \int_{-\infty}^{\infty} \varphi(x, u, s)f_x(x, u)\,dx = 0. \qquad (7.89)$$

This equation can be rewritten in another form:

$$\int_T du \int_{-\infty}^{\infty} \left\{ \int_T dt \int_{-\infty}^{\infty} \varphi_0(x', t, s)f_{xx}(x, x', u, t)\,dx' \right.$$
$$- \int_Q dt \int_{-\infty}^{\infty} h(g, t, s)f_{xg}(x, g, u, t)\,dg$$
$$\left. + \theta f_x(x, u) \right\} \varphi(x, u, s)\,dx = 0. \qquad (7.90)$$

This last equation must be satisfied for an arbitrary function $\varphi(x, u, s)$. This is possible only when the expression in the braces vanishes for arbitrary x and arbitrary $u \in T$. This means that the function φ_0 must satisfy the equation

$$\int_T dt \int_{-\infty}^{\infty} \varphi_0(x', t, s) f_{xx}(x, x', u, t) dx'$$

$$- \int_Q dt \int_{-\infty}^{\infty} h(g, t, s) f_{xg}(x, g, u, t) dg + \theta f_x(x, u) = 0,$$

$$u \in T, \quad -\infty < x < \infty. \tag{7.91}$$

Equation (7.91) is a special case of equation (7.84). Consequently, this equation, like equation (7.84), is a necessary and sufficient condition for the function φ_0 to minimize the reduced criterion (7.66). The nonlinear operator A_0 corresponding to the function φ_0 is the operator that we are seeking. This operator, like the function φ_0, depends on the parameter θ:

$$A_0 X(t) = \int_T \varphi_0(X(t), t, s, \theta) dt. \tag{7.92}$$

In the special case in which the desired output variable is equal to the useful signal:

$$H(s) = G(s),$$

the function h in (7.86) is given by the formula

$$h(g, t, s) = g\delta(s - t).$$

When we substitute this expression for the function h into equation (7.91), we obtain a condition determining the optimal function φ_0 in this case:

$$\int_T dt \int_{-\infty}^{\infty} \varphi_0(x', t, s) f_{xx}(x, x', u, t) dx'$$

$$= \int_{-\infty}^{\infty} g f_{xg}(x, g, u, s) dg - \theta f_x(x, u) = 0,$$

$$u \in T, \quad -\infty < x < \infty. \tag{7.93}$$

When we have obtained the solution of equation (7.90) or equation (7.93), we can determine the mathematical expectation of the error and the mean square error of the system as functions of the harmonizing parameter θ. The mathematical expectation of the error of the system having operator $A_0(\theta)$ is, for fixed time s, determined as follows:

$$m_E(\theta) = M[A_0 X(t) - H(s)]$$

$$= M \left[\int_T \varphi_0(X(t), t, s, \theta) dt - \int_Q h(G(t), t, s) dt \right]$$

$$= \int_T \int_{-\infty}^{\infty} \varphi_0(x, t, s, \theta) f_x(x, t) dt dx$$

$$- \int_Q \int_{-\infty}^{\infty} h(g, t, s) f_g(g, t) dt dx, \tag{7.94}$$

where $f_x(x, t)$ and $f_g(g, t)$ are one-dimensional probability densities of the random functions $X(t)$ and $G(t)$.

The mean square error of the system having operator $A_0(\theta)$ at a fixed instant of time s is determined as follows:

$$\Gamma_E(\theta) = M[\{A_0 X(t) - H(s)\}^2]$$

$$= \int_T \int_T \int_{-\infty}^{\infty} \int_{-\infty}^{\infty} \varphi_0(x, t, s, \theta) \varphi_0(x', t', s, \theta) f_{xx}(x, x', t, t)$$

$$\times dx \, dx' \, dt \, dt' - 2 \int_T \int_Q \int_{-\infty}^{\infty} \int_{-\infty}^{\infty} \varphi_0(x, t, s, \theta) h(g, u, s)$$

$$\times f_{xg}(x, g, t, u) \, dx \, dg \, du \, dt + \int_Q \int_Q \int_{-\infty}^{\infty} \int_{-\infty}^{\infty} h(g, t, s)$$

$$\times h(g', t', s) f_{gg}(g, g', t, t') \, dg \, dg' \, dt \, dt', \qquad (7.95)$$

where $f_{xx}(x, x', t, t')$ and $f_{gg}(g, g', t, t')$ are the two-dimensional probability densities of the random functions $X(t)$ and $G(t)$ respectively and $f_{xg}(x, g, t, t')$ is the two-dimensional joint probability density of the random functions $X(t)$ and $G(t)$.

Both the mathematical expectation $m_E(\theta)$ of the error and the mean square error $\Gamma_E(\theta)$ of the system with operator $A_0(\theta)$, which are determined from formulas (7.94) and (7.95), should be substituted into the criterion (7.65). Then, the criterion will be a known function Φ of the harmonizing parameter θ:

$$I = f[m_E(\theta), \Gamma_E(\theta)] = \Phi(\theta). \qquad (7.96)$$

Then, we can easily determine the value of the harmonizing parameter $\theta = \theta_0$ that minimizes or maximizes the function $\Phi(\theta)$. The optimal function $\varphi^0(X(t), t, s)$ corresponding to an extremum of the criterion (7.65) is determined from the formula

$$\varphi^0(X(t), t, s) = \varphi_0(X(t), t, s, \theta_0). \qquad (7.97)$$

The optimal output variable Y^0 of the system (corresponding to an extremum of the criterion (7.65)) is determined from the equation

$$Y^0(s) = A^0 X(t) = \int_T \varphi_0(X(t), t, s, \theta_0) \, dt. \qquad (7.98)$$

The example of the present subsection again shows us that the determination of an optimal nonlinear operator A^0 is a very complicated problem. This problem can be solved only when we have high-speed computing machines. To obtain specific results, we need to simplify the problems as much as possible by considering special cases; for example, by studying nonlinear systems with a given structure and unknown parameters.

5. Determination of an optimal nonlinear system from criteria of a general form

We have considered the following criteria for optimality: The mean square error Γ_E, a given function $f(m_E, \Gamma_E)$, of the mathematical expectation of the error and the mean square error of the system, a given function $f(I_1, \cdots, I_{n+1})$ of certain functionals $I_1, \cdots, I_{n+1}$. In the last case, we did not consider the question as to what functionals other than the mathematical expectation m_E and the mean square error Γ_E can be examples of the functionals I_i. To give other examples of such functionals I_i, let us consider the following statement of the problem.

Suppose that all the initial data coincide with the initial data assumed in the first subsection of Section 24, in which we considered the problem of determining the optimal nonlinear system with respect to the minimum of the mean square error. In the problem that we are now considering, let us take as our criterion the mathematical expectation of an arbitrary function l of the error of the system:

$$I = M[l(E)] = M[l\{Y(s) - H(s)\}], \qquad (7.99)$$

where $E = E(t)$ is the error of the system at the instant t and where $Y(t)$ and $H(t)$ are the actual and desired output variables of the system at the instant t. Let us give some examples of the function $l(E)$.

(a) $\qquad\qquad l(E) = E^2.$ (a)

In this case, the criterion (7.99) is the mean square error of the system.

(b) $\qquad l(E) = \begin{cases} 1 \text{ if } & C_1 \leqslant E \leqslant C_2, \\ 0 \text{ if } & E > C_2, \ E < C_1. \end{cases}$ (b)

In this case, the criterion (7.99) is the probability that the error of the system will not exceed allowed limits, that is, will not fall outside the interval $[C_1, C_2]$,

Thus, the present formulation of the problem differs from that of the first subsection of Section 24 only in that we are taking the more general criterion (7.99). Repeating almost verbatim the reasoning and calculations of that subsection, we can show that determination of the value of the optimal output variable Y reduces to the following operations:

(1) determination of the function $A(t, \tau, u)$ by solving the integral equation (7.33),

(2) calculation of the function $\beta(u)$ from formula (7.27),

(3) determination of the value of the output variable Y at a fixed instant t from the condition that the conditional mathematical expectation

$$M_Y[l(Y - H)/X] = \kappa(x) \int_{-\infty}^{\infty} l[\chi(t, u) - Y]f(u)$$

$$\times \exp\left\{\int_{t-T}^{t} A(t, \tau, u)x(\tau)\,d\tau - \frac{1}{2}\beta(u)\right\}du, \qquad (7.100)$$

where $\kappa(x)$ is defined by the relation (7.26), is minimized. Finding the minimum of the expression (7.100) with respect to Y is a complicated problem in the general case. In the particular case of $l(E) = E^2$, this problem is easily solved (see formula (7.30)).

It may be instructive to consider a criterion of the following form:

$$l = f\{M[l_1(Y - H)], M[l_2(Y - H)], \cdots, M[l_{n+1}(Y - H)]\},$$
(7.101)

where the l_i, for $i = 1, 2, \cdots, n + 1$, are given functions. An example of such a criterion is

$$I = \Gamma_E + km_E^2,$$
(7.102)

where k is some number, m_E is the mathematical expectation of the error, and Γ_E is the mean square error of the system. If the function f is such that

$$\frac{\partial f(m_1, m_2, \cdots, m_{n+1})}{\partial m_i} \neq 0, \quad i = 1, 2, \cdots, n + 1,$$

then, on the basis of Theorem 2b of the present chapter, we may assert that *the optimal operator belonging to the class R (corresponding to an extremum of the criterion (7.101) must ensure an extremum of the reduced criterion*

$$
\begin{aligned}
I_\theta &= \theta_1 M[l_1(Y - H)] + \theta_2 M[l_2(Y - H)] \\
&\quad + \cdots + \theta_n M[l_n(Y - H)] + M[l_{n+1}(Y - H)] \\
&= M[\theta_1 l_1(Y - H) + \theta_2 l_2(Y - H) \\
&\quad + \cdots + \theta_n l_n(Y - H) + l_{n+1}(Y - H)]
\end{aligned}
$$
(7.103)

for certain values of the harmonizing parameters $\theta_1 = \theta_{10}, \cdots, \theta_n = \theta_{n0}$.

Consequently, in the present case, we can first find the operator $A_0(\theta_1, \cdots, \theta_n)$, ensuring an extremum of the criterion (7.103) for different values of the parameters $\theta_1, \cdots, \theta_n$ and then substitute

$$Y = A_0(\theta_1, \cdots, \theta_n) X(t)$$

into the criterion (7.101). This criterion will then be a known function $\Phi(\theta_1, \cdots, \theta_n)$ of the parameters $\theta_1, \cdots, \theta_n$. Then, we need to determine by some method (for example, the method of fastest descent) the values of the harmonizing parameters

$$\theta_1 = \theta_{10}, \cdots, \theta_n = \theta_{n0},$$

corresponding to an extremum of the function Φ. The operator

$$A^0 = A_0(\theta_{10}, \cdots, \theta_{n0})$$

is the optimal operator that we are seeking, ensuring an extremum of the criterion (7.101).

The methods expounded in this chapter can be extended to the choice of optimal discrete nonlinear automatic-control systems, as was done in Chapter 5 in connection with linear discrete systems.

Chapter 8

OPTIMAL SYSTEMS WITH DECISION ELEMENTS

Throughout the preceding chapters, in posing problems of determining optimal systems, we assumed that all the required probabilistic characteristics of the useful signal $G(t)$ and the noise $Z(t)$ are known. For example, in Chapter 3, when considering problems of determining optimal linear continuous systems, we assumed in each problem that the mathematical expectations and correlation functions of the useful signal and noise were given. However, we do not always have complete information on the probabilistic characteristics of the influences. Sometimes, a portion of the probabilistic characteristics is missing due to the fact that it is difficult or impossible to obtain them. Thus, it is not always possible to obtain the required information regarding the laws of motion of objects of an opponent. The incompleteness of our information on these influences changes from case to case. In practice, we may encounter cases, for example, where we know the normalized correlation function of a stationary influence but do not know its variance in advance. It is also possible that we may not know in advance the correlation function of one or more influences. Depending on the degree of incompleteness of our information regarding the influences, various problems of determining optimal automatic-control systems arise. Let us look at some of the possible problems.

26. THE PROBLEM OF TWO CHOICES

1. An example of a problem of two choices

Let us look at the case (see Fig. 2.2) in which an input single $X(t)$, which is the sum of a useful signal $G(t)$ and a noise $Z(t)$, is applied at the input of a system. Suppose that the useful signal is a centralized stationary random function whose correlation function has the form

$$K_g(\tau) = D_g R_g(\tau),$$

where $R_g(\tau)$ is the known normalized correlation function of the useful signal and D_g is the variance (unknown in advance) of the useful signal. The noise $Z(t)$ is uncorrelated with the useful signal. Its correlation function $K_z(\tau)$ is completely known. We know that, in the course of one cycle of operation of the system, the variance of the useful signal D_g can assume only two values: $D_g = D_0$ and $D_g = D_1$. Before we switch on the automatic-control system, the variance D_g is measured by a device that operates with some error. In the general case, D_g itself cannot be measured, but some quantity (function) depending on this variance as a parameter is measured. For example, we can measure the variance of the input signal $D_x = D_g + D_z$ or the correlation function of the input signal

$$K_x(\tau) = D_g R_g(\tau) + K_z(\tau).$$

Measurements of this other quantity (function) enable us to judge as to the magnitude of the variance of the useful signal.

Let us first pose and solve the following problem: From the results of measurements, make the best decision as to the value of the variance of the useful signal in a given cycle. After solving this problem, we need to construct an optimal system that ensures an extremum of the criterion chosen. In this system, everything will be determined except a single parameter A, which depends on the unknown value of the variance D_g of the useful signal. As we know, the variance D_g can assume only two possible values D_0 and D_1, and hence the parameter A can assume one of the two values A_0 and A_1. Furthermore, from the results of the measurements, the decision element determines in the best (optimal) way the value of the variance $D_g = D_i$, for $i = 0, 1, \cdots$, and, in accordance with this value, introduces into the system the value of the parameter $A = A_h$, for $h = 0, 1$. As a special case, the parameter A can coincide quantitatively with the variance D_g.

If the variance D_g were measured without error, the parameter A would also be introduced into the system without error. However, under actual conditions, when the variance D_g is measured with some error, the parameter A is also introduced with some error. This means that cases are possible in which the decision element switched to the value $A = A_1$ of the parameter when what was required was a switch to the value $A = A_0$ (the first form of error of the decision element). We denote the conditional probability of error of this form by α. Another case of erroneous decision is also possible: The decision element is switched to the value of the parameter $A = A_0$ when what was required was a switch to the value of the parameter $A = A_1$ (the second form of error of the decision element). We denote the conditional probability of error of this kind by β. Each of these two errors causes deviations in the weight function of the control system from the optimal weight function. Consequently, these errors cause deviations from the optimal values of the criteria for comparing two systems. In the general case, an error of the first kind and an error of the second kind cause different deviations from the optimal values on the part of a criterion. We need to know the form of the dependence of the criterion I for comparing two systems on the probabilities of errors of the first and second kinds on the part of the decision element in order to choose correctly the optimal decision element. We obtain this dependence in the general form for a single particular case of the problem that we are considering.

Suppose that the unknown variance of the useful signal D_g in the problem just posed obeys the following *a priori* distribution law: $P(D_g = D_0) = p_0$, $P(D_g = D_1) = p_1$, where p_0 and p_1 are given positive numbers such that $p_0 + p_1 = 1$. Suppose that we take for the criterion for comparing two systems the probability P that the error of the system will not exceed given allowed limits. We introduce the following notation: p_{00} denotes the probability that the error of the system will not exceed given allowed limits as calculated under the assumptions that the variance of the useful signal D_g is actually equal to D_0 and that the decision element introduced into the system is the parameter A_0 corresponding to the variance D_0; p_{11} denotes the probability that the error of the system will not exceed given allowed limits as calculated under the assumptions that the variance of the useful signal D_g is equal to D_1 and that the decision element introduced into the system is the parameter A_1 corresponding to the variance D_1; p_{01} denotes the probability that the error of the system will not exceed allowed limits as calculated under the assumptions that the variance of the useful signal D_g is actually equal to D_0 and that the decision element introduced into the system is the parameter A_1 corresponding to the variance D_1; p_{10} is the probability that the error of the system will not exceed allowed limits as calculated under the assumptions that the variance of the useful system D_g is actually equal to D_1 and that the decision element introduced into the system is the parameter A_0 corresponding to the variance D_0. The probabilities p_{00} and p_{11} are values of the criterion P corresponding to optimal systems under distinct initial data regarding the influences on the system. The probabilities p_{01} and p_{10} are values of the criterion P corresponding to nonoptimal systems. Therefore,

$$p_{00} \geqslant p_{01}, \qquad p_{11} \geqslant p_{10}. \tag{8.1}$$

In the general case, inequality holds in these two relationships. Only in very rare special cases, not of practical interest, does equality hold. All the quantities p_{00}, p_{11}, p_{01}, and p_{10} are easily calculated when we have determined the optimal systems for two cases of initial data (for $D_g = D_0$

and for $D_g = D_1$). In connection with the fact that four combinations of initial data and accepted solutions are possible, the absolute possibility that the error will not exceed the allowed limits $P = P(C_1 \leqslant E \leqslant C_2)$ needs to be calculated from the formula for total probability (see formula (1.10)), which, in the present case, takes the form

$$P = P(C_1 \leqslant E < C_2) = p_{00}p_0(1 - \alpha) + p_{01}p_0\alpha$$
$$+ p_{11}p_1(1 - \beta) + p_{10}p_1\beta = (p_{01} - p_{00})p_0\alpha$$
$$+ (p_{10} - p_{11})p_1\beta + p_{00}p_0 + p_{11}p_1. \tag{8.2}$$

Here, all the quantities except the conditional probabilities of errors of the first and second kind are known. The optimal solution is the solution maximizing the function (8.2) of the variables α and β. In the given case, the function (8.2) of α and β is linear. Here, the problem reduces to choosing a solution algorithm (that is, choosing two possible values of the variance D_0 and D_1) that will maximize the linear function of the conditional probabilities of errors α and β.

Other analogous formulations of problems are possible in which the decision element is confronted with the necessity of choosing one of two values of some quantity (parameter). These problems differ from each other by the comparison criteria and specific initial data on the quantity being determined, on the noise, and on the nature of the relationship between the error and the quantity sought. Let us look at the formulation of a problem of two choices in the general case [Refs. 1, 15].

2.   Formulation of a problem of two choices

Suppose that we know the conditions of the experiment; that is, that we know the method of obtaining the input random function Y of the decision element (see Fig. 8.1) from the signal $X(t)$ and the noise $Z(t)$;

$$Y(t) = [X(t) \times Z(t)], \quad 0 \leqslant t \leqslant T. \tag{8.3}$$

Here, the symbol $[\cdots \times \cdots]$, just as in Figure (8.1), denotes the method of combining the signal and the noise before the input into the decision element and T denotes the interval of observation. The following are examples of methods of combining the signal and the noise:

$$(1) \qquad Y(t) = X(t) + Z(t) \quad \text{(addition)}, \tag{8.4}$$

$$(2) \qquad Y(t) = X(t)Z(t) \quad \text{(multiplication)}. \tag{8.5}$$

The signal $X(t)$ is a random function. It is a parameter λ that brings the randomness into this signal. An example of such a parameter is the variance D_g, of which we spoke in the preceding subsection. An

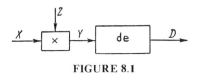

FIGURE 8.1

example of the signal $X(t)$ is the variance of the input signal into the system or the correlation function of that signal.

The parameter λ can assume only two values λ_0 and λ_1 with probabilities p_0 and p_1. The probabilistic characteristics of the noise $Z(t)$ are known. In view of all that has been said, we may assert that we know the probabilistic characteristics of the random function $Y(t)$ (that is, of the input into the decision element [de in Fig. 8.1]) under the condition that the parameter λ assumed one or the other of the two possible values. In particular, we know the joint conditional probability density $P(Y_1, \cdots, Y_n/\lambda)$ of the random variables $Y_1 = Y(t_1)$, $\cdots, Y_n = Y(t_n)$, for $0 \leqslant t_i \leqslant T$, for a given value of the parameter λ. In the given problem of two choices, we have two variants:

$$(1) \qquad P = P(y_1, \cdots, y_n/\lambda_0) = P_0,$$

$$(2) \qquad P = P(y_1, \cdots, y_n/\lambda_1) = P_1.$$

Suppose that under the given conditions we have obtained from experiment the following specific values of the input function Y in the decision element: $Y_1, \cdots, Y_n$. From these values of the random function Y we need to decide in the optimal manner which of the two possible values the parameter λ actually does assume. This is the problem of two choices in the general case.

Before we solve this problem, it will be expedient to consider the question of various errors in solution.

3. Errors in solution

Let us denote by Γ the region of possible values of the sample functions $Y_1, Y_2, \cdots, Y_n$ of the input variable Y in n-dimensional space. The acceptance of a solution in a problem of two choices means partitioning the entire region Γ of possible values $Y_1, \cdots, Y_n$ into two disjoint regions Γ_0 and Γ_1 such that $\Gamma_0 + \Gamma_1 = \Gamma$. When a combination of values of the input variable $Y_1, \cdots, Y_n$ obtained from experiment fall into the region Γ_0, we decide that $\lambda = \lambda_0$. When the points $Y_1, \cdots, Y_n$ fall into the region Γ_1, we decide that $\lambda = \lambda_1$. Here, errors of two kinds are possible. An error of the first kind consists in accepting the decision $\lambda = \lambda_1$ when the parameter λ actually assumed the value $\lambda = \lambda_0$. The conditional probability of this error, an error of the first kind, is usually denoted by α and is called the **significance level** of the tests. Sometimes, this conditional probability is called the probability of a **false alarm** (the reason for this last term will be seen if $\lambda_0 = 0$ and if $\lambda = \lambda_1$ represents the occurrence of some sort of danger). An error of the second kind consists in accepting the solution $\lambda = \lambda_0$ when the parameter λ actually assumed the value $\lambda = \lambda_1$. The conditional probability of error of the second kind is usually denoted by β. Sometimes, this conditional probability of an error of the second kind is called the probability of **erroneous all-clear**. The conditional probabilities α and β can be determined from the formulas

$$\alpha = \int_{\Gamma_1} P(y_1, \cdots, y_n/\lambda_0) dy_1 \cdots dy_n,$$

$$\beta = \int_{\Gamma_0} P(y_1, \cdots, y_n/\lambda_1) dy_1 \cdots dy_n. \tag{8.6}$$

In the first of these integrals, the integration of the conditional probability density $P(y_1, \cdots, y_n/\lambda_0)$ is over the region Γ_1 in n-dimensional space; in the second integral, the integration of the conditional probability density $P(y_1, \cdots, y_n/\lambda_1)$ is over the region Γ_0.

Let us look at the conditional probabilities of correct decisions. We denote by μ the probability of the correct decision $\lambda = \lambda_0$. The probability of the correct decision $\lambda = \lambda_1$ is called the **power of the decision** and is denoted by ε. The probabilities μ and ε can be determined from the formulas

$$\mu = \int_{\Gamma_0} P(y_1, \cdots, y_n/\lambda_0) dy_1 \cdots dy_n,$$

$$\varepsilon = \int_{\Gamma_1} P(y_1, \cdots, y_n/\lambda_1) dy_1 \cdots dy_n. \tag{8.7}$$

The probabilies α and μ on the one hand and β and ε on the other are connected by the following relationships:

$$\alpha + \mu = 1, \qquad \beta + \varepsilon = 1. \tag{8.8}$$

Obviously, the smaller the errors α and β, the better will be the decision element.

However, we still have not answered the question as to how we choose the criterion for comparing the algorithms of decision elements. What is the relationship of an error of the first kind to an error of the second kind ? Which of these errors is the more "dangerous," the more undesirable ? How can we take into consideration the different degrees of "danger" of these two kinds of error in the criterion ? We cannot give an answer to these questions that will be valid in all cases. The relationship between the degrees of "danger" of the different errors and the method of taking into account the different degrees of "danger" of errors in the criterion depend on the conditions of a specific problem. Only by taking into account the peculiar features of a particular problem and the purpose of the decision element in that particular problem can we choose the criterion correctly. For example, in the problem considered in the first subsection of this section, a suitable criterion is the criterion (8.2), which has the sense of absolute probability that the error of the system will not exceed allowed limits. In other cases, the criterion will be of a different form and will be represented by another form of dependence on the conditional probabilities α and β. Let us look at some examples, which are of practical value.

4. The Neyman-Pearson criterion

Suppose that we know the *a priori* probabilities p_0 and p_1 in a problem of two choices. We wish to consider solutions for which the absolute probability of an error of the first kind $A = p_0\alpha$ is fixed. In other words, we wish to consider not all possible partitions of the region Γ but only those partitions that satisfy the condition

$$A = p_0 \int_{\Gamma_1} P(y_1 \cdots, y_n/\lambda_0) dy_1, \cdots, dy_n = A_0. \tag{8.9}$$

To shorten our writing, we introduce a random vector Y whose components along the axes in n-dimensional space are $Y_1, \cdots, Y_n$. We denote by y the sample function of the vector Y. The components of the vector y in n-dimensional space are $y_1, \cdots, y_n$. Then, all the formulas will be written in a more compact form. For example, formula (8.9) takes the form

$$A = p_0 \int_{\Gamma_1} P(y/\lambda_0) dy = A_0. \tag{8.10}$$

Here, dy represents a small volume in the n-dimensional space $(y_1, \cdots, y_n)$. Out of all partitions satisfying condition (8.10), we propose to choose as the best (optimal) the one that corresponds to the smallest absolute error of the second kind. This is equivalent to choosing a region Γ_1 corresponding to the greatest power ε of the decision. Thus, the optimal region Γ_0 must satisfy, in addition to condition (8.10), the condition

$$E = p_1 \int_{\Gamma_1} P(y/\lambda_1) dy = \text{max}. \tag{8.11}$$

Consequently, the Neyman-Pearson criterion can be formulated as follows: The optimal solution is that solution which, for a given significance level α, ensures maximal power ε of the solution.

This criterion is completely justified in those cases in which, for some reason or other, it is necessary to restrict the probability of error of the first kind. For example, if an error of the first kind is especially dangerous, it is expedient to make the probability of occurrence of such an error very small. Once we have made such a restriction on the probability of error of the first kind, it is of course desirable to make the probability of error of the second kind as small as possible, since an error of this kind is also undesirable (although to a lesser degree than an error of the first kind).

The problem consists in finding regions Γ_0 and Γ_1 that are optimal with respect to the Neyman-Pearson criterion. Conditions (8.10) and (8.11) define from a mathematical point of view the problem of finding the conditional extremum (maximum). We need to find the maximum of the quantity E under the condition that the quantity $A = A_0$ is given.

By following the procedure expounded in Chapter 1, we can easily show that the problem of finding the maximum of the quantity E under the condition (8.10) reduces to the problem of finding the unconditional maximum of the auxiliary quantity

$$G = \gamma A + E = \gamma p_0 \int_{\Gamma_1} P(y/\lambda_0)\,dy + p_1 \int_{\Gamma_1} P(y/\lambda_1)\,dy, \qquad (8.12)$$

where γ is an undetermined Lagrange multiplier, which can be determined from condition (8.10). Let us rewrite equation (8.12) in the form

$$G = \int_{\Gamma_1} [\gamma p_0 P(y/\lambda_0) + p_1 P(y/\lambda_1)]\,dy. \qquad (8.13)$$

The optimal solution must maximize the quantity G. One can easily see that G will have its maximum value if the region Γ_1 consists of those points of the region for which the integrand, shown in the square brackets, is positive. (Points of the region Γ for which this integrand is zero can belong either to the region Γ_1 or to the region Γ_0, since this does not affect the value of G.) Specifically, exclusion of such points from the region Γ_1 decreases the value of G and inclusion of other points (for which the integrand is negative) can only decrease the value of this quantity. This means that the optimal region Γ_1 must include points of the region Γ that are determined by the inequality

$$\gamma p_0 P(y/\lambda_0) + p_1 P(y/\lambda_1) > 0, \qquad (8.14)$$

which may be rewritten as

$$\frac{P(y/\lambda_1)}{P(y/\lambda_0)} > -\gamma \frac{p_0}{p_1} = h. \qquad (8.15)$$

Here, h is a quantity known as the **threshold**. The negative sign in front of $\gamma(p_0/p_1)$ should not be disturbing, since the undetermined multiplier γ is negative.

Inequality (8.15) determines the optimal solution with respect to the

Neyman-Pearson criterion. If it is satisfied for some vector y, then the given point belongs to the region Γ_1; that is, we assume $\lambda = \lambda_1$. If the opposite inequality

$$\frac{P(y/\lambda_1)}{P(y/\lambda_0)} < -\gamma\frac{p_0}{p_1} = h \tag{8.16}$$

is satisfied, we assume that $\lambda = \lambda_0$.

In the left-hand members of inequalities (8.15) and (8.16) is the ratio of the conditional probabilities

$$\frac{P(y/\lambda_1)}{P(y/\lambda_0)} = \Lambda(y). \tag{8.17}$$

This ratio is called the **likelihood ratio**. By using the notation (8.17), we can combine inequalities (8.15) and (8.16) into a single inequality:

$$\Lambda(y)\begin{cases} > -\gamma\dfrac{p_0}{p_1} = h \to \lambda = \lambda_1, \\[2mm] < -\gamma\dfrac{p_0}{p_1} = h \to \lambda = \lambda_0. \end{cases} \tag{8.18}$$

5. Kotel'nikov's criterion

If errors of the first and second kinds are equally undesirable, it is expedient to consider that decision optimal that minimizes the unconditional probability of error

$$K = A + B = p_0\alpha + p_1\beta. \tag{8.19}$$

This criterion K was proposed by V.A. Kotel'nikov.

Thus, we need to find a partition of the region Γ that minimizes the criterion (8.19). To do this, we substitute the expressions for α and β given by (8.6) into Kotel'nikov's criterion and we obtain

$$K = p_0\int_{\Gamma_1} P(y/\lambda_0)dy + p_1\int_{\Gamma_0} P(y/\lambda_1)dy. \tag{8.20}$$

Remembering that $\Gamma = \Gamma_1 + \Gamma_0$, we can write this equation in the form

$$\begin{aligned} K &= p_0\int_{\Gamma_1} P(y/\lambda_0)dy + p_1\int_{\Gamma} P(y/\lambda_1)dy - p_1\int_{\Gamma_1} P(y/\lambda_1)dy \\ &= p_1 + \int_{\Gamma}[p_0P(y/\lambda_0) - p_1P(y/\lambda_1)]dy. \end{aligned} \tag{8.21}$$

For the criterion K to be minimal, the second term in formula (8.21) must be minimal. We can arrange for this to be the case if the region Γ_1 consists of those points of Γ at which the integrand in (8.21) is negative. Consequently, all points at which

$$p_0 P(y/\lambda_0) - p_1 P(y/\lambda_1) < 0 \qquad (8.22)$$

belong to Γ_1. The opposite inequality defines the region Γ_0:

$$p_0 P(y/\lambda_0) - p_1 P(y/\lambda_1) > 0. \qquad (8.23)$$

Conditions (8.22) and (8.23) can be rewritten by using the likelihood ratio $\Lambda(y)$:

$$\Lambda(y) \begin{cases} > \dfrac{p_1}{p_0} = h \to \lambda = \lambda_1, \\[2mm] < \dfrac{p_1}{p_0} = h \to \lambda = \lambda_0. \end{cases} \qquad (8.24)$$

Thus, the optimal system with respect to Kotel'nikov's criterion has the same form as the optimal solution with respect to the Neyman-Pearson criterion. The difference consists in the fact that there is no undetermined multiplier γ in the case of Kotel'nikov's criterion (it is equal to unity).

6. A criterion of general form

It was stated that, under different specific conditions, it is convenient to take different criteria for comparing solutions. Therefore, we need to consider a criterion I of general form that is an arbitrary function f of the conditional probabilities α and β:

$$I = f(\alpha, \beta). \qquad (8.25)$$

The optimal solution must minimize the criterion I. This minimum coincides with the minimum of the function f as the variables α and β range over some region Q (see Fig. 8.2). The region Q consists of all points (pairs of numbers α and β) corresponding to all possible partitions of the region Γ into subregions Γ_1 and Γ_0. If the function f has a minimum and this minimum lies inside the region Q, the values of α and β minimizing the function f are determined as the solution of the system of the two equations

$$\frac{\partial f(\alpha, \beta)}{\partial \alpha} = 0, \qquad \frac{\partial f(\alpha, \beta)}{\partial \beta} = 0. \qquad (8.26)$$

However, the criterion I is usually a function f that does not have a minimum inside the region Q. Consequently, the minimum of the criterion I coincides with the smallest value of the function f on the boundary L (see Fig. 8.2) of the region Q. To find the smallest value of the function f (and the partition of the region Γ corresponding to it), we first find the boundary L of the region Q and then find the smallest value of f on that boundary.

The boundary L can be found as follows: We fix the boundary

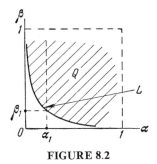

FIGURE 8.2

of the conditional probability α, taking, for example, $\alpha = \alpha_1$. For this fixed value $\alpha = \alpha_1$, we seek an extreme value (usually a minimum) of the conditional probability $\beta = \beta_1$ (see Fig. 8.2). The pair (α_1, β_1) corresponds to a point on the boundary L of the region Q. If the fixed value of the conditional probability α is allowed to vary over the entire region of admissible values of that quantity $(0 < \alpha < 1)$, we may thus determine the entire boundary L. In the fourth subsection of this section, we showed that the problem of finding Γ_1 minimizing β for fixed α has a solution given by the relations (8.15) and (8.16) or the relation (8.18). Analogously, we can show that the problem of finding the region Γ_1 maximizing the conditional probability α for a fixed value of the conditional probability β has a solution given by the relations (8.15) and (8.16) or the relation (8.18), with the direction of the inequality signs reversed. Usually, the function f attains the desired smallest value on the portion of the boundary L corresponding to the minimal value of the conditional probability β.

The solution, that is, the region Γ_1, depends on the threshold value h. We need to find this value h, which corresponds to the smallest value of f. Corresponding to each value of the threshold value h are certain values of α and β, that is, some point on the boundary L of the region Q. Variation in the value of h between certain limits causes the point α, β to be displaced along the boundary L. The smallest value of the function f can be found by seeking the values of the conditional probabilities α and β as functions of h:

$$\alpha = \alpha(h) \quad \text{and} \quad \beta = \beta(h)$$

and substituting them into the criterion I:

$$I = f[\alpha(h), \beta(h)] = \Phi(h). \tag{8.27}$$

Then, we need to find the value $h = h_0$ minimizing the function $\Phi(h)$. To do this, we need to solve the equation

$$\frac{d\Phi(h)}{dh} = 0 \tag{8.28}$$

or construct a graph of the function $\Phi(h)$ and use the graph to determine

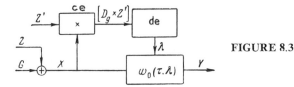

FIGURE 8.3

the value of $h = h_0$. The regions Γ_1 and Γ_0 determined by (8.15) and (8.16) for $h = h_0$ constitute the optimal solution we have been seeking for the problem in question. If the function $\Phi(h)$ has several minima, we need to choose the smallest one. The value $h = h_0$ that we have been seeking corresponds to this smallest minimum.

The case in which we need to determine the optimal solution with respect to the maximum of the criterion (8.25) does not differ in principle from the one we have been considering. The search for the maximum of the function f is easily reduced to the search for the minimum of the function $-f$. Kotel'nikov's criterion and the criterion (8.2) are very simple examples of the given criterion (8.25).

A decision element determining an optimal decision with respect to the criterion (8.25) introduces the desired value of the parameter λ into the main loop of the control system. Figure 8.3 shows the diagram of a control system with decision element. The main control loop is shown at the bottom. A single X representing the sum of a useful single G and a noise Z is applied at the input of the loop. The optimal weight function $w_0(\tau, \lambda)$ of the main control loop is determined up to the parameter λ, which depends on the variance D_g of the useful signal. To determine the variance D_g, which can assume either of two values D_0 and D_1, we use the calculating element (ce), on which a noise Z' acts. From the output of the calculating element we get a quantity $[D_g \times Z']$ that is a composite of the quantity D_g that we are seeking and the noise Z'. The output variable of the calculating element is applied at the input of the decision element (de), which produces an optimal decision from one of the formulas already given, and thus introduces into the basic control loop a parameter λ functionally related to the variance D_g of the useful signal.

7.   The case in which the *a priori* probabilities are unknown

In the preceding subsections of this section, we have assumed that we know the *a priori* probabilities p_0 and p_1 of occurrence of the values λ_0 and λ_1 of the parameter λ. The optimal decision depended in a very real way on these probabilities p_0 and p_1 (cf. formulas (8.15), (8.16), and (8.18)). However, in practice, one may encounter cases in which we do not know the *a priori* probabilities p_0 and p_1 of occurrence of the values λ_0 and λ_1 of the parameter λ. In such cases, another approach to solving the problem is necessary, such as finding a minimax decision. A minimax decision with respect to some criterion must ensure a minimum of the criterion under the most unfavorable law of distribution of the parameter λ. We may seek such a solution in the following manner: First, we need to find the optimal solution under an arbitrary distribution law of the parameter λ (under arbitrary values of the conditional probability densities p_0 and p_1 such that $p_0 + p_1 = 1$). Then we need to determine the value of the probability density p_0 (and hence of $p_1 = 1 - p_0$) at which the optimal value of the criterion is maximal. The optimal decision corresponding to this value of the probability density p_0 will be the minimax decision. In the present case, it is comparatively easy to find the minimax decision, since the overall optimal decision depends on a single variable p_0. In the general case when the parameter λ can assume a set of values $\lambda_0, \lambda_1, \cdots, \lambda_n$, the problem of finding a minimax decision is quite difficult. In solving this complex problem successfully, one can use the methods of linear and nonlinear programming.

In the present case, yet another approach to the solution of this problem is possible. It is important to note that, in the case of a minimax decision, we purposefully choose the most unfavorable probabilistic distribution of parameter λ. Sometimes, we proceed in a different way; specifically, we have given some distribution law of the unknown parameter λ. For example, we may suppose that this parameter assumes one of the two values λ_0 and λ_1 with probabilities $p_0 = 1/2$ and $p_1 = 1/2$. Of course, in this there is always some arbitrariness in the assignment of the probabilities p_0 and p_1. In fact, these values of the probabilities p_0 and p_1 differ from those chosen and, consequently, the value of the criterion chosen will differ from its actual value as obtained from experiment. The computed value of the criterion can be either greater or less than its actual value. In the case of a minimax decision the computed value of the criterion also differs from its actual value. However, a positive feature of a minimax solution is the fact that the real value of the criterion is never greater than the computed one; that is, the actual properties of the system are never worse than the computed ones (the system is evaluated with respect to the minimum of the criterion). Consequently, in the case of a minimax decision, the error in determining the criterion, the error in determining the quality of the system can be made only "from stock."

27. THE THEORY OF OPTIMAL DECISIONS

In the preceding section, we considered an example of the theoretical analysis, which reduces to a two-choice problem of statistical decisions. That example was an unusually simple one. In it, only the variance of the useful signal was an unknown probabilistic characteristic, and we knew that this variance could assume only one or the other of two values. Various generalizations of this problem are of practical interest. Let us look at some of these generalizations.

1. Examples of problems that can be solved by the methods of the theory of statistical decisions

In addition to the problem previously considered, the following problems are possible:

(1) An input signal X, which is the sum of a useful signal G and a noise Z, acts on the system (see Fig. 2.2). We know all the probabilistic characteristics of the useful signal X and the noise Z except for the variance D_g of the useful signal. With regard to this variance, we know that it can assume one of n values $D_1, D_2, \cdots, D_n$ with probabilities $p_1, p_2, \cdots, p_n$ respectively, where $p_1 + \cdots + p_n = 1$. In the present case, the usual optimal system cannot be determined, since we do not have the required probabilistic characteristics concerning the input variable X. Therefore, it is expedient to shift to an optimal system with a decision element, that is, to the system shown in Figure 8.3.

The methods expounded in the preceding chapters can be used to determine the optimal weight function of the system for the different values of the variance of the useful signal $D_1, \cdots, D_n$, after which the variance of the useful signal can be computed from experimental data. This value of the variance D_g, calculated with an error, is applied at the input of the decision element, which must produce the optimal decision regarding the actual value of the variance of the useful signal D_g; that is, it must make the optimal decision as to what value D_i, for $i = 1$, $\cdots, n$, is actually observed in experiment. This is a typical example of a many-choice problem.

(2) Suppose that we keep all the conditions of the preceding problem except that we assume that the variance of the useful signal can assume any value in an interval $[D_0, D_1]$. In this case, we speak of the problem of estimating a parameter. Here, the unknown parameter D_g may assume a continuum of values. To solve this problem we have to know the distribution law of the parameters D_g.

(3) If, in problem (1), we treat as unknown the entire correlation function $K_g(\tau)$, then the problem of estimating the function (process) arises. This problem is the most complex of all the problems that we have enumerated.

We have spoken of a single parameter D_g and a single function $K_g(\tau)$. Cases are possible when we do not have complete information regarding several parameters (for example, the variance of the useful signal D_g and the variance of the noise D_z) or regarding several functions (for example, the normalized correlation functions of the useful signal and the noise). Then, by a parameter or a function we mean a vector-valued parameter or a vector-valued function. In all of these problems, optimal decisions or minimax decisions with respect to the criteria chosen are possible. We consider one variant or another according to whether we do or do not know the distribution law of the random parameter or function.

The method of solving each of these problems and the results obtained depend to a considerable degree on the criteria chosen for comparing decisions. In the preceding, when we were studying a problem of two choices, we considered three criteria. Other criteria are also possible.

Thus, the various problems differ from each other in their initial data and the criteria. Various combinations of these initial data and criteria are possible. It would be desirable to have a single method that would enable us to solve all these problems. Such a method in fact exists. This method is the subject matter of the theory of optimal decisions (the theory of statistical decisions). We shall expound very briefly the fundamentals of the theory of statistical decisions [Refs. 1, 15, 37]. To become familiar with basic ideas of this theory, it is necessary to master a few basic concepts that are used in it.

2. Spaces of signals of a decision element

In the theory of statistical decisions, we consider random signals of an arbitrary nature. These signals can be random variables that assume one of two or several values or they can be random functions.

Let us first look at a useful signal (and for conciseness let us just call it a signal) X. Suppose that $X_1 = X(t_1), \cdots, X_k = X(t_k)$ denote the values of a specific sample function of the useful signal X at specified instants of time (where k is a finite or an infinite number). Corresponding to an arbitrary combination of values of the signal $(X_1, \cdots, X_k)$ is a vector which we denote by X. This vector belongs to a k-dimensional space $\overline{X}$. (In what follows, we shall denote the space of vectors by the same letter as the vectors themselves but with a macron.) The space $\overline{X}$ of all possible vectors X will be called, in what follows, the **signal space**. In the particular case when the useful signal $X(t, \Lambda)$ is a known function of the parameter Λ, where $\Lambda = (\Lambda_1, \cdots, \Lambda_m)$ is a random m-dimensional vector, we can use the space of the parameters Λ instead of the space of signals.

At the input of the decision element (see Fig. 8.1), is applied a combination of the signal X and the noise Z. Corresponding to an arbitrary combination of values of the noise

$$[Z_1 = Z(t_1), \ Z_2 = Z_2(t_2), \ \cdots, \ Z_k = Z(t_k)]$$

is a vector, which we denote by Z. This vector belongs to a k-dimensional space $\bar{Z}$. We shall call the space $\bar{Z}$ of all possible vectors Z the **noise space**.

In many cases, we may assume that we know the *a priori* probability density of the signal X, the probability density of the noise Z, and the method of composing the input signal Y from signal and noise. Consequently, we know the conditional probability density $P(Y/X)$, that is, the probability density of the input signal under the assumption that the sample functions of the useful signal have a given form. To each combination of values of the input signal $[Y_1 = Y(t_1), \cdots, Y_k = Y(t_k)]$ there corresponds a vector, which we shall denote by Y. This vector belongs to a k-dimensional space $\bar{Y}$. We shall call the space $\bar{Y}$ of all possible vectors Y the **input space** or the **space of observations**. The vectors X, Z, and Y are all random vectors.

A decision D is made at the output of the decision element in accordance with a definite rule (algorithm). This decision is also a random vector with components $D_1, \cdots, D_n$. We shall call the space $\bar{D}$ of all possible values of the vectors D the **decision space** or the **output space**. In the general case, the dimension of this space is not the same as the dimension of the input space. Usually, however, its dimension is the same as that of the signal space. For example, if the signal is a known function of m parameters, the space of decisions usually is m-dimensional. The coordinates $D_1, \cdots, D_n$ of the decision space are not the coordinates of the transmitted signal $X_1, \cdots, X_k$, but estimates of them. In the particular case of a problem of two choices, the decision space is a set of two points. In all cases, the decision space $\bar{D}$ is a copy of the signal space $\bar{X}$ or the parameter space $\bar{\Lambda}$ used in place of it.

The purpose of the decision element is to map the input space $\bar{Y}$ into the output space $\bar{D}$ in the optimal manner.

3. Decision functions. Loss functions

The decision element with respect to the input signal Y imparts a decision D at its output. This dependence between the input Y and the output D of the decision element can be stochastic (random) or determinate (uniquely determined). In the case of stochastic dependence, the conditional probability density $P(D/Y)$ (that is, the probability of occurrence of the decision D at the output on the assumption that the sample function Y has occurred at the input) is determined. This conditional probability density $P(D/Y)$ is called the **decision function** (decision rule). If such a decision function has been obtained, it can be achieved with the aid of a device that simulates a given stochastic dependence between the vectors Y and D. Experiment carried out on this decision element realizes the required decision function (decision rule).

In the theory of decisions, it is shown that, under broad assumptions regarding the conditions of the problem, the decision function is a nonrandom function $D = D(Y)$ that assigns to each point in the space $\bar{Y}$ a point in the space $\bar{D}$. In what follows, we shall assume that the optimal decision function is nonrandom.

To choose optimal decision functions, we need to know the criterion for comparing decision elements. We take for this criterion the so-called **risk**. This criterion is of a rather general form. It includes as special cases such familiar and, from a standpoint of practical problems, important criteria as the mean square error and the probability that the error will not exceed allowed limits. Before giving a definition of risk, we need to introduce one other important concept, that of a loss function.

Because of the influence of the noise Z, errors of decision are unavoidable for an arbitrary decision function $D = D(Y)$. In practical applications, any error is undesirable. The appearance of an error is accompanied by losses. In each specific case, these losses have their physical meaning. For example, when we are controlling an industrial process, the errors of the decision element cause losses in the quality of production, losses in the amount of energy expended, losses in time, and the like. In posing the problem of choosing an optimal decision function, it is assumed that, in accordance with the requirements imposed on the decision, the measure of the losses is chosen in the form of a **loss function** $W(X, D)$. The loss function is constructed in such a way that, if the solution D_1 is closer to the signal X than is the decision D_2, then

$$W(X, D_1) \leqslant W(X, D_2).$$

We usually attribute zero losses to the correct solution; that is, we usually take $W(X, X) = 0$. The loss function is, by virtue of the foregoing assumptions, positive; that is, it satisfies the inequality $W(X, D) \geqslant 0$.

A loss function is a subjective category. The investigator chooses or defines it as he sees fit. However, in choosing the loss function, we need to keep objective circumstances in mind as much as possible; the purpose of the system, the nature of the initial data regarding the signals, the possibilities that exist when one is constructing a decision element. The loss function (and the risk, which is defined in terms of the loss function) must reflect as much as possible the purpose of the decision element and the system of which it is a part. The complexity of the decision function (or decision element) depends on the form of the loss function and the nature of the initial conditions regarding the signals. We need to choose a sufficiently complicated loss function in order for it to reflect closely the purpose of the decision element and the system. On the other hand, this loss function must be sufficiently simple for us to be able to realize the decision unit with the aid of the tools at our disposal.

Most often, we take a loss function depending only on the difference $D - X$, that is, on the error of the decision element. The following are examples of loss functions:

(1) $W = W(D - X) = |D - X|.$ (8.29)

(2) $W = W(D - X) = (D - X)^2.$ (8.30)

(3) $W = W(D - X) = \begin{cases} 0 & \text{if} \quad C_1 \leqslant D - X \leqslant C_2, \\ 1 & \text{if} \quad D - X < C_1, D - X > C_2, \end{cases}$

(8.31)

where C_2 and C_1 are given numbers satisfying the inequality $C_2 > C_1$.

(4) *The simple loss function.* This function is defined by

$$W = W(D - X) = \begin{cases} 0 & \text{if} \quad D = X, \\ 1 & \text{if} \quad D \neq X, \end{cases}$$ (8.32)

where the signal space X and the decision space D consist of isolated points. If the space $\bar{X}$ and $\bar{D}$ are continuous (for example, if they are k-dimensional polyhedrons, where $k > 0$), the set of correct decisions is incomparably less than the set of erroneous decisions. Therefore, if we define the simple loss function in this case by formula (8.32), the correct decisions will be "drowned" in the sea of incorrect ones. Keeping this fact in mind, we define the simple loss function in this case by

$$W = W(D - X) = 1 - \delta(D - X)$$ (8.33)

or

$$W = W(D - X) = \begin{cases} -\infty & \text{if} \quad D = X, \\ 1 & \text{if} \quad D \neq X. \end{cases}$$ (8.33a)

Corresponding to different loss functions are different criteria for comparing decision elements and systems containing decision elements.

4.   The conditional risk.   The mean risk

The **conditional risk** r is defined as the mean value of the loss function under the assumption that signal X is at the input of the decision element. For fixed X, the loss function $W(X, D)$ is a random function. (The decision D is a random function, since it is chosen on the basis of the random input signal Y, which depends on the noise Z.) To obtain the mean loss function, we average over the set of decision

D. Thus, the conditional risk can be obtained in the form of the mathematical expectation of the loss function for a fixed signal X:

$$r = r(X) = \int_{\bar{D}} W(X, D) P(D/X) dD, \tag{8.34}$$

where $P(D/X)$ is the probability density of the decision D under the assumption that the useful signal has assumed the fixed value X. This probability density $P(D/X)$ can be expressed in terms of the decision function by using the familiar rules of probability theory. In the general case, we can write the relation

$$P(D/X) = \int_{\bar{Y}} P(D/Y) P(Y/X) dY. \tag{8.35}$$

We stated earlier that we would consider only nonrandom decision functions. In this case, to every input Y there corresponds a unique decision $D = D(Y)$. Consequently, the conditional probability density $P(D/Y)$ degenerates into the delta-function:

$$P(D/Y) = \delta[D - D(Y)]. \tag{8.36}$$

When we substitute (8.36) into (8.35), we obtain

$$P(D/X) = \int_{\bar{Y}} \delta[D - D(Y)] P(Y/X) dY. \tag{8.37}$$

Formulas (8.34) and (8.37) enable us to write the following expression for the conditional risk:

$$r = r(X) = \int_{\bar{D}} \int_{\bar{Y}} W(X, D) \delta[D - D(Y)] P(Y/X) dY dD. \tag{8.38}$$

The integration over the spaces $\bar{D}$ and $\bar{Y}$ means $(n + k)$-fold integration with respect to $Y_1, \cdots, Y_k$ and $D_1, \cdots, D_n$.

The conditional risk depends on the sample function of the signal X and hence is a random variable.

In connection with this, a more suitable criterion is usually the **unconditional risk** or the **mean risk** or simply the **risk** R, which is the conditional risk r averaged over the set $\bar{X}$ of signals X:

$$R = \int_{\bar{X}} r(X) P(X) dX, \tag{8.39}$$

where $P(X)$ is the *a priori* probability density of the signal X. Let us write the expanded expression for the risk:

$$R = \int_{\bar{X}} \int_{\bar{D}} \int_{\bar{Y}} W(X, D) \delta[D - D(Y)] P(Y/X) P(X) dY dD dX$$

$$= \int_{\bar{X}} \int_{\bar{Y}} W[X, D(Y)] P(Y/X) P(X) dY dX. \tag{8.40}$$

If the loss function $W(X, D)$, the *a priori* probability density $P(X)$, and the conditional probability density $P(Y/X)$ are given, the risk R depends only on the decision function $D(Y)$.

5.   Bayes and minimax decisions

In the theory of decisions, we consider two different fomulations of the problem. In the first formulation of the problem, we assume that we know the *a priori* probability density $P(X)$ of the signal X. In the second formulation, we assume we know nothing regarding this *a priori* probability density.

Let us first look at the first formulation of the problem. Here, we can express the mean risk R in terms of the decision function $D(Y)$ in accordance with formula (8.40). In this case, to every decision function there corresponds a unique risk (some number). It is natural to treat as optimal that decision function $D_b = D_b(Y)$ that minimizes the mean risk:

$$R\{D_b(Y)\} \min_{D(Y)} R\{D(Y)\}. \tag{8.41}$$

The decision function $D_b(Y)$ satisfying equation (8.41) is called the **Bayes decision function**. The minimal risk in this case is called the **Bayes risk**.

The mean risk and the corresponding optimal decision function depend on the form of the loss function $W(X, D)$. Consequently, there is an infinite set of different **Bayes criteria** for optimality of the type (8.40) and an infinite set of optimal decision functions. The choice of one loss function or another (of one criterion or another) must be made with consideration of the specific requirements made on the decision element and the system containing it.

The problem of determining the optimal decision function $D_b(Y)$ reduces to that of determining the function $D(Y)$ minimizing the multiple integral (8.40). This means that the problem in question is a variational problem.

Many of the problems considered in the present chapter are special cases of the general variational problem formulated in the present subsection. The existence of a Bayes decision is proved in the general theory of decisions under extremely general conditions (usually satisfied in practical problems).

Let us illustrate this with an example of a problem of two choices with a single parameter λ. In this case, the parameter λ can have only two values: $\lambda = \lambda_0$ and $\lambda = \lambda_1$, with *a priori* probabilites p_0 and p_1 respectively. Consequently, the *a priori* probability of the signal (the parameter λ in the present case) can be written in the form

$$P(\lambda) = p_0\delta(\lambda - \lambda_0) + p_1\delta(\lambda - \lambda_1).$$

In this case, the space of the signals $\bar{\lambda}$ consists of the two points $\lambda = \lambda_0$ and $\lambda = \lambda_1$. The space of decisions is a copy of the signal space and hence it, too, consists of two points, namely, D_0 and D_1. The decision D_0 consists in the fact that $\lambda = \lambda_0$, and the decision D_1 consists in the fact that $\lambda = \lambda_1$.

Let us write the expression for the mean risk in the foregoing case with an arbitrary loss function

$$
\begin{aligned}
R &= \int_{\bar{\lambda}} \int_{\bar{D}} \int_{\bar{Y}} W(\lambda, D) \delta [D - D(Y)] P(Y/\lambda) \\
&\quad \times [p_0 \delta(\lambda - \lambda_0) + p_1 \delta(\lambda - \lambda_1)] d\lambda \, dY \, dD \\
&= \int_{\bar{\lambda}} \int_{\bar{Y}} W[\lambda, D(Y)] P(Y/\lambda) [p_0 \delta(\lambda - \lambda_0) + p_1 \delta(\lambda - \lambda_1)] d\lambda \, dY.
\end{aligned}
$$

Carrying out the integration and keeping in mind the properties of the delta function, we obtain

$$
\begin{aligned}
R &= \int_{\bar{Y}_0} \sum_{i=0}^{1} W(\lambda_i, D_0) P(Y/\lambda_i) p_i \, dY \\
&\quad + \int_{\bar{Y}_1} \sum_{j=0}^{1} W(\lambda_j, D_1) P(Y/\lambda_j) p_j \, dY,
\end{aligned}
$$

where $\bar{Y}_0$ is that part of the space of outcomes $\bar{Y}$ corresponding to the decision D_0 (if $Y \in \bar{Y}_0$, we have $D(Y) = D_0$), and $\bar{Y}_1$ is that portion of the space $\bar{Y}$ that corresponds to the decision D_1 (if $Y \in \bar{Y}_1$, then $D(Y) = D_1$).

We introduce the notation $W(\lambda_i, D_j) = W_{ij}$ and we rewrite the expression obtained for the risk in the following form:

$$
\begin{aligned}
R &= \int_{\bar{Y}_0} [p_0 P(Y/\lambda_0) W_{00} + p_1 P(Y/\lambda_1) W_{10}] dY \\
&\quad + \int_{\bar{Y}_1} [p_0 P(Y/\lambda_0) W_{01} + p_1 P(Y/\lambda_1) W_{11}] dY \\
&= \int_{\bar{Y}_0} p_0 P(Y/\lambda_0) \left[W_{00} + W_{10} \frac{p_1}{p_0} \Lambda(Y) \right] dY \\
&\quad + \int_{\bar{Y}_1} p_0 P(Y/\lambda_0) \left[W_{01} + W_{11} \frac{p_1}{p_0} \Lambda(Y) \right] dY, \qquad \text{(8.42)}
\end{aligned}
$$

where $\Lambda(Y) = P(Y/\lambda_1)/P(Y/\lambda_0)$ is the likelihood ratio (cf. (8.17)). On the right side of this equation, let us add and subtract the integral

$$
\int_{\bar{Y}_0} p_0 P(Y/\lambda_0) \left[W_{01} + W_{11} \frac{p_1}{p_0} \Lambda(Y) \right] dY.
$$

Remembering that

$$
\int_{\bar{Y}} P(Y/\lambda_0) dY = \int_{\bar{Y}} P(Y/\lambda_1) dY = 1,
$$

we obtain

$$R = \int_{\bar{Y}_0} p_0 P(Y/\lambda_0) \left[W_{00} + \frac{p_1}{p_0} W_{10} \Lambda(Y) - W_{01} \right.$$

$$\left. - \frac{p_1}{p_0} W_{11} \Lambda(Y) \right] dY + p_0 W_{01} + p_1 W_{11}. \qquad (8.43)$$

As one would expect, the risk R depends on the decision function $D(Y)$, since the regions of integration $\bar{Y}_0$ and $\bar{Y}_1$ depend on this function. To find the optimal decision function, we need to determine the function $D(Y)$ that minimizes the mean risk R. One can easily see that the following decision function satisfies this condition:

$$D(Y) = \begin{cases} D_0, & \text{if} \quad W_{00} + \frac{p_1}{p_0} W_{10} \Lambda(Y) < W_{01} + \frac{p_1}{p_0} W_{11} \Lambda(Y), \\ \\ D_1, & \text{if} \quad W_{00} + \frac{p_1}{p_0} W_{10} \Lambda(Y) > W_{01} + \frac{p_1}{p_0} W_{11} \Lambda(Y). \end{cases}$$

If

$$W_{00} + \frac{p_1}{p_0} W_{10} \Lambda(Y) = W_{01} + \frac{p_1}{p_0} W_{11} \Lambda(Y),$$

we may take either of the two decisions $D = D_0$ or $D = D_1$. Here, the risk R does not change.

Thus, the mean risk R assume a minimum value if we take the following decision function:

$$D_b(Y) = \begin{cases} D_0, & \text{if} \quad \Lambda(Y) \leqslant \frac{p_0}{p_1} \frac{W_{01} - W_{00}}{W_{10} - W_{11}}, \\ \\ D_1, & \text{if} \quad \Lambda(Y) > \frac{p_0}{p_1} \frac{W_{01} - W_{00}}{W_{10} - W_{11}}. \end{cases} \qquad (8.44)$$

This decision function is a **Bayes decision.**

Let us clarify the meaning of the mean risk in the special case when the loss function is a simple loss function, that is, when

$$W_{00} = W_{11} = 0, \qquad W_{01} = W_{10} = 1.$$

In this case, the mean risk is equal to (cf. (8.42))

$$R = \int_{\bar{Y}_0} p_1 P(Y/\lambda_1) dY + \int_{\bar{Y}_1} p_0 P(Y/\lambda_0) dY$$

$$= p_0 \int_{\bar{Y}_1} P(Y/\lambda_0) dY + p_1 \int_{\bar{Y}_0} P(Y/\lambda_1) dY = p_0 \alpha + p_1 \beta, \qquad (8.45)$$

where α is the probability of a false alarm (significance level) and β is the probability of a false all-clear. Comparing (8.45) and (8.19), we note that the mean risk coincides in this case with Kotel'nikov's criterion.

Let us now show how we compute the conditional and mean risk in the case in which the signal X may assume one of m possible values (aspects) $X^1, \cdots, X^m$. (Here, the superscript denotes the number of possible values of the signal. The subscript used earlier denoted the number of the experiment ([measurement] or the number of the component of the vector X). This problem is called the **problem of many choices** in the theory of statistical decisions. To calculate the mean risk in this case, we can use the general formula (8.40). The *a priori* probability density $P(X)$ of the signal X can be written in the present case as follows:

$$P(X) = \sum_{i=1}^{m} \delta(X - X^i) P(X^i) = \sum_{i=1}^{m} \delta(X - X^i) p_i, \qquad (8.46)$$

where p_i denotes the probability of the event that the signal X assumes the value X_i. The numbers p_i must satisfy the conditions

$$0 \leqslant p_i \leqslant 1, \qquad p_1 + \cdots + p_m = 1.$$

Let us suppose that the numbers p_i have been ascertained by some method or other. The input to the decision element Y also assumes one of a finite number of possible values $Y^1, \cdots, Y^q$, where q, may, as a special case, be equal to m. The conditional probability $P(Y/X)$ can then be written in the form

$$P(Y/X^i) = \sum_{s=1}^{q} \delta(Y - Y^s) P(Y^s/X^i) = \sum_{s=1}^{q} \delta(Y - Y^s) p_{si}, \qquad (8.47)$$

where $p_{si} = P(Y^s/X^i)$ is the probability of appearance of the signal Y^s at the input to the decision element under the assumption that the useful signal X has the value X^i. This conditional probability can be obtained either by computation or by experiment. In the present case, the conditional probability $P(Y/X)$ may be assumed known if we know the matrix of the numbers p_{si}:

$$\|p_{si}\| = \begin{Vmatrix} p_{11} & p_{12} & \cdots & p_{1m} \\ p_{21} & p_{22} & \cdots & p_{2m} \\ \cdot & \cdot & \cdot & \cdot \\ p_{q1} & p_{q2} & \cdots & p_{qm} \end{Vmatrix}, \qquad (8.48)$$

that is, if we know the matrix of values of the conditional probabilities $P(Y^s/X^i)$. The numbers p_{si} depend on the combination of the useful signal X and the noise Z and on the probabilistic characteristics of the noise. In the present case, the decision function $D = D(Y^s)$ can assume only one out of m values: $D^1, \cdots, D^l$. We need to know the loss function $W(X, D)$ only for discrete values of the arguments D^j, X^i:

$$W[X^i, D^j(Y^s)] = W_{ij}, \qquad i, j = 1, \cdots, m. \qquad (8.49)$$

Consequently, the loss function can be replaced with the loss matrix

$$\|W_{ij}\| = \begin{Vmatrix} W_{11} & W_{12} & \cdots & W_{1m} \\ W_{21} & W_{22} & \cdots & W_{2m} \\ \cdot & \cdot & \cdots & \cdot \\ W_{m1} & W_{m2} & \cdots & W_{mm} \end{Vmatrix}. \tag{8.50}$$

Let us first write the expression for the conditional risk, substituting (8.47) and (8.49) into (8.38):

$$r(X^i) = \sum_{s=1}^{q} W[X^i, D(Y^s)]P(Y^s/X^i). \tag{8.51}$$

Keeping formulas (8.46), (8.51), and (8.39) in mind, we obtain an expression for the mean risk in this case:

$$R = \sum_{i=1}^{m} P(X^i) \sum_{s=1}^{q} W[X^i, D(Y^s)]P(Y^s/X^i)$$

$$= \sum_{i=1}^{m} \sum_{s=1}^{q} W[X^i, D(Y^s)]P(Y^s/X^i)P(X^i)$$

$$= \sum_{s=1}^{q} \left\{ \sum_{i=1}^{m} W[X^i, D(Y^s)]P(Y^s/X^i)P(X^i) \right\}. \tag{8.52}$$

We need to find the decision function $D(Y^s)$ minimizing the mean risk (8.52). This mean risk is a sum of q terms of the form

$$\rho_s = \sum_{i=1}^{m} W[X^i, D(Y^s)]P(Y^s/X^i)P(X^i). \tag{8.53}$$

In each term, ρ_s is the value of the decision function of the argument Y^s. Therefore, minimization of the mean risk (8.53) reduces to minimization of each term ρ_s defined by formula (8.53). Consequently, we need to consider each of the input Y^s and, for each input, we need to find the optimal decision $D(Y^s) = D^j$.

Thus, when we are considering a discrete many-choice problem, determination of the optimal decision function reduces to the following simple operations: First, we consider the input signal Y^1 and seek the optimal decision $D(Y^1)$. Then, we seek the optimal decisions $D(Y^2)$, $\cdots$, $D(Y^q)$. To determine the optimal decision $D(Y^s)$, we need to take successively $D(Y^s) = D^1$, $D(Y^s) = D^2$, $\cdots$, $D(Y^s) = D_m$ and for each of them calculate the quantity ρ_s in accordance with formula (8.53) by using the known values of $P(X^i) = p_i$ and the values of the elements of the matrices (8.48) and (8.50). Then, we choose that value D^j that minimizes the value of ρ^s. Each of the decisions D^j can, as a special case, be one of the values X^i of the useful signal.

Let us look at an example illustrating the decision procedure for a problem of many choices.

EXAMPLE.   Consider the system whose block diagram is shown in

Figure 8.4. Here, the controlled object of the main controlled loop has transfer function $1/(p + a)$. The parameter a varies in a random manner as a result of the influence of the external medium. Suppose that, on the basis of measurements, for example, measurements of the input and output signals of the controlled object, the measuring device (md) determines the current value of the parameter a. Suppose that an error Δa is made in the process. On the basis of the measured values $b = a + \Delta a$, the decision element (de) must supply a decision, the value of the parameter k minimizing the mean risk with a previously chosen loss function (loss matrix). In the present case, the space of decisions does not coincide with the signal space. However, there is a one-to-one correspondence between the elements k of the decision space and the elements a of the signal space. In the given example, the parameter a corresponds to the signal X studied in the general theory of decisions, the input b into the decision element corresponds to the input Y, and the error Δa in measurement of the parameter a corresponds to the noise Z. The noise and the signal in this problem are additive. This means that the input is the sum of the useful signal and the noise:

$$Y = X + Z \quad \text{or} \quad b = a + \Delta a.$$

Suppose that the parameter a assumes one of the three possible values

$$a^1 = 5, \qquad a^2 = 10, \qquad a^3 = 20.$$

The *a priori* probabilities $P(a^1) = p_i$ are known:

$$P(a^1) = 0.3, \qquad P(a^2) = 0.5, \qquad P(a^3) = 0.2.$$

The matrix of the conditional probabilities (8.48) is given:

$$\|p_{si}\| = \begin{Vmatrix} 0.5 & 0.1 & 0.0 \\ 0.3 & 0.6 & 0.4 \\ 0.2 & 0.3 & 0.6 \end{Vmatrix}.$$

Corresponding to this matrix is the following table:

Table 2.

	a^1	a^2	a^3
b^1	0.5	0.1	0.0
b^2	0.3	0.6	0.4
b^3	0.2	0.3	0.6

The possible values of the inputs into the decision element (the input space) are chosen as follows: $b^1 = 5$, $b^2 = 10$, $b^3 = 20$. Thus, in the present example, the numbers q and m coincide: $q = m = 3$.

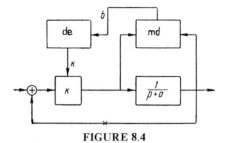

FIGURE 8.4

The decision function connects the output of the decision element k (in the general theory of decisions, it is denoted by the letter D) with the input b:

$$k = k(b).$$

In the present problem, the output k can assume one of the three values k^1, k^2, k^3. Let us determine the decision space $\bar{k}$. To do this, let us examine in greater detail the main control loop of the system (see Fig. 8.4). Let us suppose that a useful signal with constant value l and a noise that is a centralized stationary random function with spectral density $20/(\omega^2+1)$ are applied to the input of this control loop. The useful input signal G is the desired output variable of the main control loop $H(t)$; that is, $H(t) = G(t)$.

As a possible decision k^i, we take the value of the parameter k minimizing the mean square error of the main control loop when the parameter a assumed the value a^i for $i = 1, 2, 3$.

Let us find these decisions k^1, k^2, k^3. To do this, we write the formula for the mean square error in the present case:

$$\Gamma_E(a, k) = D_E(a, k) + m_E^2(a, k)$$

$$= \frac{1}{\pi} \int_0^\infty \frac{20}{\omega^2 + 1} \frac{k^2 d\omega}{(j\omega + a + k)(-j\omega + a + k)} + \frac{a^2}{(a + k)^2}$$

$$= \frac{1}{\pi} \int_0^\infty \frac{1}{[(j\omega)^2 + (1 + a + k)j\omega + a + k]}$$

$$\times \frac{20k^2 d\omega}{[(-j\omega)^2 + (1 + a + k)(-j\omega) + a + k]} + \frac{a^2}{(a + k)^2}$$

$$= I_2 + \frac{a^2}{(a + k)^2}.$$

The value of the integral I_2 can be expressed in terms of the coefficients of the polynomial in the integrand

$$(j\omega)^2 + (1 + a + k)j\omega + a + k$$

(cf. Appendix 3). In the present case,

$$I_2 = 10 \frac{k^2}{(a + k)(1 + a + k)}.$$

Consequently, the mean square error is equal to

$$\Gamma_E(a, k) = \frac{10k^2}{(a + k)(1 + a + k)} + \frac{a^2}{(a + k)^2}.$$

Seeking the minimum $\Gamma_E(a, k)$ with respect to the variable k for fixed values of the variable a ($a^1 = 5$ sec^{-1}, $a^2 = 10$ sec^{-1}, $a^3 = 20$ sec^{-1}), we find the corresponding values of the possible decisions:

$$k^1 = 0.6, \qquad k^2 = 1.0, \qquad k^3 = 2.0.$$

For loss function we take the mean square error $\Gamma_E(a, k)$ of the system for given values of the parameters a and k. In the general theory of decisions, this function was denoted by W. The function $\Gamma_E(a, k)$ is always nonnegative, and the more the value of the parameter k differs from the optimal value, the greater will be the value of this function. Consequently, it can be taken as a loss function.

Calculation of the mean square error $\Gamma_E(a, k)$ for corresponding values of the variable a and k enables us to compile a table of losses:

Table 3.

	k^1	k^2	k^3
a^1	0.89	0.95	1.2
a^2	0.95	0.92	0.95
a^3	0.96	0.91	0.88

In accordance with the procedure previously expounded, we choose the optimal decision $k^0 = k^0(b)$. Following this procedure, we need to choose the optimal decision successively for each possible value of the input b^s. First, let us perform the calculations for $b = b^1 = 5$. In this case, the value of the mean losses ρ_1 given by (8.53) is as follows: If we choose k^1,

$$\rho_1 = \Gamma_E(a_1, k^1) P(b^1/a^1) P(a^1) + \Gamma_E(a^2, k^1) P(b^1/a^2) P(a^2)$$
$$+ \Gamma_E(a^3, k^1) P(b^1/a^3) P(a^3)$$
$$= 0.89 \cdot 0.6 \cdot 0.3 + 0.95 \cdot 0.1 \cdot 0.5 + 0.96 \cdot 0.0 \cdot 0.2 = 0.17;$$

if we choose k^2

$$\rho_1 = \Gamma_E(a^1, k^2) P(b^1/a^1) P(a^1) + \Gamma_E(a^2, k^2) P(b^1/a^2) P(a^2)$$
$$+ \Gamma_E(a^3, k^2) P(b^1/a^3) P(a^3)$$
$$= 0.95 \cdot 0.6 \cdot 0.3 + 0.92 \cdot 0.1 \cdot 0.5 + 0.91 \cdot 0.0 \cdot 0.2 = 0.18;$$

if we choose k^3,

$$\rho_1 = \Gamma_E(a^1, k^3) P(b^1/a^1) P(a^1) + \Gamma_E(a^2, k^3) P(b^1/a^2) P(a^2)$$
$$+ \Gamma_E(a^3, k^3) P(b^1/a^3) P(a^3)$$
$$= 1.2 \cdot 0.6 \cdot 0.3 + 0.95 \cdot 0.1 \cdot 0.5 + 0.88 \cdot 0.0 \cdot 0.2 = 0.22.$$

Comparing the values of ρ_1 for the different values of the decision k^1, k^2, and k^3, we conclude that, for $b = b^1$, the optimal decision is $k^0 = k^1$.

In an analogous manner, we calculate ρ_3 for $b = b^3$:

$$\rho_3 = 0.298 \text{ if we choose the decision } k^1,$$
$$\rho_3 = 0.292 \text{ if we choose the decision } k^2,$$
$$\rho_3 = 0.302 \text{ if we choose the decision } k^3.$$

When we compare the values of ρ_3 for the different values of the decision k^1, k^2, k^3, we conclude, that for $b = b^3$, the optimal solution is $k^0 = k^2$.

In the same way, we can determine the optimal decision when b assumes the value b^2.

Let us look at a second formulation of the problem. Let us suppose that we have no information regarding the *a priori* probability $P(X)$ of the signal X. To construct the Bayes decision in this case, we would need to make an arbitrary assumption regarding the form of this *a priori* probability. The Bayes decision constructed for this arbitrarily chosen *a priori* probability will not be the optimal decision, since the true *a priori* probability is not the same as that chosen. Here, we need a new approach to the solution of the problem of choosing the optimal decision function.

Let us look at the conditional risk $r(X, D)$. When we shift from one signal X to another, the value of conditional risk changes. Suppose that, for a given decision function D, the maximum of the conditional risk among all X is attained with some signal X_m:

$$r(X_m, D) = \max_X r(X, D). \tag{8.54}$$

Let us compare the different decision functions with respect to the maximal conditional risk $r(X_m, D)$. We shall consider that decision function D_m optimal that corresponds to the minimal value of $r(X_m, D)$:

$$r(X_m, D_m) = \min_D r(X_m, D) = \min_D \max_X r(X, D). \tag{8.55}$$

The decision function D_m satisfying condition (8.55) is called the **minimax decision function**. The existence of a minimax decision function is proved under extremely general assumptions.

The *minimax decision* ensures the smallest risk under the worst circumstances. If we take the minimax decision, then, for an arbitrary *a priori* probability density $P(X)$, the conditional risk cannot be greater than $r(X_m, D_m)$.

There is a connection between the minimax and Bayes decisions.

In the general theory of decisions, it is proved that the following assertion holds under extremely broad conditions:

Let $P^*(X)$ be the least desired *a priori* probability density satisfying
the condition

$$R[P^*(X), D_b^*] \geqslant R[P(X), D_b],$$

where D_b^* is the Bayes decision with respect to $P^*(X)$ and D_b is the
Bayes decision with respect to any other *a priori* probability density
$P(X)$. Let D_m be the minimax decision. Then

$$D_m = D_b^*. \tag{8.56}$$

Consequently, to construct the minimax decision, we need to find the
least desirable *a priori* probability density $P^*(X)$ and then determine the
Bayes decision D_b^*.

In this formulation of the problem, as in the special case considered in Subsection 7 of the present section, another approach to
the decision is possible. One can assign the *a priori* probability density
$P(X)$ from some considerations or other. Then, the formulation of the
problem reduces to the Bayes formulation. The positive side of this
approach is the simplication of the problem. A defect is the fact that
we have no guaranteed value of the risk. In this case, the actual risk
may be either smaller or greater than the value computed for it.

6. A criterion of general form

The mean risk given by formula (8.40) is a criterion covering
many criteria that are suitable for practical calculations. However,
sensible criteria of the more general form are possible. It is expedient
to consider a criterion of the following general form:

$$I = f(R_1, \cdots, R_{n+1}), \tag{8.57}$$

where $R_i = R_i[D(Y), W_i(X, D)]$ is the mean risk (given by formula
(8.40)) corresponding to the loss function $W_i(X, D)$ and the decision
function $D(Y)$. Here, the probability densities $P(Y/X)$ and $P(X)$ are
everywhere the same (independent of i) and do not change for $i = 1$,
$\cdots, n + 1$; f is a given function of the variables $R_1, \cdots, R_{n+1}$. Using
a line of reasoning that we have frequently used in the present book
(see Chapters 1, 4, and 7), we can show that the optimal Bayes decision
function minimizing the criterion (8.49) corresponds to a minimum
(extremum) of the reduced criterion I_θ:

$$I_\theta = \theta_1 R_1 + \cdots + \theta_n R_n + R_{n+1} \tag{8.58}$$

for certain values of the harmonizing parameters $\theta_1 = \theta_{10}, \cdots, \theta_n = \theta_{n0}$.
One can easily see that if corresponding to the criteria R_i are loss func-
tions $W_i(X, D)$ for $i = 1, \cdots, n + 1$, then the reduced criterion I_θ can

be regarded as the mean risk corresponding to the function $W_\theta(X, D)$ defined by

$$W_\theta(X, D) = \theta_1 W_1(X, D) +$$
$$\cdots + \theta_n W_n(X, D) + W_{n+1}(X, D). \qquad (8.59)$$

Thus, the problem of determining the optimal decision function $D^\circ(Y)$ with respect to a criterion of the general form (8.57) reduces to the problem of determining the Bayes decision function $D_0(Y, \theta_1, \cdots, \theta_n)$ with respect to the Bayes criterion (8.59).

The values of the harmonizing parameters

$$\theta_1 = \theta_{10}, \cdots, \theta_n = \theta_{n0}$$

can be found as follows: We substitute the decision function $D_0(Y, \theta_1, \cdots, \theta_n)$ into the criterion (8.40), which then becomes a known function of the parameters $\theta_1, \cdots, \theta_n$:

$$I[D_0(Y, \theta_1, \cdots, \theta_n)] = \Phi(\theta_1, \cdots, \theta_n). \qquad (8.60)$$

Then, we determine the minimum of the function Φ and the values of the parameters

$$\theta_1 = \theta_{10}, \cdots, \theta_n = \theta_{n0},$$

corresponding to this minimum. The decision function

$$D^\circ(Y) = D_0(Y, \theta_{10}, \cdots, \theta_{n0}) \qquad (8.61)$$

is the optimal decision function that we are seeking.

It can be shown that the values of the harmonizing parameters

$$\theta_1 = \theta_{10}, \cdots, \theta_n = \theta_{n0}$$

satisfy the following equations:

$$\frac{\dfrac{\partial f}{\partial R_i}}{\dfrac{\partial f}{\partial R_{n+1}}} = \theta_{i0}, \qquad i = 1, \cdots, n, \qquad (8.62)$$

which are analogous to equations (1.167). In equations (8.62), the partial derivatives are evaluated at

$$D(Y) = D_0(Y, \theta_{10}, \cdots, \theta_{n0}).$$

If each mean risk R_i in the criterion (8.58) is defined for its own probability density $P_i(Y/X)$ and $P_i(X)$ (differing for different values of i), the reduced criterion

$$I_\theta = \theta_1 R_1 + \cdots + \theta_n R_n + R_{n+1} \qquad (8.63)$$

cannot, in the general case, be represented as the mean risk corresponding to the loss function (8.59). However, even in this case, the problem is solved in an analogous manner if there exists some way of finding the decision function yielding an extremum of the reduced criterion (8.63). Assigning different losses $W_i(X, D)$ and different functions f in the criterion (8.49) ensures a great amount of variety in the optimality criteria.

28. SYSTEMS WITH GAME DECISION ELEMENTS

In Subsection 1 of Section 26, we looked at an example of a problem of two choices. We looked at a second example of a more complex problem of many choices in Subsection 1 of Section 27. In those sections, we expounded methods of determining optimal decisions minimizing the chosen criteria of the error of the systems. An important feature of these systems with the decision elements examined in Sections 26 and 27 is the fact that a measurement of some random variable (for example, the variance of the useful input signal) was made in them and a decision was taken regarding its true value on the basis of the measurements of this random variable. Of course, this measurement was made with some error. Another formulation of the problems is possible. For example, if it is impossible to measure the randon variable in which we are interested (the variance of the useful input signal), it is necessary to construct an optimal system in some other sense. Let us look at formulations of problems of determining optimal systems under these new conditions.

1. An example of a system with game decision element

Suppose that an input signal X, which is the sum of a useful signal G and a noise Z, is applied to the system represented in Figure 2.2. All the probabilistic characteristics of the usual signal G and the noise Z are known except for the variance D_g of the useful signal. Suppose that we know that this variance can assume one of n values $D_1, \cdots, D_n$. The *a priori* probabilities, $p_1, \cdots, p_n$ of the values of this variance $D_1, \cdots, D_n$ are unknown. In the present case, we cannot determine the usual optimal system, since we do not have all the required characteristics of the input variable X. Therefore, it is expedient to shift to an optimal system with decision element. We shall assume that the system is determined up to a parameter a. For example, the system may be determined as the usual optimal system under specified initial conditions in which the variance of the useful signal D_g is an unknown parameter. In this case, the parameter a is numerically equal to D_g. Suppose that the variable parameter a of the system may assume several discrete values: $a_1, \cdots, a_m$. It is assumed that, under the given conditions, the system may be used more than once. Therefore, it is appropriate to get the best mean effect of application of this system. We can pose the problem of determining the optimal value of the parameter a_i maximizing the chosen criterion for comparing systems under the worst combination of *a priori* probabilities $p_1, \cdots, p_n$. However, the best result would be obtained in the general case if we discovered the probability densities $q_1, \cdots, q_m$ used in the system of values $a_1, \cdots a_m$ of the parameter a.

Thus, we have one of the situations considered in game theory. We may assume that one side A has at its disposal systems characterized by the values $a_1, \cdots, a_m$ of the parameter a, that is, that it has several strategies. The other side B (which may be either nature or an opponent) has at its disposal n possible values $D_1, \cdots, D_n$ of the variance of the signal G. The side A wishes to use its strategy to win as much as possible (that is to get as large as possible a value of the criterion for comparing systems). The side B wishes to use it strategy to thwart side A, that is, to make the winnings of the side A as small as possible. This is a typical conflict situation, which constitutes the subject of the mathematical theory of games [Refs. 11, 34, 35, 54].

2. Brief information from the theory of games

The theory of games is a branch of mathematics that considers conflict situations in which two or more opposing sides pursue opposing purposes and the result of each action of one side depends on the form of action (on the algorithm) of the other side. A simplified formalized model of an actual conflict situation is called a **game**. A game is conducted in accordance with fully specified rules. Chess can serve as an example of a game. We shall consider only games in which there are two sides A and B.

The result of a game is characterized by the sides' winning or losing. Wins and losses are characterized by numbers. For example, in the case of chess, a win is characterized by unity, the losing of a game is characterized by 0, and a tie by $1/2$. Simpler than chess are games with zero sum, that is, games in which the winnings of one side are equal to the losses of the other. With such games, we may consider only the winnings of one side; for example, the side A. Chess is not such a game but it can be reduced to one if we add $(-1/2)$ to all the results so that a won game is characterized by $(+1/2)$, a lost game by $(-1/2)$ and a tie by 0. The conflict situation to which the problem in the first subsection of this section reduces can also be reduced to a game with zero sum.

A *move* is defined as the choice of some one of a set of variants allowed by the rules of the game. Moves are divided into individual and random moves. An individual move is a move made on the basis of a definite algorithm. An example of an individual move is a move in chess, the choice of a definite value of a_i, for $1 \leq i \leq m$ of the parameter a in the problem just considered. A random move is a move made according to a random law. For any random move, it is necessary to indicate the probability distribution of the possible outcomes. An example of a random move is the move consisting in acceptance of the following decision: The parameter must assume the values $a_1, \cdots, a_m$ with probabilities $p_1, \cdots, p_m$ respectively (where $p_1 + \cdots + p_m = 1$).

An important concept in the theory of games is that of a strategy. The **strategy** of a player is the set of rules determining unambiguously the choice of variant for each individual move of that player, depending on the situation that arises in the course of the game. After choosing a strategy, a player may fail to participate in a game if he gives the strategy chosen to a controlling machine in the form of a program. We shall consider only finite games, that is, games in which each player has only a finite number of strategies. Suppose that player A has strategies $A_1, \cdots, A_m$ and player B has strategies $B_1, \cdots, B_n$. If the game contains only individual moves, then the choice of the strategies A_i and B_j determine uniquely the winnings of the side A. Let us denote these winnings by a_{ij}. On the other hand, if the game also contains random moves, then the winnings of the side A, with the strategies A_i and B_j, constitute a random variable. In this case, we consider the average gain, that is, the mathematical expectation of the gain and denote it by the same symbol a_{ij}. All values of the gain a_{ij} can be written in the form of a rectangular matrix (table) called the **game matrix** (see Table 4). If the matrix of the game has m rows and n columns, then the game is called an $m \times n$ game. The matrix of the game is denoted briefly by $||a_{ij}||$.

Table 4.

B A	B_1	B_2	$\cdots$	B_n
A_1	a_{11}	a_{12}	$\cdots$	a_{1n}
A_2	a_{21}	a_{22}	$\cdots$	a_{2n}
$\vdots$		$\cdot$	$\cdots$	$\cdot$
A_m	a_{m1}	a_{m2}	$\cdots$	a_{mn}

The theory of games solves the problem of producing recommendations for the appropriate behavior of players in conflict situations. It determines the optimal strategies of each of them.

The **optimal strategy** of a player A is defined as that strategy that, under numerous repetitions of the game, ensures him the maximal possible mean gain under the assumption that the player B (the opponent) does everything possible to prevent this.

One criterion for comparing strategies is the mathematical expectation of the gain. Other comparison criteria are also possible. For example, we may take for such a criterion the probability that the gain will not be less than a given amount. This criterion is of no less practical value than the mathematical expectation. However, it is more complicated and hence it presents more difficulties.

The upper and lower pure values. Consider an $m \times n$ game with matrix of the general form $||a_{ij}||$, where i denotes the row position and j denotes the column position. Let us determine the optimal strategy of the player A. To do this, let us analyze his strategies. When he chooses a strategy A_i, the player A must remember that the opponent will answer to this strategy with a strategy B_j that will minimize the gain a_{ij} of the player A. Suppose that the minimal value of the gain α_i:

$$\alpha_i = \min_j \alpha_{ij}.$$

The player A must choose out of all his strategies the one that corresponds to the maximum of the numbers α_i. Let us denote this maximal value by α:

$$\alpha = \max_i \alpha_i.$$

Consequently, we may write

$$\alpha = \max_i \min_j \alpha_{ij}.$$

The quantity α is called the **lower pure value** of the game or the **maximin**. The number α corresponds to a definite row of the matrix. The strategy of the player A determined by this row is called the **maximin strategy**. By employing the maximin strategy, the player A ensures that his gain will be no less than α (for an arbitrary strategy of the player B). With another strategy, his gain may be less than α.

The player B reasons in an analogous manner. He, too, is interested in maximizing his gain and, consequently, reducing the gain of the player A to a minimum. The player B, in choosing the strategy B_j, must assume that the player A will respond to it with the strategy A_i that maximizes the gain a_{ij}. Let us denote this value of the gain by β_j:

$$\beta_j = \max_i \alpha_{ij}.$$

Furthermore, he must find the minimum of the values B_j. Let us denote this minimal value by β:

$$\beta = \min_j \beta_j.$$

Consequently, we may write

$$\beta = \min_j \max_i \alpha_{ij}.$$

The quantity β is called the **upper pure value** of the game, or the **minimax**. The corresponding strategy is called the **minimax strategy**. This strategy ensures that the loss on the part of the player B will not exceed β.

It follows from the way in which the numbers α and β are chosen that $\alpha \leqslant \beta$. Let us look at an example of a 3 × 4 game matrix (see Table 5). Here, $\alpha_1 = 0.1$, $\alpha_2 = 0.1$, $\alpha_3 = 0.2$; $\beta_1 = 0.9$, $\beta_2 = 0.8$, $\beta_3 = 0.7$, $\beta_4 = 0.8$. The lower pure value of the game $\alpha = 0.2$. The upper pure value of the game $\beta = 0.7$. The maximin strategy is A_3, the minimax strategy B_3.

Table 5.

B A	B_1	B_2	B_3	B_4
A_1	0.9	0.8	0.4	0.1
A_2	0.1	0.2	0.5	0.8
A_3	0.2	0.2	0.7	0.3

If the lower pure value of the game α is equal to the upper pure value of the game β, their common value is called the **pure value** of the game γ. Let us give an example of a game matrix with pure value of the game (see Table 6). Here, the lower pure value of the game is equal to 0.4, the upper pure value is also 0.4. Consequently, the game has pure value $\gamma = 0.4$. The element $a_{23} = 0.4$ is the minimal value in the second row and the maximal value in the third column. Such an element is called a **saddle point** of the matrix. In this case, the strategies A_2 and B_3 are called optimal strategies and the set that they comprise is called the **solution** of the game.

Table 6.

B A	B_1	B_2	B_3	B_4
A_1	0.5	0.5	0.3	0.2
A_2	0.7	0.6	0.4	0.5
A_3	0.8	0.3	0.3	0.6
A_4	0.7	0.2	0.2	0.7

Among finite games that one encounters in practice, only rarely does one encounter games with a saddle point. One encounters games without a saddle point more frequently. In such games, the lower pure value is not equal to the upper pure value of the game. The player A can ensure a gain for himself greater than α if he does not take one "pure" strategy but alternates in a random manner between several strategies.

Combined strategies, which are an application of several *pure strategies* that alternate with a definite frequency ratio, are called **mixed strategies**. A pure strategy is the special case of a mixed strategy in which one strategy is used with probability 1 and the others with probability 0.

In this connection, we have a theorem proved by von Neumann: *Every finite game has at least one solution in the region of mixed strategies.* Consequently, every finite game has a pure value (or, simply, a value) γ. Obviously,

$$\alpha \leqslant \gamma \leqslant \beta.$$

If a mixed strategy of a player A consists in taking pure strategies A_1, $\cdots$, A_m with frequencies (probabilities) $p_1, \cdots, p_m$, we denote it as follows:

$$S_A = \left(\begin{array}{ccc} A_1 & \cdots & A_m \\ p_1 & \cdots & p_m \end{array} \right).$$

A mixed strategy of the player B is denoted analogously:

$$S_B = \left(\begin{array}{ccc} B_1 & \cdots & B_n \\ q_1 & \cdots & q_n \end{array} \right),$$

where q_i is the frequency (probability) with which the pure strategy B_j is used. Of course, the numbers p_i and q_j are subject to the conditions

$$p_1 + \cdots + p_m = 1, \qquad q_1 + \cdots + q_n = 1.$$

In the general case, the problem of finding the solution of an $m \times n$ game is a difficult one. The larger the values of m and n, the more complicated this problem will be. There are different methods of solving such problems. Let us show how the problem of finding an optimal mixed strategy can be reduced to a linear-programming problem.

Suppose that, in an $m \times n$ game with given matrix $||a_{ij}||$, we are required to find two optimal mixed strategies of the players A and B:

$$S_A^0 = \left(\begin{array}{ccc} A_1 & \cdots & A_m \\ p_1 & \cdots & p_m \end{array} \right), \qquad S_B^0 = \left(\begin{array}{ccc} B_1 & \cdots & B_n \\ q_1 & \cdots & q_n \end{array} \right).$$

The optimal strategy S_A^0 of the player A ensures that his gain will be no less than γ for any course his opponent may take. An analogous assertion is valid with regard to the player B. Let us suppose that the value of the game γ is greater than 0. This can always be arranged by adding to all elements of the matrix $||a_{ij}||$ a sufficiently large positive number k. This will increase the value of the gain, but the solution will remain unchanged.

Suppose that the player A has chosen an optimal strategy S_A^0. Then, the mean gain under the strategy B_j of the opponent is equal to

$$a_j = p_1 a_{1j} + \cdots + p_m a_{mj}, \qquad j = 1, \cdots, n.$$

Any of the numbers a_j is at least equal to the value of the game γ:

$$\left.\begin{array}{c} p_1 a_{11} + \cdots + p_m a_{m1} \geqslant \gamma, \\ \cdots\cdots\cdots\cdots\cdots \\ p_1 a_{1n} + \cdots + p_m a_{mn} \geqslant \gamma. \end{array}\right\} \qquad (8.64)$$

These inequalities can be rewritten in the following form:

$$\left.\begin{array}{c} a_{11} x_1 + \cdots + a_{m1} x_m \geqslant 1, \\ \cdots\cdots\cdots\cdots\cdots \\ a_{1n} x_1 + \cdots + a_{mn} x_m \geqslant 1, \end{array}\right\} \qquad (8.65)$$

where $x_1 = p_1/\gamma, \cdots, x_m = p_m/\gamma$. Consequently,

$$x_1 \geqslant 0, \cdots, x_m \geqslant 0, \qquad (8.66)$$

$$x_1 + \cdots + x_m = \frac{1}{\gamma}. \qquad (8.67)$$

The maximum of the quantity γ corresponds to the minimum of the sum

$$x_1 + \cdots + x_m.$$

Thus, the problem of finding a solution of the game reduces to determining the set of values $x_1, \cdots, x_m$ satisfying inequalities (8.65) and (8.66) and minimizing the linear function

$$L = x_1 + \cdots + x_m. \qquad (8.68)$$

This problem is a special case of the problem of linear programming.

We have considered the case in which the mean gain (mathematical expectation of the gain) is chosen as comparison criterion. Other formulations of problems are possible with different criteria.

Suppose that we take for such a criterion the probability P that the gain of the player A will be no less than a given value a. In this case, the problem of finding the optimal strategy maximizing P can be solved as follows:

Let us suppose that the player A has chosen the optimal strategy in this new sense. Then, the probability P under the strategy B_j of the opponent is equal to

$$P_j = p_1 \delta_{1j} + \cdots + p_m \delta_{mj},$$

where

$$\delta_{ij} = \begin{cases} 1 & \text{if } a_{ij} \geqslant a, \\ 0 & \text{if } a_{ij} < a. \end{cases}$$

Each of the numbers P_j is at least equal to P (the value of the game):

$$p_1 \delta_{11} + \cdots + p_m \delta_{m1} \geqslant P,$$
$$\cdots\cdots\cdots\cdots\cdots\cdots$$
$$p_1 \delta_{1n} + \cdots + p_m \delta_{mn} \geqslant P.$$

These inequalities can be rewritten in the form

$$\left.\begin{aligned}
\delta_{11} x_1 + \cdots + \delta_{m1} x_m &\geqslant 1, \\
\cdots\cdots\cdots\cdots\cdots\cdots \\
\delta_{1n} x_1 + \cdots + \delta_{mn} x_m &\geqslant 1,
\end{aligned}\right\} \tag{8.69}$$

where

$$x_1 = \frac{p_1}{P}, \quad \cdots, \quad x_m = \frac{p_m}{P}.$$

Consequently,

$$x_1 \geqslant 0, \quad \cdots, \quad x_m \geqslant 0, \tag{8.70}$$

$$L = x_1 + \cdots + x_m = \frac{1}{P}. \tag{8.71}$$

Thus, the problem of finding the solution of the game in this case reduces to determining the set of values $x_1, \cdots, x_m$ satisfying inequalities (8.70) and (8.71) and minimizing the value of the linear function (8.68). The problem has again been reduced to a special form of linear-programming problem.

As a criterion for comparing solutions, we may also take the quantity

$$\Delta = m^2 + kD,$$

where m is the mathematical expectation of the gain, D is the variance of the gain, and k is a negative number. The value of the coefficient k is chosen in the light of the distribution law of the gain. In this case, the gain of the player A depends nonlinearly on the unknown quantities $p_1, \cdots, p_m$. Hence, the problem of finding the optimal strategy reduces to a nonlinear-programming problem.

The following subsections of this section are devoted to linear and nonlinear programming.

3. Linear programming

Many problems of determining optimal systems and optimal decisions reduce to linear-programming problems. This branch of mathematics has been developed at an extremely rapid rate in the last few years. The first works in linear programming belong to the Soviet mathematician L. V. Kantorovich (1938). Let us formulate the linear-programming problem.

We are required to find the greatest (or smallest) value of the linear function

$$L = L(x_1, \cdots, x_n) = p_1 x_1 + \cdots + p_n p_n \qquad (8.72)$$

subject to the following restrictions on the variables $x_1, \cdots, x_n$:

$$
\begin{aligned}
a_{11} x_1 + \cdots + a_{n1} x_n &= b_1, \\
&\cdots\cdots\cdots\cdots \\
a_{1m} x_1 + \cdots + a_{nm} x_n &= b_m, \\
d_{11} x_1 + \cdots + d_{n1} x_n &\leqslant e_1, \\
&\cdots\cdots\cdots\cdots \\
d_{1r} x_1 + \cdots + d_{nr} x_n &\leqslant e_r.
\end{aligned}
\right\} \qquad (8.73)
$$

These relations determine the region G of variation of the variables $x_1, \cdots, x_n$. They can be transformed [Refs. 16, 57] in such a way that the number m of equations becomes equal to zero. Specifically, these m equations can be replaced with the inequalities

$$
\begin{aligned}
a_{11} x_1 + \cdots + a_{n1} x_n + x_{n+1} &\leqslant b_1, \\
&\cdots\cdots\cdots\cdots \\
a_{1m} x_1 + \cdots + a_{nm} x_n + x_{n+1} &\leqslant b_m, \\
x_{n+1} &\leqslant 0.
\end{aligned}
$$

The linear function L (of the $n + 1$ variables $x_1, \cdots, x_{n+1}$) then takes the form

$$L = p_1 x_1 + \cdots + p_n x_n + 0 \cdot x_{n+1}.$$

The symbol $\leqslant$ in inequalities (8.73) can always be replaced with the symbol $\geqslant$ if this should become necessary. This change is made by multiplying both sides of the inequalities by -1. In specific problems, we use whichever form is more convenient. One can easily see that conditions (8.66) and (8.69) are special cases of conditions (8.73) and that the linear functions (8.68) and (8.71) are special cases of the linear function (8.72).

In the present section, it will be more convenient for us to assume that the number m of equations in conditions (8.73) is zero. Consequently, these conditions may be written as

$$
\begin{aligned}
d_{11} x_1 + \cdots + d_{n1} x_n &\leqslant e_1, \\
&\cdots\cdots\cdots\cdots \\
d_{1r} x_1 + \cdots + d_{nr} x_n &\leqslant e_r.
\end{aligned}
\right\} \qquad (8.74)
$$

This formulation of the linear-programming problem can be given a geometrical interpretation. The linear-programming problem consists in finding the greatest value of a linear function of the variables x_i whose domain of definition is the polyhedron (8.74) in n-dimensional space $(x_1, \cdots, x_n)$. The polyhedron defined by the linear inequalities (8.74) is called **the polyhedron of the restrictions.**

It should be noted that the function L does not have a maximum in $(n+1)$-dimensional space. Therefore, the methods of classical analysis are not applicable here. The maximum (or minimum) value that L attains on the polyhedron-shaped region defined by inequalities (8.74) is attained on the boundary of that region. In fact, it can attain this maximum only at vertices of the polyhedron (8.74), since the function L is also a linear function of the variables $x_1, \cdots, x_n$ on the sides (faces) of this polyhedron. (If a point happens to be on a side of the polyhedron (8.74), this means that one of the conditional inequalities (8.74) is an equation. Consequently, one variable x_i can be expressed in terms of the other variables and substituted into the remaining inequalities. This converts the function L to a linear function of $n-1$ variables. The inequalities remain linear inequalities.)

At the present time, methods have been developed enabling us to solve linear-programming problems [Refs. 16, 25, 57]. Here, we shall expound the gradient method, which follows from the method of fastest descent as described in Chapter 3. The outline of this method is as follows:

First, we choose, on the basis of some considerations or other, a first approximation of the variables $x_1 = x_{11}, \cdots, x_n = x_{n1}$. For simplicity, we assume that each $x_{i1} = 0$. We then determine the direction of the gradient of the function L at the point $(x_{11}, \cdots, x_{n1})$. The components of the gradient along the axes $x_1, \cdots, x_n$ are equal respectively to

$$\frac{\partial L}{\partial x_1} = p_1, \cdots, \frac{\partial L}{\partial x_n} = p_n. \tag{8.75}$$

As one can see from equations (8.75), the gradient of the function L in the present case keeps the same value (both as regards magnitude and direction) throughout the entire polyhedron of the restrictions (and throughout the entire space $x_1, \cdots, x_n$). Then, we move along the direction of the gradient vector, that is, along the line described by the equations

$$x_1 = p_1 \varepsilon, \cdots, x_n = p_n \varepsilon,$$

increasing ε from zero to the value at which one of the inequalities (8.74) becomes an equation. Let us suppose that the inequality

$$(d_{i1} p_1 + \cdots + d_{in} p_n) \varepsilon \leqslant e_i$$

is the first to become an equation:

$$(d_{i1} p_1 + \cdots + d_{in} p_n) \varepsilon = e_i. \tag{8.76}$$

Satisfaction of equation (8.76) for some $\varepsilon = \varepsilon_1$ means that motion along the gradient vector was carried out by reaching the ith face of the polyhedron (8.74) at the point

$$x_{12} = p_1\varepsilon_1, \quad \cdots, \quad x_{n2} = p_n\varepsilon_1, \tag{8.77}$$

where the factor ε_1 is defined by equation (8.76):

$$\varepsilon_1 = \frac{e_i}{d_{i1}p_1 + \cdots + d_{in}p_n}. \tag{8.78}$$

Further motion made in order to find the greatest value of the function L must be made along the ith face of the polyhedron of the restrictions in the direction of the gradient of the function L (in that face). In that face, the function L depends on $n - 1$ variables, since we can eliminate one variable by using the equation for the ith face:

$$d_{i1}x_1 + \cdots + d_{in}x_n = e_i. \tag{8.79}$$

It follows from equation (8.79) that

$$x_n = -\frac{d_{i1}}{d_{in}}x_1 - \cdots - \frac{d_{i,n-1}}{d_{in}}x_{n-1} + \frac{e_i}{d_{in}}. \tag{8.80}$$

If we substitute (8.80) into (8.72), we obtain

$$L = \left(p_1 - p_n\frac{d_{i1}}{d_{in}}\right)x_1 + \cdots$$

$$\cdots + \left(p_{n-1} - p_n\frac{d_{i,n-1}}{d_{in}}\right)x_{n-1} + p_n\frac{e_i}{d_{in}}. \tag{8.81}$$

The components of the gradient of the function L along the axes x_1, $\cdots$, x_{n-1} are now equal to

$$\frac{\partial L}{\partial x_1} = p_1 - p_n\frac{d_{i1}}{d_{in}}, \quad \cdots, \quad \frac{\partial L}{\partial x_{n-1}} = p_{n-1} - p_n\frac{d_{i,n-1}}{d_{in}}. \tag{8.82}$$

Motion in the direction of the gradient (8.82) must now be begun from the point (8.77).

The coordinates of the points during the second stage of the motion along the direction of the gradient of the function L can be expressed in the form

$$\left.\begin{array}{l} x_1 = p_1\varepsilon_1 + \left(p_1 - p_n\dfrac{d_{i1}}{d_{in}}\right)\varepsilon, \\[6pt] \cdots\cdots\cdots\cdots\cdots\cdots\cdots\cdots\cdots\cdots \\[6pt] x_{n-1} = p_{n-1}\varepsilon_1 + \left(p_{n-1} - p_n\dfrac{d_{i,n-1}}{d_{in}}\right)\varepsilon, \\[6pt] x_n = -\dfrac{d_{i1}}{d_{in}}x_1 - \cdots - \dfrac{d_{i,n-1}}{d_{in}}x_{n-1} + \dfrac{e_i}{d_{in}}. \end{array}\right\} \tag{8.83}$$

We again let ε increase from 0 until one of inequalities (8.74) becomes an equation at $\varepsilon = \varepsilon_2$. Suppose that the sth inequality is the one that first becomes an equation:

$$d_{s1}x_1 + \cdots + d_{sn}x_n = e_s. \tag{8.84}$$

From equations (8.83) and (8.84), we find the value of the factor $\varepsilon = \varepsilon_2$. Then, we use formulas (8.83) to determine the coordinates of the point representing the end of the second stage in our search for the largest value of the function L; that is, we find the third approximation of the variables $x_1, \cdots, x_n$.

We then find the fourth and successive approximations in an analogous manner.

The search process terminates when the motion along the gradient vector in the next stage leads immediately to violation of the restrictions (8.74).

The search for the minimum of the function L is carried out in an analogous manner.

An algorithm of the method of linear programming can be achieved on a digital computer. The problems of linear programming can be solved (although with a lesser degree of accuracy) with the aid of machines of continuous operation.

EXAMPLE.   Suppose that

$$L = x_1 + \frac{4}{3}x_2. \tag{a}$$

The polyhedron of the restrictions is defined by the inequalities

$$\left. \begin{aligned} \frac{1}{3}x_1 + \frac{1}{2}x_2 &\leqslant 1, \\[2mm] \frac{1}{2}x_1 + \frac{1}{4}x_2 &\leqslant 1, \\[2mm] x_1 \geqslant 0, \quad x_2 &\geqslant 0. \end{aligned} \right\} \tag{b}$$

As our first approximation, we take the following values of the variables:

$$x_{11} = 0, \quad x_{21} = 0.$$

Let us determine the components of the gradient of the function L:

$$\frac{\partial L}{\partial x_1} = 1, \quad \frac{\partial L}{\partial x_2} = \frac{4}{3}.$$

Now, let us move from the point $(0, 0)$ in the direction of the gradient; that is, let us increase the factor ε in the formulas

$$x_1 = \varepsilon, \quad x_2 = \frac{4}{3}\varepsilon,$$

starting with the value zero, and let us see which of inequalities (b) first reduces to an equality. Direct verification shows that the inequality

$$\frac{1}{3}x_1 + \frac{1}{2}x_2 \leqslant 1 \tag{c}$$

first becomes an equality with $\varepsilon = \varepsilon_1 = 1$.

The second approximation of the variables is determined in accordance with formulas (8.77):

$$x_{12} = 1 \cdot 1 = 1, \quad x_{22} = \frac{4}{3} \cdot 1 = \frac{4}{3}.$$

We then need to move along the face defined by the equation

$$\frac{1}{3}x_1 + \frac{1}{2}x_2 = 1.$$

From this equation we obtain

$$x_2 = 2\left(1 - \frac{1}{3}x_1\right). \tag{d}$$

Consequently, the function L takes the following form on that face:

$$L = x_1 + \frac{4}{3} \cdot 2\left(1 - \frac{1}{3}x_1\right) = \frac{1}{9}x_1 + \frac{8}{3}.$$

One can easily see that increase in x_1 corresponds to motion toward the greatest value of the function L in this section. (Here, the gradient of the function L coincides with its derivative with respect to x_1 and is equal to $\partial L/\partial x_1 = 1/9$). Consequently, we need to set

$$x_1 = x_{12} + \frac{1}{9}\varepsilon = 1 + \frac{1}{9}\varepsilon. \tag{e}$$

Let us increase the factor ε until the inequality

$$\frac{1}{2}x_1 + \frac{1}{4}x_2 \leqslant 1$$

becomes equality:

$$\frac{1}{2}x_1 + \frac{1}{4}x_2 = 1. \tag{f}$$

From (d) and (f) we obtain

$$\frac{1}{2}x_1 + \frac{1}{4} \cdot 2\left(1 - \frac{1}{3}x_1\right) = 1. \tag{g}$$

Substitution of (e) into (g) enables us to write the equation for the value of the factor $\varepsilon = \varepsilon_2$:

$$\frac{1}{2}\left(1 + \frac{1}{9}\varepsilon\right) + \frac{1}{2}\left[1 - \frac{1}{3}\left(1 + \frac{1}{9}\varepsilon\right)\right] = 1.$$

From this we determine the unknown value $\varepsilon_2 = 9/2$. Consequently, the third approximation for the variables x_1 and x_2 is

$$x_{13} = x_{12} + \frac{1}{9}\varepsilon_2 = 1 + \frac{1}{9} \cdot \frac{9}{2} = 1.5,$$

$$x_{23} = 2\left(1 - \frac{1}{3}x_{13}\right) = 1.$$

Direct verification shows that further motion on the point $(1.5.1)$ in the direction of the gradient of the function L takes us out of the polyhedron of the restrictions (b). Consequently, the third approximation is the last.

Thus, the values of the variables $x_1 = 1.5$, $x_2 = 1.0$ correspond to the greatest value of the function L in this example. This greatest value is easily computed to be

$$L_{max} = 1.5 + \frac{4}{3} \cdot 1 = 2\frac{5}{6}.$$

4. Nonlinear programming

In the preceding subsection, we considered a linear-programming problem. In that problem, both the value function (8.72) and the conditions (8.73) defining the region G of variation of the variables $x_1, \cdots,$ x_n were linear. In practice, we also encounter problems in which either the value function $F(x_1, \cdots, x_n)$ or the conditions determining the region G of variation of the parameters $x_1, \cdots, x_n$ are nonlinear. In such a case, we get a nonlinear programming problem. The case in which both the function F and the condition determining the region G are nonlinear also belongs to nonlinear programming. Nonlinear programming problems are considerably more complex than linear programming problems. At the present time, we do not have general methods enabling us to solve nonlinear programming problems of a general form. Sometimes, mathematicians have succeeded in reducing nonlinear programming problems to linear programming problems by replacing the nonlinear function F with a piecewise-linear function and by replacing the nonlinear relations defining the region G with a polyhedron of the type (8.73). However, this method is not always applicable and it usually involves quite laborious calculations.

Let us look at the following formulation of a nonlinear programming problem that is of practical interest. Suppose that the quality index (the value function) is a given nonlinear function $F(x_1, \cdots, x_n)$. Without loss of generality, let us assume that it can be represented as a given function of several linear forms $L_1, \cdots, L_{k+1}$, that is, $F(x_1, \cdots,$ $x_n) = \Phi(L_1, \cdots, L_{k+1})$. Suppose that we are required to find the greatest value of the function $F(x_1, \cdots, x_n)$ under conditions (8.73). Before solving this problem, let us clarify why we replace the function $F(x_1, \cdots, x_n)$ with the function $\Phi(L_1, \cdots, L_{k+1})$. The reason is that, in many practical problems, the number of the variables n is quite great. This circumstance considerably complicates the process of solving the problem posed. Therefore, it is convenient to shift whenever we can from the function F of a large number of variables to the function Φ, which depends on a smaller number of variables L_i:

$$L_i = q_{i0} + q_{i1}x_1 + \cdots + q_{in}x_n,$$

$$i = 1, \cdots, k+1, \quad k < n, \quad j = 0, 1, \cdots, n,$$

where the q_{ij} are given numbers.

As will be clear from what follows, this change simplifies the procedure for finding the solution. We give two examples illustrating this device of shifting to a smaller number of variables.

EXAMPLE 1. $F(x_1, x_2, x_3) = x_1^2 + x_2^2 + x_3^2 + 2x_2x_3$. This function of the three variables x_1, x_2, x_3 can be represented as a function of two other variables L_1, L_2:

$$F(x_1, x_2, x_3) = \Phi(L_1, L_2) = \frac{L_1^2 + L_2^2}{2},$$

where

$$L_1 = x_1 + x_2 + x_3, \quad L_2 = x_1 - x_2 - x_3.$$

Here, $n = 3$ and $k = 1$.

EXAMPLE 2. $F(x_1, x_2) = x_1^2 + x_2^2$. This function of two variables cannot be represented as a function of a smaller number of variables L_i. In the present example, we can set $L_1 = x_1$ and $L_2 = x_2$. Here, $n = 2$ and $k = 1$.

The greatest value of the function F in the region G of variation of the variables $x_1, \cdots, x_n$ that is defined by conditions (8.73) coincides with the greatest value of the function Φ in the region Q of variation of the variables $L_1, L_2, \cdots, L_{k+1}$, which is also determined in the last analysis by conditions (8.73). The greatest value of the function Φ can be attained either within the region Q or on its boundary S.

In practical problems, the greatest value of Φ is usually attained on the boundary of the region Q. The solution of the problem when the greatest value of Φ is attained inside the region Q presents no difficulties (see [Refs. 8, 9]), and hence we shall not stop for that case.

Thus, let us assume that the function Φ does not have a maximum inside the region and that it attains its greatest value on the boundary S of that region. The problem of determining the greatest value of the function Φ cannot be solved by the methods of classical analysis. In this connection, the following method, consisting of two stages, is proposed:

In the first stage, we determine the boundary S of the region Q, in the second the greatest value of the function Φ on the boundary S.

Here, we can use the idea and procedure expounded in [Refs. 3, 4, 7, 9] as applied to a problem of a different nature.

To determine the boundary S for fixed values of the variables

$$L_1 = C_1, \quad \cdots, \quad L_k = C_k \tag{8.85}$$

we need to determine the greatest and smallest values of the variable L_{k+1} (see Fig. 8.5), where $k = 1$.

Since the greatest and smallest values of L_{k+1} are determined in analogous ways, in what follows we shall speak only of the greatest values of L_{k+1} (that is, of a single half-branch of the boundary S). Consequently, to find a single point on the boundary S, we need to determine the greatest value of the linear form L_{k+1} under conditions (8.73) and (8.85). This is a typical problem of linear programming. Conditions (8.85) differ in no essential way from conditions (8.73). Only the number of the equations has increaseed by k. When we know the different values of the parameters $C_1, \cdots, C_k$, we can obtain the corresponding points of the boundary S. If these points cover the entire boundary S densely enough (which is possible if we take a sufficiently small mesh in choosing a grid of values of the parameters $C_1, \cdots, C_k$), we may consider the first stage complete.

In what follows, we shall need to find the greatest value of the function Φ on the boundary S. This problem is easily solved if the number of dimensions k of the boundary S is not great. The greatest value of Φ can be approximated by comparing the values at points of the grid formed by discrete values of the numbers $C_1, \cdots, C_k$. If the number k of dimensions of the boundary S is great, obtaining a dense grid of values of the function Φ on the boundary S becomes a prohibitively laborious problem, one that cannot always be solved in reasonable periods of time even by using present-day high-speed computing machines.

We note that, in this case, the problem of determining the greatest value of the function Φ reduces to determining the maximum of the function

$$f = f(C_1, \cdots, C_k) = \Phi[C_1, \cdots, C_k, L_{k+1}(C_1, \cdots, C_k)],$$

where $L_{k+1}(C_1, \cdots, C_k)$ is the greatest (or smallest) value of the linear

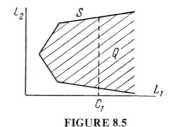

FIGURE 8.5

form L_{k+1} under conditions (8.73) and (8.85). The greatest value of the function Φ on the boundary S coincides in the general case with the maximum value of that function; that is, the greatest value is attained inside the region of variation of the parameters C_i. To determine the maximum of the function $f = f(C_1, \cdots, C_k)$, we can use the method of fastest descent. A combination of the method previously expounded for determining the boundary S of the region Q and the function $f = f(C_1, \cdots, C_k)$ with the method of fastest descent, enabling us to determine the maximum of the function f, makes it possible to avoid calculation of the values of the function f at a large number of points densely covering the entire region S of variation of the variables $C_1, \cdots, C_k$ and to replace these laborious calculations with more economical calculations according to the following plan:

Suppose that, on the basis of some considerations or other, we have chosen a first approximation of the variables $C_1 = C_{11}, C_2 = C_{21}, \cdots, C_k = C_{k1}$, which corresponds to the function $f_1 = f(C_{11}, C_{21}, \cdots, C_{k1})$. We then determine the direction of the gradient at that point. As we know, this direction is determined by a vector in the space $C = (C_1, C_2, \cdots, C_k)$, whose projections onto the axes $C_1, \cdots, C_k$ are equal respectively to $\partial f/\partial C_1, \cdots, \partial f/\partial C_k$.

The partial derivatives $\partial f/\partial C_i$ can be determined in an analogous manner if we can obtain a simple analytical reationship $f = f(C_1, \cdots, C_k)$. However, we cannot count on this, since, as a rule, the relationship $f = f(C_1, \cdots, C_k)$ is complicated and, in addition, we may not be able to find it in explicit form. Thus, in the general case the derivatives $\partial f/\partial C_i$ should be approximated as the ratio of the finite increments

$$\frac{\partial f}{\partial C_i} \simeq \frac{\Delta f_i}{\Delta C_i},$$

where

$$\Delta f_i = f(C_{11}, \cdots, C_{i-1,1}, C_i + \Delta C_i, C_{i+1,1}, \cdots, C_{k1}) - f(C_{11}, \cdots, C_{k1}).$$

When we have determined the gradient of the function f at the point $(C_{11}, \cdots, C_{k1})$, we move in the space C in the direction of this gradient vector; that is, we consider the values of the function f at the following values of the variables $C_1, \cdots, C_k$:

$$C_1 = C_{11} + \frac{\partial f}{\partial C_1}\,\varepsilon, \cdots, C_k = C_{k1} + \frac{\partial f}{\partial C_k}\,\varepsilon,$$

where $\partial f/\partial C_i$ (for $i = 1, 2, \cdots, k$) are calculated for $C_1 = C_{11}, \cdots, C_k = C_{k1}$.

The motion in the direction chosen is terminated at the value $\varepsilon = \varepsilon_1$ at which the function

$$\xi_1(\varepsilon) = f\left(C_{11} + \frac{\partial f}{\partial C_1}\,\varepsilon, \cdots, C_{k1} + \frac{\partial f}{\partial C_k}\,\varepsilon\right)$$

attains its maximum value. The maximum of the function $\xi_1(\varepsilon)$ can be determined graphically. The values of the variables

$$C_1 = C_{12} = C_{11} + \frac{\partial f}{\partial C_1} \varepsilon_1, \cdots, C_k = C_{k2} = C_{k1} + \frac{\partial f}{\partial C_k} \varepsilon_1$$

are taken as our second approximation. The value of the function $f = f_2 = f(C_{12}, \cdots, C_{k2})$ is taken as our second approximation of the function f. We then find the third and subsequent approximations of the variables $C_1, \cdots, C_k$ and the function f in the manner previously indicated. The $(\nu + 1)$st approximation is determined according to the formulas

$$C_{1, \nu+1} = C_{1\nu} + \frac{\partial f}{\partial C_1} \varepsilon_\nu, \cdots, C_{k, \nu+1} = C_{k, \nu} + \frac{\partial f}{\partial C_k} \varepsilon_k.$$

Here, $\varepsilon = \varepsilon_k$ corresponds to the maximum of the function

$$\xi_\nu(\varepsilon) = f\left(C_{1\nu} + \frac{\partial f}{\partial C_1} \varepsilon, \cdots, C_{k\nu} + \frac{\partial f}{\partial C_k} \varepsilon\right).$$

The $(\nu + 1)$st approximation of the function f is determined in accordance with the formula

$$f_{\nu+2} = f(C_{1, \nu+1}, \cdots, C_{k, \nu+1}).$$

The process of searching for the maximum of the function f is terminated when two successive approximations of f differ only negligibly from each other. In the general case, the function f can have several maxima. In this case, we need to find the *maximum maximorum*. It should be noted that the greatest value of f is, in the general case, attained inside the region S of variation of the parameters $C_1, \cdots, C_k$; that is, it coincides with the maximum of that function. Only in special rare cases is the maximum value of f attained on the boundary of the region S. This assertion follows from the fact that, in the general case, the function $F(x_1, \cdots, x_n)$ attains its greatest value on a face but not at a vertex of the polyhedron defined by conditions (8.73).

Relying on the foregoing exposition, we can recommend the following sequence of operations for determining the maximum of the function f:

(1) Choice of a first approximation of the variables $C_1 = C_{11}, \cdots, C_k = C_{k1}$;

(2) Calculation of the value of the first approximation of the function $f = f_1 = f(C_{11}, \cdots, C_{k1})$:

(3) Calculation of the components of the gradient vector of the function f at the point of first approximation $\partial f / \partial C_1, \cdots, \partial f / \partial C_k$;

(4) Calculation of the function

$$\xi_1(\varepsilon) = f\left(C_{11} + \frac{\partial f}{\partial C_1} \varepsilon, \cdots, C_{k1} + \frac{\partial f}{\partial C_k} \varepsilon\right)$$

for increasing values of the parameter $\varepsilon = l\Delta\varepsilon$, for $l = 1, 2, \cdots$, (the step $\Delta\varepsilon$ is chosen with an eye to the nature of the function f as can be determined in the computational process: The more smoothly the function f varies, the greater we can choose the step $\Delta\varepsilon$);

(5) Determination of the value of the parameter $\varepsilon = \varepsilon_1$ from the requirement that the function $\xi_1(\varepsilon)$ be maximized;

(6) Determination of the second approximation of the variables

$$C_{12} = C_{11} + \frac{\partial f}{\partial C_1} \varepsilon_1, \cdots, C_{k2} = C_{k1} + \frac{\partial f}{\partial C_k} \varepsilon_1;$$

(7) Determination of the second approximation of the function $f_2 = f(C_{12}, \cdots, C_{k2})$;

(8) Determination of the difference of two successive approximations of the function $f_2 - f_1$, and so on.

The calculations are terminated when the difference

$$f_{p+1} - f_p = f(C_{1, p+1}, \cdots, C_{k, p+1}) - f(C_{1p}, \cdots, C_{kp})$$

becomes negligibly small. The necessary number of approximations with this method is usually small. The calculations with this method can easily be programmed for a digital computing machine.

Naturally, we may wonder whether we cannot use the method of fastest descent directly to determine the greatest value of the function $F(x_1, \cdots, x_n)$ under conditions (8.37). In principle, this approach is also possible. However, it leads to considerably more complicated calculations when the number n of variables $x_1 \cdots, x_n$ is much greater than the number k of the variables $C_1, \cdots, C_k$ or the number of inequalities (and equations) in conditions (8.73) is great.

The significant increase in the number of calculations in the first case requires no clarification. In the second case, the significant increase is due to the fact that direct use of the method of fastest descent necessitates verifying, at each step when we increase ε by the amount $\Delta\varepsilon$, whether conditions (8.73) are or are not satisfied. Furthermore, the move from one face of the polyhedron (8.73) to another is accompanied by a change in the form of the function of $n - m$ variables. This complicates programming of the calculations. Consequently, the number of calculations in determining each approximation increases and so does the number of approximations. On the other hand, when the number of inequalities in conditions (8.73) is small and when $k + 1 = n$, the two methods are about equally difficult.

Let us give an example to clarify the method just expounded of solving nonlinear programming problems.

EXAMPLE. Determine the greatest value of the function $F(x_1, x_2, x_3) = x_1(x_2 + x_3)$ under the conditions

$$x_1 + 2x_2 + 3x_3 \leqslant 60, \qquad x_1 \geqslant 0, \qquad x_2 \geqslant 0, \qquad x_3 \geqslant 0. \qquad \text{(a)}$$

The given function F of the three variables x_1, x_2, x_3 can be represented as a function Φ of the two linear forms L_1 and L_2, where $L_1 = x_2 + x_3$ and $L_2 = x_1$. Here $\Phi(L_1, L_2) = L_1 L_2$. In this example, the function Φ is a monotonic increasing function. Consequently, it has no interior maxima and it attains its greatest value on the boundary S. Following the procedure previously described, let us determine the boundary S of the region Q of variation of the linear forms L_1 and L_2. In the present case, this boundary is some curve (i.e., one-dimensional space).

To determine the boundary S, we need various values of the linear form L_1. We then need to determine the greatest and smallest values of L_2. The question arises as to how we can find the values of L_1. The smallest and greatest values of the linear form L_1 under conditions (a) are easily determined by the methods of linear programming. Specifically, $0 \leqslant L_1 \leqslant 30$. Let us take some value $L_1 = C_1$, where $0 \leqslant C_1 \leqslant 30$, and let us find the greatest value of L_2. (The smallest value of L_2 is of no interest in this example, since the function Φ is a monotonic increasing function of the variable L_2.) This greatest value is easily found by the methods of linear programming (or by other methods) and can be expressed in terms of C_1 in the following form:

$$L_{2\ max} = 60 - 2C_1 \ .$$

The function Φ can, in the portion of the boundary S that we are interested in, be expressed in terms of the parameter C_1 as follows:

$$\Phi = C_1 (60 - 2C_1) \ .$$

One can easily see that the function Φ attains a maximum on the boundary S when $C_1 = C_{10} = 15$. Then, we can easily determine all quantities that we are interested in:

$$\Phi_{max} = F_{max} = 15(60 - 2 \cdot 15) = 450 \ ,$$
$$x_{10} = L_{2\ max} = 60 - 2 \cdot 15 = 30 \ .$$

In accordance with (a), the values x_{20} and x_{30} are determined from the equations

$$x_2 + x_3 = L_{10} = C_{10} = 15, \quad 30 + 2x_2 - 3x_3 = 60.$$

Solution of these equations yields the following values for x_{20} and x_{30}:

$$x_{20} = 15, \quad x_{30} = 0.$$

Chapter 9

ADAPTIVE AUTOMATIC-CONTROL SYSTEMS

29. GENERAL DISCUSSION

We know from the material of the preceding chapters that if we are given the probabilistic characteristics of the influences on the system and the class of admissible systems, then the best system is the optimal system chosen according to the corresponding criterion. In the case in which some of the parameters of the probabilistic characteristics of the influences are unknown, the best system is the optimal system with optimal decision element. This system consists of two loops: (a) The basic control loop, usually closed, and (b) a supplementary open loop with decision element.

Cases are also possible when, in the first place, we do not know the parameters of the probabilistic characteristics of the influences, and, in the second place, these unknown parameters vary with time in accordance with a random law. Ordinary optimal systems and optimal systems with decision elements do not ensure for them an extremum of the criterion chosen. In such cases, it is convenient to shift to adaptive systems.

Furthermore, it is not always possible to give precisely the class of admissible systems. Because of a random scattering of the characteristics of the different components in the system or because of incalculable random influences of the surrounding medium on parts of the system, the dynamic characteristics of a control system undergo random changes. If these random changes in the dynamic characteristics of the system have an appreciable influence on the quality of the operation of the system, then we cannot choose in a unique fashion the desired system from the class of admissible systems.

In this last case, the procedure previously explained for determining the optimal systems is not applicable: It does not enable us to determine the system ensuring an extremum of the criterion chosen. Again in this case we need to shift to adaptive automatic-control systems.

An adaptive system must itself, in the course of its operation, determine the needed (time-variable) probabilistic characteristics of the influences, and change its parameters with the purpose of letting them approximate the optimal ones or else it must determine, in the course of its operation, its own parameters and change them with the purpose of having them approximate the optimal ones. Thus, an adaptive system, in the course of its operation, must automatically make precise the information regarding either the probabilistic characteristics on the influences or its own parameters or both.

Consequently, an adaptive system can be regarded as a system that automatically keeps its parameters around their optimal values in accordance with the changing probabilistic characteristics of the influences and with the varying dynamical characteristics of the elements of that system.

At the present time, we still do not have a single, generally accepted, definition of adaptive systems. We shall give the most general and, in our view, successful definition of an adaptive automatic-control system. As a preliminary, let us clarify some other concepts.

By a controlled process we mean an automatic-control system and the conditions under which it is used (the influences). The **initial** or *a priori* **information** is defined as the set of facts regarding the controlled process that we have from the very beginning of the operation of the system. The **working information** is defined as the set of facts regarding the controlled process that are obtained during the course of operation of the system.

If the initial information is complete (as was the case, for example, in the problems examined in Chapters 2, 3, etc.), we can define and make an ordinary optimal system that, in the course of its operation, does not change its parameters or else changes them according to a law known in advance and then ensures an extremum of the criterion chosen.

On the other hand, if the initial information is incomplete, to ensure an extremum of the criterion chosen, it is necessary to change the parameters of the system during the course of its operation, using the working information to do so.

In what follows, *we shall apply the term* **adaptive automatic-control system** *to a system that does not require for its construction and operation complete initial information regarding the controlled process, yet ensures a value of the criterion chosen close to its external value.*

Here, it is a question not of the absolute but the relative amount of initial information. This means that *the necessary initial information in adaptive systems is less than in nonadaptive systems* that carry out the same functions and ensure the same value of the criterion. With the same insufficient initial information, adaptive systems ensure a higher value of the criterion chosen than nonadaptive systems, since they are able to adjust to changing external conditions, change their parameters when these external conditions change, and, in short, adapt themselves to the new situation.

Adaptive automatic-control systems constitute a progressive class of automatic-control systems. Further development of automatic-control systems will proceed along the path of harmonious combination of non-adaptive and adaptive automatic-control systems.

If the loop of an adaptive system operated without error, it would be easy to answer the question as to what system we should apply in each particular case. When the initial information regarding the con-trolled process is complete, we need to use a nonadaptive system. On the other hand, if the initial information regarding the controlled pro-cess is incomplete, we need to use an adaptive system. However, the loop of the adaptive system introduces supplementary errors, which may result in the actual adaptive system being worse than the non-adaptive system. At the present time, there are no general methods enabling us to decide in every particular case which kind of system, adaptive or nonadaptive, is the more appropriate.

The efforts of scientists and designers are at the present time directed

(a) toward the development of specific adaptive systems,

(b) toward the development of principles of construction of adap-tive systems,

(c) toward the finding of appropriate criteria for estimating the accuracy of operation of these systems,

(d) toward ways of automatic calculation of the criteria for esti-mating the systems,

(e) toward the development of methods of attaining an extremum of the criterion chosen,

(f) toward the development of methods of investigating specific adaptive systems,

(g) toward the manufacture of units of adaptive systems.

For convenience in studying and investigating adaptive systems, it is expedient to classify them as

(1) extremal-regulation systems,

(2) systems adapting themselves to a standard.

Systems of extremal-regulation are defined as adaptive systems in which the working information is the deviations from the extremum of the criterion chosen for comparing systems. Usually, the criterion is a function $F(x_1, \cdots, x_n)$ of the parameters $x_1, \cdots, x_n$ of the system. To construct a system of extremal regulation, it is not necessary that we know the function $F(x_1, \cdots, x_n)$. It is sufficient to know that the criterion is a function of the parameters $x_1, \cdots, x_n$ with an extremum in the working region of variation of these parameters and to know the approximate form of that function. The system itself carries out the necessary operations for determining the instantaneous values of the criterion (or the increments in the criterion) and for finding the extremum of the criterion. The system changes its parameters in such a way that they approximate the values corresponding to the extremum of the function F. In different systems, the function F can have different physical meanings. For example, it can be the mean square error, the probability that the error will not exceed allowed limits, the coefficient of useful action, and the like.

In certain cases, the criterion for comparing systems is a functional of some characteristic of the system. An example is the mean square error, which is a functional of the weight function of the system (see Chapter 1). However, as of the present, this case can only be considered theoretically possible. In practice, the criterion for comparing systems is expressed in the form of a function of the parameters of the system. In what follows, we shall consider systems of extremal regulation that adapt themselves to the extremum of a criterion that is a function of certain parameters of the system.

Systems of extremal regulation do not use the working information regarding factors causing displacement of the extremum of the criterion. The only information they use regards the deviations from this extremum. When these systems are properly implemented, they operate satisfactorily in the presence of different factors causing a displacement of the extremum of the criterion. There is a certain analogy between systems of extremal regulation and nonadaptive systems that operate according to the principle of using the deviation of the output variable. In both cases, the deviation of some quantity from the desired value is a signal causing necessary changes in the system. In an adaptive system, this is the deviation of the criterion from its extremal value, and in a nonadaptive system it is the deviation of the output variable from some value; for example, zero. In both cases, the system obtains no information regarding the factors causing undesired deviations.

However, there are also profound differences between these two systems. The way they obtain information regarding the deviations of the quantities in question from the desired values is different in the two cases and so is the way they react to the information obtained. In a nonadaptive system, the desired value of the ouput variable is usually determined easily. For example, in a stabilizing system, this value is a constant known in advance; in a system of program control, it is a quantity, known in advance, that varies with time; in a serro mechanism, it is a quantity, unknown in advance, that can be measured with some error by a measuring element (or the measuring element immediately causes a deviation in the output variable from the desired output variable). In an adaptive system, we need to obtain a criterion. In the general case, this problem is more complicated than the problem of obtaining the desired output variable. In the general case, the criterion is obtained as a result of measuring the output and input variables of the system and then carrying out calculations according to some formula or other. Here, we use a calculating device. However, knowing the criterion at a given instant is not enough to control a system of extremal regulation. It is necessary to know the deviation of the current value of the criterion from its extremal value. Consequently, in a system of extremal regulation, there must be a mechanism that automatically seeks the extremum of the criterion and makes changes in the system so that it will approximate this extremum. Thus, the problem of obtaining working information in adaptive systems is considerably more complicated than the analogous problem in nonadaptive systems. The working information obtained in these systems is used in different ways. In nonadaptive systems, this information is used to formulate the controlling signals of the system; in systems of extremal regulation, it is used to change the parameters of the system.

Figure 9.1 shows a diagram of a system of extremal regulation. The main control loop (mcl) transforms the input signal X into an output signal Y in accordance with the operator of the system, which depends upon the changed parameter x_1. The loop of an adaptive system includes a calculating element (ce), a mechanism for motion to the extremum (mme) and connecting lines. The working information (the input variable X, the output variable Y, the current value of the variable parameter, and the like) and the initial information (ii) are applied at the input of the calculating element. In different systems, different working information is used. In one system, we may use information regarding the input X and the output Y or other intermediary signals of the basic control loop. In another system, information regarding the output variable or the parameter x_1 may be sufficient. Figure 9.1 shows one variation of the feeding of information to the input of the calculating element. By using the initial and working information regarding the controlled process, the calculating element calculates the

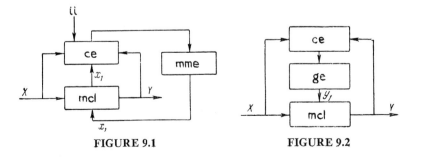

FIGURE 9.1   **FIGURE 9.2**

comparison criterion $F(x_1)$ as a function of the parameter x_1 and it calculates other characteristics (for example, the derivative $\partial f/\partial x_1$) if they are needed.

The mechanism of motion to the extremum obtains the necessary information from the calculating device, and, in accordance with this information, it makes a change in the parameter x_1 in the direction of motion toward the value x_{1e} corresponding to the extremum of the criterion chosen. If several parameters $x_1, \cdots, x_n$ are adjusted in the basic control loop, the mechanism of moving to the extremum consists of n channels. Each channel makes an adjustment of the corresponding parameter x_1. There may be an interrelationship between the different channels.

We shall refer to an adaptive system whose working information includes the information regarding the deviations of the characteristics of the main control loop as a *system that adapts itself to a standard*. The purpose of these systems is to ensure the required quality indices of the control process under varying (or incompletely known) characteristics of the main control loop. Thus, systems that adapt themselves to a standard maintain their characteristics about their optimal values if external factors tend to change these characteristics in one direction or another. The diagram of a system that adapts itself to a standard is shown in Figure 9.2. The input and output of the main control loop are applied to the calculating element, which determines the required characteristic of the system (the frequency characteristic, the weight function, the coefficient of amplification, the coefficient of damping of oscillations, and the like). The characteristic of the system thus determined is compared with a standard system and, in accordance with the results of this comparison, a command is given to the governing element (ge), which changes the parameter y_1 in such a way that the actual characteristic of the system approaches that of the standard system. Here, the calculating element is usually simpler than in an extremal-regulation system. The input and output of the main control loop are not always applied to the input of this device. The signals from other points of this contour may be applied. If there are several parameters $y_1, \cdots, y_m$ in the system being adjusted, the governing element has m channels, each of which introduces into the system the corresponding value of the parameter y_i.

Thus, if we have only incomplete initial information regarding the influences on the system, it is convenient to shift from the usual optimal system to an extremal regulation system, which automatically changes its parameters in such a way that they ensure an extremum of the criterion chosen. On the other hand, if we have only incomplete initial information regarding the characteristics of the system, it is convenient to shift from the usual optimal system to a system that adapts itself to a standard (that is, to an optimal system that is determined in a theoretical way or one close to it). If we have incomplete initial information regarding both the influences (the external medium) and the characteristics of the system, we can use a system of extremal-regulation, but it will ensure a poorer value of the criterion than in the first of the cases just considered, since the random changes in the characteristics of the system are in this case additional noises. In such a case, the best results can be expected from a combined adaptive system in which the adaptation includes a loop representing the system of extremal regulation of the parameters $x_1, \cdots, x_n$ and another loop which is a system that adapts itself to a standard and maintains the values of the parameters $y_1, \cdots, y_m$ unchanged. However, such combined systems are very complicated and they have not been achieved at the present time.

Let us look in greater detail at systems for extremal regulation.

30. SYSTEMS FOR EXTREMAL REGULATION

It is appropriate to construct a system for extremal regulation when we have incomplete initial information regarding different kinds of influences on that system (on the input signals).

The purpose of these systems is stabilization of the variables $x_1, \cdots, x_n$ about the values $x_1 = x_{1e}, \cdots, x_n = x_{ne}$ corresponding to an extremum of the criterion $F = F(x_1, \cdots, x_n, t)$. The variables $x_1, \cdots, x_n$ are the parameters of the system. The function F depends not only on the parameters $x_1, \cdots, x_n$ but on other (uncontrolled) parameters and, in the last analysis, on the time. This dependence on the time is random with unknown probabilistic characteristics. We shall impose a restriction on the function $F(x_1, \cdots, x_n, t)$. We shall assume that, for fixed values of the parameters $x_1, \cdots, x_n$, this function changes slowly with respect to time.

At the present time, there is no general method enabling us to synthesize adaptive systems with a given purpose. Various authors have proposed different schemes of adaptive systems [Refs. 13, 15, 24, 25, 46] based on different operating principles. The investigation of systems for extremal regulation must proceed in different directions. At the present time, the following are important directions of investigation of these systems:

(a) Development of methods of finding the extremum of a criterion,

(b) investigation of stability,

(c) investigation of the time required for transition of a process,

(d) investigation of established accuracy,

(e) investigation of reliability,

(f) estimation of the gain resulting from a shift to an adaptive system.

In the present section, we shall briefly consider the first of these.

In line with the fact that we are considering only cases in which the criterion F changes slowly with time for fixed values of the parameters $x_1, \cdots, x_n$, we shall write F as a function only of the arguments $x_1, \cdots, x_n$.

To search for the extremum of a criterion, we need to know the direction in which we must change the parameters $x_1, \cdots, x_n$ in order to approximate the extremum that we are seeking. If the criterion F depends only on a single parameter x_1, then, for a positive derivative $\partial F/\partial x_1$, the value of the parameter corresponds to motion toward the maximum of the criterion, and decrease in this parameter corresponds to motion away from the maximum of this criterion. In the case of a negative derivative $\partial F/\partial x_1$, increase in the parameter x_1 corresponds to motion away from the maximum of the criterion, and decrease in the parameter x_1 corresponds to motion toward the maximum. Vanishing of the derivative $\partial F/\partial x_1$ in this case means that we have attained the maximum of the criterion (taking into account the preliminary motion toward a maximum and not a minimum; we are excluding points of inflection from consideration as exceptions). Analogous rules hold if we are seeking a minimum of the criterion. Consequently, in this special case $(n = 1)$, we can determine the required direction of change of the parameter x_1 from the sign and magnitude of the derivative. In the general case in which the criterion depends on n parameters $(n > 1)$, we need to consider the n partial derivatives $\partial F/\partial x_1, \cdots, \partial F/\partial x_n$ or the gradient of the function F:

$$\text{grad } F = \frac{\partial F}{\partial x_1} e_1 + \cdots + \frac{\partial F}{\partial x_n} e_n, \qquad (9.1)$$

where $e_1, \cdots, e_n$ are unit vectors along the axes $x_1, \cdots, x_n$ in the space $(x_1, \cdots, x_n)$.

If the adaptive system is designed to ensure a maximum of the criterion, the parameter x_i should be increased for $\partial F/\partial x_i > 0$ and decreased for $\partial F/\partial x_i < 0$. To make a decision regarding the directions of change of all the parameters, we need to know all the partial derivatives

$$\frac{\partial F}{\partial x_1}, \cdots, \frac{\partial F}{\partial x_n},$$

that is, we need to know the gradient of the function F.

We have spoken only about how to determine the direction of change of each parameter. In addition, the following questions arise: In accordance with what law should the parameters $x_1, \cdots, x_n$ be changed in the directions chosen? What parameters should be made to change rapidly and what parameters should be made to change slowly?

The brief preliminary considerations that we have presented enable us to conclude that the problem of finding an extremum of the criterion

F can be divided into three problems:

(1)   Calculation of the criterion $F(x_1, \cdots, x_n)$, which is a function of the parameters of the system $x_1, \cdots, x_n$,

(2)   determination of the gradient of the function $F(x_1, \cdots, x_n)$, that is, the gradient of the criterion,

(3)   organization of the motion to the extremum of the criterion.

Calculation of the criterion $F(x_1, \cdots, x_n)$ is a difficult problem in the general case. The difficulty lies in the fact that the criterion is a probabilistic characteristic of the error of the system (or of some other quantity). The error of the system E is equal to

$$E(t) = Y(t) - H(t),$$

where $Y(t)$ is the actual output variable of the main control loop and $H(t)$ is the desired output variable of that control loop. The actual output variable $Y(t)$ can be measured with great accuracy and fed to the calculating element. However, we cannot as a rule measure the desired output variable with a high degree of accuracy. This variable is the result of the transformation of the useful signal G, which is measurable with error $Z(t)$ (cf. Chapter 1). The error $Z(t)$ can be considerable.

In certain cases, measurement of the real output variable $Y(t)$ and the input variable $X(t)$ of the main control loop (or one of these) with a high degree of accuracy enables us to obtain the necessary information for calculating the criterion. Obtaining the criterion with a high degree of accuracy requires sufficiently protracted sample functions of the variables $Y(t)$ and $X(t)$. In the following section, we shall consider specific cases characterized by some degree of completeness of the initial information regarding the influences and we shall propose methods of obtaining (calculating) the criterion, taking into account the peculiarities associated with the case in question.

Determination of the gradient of the criterion of the function $F(x_1, \cdots, x_n)$ can be done by different methods [Refs. 13, 24, 25]. Here, we shall consider one of these, namely, the method of **synchronous detection**. With this method, we add to the basic, slowly changing components of the parameters $x_1^0, \cdots, x_n^0$ small harmonic components with unequal frequencies. Consequently, the current value of the parameter x_i is represented in this case in the form of a sum

$$x_i = x_i^0 + x_{i0} \sin \omega_i t, \quad i = 1, \cdots, n, \tag{9.2}$$

where x_i^0 is the slowly changing component and $x_{i0} \sin \omega_i t$ is the rapidly changing artificially introduced component. The criterion F from the output of the calculating element is applied to the synchronous detectors $sd_1, \cdots, sd_n$ (see Fig. 9.3). To these synchronous detectors we also add harmonic components of the form $x_{i0} \sin \omega_i t$, for $i = 1, \cdots, n$. The synchronous detectors (their role may be played, for example, by phase discriminators) carry out the operation of multiplication of the function

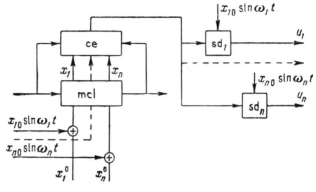

FIGURE 9.3

F by the harmonic components $x_{i0} \sin \omega_i t$ and the operation of averaging the resulting products over the time. (This averaging operation can be carried out approximately, for example, by an aperiodic component.) Consequently, the output variables of the synchronous detectors are equal to

$$u_1 = x_{10}\overline{F \sin \omega_1 t}, \quad \cdots, \quad u_n = x_{n0}\overline{F \sin \omega_n t}, \tag{9.3}$$

where the vinculum denotes the operation of averaging with respect to time over a sufficiently long time interval.

It turns out that these output variables of the synchronous detectors u_i are, up to infinitesimals of higher order, proportional to the partial derivatives $\partial F/\partial x_i$ at the point $(x_1^0, \cdots, x_n^0)$. Let us prove this, assuming that the function F can be represented in a neighborhood of the point $(x_1^0, \cdots, x_n^0)$ by a power series

$$F = F(x_1^0 + \Delta x_1, \cdots, x_n^0 + \Delta x_n) = F(x_1^0, \cdots, x_n^0)$$

$$+ \sum_{i=1}^{n} \frac{\partial F}{\partial x_i}\Delta x_i + \frac{1}{2!} \sum_{i,k=1}^{n} \frac{\partial^2 F}{\partial x_i \partial x_k}\Delta x_k \Delta x_i + \cdots, \tag{9.4}$$

where the partial derivatives are evaluated at the point $(x_1^0, \cdots, x_n^0)$. In equation (9.4), the small increments Δx_i are determined from the formulas

$$\Delta x_i = x_{i0} \sin \omega_i t, \quad i = 1, \cdots, n,$$

where the x_{i0} are small constants.

In this case, the output variables of the synchronous detectors can be written in the following form:

$$u_s = x_{s0}\overline{F \sin \omega_s t} = x_{s0}\overline{F(x_1^0, \cdots, x_n^0) \sin \omega_s t}$$

$$+ \sum_{i=1}^{n} x_{i0}\overline{\frac{\partial F}{\partial x_i} \sin \omega_i t \sin \omega_s t}$$

$$+ \frac{1}{2} x_{s0} \sum_{i,k=1}^{n} x_{i0} x_{k0} \overline{\frac{\partial^2 F}{\partial x_i n x_k} \sin \omega_i t \sin \omega_k k \sin \omega_s t} + \cdots. \qquad (9.5)$$

We assume that the quantities x_i^0 and hence the functions

$$F, \quad \frac{\partial F}{\partial x_i}, \quad \frac{\partial^2 F}{\partial x_i \partial x_k}$$

of these variables vary only negligibly during the period of that one of the time functions

$$\sin \omega_i t, \quad \sin \omega_i t \sin \omega_s t, \quad \sin \omega_i t \sin \omega_k t \sin \omega_s t$$

that is of lowest frequency. With this assumption, we can rewrite formula (9.5) in the form

$$u_s = x_{s0} \overline{F \sin \omega_s t} + x_{s0} \sum_{i=1}^{n} x_{i0} \frac{\partial F}{\partial x_i} \overline{\sin \omega_i t \sin \omega_s t}$$

$$+ \frac{1}{2} x_{s0} \sum_{i,k=1}^{n} x_{i0} x_{k0} \frac{\partial^2 F}{\partial x_i \partial x_k} \overline{\sin \omega_i t \sin \omega_k t \sin \omega_s t} + \cdots, \qquad (9.6)$$

$$s = 1, \cdots, n.$$

We know that

$$\overline{\sin \omega_s t} \simeq 0, \quad \overline{\sin \omega_i t \sin \omega_s t} \simeq \begin{cases} \dfrac{1}{2}, & \text{if} \quad i = s, \\ 0, & \text{if} \quad i \neq s. \end{cases} \qquad (9.7)$$

These equations are satisfied exactly when the averaging is carried out over intervals of time equal to a whole number of periods of the averaged functions. With an arbitrary but sufficiently great interval of averaging, equations (9.7) are approximately satisfied with a high degree of accuracy. Thus, formulas (9.6) can be written as

$$u_s = \frac{1}{2} x_{s0}^2 \frac{\partial F}{\partial x_s} + \Delta u_s, \quad s = 1, \cdots, n, \qquad (9.8)$$

where

$$\Delta u_s = \frac{1}{2} x_{s0} \sum_{i,k=1}^{n} x_{i0} x_{k0} \frac{\partial^2 F}{\partial x_i \partial x_k} \overline{\sin \omega_i t \sin \omega_k t \sin \omega_s t} + \cdots.$$

The quantities Δu_s, for $s = 1, \cdots, n$, are infinitesimals of higher order than

$$\frac{1}{2} x_{s0}^2 \frac{\partial F}{\partial x_s}.$$

(The quantities x_{s0}, for $s = 1, \cdots, n$, are infinitesimals of first order.) If the frequencies $\omega_1, \cdots, \omega_n$ are chosen in such a way that $\omega_i \neq \omega_k + \omega_s$ for arbitrary i, k, and s, then

$$\overline{\sin \omega_i t \sin \omega_n t \sin \omega_s t} \simeq 0$$

and the quantity Δu_s is an infinitesimal of at least fourth order with respect to x_{s0} or second order with respect to

$$\frac{1}{2} x_{s0}^2 \frac{\partial F}{\partial x_s}.$$

Consequently, we may assume that, for sufficiently small amplitudes in the harmonic components and for a sufficiently long period of averaging, the output variables of the synchronous detectors are proportional to the components of the gradient of the function F at the point $(x_1^0, \cdots, x_n^0)$:

$$u_s = \frac{1}{2} x_{s0}^2 \frac{\partial F}{\partial x_s}, \quad s = 1, \cdots, n. \tag{9.9}$$

This method of determining the gradient of the criterion F possesses a high protection from noise. However, it requires a great deal of time to obtain the components of the gradient with sufficient accuracy by this method. Instead of the harmonic components in (9.2), we can use random function; that is, we can take

$$\Delta x_i = X_i(t), \quad i = 1, \cdots, n, \tag{9.10}$$

where $X_i(t)$ is a stationary centralized random function and

$$M[X_i(t) X_j(t)] = 0; \tag{9.11}$$

that is, the random functions (9.10) are uncorrelated with each other. Let us also require that the random functions $X_1(t), \cdots, X_n(t)$ be stationarily connected with each other. In this case, the output variable u_3 can be determined from formula (9.6), in which we need to substitute $X_s(t)$, where $s = 1, \cdots, n$, for $x_{s0} \sin \omega_s t$:

$$u_s = \overline{F X_s(t)} + \sum_{i=1}^{n} \frac{\partial F}{\partial x_i} \overline{X_i(t) X_s(t)}$$

$$+ \frac{1}{2} \sum_{i,k=1}^{n} \frac{\partial^2 F}{\partial x_i \partial x_k} \overline{X_i(t) X_s(t) X_k(t)} + \cdots, \quad s = 1, \cdots, n. \tag{9.12}$$

Let us also suppose that the random functions $X_s(t)$ are ergodic (with respect to the mathematical expectation and the correlation function). In such a case,

$$\overline{X_s(t)} \simeq m_{x_s}(t) = 0,$$

$$\overline{X_s(t) X_i(t)} \simeq K_{x_s x_i}(0) = \begin{cases} D_s & \text{if } i = s, \\ 0 & \text{if } i \neq s, \end{cases} \tag{9.13}$$

where D_s is the variance of the random function $X_s(t)$, where $s = 1, \cdots, n$ and $i = 1, \cdots, n$.

Equations (9.13) are satisfied exactly if the averaging over the time is carried out between infinite limits (theoretically). Under actual conditions, the averaging is over some finite interval of time. If this interval is sufficiently great, equations (9.12) are approximate but accurate to a sufficient degree. Thus, formulas (9.12) can be rewritten in the form

$$u_s = D_s \frac{\partial F}{\partial x_s} + \Delta u_s, \tag{9.14}$$

where

$$\Delta u_s = \frac{1}{2} \sum_{i,\,k=1}^{n} \frac{\partial_b F}{\partial x_i \, \partial x_k} \overline{X_i(t) X_s(t) X_k(t)} + \cdots.$$

The quantities Δu_s are infinitesimals of higher order than $D_s(\partial F/\partial x_s)$. (The variances $D_1, \cdots, D_n$ of the stationary random functions $X_i(t), \cdots, X_n(t)$ are considered infinitesimals of first order.) Consequently, for sufficiently small variances $D_1, \cdots, D_n$ and for a sufficiently long period of time of averaging, the output variables of the synchronous detectors are proportional to the components of the gradient of the function F at the point $(x_1^0, \cdots, x_n^0)$:

$$u_s = D_s \frac{\partial F}{\partial x_s}, \qquad s = 1, \cdots, n. \tag{9.15}$$

After we have constructed a mechanism that determines the gradient of the criterion F, we need to choose and realize a method of organizing the motion to the extremum of the criterion. This motion to the extremum of the criterion can be realized, for example, (a) by the method of successive change of the parameters $x_1, \cdots, x_n$, (b) by the method of fastest descent, (c) by the gradient method [Refs. 24, 25, 46].

The method of successive change of the parameters is, in essence, an automated variation of the method of successive choice of parameters as expounded in Chapter 3. According to this method, we first change the parameter x in such a way as to increase the criterion for fixed values of the other parameters. Change in the parameter x_1 continues until the maximum of the criterion F is attained. Then, we fix this value of the parameter x_1 and start changing the parameter x_2 (again leaving the parameters $x_3, \cdots, x_n$ unchanged) in such a way as to increase the criterion. Change in this parameter continues until the maximum of the criteria is attained. Then, we fix this value of the parameter x_2 and proceed to make a new choice of the parameter x_3, and so on. All these operations are carried out automatically by the system. The initial data are sufficient for this. Knowledge of the components of the gradient enables us to determine the necessary direction of motion to the maximum of the criterion. If $\partial F/\partial x_s > 0$, we need to increase the parameter x_s; if $\partial F/\partial x_s < 0$, we need to decrease it.

To go, let us say, from the approximation $x_{11}, \cdots, x_{n1}$ to the second approximation $x_{12}, \cdots, x_{n2}$ takes a great deal of time. We can carry out the motion to the extremum of the criterion more rapidly by the *method of fastest descent*. This method is an automated variant of the method of the same name treated in Chapter 3. With this method, the motion to the extremum of the criterion proceeds by steps. The method of fastest descent enables us to reach the extremum of the criterion more rapidly than does the method of successive change of parameters since with this method the motion proceeds in the direction of the gradient at the beginning of each stage, that is, in the most suitable direction.

It should be noted that the fastest descent (ascent) is observed in this method only at the very beginning of each stage (after the break in the trajectory of the image point). Furthermore, at this stage the motion is no longer in the direction of the gradient, which would be optimal. Therefore, a more expedient way of moving to the extremum of the criterion is a method according to which the motion is in the direction of the gradient at every instant. Such a plan of motion to the extremum of the criterion is called the **gradient method**.

With this method, the gradient vector is determined continuously and motion is carried out in the direction of the instantaneous (corresponding to the point $(x_1, \cdots, x_n)$ in question) gradient vector. Motion of the image point in the space $(x_1, \cdots, x_n)$ proceeds continuously with this method. This method can also be performed approximately by means of a step motion with small step length.

The method of synchronous detection enables us to determine the components of the gradient continuously. Therefore, it is expedient to combine this method of determining the gradient with the gradient method of organization of motion to the extremum of the criterion.

The gradient method in its ideal form consists in making the rates of change of the regulated parameters proportional to the corresponding components of the gradient:

$$\dot{x}_i = a\frac{\partial F}{\partial x_i}, \quad i = 1, \cdots, n. \tag{9.16}$$

If we need to seek the maximum of the criterion F, we should take the factor a in formulas (9.16) positive. If we need to seek the minimum of the criterion F, we should take this factor negative. The absolute value of this factor should be chosen in such a way that the adaptive system as a whole ensures the highest qualities (the least time spent in search for the extremum, the smallest error in the result of the search, and the like).

In carrying out the gradient method, we need to keep in mind the lag in the measuring and governing devices. Therefore, in actual systems, equations (9.16) must be replaced with the following:

$$pX_i(p) = W(p)\frac{\partial F}{\partial x_i}, \quad i = 1, \cdots, n, \tag{9.17}$$

where $X_i(p)$ is the Laplace transform of the law of change of the parameter x_i with time, that is, $X_i(p) \longrightarrow x_i(t)$. $W(p)$ is the transfer function of $\partial F/\partial x_i$ (that is, of the output of the synchronous detection) into x_i.

If we consider the disturbances acting on the system, then the system of equations (9.17) must be replaced with the following:

$$pX_i(p) = W(p)\left[\frac{\partial F}{\partial x_i} + Z_i(p)\right], \quad i = 1, \cdots, n, \tag{9.18}$$

where $Z_i(p)$ is the transform of the disturbance applied to the output from the synchronous detector of the ith channel. In time variables, equations (9.18) may be written as

$$\dot{x}_i(t) = \int_0^t w(\tau)\left[\frac{\partial F}{\partial x_i} + Z_i(t - \tau)\right]d\tau, \tag{9.18a}$$

where $w(\tau)$ is the weight function of the component transforming the output of the ith synchronous detector into the rate $\dot{x}_i$ of change of the parameter x_i, and where $Z_i(t)$ is the noise applied to the output from the ith synchronous detector.

If the derivative $\partial F/\partial x_i$ changes significantly with time, we need to keep this fact in mind in formula (9.18a); that is, we need to substitute

$$\frac{\partial F}{\partial x_i} = \chi(t - \tau).$$

We have been looking at problems of calculating statistical criteria, determining the gradient, and organizing the motion to the extremum of the criterion. We considered each of these problems separately without regard to their relationship with other problems. It is desirable to consider all these problems together, combining them into a single general problem of finding the extremum of a criterion. Let us consider this general problem of finding the extremum in certain special cases. Here, our main attention will be directed to calculation of the criterion and its gradient.

31. CALCULATION OF A STATISTICAL CRITERION AND ITS GRADIENT IN ADAPTIVE SYSTEMS. MOTION TOWARD THE EXTREMUM

We stated in the preceding section that calculation of a statistical criterion in the process of operation of an adaptive system is a complicated technological problem. The methods of carrying out the calculation of the criterion depend in a very real way on the degree of completeness of our initial information regarding the influences. Therefore, it is desirable to consider some typical variants, differing from each other in nature and completeness of our initial information regarding the influences.

1. The variance of the error of the system chosen as criterion

Variant 1. We do not know the distribution law of the variance of the noise. Suppose that the block diagram of the main loop of the control has the form shown in (3.1). Suppose that the correlation function $K_g(\tau)$ of the stationary useful signal $G(t)$ is known. The correlation function $K_z(\tau)$ of the stationary noise $Z(t)$ has the form $K_z(\tau) = D_z R_z(\tau)$, where $R_z(\tau)$ is a known normalized correlation function of the noise and D_z is the unknown variance of the noise (its distribution law is also unknown). We know only that the variance of the noise changes slowly as a result random factors. During the time of a transition process, this variance can be assumed constant in the main loop.

Suppose that the mathematical expectations of both the useful signal and the noise are equal to zero: $m_g = m_z = 0$. The main control loop is designed for reproduction of the function $H(t)$, which is the result of carrying out some linear operation L over the useful signal $G(t)$. The useful signal $G(t)$ and the noise $Z(t)$ are uncorrelated; that is, $K_{gz} = 0$. Consequently, the correlation function of the input signal $X(t)$ is equal to

$$K_x(\tau) = K_g(\tau) + K_z(\tau) = K_g(\tau) + D_z R_z(\tau), \qquad (9.19)$$

and the joint correlation function $K_{xh}(\tau)$ of the functions $X(t)$ and $H(t)$ is

$$K_{xh}(\tau) = K_{gh}(\tau) = L K_g(\tau). \qquad (9.20)$$

The operation L is known and hence the joint correlation function $K_{xh}(\tau)$ is also known.

In the present case, we do not have complete initial information regarding the disturbances, since we do not know the variance of the noise. Consequently, we cannot determine the optimal system by the procedure expounded in Chapter 3. Here, it is expedient to shift to an adaptive system.

As the criterion for comparing systems, we take the variance of the error D_E. In the present case, this variance is determined in accordance with formula (3.3). Let us write (3.3), taking (9.19) and (9.20) into account. We have

$$D_E = \int_0^T \int_0^T w(\tau) w(\lambda) [K_g(\tau - \lambda) + D_z R_z(\tau - \lambda)] d\tau \, d\lambda$$

$$- 2 \int_0^T K_{gh}(\tau) w(\tau) d\tau + D_h. \tag{9.21}$$

Since the variance D_z of the noise is unknown, we denote is as follows:

$$D_z = x_1 \tag{9.22}$$

and we rewrite formula (9.21), using this new notation:

$$D_E = \int_0^T \int_0^T w(\tau) w(\lambda) [K_h(\tau - \lambda) + x_1 R_z(\tau - \lambda)] d\tau \, d\lambda$$
$$- 2 \int_0^T K_{gh}(\tau) w(\tau) d\tau + D_h. \tag{9.23}$$

Now, we can obtain the optimal weight function of the system, minimizing the variance of the error (9.23) for different values of the parameter x_1 (i.e., for different values of the variance of the noise D_z). For every fixed value of the parameter x_1, we can obtain this optimal weight function as a solution of the integral equation (3.6), which, in view of the relations (9.19), (9.20), and (9.22), can be written in the form

$$\int_0^T [K_g(\tau - \lambda) + x_1 R_z(\tau - \lambda)] w_0(\lambda, x_1) d\lambda - K_{gh}(\tau) = 0,$$
$$0 \leqslant \tau \leqslant T. \tag{9.24}$$

Of course the solution $w_0(\tau, x_1)$ of this integral equation depends on x_1 as a parameter.

If we knew the quantity x_1, the solution of equation (9.24) would determine the optimal weight function $w_0(\tau, x_1)$ and the optimal system corresponding to that weight function. But we do not know the quantity x_1. In such a case, it is expedient to construct a system with weight function $w_0(\tau, x_1)$. (In the general case, such a system can be achieved approximately.) This system must include the variable parameter x_1, as well as be the main control loop. The supplementary loop must carry out the adaptation of the parameter x_1 to its extremal value, the value $x_1 = x_{1e}$, minimizing the variance of the error (9.23) at each instant of time. Such a two-loop adaptive system is the best system, since it minimizes the criterion in question at each instant of time.

To construct an adaptive system (system for extremal regulation), we need to solve the three problems mentioned in the preceding section: (a) Calculation of the criterion F for comparing systems, (b) determination of the gradient of the criterion, and (c) ensuring of motion toward an extremum (in the present case, the minimum) of the criterion. The extreme value of the parameter x_1 of the weight function is equal to the value of the variance of the noise D_z^0 that is observed at the given instant:

$$x_{1e} = D_z^0. \tag{9.25}$$

The actual value of the variance at an arbitrary instant of time D_z^0 is unknown. The value of the parameter x_1 of the weight function can be considered known, since it can always be measured in an actual system and given to the calculating element.

At each instant, the criterion F can, when we know the value of the parameter x_1, be calculated from formula (9.21), in which we need to replace the arbitrary weight function $w(\tau)$ with $w_0(\tau, x_1)$, which is a solution of equation (9.24), and the arbitrary variance of the noise D_z with the variance D_z^0:

$$F(x_1) = D_E(x_1) = \int_0^T \int_0^T w_0(\tau, x_1)w_0(\lambda, x_1)[K_g(\tau - \lambda)$$

$$+ D_z^0 R_z(\tau - \lambda)]d\tau\, d\lambda - 2\int_0^T K_{gh}(\tau)w_0(\tau, x_1)d\tau + d\tau + D_h. \quad (9.26)$$

Here, the function

$$K_g(\tau), \quad R_z(\tau), \quad K_{gh}(\tau), \quad w_0(\tau, x_1)$$

are known and the quantity D_h is known (although this is of no significance, since this quantity is independent of the weight function of the main control loop). The only quantity in formula (9.26) that we do not know is the variance of the noise D_z.

There are various ways of obtaining the information needed for calculating the criterion. We propose the following procedure: The first term in formula (9.26) is the variance of the output variable $Y(t)$ of the main control loop. Consequently, when we feed the output variable $Y(t)$ into the calculating element, we can determine the unknown variance D_y with the required accuracy from a single sample function of sufficient duration T_s. (Let us suppose that the output variable $Y(t)$ is a random ergodic function with respect to the variance.) In the calculating element, the calculation is made according to the formula

$$D_y = \frac{1}{T_s}\int_0^{T_s} y^2(\tau)d\tau, \quad (9.27)$$

where T_s is the duration of the sample function $y(t)$ of the output variable of the main control loop. Formula (9.26) can then be rewritten in the following form:

$$F(x_1) = D_y(x_1) - 2\int_0^T K_{gh}(\tau)w_0(\tau, x_1)d\tau + D_h, \quad (9.28)$$

which brings out the dependence of the variance of the ouput variable D_y on the parameter x_1 of the main control loop.

Thus, the criterion $F(x_1)$ is calculated in accordance with formula (9.28). It is a function of a single argument x_1. Consequently, the gradient in this case coincides with the derivative $dF(x_1)/dx_1$. In this special case, the gradient method in its ideal form (see (9.16)) determines the dependence between the rate of change of the parameter x_1 and the derivative of the criterion F:

$$\dot{x}_1 = -k\frac{dF(x_1)}{dx_1}, \qquad (9.29)$$

where k is some positive number.

Figure 9.4 shows the block diagram of an extremal-regulation system that carries out the procedure expounded for calculating the criterion in accordance with formulas (9.27) and (9.28) and the gradient method of motion toward the minimum of the criterion.

Besides the main control loop connecting the input variable $X(t)$ and the output variable $Y(t)$ and characterized by the weight function $w_0(\tau, x_1)$, the system includes an adaptive loop. This loop contains elements designed for calculating the criterion $F(x_1)$, that is, the variance of the error of the system, for determining the derivative of the criterion with respect to the parameter x_1, and for carrying out the motion toward the minimum of the criterion. The criterion $F(x_1)$ is characterized by a calculating element (ce) at whose input is fed the current value of the parameter x_1 and the initial information (ii) regarding the control process (the joint correlation function $K_{gh}(\tau)$ of the useful signal $G(t)$ and the desired output variable $H(t)$, the variance D_h of the output variable, and the weight function $w_0(\tau, x_1)$, which depends on the parameter x_1). The current value of the parameter x_1 of the weight function is working information. It is fed into the computer from the main control loop.

The derivative $dF(x_1)/dx_1$ of the criterion with respect to the parameter x_1 is determined with the aid of the synchronous detector indicated in the diagram by the square with the crossed diagonal lines.

The motion toward the extremum is carried out in accordance with formula (9.29) or in accordance with the equivalent formula

$$x_1 = -k\int_{t_0}^{t}\frac{dF(x_1)}{dx_1}dt + x_1(t_0). \qquad (9.30)$$

Here, the integration is from the instant the system is put into operation to the variable value of the time t. The integration with a change of sign can be carried out, for example, on an integrating amplifier. In

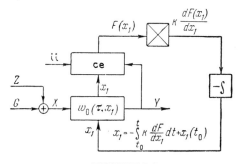

FIGURE 9.4

accordance with law (9.30), the governing element (not shown in Fig. 9.4) changes the parameter x_1 of the main control loop.

A continuous search process in accordance with the block diagram shown in Figure 9.4 ensures stability; that is, it leads the system to the minimum of the criterion F under arbitrary initial conditions. In fact, the total derivative of the criterion with respect to time is

$$\frac{dF}{dt} = \frac{\partial F}{\partial x_1}\frac{dx_1}{dt} = \frac{dF}{dx_1}\frac{dx_1}{dt}. \tag{9.31}$$

In view of the slow change in the function F for a constant value of the parameter x_1, the derivative $\partial F/\partial t$ is taken equal to zero. When we substitute (9.29) into (9.31), we obtain

$$\frac{dF}{dt} = -k\left(\frac{dF}{dx_1}\right)^2. \tag{9.32}$$

From this it is obvious that the derivative dF/dt is everywhere negative except at an extremum. Consequently, the criterion F decreases monotonically in the process of seeking the minimum.

If we keep in mind the inertia of the governing element and other components in the system (amplifiers, transforms, and the like), we must replace equation (9.29) with the following one:

$$pX_1(p) = -W(p)\frac{dF}{dx_1}(p),$$

where $X_1(p)$ is the Laplace transform of the parameter $x_1(t)$, $dF(p)/dx_1$ is the Laplace transform of the derivative $dF(t)/dx_1$, and $W(p)$ is the transfer function connecting the output of the synchronous detector with the variable x_1 (that is, with the variance of the noise D_z).

Variant 2.   We do not know the distribution law of n parameters of the correlation function of the noise.   Suppose that the initial data are the same as with variant 1 except the data regarding the noise. In the present case, let us assume that the noise Z, which is uncorrelated with the useful signal G, has a correlation function $K_z = K_z(D_1, \cdots, D_n, \tau)$ depending on n parameters $D_1, \cdots, D_n$. The parameter $D_1, \cdots, D_n$ can be the variances of the different components of the noise Z or other physical quantities. For example, if the correlation function of the noise is of the form

$$K_z = \sum_{i=1}^{n} B_i e^{-\beta_i|\tau|}, \tag{9.33}$$

then the unknown constant quantities $B_1, \cdots, B_k, \beta_1, \cdots, \beta_k$ are the parameters $D_1, \cdots, D_n$; that is,

$$D_1 = B_1, \; D_2 = B_2, \; \cdots, \; D_{\frac{n}{2}} = B_k, \; D_{\frac{n}{2}+1} = \beta_1, \; \cdots, \; D_n = \beta_k.$$

In the present variant, we do not have complete initial information regarding the noise. This means that we need to shift to an extremal-regulation system.

We take as our criterion for comparing systems the variance of the error D_E. In the present case, it is determined from formula (3.3):

$$D_E = \int_0^T \int_0^T w(\tau) w(\lambda) [K_g(\tau - \lambda) + K_z(D_1, \cdots, D_n; \tau - \lambda)]$$
$$\times \, d\tau \, d\lambda - 2 \int_0^T K_{gh}(\tau) w(\tau) d\tau + D_h. \qquad (9.34)$$

Here, we use the relationship

$$K_x(\tau) = K_g(\tau) + K_z(D_1, \cdots, D_n, \tau), \qquad (9.35)$$

which reflects the fact that the noise is uncorrelated with the useful signal. We denote the unknown fixed values of the parameters $D_1, \cdots,$ D_n by $x_1, \cdots, x_n$. In this notation, formula (9.34) becomes

$$D_E = \int_0^T \int_0^T w(\tau) w(\lambda) [K_g(\tau - \lambda) + K_z(x_1, \cdots, x_n; \tau - \lambda)]$$
$$\times \, d\tau \, d\lambda - 2 \int_0^T K_{gh}(\tau) w(\tau) d\tau + D_h. \qquad (9.36)$$

For arbitrary fixed values of the parameters $x_1, \cdots, x_n$, we can determine the optimal weight function of the main control loop minimizing the variance D_E. This optimal weight function can be obtained as the solution of the integral equation (3.6) which, by virtue of (9.19), (9.20), and (9.34) may be written in the form

$$\int_0^T [K_g(\tau - \lambda) + D_z(x_1, \cdots, x_n; \tau - \lambda)] w_0(\lambda, x_1, \cdots, x_n)$$
$$\times \, d\lambda - K_{gh}(\tau) = 0, \quad 0 \leqslant \tau \leqslant T. \qquad (9.37)$$

The solution $w_0(\tau, x_1, \cdots, x_n)$ of this integral equation depends on $x_1,$ $\cdots, x_n$ as parameters. From the weight function $w_0(\tau, x_1, \cdots, x_n)$, we construct the main loop of the adaptive system with n variable parameters $x_1, \cdots, x_n$. The supplementary loop must achieve for the parameters $x_1, \cdots, x_n$ their extremal values, that is, the values $x_i = x_{ie}$ minimizing the variance of the error (9.36) at each instant of time. The extreme values of the parameters $x_1, \cdots, x_n$ of the weight function w_0 are equal to those values of the parameters $D_1^0, \cdots, D_n^0$ of the correlation function of the noise $K_z(D_1^0, \cdots, D_n^0, \tau)$ that are observed at a given instant of time:

$$x_{i \ni} = D_i^0. \qquad (9.38)$$

The actual values of the parameters D_i^0 at an arbitrary instant of time are unknown. The values of the parameters x_i of the weight function can be measured. Therefore, we consider them known. Let us look at the problem of calculating the criterion $F(x_1, \cdots, x_m) = D_E(x_1, \cdots, x_n)$.

At each instant of time, this criterion can, for known values of the parameters $x_1, \cdots, x_n$, be calculated from formula (9.34) in which we need to replace the arbitrary weight functions $w(\tau)$ with $w_0(\tau, x_1, \cdots, x_n)$, which is a solution of equation (9.37) and, instead of arbitrary values of the parameters $D_1, \cdots, D_n$, we need to substitute the actual current values $D_1^0, \cdots, D_n^0$:

$$
\begin{aligned}
F(x_1, \cdots, x_n) &= D_E(x_1, \cdots, x_n) \\
&= \int_0^T \int_0^T w_0(\tau, x_1, \cdots, x_n) w_0(\lambda, x_1, \cdots, x_n) \\
&\quad \times [K_g(\tau - \lambda) + K_z(D_1^0, \cdots, D_n^0, \tau - \lambda)] d\tau \, d\lambda \\
&\quad - 2 \int_0^T K_{gh}(\tau) w_0(\tau, x_1, \cdots, x_n) d\tau + D_h.
\end{aligned}
\tag{9.39}
$$

The first term in (9.39) is the variance of the output variable $Y(t)$ of the main control loop. Consequently, by feeding the output variable $Y(t)$ into the calculating element, we can use a single sufficiently protracted sample function to determine the unknown variance D_y with the required degree of accuracy. Here, we assume that the output variable $Y(t)$ is a random function that is ergodic with respect to the variance.

Calculation of the variance D_y is done in accordance with formula (9.27).

Now, equation (9.39) can be rewritten in the form

$$
\begin{aligned}
F(x_1, \cdots, x_n) &= D_y(x_1, \cdots, x_n) \\
&\quad - 2 \int_0^T K_{gh}(\tau) w_0(\tau, x_1, \cdots, x_n) d\tau + D_h.
\end{aligned}
\tag{9.40}
$$

The joint correlation function of the useful signal and the desired output variable $K_{gh}(\tau)$ is known and so is the variance of desired output variable D_h. The weight function $w_0(\tau, x_1, \cdots, x_n)$ is a known function of the variable τ and the parameters $x_1, \cdots, x_n$. Consequently, the criterion F can be calculated in accordance with formula (9.40) as a function of the varying parameters $x_1, \cdots, x_n$.

We then need to solve the second problem; that is, we need to determine the gradient of the criterion F. Suppose that we are determining the components of the gradient F by the method of synchronous detection.

To move toward the extremum, let us use the gradient method. In the present case, this method in its ideal form (9.16) determines the relationship between the rate of change of the parameter x_i and the derivative of the criterion $\partial F / \partial x_i$ in accordance with the formula

$$
\dot{x}_i = -k \frac{\partial F}{\partial x_i}, \quad i = 1, \cdots, n,
\tag{9.41}
$$

where k is a positive number.

The block diagram of the extremal-regulation system, carrying out

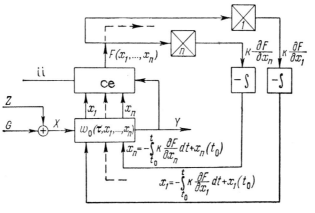

FIGURE 9.5

the method described for calculating the criterion (in accordance with formulas (9.27) and (9.40)) and the gradient method of motion toward the minimum of the variance of the error, is shown in Figure 9.5.

In addition to the main control loop characterized by the weight function $w_0(\tau, x_1, \cdots, x_n)$, the system also includes the adaptation loops. These loops contain elements designated for calculating the criterion $F(x_1, \cdots, x_n) = D_E(x_1, \cdots, x_n)$, for determining the components of the gradient of the criterion $\partial F/\partial x_i$, for $i = 1, \cdots, n$, and for carrying out the motion toward the minimum of the criterion. The criterion F is determined by the calculating element and is fed to all n channels of the adaptor system. The calculating element is fed the initial information (ii), namely, the correlation function $K_{gh}(\tau)$, the variance D_h, and the function $w_0(\tau, x_1, \cdots, x_n)$. The current values of the parameters $x_1, \cdots, x_n$ constitute working information. This working information goes from the main control loop to the calculating element.

The components of the gradient $\partial F/\partial x_i$ of the criterion are determined continuously with the aid of the synchronous detectors, indicated in Figure 9.5 by the squares with the diagonally crossed lines and the corresponding numbers.

The motion toward the minimum of the criterion is carried out in accordance with formulas (9.41) or the equivalent formulas

$$x_i = -\int_{t_0}^{t} k\frac{\partial F}{\partial x_i} dt + x_i(t_0), \quad i = 1, \cdots, n. \tag{9.42}$$

In accordance with the signals (9.42), obtained from the outputs of the integrating units, the governing elements (not shown in Fig. 9.5) change the values of the parameters $x_1, \cdots, x_n$ of the main control loop.

A continuous search process in accordance with the block diagram of Figure 9.5 ensures stability, that is, leads the system to the minimum of the criterion F for arbitrary initial conditions. In fact, the total derivative of the criterion with respect to time is

$$\frac{dF}{dt} = \frac{\partial F}{\partial x_1}\frac{dx_1}{dt} + \cdots + \frac{\partial F}{\partial x_n}\frac{dx_n}{dt}. \qquad (9.43)$$

The derivative $\varrho F/\partial t$ is, by hypothesis, close to zero. Therefore, it is omitted from (9.43). When we substitute (9.29) into (9.43), we obtain

$$\frac{dF}{dt} = -k\left[\left(\frac{\partial F}{\partial x_1}\right)^2 + \cdots + \left(\frac{\partial F}{\partial x_n}\right)^2\right]. \qquad (9.44)$$

From this it is clear that the derivative dF/dt is always nonpositive. Consequently, during the search process, the criterion F decreases monotonically to its minimal value.

The case in which noises are applied to the system at different points reduces to this variant.

Variant 3. We do not know the distribution law of the variance of the useful signal. Suppose that the block diagram of the main control loop has the form shown in Figure 3.1. Let us assume that the correlation function $K_z(\tau)$ of a steady-state noise $Z(t)$ is known. The correlation function of the useful signal has the form $K_g(\tau) = D_g R_g(\tau)$, where $R_g(\tau)$ is a known normalized correlation function of the useful signal $G(t)$ and D_g is the unknown variance of that useful signal. (We also do not know the distribution of the random function D_g.) We know only that D_g changes slowly with time under the action of random factors. Suppose that the mathematical expectations of the useful signal and the noise are both zero: $m_g = m_z = 0$. The main control loop is designed for reproduction of the function $H(t)$, which is the result of carrying out some given linear operation L that maps the steady-state signal $G(t)$ into the steady state signal $H(t)$. The useful signal $G(t)$ and the noise $Z(t)$ are uncorrelated; that is, $K_{gz} = 0$. Consequently, the correlation function of the input variable $X(t) = G(t) + Z(t)$ is determined in accordance with the formula

$$K_x(\tau) = D_g R_g(\tau) + K_z(\tau). \qquad (9.45)$$

and the joint correlation function $K_{xh}(\tau)$ of the random functions $X(t)$ and $H(t)$ is

$$K_{xh}(\tau) = K_{gh}(\tau) = L\{K_g(\tau)\} = D_g L\{R_g(\tau)\}. \qquad (9.46)$$

In the present case, we do not have complete initial information regarding the useful signal, since we do not know the variance of the useful signal. Consequently, we need to shift to an adaptive system.

We take as our criterion for comparing systems the variance of the error D_E. In the present case, it is determined in accordance with formula (3.3). Let us rewrite this formula in the light of equations (9.44) and (9.45):

$$D_E = \int_0^T\int_0^T w(\tau)w(\lambda)[D_g R_g(\tau - \lambda) + K_z(\tau - \lambda)]d\tau\,d\lambda$$
$$- 2D_g\int_0^T L\{R_g(\tau)\}w(\tau)d\tau + D_h. \qquad (9.47)$$

We use the following notation for the unknown variance of the useful signal D_g:

$$D_g = x_1. \tag{9.48}$$

In this notation, formula (9.47) becomes

$$D_E = \int_0^T \int_0^T w(\tau)w(\lambda)[x_1 R_g(\tau - \lambda) + K_z(\tau - \lambda)]d\tau\,d\lambda$$
$$- 2x_1 \int_0^T L\{R_g(\tau)\}w(\tau)d\tau + D_h. \tag{9.49}$$

Let us find the optimal weight function $w_0(\tau, x_1)$ minimizing the variance (9.49) for some fixed value of the parameter x_1 (for a fixed value of the variance D_g of the useful signal). This optimal weight function $w_0(\tau, x_1)$ is a solution of the integral equation (3.6), which, in view of the relations (9.45), (9.46), and (9.48) may be rewritten in the following form:

$$\int_0^T [x_1 R_g(\tau - \lambda) + K_z(\tau - \lambda)]w_0(\lambda, x_1)d\lambda - x_1 L\{R_g(\tau)\} = 0,$$
$$0 \leqslant \tau \leqslant T. \tag{9.50}$$

The solution $w_0(\tau, x_1)$ of this integral equation depends on x_1 as a parameter. This parameter x_1 is numerically equal to the variance of the useful signal D_g. Since the variance D_g and its distribution law are not known in advance, it is expedient in this case to construct a system with weight function $w_0(\tau, x_1)$. This system must contain the variable parameter x_1. The given system must represent the main control loop. The supplementary loop must ensure adaptation of the parameter x_1 to its extremal value; that is, to the value $x_1 = x_{1e}$ corresponding to the minimum of the variance of the error (9.49) at each instant. The extremal value of the parameter x_1 is equal to that value of the variance of the useful signal D_g^0 corresponding to a given instant:

$$x_{1e} = D_g^0.$$

Such a two-loop adaptive system is the best one in the present case, since it minimizes the variance of the error at each instant of time.

Let us look at the question of calculating a criterion in the process of operation of this adaptive system (which is an extremal-regulation system).

At each instant, the criterion $F(x_1) = D_E(x_1)$ can, when we know the value of the parameter x_1, be calculated in accordance with formula (9.47), in which we need to take not an arbitrary weight function $w(\tau)$ but the weight function $w_0(\tau, x_1)$ that is the solution of equation (9.50) and, instead of the arbitrary variance D_g of the useful signal, the variance D_g^0:

$$F(x_1) = D_E(x_1)$$
$$= \int_0^T \int_0^T w_0(\tau, \, x_1) w_0(\lambda, \, x_1) [D_g^0 R_g(\tau - \lambda) + K_z(\tau - \lambda)] d\tau \, d\lambda$$
$$- 2D_g^0 \int_0^T L\{R_g(\tau)\} w_0(\tau, \, x_1) d\tau + D_h. \tag{9.51}$$

The first term in this equation is the variance $D_y(x_1)$ of the output variable $Y(t)$ of the main control loop. This variance depends on the parameter x_1. It can be calculated from a realization of the output variable $Y(t)$ of sufficient duration. (We assume that the random function $Y(t)$ is ergodic with respect to the variance.) The second term in formula (9.51) can be represented in the form

$$- 2D_g^0 K_1(x_1), \tag{9.52}$$

where the function

$$K_1(x_1) = \int_0^T L\{R_g(\tau)\} w_0(\tau, \, x_1) d\tau$$

is a known function of the parameter x_1. Consequently, formula (9.51) can be rewritten in the form

$$F(x_1) = D_E(x_1) = D_y(x_1) - 2D_g^0 K_1(x_1) + D_h. \tag{9.53}$$

The term $2D_g^0 K_1(x_1)$ in this formula cannot be calculated, since we do not know the variable value of the variance D_g^0 of the useful signal. Herein lies the essential difference between this variant and variant 1, in which the criterion $F(x_1) = D_E(x_1)$ is completely calculated from formula (9.28).

We propose the following method for getting out of this complex predicament: Instead of the criterion $F(x_1)$, let us at once calculate its derivative, which is necessary for executing the motion to the minimum of the criterion $F(x_1)$. Let us calculate this derivative approximately. Instead of the exact formula

$$\frac{dF(x_1)}{dx_1} = \frac{dD_y(x_1)}{dx_1} - 2D_g^0 \frac{dK_1(x_1)}{dx_1} \tag{9.54}$$

let us use the approximate formula

$$\frac{dF}{dx_1} \simeq \varphi_1(x_1) = \frac{dD_y(x_1)}{dx_1} - 2x_1 \frac{dK_1(x_1)}{dx_1}. \tag{9.55}$$

The smaller the difference $x_1 - D_g^0$ the smaller will be the error in determining the derivative of the criterion with respect to the parameter x_1:

$$\varphi_1(x_1) - \frac{dF(x_1)}{dx_1} = (\acute{D}_g^0 - x_1) 2 \frac{dK_1(x_1)}{dx_1}. \tag{9.56}$$

We can determine the derivative $dD_y(x_1)/dx_1$, for example, by means of synchronous detection. The function

$$2x_1 \frac{dK_1(x_1)}{dx_1}$$

is formed with the aid of the calculating element.

Thus, instead of using the derivative of the criterion F, expressed by (9.54), we use in the system the function $\varphi_1(x_1)$ defined by formula (9.55). We carry out the motion to the minimum of the criterion $F(x_1)$ according to a modified gradient method. We substitute $\varphi_1(x_1)$ for $dF(x_1)/dx_1$ in (9.16) and get

$$\dot{x}_1 = -k\varphi_1(x_1) = -k\left[\frac{dD_y(x_1)}{dx_1} - 2x_1\frac{dK_1(x_1)}{dx_1}\right], \qquad (9.57)$$

or

$$\begin{aligned} x_1 &= -\int_{t_0}^{t} k\varphi_1(x_1)\,dt + x_1(t_0) \\ &= -\int_{t_0}^{t} k\left[\frac{dD_y(x_1)}{dx_1} - 2x_1\frac{dK_1(x_1)}{dx_1}\right]dt + x_1(t_0). \qquad (9.58) \end{aligned}$$

Let us show that the system attains an equilibrium state at $x_1 = x_{1e} = D_g^0$. An equilibrium state of a system for extremal regulation acting in accordance with formula (9.57) is defined by the relation

$$\varphi_1(x_1) = \frac{dD_y(x_1)}{dx_1} - 2x_1\frac{dK_1(x_1)}{dx_1} = 0. \qquad (9.59)$$

Let us compare this equation with the equation

$$\frac{dF_1(x_1)}{dx_1} = \frac{dD_E(x_1)}{dx_1} = \frac{dD_y(x_1)}{dx_1} - 2D_g^0\frac{dK_1(x_1)}{dx_1} = 0. \qquad (9.60)$$

obtained by differentiating (9.53). This equation (9.60) is satisfied at the value $x_1 = D_g^0$, since the minimum of the criterion F is attained at this value of the parameter x_1. It is easy to see that equation (9.59) is satisfied with $x_1 = D_g^0 = x_{1e}$. Consequently, the extremal-regulation system in which the motion to the minimum of the criterion $F(x_1)$ is carried out in accordance with formula (9.57) or (9.58) ensures under these conditions an extremal value of the parameter $x_1 = x_{1e} = D_g^0$ and the minimal value of the variance of the error of the main control loop.

A system of extremal regulation that executes motion toward the minimum of the variance D_E of the other error in accordance with the law (9.58) is shown in Figure 9.6.

In contrast with variant 1 (see Fig. 9.4), monotonic decrease in the criterion $F(x_1)$ is not ensured this time for all values of the parameter x_1. Let us see what extra condition we need to impose on the parameter x_1 for the block diagram shown in Figure 9.6 to ensure monotonic decrease of the criterion. To do this, we write the expression for the derivative of the criterion with respect to time, taking into account equation (9.54):

$$\frac{dF(x_1)}{dt} = \frac{dF}{dx_1}\frac{dx_1}{dt} = -k\frac{dF}{dx_1}\left[\frac{dD_y(x_1)}{dx_1} - 2x_1\frac{dK_1(x_1)}{dx_1}\right]. \qquad (9.61)$$

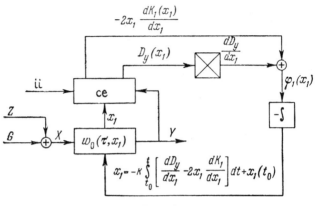

FIGURE 9.6

On the basis of (9.60), we rewrite formula (9.61) as follows:

$$\frac{dF}{dt} = -k\frac{dF}{dx_1}\left[\frac{dF}{dx_1} + 2\frac{dK_1}{dx_1}(D_g^0 - x_1)\right]$$
$$= -k\left[\left(\frac{dF}{dx_1}\right)^2 + 2\frac{dF}{dx_1}\frac{dK_1}{dx_1}(D_g^0 - x_1)\right]. \qquad (9.62)$$

It follows from this equation that the criterion F will decrease monotonically if

$$\frac{\dfrac{dK_1}{dx_1}}{\dfrac{dF}{dx_1}}(D_g^0 - x_1) < \frac{1}{2}. \qquad (9.63)$$

In particular, inequality (9.63) will be satisfied if

$$|D_g^0 - x_1| < \frac{1}{2}\frac{\left|\dfrac{dF}{dx_1}\right|}{\left|\dfrac{dK_1}{dx_1}\right|}. \qquad (9.64)$$

Variant 4.   We do not know the distribution law of n parameters of the correlation function of the useful signal. Suppose that the block diagram of the main control loop has the form shown in Figure 3.1. All the initial data regarding the influences are the same as in Variant 3 except that the correlation function of the useful signal now has the more complicated form

$$K_g(\tau) = D_1 R_1(\tau) + \cdots + D_n R_n(\tau), \qquad (9.65)$$

where $D_1, \cdots, D_n$ are positive quantities with unknown distribution laws and $R_1(\tau), \cdots, R_n(\tau)$ are known functions of τ. The quantities $D_1, \cdots, D_n$ change slowly with time under the influence of random factors.

In the present case, the correlation function of the input variable $X(t)$ is determined according to the formula

$$K_x(\tau) = D_1 R_1(\tau) + \cdots + D_n R_n(\tau) + K_z(\tau), \qquad (9.66)$$

and the joint correlation function $K_{xh}(\tau)$ of the random function $X(t)$ and $H(t)$ is

$$K_{xh}(\tau) = K_{gh}(\tau) = D_1 L\{R_1(\tau)\} + \cdots + D_n L\{R_n(\tau)\}. \qquad (9.67)$$

In the present variant, we do not have complete initial information regarding the useful signal, since we do not know the quantities D_i, which usually have the meaning of variances of the individual components $X_i(t)$ of the useful signal

$$X(t) = X_1(t) + \cdots + X_n(t).$$

We take as criterion the variance of the error of the system D_E. In the present case, this criterion is determined from formula (3.3). On the basis of equations (9.66) and (9.67) this formula becomes

$$D_E = \int_0^T \int_0^T w(\tau) w(\lambda) [D_1 R_1(\tau - \lambda) + \cdots + D_n R_n(\tau - \lambda)$$
$$+ K_z(\tau - \lambda)] d\tau\, d\lambda - 2D_1 \int_0^T L\{R_1(\tau)\} w(\tau) d\tau$$
$$- \cdots - 2D_n \int_0^T L\{R_n(\tau)\} w(\tau) d\tau + D_h. \qquad (9.68)$$

We use the following notation for the unknown quantities D_i (the variances):

$$D_i = x_i. \qquad (9.69)$$

In this notation, formula (9.68) becomes

$$D_E = \int_0^T \int_0^T w(\tau) w(\lambda) \left[\sum_{i=1}^n x_i R_i(\tau - \lambda) + K_z(\tau - \lambda) \right] d\tau\, d\lambda$$
$$- 2 \sum_{i=1}^n x_i \int_0^T L\{R_i(\tau)\} w(\tau) d\tau + D_h. \qquad (9.70)$$

Let us find the optimal weight function $w_0(\tau, x_1, \cdots, x_n)$ minimizing the variance (9.70) for certain fixed values of parameters $x_1, \cdots, x_n$ (for fixed values of the quantities $D_1, \cdots, D_n$). This optimal weight function $w_0(\tau, x_1, \cdots, x_n)$ is a solution of the integral equation (3.6), which, by virtue of equations (9.66), (9.67), and (9.69), may be written in the form

$$\int_0^T \left[\sum_{i=1}^n x_i R_i(\tau - \lambda) + K_z(\tau - \lambda) \right] w_0(\lambda, x_1, \cdots, x_n) d\lambda$$
$$- \sum_{i=1}^n x_i L\{R_i(\tau)\} = 0, \quad 0 \leqslant \tau \leqslant T. \qquad (9.71)$$

The solution $w_0(\tau, x_1, \cdots, x_n)$ of this integral equation depends on x_1, $\cdots$, x_n as parameters. These parameters are numerically equal to the corresponding variables $D_1, \cdots, D_n$, characterizing the correlation function of the useful signal. Since the quantities $D_1, \cdots, D_n$ and their distribution laws are unknown, in this case it will be expedient to construct an adaptive system whose main loop has the weight function $w_0(\tau, x_1, \cdots, x_n)$. The parameters $x_1, \cdots, x_n$ of the main control loop can be changed during the course of operation of the system. The supplementary loops must ensure adaptation of the parameters $x_1, \cdots,$ x_n to their extremal values, that is, to the values $x_i = x_{ie}$ corresponding to a minimum of the variance of the error (9.70) at each instant. The extremal values of the parameters x_i are equal to the corresponding values of the quantities D_i^0 at any instant of time:

$$x_{ie} = D_i^0, \quad i = 1, \cdots, n. \tag{9.72}$$

Such a multiple-loop adaptive system minimizes the variance in the error at each instant of time.

Let us look at the question of calculation of the criterion and determination of the gradient of the criterion during the course of operation of this extremal-regulation system.

At each given instant of time, the criterion $F(x_1, \cdots, x_n) = D_E(x_1,$ $\cdots, x_n)$ can, for known values of the parameters $x_1, \cdots, x_n$, be calculated in accordance with formula (9.68). In this formula, we need to replace the arbitrary weight function $w(\tau)$ with the weight function $w_0(\tau, x_1, \cdots, x_n)$, which is a solution of equation (9.71), and we need to replace the arbitrary values of the quantities $D_1, \cdots, D_n$ with the quantities $D_1^0, \cdots, D_n^0$:

$$
\begin{aligned}
F(x_1, \cdots, x_n) &= D_E(x_1, \cdots, x_n) \\
&= \int_0^T \int_0^T w_0(\tau, x_1, \cdots, x_n) w_0(\lambda, x_1, \cdots, x_n) \\
&\quad \times \left[\sum_{i=1}^n D_i^0 R_i(\tau - \lambda) + K_z(\tau - \lambda) \right] d\tau \, d\lambda \\
&\quad - 2 \sum_{i=1}^n D_i^0 \int_0^T L\{R_i(\tau)\} w_0(\tau, x_1, \cdots, x_n) d\tau + D_h. \tag{9.73}
\end{aligned}
$$

The first term in (9.73) is the variance $D_y(x_1, \cdots, x_n)$ of the output variable $Y(t)$ of the main control loop. It can be calculated from a sufficiently protracted sample function of the output variable $Y(t)$. The second term in formula (9.73) can be represented as:

$$- 2 \sum_{i=1}^n D_i^0 K_i(x_1, \cdots, x_n), \tag{9.74}$$

where

$$K_i(x_1, \cdots, x_n) = \int_0^T L\{R_1(\tau)\} w_0(\tau, x_1, \cdots, x_n) d\tau$$

is a known function of the parameters $x_1, \cdots, x_n$. Consequently, formula (9.73) can be written as

$$F(x_1, \cdots, x_n) = D_E(x_1, \cdots, x_n)$$

$$= D_y(x_1, \cdots, x_n) - \sum_{i=1}^{n} D_i^0 K_i(x_1, \cdots, x_n) + D_h. \qquad (9.75)$$

The term

$$-2 \sum_{i=1}^{n} D_i^0 K_i(x_1, \cdots, x_n)$$

in this formula cannot be calculated, since we do not know the current values of the quantities $D_1^0, \cdots, D_n^0$.

Just as in the preceding variant, we shall calculate not the criterion $F(x_1, \cdots, x_n)$ but its gradient, which is necessary for carrying out the motion toward the minimum of the variance D_E. We cannot calculate the gradient exactly. Therefore, let us calculate it approximately. Instead of the exact formula

$$\frac{\partial F}{\partial x_j} = \frac{\partial D_y}{\partial x_j} - 2 \sum_{i=1}^{n} D_i^0 \frac{\partial K_i}{\partial x_j}, \qquad (9.76)$$

containing the unknown quantities D_i^0, we shall use the approximate formulas

$$\frac{\partial F}{\partial x_j} \simeq \varphi_j(x_1, \cdots, x_n) = \frac{\partial D_y}{\partial x_j} - 2 \sum_{i=1}^{n} x_i \frac{\partial K_i}{\partial x_j}. \qquad (9.77)$$

The derivatives $\partial D_y/\partial x_i$ can be determined, for example, by means of synchronous detection. The function

$$-2 \sum_{i=1}^{n} x_i \frac{\partial K_i}{\partial x_j}$$

can be formed by the calculating element, which receives the working information regarding the values of the parameters x_i of the main control loop. Thus, instead of the partial derivatives (9.76) of the criterion F with respect to the parameters x_j in the adaptive system, we use the functions $\varphi_j(x_1, \cdots, x_n)$ defined by formula (9.77).

The motion toward the minimum of the variance D_E is made according to a modified gradient method determined by the relations

$$\dot{x}_j = -k\varphi_j(x_1, \cdots, x_n) = -k\left[\frac{\partial D_y}{\partial x_j} - 2 \sum_{i=1}^{n} x_i \frac{\partial K_i}{\partial x_j} \right] \qquad (9.78)$$

or

$$x_j = -k \int_{t_0}^{t} \left[\frac{\partial D_y}{\partial x_j} - 2 \sum_{i=1}^{n} x_i \frac{\partial K_i}{\partial x_j} \right] dt + x_j(t_0). \qquad (9.79)$$

Despite the fact that here the motion toward the extremum is not made precisely according to the gradient method, the equilibrium state of the system is attained at $x_i = x_{ie} = D_i^0$. To determine the values of the parameters corresponding to the equilibrium state of the system, we need to set the derivatives $\dot{x}_j$ (see (9.79)) equal to zero:

$$\frac{\partial D_y}{\partial x_j} - 2 \sum_{i=1}^{n} x_i \frac{\partial K_1}{\partial x_j} = 0, \quad j = 1, \cdots, n. \qquad (9.80)$$

Let us compare the system of equations (9.80) with the equations

$$\frac{\partial D_y}{\partial x_j} - 2 \sum_{i=1}^{n} D_i^0 \frac{\partial K_i}{\partial x_j} = 0, \quad j = 1, \cdots, n, \qquad (9.81)$$

obtained by differentiating (9.75) with respect to x_j. Equations (9.81) are satisfied at the values of the parameters $x_j = D_j^0$, since these values of the parameters correspond to the minimum of the variance of the error. This means that

$$\left[\frac{\partial D_y}{\partial x_j} - 2 \sum_{i=1}^{n} D_i^0 \frac{\partial K_i}{\partial x_j} \right]\Bigg|_{\substack{x_1 = D_0^1 \\ \cdots \\ x_n = D_n^0}} = 0. \qquad (9.82)$$

It follows from these equations that equations (9.80) are satisfied by the

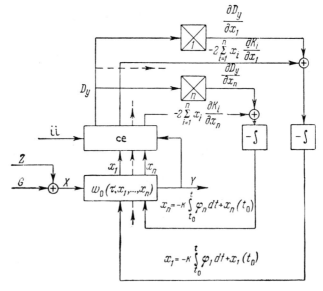

FIGURE 9.7

following values of the parameters: $x_i = D_i^2$, for $i = 1, \cdots, n$.

This means that the extremal-regulation system in which the motion toward the minimum of the criterion $F(x_1, \cdots, x_n) = D_E(x_1, \cdots, x_n)$ is carried out in accordance with formulas (9.78) ensures under these conditions the extremal values of the parameters $x_j = x_{je} = D_j^2$ and the minimum of the variance of the error of the main control loop

$$D_{E\ \min} = D_E(D_1^2, \cdots, D_n^2).$$

The block diagram of an extremal-regulation system performing the motion toward the minimum of the variance in the error D_E in accordance with the law (9.79) is shown in Figure 9.7.

In contrast with Variant 2 (see Fig. 9.5), monotonic decrease of the criterion $F = D_E$ is not ensured for all initial values of the parameters $x_1, \cdots, x_n$. We can obtain relations analogous to inequality (9.63) that do ensure monotonic decrease of the criterion F.

Variant 5. We do not know the distribution law of the variances of the useful signal and the noise. An input signal $X(t)$, constituting the sum of a useful signal $G(t)$ and a noise $Z(t)$ acts on the system (see Fig. 3.1). The mathematical expectations of the useful signal and the noise are equal to zero. We know that the noise and the useful signal are uncorrelated. The desired output variable $H(t)$ is the result of the application of a given linear operator L of the useful signal:

$$H(t) = L\{G(t)\}.$$

The correlation functions of the useful signal and noise are of the form

$$K_g(\tau) = D_g R_g(\tau), \quad K_z(\tau) = D_z R_z(\tau),$$

where D_g and D_z are the unknown variances of the useful signal and noise respectively and $R_g(\tau)$ and $R_z(\tau)$ are given normalized correlation functions of the useful signal and noise. The correlation function $K_x(\tau)$ of the output variable $X(t)$ and the joint correlation function $K_{xh}(\tau)$ of the input variable and the desired output variable are determined in this case in accordance with the formulas

$$K_x(\tau) = D_g R_g(\tau) + D_z R_z(\tau), \tag{9.83}$$

$$K_{xh}(\tau) = D_g L\{R_g(\tau)\}. \tag{9.84}$$

In the present case, we do not have complete initial information regarding the useful signal and noise. It is expedient to shift to an adaptive system.

We take as our criterion the variance in the error of the system D_E. We determine it in accordance with formula (3.3), keeping (9.83) and (9.84) in mind:

$$D_E = \int_0^T \int_0^T w(\tau)w(\lambda)[D_g R_g(\tau - \lambda) + D_z R_z(\tau - \lambda)]\,d\tau\,d\lambda$$
$$- 2D_g \int_0^T L\{R_g(\tau)\}w(\tau)\,d\tau + D_h. \tag{9.85}$$

We denote the unknown variances D_g and D_z as follows:

$$D_g = x_1, \quad D_z = x_2. \tag{9.86}$$

In this notation, formula (9.85) becomes

$$D_E = x_1 \left\{ \int_0^T\!\!\int_0^T w(\tau)w(\lambda)\left[R_g(\tau - \lambda) + \frac{x_2}{x_1}R_z(\tau - \lambda) \right] d\tau\, d\lambda \right.$$
$$\left. - 2\int_0^T L[R_g(\tau)]w(\tau)d\tau \right\} + D_h. \tag{9.87}$$

We define

$$\frac{x_2}{x_1} = y_1. \tag{9.88}$$

Equation (9.87) then becomes

$$D_E = x_1 \left\{ \int_0^T\!\!\int_0^T w(\tau)w(\lambda)[R_g(\tau - \lambda) + y_1 R_z(\tau - \lambda)] d\tau\, d\lambda \right.$$
$$\left. - 2\int_0^T L[R_g(\tau)]w(\tau)d\tau \right\} + D_h. \tag{9.89}$$

Let us find the optimal weight function $w_0(\tau, y_1)$, which minimizes the variance (9.89) for some fixed value of the parameter y_1 (for a fixed value of the ratio $x_2/x_1 = D_r/D_g$). This optimal weight function $w_0(\tau, y_1)$ is a solution of the integral equation (3.6), which, in view of the relations (9.83), (9.84), (9.86), (9.88), and (9.89), may be written as

$$\int_0^T [R_g(\tau - \lambda) + y_1 R_z(\tau - \lambda)]w_0(\lambda, y_1)d\lambda - L[R_g(\tau)] = 0,$$
$$0 \leqslant \tau \leqslant T. \tag{9.90}$$

The solution $w_0(\tau, y_1)$ of this integral equation depends on y_1 as a parameter. This parameter is numerically equal to the ratio of the variance of the noise to the variance of the useful signal.

Since the distribution law of the quantities D_g and D_z and hence of the quantity y_1 is known, it will be expedient in this case to construct an adaptive system whose main loop has weight function $w_0(\tau, y_1)$ with variable parameter y_1. The supplementary loop must carry out an adaptation of the parameter y_1 to its extremal value, that is, to the value $y_1 = y_{1e}$, corresponding to the minimum of the variance in the error D_E at each instant of time. The extremal value of the parameter y_1 is equal to the value of the ratio of the variances D_z^0/D_g^0 at the given instant of time:

$$y_1 = \frac{D_z^0}{D_g^0}. \tag{9.91}$$

Let us look at the question of calculating the criterion in the course of operation of this extremal-regulation system. For a known value of the parameter y_1, the variance D_E can, at each instant of time, be calculated from formula (9.85) with the arbitrary weight function $w(\tau)$ replaced by the particular weight function $w_0(\tau, y_1)$, which is a solution of equation (9.90), and the arbitrary variances D_g and D_z replaced with the particular variances D_g^0 and D_z^0 corresponding to the given current time:

$$D_E(y_1) = F(y_1)$$
$$= \int_0^T \int_0^T w_0(\tau, y_1) w_0(\lambda, y_1)[D_g^0 R_g(\tau - \lambda) + D_z R_z(\tau - \lambda)]d\tau\, d\lambda$$
$$- 2D_g^0 \int_0^T L[R_g(\tau)]w_0(\tau, y_1)d\tau + D_h. \tag{9.92}$$

This first term in (9.92) is the variance $D_y(y_1)$ of the output variable $Y(t)$ of the main control loop. This variance can be calculated from a sample function of the output variable if we assume that the random function $Y(t)$ is ergodic with respect to the variance. The second term in formula (9.92) can be represented in the form

$$- 2D_g^0 K_1(y_1), \tag{9.93}$$

where the function

$$K_1(y_1) = \int_0^T L[R_g(\tau)]w_0(\tau, y_1)d\tau$$

is a known function of the parameter y_1. Consequently, formula (9.92) can be represented in the form

$$F(y_1) = D_E(y_1) = D_y(y_1) - 2D_g^0 K_1(y_1) + D_h. \tag{9.94}$$

This formula coincides formally with formula (9.53). However, the situation here is quite different from that of Variant 3. In the case of Variant 3, the extremal value of the parameter x_1 coincides with the current value of the variance of the useful signal D_g^0. In the present case, the extremal value of the parameter y_1 is determined by equation (9.91). This fact complicates the solution of the problem.

The term $-2D_g^0 K_1(y)$ in formula (9.94) cannot be calculated, since we do not know the current value of the variance of the useful signal. Consequently, we cannot calculate the criterion $F(y_1)$. Let us proceed in a manner analogous to the procedure in Variant 3. We first calculate the derivative of the criterion with respect to the parameter y_1. This derivative we shall calculate approximately. First, we express $x_1 = D_g$ in terms of y_1. To do this, we use the relation

$$\int_0^T \int_0^T [D_g R_g(\tau - \lambda) + D_z R_z(\tau - \lambda)]w_0(\tau, y_1)w_0(\lambda, y_1)d\tau\, d\lambda = D_y(y_1),$$

which can be rewritten in the form

$$D_g K_2(y_1) + D_z K_3(y_1) = D_y(y_1), \tag{9.95}$$

where

$$K_2(y_1) = \int_0^T \int_0^T R_g(\tau - \lambda) w_0(\tau, y_1) w_0(\lambda, y_1) d\tau \, d\lambda,$$

$$K_3(y_1) = \int_0^T \int_0^T R_z(\tau - \lambda) w_0(\tau, y_1) w_0(\lambda, y_1) d\tau \, d\lambda.$$

The value of the variance $D_y(y_1)$ has already been calculated. The quantities $K_2(y_1)$ and $K_3(y_1)$ can be calculated for each particular value of the parameter y_1. Consequently, we may express $D_g = x_1$ in terms of y_1 by using the formula

$$D_g = x_1 = \frac{D_y(y_1)}{K_2(y_1) + y_1 K_3(y_1)}. \tag{9.96}$$

Instead of the exact formula giving the derivative of the criterion with respect to the parameter y_1, that is, the formula

$$\frac{dF(y_1)}{dy_1} = \frac{dD_y(y_1)}{dy_1} - 2D_g^0 \frac{dK_1(y_1)}{dy_1} \tag{9.97}$$

we use the approximate formula

$$\frac{dF(y_1)}{dy_1} \simeq \varphi_1(y_1) = \frac{dD_y(y_1)}{dy_1} - 2 \frac{D_y(y_1)}{K_2(y_1) + y_1 K_3(y_1)} \frac{dK_1(y_1)}{dy_1}. \tag{9.98}$$

The approximate nature of the formula (9.98) consists in the fact that instead of the actual current variance D_g^0, we now take the variance D_g corresponding to the parameter y_1. (The variance D_g and the parameter y_1 are connected by (9.96)).

Motion toward the minimum of the criterion $F(y_1)$ is carried out according to a modified gradient method. In equation (9.16), we substitute $\varphi_1(y_1)$ for $dF(y_1)/dy_1$ and we set

$$\dot{y}_1 = -k\varphi_1(y_1)$$
$$= -k \left[\frac{dD_y(y)}{dy_1} - 2 \frac{D_y(y_1)}{K_2(y_1) + y_1 K_3(y_1)} \frac{dK_1(y_1)}{dy_1} \right] \tag{9.99}$$

or

$$y_1 = -k \int_{t_0}^t \varphi_1(y_1) dt + y_1(t_0). \tag{9.100}$$

The equilibrium state of the extremal-regulation system operating according to formula (9.99) is attained when

$$\varphi_1(y_1) = \frac{dD_y(y_1)}{dy_2} - 2 \frac{D_y(y_1)}{K_2(y_1) + y_1 K_3(y_1)} \frac{dK_1(y_1)}{dy_1} = 0. \tag{9.101}$$

Let us compare this equation with the equation

$$\frac{dF(y_1)}{dy_1} = \frac{dD_E(y_1)}{dy_1} = \frac{dD_y(y_1)}{dy_1} - 2D_g^2 \frac{dK_1(y_1)}{dy_1} = 0. \tag{9.102}$$

which is obtained by differentiating (9.94). Equation (9.102) is satisfied when $y_1 = y_{1e} = D_z^0/D_g^0$, since the minimum of the criterion F is attained at that value of the parameter y_1.

Equation (9.101) is satisfied when $y_1 = y_{1e} = D_z^0/D_g^0$, since equation (9.96) implies

$$\frac{D_y(y_{1e})}{K_2(y_{1e}) + y_{1e}K_3(y_{1e})} = D_g^0.$$

Consequently, the extremal-regulation system in which the motion toward the minimum of the criterion $F(y_1)$ is carried out in accordance with formula (9.99) or (9.100) ensures under these conditions the extremal value of the parameter $y_1 = y_{1e} = D_z^0/D_g^0$ and the minimal value of the variance in the error of the main control loop.

The block diagram of an extremal-regulation system executing the motion toward the minimum of the variance in the error D_E in accordance with the law (9.100) is shown in Figure 9.8.

2. Probability that the error of the system will not exceed the allowed limits chosen as criterion

We have considered systems that adapt themselves to the minimum of the variance in the error. It is possible to construct systems that adapt themselves to the extrema of other statistical criteria. As an example, let us consider a system that adapts itself to the maximum probability that the error will not exceed allowed limits.

Suppose that a signal $X(t)$, constituting the sum of a useful signal $G(t)$ and a noise $Z(t)$, uncorrelated with each other, is applied at the input of the main control loop (see Fig. 3.1). The mathematical expectation m_g of the useful signal, the correlation function $K_g(\tau)$ of the useful signal, and the normalized correlation function of the noise $K_z(\tau)$

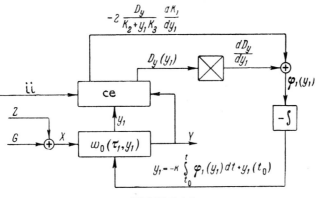

FIGURE 9.8

are known. The mathematical expectation and the variance of the noise and their distribution laws are unknown. The desired output variable $H(t)$ is the result of an application of a known linear operator L to the useful signal:

$$H(t) = L\{G(t)\}.$$

As criterion, we take the probability that the normally distributed error will not exceed allowed limits:

$$P = P(C_1 \leqslant E \leqslant C_2)$$
$$= \frac{1}{\sqrt{2\pi D_E}} \int_{C_1}^{C_2} \exp\left\{-\frac{(E - m_E)^2}{2D_E}\right\} dE, \qquad (9.103)$$

where the mathematical expectation m_E of the error is defined by formula (1.95a) and the variance D_E of the error is defined by formula (1.96a), in which we need to set $\tau = 0$. In the particular case in question, formulas (1.95a) and (1.96a) take the forms

$$m_E = \int_0^T (m_g + m_z) w(\tau) d\tau - L\{m_g\}, \qquad (9.104)$$

$$D_E = \int_0^T \int_0^T [K_g(\tau - \lambda) + D_z R_z(\tau - \lambda)] w(\tau) w(\lambda) d\tau d\lambda$$
$$- 2 \int_0^T K_{gh}(\tau) w(\tau) d\tau + D_h. \qquad (9.105)$$

Since mathematical expectation m_z and the variance D_z are unknown, we use the notations

$$m_z = x_1, \quad D_z = x_2. \qquad (9.106)$$

In this notation, formulas (9.104) and (9.105) become

$$m_E = \int_0^T (m_g + x_1) w(\tau) d\tau - L\{m_g\}, \qquad (9.107)$$

$$D_E = \int_0^T \int_0^T K_g(\tau - \lambda) + x_2 R_z(\tau - \lambda)] w(\tau) w(\lambda) d\tau d\lambda$$
$$- 2 \int_0^T K_{gh}(\tau) w(\tau) d\tau + D_h. \qquad (9.108)$$

Now, we can determine the optimal weight function of the system, which maximizes the probability (9.103) for various values of the parameters x_1 and x_2 (for various values of the mathematical expectation m_z and variance D_z of the noise). This optimal weight function $w_0(\tau, x_1, x_2)$ can be obtained for fixed values of the parameters x_1 and x_2 by the method expounded in Section 15 of Chapter 4. The quantities x_1 and x_2 are unknown. Therefore, it is expedient to construct an extremal regulation system whose main control loop has weight function $w_0(\tau, x_1, x_2)$ or a weight function close to it. The supplementary loops must adapt the parameters x_1 and x_2 to their extremal values x_1 and x_{1e} and

$x_2 = x_{2e}$, corresponding to the maximum of the probability (9.103) at each instant of time. Such a multiple-loop adaptive system is the best system, since it maximizes the criterion chosen at each instant of time.

The extremal values of the parameters x_1 and x_2 of the weight function $w_0(\tau, x_1, x_2)$ are equal to the values of the mathematical expectation and variance of the noise that are observed at the given instant:

$$x_{1e} = m_z^0, \quad x_{2e} = D_z^0. \qquad (9.109)$$

The actual values of the mathematical expectation m_z^2 and variance D_z^2 of the error at the current instant of time are unknown. The values of the parameters x_1 and x_2 of the main loop are continuously measured and are fed into the calculating element.

At each instant, the criterion P can be calculated in accordance with formulas (9.103) through (9.105), in which we take, instead of an arbitrary weight function $w(\tau)$, the weight function $w_0(\tau, x_1, x_2)$ and, instead of arbitrary m_z and D_z, the values of m_z^2 and D_z^0. Formula (9.103) remains invariant when we do this and formulas (9.104) and (9.105) take the forms

$$m_E(x_1, x_2) = \int_0^T (m_g + m_z^0) w_0(\tau, x_1, x_2) d\tau - L\{m_g\}, \qquad (9.110)$$

$$
\begin{aligned}
D_E(x_1, x_2) \\
= \int_0^T \int_0^T [K_g(\tau - \lambda) + D_z^0 R_z(\tau - \lambda)] w_0(\tau, x_1, x_2) w_0(\lambda, x_1, x_2) d\tau \, d\lambda \\
- 2 \int_0^T K_{gh}(\tau) w_0(\tau, x_1, x_2) d\tau + D_h.
\end{aligned}
\qquad (9.111)
$$

In these formulas, the only unknowns are m_z and D_z. However, these two quantities can be calculated if we use the information regarding the output variable $Y(t)$ of the main control loop. From a sample function of the ergodic random function $Y(t)$ we can determine the mathematical expectation $m_y(x_1, x_2)$ and variance $D_y(x_1, x_2)$ of that random function:

$$m_y(x_1, x_2) = \frac{1}{T_s} \int_0^{T_s} y(\tau) d\tau, \qquad (9.112)$$

$$D_y(x_1, x_2) = \frac{1}{T_s} \int_0^{T_s} [y(\tau) - m_y(x_1, x_2)]^2 d\tau, \qquad (9.113)$$

where T_s is the duration of the sample function $y(t)$ of the output variable $Y(t)$. The mathematical expectation $m_y(x_1, x_2)$ and variance $D_y(x_1, x_2)$ of the output variable $Y(t)$, which are determined from formulas (9.112) and (9.113), depend on the parameters x_1 and x_2 of the main control loop, since the sample function $y(t)$ of the random function $Y(t)$ depends on these parameters. Formulas (9.110) and (9.111) can now be written in the following forms:

$$m_E(x_1, x_2) = m_y(x_1, x_2) - L\{m_g\}, \tag{9.114}$$

$$D_E(x_1, x_2) = D_y(x_1, x_2) - 2\int_0^T K_{gh}(\tau)w_0(x_1, x_2)d\tau + D_h. \tag{9.115}$$

Thus, the criterion P can be calculated from formulas (9.103), (9.114), and (9.115). It is a function of the two parameters x_1 and x_2.

To carry out the motion toward the maximum of the criterion (9.103), we need to determine the components of the gradient of that criterion; that is, we need to determine the partial derivatives

$$\frac{\partial P(x_1, x_2)}{\partial x_1}, \quad \frac{\partial P(x_1, x_2)}{\partial x_2}.$$

Let us suppose that these partial derivatives are determined with the aid of synchronous detectors. Motion toward the maximum of the criterion P can be achieved, for example, by means of the gradient method in its ideal form (9.116):

$$\left.\begin{aligned}
\dot{x}_1 &= k\frac{\partial P(x_1, x_2)}{\partial x_1}, \\
\dot{x}_2 &= k\frac{\partial P(x_1, x_2)}{\partial x_2},
\end{aligned}\right\} \tag{9.116}$$

where k is a positive number.

The block diagram of an extremal-control system that calculates, by the method described, the criterion in accordance with formulas (9.103), (9.112) through (9.115) and the gradient method of motion toward the maximum of the criterion P is shown in Figure 9.9. This system includes the main control loop with weight function $w_0(\tau, x_1, x_2)$ and two adaptation loops. The criterion $P(x_1, x_2)$, when it comes from the calculating element is fed to the inputs of the synchronous detectors. From the outputs of the synchronous detectors, the partial derivatives $\partial P/\partial x_1$ and $\partial P/\partial x_2$ of the criterion with respect to the parameters are fed to the integrating components. The signals x_1 and x_2 are formed at the outputs of the integrating components in accordance with formulas (9.116) or the equivalent formulas

$$\left.\begin{aligned}
x_1 &= k\int_{t_0}^t \frac{\partial P}{\partial x_1}dt + x_1(t_0), \\
x_2 &= k\int_{t_0}^t \frac{\partial P}{\partial x_2}dt + x_2(t_0).
\end{aligned}\right\} \tag{9.117}$$

Here, t_0 is the instant at which the system is put into operation and t is a variable instant of time.

In accordance with the law (9.117), the governing elements (not shown in Fig. 9.9) change the parameters x_1 and x_2 of the main control loop.

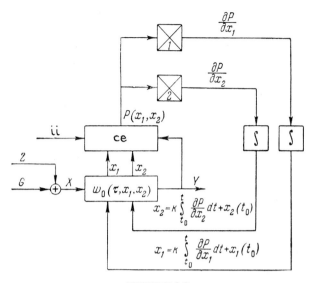

FIGURE 9.9

A continuous search process in accordance with the diagram shown in Figure 9.9 ensures monotonic increase in the criterion P under arbitrary initial conditions. To see this, let us express the derivative of the criterion P with respect to time in terms of the derivatives of the criterion with respect to the parameters:

$$\frac{dP}{dt} = \frac{\partial P}{\partial x_1}\dot{x}_1 + \frac{\partial P}{\partial x_2}\dot{x}_2. \qquad (9.118)$$

From (9.117) and (9.118), we obtain

$$\frac{dP}{dt} = k\left[\left(\frac{\partial P}{\partial x_1}\right)^2 + \left(\frac{\partial P}{\partial x_2}\right)^2\right]. \qquad (9.119)$$

From this it is obvious that the derivative is everywhere positive if the parameters x_1 and x_2 are not extremal. This in turn means that the criterion increases monotonically in our process of seeking its maximum.

In the present section, we have considered cases characterized by some criterion or other for comparing systems or by some sort of incompleteness in the initial information regarding the influences on the system. The method expounded can be used to construct block diagrams of extremal-regulation systems in other cases as well.

A characteristic feature of the adaptive systems that we have just considered is the fact that they ensure an absolute extremum of the criterion chosen if we make no errors in the searching process. This is achieved by a preliminary choice of weight function $w_0(\tau, x_1, \cdots, x_n)$ of the main control loop. It is convenient to call such adaptive systems **optimal adapting systems.** A non-optimal adaptive system or simply an adaptive system can include the main control loop with another weight function $w(\tau, x_1, \cdots, x_m)$ chosen from other conditions of some sort or other. For example, such a weight function $w(\tau, x_1, \cdots, x_m)$ may be the weight function of some existent system with variable parameters $x_1, \cdots, x_m$.

CONCLUSION

In this book, we have considered various problems of determining optimal automatic-control systems. The material in it enables us to conclude that the problem of determining the optimal system out of a class of admissible linear systems can be solved in a simple manner by using contemporary computation techniques. On the other hand, the problem of determining the optimal nonlinear system in the class of admissible nonlinear systems is difficult to solve and cannot always be solved within restricted time limits even with the aid of present-day mathematical computing machines. Therefore, it is expedient to find simple methods of determining optimal nonlinear systems of some particular form or other.

The theory of optimal systems has great practical significance, consisting in the following:

(a) The optimal characteristics, obtained by a theoretical approach, of automatic-control systems (the weight function, the frequency characteristics, combination of parameter, and the like) and the value of the criterion corresponding to these optimal characteristics enable us to evaluate existent systems of a given type, that is, to compare them with the ideal optimal system.

(b) If the existent systems deviate significantly from the optimal system as regards the value of the criterion, the optimal system enables us to note the direction in which we should change the characteristics of the existent systems in order to have them approximate the characteristics of the optimal system.

(c) The theory of optimal systems enables us to determine the maximal possible value of the criterion that can be attained with the aid of actual systems. Consequently, this theory can serve as a scientific basis in the development of technological requirements on projected systems.

(d) The theory of optimal systems can be used in the choice of the direction of perspective projection and construction of new automatic-control systems.

(e) The theory of optimal systems can be used in the projection of newer, perfected systems. In this connection, the time required to find a satisfactory result can be shortened.

(f) The theory of optimal systems must serve as the basis for projecting and using adaptive and self-organizing automatic-control systems.

(g)   The theory of optimal systems can be used to study living organisms, since many characteristics of individual organs and the relationships between them in a living organism are optimal in some sense (with respect to some criterion). The theory of optimal systems enables us to show the appropriateness exhibited in the construction of various organisms in the past and present and to predict the development of these or other forms in the future (for example the change of forms under the influence of specific changes in the conditions of the external medium).

At the present time, the methods of synthesis proper, that is, the methods of realization of systems with nearly optimal characteristics are insufficiently developed. This direction of scientific work is extremely perspective. The higher the technological level, the greater the possibilities are for synthesis proper. The application of new materials and the use of new physical phenomena in technology will broaden the possibilities of achieving nearly optimal systems.

Finally, the use of computing machines in the construction of automatic-control systems opens broad possibilities for the realization of systems, including nearly optimal ones.

APPENDICES

APPENDIX I

Values of the function $\Phi(u) = \dfrac{1}{\sqrt{2\pi}} \displaystyle\int_0^u e^{-t^2/2}dt$

u	$\Phi(u)$	u	$\Phi(u)$	u	$\Phi(u)$	u	$\Phi(u)$
0.00	0.0000	0.30	0.1179	0.60	0.2257	0.90	0.3159
0.01	0.0040	0.31	0.1217	0.61	0.2291	0.91	0.3186
0.02	0.0080	0.32	0.1255	0.62	0.2324	0.92	0.3212
0.03	0.0120	0.33	0.1293	0.63	0.2357	0.93	0.3238
0.04	0.0160	0.34	0.1331	0.64	0.2389	0.94	0.3264
0.05	0.0199	0.35	0.1368	0.65	0.2422	0.95	0.3289
0.06	0.0239	0.36	0.1406	0.66	0.2454	0.96	0.3315
0.07	0.0279	0.37	0.1443	0.67	0.2486	0.97	0.3340
0.08	0.0319	0.38	0.1480	0.68	0.2517	0.98	0.3365
0.09	0.0359	0.39	0.1517	0.69	0.2549	0.99	0.3389
0.10	0.0398	0.40	0.1554	0.70	0.2580	1.00	0.3413
0.11	0.0438	0.41	0.1591	0.71	0.2611	1.01	0.3437
0.12	0.0478	0.42	0.1628	0.72	0.2642	1.02	0.3461
0.13	0.0517	0.43	0.1664	0.73	0.2673	1.03	0.3485
0.14	0.0557	0.44	0.1700	0.74	0.2703	1.04	0.3508
0.15	0.0596	0.45	0.1736	0.75	0.2734	1.05	0.3531
0.16	0.0636	0.46	0.1772	0.76	0.2764	1.06	0.3554
0.17	0.0675	0.47	0.1808	0.77	0.2794	1.07	0.3577
0.18	0.0714	0.48	0.1844	0.78	0.2823	1.08	0.3599
0.19	0.0753	0.49	0.1879	0.79	0.2852	1.09	0.3621
0.20	0.0793	0.50	0.1915	0.80	0.2881	1.10	0.3643
0.21	0.0832	0.51	0.1950	0.81	0.2910	1.11	0.3665
0.22	0.0871	0.52	0.1985	0.82	0.2939	1.12	0.3686
0.23	0.0910	0.53	0.2019	0.83	0.2967	1.13	0.3708
0.24	0.0948	0.54	0.2054	0.84	0.2995	1.14	0.3729
0.25	0.0987	0.55	0.2088	0.85	0.3023	1.15	0.3749
0.26	0.1026	0.56	0.2123	0.86	0.3051	1.16	0.3770
0.27	0.1064	0.57	0.2157	0.87	0.3078	1.17	0.3790
0.28	0.1103	0.58	0.2190	0.88	0.3106	1.18	0.3810
0.29	0.1141	0.59	0.2224	0.89	0.3133	1.19	0.3830

Appendix I—continued

u	$\Phi(u)$	u	$\Phi(u)$	u	$\Phi(u)$	u	$\Phi(u)$
1.20	0.3849	1.55	0.4394	1.90	0.4713	2.48	0.4934
1.21	0.3869	1.56	0.4406	1.91	0.4719	2.50	0.4938
1.22	0.3888	1.57	0.4418	1.92	0.4726	2.52	0.4941
1.23	0.3907	1.58	0.4429	1.93	0.4732	2.54	0.4945
1.24	0.3925	1.59	0.4441	1.94	0.4738	2.56	0.4948
1.25	0.3944			1.95	0.4744	2.58	0.4951
1.26	0.3962	1.60	0.4452	1.96	0.4750		
1.27	0.3980	1.61	0.4463	1.97	0.4756		
1.28	0.3997	1.62	0.4474	1.98	0.4761	2.60	0.4953
1.29	0.4015	1.63	0.4484	1.99	0.4767	2.62	0.4956
		1.64	0.4495			2.64	0.4959
1.30	0.4032	1.65	0.4505			2.66	0.4961
1.31	0.4049	1.66	0.4515	2.00	0.4772	2.68	0.4963
1.32	0.4066	1.67	0.4525	2.02	0.4783	2.70	0.4965
1.33	0.4082	1.68	0.4535	2.04	0.4793	2.72	0.4967
1.34	0.4099	1.69	0.4545	2.06	0.4803	2.74	0.4969
1.35	0.4115			2.08	0.4812	2.76	0.4971
1.36	0.4131	1.70	0.4554	2.10	0.4821	2.78	0.4973
1.37	0.4147	1.71	0.4564	2.12	0.4830		
1.38	0.4162	1.72	0.4573	2.14	0.4838		
1.39	0.4177	1.73	0.4582	2.16	0.4846	2.80	0.4974
		1.74	0.4591	2.18	0.4854	2.82	0.4976
1.40	0.4192	1.75	0.4599			2.84	0.4977
1.41	0.4207	1.76	0.4608			2.86	0.4979
1.42	0.4222	1.77	0.4616	2.20	0.4861	2.88	0.4980
1.43	0.4236	1.78	0.4625	2.22	0.4868	2.90	0.4981
1.44	0.4251	1.79	0.4633	2.24	0.4875	2.92	0.4982
1.45	0.4265			2.26	0.4881	2.94	0.4984
1.46	0.4279	1.80	0.4641	2.28	0.4887	2.96	0.4985
1.47	0.4292	1.81	0.4649	2.30	0.4893	2.98	0.4986
1.48	0.4306	1.82	0.4656	2.32	0.4898		
1.49	0.4319	1.83	0.4664	2.34	0.4904		
		1.84	0.4671	2.36	0.4909	3.00	0.49865
1.50	0.4332	1.85	0.4678	2.38	0.4913	3.20	0.49931
1.51	0.4345	1.86	0.4686			3.40	0.49966
1.52	0.4357	1.87	0.4693	2.40	0.4918	3.60	0.499841
1.53	0.4370	1.88	0.4699	2.42	0.4922	3.80	0.499928
1.54	0.4382	1.89	0.4706	2.44	0.4927	4.00	0.499968
				2.46	0.4931	4.50	0.499997
						5.00	0.499999

APPENDIX II

Values of the function $\Phi'(u) = \dfrac{1}{\sqrt{2\pi}} e^{-u^2/2}$

	0	1	2	3	4	5	6	7	8	9
0.0	0.3989	0.3989	0.3989	0.3988	0.3986	0.3984	0.3982	0.3980	0.3977	0.3973
0.1	0.3970	0.3965	0.3961	0.3956	0.3951	0.3945	0.3939	0.3932	0.3925	0.3918
0.2	0.3910	0.3902	0.3894	0.3885	0.3876	0.3867	0.3857	0.3847	0.3836	0.3825
0.3	0.3814	0.3802	0.3790	0.3778	0.3765	0.3752	0.3739	0.3726	0.3712	0.3697
0.4	0.3683	0.3668	0.3653	0.3637	0.3621	0.3605	0.3589	0.3572	0.3565	0.3528
0.5	0.3521	0.3503	0.3485	0.3467	0.3448	0.3429	0.3410	0.3391	0.3372	0.3352
0.6	0.3332	0.3312	0.3292	0.3271	0.3251	0.3230	0.3209	0.3187	0.3166	0.3144
0.7	0.3123	0.3101	0.3079	0.3056	0.3033	0.3011	0.2989	0.2966	0.2943	0.2920
0.8	0.2897	0.2874	0.2850	0.2827	0.2803	0.2780	0.2756	0.2732	0.2709	0.2685
0.9	0.2661	0.2637	0.2613	0.2589	0.2565	0.2541	0.2516	0.2492	0.2468	0.2444
1.0	0.2420	0.2396	0.2371	0.2347	0.2323	0.2299	0.2275	0.2251	0.2227	0.2203
1.1	0.2179	0.2155	0.2131	0.2107	0.2083	0.2059	0.2036	0.2012	0.1989	0.1965
1.2	0.1942	0.1919	0.1895	0.1872	0.1849	0.1826	0.1804	0.1781	0.1758	0.1736
1.3	0.1714	0.1691	0.1669	0.1647	0.1626	0.1604	0.1582	0.1561	0.1539	0.1518
1.4	0.1497	0.1476	0.1456	0.1435	0.1415	0.1394	0.1374	0.1354	0.1334	0.1315
1.5	0.1295	0.1276	0.1257	0.1238	0.1219	0.1200	0.1182	0.1163	0.1145	0.1127
1.6	0.1109	0.1092	0.1074	0.1057	0.1040	0.1023	0.1006	0.0989	0.0973	0.0957
1.7	0.0941	0.0925	0.0909	0.0893	0.0878	0.0863	0.0848	0.0833	0.0818	0.0804
1.8	0.0790	0.0775	0.0761	0.0748	0.0734	0.0721	0.0707	0.0694	0.0681	0.0669
1.9	0.0656	0.0644	0.0632	0.0620	0.0608	0.0596	0.0584	0.0573	0.0562	0.0551

Appendix II—continued

	0	1	2	3	4	5	6	7	8	9
2.0	0.0540	0.0529	0.0519	0.0508	0.0498	0.0488	0.0478	0.0468	0.0459	0.0449
2.1	0.0440	0.0431	0.0422	0.0413	0.0404	0.0396	0.0387	0.0379	0.0371	0.0363
2.2	0.0355	0.0347	0.0329	0.0332	0.0325	0.0317	0.0310	0.0303	0.0297	0.0290
2.3	0.0283	0.0277	0.0270	0.0264	0.0258	0.0252	0.0246	0.0241	0.0235	0.0229
2.4	0.0224	0.0219	0.0213	0.0208	0.0203	0.0198	0.0194	0.0189	0.0184	0.0180
2.5	0.0175	0.0171	0.0167	0.0163	0.0158	0.0154	0.0151	0.0147	0.0143	0.0139
2.6	0.0136	0.0132	0.0129	0.0126	0.0122	0.0119	0.0116	0.0113	0.0110	8.0107
2.7	0.0104	0.0101	0.0099	0.0096	0.0093	0.0091	0.0088	0.0086	0.0084	0.0081
2.8	0.0079	0.0077	0.0075	0.0073	0.0071	0.0069	0.0067	0.0065	0.0063	0.0061
2.9	0.0060	0.0058	0.0056	0.0055	0.0053	0.0051	0.0050	0.0048	0.0047	0.0046
3.0	0.0044	0.0043	0.0042	0.0040	0.0039	0.0038	0.0037	0.0036	0.0035	0.0034
3.1	0.0033	0.0032	0.0031	0.0030	0.0029	0.0028	0.0027	0.0026	0.0025	0.0025
3.2	0.0024	0.0023	0.0022	0.0022	0.0021	0.0020	0.0020	0.0019	0.0018	0.0018
3.3	0.0017	0.0017	0.0016	0.0016	0.0015	0.0015	0.0014	0.0014	0.0013	0.0013
3.4	0.0012	0.0012	0.0012	0.0011	0.0011	0.0010	0.0010	0.0010	0.0009	0.0009
3.5	0.0009	0.0008	0.0008	0.0008	0.0008	0.0007	0.0007	0.0007	0.0007	0.0006
3.6	0.0006	0.0006	0.0006	0.0005	0.0005	0.0005	0.0005	0.0005	0.0005	0.0004
3.7	0.0004	0.0004	0.0004	0.0004	0.0004	0.0004	0.0003	0.0003	0.0003	0.0003
3.8	0.0003	0.0003	0.0003	0.0003	0.0003	0.0002	0.0002	0.0002	0.0002	0.0002
3.9	0.0002	0.0002	0.0002	0.0002	0.0002	0.0002	0.0002	0.0002	0.0001	0.0001

APPENDIX III

Integral formulas

$$I_n = \frac{1}{2\pi} \int_{-\infty}^{\infty} \frac{g_n(i\omega)}{h_n(i\omega)\, h_n(-i\omega)}\, d\omega \qquad (n = 1, 2, \cdots, 7),$$

where

$$h_n(x) = a_0 x^n + a_1 x^{n-1} + \cdots + a_n,$$
$$g_n(x) = b_0 x^{2n-2} + b_1 x^{2n-4} + \cdots + b_{n-1}.$$

Assuming that all the roots of $h_n(x)$ lie in the left half-plane, we obtain

$$I_1 = \frac{b_0}{2a_0 a_1},$$

$$I_2 = \frac{-b_0 + \dfrac{a_0 b_1}{a_2}}{2a_0 a_1},$$

$$I_3 = \frac{-a_2 b_0 + a_0 b_1 - \dfrac{a_0 a_1 b_2}{a_3}}{2a_0(a_0 a_3 - a_1 a_2)},$$

$$I_4 = \frac{b_0(-a_1 a_4 + a_2 a_3) - a_0 a_3 b_1 + a_0 a_1 b_2 + \dfrac{a_0 b_3}{a^4}(a_0 a_3 - a_1 a_2)}{2a_0(a_0 a_3^2 + a_1^2 a_4 - a_1 a_2 a_3)},$$

$$I_5 = \frac{M^5}{2a_0 \Delta_5},$$

$$\begin{aligned}
M_5 = \; & b_0(-a_0 a_4 a_5 + a_1 a_4^2 + a_2^2 a_5 - a_2 a_3 a_4) \\
& + a_0 b_1(-a_2 a_5 + a_3 a_4) + a_0 b_2(a_0 a_5 - a_1 a_4) \\
& + a_0 b_3(-a_0 a_3 + a_1 a_2) \\
& + \frac{a_0 b_4}{a_5}(-a_0 a_1 a_5 + a_0 a_3^2 + a_1^2 a_4 - a_1 a_2 a_3),
\end{aligned}$$

$$\begin{aligned}
\Delta_5 = \; & a_0^2 a_5^2 - 2a_0 a_1 a_4 a_5 \\
& - a_0 a_2 a_3 a_5 + a_0 a_3^2 a_4 + a_1^2 a_4^2 + a_1 a_2^2 a_5 - a_1 a_2 a_3 a_4,
\end{aligned}$$

$$I_6 = \frac{M_6}{2a_0 \Delta_6},$$

$$\begin{aligned}
M_6 = \; & b_0(-a_0 a_3 a_5 a_6 - a_0 a_4 a_5^2 - a_1^2 a_6^2 + 2a_1 a_2 a_5 a_6 \\
& + a_1 a_3 a_4 a_6 - a_1 a_4^2 a_5 - a_2^2 a_5^2 - a_2 a_3^2 a_6 + a_2 a_3 a_4 a_5) \\
& + a_0 b_1(-a_1 a_5 a_6 + a_2 a_5^2 + a_3^2 a_6 - a_3 a_4 a_5) \\
& + a_0 b_2(-a_0 a_5^2 - a_1 a_3 a_6 + a_1 a_4 a_5) \\
& + a_0 b_3(a_0 a_3 a_5 + a_1^2 a_6 - a_1 a_2 a_5) \\
& + a_0 b_4(a_0 a_1 a_5 - a_0 a_3^2 - a_1^2 a_4 + a_1 a_2 a_3)
\end{aligned}$$

$$+ \frac{a_0 b_5}{a_6} \left(a_0^2 a_5^2 + a_0 a_1 a_3 a_6 - 2a_0 a_1 a_4 a_5 - a_0 a_2 a_3 a_5 \right.$$
$$\left. + a_0 a_3^2 a_4 - a_1^2 a_2 a_6 + a_1^2 a_4^2 + a_1 a_2^2 a_5 - a_1 a_2 a_3 a_4 \right),$$

$$\Delta_6 = a_0^2 a_5^3 + 3a_0 a_1 a_3 a_5 a_6 - 2a_0 a_1 a_4 a_5^2 - a_0 a_2 a_3 a_5^2 - a_0 a_3^3 a_6$$
$$+ a_0 a_3^2 a_4 a_5 + a_1^3 a_6^2 - 2a_1^2 a_2 a_5 a_6 - a_1^2 a_3 a_4 a_6$$
$$+ a_1^2 a_4^2 a_5 + a_1 a_2^2 a_5^2 + a_1 a_2 a_3^2 a_6 - a_1 a_2 a_3 a_4 a_5,$$

$$I_7 = \frac{M_7}{2a_0 \Delta_7},$$

$$M_7 = b_0 m_0 + a_0 b_1 m_1 + a_0 b_2 m_2 + \cdots + a_0 b_6 m_6,$$

$$m_0 = a_0^2 a_6 a_7^2 - 2a_0 a_1 a_6^2 a_7 - 2a_0 a_2 a_4 a_7^2 + a_0 a_2 a_5 a_6 a_7$$
$$+ a_0 a_3 a_5 a_6^2 + a_0 a_4^2 a_5 a_7 - a_0 a_4 a_5^2 a_6 + a_1^2 a_6^3$$
$$+ 3a_1 a_2 a_4 a_6 a_7 - 2a_1 a_2 a_5 a_6^2 - a_1 a_3 a_4 a_6^2 - a_1 a_4^3 a_7$$
$$+ a_1 a_4^2 a_5 a_6 + a_2^3 a_7^2 - 2a_2^2 a_3 a_6 a_7 - a_2^2 a_4 a_5 a_7$$
$$+ a_2^2 a_5^2 a_6 + a_2 a_3 a_4^2 a_7 - a_2 a_3 a_4 a_5 a_6 - a_2 a_3^2 a_6^2,$$

$$m_1 = a_0 a_4 a_7^2 - a_0 a_5 a_6 a_7 - a_1 a_4 a_6 a_7 + a_1 a_5 a_6^2 - a_2^2 a_7^2$$
$$+ 2a_2 a_3 a_6 a_7 + a_2 a_4 a_5 a_7 - a_2 a_5^2 a_6 - a_3^2 a_6^2 - a_3 a_4^2 a_7 + a_3 a_4 a_5 a_6,$$

$$m_2 = a_0 a_2 a_7^2 - a_0 a_3 a_6 a_7 - a_0 a_4 a_5 a_7$$
$$+ a_0 a_5^2 a_6 - a_1 a_2 a_6 a_7 + a_1 a_3 a_6^2 + a_1 a_4^2 a_7 - a_1 a_4 a_5 a_6,$$

$$m_3 = -a_0^2 a_7^2 + 2a_0 a_1 a_6 a_7$$
$$+ a_0 a_3 a_4 a_7 - a_0 a_3 a_5 a_6 - a_1^2 a_6^2 - a_1 a_2 a_4 a_7 + a_1 a_2 a_5 a_6,$$

$$m_4 = a_0^2 a_5 a_7 - a_0 a_1 a_4 a_7 - a_0 a_1 a_5 a_6 - a_0 a_2 a_3 a_7$$
$$+ a_0 a_3^2 a_6 + a_1^2 a_4 a_6 + a_1 a_2^2 a_7 - a_1 a_2 a_3 a_6,$$

$$m_5 = a_0^2 a_3 a_7 - a_0^2 a_5^2 - a_0 a_1 a_2 a_7 - a_0 a_1 a_3 a_6 - 2a_0 a_1 a_4 a_5$$
$$+ a_0 a_2 a_3 a_5 - a_0 a_3^2 a_4 + a_1^2 a_2 a_6 - a_1^2 a_4^2 - a_1 a_2^2 a_5 + a_1 a_2 a_3 a_4,$$

$$m_6 = \frac{1}{a_7} \left(a_0^2 a_1 a_7^2 - 2a_0^2 a_3 a_5 a_7 + a_0^2 a_5^3 - 2a_0 a_1^2 a_6 a_7 \right.$$
$$+ a_0 a_1 a_2 a_5 a_7 + 3a_0 a_1 a_3 a_5 a_6 - 2a_0 a_1 a_4 a_5^2 + a_0 a_2 a_3^2 a_7$$
$$- a_0 a_2 a_3 a_5^2 - a_0 a_3^3 a_6 + a_0 a_3^2 a_4 a_5 + a_1^3 a_6^2 + a_1^2 a_2 a_4 a_7$$
$$- 2a_1^2 a_2 a_5 a_6 - a_1^2 a_3 a_4 a_6 + a_1^2 a_4^2 a_5 - a_1 a_2^2 a_3 a_7$$
$$\left. + a_1 a_2^2 a_5^2 + a_1 a_2 a_3^2 a_6 - a_1 a_2 a_3 a_4 a_5 \right),$$

$$\Delta_7 = -a_0^3 a_7^3 + 3a_0^2 a_1 a_6 a_7^2 + a_0^2 a_2 a_5 a_7^2 + 2a_0^2 a_3 a_4 a_7^2$$
$$- 3a_0^2 a_3 a_5 a_6 a_7 - a_0^2 a_4 a_5^2 a_7 + a_0^2 a_5^3 a_6 - 3a_0 a_1^2 a_6^2 a_7 - 3a_0 a_1 a_2 a_4 a_7^2$$
$$+ a_0 a_1 a_2 a_5 a_6 a_7 + 3a_0 a_1 a_3 a_5 a_6^2 - a_0 a_1 a_3 a_4 a_6 a_7$$
$$+ 2a_0 a_1 a_4^2 a_5 a_7 - 2a_0 a_1 a_4 a_5^2 a_6 - a_0 a_2^2 a_3 a_7^2$$
$$+ 2a_0 a_2 a_3^2 a_6 a_7 + a_0 a_2 a_3 a_4 a_5 a_7 - a_0 a_2 a_3 a_5^2 a_6$$
$$- a_0 a_3^3 a_6^2 - a_0 a_3^2 a_4^2 a_7 + a_0 a_3^2 a_4 a_5 a_6 + a_1^3 a_6^3 + 3a_1^2 a_2 a_4 a_6 a_7$$
$$- 2a_1^2 a_2 a_5 a_6^2 - a_1^2 a_3 a_4 a_6^2 - a_1^2 a_4^3 a_7 + a_1^2 a_4^2 a_5 a_6$$
$$+ a_1 a_2^3 a_7^2 - 2a_1 a_2^2 a_3 a_6 a_7 - a_1 a_2^2 a_4 a_5 a_7$$
$$+ a_1 a_2^2 a_5^2 a_6 + a_1 a_2 a_3^2 a_6^2 + a_1 a_2 a_3 a_4^2 a_7 - a_1 a_2 a_3 a_4 a_5 a_6.$$

APPENDIX IV

Ф-номограм

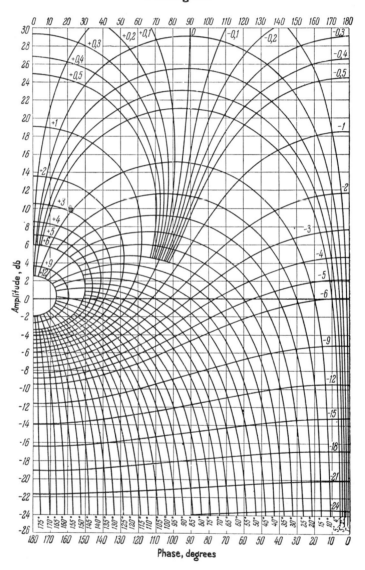

APPENDIX V

(*P*, *Q*)-номограм

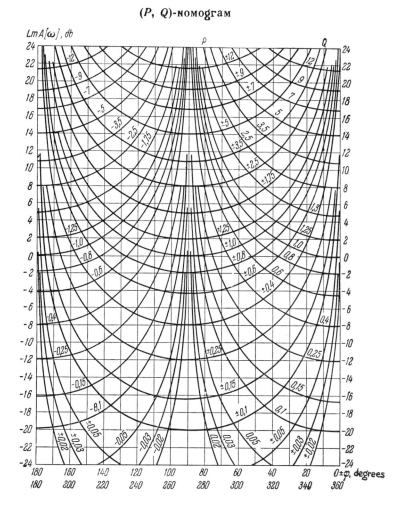

Bibliography

1. Amiantov, I. N., Primeneniye teorii resheniy k zadacham obnaryuzheniya signalov i vydeleniya signalov iz shuma (Application of the theory of decisions to problems of discovering signals and distinguishing them from noise), author's summary of his dissertation for the degree of candidat in physical and mathematical sciences, 1959.
2. Andreyev, N. I., Opredeleniye korrelyatsionnoy funktsii oshibki na vykhode lineynoy sistemy s postoyannymi koeffitsiyentami, esli na vkhod etoy sistemy podayetsya nestatsionarnoye vozmushcheniye (Determination of the correlation function of the error at the output of a linear system with constant coefficients if a nonstationary disturbance is applied at the input of that system), *Sbornik nauchnykh trudov*, Voyennovozdushnaya inzhenernaya Akademiya im. Zhukovskogo (Zhukovskiy Military Air Engineering Academy), Vol. 1, 1954.
3. Andreyev, N. I., Opredeleniye optimal'noy lineynoy dinamicheskoy sistemy po kriteriyu ekstremuma funktsionala chastnogo vida (Determination of an optimal linear dynamic system with respect to the criterion of maximizing or minimizing a functional of a special form), *Avtomatika i telemekhanika*, **18**, No. 7 (1957).
4. Andreyev, N. I., K teorii opredeleniya optimal'noy dinamicheskoy sistemy (On the theory of determining an optimal dynamic system), *Avtomatika i telemekhanika*, **19**, No. 12 (1958).
5. Andreyev, N. I., Obshcheye usloviye ekstremuma zadannoy funktsii srednekvadratichnoy oshibki i kvadrata matematicheskogo ozhidaniya oshibki dinamicheskoy sistemy (The general condition of an extremum of a given function of the mean-square error and of the square of the mathematical expectation of the error of a dynamical system), *Avtomatika i telemekhanika*, **20**, No. 7 (1959).
6. Andreyev, N. I., Opredeleniye optimal'noy vesovoy funktsii impul'snoy sistemy, obespechivayushcheye ekstremum nekotorogo funktsionala (Determination of the optimal weight function of a sampled-data system ensuring an extremum of a functional), *Avtomatika i telemekhanika*, **21**, No. 4 (1960).
7. Andreyev, N. I., Metod opredeleniya optimal'noy dinamicheskoy sistemy po criteriyu ekstremuma funktsionala, predstavlyayushchego soboy zadannuyu funktsiyu ot neskol'kikh drugikh funktsionalov (A method of determining an optimal dynamic system with respect to the criterion of minimization or maximization of a functional that is a given function of other functionals), *Trudy 1-go Mezhdunarodnogo kongressa po avtomaticheskomu upravleniyu* (Proceedings of the First International Congress on Automatic Control), Izd-vo Akad. nauk, USSR, 1961.
8. Andreyev, N. I., O metode resheniya nekotorykh zadach nelineynogo programmirovaniya (On a method of solving certain nonlinear programming problems), Izv. Akad. nauk, USSR, *Tekhnicheskaya kibernetika* (technical cybernetics), No. 1 (1963).

9. Andreyev, N. I., Nelineynoye programmirovaniye v zadachakh issledovaniya optimal'nykh sistem avtomaticheskogo upravleniya (Nonlinear programming in problems of investigating optimal automatic-control systems), *Trudy 2-go mezhdunarodnogo kongressa po avtomaticheskomu upravleniyu* (Proceedings of the Second International Congress on Automatic Control), Izd.-vo Akad. nauk, USSR, 1964.

10. Andreyev, N. I., Vychisleniye statisticheskikh kriteriyev v samonastraivayushchikhsya sistemakh (Calculation of statistical criteria in adaptive systems), *Tezisy doklada na III Vsesoyuznom soveshchanii po avtomaticheskomu upravleniyu (tekhnicheskoy kibernetike)* (Theses of an address at the third All-Union Council on Automatic Control [technological cybernetics]), Odessa, 1965.

11. Blackwell, D., and Girshick, M. A., *Theory of Games and Statistical Decisions*, New York, Wiley, 1954.

12. Booton, R. C., An optimization theory for time-varying linear systems with nonstationary statistical inputs, *Proc. IRE*, **40**, No. 8 (1952).

13. Chinayev, P. I., *Samonastraivayushchiyesya sistemy. Raschet i proyektirovaniye* (Adaptive systems. Calculation and projection), Mashgiz, 1963.

14. Fel'dbaum, A. A., *Optimal Control Systems*, New York, Academic Press, 1965 (translation of *Osnovy teorii optimal'nykh avtomaticheskikh sistem*).

15. Fel'dbaum, A. A., Dudykin, A. D., Manovtsev, A. P., and Mirolyubov, N. N., *Teoreticheskiye osnovy svyazi i upravleniya* (Theoretical bases of connection and control), Fizmatgiz, 1963.

16. Gass, S. I., *Linear Programming*, 2nd ed., New York, McGraw-Hill, 1964.

17. Gel'fand, I. M., and Shilov, G. Y., *Generalized Functions*, Vol. I, *Properties and Operations*, New York, Academic Press, 1964 (translation of *Obobshcheniyye funktsii i deystviya nad nimi*).

18. Gnedenko, B. V., *Theory of Probability*, 4th ed., New York, Chelsea, 1963 (translation of *Kurs teorii veroyatnostey*).

19. Kantorovich, L.V., Funktsional'nyy analiz i prikladanaya matematika (Functional analysis and applied mathematics), *Uspekhi matematicheskikh nauk*, **3**, No. 6 (1948).

20. Kazakov, I. Y., and Dostupov, B. G., Statisticheskaya dinamika nelineynykh avtomaticheskikh sistem (Statistical dynamics of nonlinear automatic systems), Fizmatgiz, 1962.

21. Kochetkov, Y. A., Optimal'naya approksimatsiya kvadratichnogo signala (Optimal approximation of a square signal), Izv Akad. nauk, USSR, *Tekhnicheskaya kibernetika* (Technical cybernetics), No. 6 (1963).

22. Kolmogorov, A. N., Analiticheskiye metody v teorii veroyatnostey (Analytical methods in probability theory), *Uspekhi matematicheskikh nauk*, No. 5 (1938).

23. Kolmogorov, A. N., Interpolirovaniye i ekstrapolirovaniye statsionarnykh sluchaynykh posledovatel'nostey (Interpolation and extrapolation of stationary random sequences), *Izv. Akad. nauk*, USSR, ser. matem, **5**, No. 1 (1941).

24. Krasovskiy, A. A., *Dinamika nepreryvnykh samonastraivayushchikhsya sistem* (Dynamics of continuous adaptive systems), Fizmatgiz, 1963.

25. Krasovskiy, A. A., and Pospelov, G. S., *Osnovy avtomatiki i tekhnicheskoy kibernetiki* (The foundations of automation and technological cybernetics), Gosenergoizdat, 1962.

26. Krut'ko, P. D., *Statisticheskaya dinamika impul'snykh sistem* (Statistical dynamics of sampled-data systems), Sovetskoye radio, 1963.

27. Kukhtenko, V. I., K raschetu korrektiruyushchikh tsepey sistem avtomaticheskogo upravleniya po kriteriyu minimuma srednekvadraticheskoy oshibki (On the calculation of correcting circuits of automatic-control systems with respect to the criterion of minimization of mean-square error), *Avtomatika i telemekhanika*, **20**, No. 9 (1959).

28. Kurosh, A. G., *Kurs vysshey algebry* (Course of higher algebra), Gostekhizdat, 1955.

29. Kuznetsov, P.I., Stratonovich, P.L., and Tikhonov, V.I., Prokhozhdeniye sluchay-nykh funktsiy cherez lineynyye sistemy (The passing of random functions through linear systems), *Avtomatika i telemechanika*, **15**, No. 3 (1954).
30. Lampard, D. G., Generalization of the Wiener-Khinchin theorem to nonstationary processes, *J. Appl. Rhysics*, **25**, No. 6 (1954).
31. Laning, J. H., Jr., and R. H. Battin, *Random Processes in Automatic Control*, New York, McGraw-Hill, 1956.
32. Lavrent'yev, M. A., and Lyusternik, L. A., *Kurs variatsionnogo ischisleniya* (Course of calculus of variations), Gostekhizdat, 1950.
33. Lifshitz, N. A., and Pugachev, V. N., *Veroyatnostnyy analiz sistem avtomati-cheskogo upravleniya* (Probabilistic analysis of automatic-control systems), Sovetskoye radio, 1963.
34. Luce, R. D., and Raiffa, H., *Games and Decisions*, New York, Wiley, 1957.
35. McKinsey, J. C. C., *Introduction to the Theory of Games*, New York, McGraw-Hill, 1952.
36. Mikhlin, S. G., *The Problem of the Minimum of a Quadratic Functional*, San Francisco, Holden-Day, 1965 (translation of *Problema minimuma kvadratich-nogo funktsionala*).
37. Mishkin, E., and Braun, L., eds., *Adaptive Control Systems*, New York, McGraw-Hill, 1961.
38. Pélegrin, M. J., *Calcul Statistique des Systèmes Asservis*, Publications Scienti-fiques et Techniques du Ministére de l'Air, Paris, 1953.
39. Perov, V. P., *Statisticheskiy sintez impul'snykh sistem* (Statistical synthesis of sampled-data systems), Sovetskoye radio, 1959.
40. Popov, Y. P., and Pal'tov, I. P., *Priblizhennyye metody issledovaniya neliney-nykh avtomaticheskikh sistem* (Approximate methods of investigating nonlinear automatic systems), Fizmatgiz, 1960.
41. Privalov, I. I., *Integral'nyye uravneniya* (Integral equations), ONTI, 1935.
42. Pugachev, V.S., *Osnovy obshchey teorii sluchaynykh funktsiy* (The fundamentals of the general theory of random functions), Trudy Akademii art. nauk, 1952.
43. Pugachev, V. S., Obshchaya teoriya korrelyatsii sluchaynykh funktsiy (The gen-eral theory of correlation of random functions), *Izd-vo Akad. nauk*, USSR, ser. matem., **17**, No. 5 (1953).
44. Pugachev, V. S., Obshchaya teoria sinteza dinamicheskikh sistem s uchetom sluchaynykh vozmushcheniy (The general theory of synthesis of dynamical systems with consideration of random disturbances), *Sbornik nauchnykh trudov, Voyennovozdushnaya inzhenernaya Akademiya im. Zhukovskogo* (Zhukovskiy Military Air Engineering Academy), Vol. 1, 1954.
45. Pugachev, V. S., Obshcheye usloviye minimuma sredney kvadraticheskoy oshibki dinamicheskoy sistemy (The general theory of the minimum of the mean square error of a dynamical system), *Avtomatika i telemekhanika*, **17**, No. 4 (1956).
46. Pugachev, V. S., Kazakov, I. Y., Gladkov, D. I., Yevlanov, L. G., Mal'chikov, S. V., Mishakov, A. F., Sedov, V. D., and Sokolov, V. I., *Osnovy avtomatich-eskogo upravleniya* (Foundations of automatic control), Fizmatgiz, 1963.
47. Pugachev, V. S., *Theory of Random Functions*, Reading, Massachusetts, Addison-Wesley, 1965 (translation of *Teoriya sluchaynykh funktsiy i yeye primeneniye k zadacham avtomaticheskogo upravleniya*).
48. Semenov, V. M., K teorii ekstrapolirovaniya sluchaynykh protsessov (On the theory of extrapolation of random processes), *Sbornik nauchnykh trudov, Voyennovozdushnaya inzhenernaya Akademiya im. Zhukovskogo* (Zhukovskiy Military Air Engineering Academy), Vol. 1, 1954.
49. Shatalov, A. S., *Strukturnyye metody v teorii upravleniya i elektroavtomatike* (Structural methods in control theory and in electroautomation), Gosenergoizdat, 1962.
50. Smirnov, V. I., *Course of Higher Mathematics*, 5 vols., Reading, Massachusetts, Addison-Wesley, 1964 (translation of *Kurs vysshey matematiki*).

51. Solodov, A. V., *Linear Automatic Control Systems*, New York, Gordon and Breach, 1966 (translation of *Lineynyye sistemy avtomaticheskogo upravleniya s peremennymi parametrami*).
52. Solodovnikov, V. V., *Statistical Dynamics of Linear Automatic Control Systems*, Princeton, New Jersey, Van Nostrand, 1965 (translation of *Statisticheskaya dinamika lineynykh sistem avtomaticheskogo upravleniya*).
53. Tsypkin, Y. Z., *Teoriya lineynykh impul'snykh sistem* (Theory of linear sampled-data systems), Fizmatgiz, 1963.
54. Venttsel', E. S., *Lectures on Game Theory*, New York, Gordon and Breach, 1962 (translation of *Elementy teorii igr*).
55. Wiener, N., *Extrapolation, Interpolation and Smoothing of Stationary Time Series*, New York, Wiley, 1949.
56. Yaglom, A. M., *Introduction to the Theory of Stationary Random Functions*, Englewood Cliffs, New Jersey, Prentice-Hall, 1962 (translation of *Vvedeniye v teoriyu statsionarnykh sluchaynykh funktsiy*).
57. Yudin, D. V., and Gol'shteyn, Y. G., *Zadachi i metody lineynogo programmirovaniya* (Problems and methods of linear programming), Izd-vo "Sovetskoye radio," 1961.
58. Zadeh, L. A., Optimum nonlinear filters, *J. Appl. Physics*, **24**, No. 4 (1953).
59. Zadeh, L. A., and Ragazzini, J. R., Extension of Wiener's theory of prediction, *J. Appl. Physics*, **21**, No. 7 (1950).

Index